THE
RATIONALE OF
PUNISHMENT

Titles on Philosophy in Religion in Prometheus's Great Books Series

See the back of this volume for a complete list of titles in
Prometheus's Great Books in Philosophy and Great Minds series.

THE RATIONALE OF PUNISHMENT

JEREMY BENTHAM

EDITED BY JAMES T. MCHUGH

GREAT BOOKS SERIES

Prometheus Books
59 John Glenn Drive
Amherst, New York 14228-2119

Published 2009 by Prometheus Books

Inquiries should be addressed to
Prometheus Books
59 John Glenn Drive
Amherst, New York 14228–2119

716–691–0133 ext. 210 FAX: 716–691–0137
WWW.PROMETHEUSBOOKS.COM

13 12 11 10 09   5 4 3 2 1

Library of Congress Cataloging-in-Publication Data

Bentham, Jeremy, 1748–1832.

The rationale of punishment / by Jeremy Bentham ; with Pierre Étienne
Louis Dumont and Richard Smith ; edited by James T. McHugh.
    p. cm.

Includes bibliographical references.

ISBN 978-1-59102-627-3 (pbk. : alk. paper) 1. Punishment—Philosophy.
I. Dumont, Etienne, 1759–1829. II. Smith, Richard, of the Stamps and Taxes
Office. III. McHugh, James T., 1961—IV. Title.

K5103.B46 2009
364.601—dc22

2009013380

Printed in the United States of America on acid-free paper

BIOGRAPHY

Jeremy Bentham was born in London on February 15, 1748, to a family of comfortable means. His was the life of a child prodigy who read Latin at three years of age and at twelve was enrolled in Oxford University, where he received his undergraduate degree at the age of sixteen. Thereafter, he studied law at Lincoln's Inn, Westminster. Inheritances from his parents afforded Bentham the opportunity to pursue a life of study and writing. While in his midforties, he dedicated himself to the critical analysis and reform of moral, political, religious, legal, educational, and economic institutions as they existed in England.

Though he found the judicial system to be hypocritical and corrupt, Bentham's fascinations with the fundamental ideals of the law steered him toward philosophy and science in an effort to develop standards that could ground the social order. His reformist tendencies proved to be a significant factor in the development of his now famous system of ethics known as utilitarianism, wherein human action was to be judged by the amount of pleasure and pain it produced.

Among Bentham's published works are *La Théorie des Peines et des Récompenses* (written in 1775 and translated into English as *The Rationale of Reward* [1825] and *The Rationale of Punishment* [1830]), A Fragment on Government (1776), *An Introduction to the Principles of Morals and Legislation* (1781), *The Rational of Judicial Evidence* (edited by John Stuart Mill in 1825), and two volumes on *Constitutional Code* (ca. 1830). Bentham died in London on June 16, 1832.

Pierre Étienne Louis Dumont was born on July 18, 1759, in Geneva. He was a French-speaking Swiss political writer, religious minister, and an advocate for liberal reform who was forced to flee Geneva when its aristocratic faction came to power in 1781. He eventually traveled to London, where he became a friend and associate of many leading political reformers, including Richard Sheridan, Lord Shelburne, and Sir Samuel Romilly. In 1788 he met Bentham and became enamored of his utilitarian ideas, dedicating himself to the task of transcribing and translating many of Bentham's writings, including in terms of filling considerable lacunae. He traveled to Paris before and during the French Revolution and continued to work on behalf of promoting Genevese democracy, returning to that city when its independence was restored in 1814 and becoming leader of its Supreme Council. He continued to edit and publish French versions of the works of Bentham until shortly before his death while traveling in Milan on September 29, 1829.

Richard Smith (circa 1780–1850) was a British civil servant who worked for the Bureau of Taxation and became an ardent supporter of Bentham and his utilitarian ideas. He devoted great energy to copying many of Bentham's manuscripts and editing much of his writing. Upon Bentham's death, Smith worked with the literary executor of Bentham's estate, John Bowring, to help edit and publish a collected edition of his works that first appeared in 1846.

ACKNOWLEDGMENTS

This project was accomplished with the assistance of many sources. The Library Research Annex of the University of Vermont's Bailey-Howe Library (with the direct help of the Executive Assistant to the Dean of Library and Information Technology, Judith McHugh) provided an invaluable copy of the 1830 edition of The Rationale of Punishment that is the primary source for this edition. Even more significant was the invaluable accessibility that I was given for comparing that text with the original manuscripts and transcriptions of Bentham's treatise through the kindness of the Special Collections Library of University College, London and its extremely helpful and highly professional staff. Additional, and much appreciated, support was provided by the Murray Green Library of Roosevelt University, the McCormick Special Collections Library of Northwestern University, the Baker-Berry Library of Dartmouth College, the Louis L. Biro Library of the John Marshall Law School, the library of the University of Illinois at Chicago, La Bibliothèque Nationale in Paris, the Library of Congress in Washington, and all of their respective staffs.

Roosevelt University also provided funding through a Summer Research Grant that made possible my research trips to London and Paris, without which travel this project would not have been possible. The resources of both the Office of International Affairs at American University (and the support of my colleagues in that office) and that university's Legal Affairs Department also were very important to the final success of this project, as was the assistance and encouragement of the editorial staff of Prometheus Books. Of course, the ongoing encouragement of my family (especially my parents, who finally have come to believe in the permanence of my current career choice) is deeply appreciated, as it has been throughout my life.

CONTENTS

BOOK I—GENERAL PRINCIPLES

EDITOR'S INTRODUCTION

A TIMELY REASSESSMENT

Some treatises are undeservedly overlooked. In relation to that claim, *The Rationale of Punishment* might reasonably be considered to be the most under appreciated published treatise of early utilitarianism. Its importance rests upon three considerations. First, it offers the most thorough elaboration upon that area of practical application for utilitarian thought that has been, arguably, its most effective subject: penal law and policy. In that context, it extends those writings upon this subject that, previously (at least in terms of date of publication), had been given their most important exposition within Jeremy Bentham's seminal text, *An Introduction to the Principles of Morals and Legislation*. While it extends upon the themes of that famous book, *The Rationale of Punishment* also explores, with greater specificity and imagination, the justifications and consequences of punishment as based upon reason, rather than revenge. It also illustrates the applicability of the properties of punishment (adding "simplicity of description") that were introduced within *An Introduction to the Principles of Morals and Legislation*.

Second, the final published version of this treatise that emerged in 1830 no longer represents solely the ideas of Bentham but, instead, provides a seminal text of a broader, "second generation" of utilitarian scholarship, alongside John Austin's *The Province of Jurisprudence Determined*. This approach of this generation of scholars differed from the origins of the utilitarian school in an apparent tendency to include considerations of normative and subjective moral principles as a supplemental aspect of its precepts. They helped to transform this utilitarian critique of penal law and policy from one that was based upon an extrinsic to an intrin*s*ic concept of "good" and "evil."[1]

Third, it offers an unstated, yet perceivable, theoretical goal for the pursuit of reform in penal law and policy. That idealistic goal offers an arguably clearer (though practically unattainable) standard for measuring the success of a particular form of punishment, criminal statute, or judicial ruling than other utilitarian proposals—one that is particularly relevant to the spirit of political and legal reform that particularly motivated nineteenth-century utilitarians who succeeded Bentham. It is a standard that

11

treats punishment as an intrinsic evil that is undesirable not because of a lack of preference for it as a relative choice among painful or pleasurable options but because it is internally undesirable as a general principle. Therefore, punishment ought not to be inflicted unless it is absolutely necessary to prevent a measurably greater evil. That approach may be compared to the concept of hedonistic utilitarianism that initially emerged during the late nineteenth century. The utilitarian account of punishment provided by this book may make more sense from an intrinsic, rather than a strictly extrinsic, perspective, despite the obvious assumption that criminals prefer to avoid the pain of punishment over the pleasure of their crimes as an intuitive preference, rather than something that is good or bad in itself.[2]

Therefore, in connection with this third consideration, an alternative interpretation of utilitarian penal law and policy as provided by this book is that it offers a different assumption and standard regarding the nature of punishment as something that is objectively evil, rather than an intuitive preference. Therefore, in an ideal world, if penal policy works, perfectly, its implementation ultimately would result in its redundancy. That interpretation of utilitarian penal policy as derived from *The Rationale of Punishment* might appear to reflect some of the principles associated with the interpretation known as "negative utilitarianism," which advances the proposition that the reduction of pain is a superior goal for the utilitarian reformer than the promotion of pleasure.[3] However, in the case of penal law and policy, the standard is not based upon a competition between pain and pleasure but, instead, an attempt to reduce two parallel forms of pain: the pain caused by crime and the pain imposed by punishment. That competition implicitly underscores the overall tone and pattern of *The Rationale of Punishment* and reinforces the editorial contributions made by the collaborators who were responsible for its ultimate publication.

AN OVERLOOKED AND UNDERAPPRECIATED TREATISE

The Rationale of Punishment is an incomplete reflection of the totality of Jeremy Bentham's writings and ideas concerning the theory of punishment and penal law. Nonetheless, as an example of applied philosophy, its importance continues to be potentially great. Furthermore, it is not a mere extension of similar arguments found within *Introduction to the Principles of Morals and Legislation*. It offers the most comprehensive application of utilitarian theory to one of the most important areas of public policy in the modern world. Although not as well known as the more concise treatment offered within *Introduction to the Principles of Morals and Legislation*, its lack of recognition may be the result of oversight, of the continental origins of its publication, or of the uncertainty surrounding the possibly collaborative nature of its overall manuscript.

Therefore, it is possible to argue that Jeremy Bentham's *The Rationale of Punishment* is his most important published work of applied philosophy. That claim might be regarded as audacious under normal circumstances. As already noted, this particular book has not been published since 1830, although it was reproduced within Bentham's collected works that were posthumously edited and published by John Bowring in 1846.[4] This book is based upon incomplete manuscripts that, ultimately, were compiled and prepared by not one but two different editors, one of whom first published a version of it in French. Bentham's original manuscripts for this book were written between 1774 and 1776, although the surviving manuscripts in his handwriting are relatively few, with most of the available manuscript pages being transcripts prepared by Richard Smith.[5]

An objection to this audacious claim regarding the importance of this book might be prompted by a preliminary observation that it appears, upon cursory examination, to replicate the same essential arguments as provided within one of Bentham's most famous books, *Introduction to the Principles of Morals and Legislation*.[6] Therefore, an understandable concern that could be raised in terms of whether or not a new edition of this book is even warranted (let alone whether or not it can approach a bold claim concerning its alleged importance) might be based upon its supposed lack of novelty. It is necessary, therefore, to address this preliminary and fundamental challenge regarding the very relevance of *The Rationale of Punishment* as an original and significant contribution to utilitarian thought, in particular, and political philosophy, in general.

One objection to the publication of *many* of Bentham's works is the charge of redundancy.[7] That charge may be slightly exaggerated, specifically in the area of punishment. Certainly, the scope of Bentham's writings upon this subject is copious and varied, especially regarding the subtopics that fall under it. Furthermore, his writings regarding his specific plans for reform of the actual implementation of punishment (culminating in his proposals for a penal system, the Panopticon)[8] extended into many years of practical schemes and active promotion.

But in terms of general themes, this charge of redundancy is, arguably, acceptable. Both books do emphasize the theme of punishment as a form of pain and, thus, as being, objectively and extrinsically, "evil"—although *The Rationale of Punishment* seems to use that phrase in an arguably more intrinsic sense, a claim that will be addressed elsewhere. As a result of this shared emphasis, both books also stress, therefore, the application of general utilitarian principles to this subject. The essential arguments of both books contend that a balance should be sought between the infliction of pain upon criminals (or in constraining potential criminals) and the pleasure that unconstrained criminals would derive from their crimes, as well as the pleasure of society, in general, of being free from the infliction of those crimes. Because deterrence can achieve a maximum of pleasure with a minimum of pain, that overall role of a penal system is particularly stressed within both books.[9]

Both books also make the same general utilitarian assumptions regarding human nature and apply them to potential and actual criminals. The contention is that criminals make rational calculations of the pleasure to be gained from committing a crime and weigh that possibility against the potential pain to be experienced from the punishment they will receive if they are caught. If a situation cannot be addressed in that way (for example, if a crime actually was not committed, if the punishment will not work, or if the cost of the punishment exceeds its reward to society), the situation is deemed to be "unmeet for punishment."[10]

Perhaps, most significantly, both books insist on a rule of proportionality, including incentives for criminals to choose to commit a less serious crime over the option of committing a more serious crime, such as murdering, as well as robbing, a victim. Likewise, the most coercive penalties (especially "afflictive" punishments, such as the death penalty) should be avoided in favor of less coercive alternatives, again as an attempt to diminish pain and maximize pleasure. In support of that principle, both books enumerate the same thirteen rules that provide a method for determining that proportionality.

Furthermore, the other significant parallel that supports the proposition that *The Rationale of Punishment* is redundant in relation to *Introduction to the Principles of Morals and Legislation* is the list of qualities that legitimate punishment (under a theory of utilitarianism) should possess. Those qualities, as listed in different locations within the text of *The Rationale of Punishment,* include "variability," "equability," "commensurability," "characteristicalness [sic]," "exemplarity," "frugality," "subserviency [sic] to reformation," "efficacy with respect to disablement," "subserviency to compensation," "popularity," "simplicity of description," and "remissibility." The only addition that this book makes to the list described within *Introduction to the Principles of Morals and Legislation* is the category of "simplicity of description," although that theme is implied by other passages within that book. Likewise, Bentham demonstrates, within both books, his obsession with categorization, making all elements of his system

identifiable in terms of type, purpose, and other shared and unshared properties. It is this aspect of his approach that has given his utilitarian philosophy a veneer of a scientific approach that would be found to be so
appealing to other, including later, utilitarian scholars, especially in the area
of law and jurisprudence.[11]

However, despite the acknowledgement of these broad similarities,
The Rationale of Punishment is not a mere recapitulation and occasional
elaboration upon those same themes found within *Introduction to the Principles of Morals and Legislation*. Its differences are subtle but they also are
profound. In order to appreciate that distinction, it is important to examine,
further, the characteristics that distinguish these works from each other and
from other publications of the Bentham canon.

An Indirect Collaboration

The source of these distinctions may be found in the claim that the definitive version of *The Rationale of Punishment* that was published in 1830
(and largely reprinted within the subsequent *Complete Works* that were
compiled under John Bowring) may not represent the exclusive interpretations of a single contributor. Many of Bentham's books were the result of a
compiling of manuscripts on various subjects by other utilitarian scholars.
Although these scholars were devoted followers of Bentham who sought to
repeat, rather than transform, his ideas, their imprint could have had a significant influence upon the final published version of these books.[12] It is the
nature of political communication that all reality must be translated through
various media, including the media of the human senses and the medium of
the brain's own ability to transcribe ideas, internally.[13] Therefore, the
process of transcribing, compiling, editing, and, potentially, interpreting
and adding to these manuscripts could have resulted in an entire category
of published materials that reflect not just Bentham's specific ideas but the
evolution of his thought through the auspices of a second generation of utilitarian scholars.[14]

The Rationale of Punishment arguably falls under that category. This
book resulted from the compilation of a series of manuscripts and notes, most
of which, as previously noted, had been written by Bentham between 1774
and 1776.[15] These manuscripts were assembled and edited, primarily, by two
persons: Richard Smith and Etienne Dumont. These two men would play
such an intimate role in the process of publishing many of Bentham's writings in this area that it may be reasonable to regard them almost as collaborators on certain published works, including *The Rationale of Punishment*.[16]

Etienne Dumont was a former religious minister and a political refugee from Geneva who had come under the patronage (like Bentham) of the Marquis of Lansdowne. Dumont met Bentham, became acquainted with his writings in French, and quickly became one of his most ardent and active supporters. The correspondence that took place between the two men bears evidence of that relationship. Dumont was captivated by Bentham's utilitarian doctrines and felt that they were particularly adaptable (perhaps more adaptable) to the Continent than to Britain. He became, therefore, very active in translating Bentham's writings for publication on the Continent and relatively more successful, in that respect, than Bentham had been within the United Kingdom.[17]

Dumont's most notable contribution to Bentham's writings appears to have been in consolidating and reorganizing his manuscripts, which often suffered from wordiness, redundancy, and extensive analogies. In the process of that consolidation, however, it is not clear whether he substantively reshaped these writings, including in terms of interpretation. He published three editions of this treatise as part of a two-volume set with a French version of *The Rationale of Reward* in 1811, 1818, and 1832. Certainly, a careful reading of the French editions of these books (particularly the 1818 edition, which appears to have been the one that was most directly consulted by Richard Smith) indicates that they were not direct translations of the manuscripts that appear within the 1830 English edition.[18]

Much less is known about the contributions of Richard Smith. He was diligent in transcribing Bentham's original manuscripts, especially on the subject of punishment and penal law. Most of the available manuscripts that offer an "original" text for *The Rationale of Punishment* are, in fact, supposedly copies of Bentham's original manuscripts that were transcribed by Smith. He also reportedly was responsible for many of the transcriptions that were included within the collected works that were edited by John Bowring after Bentham's death. Despite his primary professional responsibilities as a government bureaucrat, Smith may have become a crucial medium through which many of Bentham's ideas have been revealed.[19]

As already inferred, a principal objection to the relevance of *The Rationale of Punishment* is that it accomplishes little more than an expansion upon themes and ideas that have been addressed, more than sufficiently, in *Introduction to the Principles of Morals and Legislation*. But there are three crucial distinctions that make *The Rationale of Punishment* an indispensable contribution, not only for utilitarian philosophy but for the critique of penal law, especially within countries that have adopted the institutional framework of the common law system. First, its scope, while occasionally repetitive and pedantic (which is typical of Bentham's writing), is comprehensive. This point can be illustrated through a comparison of *The Rationale of Punishment* with those sections of *Introduction to the Principles of Morals and Legislation* that seem to parallel it.

Each subject that is addressed in both books is addressed in greater detail, with more explanation, and with reference to more analogies in *The Rationale of Punishment*. This process sometimes resulted in mere elaboration. However, sometimes it resulted in a more substantive expansion. For example, chapter VII of book I of *The Rationale of Punishment* offers a far more extensive discussion of analogy as a basis for punishment than any of Bentham's other published sources on punishment, while the entirety of book IV attempts to provide a seamless demonstration of the application of Bentham's general theory to every conceivable category of punishment and penal law.

Second, the focus of *The Rationale of Punishment* is as dedicated to the role of the judge within this system as it is to the role of the legislator, which is a very significant departure from the overall theme of *Introduction to the Principles of Moral and Legislation*.

Many examples of this distinctive focus upon the role of the judge can be found within *The Rationale of Punishment*. A good one occurs in book VI, chapter I, in which the discretion of the judge is evaluated in terms of an analytical framework of options that are intended to replace the presumably arbitrary inclinations of judges that they often would support by reference to the "ancient principles" that Blackstone expounded within his classic writings upon the subject.[20] Indeed, throughout this book, references to the "improper" role of judges in assigning punishment are mentioned by Bentham. Just one passing example is his reference to "misseated" punishment: "When, in so far as by appointment of the legislator or of the Judge, acting (as in all cases of unwritten or judge-made law) in the place of the legislator, punishment is inflicted on any person by whom no part has been borne in the offence, it may be said to be mis-seated [*sic*]: seated in a place which is not its proper place."[21]

Third, it offers an overarching comment on the penal law that comes closer to approaching a moral, rather than a strictly rational, tone than generally can be found (or is supposed to be found) within Bentham's other writings. Bentham's utilitarianism was adamantly opposed to normative moral systems and arguments. Therefore, this claim may require an acceptance of the collaborative (and not just editorial) contributions of Dumont and Smith to the final published version of *The Rationale of Punishment*. It is supported particularly by the generally critical spirit of the work—not simply a critique of the lack of reason supporting the traditional reverence for common-law norms but also a commentary on the apparent, specific examples of cruelty that the penal system has, in fact, produced. The tone of the first chapter and its description of punishment as an absolute, but necessary, "evil" offer such an indication. Bentham uses similar language within *Introduction to the Principles of Morals and Legislation*. But a distinctively different emphasis within *The Rationale of Punishment* is subtly present.

> Punishment then is an *evil*—that is, a physical evil; either of pain, or a loss of pleasure, or else of that situation or condition of the party affected, which is the immediate cause of such pain or loss of pleasure. It is an evil resulting from the *direct* intention of another. It is not punishment, if it be obliquely intentional on the part of the person from whose agency it results, but an evil of some other nature, but which, however, is not in all cases distinguished by a specific name.[22]

Another example of this tone can be found within chapter III of book I, which addresses the theme of analogous punishment.

> In the fabrication of base coin, the art of the delinquent may furnish an analogous source of punishment. He has made an impression upon the metal he has employed;—a like impression may be made on some conspicuous part of his face. This mark may be either evanescent or indelible, according as the imprisonment by it is to be accompanied is either temporary or perpetual.[23]

It is possible to argue that Bentham was deliberately employing sarcasm, in this instance, to reinforce his overarching conviction on this matter, which Dumont distinctly implies. But another distinct possibility is that Dumont or, perhaps, even Smith reconstructed these analogies to be portrayed in such a brutal way. They may have been appalled at Bentham's suggestion that torture could be justified under certain circumstances (such as uncovering guilt and protecting the innocent from unwarranted punishment) and so sought to present these specific passages in a way that might suggest this satirical interpretation.[24]

THE HEDONIC CRITIQUE AND A UTILITARIAN THEORY AND "TONE" OF LEGAL JUSTICE

Bentham's utilitarianism has been criticized, traditionally, for lacking a fundamental conception of justice.[25] This absence supposedly was rectified within the utilitarian writings of John Stuart Mill. This criticism is grounded upon the "hedonic" calculus that informed Bentham's principles and their application. The underlying assumption of that calculus is that every human is motivated to pursue a pleasure that is self-defined and, therefore, necessarily subjective. A calculation based upon objective criteria of pleasure or happiness is not only impossible to determine but also must be based upon normative standards that cannot be proven but, merely, asserted.[26]

That hedonic impression of early utilitarian thought, in particular, has been a source of philosophical criticism. According to this objection, Bentham and his method created a philosophical matrix that would permit (if not necessitate) the sacrifice of the good of a minority of people to a competing and, very possibly, mutually exclusive good of the majority. Some scholars have argued that this conclusion is not, necessarily, true. But even if such an interpretation of Bentham's direct writings becomes widely accepted, the writings, themselves, make no such express allowance.[27]

Therefore, an assumption is present, throughout his most popular writings that touch upon crime and punishment, that crime always will be present to some degree. That presence would remain, even if deterrence and improved socio political and economic circumstances prompt its decline. That assumption emphasizes the measurable effectiveness of punishment as a necessary infliction of pain, rather than as a deviation from an ideal avoidance of pain and it remains, admittedly, present within *The Rationale of Punishment*.[28]

Nonetheless, a different tone is present within that particular treatise. This tone appears to reflect a more skeptical attitude regarding the necessity of certain types of punishment (and, at times, punishment, itself) than Bentham's previous publications on the subject. The word "publications," rather than "writings," must be stressed in this respect; while the definitive English publication of *The Rationale of Punishment* did not appear until 1830, it was based upon a collection of manuscripts, many of which were written as early as 1775, around the time of the publication of *A Fragment on Government*. That early period of Bentham's philosophical development, in particular, was one of certainty in the rational superiority of utility. It was, for him, a tool of political and legal policy that could transcend the arbitrary principles that had been responsible for English jurisprudence, especially as previously expounded by the writings of Sir William Blackstone.[29]

But the tone of *The Rationale of Punishment*, as a published whole, exhibits, at times, a sense of moral sympathy for victims of crime. More interestingly, it appears, at times, to exhibit a certain amount of sympathy for the subjects of punishment, too. This sentiment is, entirely, consistent with Bentham's utilitarianism in terms of the regrettable quality of pain. However, pain appears to be presented as an inevitable quality, also, within his writings. Therefore, a tendency to treat pain as not only unfortunate but undesirable arguably offers a subtle, yet powerful, distinction in connection with his writings, although the detection of such moral qualms are, admittedly, a contentious interpretation of Bentham's utilitarianism.[30] Therefore, it also is possible to contend that such a presence may not have been the result of Bentham's unadulterated intention. The presence of any indication of that latter tendency within various passages of *The Rationale of Punishment* may be a result of an editorial contribution on the part of those disciples who compiled, translated, edited, and completed this text from the disparate manuscripts of its original author.

The effect of translation, alone, can account for differences in the meaning that can be conveyed from a written treatise. As previously noted, *The Rationale of Punishment* originally was the result of the editorial efforts of Pierre Étienne Louis Dumont. Although he was an enthusiastic convert to utilitarianism and a devoted disciple of Bentham, Dumont represented a continental perspective. Reportedly, he never sought to do more than translate Bentham's works. However, he was compelled to condense certain writings (a particular necessity, at times, given the pedantic nature of Bentham's writing style) as well as supplement omissions.[31] This sort of supplementary work may have been influenced by his previous career as he had prepared for the Calvinist ministry in Geneva. Certainly, his devotion for that city remained with him, especially as he strived to develop a liberal penal code with assistance from the advice that Bentham provided him on the subject, especially between 1816 and 1829.[32]

Dumont developed a close relation with Bentham in other ways, too, especially as he sought to spread his works, throughout the Continent. His praise for Bentham's manuscripts could be exultant.[33] Unfortunately, this amity would deteriorate, late in both of their lives, reportedly as a result of Bentham's belief that Dumont had misinterpreted many of his theoretical concepts, although other, more personal anecdotes also are offered as an explanation of this rift.[34] Even before that rift occurred, there were practical difficulties in their working relations, with Dumont frequently entreating Bentham to provide additional assistance and insight for the purpose of interpreting his manuscripts, while Bentham complained that Dumont was supposed to "take my half-finished manuscripts as he found them—half English, half English-French, and make what he could of them in Genevan-French, without giving me any further trouble about the matter. Instead of that, the lazy rogue comes to me with everything that he writes, and teazes [*sic*] me to fill up every gap he has observed."[35]

Dumont, for his part, described the difficulties in preparing Bentham's manuscripts for publication (such as his efforts on behalf of the *Bibliothèque britannique*) because they were so "fort obscurs et sans ordre."[36] The result could be a confusion regarding the ultimate source for some of these ideas as presented within the final versions of these writings as Dumont presented them, especially because Bentham professed "that there has been no time for anything like a compleat [*sic*] review: so that I may not be charged with the responsibility of ideas that, whether they were mine or no are not so *now*."[37] Bentham elsewhere acknowledged the practical need to give Dumont latitude in publishing his writings concerning reform of the penal code,[38] especially given the practical necessities imposed by the process of translation, as Dumont reminded Bentham, more than once.[39] Nonetheless, Bentham professed general contentment with the published French versions of his works in this area, despite these difficulties.[40]

Dumont's love of republican liberty also may be surmised from his devotion to the cause of liberty for his native city—an attitude shared by his fellow citizen Jean Jacques Rousseau.[41] He was forced to leave that city because of "political troubles" and became a friend of another of Bentham's devoted disciples and political proponents, Sir Samuel Romilly.[42] His devotion to this political cause for his native city was revealed through his efforts to persuade the French government to help restore Genovese sovereignty by repudiating the treaty between France and Switzerland that prevented the republic from enacting new laws without the consent of the parties to this treaty. Therefore, it is conceivable that Dumont may have been affected by both republican thought and a strong Christian conception of good and evil, especially as he also served as a writer for Honoré Gabriel Riquetti, Comte de Mirabeau.[43] That experience may have influenced his approach to the task of translating, editing, and completing select texts of Bentham, despite his attraction for the dispassionate methods that his utilitarian philosophy represented.[44]

Also as previously noted, much less is known about Richard Smith. He was a civil servant and another of Bentham's young and enthusiastic disciples. He was mentioned as being in the employ of the "Stamps and Taxes Office" of the British government, although the precise capacity is not certain.[45] Obviously, his enthusiasm extended to a willingness to engage in an involved process of transcribing manuscripts, translating previously published French texts, and preparing this material for publication. He is credited with having edited many of the texts for John Bowring's early definitive edition of Bentham's works, although the quality of that effort has been subject to criticism.[46] The responsibility for comparing original English manuscripts with Dumont's French translations represented a particularly impressive effort, especially in the frequent cases in which no original manuscript was available for engaging in such a comparison.

Bentham noted this difficulty, particularly as Smith's translations were based upon Dumont's manuscripts, rather than his final published French edition, which Smith never read.[47] Nonetheless, Bentham indicated great trust in Smith's abilities. He described him as a "very worthy man" and was concerned that his work on these manuscripts and translations "might be prejudicial to him, were the part he takes in it known to higher powers,"[48] presumably because of his position as a civil servant who was supposed to be, officially, neutral regarding matters of public policy.

The process of translation, by itself, is a persistent source of reinterpretation. Not only can words acquire different meanings, but syntax, emphasis, phrasing, and structural features can be understood in ways that are subtly different from one language to another one.[49] The symbolic effect of language also is severely affected by translation, thus exacerbating this effect. Language is epistemological, affecting the very manner in which people think, as well as communicate.[50] Therefore, differences regarding the understanding of ideas and the conveying of "tone" are readily understood within that linguistic context. Bentham also recommended Smith to Dumont while acknowledging that the two disciples had never met and that Dumont was, most likely, unaware of Smith's credentials for performing this sort of work. At the same time, Bentham noted potential conflicts of interpretation between the two editors but sought to assure Dumont that he was aware of them and taking steps to correct any such discrepancies.[51] However, Bentham also acknowledged that Smith's task would be complicated by other problems of interpretation, given the fact that, regarding the subject of punishment and penal policy, Bentham's "present opinions being on I know not how many points so different from what they were then."[52]

Translation between the English and French languages can be particularly susceptible to these challenges, especially regarding highly theoretical concepts, such as the law provides.[53] For example, the English word representing "right" is translated as "*droit*" in French. However, that French word also can be translated, back into English, as "right" or "legal authority," or, even, as "law" in general. Furthermore, concepts such as a "civil right," as distinct from a "human right," cannot be readily translated into French. That distinction does not exist, technically, within the French language. There is a single category of "rights," in the theoretical legal sense, within that linguistic tradition; the term "*droit civile*" refers to the civil law system, rather than civil rights, in French. Many other, less dramatic but equally significant differences in meaning (especially both legally and philosophically) result from translation between these two languages.[54]

But, aside from the inevitable influence of translation regarding the tone of a manuscript, it is possible to argue that other forces are at work, in this respect, regarding this more thorough exposition of utilitarian thought concerning penal law and policy. First, this book was not, solely, the product of translation and transcription of an original manuscript. Dumont provided text for the frequent lacunae found within these manuscripts. It is possible that Smith provided additional lacunae to account for gaps that may have been found between the original manuscripts and Dumont's published edition.[55] Even though Bentham reportedly reviewed the completed text and approved of it as reflecting his ideas, accurately, it is highly conceivable that the subtle subtext that this rephrasing presented was not, necessarily, noticed or appreciated by him, especially when he reviewed the final French draft. Even after reviewing the retranslation back into English that Smith provided (excepting the surviving Bentham manuscripts that he merely transcribed), it is not apparent that such a subtle shift in emphasis or interpretation would, necessarily, have been noticed by the primary author. This expectation could be strengthened by the fact that the primary author was, at this point, not only advanced in age but also within two years of his death.

It is feasible that Bentham's emphasis, upon reviewing these reconstructed editions, would have been upon the accurate reflection of the essential thesis regarding both pain and its measurement. The concept that pain must be measured upon the basis of several different criteria adds a normative content to a system that remains subjective and, also (as loosely articulated), "scientific." That principle has been, of course, the basis upon which Bentham sought to remove nonrational influences from the process of public policy and law. But traits such as "intensity" and "popularity" necessarily suggest potential value judgments that, while not generally entertained by Bentham, may have influenced the approach of Dumont and Smith toward the interpretation and reconstruction of this treatise.

Book III, chapter I uses the word "privilege" within the manuscript (reportedly in Bentham's handwriting) after crossing out the word "rights," in referring to corporation privileges. It appears in Dumont's edition as *droits*, which can be translated as either "rights" or "privileges" or, more generally, "law." Book III, chapter V reveals a tendency to emphasize different words and phrases between the two disciples, such as Smith's emphasis (in the apparent absence of Bentham's manuscript) upon the word "incorporeal," which Dumont does not emphasize, and Dumont's emphasis upon the phrase *"entité actuels."* Likewise, rather than using the word "*rang*," Dumont employs the broader word "*dignité*" (with its, arguably, more particular continental meaning) while Smith's edition, at that parallel point of the text, uses the more precise word of "rank." Book V, chapter III is particularly interesting in this respect, because it is written in the third person within the editions of both Smith and Dumont. In its explanation of the benefits of the idea for a prison (Bentham's Panopticon), it offers a portrait that does not merely emphasize its efficiency but also suggests compassion toward its inmates. Indeed, the manuscript in Smith's handwriting added a phrase (not found within Dumont's edition) that, though not included within the published text, exemplified this sense of sympathy upon his part: "The Porter will be no stronger than his flock: they are objects of him daily: they are the objects of his daily solicitude; he watches the prospect of their amendment and stands as their mediator and patron between them and their superior."[56] Likewise, Dumont's edition adds a moral commentary within this chapter (which was translated by Smith and included within his edition) when he quotes Molière: "Oh Virtue! where wilt thou hide thyself."[57]

These extracts offer only a few examples of the somewhat more intrinsic and moral tone of this work. The overall text is replete with additional (though, admittedly, often equally subtle) examples, as well as an underlying sentiment that appears to be present throughout it. Again, tone is an exacerbating quality to demonstrate, let alone prove, empirically.[58] Nonetheless, certain specific examples of the text offer more tangible insights in this respect. The most explicit evidence of this nuanced contribution to the interpretation of utilitarian thought within this book is provided within book I, chapter VIII. Dumont added a lengthy note to that chapter, carefully noted by Smith, which appears to qualify the amoral calculus of Bentham's method. Although it has been observed that Bentham read the editions of both Dumont and Smith and did not object to them, this note deviates from the tone of Bentham's previous writings on this subject. Dumont added this note to the end of the chapter that addressed analogous punishment, seemingly as a corrective to the harsh nature of many of the examples of punishment (described in the spirit of "an eye for an eye") that were described under this category.

> Everything ought also to be avoided which as an appearance of great study and refinement. Punishment ought only to be inflicted of necessity, and with feelings of regret and repugnance. The multitude of instruments possessed by a surgeon, may be contemplated with satisfaction, as intended to promote the cure and lessen the weight of our sufferings. The same satisfaction will not, however, be felt in contemplating a variety of punishments, and they will most likely be considered as degrading to the character of the legislator.[59]

Other, more subtle examples of this interpretive license can be found throughout the text. Book IV (which addresses "mis-seated punishment") offers, perhaps, the best examples. It provides descriptions of punishments that are imposed upon or, otherwise, adversely affect persons other than the offenders and evaluates the effect of such punishments. Bentham insists that avoidable punishments of this category do not conform to the purposes of utility, especially because they constitute an evil that produces no good result, either in terms of "reformation, determent, disablement."[60] Nonetheless, he entertains the possibility of a greater good resulting from an unavoidable inflicting of pain upon those persons who are not directly connected to an offence, although he disproves that possibility through various examples. Nonetheless, Bentham does address possible exceptions to this deficiency, even extending the theme to the "punishment" inflicted upon innocent civilians in time of war.

> In speaking of vicarious punishment, in order to avoid the confusion that might be produced by its liability to be ranked under this head, it may be necessary to mention a case belonging to the subject of international law. The case of reprizals [*sic*] in war. By a foreign nation, innocent persons are subjected to the most rigorous punishment—to confinement, and even to death, the real author of the offence not being in the jurisdiction of the foreign state. The exercise of this power is justified by necessity, as a means of preventing the infliction of injuries not warranted by the rules of war.
>
> This is not strictly speaking vicarious punishment. The reprizals inflicted on his subjects, operate upon the Sovereign himself, either by the compassion felt for their suffering, or by the fear, if patiently submitted to, of alienating the affections of his people. It is more particularly useful between contending armies. Honour is the principal sanction of the laws of war, but the power of making reprizals is a very necessary coadjutor. In these cases, what humanity dictates, is, that the sufferings inflicted on the innocent should be the least possible, consistent with the production of the desired effect, that they should be remissible, and that the utmost degree of publicity should be given to them, either by public declarations or in any other more effectual manner.[61]

Dumont's edition added, at this point, a further comment: "This law is yet justified by necessity, so to speak, in the case where there is not another method for repressing unusual violence, or for stopping acts of injustice."[62] It appears to be an admission of the overall distasteful quality of punishment. It arguably represents an underlying desire to avoid punishment, entirely, if the circumstances of a grossly imperfect society could allow for that possibility.

Ironically, a better indication of this shift in tone may be provided by those passages in which the different editions diverge. Again, book IV offers an excellent example. At one point, section 5 offers two versions. Neither of these versions can be compared to the original manuscript, which is missing for this section. Nonetheless, Smith's version may have been based upon Bentham's manuscript, especially given the fact that the remainder of the manuscript is in his handwriting and the fact that he does not translate Dumont's edition, suggesting that the parallel passage may represent a lacuna on his part. On the other hand, in the absence of a manuscript for the entire chapter, it is very possible that Smith's edition was compelled to provide a bridge at this point in the text. That bridge would have to be based either upon Dumont's previous version or upon Smith's best estimate of Bentham's meaning for this text as filtered through his own perspective as a disciple of Bentham's utilitarianism. Therefore, differing versions that are derived from the English and French drafts may suggest this sort of original contribution upon the part of the compilers.

> The end of punishment, is to restrain a man from delinquency. The question is, whether it be an advantageous way of endeavouring at this, to punish in any, and what cases, in any, and what mode, to any, and what degree, his wife, his children, or other descendants; that is, with a direct intention to make them sufferers.
>
> If a man can be prevented from running into delinquency, by means of punishment hung over the heads of persons thus connected with him, it is not, as in the cases above-mentioned, because it is expected that they should have it in their power to restrain him, by any coercion, physical or mental, of their imposing. It is not that they are likely to have it in their power, by anything they can do. In the case of the wife, it is not very likely: in the case of children already born, it is still less likely: in the case of children not yet born, it is impossible. What is expected to work upon him, is the image of what they may he made to *suffer*. The punishment then upon theme may be, and it is expected will be, without any act of theirs, a punishment upon him. It will produce in him a pain of sympathy.
>
> First, we will consider the case of the wife, where the punishment consists in being made to lose what is already in specific prospect: viz. The immoveable property in which she had her dower.
>
> It has been doubted whether it were possible for a man to love another better than himself; that is to be affected, not merely momentarily, but for a length of time together, more by the pains and pleasures of another than by his own. Some have denied the possibility, all will admit that it is extremely rare. Suppose it then to happen in one case out of five hundred, and to do all possible honour to the marriage state, let us suppose that this person whom a man loves better than he does himself, is never any other than his wife. But it is not so many as half the number

of men of an age to commit crimes, that have wives. Nor is there above one in a hundred who has lands of which a wife is endowed. Upon this calculation, there is not above one man in 50,000 of those that are liable to this mode of punishment, on whom it would operate in as great a degree as if laid on himself. In the remaining 49,999 instances, in order to produce the same effect, more punishment must be laid upon the innocent wife, than would need to be laid upon the offending husband. Let us suppose, for the purpose of the argument, that every man loves his wife half as much as he does himself, on this supposition, ten degrees or grains (or by what other name soever it shall be thought proper to call so many aliquot parts of punishment, must be laid upon the wife, in order to produce) the effect of five grains laid directly upon the husband. On this supposition, then in 49,999 out of 50,000, half the punishment that is laid on in this way, is laid in waste.

What has been said with regard to the wife, may, without any very considerable variation, be applied to the children. In this latter case, however, generally speaking, the affection is likely to be more uniform and certain, and consequently the contemplation of the suffering they may be exposed to more certainly effacious [*sic*], in restraining the commission of the act intended to be guarded against. The same method, making due allowance on this score, will therefore apply to this, as to the preceding case.

What follows from this, therefore, is that till the whole stock of direct punishment be exhausted upon the offender himself; none ought in this way to be attempted to be applied through the medium of the innocent.

* It will not, it is hoped, be understood that any stress is meant to be laid upon the particular number here employed: the reader may put in numbers for himself: they are merely given as a specimen of the manner in which such an enquiry ought to be conducted.[63]

Dumont's version of this passage is different. Again, it could represent a necessary supplement to a missing original manuscript. Therefore, this difference could be a reflection of different attempts upon the part of Smith and Dumont to deduce an interpretation of this utilitarian theme of Bentham as *they*, each, interpreted it.

Let us not enter into this polemic. Let us leave alone this shameful jargon. Let us see what one could say for justifying these transitive punishments.

After my personal punishment, a punishment which falls upon those who are my loved ones is again a punishment against me. I participate in the suffering of those to whom I am attached with the most kindness. I can face the evils that would be only for me: I can be restrained by the fear to involve in my ruin those who are the first objects of my affections.

Punishments against the family of a delinquent are thus punishments against himself.

This principle is true: but is it good? does it conform to utility?

Asking whether a sympathetic punishment is as effective as a direct punishment is to ask whether the attachment that one bears for others is as strong as self-love.

If self-love is the stronger sentiment, it follows that one must resort to sympathetic punishments only after having suffered all that human nature can suffer in inflicting direct punishments. No torture is so cruel that one must not employ, before punishing the wife for the deeds of the husband, and the children for the deeds of the father.[64]

Therefore, other language within Smith's final published edition of the book understandably reflects a similar tension. It would be reasonable to expect that he certainly would be faithful to Bentham's text in all instances in which the original manuscripts is available. However, in the absence of a verbatim record, his own understanding of the meaning (and the overall goal) of these ideas would need to be substituted, as any attempt at reconstruction inevitably tends to produce.

Were we indeed to enquire minutely into the distinction between the nature of the political and moral sanctions, it would come out that, of the evils which when considered as issuing from the moral sanction I have stiled [sic] casual evils, some are even more likely to be brought upon a man by the action of one of these sanctions, and some others by that of the other. But as to the species of the evil, this is all the distinction we shall be able to make out; for there is not any evil which the exertion of one of these forces may bring upon a man, but which may also be brought upon him by the action of the other.

The most studied and artificial torments, for instance, that can be invented by a political magistrate, and the most unlikely for a man to be exposed to suffer by the unassisted powers of nature, or even from the unauthorized resentment of an individual, are what he may by accident be exposed to from the latter source. It may be for want of some evidence that an individual might furnish, and from ill-will forbears to furnish, that I may have been doomed to these torments by a Judge; or if the like torments be supposed to be inflicted by the unauthorized violence of an enemy, they may be attributed in the first place indeed to the vengeance of that enemy; but in the second place, to the dis-esteem [sic] and ill-will borne me by some stranger, who having it in his power to rescue me, yet exasperated against me on account of some real or supposed instance of immorality in my behaviour, chose rather to see me suffer than to be at the pains of affording me his assistance.

On the other hand, the whole sum of the evils depending upon the moral sanction, to wit, not only the casual evils, but the sense of infamy which constitutes the characteristic evil, is liable in many instances to be brought upon a man by the doom of the political magistrate. This is what we have found it unavoidably necessary, on various occasions, to give imitation of, and what we shall have need more particularly to enlarge upon hereafter.[65]

Therefore, a subtle moral tone within the published editions of both Dumont and, ultimately, Smith that reveals a subtle moral vision (despite Bentham's disinclination in this respect) is very possible. This distinction may be subtle but it reoccurs, persistently. Furthermore, it is not, necessarily, consistent; the tone often seems to shift from analysis to commentary. Of course, Bentham disapproved of the arbitrary nature of eighteenth-century English law as it had been conveyed to him through the Inns of Court, the writings of Blackstone on the common law, and the penal policies of the British government. But *The Rationale of Punishment* appears, within certain places, to exhibit a feeling of regret regarding the need for punishment as, perhaps, a "necessary evil."

The way in which capital punishment is addressed within this book appears, likewise, to betray a sentiment that strays from the dispassionate calculation toward a sense of moral disapproval. A subtle sense of regret also appears to accompany the descriptions of this ultimate punishment within both editions. This chapter is missing from the manuscripts and appears at a different location of the text within Dumont's edition. But the sentiment is similar within the published English version.

> The only reason that can be given by any government, that persists in continuing to employ a mode of punishing so highly penal, is, that the habitual condition of the people is so wretched that they are incapable of being restrained by a more lenient kind of punishment.
>
> Will it be said that crimes are more frequent in countries in which punishments such as those in question are unknown. The contrary is the fact. It is under such laws that the most ferocious robbers are found: and this is readily accounted for. The fate with which they are threatened hardens them to the feelings of others as well as their own. They are converted into the most bitter enemies, and every barbarity they inflict is considered as a sort of reprisal.
>
> Upon this subject, as upon so many others, Montaigne was far beyond the age in which he lived. All beyond simple death (he says) appears to me to be cruelty. The legislator ought not to expect that the offender that is not to be deterred by the apprehension of death, and by being beheaded and hanged, will be more effectually deterred by the dread of being exposed to a slow fire, or the rack. And I do not know indeed but that he may be rendered desperate.*

*Liv. ii. ch. 27.—*Cowardice the mother of cruelty.*

Et lapus et turpes instant morientibus ursi Et quæcunque minor nobilitate fera est.

OVID.[66]

The last paragraphs of this chapter offer a description of torture and capital punishment as practiced in the West Indies against slaves. It does not comment, directly, upon the morality of slavery, itself. However, it does strongly suggest a tone of normative moral disapproval that is, generally, missing from Bentham's treatises.

> At the same time, what admits of very little doubt is, that the defenders of these punishments, in order to justify them, exaggerate the miseries of slavery, and the little value set by the slaves upon life. If they were really reduced to such a state of misery as to render necessary laws so atrocious, even such laws would be insufficient for their restraint; having nothing to lose, they would be regardless of all consequences; they would be engaged in perpetual insurrections and massacres. The state of desperation to which they would be reduced would daily produce the most frightful disorders. But if existence is not to them a matter of indifference, the only pretence that there is in favour of these laws falls to the ground. Let the colonists reflect upon this; if such a code be necessary, the colonies are a disgrace and an outrage on humanity: if not necessary, these laws are a disgrace to the colonists themselves.[67]

Dumont's edition, interestingly, adds some text that is not found within Smith's edition. Its religious references are significant in this respect and may reflect his previous career as a Calvinist minister. It may suggest, further, a relationship between utilitarian and Christian principles that Bentham might not have pursued.

> Everyone knows the reasons for abolishing this category of death among Christian nations. *Felix culpa*, we would say, along with a father of the Church, in another sense, if the same reasoning had been used to abolish all other cruel tortures. The exposition of ferocious animals is one which the Gospels well sought to destroy. It was sustained under the Christian emperors. Valentinian would throw criminals into the pit of two bears, which, by a barbarian derision, was given the name of Scrap of Gold and of Innocence: and even to reward the services of one of these animals, when in contemplation of this ferocious appetite, he would set it at liberty in the forest. *Gibbon*, vol. IV, chap. XXV.[68]

Another section of text that appears within Dumont's edition adds a reference that, again, is omitted from Smith's edition and that suggests a concern for normative moral outcomes that is not usual for Bentham's writings.

> This is a work cited by Mallebranche. (*Recherche de la vérité*, book II, chap. VII.)
>
> 'Around seven or eight ago one could have seen, at the Incurables, a young man who was born insane, whose body had been broken in the same places in which one broke criminals. He lived nearly twenty years in that state: several people saw him there, and the late Queen Mother, having gone to visit the hospital, had been curious to see him, and even to touch the arms and legs of this young man at the places which had been fractured. According to the principles I have just established, the cause of this disastrous accident was that his mother, seeing how one broke a criminal, was content to see it carried out. All the blows inflicted upon this poor wretch, struck with imaginative force by this mother, and consequently upon the tender and delicate brain of this child, etc.[69]

Although the reason for this discrepancy cannot be known, absolutely, it is possible to surmise possible explanations. Bentham may have objected to the strong moral disapproval of these lacunae passages when Smith was preparing his edition (a disapproval he, apparently, did not convey when he approved of Dumont's French edition when it was first prepared for publication) and so Smith removed them. Nonetheless, they reinforce the moral tone that is found within other parts of this chapter and, indeed, both editions of this book. They further suggest that both Dumont and Smith may have engaged in an inevitable process of shifting, if only subtly, the emphasis of this application of utilitarian thought.

Part of the difficulty with this interpretation is based upon the larger context of Bentham's own perception of utility. One perception is that a utilitarian approach toward all public policy treats it as a "zero-sum game" in which the "greatest happiness" principle is the guiding force. However, other examples of Bentham's writing suggest that individual happiness is the ideal goal. Therefore, in a perfect society, the pleasure of all could be advanced and the infliction of pain upon any person could be avoided.[70]

That interpretation admittedly contrasts with a widely accepted notion of the overriding benefit of the community as a utilitarian theme that is emphasized in other writings by Bentham, especially *The Fragment on Government*. The promotion of the general benefit, according to that interpretation, may require the negation of a particular benefit to a group within that community. Thus the needs of the majority clearly appear to override the needs and, indeed, the individual rights of the minority.[71] On the other hand, in other writings, such as the *Pannomial Fragments*, Bentham appears to have emphasized individual desires to avoid various evils as a prime motivator and goal. The interest of the community is one that each member must accept or it is not, properly, a communal interest. This problem of tautology is one that early utilitarianism appeared unable to reconcile.[72] Therefore, it is possible that Bentham's disciples may have favored, indirectly, an approach to the editing and publication of Bentham's fragmented manuscripts that attempted to overcome that apparent contradiction.

Another way to approach this difficulty could have been through an emphasis upon the theme of the "natural harmony of interests." That theme was particularly evident within Bentham's writings on economic principles. However, it may not be useful as a means for understanding the interpretation of his penal theories because it appeared to be much less applicable to other areas of legislation, including punishment.[73] Bentham recognized the difficulties of this concept by acknowledging the competition of potentially conflicting understandings and goals of pleasure.[74] One solution is "forceable [sic] renunciation," though Bentham was, again, inconsistent on acknowledging this matter.[75] Bentham made this explicit point within other writings regarding penal policy.[76]

Overall, it is possible that Bentham's immediate disciples preferred the moral to the legal sanction so they made that preference a feature of their editorial interpretation of his unpublished writings. Given that premise, it is clearly understandable that Dumont made Le Théorie des Peines a companion to La Théorie des Recompenses. That approach may not be definitive but it also is far from inconsistent with other areas of Bentham's written work. Indeed, for Bentham, education became a particularly prominent strategy for reconciling these conflicting interests and, presumably, eliminating the need for government to inflict pain through punishment.[77] Penal legislation would become the "silken thread" that would guide, rather than compel, members of society toward compliance with the greatest pleasure of the community as a whole.[78] After all, the Panopticon was conceived for this purpose of rehabilitation through reeducation.[79]

PUNISHMENT AS AN INTRINSIC EVIL

Therefore, The Rationale of Punishment was especially relevant to Bentham and, even more so, for his disciples (including Dumont and Smith) who sought to apply it toward the ongoing process of political and legal reform within Great Britain and elsewhere. Yet, that book has not been republished in a thoroughly new edition for more than 175 years. That lack of apparent interest by both the popular and scholarly communities has been unfortunate because they have overlooked the profound contribution that this book offers toward that goal. Not only has it expanded upon the application of utilitarian principles to the realm of penal law but it also contributes to an understanding of the evolution of early utilitarianism. That understanding addresses the controversy, within this philosophical tradition, of the nature of "pain" as merely an analytically extrinsic "evil" or as an intrinsically "evil" condition that a government should, in a "perfect world," seek to avoid, entirely. The contention that a "second generation" of utilitarian thought helped to modify this aspect of its principles in this respect warrants further study and consideration.

The Rationale of Punishment ought to be as relevant to twenty-first-century public policy as it was to eighteenth- and early nineteenth-century policy. The adoption of "minimum sentencing laws," especially during the 1980s and 1990s, was prompted by concerns over rising crime rates.[80] Interestingly, rising crime rates in late eighteenth-century Great Britain led to a similar response, culminating in the infamous "Black Acts" that resulted in dozens of capital offences and a multitude of petty criminals who were sentenced to death under them.[81] The utilitarian movement was motivated, in large part, by the desire to find a philosophical critique of this excess that would offer an alternative without resorting to the sort of desert-oriented subjective moral standards that often had been used to justify these excessive punishments. Deterrence is the motive for punishment that has attracted the most attention in this respect; therefore, reference to a deterrent-based approach to punishment often receives overwhelming attention within scholarly treatments of utilitarian assessments of penal law and policy.[82] This tendency tends to persist, even though Bentham and other utilitarians have addressed other, reductionist purposes of punishment, including immediate protection of society and crime victims and the goal of rehabilitating criminals.[83]

The long-term attempt to replace a retributivist penal policy, based upon a subjective morality, with a reductionist (particularly a deterrence-oriented) policy that is claimed to be based upon "scientific" evaluations of human motivations, has prompted critical responses. One of the most persistent criticisms of utilitarian approaches to punishment concern the relationship that is drawn by some commentators between the trade-off of "pain" and "pleasure." This criticism is particularly directed toward a "rule utilitarian" perspective, as opposed to an "act utilitarian" perspective that trusts the rational choices of individual agents to produce "best consequences."[84] This rule-utilitarian approach is instrumentally oriented and attempts to arrive at a systemic arrangement of maximum good through institutional means that are imposed upon society. Conceivably, it is argued (though Bentham never explicitly makes this claim) that this utilitarian approach to penal law would tolerate the possibility of punishing an innocent person if the effect (in terms of promoting deterrence or increasing public feelings of security) produces a greater "good."[85] Indeed, it is argued that the utilitarian conceivably would approve of the punishment of a person who is known to be innocent as a calculated imposition of "pain" to achieve a greater social "pleasure."[86]

Another criticism leveled against the utilitarian approach to punishment (especially in terms of its seeming emphasis upon deterrence as a prime goal of penal policy) is its lack of a persuasive normative moral standard to counter the claims made upon a retributivist approach. The argument that punishment is a response to a social judgment about the offence committed toward the individual victim or the community (particularly in terms of desert) can be a powerful one, especially on an emotional level. Communitarian defenses of retributive penal policies can be particularly ardent in this respect.[87] The contrast of crime retribution with the utilitarian emphasis upon crime reduction and its seemingly sterile calculations can make that utilitarian argument seem unappealing, even if it is more satisfying from a purely intellectual position.[88]

Much of that criticism may be based upon a belief that the utilitarian vision of the human condition is grounded in a form of relativism, especially in terms of the hedonistic approach most often associated with Bentham and later utilitarians, such as John Stuart Mill[89] and Henry Sidgwick.[90] It also may be prompted by a related caricature of utilitarian reasoning that would lead to logical conclusions that could seem highly objectionable. This caricature contrasts this approach with concerns for the value of truth regarding the committing of crimes and subsequent determinations of guilt, innocence, and the ultimate justification of any act of punishment.[91] Yet a response to that criticism raises a potential paradox because the identification of a utilitarian principle that is grounded upon an intrinsic "higher morality" may undermine the utilitarian claim that it avoids the subjective and, arguably, arbitrary standards that motivate retributive claims.[92]

But because Bentham is perceived to have embraced a hedonistic interpretation of pleasure (as prominent scholars such as G. E. Moore have contended),[93] his calculations also are perceived to have accepted the relativism of individual definitions of pleasure. This interpretation is based upon a further contention that pleasure, itself, is intrinsically good (even if different sensations of pleasure do not even feel alike),[94] regardless of the motivation or form. These calculations could, legitimately (and admittedly within his own writings), extend to punishment derived from motivations that a subjective moral appraisal might conclude to be "base" or "cruel," including in terms of the approval of certain severe types of punishment. That emphasis can, understandably, create the impression that punishment should be tolerated as a means for reaching this maximum pleasure and be justified solely upon that basis, rather than upon considerations of subjective and unproven "higher truths," including, conceivably, matters of actual guilt or innocence.[95]

However, within *Introduction to the Principles of Morals and Legislation*, Bentham makes reference to a more detailed treatment of this subject that would provide a more considered application of utility to penal law and practice. That book presents these ideas in a slightly different, but potentially profound, manner and which are, arguably, relevant to the more focused arguments provided within *The Rationale of Punishment*. This difference of approach might offer a persuasive response to critics of the reductionist-based preferences of utilitarians. It also might address matters of guilt and innocence (and other "moral" considerations) in a way that challenges the ethical claims of advocates of retributivist approaches to punishment. It also could undermine, simultaneously, the perception of Bentham's calculations of pain and pleasure as being based upon a strictly hedonistic appreciation of this central concept.[96]

PROPORTIONALITY AND THE GOAL OF ELIMINATING THE NEED FOR PUNISHMENT

Reconciling competing "pleasures" is the key to public policy. The pursuit of pleasure by some persons can inflict pain upon other persons. A business transaction can result in a better deal (and more pleasure) for one participant than another one.[97] A crime can bring pleasure to the criminal but also can impose pain upon not only the immediate victims but to society (especially in terms of feelings of fear and insecurity) in general. The state has a responsibility to prevent the greater pain to individual and societal victims of crime by imposing the pain of punishment upon the people who commit these acts. However, that necessary imposition of pain should not be excessive; it should alleviate the pain that the initial act (or the potential of a repeat of that act) imposes, but it should not be more painful than necessary, since maximizing pleasure, for as many persons as possible, is the ultimate responsibility and goal of the state.[98]

Therefore, punishment should be "proportional" to the crime. "Proportionality" is, by definition, the establishment of a proper relationship between two or more competing conditions or goals. It involves a trade-off, for the utilitarian, which should result, ultimately, in more "pleasure" than "pain," both quantitatively and qualitatively. It should provide pleasure for the greater number of people but it also should provide the greatest possible quality of pleasure. By Bentham's own admission, this calculation of the quality of pain and pleasure is not an easy one. Nonetheless, it is one that must be applied to each agent who is included in these calculations.[99]

But Bentham appears to have treated the state, as an agent that also participates in this process, very differently. This distinction between the agents who commit crimes and the agent that punishes them is made apparent through the general way in which Bentham addressed his subjects. That approach includes the greater emphasis he appeared to place upon the need for justification that he applied to acts of the state in relation to actions of the sum of individual members of society who are governed by that state. Thus the state is, arguably, held to a "higher standard." Its monopoly of legitimate violence is not only necessarily constrained but it actually constitutes a pursuit of "pleasure," on behalf of society, in general (through penal imposition of pain), that is ethically inferior to the pursuit of pleasure by individual subjects of the law.[100]

Bentham expressed this distinction within the first paragraph of *The Rationale of Punishment* when he declared that "[p]unishment, whatever shape it may assume, is an *evil*."[101] The use of this word, assuming that it appears that way in the original manuscript, is particularly significant when contrasted with the emphasis that Bentham chose to employ in other references to penal law and policy within his writings.[102] The fact that this sentence appears to be so emphatic in designating punishment in that way may be very significant.

Bentham also used the word "evil" in reference to punishment in other sources, most notably in *Introduction to the Principles of Morals and Legislation*.[103] However, his use of this word within *The Rationale of Punishment* was more pointed and consistent. A footnote near the beginning of chapter XIII of *The Principles of Morals and Legislation* (at the precise point at which he refers to punishment as "evil")[104] indicates Bentham's intention to clarify this distinction. It also indicates his intention to address this general topic in much greater length and detail, and the subsequent publishing of these manuscripts under the direction of Etienne Dumont. This fact, and the tone of the subsequent manuscripts and book that were promised, might reveal a desire and, ultimately, a tendency, on Bentham's part, to treat punishment not only as a different category of pain but, perhaps, as a qualitatively different *kind* of pain.

Bentham, in using this word "evil," may not have been designating pain as merely instrumentally bad. This possibility exists, even though the explanation of this "evil" as "resulting to an individual from the direct intention of another, on account of some act that appears to have been done, or omitted"[105] appears to confirm that instrumentalist application.[106] Nonetheless, it also may connote an *intrinsic* valuation and designate punishment as a condition that transcends a normal understanding of "pain." Under that circumstance, its complete elimination, and not merely its reduction in relation to various pleasures or its role in advancing certain types of societal pleasures, would constitute an ideal goal, in itself, even if its implementation or threat of implementation can result in an instrumental good. That intrinsic, in addition to the instrumentalist, designation, offers a more profound meaning to Bentham's claim that "[a]ll punishment being in itself evil, upon the principle of utility, if it ought at all to be admitted, it ought only to be admitted in as far as it promises to exclude some greater evil."[107]

The *ideal* utilitarian society, from this perspective, is one in which this state-produced "pain" is *entirely* eliminated. Therefore, the government of such a society is one that has conceived of a means to promote "pleasure" in a way that not only eliminates causes and consequences of "pain" but also avoids, if at all possible, inflicting *any* "pain" as an end in itself. That goal is, of course, practically unattainable. But it does serve as the measurement of relative success in terms of applying utilitarian principles regarding matters of public policy, including penal policy. The government that is able to promote more pleasure and less pain than another government is, therefore, superior in this respect and comes closest to achieving the utilitarian ideal.

A logical conclusion can be drawn, in this respect, concerning the ideal conclusion of utilitarian philosophy. This conclusion could be reached, analogously, through an external, nonutilitarian philosophical appeal to the platonic conceptualization of "forms." This unarticulated suggestion of the theoretical possibility of an ideal utilitarian society, free from *any* punishment, is, admittedly, unattainable in the "real" world of Plato's "shadows." But it *is* attainable to the philosopher as a rationally conceived "form." Plato's normative quest for an ideal republic that cannot be experienced but only perceived through a superior application of reason offers a potentially appropriate model for understanding Bentham's apparent, though unstated, allusion to a modern unattainable philosophical and political goal.[108] A state that can promote pleasure without ever imposing pain arguably offers a similar standard for evaluating the ultimate ethical appropriateness of all penal actions of government.

Arguably, this approach to the interpretation of utilitarianism also offers a potential Aristotelian dimension. "Pleasure" can be identified as the ultimate end, or *telos*, of a modern government. If the utilitarian conceptualization of a state's *telos* is the promotion of pleasure, then the best possible government is one that achieves that end as perfectly as possible, thus avoiding the imposition of any pain. Even if no state is capable of attaining that end, perfectly, it is better than another state if it can promote the pleasure of society through the application of less pain than another state.[109]

Penal law rests upon the assumption that certain persons will seek their particular "pleasures" in a manner that will inflict various types of "pain" upon other persons and, indirectly, upon the general society. It also assumes that the only effective way to eliminate the "pain" that these persons will inflict in the course of this pursuit of their own "pleasure" is for that government to counter that "pain" with its own infliction of "pain." Because inflicting "pain" is, theoretically, anathema to the government that faithfully observes the utilitarian model, it is an action that is made necessary only because failure to inflict that "pain" upon the criminal will result in even greater "pain" to that person's victims and the generally well-being of society.[110]

Punishment is, therefore, a "necessary evil," because it imposes "pain," ironically, as a means of eliminating "pain" and, thus, increasing the capacity for the greatest number of persons to pursue "pleasure." Consequently, the logical result of this utilitarian conceptualization of penal law and policy is an approach that is both constrained and *absolutely* reluctant. If punishment is, indeed, "evil," then the ability of the state to advance pleasure for society without any recourse to it constitutes an ideal—perhaps, even, a "moral" ideal. That approach arguably constitutes, in turn, a platonic "form" or, perhaps, even a pre-Socratic notion of an ultimate "virtue," signified by the ideal of *archē* (a concept that also is conceived as an appeal to "first principles") from which all other moral concepts can be derived.[111]

These themes of "constraint" and "reluctance" lie, by implication, at the core of the utilitarian principle of proportionality of punishment, even though it is not explicitly identified or acknowledged in those terms. Ideally, no punishment should be inflicted upon anyone. If, however, that ideal is unattainable, then only the absolute least amount of "pain" (in the form of punishment) must be imposed in order to achieve the greater pleasure that this action seeks to achieve. In that way, the "pain" of punishment becomes proportional to the "pleasure" that it produces: minimal "pain" results in "maximum pleasure, so the utilitarian ideal is realized.[112]

Bentham distinguished different types of "pleasure" and assigned a hierarchy of preferential status regarding them. Interestingly, this approach appears to deviate from the more rigidly empirical emphasis that generally defines utilitarian thought. Rather than relying upon the initial *ontological* premise that all humans avoid pain and seek pleasure, regardless of qualitative differences in defining the conditions that constitute "pain" and "pleasure" for each person, Bentham appears to have attempted to avoid a simplistically homogeneous categorization of "pleasures." Some types of pleasure are alleged to be more useful than other types and, thus, preferential as a basis for determining the sorts of "pleasure" that a government generally should promote for society. These pleasures include ones that are achieved through the necessary imposition of "pain" upon persons whose actions would interfere with the experience of "pleasures" for other persons.[113]

Punishment, itself, can be used as a means of promoting a more useful "pleasure" for the persons upon whom it is imposed. But it is the actual calculation of appropriate, or proportional, punishment that becomes the core of the thesis of *The Rationale of Punishment*. Bentham places particular emphasis upon the quantification of this process, especially in terms of the varying, contributory sources of pleasure and pain that are considered. The pain of the offence must be weighed against the pain of the punishment, while the pleasure of the offender in committing the relevant offence is weighed against the pleasure of the public in preventing the crime or ameliorating its effects.[114]

This last category can be most significant. Bentham noted that the public desire to advance its "pleasure" regarding freedom from crime or the apprehension of crime, in terms of strict proportionality, might not be precisely attainable. Bentham acknowledged that "an error on the minimum side," in this respect, constitutes the "greatest danger" because it would render a punishment ineffective.[115] But Bentham then minimized the likelihood that this error will occur. It is the possibility of punishing too severely that constituted, for him, the outcome that should be most carefully avoided. The lack of strict proportionality ought, from Bentham's perspective, to favor the offender, again implying not just a pragmatic concern but suggesting the pain of punishment must be avoided as much as possible, if not entirely.

> An error on the maximum side [of punishment], on the contrary, is that to which the legislators and men in general are naturally inclined—antipathy, or a want of compassion for individuals who are represented as dangerous or vile, pushes them onward to an undue severity. It is on this side, therefore, that we should take the most precautions, as on this side there has been shewn [*sic*] the greatest disposition to err.[116]

Despite his pragmatic calculations, Bentham displayed a tendency to minimize punishment that suggests the possibility of characterizing this area of law and public policy as truly constituting an intrinsic, rather than merely an instrumental, evil. Granted, a few utilitarian commentators also have used the term "intrinsic evil" in reference to the general concept of punishment. However, their actual application of the concept generally has been directed toward a description of its instrumental or extrinsic effect.[117] They have not treated it as an evil in itself.

Of course, it also is far from clear that Bentham ever contemplated even the possibility of regarding punishment as a truly *intrinsic* evil, either. But it may be extremely useful to "tease" such an understanding out of his analysis, especially as it is presented within *The Rationale of Punishment*. That understanding could overcome the unfortunately persistent and misplaced criticism that a utilitarian scheme of penal law and policy treats punishment as merely a competing form of pain and an instrument to maximize pleasure that could justify the punishment of an innocent person. That conclusion clearly appears to be contrary to the spirit of this book and Bentham's entire intent regarding the reform of penal law.[118]

PENAL POLICY AND THE IDEAL GOAL OF THE ULTIMATE REDUCTION OF ALL PAIN

Furthermore, this understanding could provide a clearer standard. By establishing the intrinsic evil of punishment as a means of using its complete elimination as the ideal against which all penal law and policy can be measured, the proper proportionality of specific acts of punishment can be more readily evaluated. If punishment is intrinsically evil (so it should be avoided as much as absolutely possible), then the imposition of *any* punishment can be assessed in terms of whether or not a lesser punishment can achieve the same effect.[119] Also, this approach could gain the moral advantage that retributivist approaches to punishment enjoy in terms of an appeal to a higher ethical ideal (punishment as an absolute evil in itself) that can counter subjective claims that punishment is a moral consequence of desert. Utilitarian critiques of penal law and policy would not be perceived as calculations of sterile, rationally derived trade-offs of relative causes and consequences of pain and pleasure.[120] Instead, it can gain the dimension of appealing to a (admittedly utopian) desire to attain a higher goal of a platonic form in which all pleasure can be advanced and all pain can be abolished.

This argument might appear to be consistent with a variation of the philosophical tradition known as "negative utilitarianism." That variation also is based upon the maxim that, as an ideal goal, all pain should be avoided as an ethically simpler and more lucid path toward the ultimate maximization of human happiness. That argument consequently advances a perspective that the avoidance of pain is a qualitatively superior motivation than the pursuit of pleasure. A criticism of that approach has posited the notion that this desire would lead, logically, to a conclusion that it is better to eliminate human existence (thus avoiding the inevitable pain that accompanies it) than to promote it.[121]

That sort of extreme interpretation is inconsistent with the argument that is offered in connection with *The Rationale of Punishment*. As a matter of practical policy (in this case, in terms of penal law), the ideal by which the success of the action of the state toward crime and other offences is measured is one that evaluates whether pain in all forms (either as the motive for crime, its consequences for its direct and indirect victims, or the results of the actions taken against the offenders) has been avoided as much as absolutely possible. This policy emphasizes, as a rule, the elimination of pain as the means to achieve greater pleasure, particularly in terms of the elimination of crime as a means of promoting a more beneficial society.[122] The contest between the pain of crime and the pain of punishment is, therefore, a reflection of that emphasis. Rather than consider the expansive and nebulous promotion of the human condition as a whole, it ponders the more pragmatic management of a particular expression of human activity.[123]

In this case, though, the measure of success is guided by an ideal (the elimination of pain will permit the promotion of human pleasure) as an unstated but logically derived goal. Of course, that goal is never, actually, claimed by the author or contributors; on the contrary, any such goal as the elimination of the need for actual punishment is tacitly accepted as practically unachievable by Bentham and his editorial collaborators. Nonetheless, this idealist interpretation of the ultimate goal of a utilitarian penal policy is consistent with the tone that appears to emerge from this broader treatment of the subject. It may reflect a variation upon the interpretive theme of negative utilitarianism but it also reflects both an idealistic and a pragmatic philosophical approach to promoting actual legal and political reform that is particularly reflective of those "second generation" utilitarians who carried this tradition into the early and mid-nineteenth century.[124]

CONCLUSION

Therefore, *The Rationale of Punishment* is a book that persists in its relevance to modern society. That relevance is aided by the way in which the three considerations that have been posited enhance the understanding of this theory and its applicability to actual policy in this area. First, this book is more relevant than its limited publication history suggests. Second, its collaborative nature provides an interpretation that transcends a unitary philosophical perspective and suggests, instead, a step in an evolution of thought that can be further adjusted in response to actual experiences as well as theoretical ideals. Third, it provides a more rigorous (though, admittedly, impossibly idealistic) standard by which to measure the effectiveness of a particular penal policy, law, ruling, or practice as based upon an interpretation of punishment as intrinsically bad and, so, as a necessary evil that an ideal society should seek to eliminate.

This book does not offer only prescriptions but a change in attitude as the means of affecting that ultimate end. It is, therefore, a model of applied philosophy that should be reexamined and adapted to the debates that continue regarding the desire to prevent crime, compensate its victims, avoid unattractive and potentially self-destructive tendencies of human vindictiveness, and promote the paramount vision of a truly good society. *The Rationale of Punishment* may not be an absolutely comprehensive account of all of Bentham's manuscripts on the subject nor a thoroughly representative example of the evolving influence that subsequent generations of utilitarian scholars could bring to his ideas within this subject area. However, it may provide a more definitive understanding of the theory of punishment than any other primary treatise of utilitarian thought has yet provided.

ADVERTISEMENT

The following account is given by M. Dumont of his labours, with respect to the two volumes published by him at Paris in 1811, under the title of *Théorie des Peines et des Récompenses*. Of this work, three editions have been printed in France, and one in England.[125]

"When I published in Paris in 1802 *Les Traités de Législation Civile et Pénale*, in three volumes, I announced other works of the same kind, which I had, in the same manner, extracted from the manuscripts of Mr. Bentham, but which were not then ready for the press.

"Success has encouraged my labours:[126] three thousand copies were distributed more rapidly than I had dared to hope would be the case with the first work of a foreign author, but little know upon the continent. I have reason also to think that all recent as this work is, it has not been without its influence, since it has been frequently quoted[127] in many official compositions relating to civil or criminal codes.

"But circumstances which prevented those new volumes from entering upon the same course of circulation as the preceding have sometimes cooled[128] my zeal, and I should willingly have resigned the task I had imposed upon myself, if the author would have undertaken it himself. Unhappily, he is as little disposed so to do as ever, and if these works do not appear in the French dress which I have given them, it is most probable that they will remain shut up in his cabinet.

"They have lain there thirty years: the manuscripts from which I have extracted *La Théorie des Peines*, were written in 1775. Those which have supplied me with *La Théorie des Récompenses*, are a little later: they were not thrown aside as useless, but laid aside as rough hewn materials, which might at a future day be polished, and form part of a general system of legislation—or as studies which the author had made for his own use.[129]

"These manuscripts, though much more voluminous than the work I have presented to the public, are very incomplete. They offered to me often different essays upon the same subject, of which it was necessary to take the substance and unite them into one. In some chapters I had nothing but marginal notes to direct me. For the fourth book of *Théorie des Peines*, I was obliged to collect and prepare a variety of fragments. The discussion upon the punishment of death was unfinished. At one time, the author intended to treat of this subject anew, but this intention has not been carried into effect. He had prepared nothing upon transportation—nothing upon

Penitentiaries. The idea of the Panopticon was as yet unformed. I have derived the foundations of these two important chapters from a work of Mr. Bentham's, since published (Letters to Lord Pelham, &c. &c.).[130] I have taken all that suited my general method of treating the subject, by separating it from all controversy.

"After these explanations, it will not be a matter of surprise,[131] if the facts and allusions do not always accord with the date of the original manuscripts. I have freely used the rights of an Editor—according to the nature of the text and the occasion, I have translated, commented, abridged, or supplied, but it need hardly be repeated, after what was said in the preliminary discourse to the former publication, that this co-operation on my part has had any reference to the details only, and ought not to diminish the confidence of the readers; it is not my work that I present to them, it is, as faithfully as the nature of things will permit, the work of Mr. Bentham.

"It has been said, that these additions, these changes, should bear some distinctive mark; but though this species of fidelity is desirable, it is impossible. It is only necessary to imagine what is the labour of finishing a first sketch, of completing unfinished and unreviewed manuscripts, sometimes consisting of fragments and simple notes, in order to comprehend, that it required a continued freedom, a species of imperceptible infusion, if I may so speak, which it is scarcely possible for the individual himself to remember. This is, however, of no importance.[132] It may be believed that the author has not found his ideas disfigured or falsified, since he has continued to entrust me with his papers.

"I must however declare, that he has altogether refused to share my labour, and that he will not, in any manner, be responsible for it. As he has never been satisfied with a first attempt, and has never published anything which he has not written at least twice over, he has foreseen that the revision of so old an essay, would lead him too far away from, and be incompatible with, his present engagements. In this manner he has justified his refusal; but he has authorised me to add, that any change which he might make would bear only upon the *form*; as respects the *principles*, his opinions have not changed: on the contrary, time and reflection have given them additional[133] strength.

"That Mr. Bentham, who is too particular about his productions, should not deem these worthy of public notice, will not astonish those who know all that he requires of himself, and the ideas which he has formed for himself of a complete work.

"A perfect book would be that which should render useless all which had been written in time past, or that could be written in future time, upon the same subject. With respect to the second condition, it is not possible to decide when it is accomplished, without pretending to measure the power of the human mind; with respect to the first, we can more easily decide by a comparison with the works which have gone before.

"This comparison has supported me against a just distrust of my own powers. After the author had refused me all assistance,[134] and had expressed his doubts upon the merit of his own work, I was led to reperuse [*sic*] and reconsider the most celebrated works upon this subject, and even those which had been less distinguished, and then I could hesitate no longer.[135]

"I was tempted, at one time, to collect every thing dispersed through *L'Esprit des Lois* upon the subject of Rewards and Punishments. This collection would have been contained in ten or a dozen pages. By thus collecting the whole together, it would have been possible to judge of the correctness of that expression of D'Alembert, so often repeated in France, that *Montesquieu had said all, that he had abridged all, because he had seen all.* Among a multitude of vague and undefined thoughts upon these subjects, of which some are erroneous, there are certainly some which are judicious and profound, as in everything we possess of this illustrious writer. But he has not developed the Rationale of Rewards[136] and Punishments,— indeed, this was not his design,[137] and nothing would be more unjust than to criticise him for not having done what he did not intend to perform.

"Beccaria has done more: he first examined the efficacy of punishments, by considering their effect upon the human heart; by calculating the force of the motives by which individuals are impelled to the commission of crimes; and of those opposite motives which the law ought to present. This species of analytical merit was, however, less the cause of his great success, than the courage with which he attacked established errors, and that eloquent humanity which spreads so lively over his work; but after this, I scruple not to say, that he is destitute of method, that he only glances at the most important questions, that he carefully shuns all practical discussion in which it would have been evident, that he was unacquainted with the science of Jurisprudence.[138] He announces two distinct objects: crimes and punishments; he adds to these, occasionally, Procedure; and these three vast subjects with difficulty furnish out matter for one little volume.

"After Montesquieu and Beccaria, we may leave in peace a whole library of books, more or less valuable, but which are not distinguished by any great character of originality; not but that we should find in them correct and judicious views, interesting facts, valuable criticisms upon laws, many of which no longer exist, and to the disappearance of which these works have contributed. I intend not here to enter in detail either upon their criticism or eulogium. It is enough for me to observe, that none have laid down the Rationale of Rewards and Punishments, or could be employed as a general guide.

"In the volumes formerly published, the Rationale of Punishment was only sketched out—a general map only was given of the department of Criminal Law, of which this work exhibits a topography.

"To prevent frequent reference, and to render this work complete in itself, I have borrowed some chapters from the preceding work, making considerable additions to them, and giving them a different form.[139]

"At the risk, however, of inspiring my readers with a prejudice unfavourable to my work, I must acknowledge that its object, how important soever it may be in relation to its consequences, is anything but interesting in its nature. I have been sensible of this during the progress of my labour, and I have not completed it without having often to conquer myself. A philosophical interest alone must suffice; the descriptions of punishments, and the examination of punishments,[140] which follow each other without cessation in a didactic order, do not allow of a variety of style, do not present any pictures upon which the imagination can repose with pleasure.

"'Felices ditant hæc ornamenta libellos, Non est conveniens luctibus ille color.'

"Happily, the subject of Rewards, by its novelty, and by the ideas of virtues, talents, and services, which it causes to pass in review, will conduct the readers by more agreeable routes.—The Tartarus and Elysium of legislation, so to speak, are here disclosed; but in entering into this Tartarus, it is only to lighten its torments, and we are careful not to engrave upon its portals the terrible inscription of the poet,

"'Lasciate speranza, voi ch'entrate.'"

In preparing the Rationale of Punishment* for its appearance before the English public, the Editor has taken the second volume, published by M. Dumont, as the ground-work of his labours, but having availed himself, whenever he could, of the original manuscripts, his will in many instances not be found a literal translation of M. Dumont's work.   EDITOR.[141]

BOOK I.
GENERAL PRINCIPLES.

CHAPTER I.
DEFINITIONS AND DISTINCTIONS.

To[142] afford a clear apprehension of the subject of the following work, which subject is Punishment, it is necessary that what punishment *is*, and what punishment *is not*, should be clearly understood. For this purpose it will be proper to distinguish it from those objects with which it is in danger of being confounded, and also to point out the different shapes which it may assume.[143]

Punishment, whatever shape it may assume, is an evil.[144] The matter of *evil*, therefore, is the sort of matter here in question:—the matter of evil in almost all the shapes of which it is susceptible. In considering this matter, two objects, constant accompaniments one to the other, will require to be distinguished;—viz. 1. The act by which the evil is considered as being produced; and, 2. What is considered as being the result of that same act, the evil itself which is thus produced.[145]

The English language affords but one single worded appellative in common use for designating both these objects; viz. *Punishment.**

Punishment[146] may be defined—an evil resulting to an individual from the direct intention of another, on account of some act that appears to have been done or omitted. The propriety of this definition will appear, and its use be manifested, by taking it to pieces, and examining its several constituent parts.

---

*In the French, there exists for the designation of the act one name, viz. *punition—acte de punition*; and for the designation of the evil, the result or produce of that act, another name, viz. *peine*.

But though exempt from the ambiguity by which, as above, the English language is deteriorated, the French labours under another. By the word *peine*, the result is indeed secured against being confounded with the act that caused it. But, on the other hand, the use of this word is not confined to the case in which the object is designated by it is the result of an act emanating from the will of a sentient being; it is at least as frequently employed to designate the object itself, without regard to the cause by which it has been produced.

Besides being too broad in one direction, the import of it is too narrow in another. It is synonymous to, and not more than coextensive with, *douleur*: it fails of including that modification of evil which is of the purely negative cast, consisting of the absence, certain or more or less probable, of this or that modification of pleasure.

[Manuscript does not include this note. It may have been included by Dumont, rather than originally written by Bentham, as it appears in the 1830 edition, p. 2.]

Punishment then is an *evil*[147]—that is, a physical evil; either a pain, or a loss of pleasure, or else of that situation or condition of the party affected, which is the immediate cause of such pain or loss of pleasure.[148] It is an evil resulting from the *direct* intention of another. It is not punishment, if it be obliquely intentional on the part of the person from whose agency it results, but an evil of some other nature, but which, however, is not in all cases distinguished by a specific name.

It is an evil resulting to a person from the direct intention of another, *on account of* some act that has been done or omitted. An evil resulting to an individual, although it be from the direct intention of another, if it be not on account of some act that has been done or omitted, is not a punishment. If, out of *wantonness*, for the sake of *sport*, or out of *ill-will*, resulting from an *antipathy* you entertain against a man's person, without having any particular act of his to ground it upon, you do him a mischief, the evil produced in this case is what nobody would understand to come under the name of punishment.[149]

But so it be on account of some act that has been done, it matters not by whom the act was done. The most common case is for the act to have been done by the same person by whom the evil is suffered. But the evil may light upon a different person, and still bear the name of punishment. In such case it may be styled punishment *in alienam personam*, in contradistinction to the more common case in which it may be styled punishment *in propriam personam*. Whether the act be ultimately or only mediately [*sic*] intentional, it may consistently enough with common usage bear the name of punishment. Though according as it was, in the one or the other way that the intention happened to regard it, the act will assume a different name, as we shall have occasion to mention presently.

It must be on account of some act that at least *appears* to have been done; but whether such an act as appears to have been done, or any act, actually was done, is not material.

By the denomination thus given to the act, by the word punishment, taken by itself, no limitation is put to the description of the person of the agent; but on the occasion of the present work; this person is all along considered as a person invested for this purpose with the authority of the state; a legislator appointing the species of evil to be inflicted in a species of case; or a judge appointing the individual lot of evil to be inflicted in this or that individual case.[150]

Vengeance, antipathy, amendment, disablement, determent, self-defence, self-preservation, safe custody, restraint, compulsion, torture, compensation in the sense in which it means a particular mode of satisfaction for injury or damage—burthen in any such phrase as that of imposition of a burthen, and taxation: by all these several words ideas are presented which will require in each instance to be compared, and, in most instances, to be distinguished from the ideas presented by the word *punishment*.[151]

Take whatever portion of the matter of evil is upon the carpet, whether the term punishment shall or shall not with the propriety be applied, depends upon the position in which the actual result stands with reference to the time in which the *will* or intention of the agent acts.

Intentional or unintentional: if intentional, directly or indirectly, or, to use another word, collaterally intentionally; if directly, ultimately, or but mediately [*sic*] intentional; such are the modifications which the matter of evil may be considered as receiving, when considered in the character of an object to which the will or intention turns itself.

In some cases, the man in power, or some person or persons, having, as he supposes, received at the hands of some person or other, evil in some shape or other, the object which he has in view, in the infliction of the evil in question, is an enjoyment of a certain kind, which he derives, or expects to derive, from the contemplation of the evil just sustained. In this case, the act in question is termed the act of *vengeance.*

So far as this, and this alone, is his object, this evil thus produced is not only directly but ultimately intentional.

Whether in the character of a sole object, a result of this nature be a fit object for the man in power to propose to himself, is indeed a very important question, but one which has no place here: punishment, by being misapplied, is not the less punishment.

Laying out of the above case the supposed antecedent evil, you have no longer an act of vengeance, but an act performed for the mere gratification of *antipathy.* But by the supposition having for its author or agent the legislator or the Judge, it is still not the less an act of punishment.

Of the cases in which the act productive of the evil, intentionally produced by the hand of power, is termed an act of punishment, the most common class is that which is composed of those in which, on the part of the agent, the evil thus produced is, though intentional, and even directly intentional, yet not ultimately, but only mediately intentional.

In this case, the ultimately intentional object—the object in relation to which the act of punishment is intended to minister in the character of a means to an end—may be either an act of the negative or the positive* cast.

When the act to which the punishment is annexed is of the positive case, the ultimately intentional object aimed at by the act of punishment is

---

*Note.—To him who would understand what he hears of what he says, positive and negative are adjuncts; the use of which is not more necessary in electricity and galvanism than in law, and especially in penal law.

of the opposite cast: and so when the offence is negative, the result, the production of which is aimed at by the punishment, is positive.

If the offence be of the positive cast, then come the following string of appellatives, expressive of the results, the production of which is in different ways aimed at: viz. 1. Amendment or reformation: 2. Disablement: 3. Determent: 4. Self-defence: 5. Self-preservation: 6. Safe custody: and 7. Restraint.

If the offence be of the negative cast, then comes another string of appellatives, expressive, as above, of the results aimed at: viz. 1. Compulsion or constraint: 2. Torture: 3. Compensation, in the sense in which it is equivalent to *satisfaction*, rendered in consideration of injury resulting from an offence, or in consideration of damage produced without intentional injury: 4. Taxation.

Whether the result aimed at be of the negative or positive cast, the terms, coercion, obligation, burthen, or the phrase *imposition* of a burthen, are competent to the designation of it.

Amendment, or reformation, and *disablement*, are words expressive of the result aimed at, in so far as the conduct of the supposed delinquent is concerned. In the case of *amendment* or *reformation*, the obnoxious act is regarded as being of such a nature, that by a single instance of its being committed, such a degree of disorder in the moral constitution is indicated, as requires a general change to remove it, and bring the patient to a state of ordinary purity.[152]

For if any offences of the negative class being to be found which exhibit any such degree of malignity,—the use of the terms amendment and reformation is nearly confined to the case when the obnoxious act, the prevention of which is the ultimate end of the punishment, is of the positive kind.

Disablement is a term for which, with reference to an act of the negative kind, a place is hardly to be found. Doing nothing is a sort of offence to which every man is so competent, that all endeavours on the part of Government to disable a man from committing it may be set at defiance.

Determent is a result equally applicable to the case either of a positive or negative offence. It is moreover equally applicable to the situation of the already punished delinquent, and that of other persons at large; nor does it involve, on the part of the punished delinquent, the supposition of any such general disorder as is implied by the words *amendment* or *reformation*.

When the ultimately intentional result is amendment or reformation, it is by the impression made by the action of the evil on the will of the offender that, in so far as it is produced, the result is considered as being produced. In this case the *act of punishment* is also termed an act of *correction*.

When the ultimately intentional result is disablement, it is by depriving the offender of the power of committing obnoxious acts of the like description, that, in so far as it is produced, the result is considered as being produced. In this case, the course taken to produce the result may either be such the nature of which is to produce it only for a time, as is done by temporary imprisonment, confinement, or deportation; or for ever, as would in some cases be done by mutilation.

In so far as by the act of punishment exercised on the delinquent, other persons at large are considered as deterred from the commission of acts of the like obnoxious description, and the act of punishment is in consequence considered as endued with the quality of *determent*. It is by the impression made on the will of those persons, an impression made in this case not by the act itself, but by the idea of it, accompanied with the eventual expectation of a similar *evil*, as about to be eventually in their own instances, that the ultimately intentional result is considered as produced: and in this case it is also said to be produced by the *example*, or by the force of *example*.

Between self-defence and punishment, the relation is of this sort,—viz. that to the same act which ministers to the one of those purposes, it may happen to minister to the other. This coincidence may have place in either of two ways: an act which has self-defence for its direct object and result, may have punishment for its collateral result; or an act which has punishment for its direct object and result, may have self-defence for its collateral result.

In repelling a personal assault, it may happen to an individual, intentionally or unintentionally, to inflict on the assailant, a suffering by any amount greater than that of any which, by the assault, was inflicted on himself: if unintentionally, self-defence was not only the sole ultimately intentional, but the sole intentional result: but the suffering of the assailant, though not the collaterally intentional, was not in effect less truly the collateral result.

On the other hand, in inflicting punishment on a delinquent, it may happen to the *man in authority* to be exercising on his own behalf an act of *self-defence*: in regard to all offences, such as *rebellion* and *treason*, which have for their object or their effect the subversion of the government, or the weakening of its powers. But it is only in reference to such offences that an act of punishment can, with reference to the constituted authorities, be with propriety called an act of self-defence.

But if in lieu of the constituted authorities, the members of the community at large be considered as the persons by whom the punishment is inflicted; then is all punishment an act of *self-defence*, in relation to the particular species of evil with which the offence thus punished is pregnant: an act tending to defend the community against offences of the sort in question, with their attendant evils, viz. by means of reformation, disablement, and determent, one or more of them as above.[153]

In the signification of the word *self-defence*, it is implied that the evil against which the party is endeavouring to guard himself has for its cause an act done by some sentient being, with the intention of producing that same evil.

The word self-preservation, is alike applicable whatsoever be the source or quarter from which the evil is considered as about to come. In so far, therefore, as the act of punishment is with propriety capable of being termed an act of self-defence, it is, with the same propriety, capable of being termed an act of *self-preservation*.

Between safe custody and punishment, the relation is of this sort:—To one and the same operation or factitious state of things it may happen to be productive of both of these effects. But in the instance of the same individual, it is only to a limited degree that there can be a sufficient reason for making provision for both at the same time.

To a considerable extent imprisonment with propriety may be, and everywhere is applied, under the name and to the purpose of punishment. In this case, safe custody is in part the same thing with the intended punishment itself; in part a concomitant necessary to the existence and continuance of whatsoever inflictions it may be deemed proper to add to those which are inseparable from the safe custody of itself.

But in another case, imprisonment, or an infliction of the same name at least as that which is employed as above, for the purpose of punishment, is to a great extent administered ultimately for the purpose of eventual forthcomingness [*sic*], and mediately for the purpose of safe custody, though no such thing as punishment is, or at least ought to be, intended, because no ground for punishment has as yet been, and perhaps never may be, established.

Between restraint and punishment the relation is of this sort. In some shape or other, restraint is the *directly* intentional result of every prohibitive law. The evil, whatever it be that constitutes an inseparable accompaniment of the state thus denominated, is a collaterally intentional result of that same law. The evil of the restraint may be very moderate, but still by every general prohibitive law; evil in some shape or other, in some quantity or other, must come.

At the same time, restraint is, in a great variety of shapes, capable of being employed in the character of a punishment. As a punishment, restraint is not incapable of being employed for the purpose of securing submission to restraint. But in this case, the coincidence is but verbal, and arises from the generality of the word restraint. In the character of a punishment we cannot employ the restraint collaterally resulting from the negative act, the production of which is the object of the prohibition in the character of the eventual punishment, to secure obedience to that same prohibitive law. To prevent a man from stealing, a law threatening to prevent him from stealing, would be but an indifferent resource. To secure, by means of eventual punishment, restraint in this shape, you must employ restraint in some other shape; for example, the restraint attached to imprisonment.

Between compulsion and punishment, the relation is of this sort. In the case of compulsion, as in the case of restraint, the act in question is the act which is regarded as the efficient cause of the evil, the prevention of which is the ultimate object of the act of punishment. What *restraint* is in the case when the act in question is of the positive case, *compulsion* is in the case when the act is of the negative cast.

Between torture and punishment, the relation is of this sort. The term torture is employed, and perhaps with nearly equal frequency, in two different senses. In its most extended sense it is employed to designate pain, especially pain of body, when considered as being intense in its degree, and this without reference to the cause by which it is produced.

In its more restricted sense, being that in which it is most apt to be employed, when considered as the result of law, it is employed to signify pain of body in its degree intense as above, employed in due course of law, or, at any rate, by the hand of power, in the character of an instrument of compulsion.

But the account given of it when employed in this sense wants much, as yet, of being complete. The compulsion, or constraint, may be produced by the mere apprehension of the punishment which is denounced.

By this circumstance, torture stands distinguished not only from compulsion itself, but from any lot of punishment considered as applied to the purpose of compulsion in the ordinary mode.

The notion of torture is not included in a punishment attached to an act of disobedience, of which no remission is allowed; but suppose the same lot of pain attached to the same offence, with power to remit any part of it, in case of and immediately upon compliance with the requisition of the law; and here the punishment comes under the notion and denomination of torture.

Between compensation, or satisfaction and punishment, the relation is of this sort: in all cases, if compensation be the end in view, so far as concerns pecuniary compensation, by whatsoever is done for the purpose of compensation, the effect of pecuniary punishment is produced likewise. More suffering, however, will in general be produced by what is taken for the purpose of punishment; it will be accompanied by the regret produced by the idea of the advantage not only reaped by an adversary, but reaped at one own's [*sic*] expense.

On the other hand, by the contemplation of the suffering inflicted by punishment on the delinquents, good in the shape of compensation, or say vindictive satisfaction, is administered to the party injured.

Between taxation and punishment of the pecuniary kind, for it is only in this form that they can be compared, the relation is of this sort: they both consist in the application of compulsion to the extracting out of the pocket in question a certain sum; the difference between them consists in the end in view. In the case of taxation, the object is the obtainment of a certain sum; in the case of punishment, the object is the prevention of the obnoxious act, to the commission of which the obligation of paying the money is attached in the character of a punishment. In the case of taxation, the wish of the legislator is, that the money may be paid; and, consequently, if it be to the performance of a certain act that the obligation of paying the money is annexed, his wish is that the act may be performed.

As in the two cases the result intended is opposite, the actual results are accordingly incompatible, in so far as either result is obtained, the other is missed. Whether the effect of any given law shall be taxation, or effectual prohibition, depends in the instance of each individual upon the value, which, in the case in question, he is called upon to pay, compared with the value in his estimation of the advantage which stands annexed to the exercise of the act; if the advantage appear the greater, he pays the money and exercises the act; if the value of the money to be eventually paid appear the greater, he obeys the prohibitory [sic] law, and abstains from the performance of the act.

When the face assumed by any law is that of a prohibition, if the penalty be nothing but pecuniary and the amount is fixed, while the profits of the offence are variable, the probability is that in many instances the penalty even if levied, which could not be without detection, prosecution, and conviction, would but operate as a taxed licence.

This circumstance is so obvious, that one would have thought it could not have been overlooked; had it, however, been observed with any tolerable steadiness in England, the law of that country would wear a face widely different from that which it wears at present.

In relation to all these several results or concomitants* of punishment,

---

* The distinctions between these several objects may be illustrated by an example.

In 1769, a jury gave a verdict of 4,000£ damages against the Earl of Halifax, for the wrongful imprisonment of John Wilkes, Esq. on suspicion of being the author of a state libel. It may be inquired, what sort of act did the jury perform, when by giving this verdict they appointed the sum in question to be paid by the one person to the other?

It was intended to be an act of punishment. If any juryman being angry with Lord Halifax also intended to produce pain in him, on account of the pleasure he took in thinking of that pain; in the case of such jury man it was an act of vengeance; being done, however, on account of an act that had been done, viz. the imprisonment of Mr. Wilkes, it was not an act of antipathy.

one observation useful to be borne in mind, that it may operate as a preservative against much error, is—that it is but in very few, if any of these instances, that from the name by which the object is here designated, any true judgment can be formed on any such question as whether and how far the object is a fit object of pursuit or aim in the character of an end.

Take any one of them for example,—if taken by itself that object be of the nature of good, yet in the first place, that good may be in any degree minute; in the next place, to the quantity of evil with which it may happen to it to be followed, there are no limits: and thus it is that false must be that proposition, which without leaving room for exceptions, should pronounce the attainment of that object to be universally an end fit to be aimed at, whether through the intervention of punishment, or any other means; and conversely.

Of the distinctions here pointed out between punishment and the several objects that are of kin to it, five distinguishable practical uses may be made.

1. They may serve as a memento to the legislator, to see on every occa-

---

If the juryman did it with a view of deterring Lord Halifax, or any one who might occupy that nobleman's place in future, from doing acts of the like kind, and of preventing the mischief apprehended from such acts, it was in him an act for amendment and determent. It could not, however, operate for the purpose of disablement, the paying of a sum of money, having no tendency to disable Lord Halifax, or those holding the same office, from imprisoning others who might become the objects of their dislike.

It was not an act of immediate self-defence, for self-defence implies attack, that is, implies that there is some person who is actually using his endeavours to do mischief to the party defending himself. If, however, any juryman thinking himself in danger of suffering in the like, or any other manner from Lord H., and persons liable to act as he did, joined in the verdict with the view of preserving himself from such suffering, to wit, by means of the restraint which the fear of similar punishment might be expected to impose on Lord Halifax and such other persons, on the part of such juryman it was an act of self-preservation.

The payment of the fine imposed could contribute nothing to the purposes of safe custody of physical restraint, neither was it an act of compulsion, for it was not designed as a means of compelling him to do anything.

It was not an act of torture; the penalty, if paid, was paid instantaneously; the act of paying ceasing of itself, and not being capable of being protracted so as to be made to cease only at a future given instant.

If any juryman did it with the view of making Mr. Wilkes amends for the pain he had suffered by the supposed injury in question, in such juryman it was an act of compensation; and if the juryman who intended to make compensation to Mr. Wilkes also thought that it was right to tax Lord Halifax to the amount of the compensation proper to be given to Mr. Wilkes, it was an act of taxation.

[This note does not appear within the final draft of the original manuscript as transcribed by Smith. It does appear, however, as part of an apparent earlier draft in nearly identical form to the version that appears in the 1830 edition, pp. 14–15, which was, apparently, derived from a note included within the first chapter of Dumont's version of the first chapter, *Théorie des peines*, pp. 6–7. The draft by Smith included the following comment: "Was it an act of vengeance, restraint, prevention, compensation, or self-preservation? B. says it could have been all." Back of RP MSS 141/1: 5.]

sion that for the several objects which may have place and present a demand for legislative provision; due and adequate provision is accordingly made.

2. To preserve him from the delusion which would have place, wheresoever it happens that by one and the same lot of evil, due and adequate provision may be made for two or more of these purposes, if by the difference of their respective denominations, he were led to give birth to two or more lots of evil for the purpose of effecting the good, for the effectuation of which one of them would suffice.

3. That in each instance, in comparing the end he has in view with the means which he proposes to employ for the attainment of it, the view he takes of such proposed means may be sufficiently clear, correct, and complete, to enable him to form a correct judgment of the mode and degree in which they promise to be conducive to the attainment of the end.

4. That he may be upon his guard against the sort of rhetorical artifice which operates by substituting for the proper name of the object or result in question, according to the purpose in view, the name of some other object or result, the name of which is either more or less popular than the proper one.

5. That while in pursuit of any one of these objects, in the character of an *end*, he employs such means as to his conception appear conducive to that end, he may be correctly and completely aware of any tendency which such arrangements may have to be conducive or obstructive, with reference to any other of these same ends.

CHAPTER II.
CLASSIFICATION.[154]

I n a former work it has been shewn* [*sic*] that offences against individuals may be ranged under four principal heads; offences against the *person*, *property*, *reputation*, and *condition*. The same division may be applied to punishments; an individual can only be punished by affecting his person, his property, his reputation, or his condition.[155]

The circumstance which renders these two classifications similar is this—punishments and offences are both evils caused by the free agency of man.[156] In as many points as we are liable to be injured by the hand of an offender, in so many points is the offender himself exposed to the sword of justice. The difference between punishments and offences is not then in their nature, which is, or may be, the same; but in the legality of the one, and the illegality of the other, offences are prohibited, punishments are instituted by the laws. Their effects also are diametrically opposite. An offence produces an evil both of the *first* and *second order*;† it causes suffering in an individual which he was unable to avoid, and it spreads an alarm more or less general. A punishment produces an *evil* of the *first order*, and a *good* of the *second order*. It inflicts suffering upon an individual who has incurred it voluntarily, and in its secondary effects it produces only good, it intimidates the ill-disposed, it re-assures the innocent, and becomes the safeguard of society.

Those punishments which immediately affect the person in its active or passive powers, constitute the class of corporal punishments, they may be divided into the following different kinds.

Introduction to Principles of Morals and Legislation, vol. ii, page 63.

†See *Principles of Morals and Legislation*, ch. 12, vol. i, page 254, 'Of the Consequences of a Mischievous Act,'—"The mischief of an offence may frequently be distinguished, as it were, into two shares or parcels; the one containing what may be called the primary; the other what may be called the secondary. That share may be termed *primary* which is sustained by an assignable individual, or a multitude of assignable individuals. That share may be termed secondary, which, taking its origin from the former, extends itself rather over the whole community, or over some other multitude of unassignable individuals."

For the full development of this subject, reference may be made to the chapter indicated. [A much more detailed treatment is provided throughout *IPML*, ch. 12.]

1. Simply afflictive punishments.
2. Complexly afflictive punishments.
3. Restrictive punishments.
4. Active or laborious punishments.
5. Capital punishments.

Punishments which affect property, reputation, or condition, possess this quality in common, they deprive the individual of some advantage which he before enjoyed; such are *privative* punishments, *losses*, and *forfeitures*. The punishments of this class are very various, they extend to every possible kind of possession.

Hence we perceive that all punishments may be reduced to two classes.

1. Corporal punishments.
2. Privative punishments, or punishments by loss or forfeiture.

CHAPTER III.
OF THE ENDS OF PUNISHMENT.[157]

W hen any act has been committed which is followed, or threatens to be followed, by such effects as a provident legislator would be anxious to prevent, two wishes naturally and immediately suggest themselves to his mind: first, to obviate the danger of the like mischief in future: secondly, to compensate the mischief that has already been done.[158]

The mischief likely to ensue from acts of the like kind may arise from either of two sources,—either the conduct of the party himself who has been the author of the mischief already done, or the conduct of such other persons as may have adequate motives and sufficient opportunities to do the like.

Hence the prevention of offences divides itself into two branches: *Particular prevention*, which applies to the delinquent himself; and *general prevention*, which is applicable to all the members of the community without exception.

Pain and pleasure are the great springs of human action.[159] When a man perceives or supposes pain to be the consequence of an act, he is acted upon in such a manner as tends, with a certain force, to withdraw him, as it were, from the commission of that act. If the apparent magnitude, or rather value* of that pain be greater than the apparent magnitude or value of the pleasure or good he expects to be the consequence of the act,[160] he will be absolutely prevented from performing it. The mischief which would have ensued from the act, if performed, will also by the means be prevented.

With respect to a given individual, the recurrence of an offence may be provided against in three ways:—

1. By taking from him the physical power of offending.
2. By taking away the desire of offending.
3. By making him afraid of offending.

In the first case, the individual can no more commit the offence; in the second, he no longer desires to commit it; in the third, he may still wish to

---

*I say *value*, in order to include the circumstances of *intensity*, *certainty*, and *duration*, which magnitude, properly speaking, does not. This may serve to obviate the objections made by Locke (book II, ch. 21) against the proposition, that man is determined by the greater apparent good.

commit it, but he no longer dares to do it. In the first case, there is a physical incapacity; in the second, a moral reformation; in the third, there is intimidation or terror of the law.

General prevention is effected by the denunciation of punishment, and by its application, which, according to the common expression, *serves for an example*. The punishment suffered by the offender presents to every one an example of what he himself will have to suffer if he is guilty of the same offence.

General prevention ought to be the chief end of punishment, as it is its real justification. If we could consider an offence which has been committed as an isolated fact, the like of which would never recur, punishment would be useless. It would be only adding one evil to another. But when we consider that an unpunished crime leaves the path of crime open not only to the same delinquent, but also to all those who may have the same motives and opportunities for entering upon it, we perceive that the punishment inflicted on the individual becomes a source of security to all. That punishment, which, considered in itself, appeared base and repugnant to all generous sentiments, is elevated to the first rank of benefits, when it is regarded not as an act of wrath or of vengeance against a guilty or unfortunate individual who has given way to mischievous inclinations, but as an indispensable sacrifice to the common safety.[161]

With respect to any particular delinquent, we have seen that punishment has three objects,—incapacitation, reformation, and intimidation. If the crime he has committed is of a kind calculated to inspire great alarm, as manifesting a very mischievous disposition, it becomes necessary to take from him the power of committing it again. But if the crime, being less dangerous, only justifies a transient punishment, and it is possible for the delinquent to return to society, it is proper that the punishment should possess qualities calculated to reform or to intimidate him.

After having provided for the prevention of future crimes, reparation still remains to be made, as far as possible, for those which are passed, by bestowing a compensation on the party injured; that is to say, bestowing a good equal to the evil suffered.

This compensation, founded upon reasons which have been elsewhere developed,* does not at first view appear to belong to the subject of punishments, because it concerns another individual than the delinquent. But these two ends have a real connexion [*sic*]. There are punishments which have the double effect of affording compensation to the party injured, and of inflicting a proportionate suffering on the delinquent; so that these two ends may be effected by a single operation. This is, in certain cases, the peculiar advantage of pecuniary punishments.

---

* Traités, &c. tom. ii, p. 310.

CHAPTER IV.[162]
CASES UNMEET
FOR PUNISHMENT.[163]

All punishment being in itself evil, upon the principle of utility, if it ought at all to be admitted, it ought only to be admitted in as far as it promises to exclude some greater evil.[164]

It is plain, therefore, that in the following cases punishment ought not to be inflicted:—1. Where it is *groundless*: 2. Where it must be *inefficacious*; because it cannot act so as to prevent the mischief: 3. Where it is *unprofitable* or too *expensive*: 4. Where it is *needless*; because the mischief may be prevented or cease itself without it.[165]

SEC. I.—CASES IN WHICH PUNISHMENT IS GROUNDLESS.

1. Where there has never been any mischief, as in the case of consent: Such consent, provided it be free and fairly given, being the best proof that can be obtained, that at least no immediate mischief upon the whole has been done to the party who gives it.

2. Where the mischief is *outweighed* by the production of a benefit of greater value, as in precautions against instant calamity, and the exercise of domestic, judicial, military, and supreme powers.

SEC. II.—CASES IN WHICH PUNISHMENT MUST BE INEFFICACIOUS.

These are, 1. Where the penal provision is *not established* until after the act is done. Such are the cases of an *ex post facto* law, and of a sentence beyond the law. 2. Where the penal provision, though established, is *not conveyed* to the notice of the person on whom it is intended to operate, as from want of due promulgation. 3. Where the penal provision, though it were conveyed to the individual's notice, *could produce no effect* with respect to preventing his engaging in the act prohibited: as in the cases of extreme *infancy*, *insanity*, and *intoxication*.[166] 4. Where the penal provision; though present to the party's notice, does not produce its effect, because he knows not the act he is about to engage in is of the number of those to which the penal provision relates. 5. Where, though the penal clause might exert a full and prevailing influence were it to act alone, yet by the *predominant* influence of some opposite cause upon the will, such as physical danger or threatened mischief, it must necessarily be ineffectual. 6. Where, though the penal clause may exert a full and prevailing influence over the *will* of the party, yet his *physical faculties* (owing to the predominant influence of some physical cause) are not in a condition to follow the determination of his will: insomuch that the act is absolutely involuntary, as through *compulsion* or *restraint*.[167]

SEC. III.—CASES WHERE PUNISHMENT IS UNPROFITABLE.

If the evil of the punishment exceed the evil of the offence, the punishment will be unprofitable, the legislator will have produced more suffering than he has prevented. He will have purchased exemption from one evil at the expense of a greater.

The evil resulting from punishment divides itself into four branches:—1. The evil of *coercion* or *restraint*, or the pain which it gives a man not to be able to do the act, whatever it be, which, by the apprehension of the punishment, he is deterred from doing. 2. The evil of *apprehension*, or the pain which a man, who has exposed himself to punishment, feels at the thoughts of undergoing it. 3. The evils of *sufferance*, or the pain which a man feels, in virtue of the punishment itself, from the time when he begins to undergo it. 4. The pain of sympathy, and the other *derivative* evils resulting to the persons who are in *connection* with those who suffer from the preceding causes.[168]

SEC. IV.—CASES WHERE PUNISHMENT IS NEEDLESS.

A punishment is needless, where the purpose of putting an end to the practice may be attained as effectually at a cheaper rate, by instruction for instance, as well as by terror; by informing the understanding, as well as by exercising an immediate influence on the will. This seems to be the case with respect to all those offences which consist in the disseminating pernicious principles in matters of *duty*, of whatever kind the duty may be, whether political, moral, or religious. And this, whether such principles be disseminated *under*, or even *without* a sincere persuasion of their being beneficial. I say even *without*; for though, in such a case, it is not instruction that can prevent the individual form endeavouring to inculcate his principles, yet it may prevent others from adopting them: without which, the endeavours to inculcate them will do no harm. In such a case, the sovereign will commonly have little occasion to take an active part: if it be the interest of *one* individual to inculcate opinions that are pernicious, it will surely be the interest of other individuals to expose them. But if the sovereign must needs take a part in the controversy, the pen is the proper weapon wherewith to combat error, and not the sword.[169]

On the other hand, as to the evil of the offence, this will, of course, be greater or less according to the nature of each offence. The proportion between the one evil and the other will therefore be different in the case of each particular offence. The cases, therefore, where punishment is unprofitable on this ground, can by no other means be discovered, than by an examination of each particular offence.

These considerations ought at all times to be present to the mind of the legislator, whenever he establishes any punishment. It is from them that he will derive his principal reasons for general amnesties, on account of the multitude of delinquents: for the preservation of a delinquent, whose talents could not be replaced, or whose punishment would excite the public displeasure, or the displeasure of foreign powers.

CHAPTER V.[170]

EXPENSE OF PUNISHMENT.

*E*xpense of Punishment.—This expression, which has not yet been introduced into the common use, may at first sight be accused of singularity and pedantry. It has however been chosen upon reflection as the only one which conveys the desired idea, without conveying at the same time an anticipated judgment of approbation or disapprobation. The pain produced by punishments, is as it were a capital hazarded in[171] expectation of profit. This profit is the prevention of crimes. In this operation everything ought to be taken into the calculation of profit and loss; and when we estimate the profit, we must subtract the loss; from which it evidently results that the diminution of the expense, or the increase of the profit, equally tend to the production of a favourable balance.[172]

The term *expense* once admitted naturally introduces that of *economy* or *frugality*. The mildness or the rigour of punishments is commonly spoken of: these terms include a prejudice in the one case of favour, in the other of disfavour, which prevents impartiality in their examination. But to say that a punishment is economic, is to use the language of reason and calculation.

We should say then that a punishment is *economic*, when the desired effect is produced by the employment of the least possible suffering. We should say that is too *expensive*, when it produces more evil than good; or when it is possible to obtain the same good by means of a less punishment.

In this place distinction should be made between the *real* and the *apparent* value of a punishment.

By the real value, I mean that which it would be found to have by one who, like the legislator, is in a condition accurately to trace and coolly to estimate it through all its parts, exempt from the delusions which are seen to govern the uninformed and unthinking part of mankind; knowing, beforehand, upon general principles, what the delinquent will know afterwards by particular experience.

By the apparent value of a punishment, I mean that which it appears to a delinquent to have at any time previous to that in which he comes to experience it; or to a person under temptation to become a delinquent previous to the time at which, were he to become so, he would experience it.

The real value of the punishment constitutes the expense.[173] The apparent value influences the conduct of individuals. It is the real punishment that is the expense—the apparent punishment that gives the profit.

The profit of punishments has reference to the interests of two parties—the public, and the party injured. The expense of the punishment adds to this number a third interest, that of the delinquent.[174]

It ought not to be forgotten, although it has been too frequently forgotten, that the delinquent is a member of the community, as well as any other individual—as well as the party injured himself; and that there is just as much reason for consulting his interest as that of any other. His welfare is proportionably [*sic*] the welfare of the community—his suffering the suffering of the community. It may be right that the interest of the delinquent should in part be sacrificed to that of the rest of the community; but it never can be right that it should be totally disregarded.[175] It may be prudent to hazard a great punishment for the chance of obtaining a great good: it would be absurd to hazard the same punishment where the chance is much weaker, and the advantage much less. Such are the principles which direct men in their private speculations. Why should they not guide the legislator?[176]

Ought any real punishments to be inflicted? Most certainly. Why? For the sake of producing the *appearance* of it. Upon the principle of utility, except as to so much as is necessary for reformation and compensation, for this reason, and for no other whatever. Every particle of real punishment that is produced more than what is necessary for the production of the requisite quantity of apparent punishment, is just so much misery run to waste. Hence the real punishment ought to be as small, and the apparent punishment as great as possible.[177] If hanging a man in *effigy*, would produce the same salutary impression of terror upon the minds of the people, it would be folly or cruelty ever to hang a man *in person.**

If delinquents were constantly punished for their offences, and nobody else knew of it, it is evident that, excepting the inconsiderable benefit which might result in the way of disablement, or reformation, there would be a great deal of mischief done, and not the least particle of good. The *real* punishment would be as great as ever, and the *apparent* would be nothing. The

---

*At the Cape of Good Hope, the Dutch made use of a stratagem which could only succeed among Hottentots. One of their officers having killed an individual of this inoffensive tribe, the whole nation took up the matter and became furious and implacable. It was necessary to make an example to pacify them. The delinquent was therefore brought before them in irons, as a malefactor: he was tried with great form, and was condemned to swallow a goblet of ignited brandy. The man played his part;—he feigned himself dead, and fell motionless. His friends covered him with a cloak, and bore him away. The Hottentots declared themselves satisfied. "The worst we should have done with the man," they said, "would have been to throw him into the fire; but the Dutch have done better—they have put the fire into the man."— *Lloyd's Evening Post*, for August or September 1776.

punishment would befal [*sic*] every offender as an unforeseen evil. It would never have been present to his mind to deter him from the commission of crime. It would serve as an example to no one.

Delinquents may happen to know nothing of the punishment provided for them in either of two cases.—1. When it is inflicted without having been previously made known.—2. When, though promulgated, it has not been made known to the individual. The latter of these cases may be the case where the punishment is appointed by *statute*—or as it is called, *written* law. The former must happen in all new cases where the punishment is appointed in the way of *common* or *unwritten* law.

The punishment appointed by the law may be presented to the mind in two ways:—1. By its legal denunciation and description:—2. By its public execution, when it is inflicted with suitable notoriety.

The notion entertained of a punishment ought to be exact, or, as the logicians would say, adequate; that is, it should present to the mind not only a part, but the whole of the sufferings it includes. The denunciation of a punishment ought therefore to include all the items of which it is composed, since that which is not known cannot operate as a motive.

Hence we may deduce three important maxims:—

1. That a punishment that is more easily learnt, is better than one that is less easily learnt.

2. That a punishment that is more easily remembered, is better than one that is less easily remembered.

3. That a punishment that appears of greater magnitude in comparison of what it really is, is better than one that appears of less magnitude.[178]

CHAPTER VI.
MEASURE OF PUNISHMENT.

Adsit

Regula, peccatis quæ pœnas irroget æquas.
Ne scutica dignum, horribili sectere flagello.

Hon. *L.* 1. *Sat.* iii.[179]

Establish a proportion between crimes and punishments—has been said by Montesquieu, Beccaria, and many others.[180] The maxim is, without doubt, a good one, but whilst it is thus confined to general terms, it must be confessed it is more oracular than instructive. Nothing has been accomplished till wherein this proportion consists has been explained, and the rules have been laid down by which it may be determined that a certain measure of punishment ought to be applied to a certain crime.[181]

Punishments may be too small or too great; and there are reasons for not making them too great. The terms *minimum* and *maximum* may serve to mark the two extremes of this question, which require equal attention.

With a view of marking out the limits of punishment on the side of the first of these extremes, we may lay it down as a rule:—[182]

1. That the value of the punishment must not be less in any case than what is sufficient to outweigh that of the profit of the offence.[183]

By the profit of the crime, must be understood not only pecuniary profit, but every advantage, real or apparent, which has operated as a motive to the commission of the crime.

The profit of the crime is the force which urges a man to delinquency—the pain of the punishment is the force employed to restrain him from it. If the first of these forces be the greater, the crime will be committed;*[184] if the second, the crime will not be committed. If then a man, having reaped the profit of a crime, and undergone the punishment, finds the former more than equivalent to the latter, he will go on offending for ever; there is nothing to restrain him. If those, also, who behold him, reckon that the balance of gain is in favour of the delinquent, the punishment will be useless for the purposes of example.

The Anglo-Saxon laws, which fixed a price upon the lives of men; 200 shillings for the murder of a peasant, six times as much for that of a

---

*That is to say, committed by those who are only restrained by the laws, and not by any other tutelary motives, such as benevolence, religion, or honour.

nobleman, and thirty-six times as much for that of the king, evidently transgressed against this rule. In a great number of cases, the punishment would appear nothing, compared with the profit of the crime.[185]

The same error is committed[186] whenever a punishment is established which reaches only to a certain fixed point, which the advantage of the crime may surpass.

Authors[187] of celebrity have been found desirous of establishing a rule precisely the reverse, they have said that the greatness of temptation is a reason for lessening the punishment; because it lessens the fault; because the more powerful the seduction, the less reason is there for concluding that the offender is depraved. Those, therefore, who are overcome, in this case, naturally inspire us with commiseration.*[188]

This may all be very true, and yet afford no reason for departing from the rule. That it may prove effectual, the punishment must be more dreaded than the profit of the crime desired. Besides, an inefficacious punishment is doubly mischievous;—mischievous to the public, since it permits the crime to be committed,—mischievous to the delinquent, since the punishment inflicted upon him is just so much[189] misery in waste. What should we say[190] to the surgeon, who, that he might save his patient a small degree of pain, should only half cure him? What should we think of his humanity, if he should add to his disease the torment of a useless operation?

It is, therefore, desirable that punishment should correspond to every degree of temptation; at the same time, the power of mitigation might be reserved in those cases where the nature of the temptation itself indicates the absence of confirmed depravity, or the possession of benevolence—as might be the case should a father commit a theft that he might supply his starving family with bread.†

---

*One is astonished that a writer of such consummate genius as Adam Smith should have fallen into this mistake; speaking of smuggling, he says: "The law, contrary to all the ordinary principles of justice, first creates the temptation, and then punishes those who yield to it; and it commonly enhances the punishment, too, in proportion to the very circumstance which ought certainly to alleviate it—the temptation to commit the crime."—*Wealth of Nations, b.* 5, *ch.* ii. [This note is not found within Dumont's edition.]

†It is easy to estimate the profit of a crime in cases of rapacity, but how are we to ascertain it in those of malice and enmity?

The profit may be estimated by the nature of the mischief that the offender has done to his adversary. Has his conduct been more offensive than painful? The profit is the degree of humiliation that he believes his adversary to have undergone. Has he mutilated or wounded him? The profit is the degree of suffering he has inflicted.

In this, in his own opinion, consists the profit of his offense: if then he is punished in an analogous manner, he is struck in the most sensible part, which has, so to speak, been pointed out by himself; for it is not possible but that the mischief which he has chosen as the instrument of his vengeance, must appear hurtful to himself.

Rule II.[191] The *greater the mischief of the offence, the greater is the expense it may be worth while to be at, in the way of punishment.*[192]

This rule is so obvious in itself, that to say anything in proof of it would be needless; but how few are the instances in which it has been observed. It is not long since that women were condemned to be burnt alive for uttering bad money. The punishment of death is still lavished on a multitude of offences of the least mischievous description. The punishment of burning is still in use in many countries for offences which might safely be left to the restraint of the moral sanction. If it can be worth while to be at the expense of so terrible a punishment as that of burning alive, it ought to be reserved for murder or incendiarism [*sic*].

It will be said, perhaps, that the intention of legislators has always been to follow this rule, but that their opinions, as well as those of the people, have fluctuated respecting the relative magnitude and nature of crimes. At one period, witchcraft was regarded as the most mischievous offence. Sorcerers, who sold their souls to the devil, were objects of abhorrence. A heretic, the enemy of the Almighty, drew down divine wrath upon a whole kingdom. To steal property consecrated to divine uses was an offence of a more malignant nature than ordinary theft, the crime being directed against the Divinity. A false estimate being made of these crimes, an undue measure of punishment was applied to them.

Rule III.[193] *When two offences come in competition, the punishment for the greater offence must be sufficient to induce a man to prefer the less.*[194]

Two offences may be said to be in competition, when it is in the power of an individual to commit both. When thieves break into a house, they may execute their purpose in different manners; by simply stealing, by theft accompanied with bodily injury, or murder, or incendiarism. If the punishment is the same for simple theft, as for theft and murder, you give the thieves a motive for committing murder, because this crime adds to the facility of committing the former, and the chance of impunity when it is committed.[195]

The great inconvenience resulting from the infliction of great punishments for small offences, is, that the power of increasing them in proportion to the magnitude of the offence is thereby lost.*

---

*Montesquieu, after having recommended this rule of proportion, adds, "Quand il n'y a point de difference dans la peine, il faut en mettre, dans l'esperance de la grace; en Angleterre, on n'assassine point (il auroit du dire *peu*), parce que les voleurs peuvent esperer d'être transportés dans les colonies, non pas les assassins."—*Esprit des Lois, lib.* 6, *ch.* xvi.

This expectation of favour, no doubt, contributes to the effect of which he speaks, but why should this manifest imperfection in the laws remain, that it may be corrected by an arbitrary act of the sovereign? If an uncertain advantage produces this measure of good, a certain advantage would operate more surely.

Rule IV. *The punishment should be adjusted in such manner to each particular offence, that for every part of the mischief there may be a motive to restrain the offender from giving birth to it.*

Thus, for example, in adjusting the punishment for stealing a sum of money, let the magnitude of the punishment be determined by the amount of the sum stolen. If for stealing ten shillings an offender is punished no more than for stealing five; the stealing of the remaining five of those ten shillings is an offence for which there is no punishment at all.[196]

The last object is, whatever mischief is guarded against, to guard against it at as cheap a rate as possible; therefore,—

Rule V. *The punishment ought in no case to be more than what is necessary to bring it into conformity with the rules here given.*

Rule VI.[197] *That the quantity of punishment actually inflicted on each individual offender, may correspond to the quantity intended for similar offenders in general, the several circumstances influencing sensibility ought to be taken into the account.*[198]

The same *nominal* punishment is not, for different individuals, the same *real* punishment. Let the punishment in question be a fine: the sum that would not be felt by a rich man, would be ruin to a poor one.[199] The same ignominious punishment that would fix an indelible stigma upon a man of certain rank, would not affect a man of a lower rank. The same imprisonment that would be ruin to a man of business, death to an old man, and destruction of reputation to a woman, would be as nothing, or next to nothing, to persons placed in other circumstances.

The law may, by anticipation, provide that such or such a degree of mitigation shall be made in the amount of the punishment, in consideration of such or such circumstances influencing the sensibility of the patient— such as age, sex, rank, &c.[200] But in these cases considerable latitude must be left to the Judges.*

Of[201] the above rules of proportion, the four first may serve to mark out the limits on the minimum side; the limits *below* which a punishment ought not to be diminished; the fifth will mark out the limits on the maximum side, the limits above which it ought not to be increased.

The minimum of punishment is more clearly marked than its maximum. What is *too little* is more clearly observed than what is *too much.* What is not sufficient is easily seen, but it is not possible so exactly to distinguish an excess. An approximation only can be attained. The irregularities in the force of temptations, compel the legislator to increase his punishments till they are not merely sufficient to restrain the ordinary desires of men; but also the violence of their desires when unusually excited.

---

*See Introduction to Morals and Legislation, circumstances influencing sensibility.

The greater danger lies in an error on the minimum side, because in this case the punishment is inefficacious; but this error is least likely to occur, a slight degree of attention sufficing for its escape; and when it does exist, it is at the same time clear and manifest, and easy to be remedied. An error on the maximum side, on the contrary, is that to which legislators and men in general are naturally inclined—antipathy, or a want of compassion for individuals who are represented as dangerous and vile, pushes them onward to an undue severity. It is on this side, therefore, that we should take the most precautions, as on this side there has been shewn the greatest disposition to err.[202]

By way of supplement and explanation to the first rule, and to make sure of giving to the punishment the superiority over the offence, the three following rules may be laid down.

Rule VII.—*That the value of the punishment may outweigh the profit of the offence, it must be increased in point of magnitude, in proportion as it falls short in point of certainty.*

Rule VIII.—*Punishment must be further increased in point of magnitude, in proportion as it falls short in point of proximity.*[203]

The profit of a crime is commonly more certain than its punishment, or what amounts to the same thing, appears so to the offender. It is generally more immediate, the temptation to offend is present; the punishment is at a distance. Hence there are two circumstances which weaken the effect of punishment, its *uncertainty* and its *distance.*

Suppose the profit of a crime equal to 10£ sterling, suppose the chance of punishment as one to two. It is clear that if the punishment, supposing that it were to take place, is not more than 10£ sterling, its effect upon a man's mind whilst it continues uncertain, is not equal to a certain loss of 10£ sterling: it is only equal to a certain loss of 5£ sterling. That it may be rendered equal to the profit of the crime, it must be raised to 20£.

Unless men are hurried on by outrageous passion, they do not engage in the career of crime without the hope of impunity. If a punishment were to consist only in taking from an offender the fruit of his crime, and this punishment were infallible, there would be no more such crimes committed; for what man would be so insensate as to take the trouble of committing a crime with the certainty of not enjoying its fruits, and the shame of having attempted it? But as there are always some chances of escape, it is necessary to increase the value of the punishment, to counterbalance these chances of impunity.[204]

It is therefore true, that the more the certainty of punishment can be augmented, the more it may be diminished in amount. This is one advantage resulting from simplicity of legislation, and excellence of legal procedure.

For the same reason, it is necessary that the punishment should be as near, in point of time, to the crime as possible; because its impression upon the minds of men is weakened by distance; and because this distance adds to the uncertainty of its infliction, by affording fresh chances of escape.

Rule IX.—*When the act is conclusively indicative of a habit, such an increase must be given to the punishment as may enable it to outweigh the profit, not only of the individual offence, but of such other like offences as are likely to have been committed with impunity by the same offender.*[205]

Severe as this conjectural calculation may appear, it is absolutely necessary in some cases. Of this kind are fraudulent crimes; using false weights or measures, and issuing base coin. If the coiner was only punished according to the value of the single crime of which he is convicted,[206] his fraudulent practice would, upon the whole, be a lucrative one. Punishment would therefore be inefficacious if it did not bear a proportion to the total gain which may be supposed to have been derived, not from one particular act, but from a train of actions of the same kind.

There may be a few other circumstances or considerations which may influence, in some small degree, the demand for punishment; but as the propriety of these is either not so demonstrable, or not so constant, or the application of them not so determinate, as that of the foregoing, it may be doubted whether they are worth putting on a level with the others.[207]

Rule X.—*When a punishment, which in point of quality is particularly well calculated to answer its intention, cannot exist in less than a certain quantity, it may sometimes be of use, for the sake of employing it, to stretch a little beyond that quantity which, on other accounts, would be strictly necessary.*

Rule XI.—*In particular, this may be the case where the punishment proposed is of such a nature as to be particularly well calculated to answer the purpose of a moral lesson.*

Rule XII.—*In adjusting the quantum of punishment, the circumstances by which all punishments may be rendered unprofitable ought to be attended to.*

And lastly, as too great a nicety in establishing[208] proportions between punishment and crime would tend to defeat its own object, by rendering the whole matter too complex; we may add:—

Rule XIII.—*Among provisions designed to perfect the proportion between punishments and offences, if any occur which by their own particular good effects would not make up for the harm they would do by adding to the intricacy of the Code, they should be omitted.*

The observation of rules of proportion between crimes and punishments has been objected to as useless, because they seem to suppose, that a spirit of calculation has place among the passions of men, who, it is said, never calculate. But dogmatic[209] as this proposition is, it is altogether false. In matters of importance every one calculates. Each individual calculates with more or less correctness, according to the degrees of his information, and the power of the motives which actuate him, but all calculate. It would be hard to say that a madman does not calculate. Happily, the passion of cupidity, which on account of its power, its constancy, and its extent, is most formidable to society; is the passion which is most given to calculation. This, therefore, will be more successfully combated, the more carefully the law turns the balance of profit against it.

CHAPTER VII.[210]
OF THE PROPERTIES TO BE GIVEN TO A LOT OF PUNISHMENT.

I t has been shewn what rules ought to be observed in adjusting the proportion between punishment and offences. The properties to be given to a lot of punishment in every instance will of course be such as it stands in need of, in order to be capable of being applied in conformity to those rules: the *quality* will be regulated by the *quantity*.[211]

SEC. I. VARIABILITY.

The first quality desirable in a lot of punishment is *variability*; that it be susceptible of degrees both of intensity and duration.

An *invariable* punishment cannot be made to correspond to the different degrees of the scale of punishment: it will be liable to err either by excess or defect:—in the first case it would be too expensive, in the second inefficacious.

Acute corporeal punishments are extremely variable in respect of intensity, but not of duration. Penal labour is variable in both respects, in nearly equal degrees.

Chronic punishments, such as banishment and imprisonment, may be easily divided as to their duration: they may also be varied as to their intensity. A prison may be more or less severe. Banishment may be directed to a genial or ungenial [*sic*] clime.

SEC. II. EQUABILITY.[212]

A second property, intimately connected with the former, may be titled *equability*. It will avail but little that a mode of punishment (proper in all other respects) has been established by the legislature, and that capable of being screwed up or let down to any degree that can be required, if, after all, whatever degree of it be pitched upon, that same degree shall be liable, according to circumstances, to produce a very heavy degree of pain, or a very slight one, or even none at all. An equable punishment is free from this irregularity: an unequable [*sic*] one is liable to it.

Banishment is unequable. It may either prove a punishment or not, according to the temper, the age,[213] the rank, or the fortune of the individuals. This is also the case with *pecuniary* or *quasi pecuniary* punishment, when it respects some particular species of property which the offender may or may not possess. By the English law there are several offences which are punished by a total forfeiture of moveables, not extending to immoveables [*sic*]. In some cases this is the principle punishment—in others, even the only one. The consequence is, that if a man's fortune happens to consist in moveables, he is ruined; if in immoveables, he suffers nothing.

In the absence of other punishment, it may be proper to admit an unequable punishment. The chance of punishing some delinquents is preferable to universal impunity.

One mode of obviating the evil of inequality consists in the providing of two different species of punishment, not to be used together, but that the one may be substituted for and supply the defects of the other: for example, corporeal may be substituted for pecuniary punishment, when the poverty of the individual prevents the application of the latter.

An uncertain punishment is unequable. Complete certainty supposes complete equability; that is to say, that the same punishment shall produce in every case the same degree of suffering. Such accuracy is however evidently unattainable, the circumstances and sensibility of individuals being so variable and so unequal. All that can be accomplished is to avoid striking and manifest inequality. In the preparation of a penal code, it ought constantly to be kept in view, that according to circumstances, of condition, fortune, age, sex, &c. the same nominal is not the same real punishment. A fixed fine is always an unequable punishment; and the same remark is applicable to corporeal punishments. Whipping is not the same punishment when applied to all ages and ranks of persons. In China, indeed, every one is submitted to the bamboo, from the water-carrier to the mandarin; but this only proves, that among the Chinese the sentiments of honour are unknown.

SEC. III. COMMENSURABILITY.

Punishments are commensurable when the penal effects of each can be measured, and a distinct conception formed, of how much the suffering produced by the one falls short of or exceeds that produced by another.[214] Suppose a man placed in a situation to choose between several crimes,— he can obtain a sum of money by theft, by murder, or by arson: the law ought to give him a motive to abstain from the greatest crime; he will have that motive, if he see that the greatest crime draws after it the greatest punishment: he ought, therefore to be able to compare these punishments among themselves, and measure their different degrees.

If the same punishment of death is denounced for these three crimes, there is nothing to compare; the individual is left free to choose that crime which appears most easy of execution, and least liable to be detected.

Punishments may be made commensurable in two ways: 1. By adding to a certain punishment another quantity of the same kind; for example, to five years of imprisonment for a certain crime, two more years for a certain aggravation: 2. By adding a punishment of a different kind, for example, to five years of imprisonment for a certain crime, a mark of disgrace for a certain aggravation.[215]

SEC. IV. CHARACTERISTICALNESS.

Punishment can act as a preventative only when the idea of it, and of its connection with the crime, is present to the mind. Now, to be present, it must be remembered, and to be remembered it must have been learnt. But of all punishments that can be imagined, there are none of which the connection with the offence is either so easily learnt, or so efficaciously remembered, as those of which the idea is already in part associated with some part of the offence, which is the case when the one and the other have some circumstance that belongs to them in common.[216]

The law of retaliation is admirable in this respect. *An eye for an eye, and a tooth for a tooth.* The most imperfect intelligence can connect these ideas. This rule of retaliation is however rarely practicable; it is too unequable and too expensive; recourse must therefore be had to other sources of analogy. We shall therefore recur to this subject in the next chapter.[217]

SEC. V. EXEMPLARITY.

A mode of punishment is exemplary in proportion to its *apparent*, not to its *real* magnitude. It is the apparent punishment that does all the service in the way of example. A real punishment, which should produce no visible effects, might serve to intimidate or reform the offender subjected to it, but its use, as an example to the public, would be lost.

The object of the legislator ought therefore to be so far as it may be safely practicable, to select such modes of punishment, as, at the expense of the least *real*, shall produce the greatest *apparent* suffering; and to accompany each particular mode of punishment with such *solemnities* as may be best calculated to further this object.

In this point of view, the *auto-da-fes* would furnish most useful models for acts of justice. What is a public execution? It is a solemn tragedy which the legislator presents before an assembled people,—a tragedy truly important, truly pathetic, by the sad reality of its catastrophe, and the grandeur of its object. The preparation for it—the place of exhibition—and the attendant circumstances, cannot be too carefully selected, as upon these the principal effect depends. The tribunal, the scaffold, the dresses of the officers of justice, the religious service, the procession, every kind of accompaniment, ought to bear a grave and melancholy character. The executioners might be veiled in black, that the terror of the scene might be heightened, and these useful servants of the state screened from the hatred of the people.

Care must however be taken lest punishment become unpopular and odious through a false appearance of rigour.[218]

SEC. VI. FRUGALITY.

If any mode of punishment is more apt than another to produce superfluous and needless pain, it may be styled *unfrugal* [*sic*]; if less, it may be styled *frugal*. The perfection of frugality in a mode of punishment is where not only no superfluous pain is produced on the part of the person punished, but even that same operation by which he is subjected to pain, is made to answer the purpose of producing pleasure on the part of some other person.

Pecuniary punishments possess this quality in an eminent degree; nearly all the evil felt by the party paying, turns to the advantage of him who receives.

There are some punishments, which, with reference to the public expense, are particularly unfrugal: for example, mutilations, applied to offences of frequent occurrence, such as smuggling. When an individual is rendered unable to work, he must be supported by the state, or rendered dependent upon public charity, and thus fixed as a burthen upon the most benevolent.

If the statement of Filangieri is correct, there were constantly in the state prisons of Naples more than forty thousand idle prisoners. What an immense loss of productive power! The largest manufacturing town in England scarcely employs a greater number of workmen.[219]

By the military laws of most countries, deserters are still condemned to death. It costs little to shoot a man; but everything which he might be made to produce, is lost; and to supply his place a productive labourer must be converted into an unproductive one.

SEC. VII. SUBSERVIENCY[200] TO REFORMATION.[221]

All punishment has a certain tendency to deter[222] from the commission of offences; but if the delinquent, after he has been punished, is only deterred by fear from the repetition of his offence, he is not reformed. Reformation implies a change of character and moral dispositions.

Hence those punishments which are calculated to weaken the seductive, and to strengthen the preserving motives, have an advantage over all others with respect to those offences to which can be applied.

There are other punishments which have an opposite tendency, and which serve to render those who undergo them still more vicious. Punishments which are considered infamous, are extremely dangerous in this respect, particularly when applied to slight offences and juvenile offenders. *Diligentius enim vivit, cui aliquid integri superset. Nemo dignitati perditæ parcit. Impunitatis genus est jam non habere pœnæ locum.**

Of this nature also, in a high degree, is the punishment of[223] imprisonment, when care is not taken to prevent the indiscriminate association of prisoners; but the juvenile and the hoary delinquents are allowed to meet and to live together. Such prisons, instead of places for reform, are schools of crime.[224]

SEC. VIII. EFFICACY WITH RESPECT TO DISABLEMENT.[225]

A punishment which takes away the power of repeating the crime, must be very desirable, if not too costly. Imprisonment, whilst it continues, has this effect in a great measure. Mutilation sometimes reduces the power of committing crimes almost to nothing, and death destroys it altogether. It will, however, be perceived, that whilst a man is disabled from doing mischief, he is also in great measure disabled from doing good to himself or others.

In some extraordinary cases the power of doing mischief can only be destroyed by death: as, for example, the case of civil war, when the mere existence of the head of a party is sufficient to keep alive the hopes and exertions of his partisans. In such a case, however, the guilt of the parties is often problematic, and the punishment of death savours more of vengeance than of law.

---

*Senec. de Clem. chap. xxii.

There are however cases in which the ability to do mischief may be taken away with great economy of suffering. Has the offence consisted in an abuse of power, in an unfaithful discharge of duty, it is sufficient to depose the delinquent, to remove him from employment, the administration, the guardianship, the trust, he has abused. This remedy may equally be employed in domestic and political government.[226]

SEC. IX. SUBSERVIENCY TO COMPENSATION.[227]

A further property desirable in a lot of punishment is, that it may be convertible to profit.

When a crime is committed, and afterwards punished, there has existed two lots of evil—the evil of the offence, and the evil of the punishment.[228] Whenever then the evil of the offence falls upon a specific person, if the punishment yield a profit, let the profit arising from it be given to that person. The evil of the offence will be removed, and there will then only exist one lot of evil instead of two. When there is no specific party injured, as when the mischief of the crime consists in alarm or danger, there will be no specific injury to be compensated; still, if the punishment yield a profit, there is a clear balance of good gained.

This property is possessed in a more eminent degree by pecuniary than by any other mode of punishment.[229]

SEC. X. POPULARITY.[230]

In the rear of all of these properties may be introduced that of *popularity*— a very fleeting and indeterminate kind of property, which may belong to a lot of punishment one moment, and be lost by it the next. This[231] property, in strictness of speech, ought rather to be called *absence of unpopularity*; for it cannot be expected, in regard to such a matter as punishment, that any species or lot of it should be positively acceptable and grateful to the people; it is sufficient, for the most part, if they have no decided aversion to the thoughts of it.

The use of inserting this property in the catalogue is, that it may serve as a memento to the legislator not to introduce, without a cogent necessity, any mode or lot of punishment towards which any violent aversion is entertained by the body of the people, since it would be productive of useless suffering—suffering borne not by the guilty, but the innocent; and among the innocent by the most amiable, by those whose sensibility would be shocked, whose opinions would be outraged, by the punishment which would appear to them violent and tyrannical.[232] The effect of such injudicious conduct on the part of a legislator would be to turn the tide of popular opinion against himself: he would lose the assistance which individuals voluntarily lend to the execution of the laws which they approve: the people would not be his allies but his enemies. Some would favour the escape of the delinquent; the injured would hesitate to prosecute, and witnesses to bear testimony against him. By[233] degrees a stigma would attach to those who assisted in the execution of the laws. Public dissatisfaction would not always stop here; it would sometimes break out into open resistance to the officers of justice and the execution of such laws. Successful resistance would be considered a victory, and the unpunished delinquent would rejoice over the weakness of the laws disgraced by his triumph.[234]

The unpopularity of particular punishments almost always depends upon their improper selection. The more completely the penal code shall become conformed to the rules here laid down, the more completely will it merit the enlightened approbation of the wise, and the sentimental approval of the multitude.[235]

SEC. XI.[236] SIMPLICITY OF DESCRIPTION.[237]

A mode of punishment ought also to be as simple as possible in its description; it ought to be entirely intelligible; and that not only to the enlightened, but to the most unenlightened and ignorant.[238]

It will not always be proper, however, to confine punishments to those of a simple description; there are many offences in which it will be proper that the punishment should be composed of many parts, as of pecuniary fine, corporal suffering, and imprisonment. The rule of *simplicity* must give way to superior considerations. It has been placed here that it may not be lost sight of. The more complex punishment is, the greater reason is there to fear that it will not be present as a whole to the mind of an individual in the time of temptation; of its different parts he may never have known some—he may have forgotten others. All the parts will be found in the *real* punishment, but they have not been perceived in the *apparent*.[239]

The name of a punishment is an important object. Enigmatical names spread a cloud over the mass of punishments which the mind cannot dissipate. The English laws are frequently defective in this respect. A *capital felony* includes different lots of punishment, the greater part unknown, and consequently inefficacious. A *felony with benefit of clergy*, is equally obscure: the threatening of the law does not convey any distinct idea to the mind;—the first idea which the term would offer to an uninstructed person, would be that it had some reference to a reward. A *præmunire* is not more intelligible; even those who understand the Latin word are far from comprehending the nature of the punishment which it denounces.

Riddles of this kind resemble those of the sphinx—those are punished who do not decypher [*sic*] them.

SEC. XII. REMISSIBILITY.[240]

Remissibility is the last of all the properties that seem to be requisite in a lot of punishment. The general presumption is, that when punishment is applied, punishment is needful: that it ought to be applied, and therefore cannot be remitted. But in very particular, and those very deplorable cases, it may by accident happen otherwise. Punishment may have been inflicted upon an individual whose innocence is afterwards discovered. The punishment which he has suffered cannot, it is true, be remitted, but he may be freed from as much of it as is yet to come. There is however little chance of there being any yet to come, unless it be so much as consists of *chronical* [*sic*] punishment; such as imprisonment, banishment, penal labour, and the like. So much as consists in *acute* punishment, where the penal process itself is over presently, however permanent the punishment may be in its effects may be considered as irremissible [*sic*]. This is the case, for example, with whipping, branding, mutilation, and capital punishment.[241] The most perfectly irremissible of any is capital punishment. In all other cases means of compensation may be found for the sufferings of the unfortunate victim, but not in this.[242]

The foregoing catalogue of properties desirable in a lot of punishment, is far from unnecessary. On every occasion, before a right judgment can be formed, it is necessary to form an abstract idea of all the properties the object ought to possess. Unless this is done, every expression of approbation or disapprobation can arise only from a confused feeling of sympathy or antipathy. We now possess clear and distinct reasons for determining our choice of punishments. It remains only to observe in what proportion a particular punishment possesses these different qualities.

If a conclusion is drawn from one of these qualities alone, it may be subject to error; attention ought to be paid not to one quality alone, but to the whole together.

There is no one lot of punishment which unites all of these desirable qualities; but, according to the nature of the offences, one set of qualities are more important than another.

For great crimes, it is desirable that punishments should be exemplary and analogous. For lesser crimes, the punishments should be inflicted with a greater attention to their frugality, and their tendency to moral reformation. As to crimes against property, those punishments which are convertible to profit are to be preferred, since they may be rendered subservient to compensation for the party injured.

NOTE BY DUMONT

I subjoin to this chapter an example of the progressive march of thought, and of the utility of these enumerations to which every new observation may be referred, so that nothing may be lost.

I have sought out from the works of Montesquieu all the qualities which he appears to have regarded as necessary in a lot of punishment. I have found only four, and these are either expressed by indefinite terms or periphrasis.—

1. He says, that *Punishments should be drawn from the nature of the crimes*; and he appears to mean, that they should be characteristic.

2. That they should be *moderate*; an expression which is indeterminate, and does not yield any point of comparison.

3. That they should be *proportional to the crime.*—This proportion has reference, however, rather to the quantity of the punishment than to its quality. He has neither explained in what it consists, nor given any rule respecting it.

4. That they should be *modest.*

Beccaria has mentioned *four* qualities:—

1. He requires that punishments should be *analogous to the crimes*; but he does not enter into any detail upon this analogy.

2. That they should be *public*; and he means by that *exemplary*.

3. That they be *gentle*; an improper and unsignificant [*sic*] term, whilst his observations upon the danger of excess in punishment are very judicious.

4. That they should be *proportional*; but he gives no rule for this proposition.

He requires, besides this, that they should be *certain, prompt,* and *inevitable*; but these circumstances depend upon the forms of procedure in the application of punishment, and not upon its qualities.

In his commentary upon Beccaria, Voltaire often recurs to the idea of rendering punishments profitable.—"A dead man is good for nothing."

One of the heroes of humanity, the good and amiable Howard, had continually in view the amendment of delinquents.

Confining our attention to those who are considered as oracles in this branch of science, we cannot but observe that between these scattered ideas, and vague conceptions, which have not yet received a name, and a regular catalogue in which these qualities are distinctly presented to us, with names and definitions, there is a wide interval. By thus placing them under one point of view, another advantage is gained—their true worth and comparative importance is determined. Montesquieu was dazzled by the merit of analogy in a punishment, and has attributed to it wonderful effects which it does not possess.—*Esprit des Lois*, xii. 4.

These considerations appear to afford a sufficient answer to the objection often raised against the methodic [*sic*] forms employed by Mr. Bentham. I refer to his divisions, tables, and classifications, which have been called his *logical apparatus*. All this, it has been said, is only the scaffold, which ought to be taken down when the building is erected. But why deprive his readers of the instruments which the author has employed? Why hide from them his analytical labours and process of invention? These tables form a machine for thought,—*organum cogitativum*. The author discloses his secret; he associates his readers with him in his labour; he gives them the clue which has guided him in his researches, and enables them to verify his results. The singularity is this—the extent of the service diminishes its value.

I am sensible that by employing these logical methods, as a secret, by not exhibiting, so to speak, the skeleton, the muscles, the nerves, much would be gained in elegance and interest. By using the method of analysis, everything is announced beforehand—there is nothing unexpected;—the whole is clear; and there are[243] no points of surprise—no flashes of genius to dazzle for a moment, and then leave you in darkness. It requires courage to follow up so severe a method, but it is the only method which can completely satisfy the mind.

CHAPTER VIII.[244]
OF ANALOGY BETWEEN CRIMES AND PUNISHMENTS.

Analogy is that relation, connexion, or tye [sic] between two objects, whereby the one being present to the mind, the idea of the other is naturally excited.

Likeness is one source of analogy, contrast another.* That a punishment may be analogous to an offence, it is necessary that the crime should be attended with some striking characteristic circumstances, capable of being transferred upon the punishment.

These characteristic circumstances will be different in different crimes. In some cases they may arise from the instrument whereby the mischief has been done; in others, from the means employed to prevent detection.

The examples which follow are only intended clearly to explain this idea of analogy. I shall point out[245] the analogy between certain crimes and certain punishments, without absolutely recommending the employment of those punishments in all cases. It is not a sufficient reason for the adoption of a punishment that it is analogous; other considerations ought to be always regarded.[246]

SEC. I.—FIRST SOURCE OF ANALOGY.
The same Instrument used in the Crime as in the Punishment.

Incendiarism, inundation, poisoning—in these crimes the instrument employed is the first circumstance which strikes the mind. In their punishment, the same instrument may be employed.

With respect to incendiarism, we may observe, that this crime should be considered as limited to those cases in which some individual has perished by fire: if no life has been lost, nor any personal injury been suffered, the offence ought to be treated as an ordinary waste;[247] whether an article of property has been destroyed by fire, or any other agent, does not make any difference. The

---

*Thus from the idea of a giant, the mind passes on to every thing that is great. The Liliputians called Gulliver the Manmountain. Or, from the idea of a giant the mind may pass to that of a dwarf.

amount of the damage ought to be the measure of the crime. Does a man set fire to a solitary and uninhabited house; this would be an act of destruction, and ought not to be ranked under the definition of incendiarism.*

If the punishment of fire had been reserved for incendiaries, the law would have had in its favour both reason and analogy; but in the legislation of barbarous times, it has been generally employed throughout Europe, for three sorts of offence: magic, a purely imaginary offence: heresy, a simple difference of religious opinion, perfectly innocent, often useful, and with respect to which, the only effect of punishment is to produce falsehood, the third offence, resulting in a harmless deprivation that is sufficiently rebuked through shame.†[248]

Fire may be employed as an instrument of punishment, without occasioning death. This punishment is variable in its nature through all the degrees of severity of which there can be any need. It would be necessary carefully to determine in the text of the law, the part of the body which ought to be exposed to the action of the fire; the intensity of the fire; the time during which it is to be applied, and the paraphanalia [*sic*] to be employed to increase the terror of the punishment. In order to render the description more striking, a print might be annexed in which the operation should be represented.

Inundation is an offence less common than incendiarism, in some countries it is altogether unexampled, it can only be perpetrated in countries that are intersected by water, confined by artificial banks. It is susceptible of every degree of aggravation from the highest to the lowest. If the

---

*The employment of this means of destruction ought, however, to be considered an aggravation, if there has been any danger of the fire communicating to contiguous objects.

†Torment by fire, other times applied in France to this offense, finds its origin in false reasoning, drawn from the history of the Jewish people. One belief is to imitate Providence, which had destroyed by fire two culpable cities.

But, first, theologians of all persuasions agree that miraculous dispensations of divine justice cannot provide a rule for ordinary and permanent institutions of human legislatures; no more than murmurings against authority (15,000 persons were put to death for murmuring against Moses—see the story of Korah, Dathan, and Abiran, Num. 1:16) and mockery of elders (the offense for which 42 children were torn to pieces by bears upon the prayer of Elisha, 2 Kings 11) can achieve the rank of capital crimes.

Second, if God willed that this punishment should be punished by fire, it would have begun through his people; but Jewish law commands the death penalty in generous terms; likewise, punishment by fire was excluded, since within the following verse, for a sort of incest, it is positively proscribed. Leviticus XX, 13–14.

Third, it is not said that this offense had been the only one for which these cities had been destroyed: the text generally imputes all sorts of iniquities and wickedness.

Fourth, it was not simply the same offense of impurity that had been the crime of the Canaanites: the had been guilty of a violation of hospitality and personal violence: two grievances that were so strong that they completely changed the nature of the offense.

offence consist merely in inundation, in effect it amounts only to a simple destruction of property. It is by the destruction of life that this crime is raised to that degree of atrocity which requires severe punishment.

A most evident[249] analogy points out the means of punishment, that is, the drowning of the criminal, with such accompanying circumstances as will add to the terror of the punishment. In a penal code, which should not admit the punishment of death, the offender might be drowned and then restored to life. This might be made part of the punishment.

It may be asked, ought poison to be employed as a means of punishment for a poisoner?

In some respects there is no punishment more suitable. Poisoning is distinguished from other murders, by the secrecy with which it may be perpetrated, and the cool determination which it supposes. Of these two circumstances, the first increases the force of temptation and the evil of the crime; the second, proves that the criminal, attentive to his own interest, is capable of serious reflection upon the nature of the punishment. The idea of perishing by the same kind of death which he prepares, is the more frightful for him. In every step of his preparations his imagination will represent to him his own lot. In this point of view the analogy would produce its full effect.[250]

There are, however, many difficulties; poisons are uncertain in their operation. It would be necessary therefore to fix a time after which the punishment should be abridged by strangulation. If the effect of the poison should be to produce sleep, the punishment may not be sufficiently exemplary. If it produce convulsions and distortions, it may prove hateful.

If the poison administered by the criminal has not proved fatal, he may be made to take an antidote before the penal poison has produced death. The dose and the time may be fixed by the Judges, according to the report of skilful physicians.

The horror attached to this crime would most probably render this punishment popular. And if there is one country in which this crime is more common than others, it is there that this punishment, which possesses so striking an analogy with the crime, would be the most suitable.[251]

SEC. II.—SECOND SOURCE OF ANALOGY.
For a Corporal Injury a similar Corporal Injury.

"An eye for an eye, a tooth for a tooth." In crimes producing irreparable bodily injuries, the part of the body injured will afford the characteristic circumstance. The analogy will consist in making[252] the offender suffer an evil similar to that which he has maliciously and wilfully inflicted.[253]

It will, however, be necessary to provide for two cases—that in which the offender does not possess the member of which he has deprived the party he has attacked, and that in which the loss of the member would be more or less prejudicial to him than to the party injured.

If the injury has been of an ignominious nature, without permanent mischief—Similar ignominy may be employed in the punishment, when the rank of the party and other circumstances permit.[254]

[255]SEC. III.—THIRD SOURCE OF ANALOGY.
Punishment of the Offending Member.

In crimes of deceit, the tongue and the hand are the usual instruments. An exact analogy in the punishment may be drawn from this circumstance.

In punishing the crime of forgery, the hand of the offender may be transfixed by an iron instrument fashioned like a pen, and in this condition he may be exhibited to the public previously to undergoing the punishment of imprisonment.

In the utterance of calumny, and the dissemination of false reports, the tongue is the instrument employed. The offender might in the same manner be publicly exposed with his tongue pierced.*

These punishments may be made more formidable in appearance than in reality, by dividing the instruments in two parts, so that the part which should pierce the offending member, need not be thicker than a pin, whilst the other part of the instrument may be much thicker, and appear to penetrate with all its thickness.[256]

Punishments of this kind may appear ridiculous, but the ridicule which attaches to them enhances their merit. This ridicule will be directed against the cheat, whom it will render more despicable, whilst it will increase the respect due to upright dealing.

[257]SEC. IV.—FOURTH SOURCE OF ANALOGY.
Imposition of Disguise assumed.

Some offences are characterized by the assumption of a disguise to facilitate their commission:—a mask, or crape over the face, has commonly been

---

*By the same observation, the thinnest needle, ending in two knots, is sufficient for impeding language from returning to the mouth. [This note appeared as an in-text note, following the previous paragraph, within Dumont's edition, *Théorie des peines*, vol. I, p. 67. It does not appear within Smith's 1830 edition.]

used. This circumstance constitutes an aggravation of the offence; it increases the alarm produced, and diminishes the probability of detection; and hence arises the propriety of additional punishment. Analogy would recommend the imprinting on the offender a representation of the disguise assumed. This impression might be made either evanescent or indelible, according as the imprisonment by which it may be accompanied, is to be either temporary or otherwise. If evanescent, it might be produced by the use of a black wash. If indelible, by tattooing. The utility of this punishment would be most particularly felt in cases of premeditated murder, rape, irreparable personal injury, and theft, when accompanied with violence and alarm.

[258]SEC. V.—OTHER SOURCES OF ANALOGY.

There are other characteristic circumstances, which do not, like the foregoing, fall into classes; which may, however, according to the nature of the different offences, be employed as a foundation for analogy.

In the fabrication of base coin, the art of the delinquent may furnish an analogous source of punishment. He has made an impression upon the metal he has employed;—a like impression may be made on some conspicuous part of his face. This mark may be either evanescent or indelible, according as the imprisonment by which it is to be accompanied is either temporary or perpetual.

At Amsterdam, vagabonds and idle persons are committed to the House of Corrections, called the Rasp House. It is said, that among other species of forced labour, in which such characters are employed, there is one reserved for those who are incorrigible by other means; which consists in keeping a leaky vessel, in which the idle prisoner is placed, dry, by means of a pump at which he must work, if he would keep himself from being drowned. Whether this punishment is in use or not, it is an example of an analogous punishment carried to the highest degree of rigour. If such a method of punishment is adopted, it ought to be accompanied with precise regulations for adjusting the punishment to the strength of the individual undergoing it.

[259]The place in which a crime has been committed may furnish a species of analogy. Catherine II condemned a man who had committed some knavish trick at the Exchange, to sweep it out every day that it was used, during six months.

NOTE BY DUMONT[260]

I am not aware of any objection having been urged against[261] the utility of analogy in punishments: whilst it is spoken of only in general terms,[262] everybody acknowledges its propriety: when we proceed to apply the principle, the imagination being the chief judge of the propriety of its application, the diversity of opinion is infinite. Hence some persons have been struck with extreme repugnance in contemplating the analogous punishments proposed by Mr. Bentham,*[263] whilst others have considered them only as fit subjects for ridicule and caricature.

Success depends upon the choice of the means employed. Those sources of analogy ought therefore to be avoided which are not of a sufficiently grave character to be used as punishments; but, it may be observed, that with relation to certain offenses, those, for instance, which are accompanied by insolence and insult, that an analogous punishment which excites ridicule, is well calculated to humble the pride of the offender, and gratify the offended party.

Everything ought also to be avoided which has an appearance of great study and refinement. Punishment ought[264] only to be inflicted of necessity, and with feelings of regret and repugnance. The multitude of instruments possessed by a surgeon, may be contemplated with satisfaction, as intended to promote the cure and lessen the weight of our sufferings. The same satisfaction will not, however, be felt in contemplating a variety of punishments, and they will most likely be considered as degrading[265] to the character of the legislator.

With these precautions, analogy is calculated to produce only good effects. It puts us in the track of discovering the most economical and efficacious punishments. I cannot resist the pleasure of citing an example furnished me by a Captain in the English Navy:—He had not studied the principles of Mr. Bentham, but he knew how to read the human heart.

The leave of absence generally granted to sailors, was for twenty-four hours: if they exceeded this time, the ordinary punishment was the cat-o'-nine-tails.[266] The dread of this punishment[267] was a frequent cause of desertions. Many Captains, in order to prevent both these offenses, refused all leave of absence to their sailors, so that they were kept on shipboard for years together. The individual to whom I refer, discovered a method of reconciling the granting of leave with the security of the service. He made a simple change in the punishment:—Every man who exceeded his prescribed time of leave, lost his right to a future leave, in proportion to his fault. If he remained on shore more than twenty-four hours, he lost one turn;[268] and so of the rest. The experiment was perfectly successful. The fault became less frequent,[269] and desertions were unknown.

---

*Traités de Legislation, vol. II, p. 352.

CHAPTER IX.[270]
OF RETALIATION.[271]

[272]

IF the law of retaliation were admissible in all cases, it would very much abridge the labours of the legislators. It would make short work of the business of laying out a plan of punishment:—a word would supply the place of a volume.*[273]

Before we say anything as to the advantage of the rule, it will be proper to state with precision what is meant by it. The idea given of it in Blackstone's Commentaries, seems to be a correct one;—it is that rule which prescribes, in the way of punishment, the doing to a delinquent the same hurt he has done (one might perhaps add, or attempted to do) to another. If the injury were done to the person, the delinquent should be punished in his person: if to property, in his property: if to the reputation, in his reputation.[274] This is the general scheme; but this, however, in itself, is not quite enough. To make the punishment come incontestably under the law of retaliation, the identity between the subject of the offence and that of the punishment should be still more specific and determinate. If, for example, the injury were to a man's house, for instance, by the destruction of his house, then the delinquent should have his house destroyed: if to his reputation, by causing him to lose a certain rank, then the delinquent should be made to lose the same rank: if to the eyes, then the criminal should be made to lose his eyes: if to his lip, then to lose his lip: and in short, the more specific and particular the resemblance between the subject of the offence and of the punishment, the more strictly and incontestibly [sic] it would appear to come under the rule. It is when the person is the subject of the injury, that the resemblance is capable of being rendered the most minute; for it is in this case that by means of the strict identity of the part affected, "*the hurt*" is capable of being rendered the most accurately the "*same.*" *An eye for an eye, and a tooth for a tooth*, are the familiar instances that are put of the law of retaliation. In this case, too, the identity may be pushed still further, by affecting the same part in the same manner; the sameness of the hurt depending on the identity of the one circumstance as well as of the other.

---

*The law of retaliation was often adopted in the early attempts at legislation. Among the laws of Alfred we find the following article:—"Si quis alterius occulum effoderit, compenset proprio, dentem prodente, manum pro manu, pedem pro pede, adustionem pro adustione, vulnus pro vulnere, vimen pro vimine."—*Wilk. Ll. Ang. Sax.* p. 30. Art. 19.

Thus, if the injury consisted in the burning out of an eye, the punishment will be more strictly the same, if it be effected by burning rather than cutting out the eye of the delinquent.[275]

The great merit of the law of retaliation is its simplicity. If it were capable of universal adoption, the whole penal code would be contained in one law:—"Let every offender suffer an evil similar to that which he has inflicted."

No other imaginable plan can for its extent find so easy an entrance into the apprehension, or sit so easy on the memory. The rule is at once so short and so expressive, that he who has once heard it, is not likely to forget it, or ever to think of a crime, but he must think also of its punishment. The stronger the temptation to commit an offence, the more likely is its punishment to be an object of dread. Thus the defence is erected on the side of danger.

One advantage that cannot be denied to this mode of punishment is its popularity, requiring little expense of thought, it will generally be found to possess the judgment of the multitude in its favour. Should they in any instance be disposed to quarrel with it, they will still be ready enough probably to own it to be consonant to justice: but that justice, they will say, is rigid justice, or to vary the jargon, justice in the abstract. All this while, with these phrases on their lips, they would perhaps prefer a milder punishment, as being more consonant to mercy, and, upon the whole, more conducive to the general happiness: as if justice, and especially penal justice, were something distinct from, and adverse to, that happiness. When, however, it happens not to give disgust by its severity, nothing can be more popular than this mode of punishment. This may be seen in the case of murder, with respect to which the attachment to this mode of punishment is warm and general. Blood (as the phrase is)[276] will have blood. Unless a murderer be punished with death, the multitude of speculators can seldom bring themselves to think that the rules of justice are pursued.[277]

The law of retaliation is, however, liable to a variety of objections, one of which, so far as it applies, is conclusive against its adoption.[278] In a great variety of cases it is physically inapplicable. Without descending far into detail, a few instances may suffice as examples. In the first place, it can never be applied when the offence is merely of a public nature, the characteristic quality of such offences being, that no assignable individual is hurt by them. If a man has been guilty of high treason, or has engaged in criminal correspondence with an enemy, or has, from cowardice, abandoned the defence of a post entrusted to him; how would it be possible to make him suffer an evil similar to that of which he has been the cause.

It is equally inapplicable to offences of the semi-public class—to offences which affect a certain district,[279] or particular class of the community. The mischief of these offences often consists in alarm and danger, which do not affect one individual alone, and therefore do not present any opportunity for the exercise of retaliation.

With respect to self-regarding offences, consisting of acts which offend against morality, the application of this law would be absurd. The individual has chosen to perform the act, to do the same thing to him would not be to punish him.[280]

In offences against reputation, consisting, for instance, in the propagation of false reports affecting the character, it would be useless as a punishment to direct a similar false report to be propagated affecting the character of the delinquent. The like evil would not result from the circulation of what was acknowledged to be false.

In offences against property, the punishment of retaliation would at all times be defective in point of exemplarity and efficacy, and, in many cases, altogether inapplicable; those who are most apt to injure others in this respect, being, by their poverty, unable to suffer in a similar manner.

For a similar reason it cannot be constantly applied to offences affecting the civil condition of individuals, to say nothing of the reasons that might render it ineligible if it were possible to be applied.

These exceptions reduce its possible field of action to a very small extent, the only classes of offences to which it will be found applicable, with any degree of constancy, are those that affect the person, and even here must be assumed what scarcely ever exists, a perfect identity of circumstances. Even in this very limited class of cases, it would be found to err on the side of excessive severity. Its radical defect is, its inflexibility. The law ought so to apportion the punishment as to meet the several circumstances of aggravation or extenuation that may be found in the offence: retaliation is altogether incompatible with any such apportionment.

The class of people among whom this mode of punishment is most likely to be popular, are those of a vindictive character. Mahomet found it established among the Arabians, and has adopted it in the Koran, with a degree of approbation, that marks the extent of his talent for legislation. "O you who have a heart, you will find in the law of retaliation, and in the fear that accompanies it, universal security."—(Vol. I, ch. ii, *On the Law*.) Either from weakness or ignorance, he encouraged the prevailing vice which he ought to have checked.

CHAPTER X.[281]

POPULARITY.

To[282] prove that an institution is agreeable to the principle of utility, is to prove, as far as can be proved, that the people *ought* to like it: but whether they *will* like it or no after all, is another question.[283] They would like it if, in their judgments, they suffered themselves to be uniformly and exclusively governed by that principle. By this principle they do govern themselves in proportion as they are humanized and enlightened; accordingly, the deference they pay to its dictates is more uniform in this intelligent and favoured country than perhaps in any other.[284] I speak here, taking the great mass of the people upon this occasion, into the account; and not confining my views, as is too commonly the case, to men of rank and education.[285]

Even in this country, however, their acquiescence is far from being as yet altogether uniform and undeviating: in some instances their judgments are still warped[286] by antipathies or prejudices unconnected with the principle of utility, and therefore irreconcileable [*sic*] to reason. They are apt to bear antipathy to certain offences without regard to even[287] their imputed mischievousness, and to entertain a prejudice against certain punishments without regard to their eligibility with respect to the ends of punishment.[288]

The variety of capricious objections to which each particular mode of punishment is exposed, has no other limits than the fecundity of the imagination: with some slight exceptions, they may[289] however be ranged under one or other of the following heads:—*Liberty—Decency—Religion—Humanity*.[290] What I mean by a capricious objection, is an objection which derives the whole of its apparent value from the impression that is apt to be made by the use of those hallowed expressions: the caprice consists in employing them in a perverted sense.

[291]1. *Liberty*.—Under this head there is little to be said. All punishment is an infringement on liberty: no one submits to it but from compulsion. Enthusiasts, however, are not wanting, who, without regarding this circumstance, condemn certain modes of punishment, as, for example, imprisonment accompanied with penal labour, as a violation of the natural rights of man. In a free country like this, say they, it ought not to be tolerated, that even malefactors should be reduced to a state of slavery. The precedent is dangerous and pernicious. None but men groaning under a despotic gov-

ernment can endure the sight of galley-slaves.[292]

When the establishment of the penitentiary system was proposed,[293] this objection was echoed and insisted on, in a variety of publications that appeared on that occasion. Examine this senseless clamour, it will resolve itself into a declaration that liberty ought to be left to those that abuse it, and that the liberty of malefactors is an essential part of the liberty of honest men.

2. *Decency.*—Objections drawn from the topics of decency are confined to those punishments, of which the effect is to render those parts which it is inconsistent with decency to expose, the objects of sight or of conversation.

Who can doubt, that in all punishments, care should be taken that no offence be given to modesty. But modesty, like other virtues, is valuable only in proportion to its utility. When the punishment is the most appropriate, though not either in its description or its execution altogether reconcileable [*sic*] with modesty, this circumstance ought not, as it appears to me, to stand in the way of the attainment of any object of greater utility.[294] Castration, for example, seems the most appropriate punishment in the case of rape, that is to say, the best adapted to produce a strong impression on the mind at the moment of temptation. Is it expedient, then, on account of such scruples of modesty, that another punishment, as, for example, death, should be employed which is less exemplary, and, consequently, less efficacious?*

3. *Religion.*—Among Christians there are some sects who conceive that the punishment of death is unlawful: life, they say, is the gift of God, and man is forbidden to take it away.

We shall find in the next book, that very cogent reasons are not wanting for altogether abolishing capital punishment, or, at most, for confining it to extraordinary cases. But this pretence of unlawfulness is a reason drawn from false principles.[295]

Unlawful, means *contrary to some law*. Those, who, upon the occasion in question, apply this expression to the punishment of death, believe themselves, or endeavour to make others believe, that it is contrary to some Divine law: this Divine law is either revealed or unrevealed; if it be

---

*It is said, that in one of the cities of Greece, among the young women, instigated by I know not what disease of the imagination, the practice of suicide was for a time extremely prevalent. The magistrates, alarmed by its frequency, ordered that as a sort of posthumous punishment, their bodies, in a state of nudity, should be drawn through the public places. Into the truth of the relation, it is needless to inquire; but the narrator adds, the offense thenceforth altogether ceased. Here, then, is an instance of the utility of a law offensive to modesty, proved by its efficacy: for what higher degree of perfection can be looked for in any penal law than that of preventing the offense. [This note is presented as a separate paragraph at the conclusion of the parallel section of Dumont's edition, *Théorie des peines*, vol. I, p. 81.]

revealed, it must be found in the text of those books which are understood to contain the expressions of God's will; but as there exists no such text in the New Testament, and as the Jewish law expressly ordains capital punishment, the partizans [sic] of this opinion must have recourse to some Divine law not revealed—to a natural law—that is to say, to a law deduced from the supposed will of God.

But if we presume that God wills[296] anything, we must suppose that he has a reason for so doing, a reason worthy of himself, which can only be the greatest happiness of his creatures. In this point of view, therefore, the Divine will cannot require anything inconsistent with general utility.

If it be pretended that God can have any will not consistent with utility, his will becomes a fantastic and delusive principle, in which the ravings of enthusiasm, and the extravagancies of superstition, will find sanction and authority.[297]

In many cases, religion has been to such a degree perverted as to become a bar to the execution of penal laws: as in the case of sanctuaries opened for criminals, in the Romish churches.[298]

Theodosius I forbade all criminal proceedings during Lent, alleging, as a reason, that the judges ought not to punish the crimes of others whilst they were imploring the Divine forgiveness for their own transgressions. Valentinian I directed that at Easter all prisoners should be discharged, except those that were accused of the most malignant offences.[299]

Constantine prohibited, by law, the branding of criminals on the face, alleging, that it is a violation of the law of nature to disfigure the majesty of the human face—the majesty of the face of a scoundrel!

The Inquisition, says Bayle, that it might not violate the maxim, *Ecclesia non novit sanguinem*, condemned its victims to be burnt alive. Religion has had its quibbles as well as the law.

[300]4. *Humanity.*—Attend not to the sophistries of reason, which often deceive, but be governed by your hearts, which will always lead you to right.[301] I reject, without hesitation, the punishment you propose, it violates natural feelings, it harrows up[302] the susceptible mind, it is tyrannical and cruel. Such is the language of your sentimental orators.

But abolish any one penal law merely because it is repugnant to the feelings of a humane heart, and, if consistent, you abolish the whole penal code, there is not one of its provisions that does not, in a more or less painful degree,[303] wound the sensibility.

All punishment is in itself necessarily odious; if it were not dreaded, it would not effect its purpose; it can never be contemplated with approbation, but when considered in connection with the prevention of the crime against which it is denounced.[304]

I reject sentiment as an absolute Judge, but under the control of reason it may not be a useless monitor. When a penal dispensation is revolting to the public feeling, this is not of itself a sufficient reason for rejecting it, but it is a reason for subjecting it to a rigorous scrutiny. If it deserves the antipathy it excites, the causes of that antipathy may be easily detected.[305] We shall find that the punishment in question is mis-seated or superfluous, or disproportionate to the offence, or that it has a tendency to produce more mischief than it prevents.[306] By this means we arrive at the seat of error. Sentiment excites to reflection, and reflection detects the impropriety of the law.[307]

The species of punishment that command the largest share of public approbation are such as are analogous to the offence. Punishments of this description are commonly considered just and equitable; but what is the foundation of this justice and equity I know not. The delinquent suffers the same evil he has caused. Ought the law to imitate the example it condemns? Ought the Judge to imitate the malefactor in his wickedness? Ought a solemn act of justice to be the same in kind as an act of criminality?

This circumstance satisfies the multitude;[308] the mouth of the criminal is stopped, and he cannot accuse the law of severity, without at the same time being equally self-condemned.[309]

Fortunately, the same bent of the imagination that renders this mode of punishment popular, renders it at the same time appropriate. The analogy that presents itself to the people, presents itself, at the moment of temptation, to the delinquent, and renders it a peculiar object of dread.[310]

[311]It is of importance to detect and expose erroneous conceptions, even when they happen to accord with the principle of utility. The coincidence is a mere accident; and whoever on any one occasion[312] forms his judgment, without reference to this principle, prepares himself upon any other to decide[313] in contradiction to it. There will be no safe and steady guide for the understanding in its progress till men shall have learnt to trust to this principle alone, to the exclusion of all others. When the judgment is to decide, the use of laudatory or vituperative expressions, is the mere babbling of children. They ought to be avoided in all philosophical disquisitions, where the object ought to be to instruct and convince the understanding, and not to inflame the passions.[314]

BOOK II.
OF CORPORAL PUNISHMENTS.

CHAPTER I.
SIMPLE AFFLICTIVE*
PUNISHMENTS.

A punishment is simply afflictive when the object aimed at is to produce immediate temporary suffering, and is so called to distinguish it from other classes of corporeal punishments in which the suffering produced is designed to be more permanent. Simple afflictive punishments are distinguished from one another by three principle circumstances:—the part affected, the nature of the instrument, and the manner of its application.[315]

To enumerate all the varieties of punishment which might be produced by the combination of these different circumstances, would be an useless as well as an endless task. To enumerate the several parts of a man's body in which he is liable to be made to suffer, would be to give a complete body of natural history. To attempt to enumerate the different manners in which those instruments may be applied to such a purpose, would be to attempt to exhaust the inexhaustible variety of motions and situations.

Among the indefinite multitude of punishments of this kind that might be imagined and described, it will answer every purpose if we mention some of those which have been in use in this and other countries.[316]

The most obvious method of inflicting this species of punishment, and which has been most commonly used, consists in exposing the body to blows or stripes. When these are inflicted with a flexible instrument, the operation is called whipping. When a less flexible instrument is employed, the effects are different; but the operation is seldom[317] distinguished by another name.

---

*I am sensible how imperfectly the word *afflictive* is calculated to express the particular kind of punishment I have here employed to express, in contradistinction to others; but I could find no other word in the language that would do it better. It may be some reason for employing it thus, that in French it is employed in a sense nearly, if not altogether, as confined:† and the pains it is the nature of the punishments in question to produce, Cicero expresses by a word of the same root:—"*Adfictatio*" (says that orator in his Tusculan Disputations, when he is defining and distinguishing the several sorts of pain,) "*est ægritudo cum vexatione corporis.*"‡

†Causes Celèbres, chap. iv. p. 229.—ed. Amsterd. 1764.

‡Lib. iv. c. 8.

[This note apparently was added by Richard Smith, as it does not appear within the manuscript or Dumont's edition. RP MSS 141/45.]

In Italy, and particularly in Naples, there is a method, not uncommon, of punishing pickpockets, called the *Strappado*. It consists in raising the offender by his arms, by means of an engine like a crane, to a certain height, and then letting him fall, but suddenly stopping his descent before he reaches the ground. The momentum which his body has acquired in the descent, is thus made to bear upon his arms, and the consequence generally is, that they are dislocated at the shoulder: to prevent the permanent evil consequences, a surgeon is then employed to reset them.

There were formerly in England two kinds of punishment of this class, discarded now even from the military code, in which they were longest retained. The one called *Picketing*, which consisted in suspending the offender in such manner that the weight of his body was supported to principally by a spike, on which he was made to stand with one foot: the other, the *Wooden Horse*, as it was called, was a narrow ledge or board, on which the individual was made to *sit* astride; and the inconvenience of which was increased by suspending weights to his legs.[318]

Another species of punishments formerly practised in this country, but now rarely used, consisted in subjecting the patient to frequent immersions in water, called ducking. The individual was fastened to a chair or stool, called the ducking-stool, and plunged repeatedly. In this case the punishment was not of the acute, but of the uneasy kind. The physical uneasiness arises partly from the cold, partly from temporary stoppage of respiration. It has something of the ridiculous mixed with it, and was most generally applied to scolding women, whose tongues disturbed their neighbours. It is a relict of the simplicity of the olden time. It is still occasionally resorted to, when people take the administration of the laws into their own hands; and is not uncommonly the fate of the pickpocket who is detected at a fair or other place of promiscuous resort.[319]

The powers of invention have been principally employed in devising instruments for the production of pain, by those tribunals which have sought to extort proofs of his criminality from the individual suspected. They have been prepared for all parts of the body, according as they have wished to stretch, to distort, or to dislocate them. Screws for compressing the thumbs; straight boots, for compressing the shins, with wedges driven in by a mallet; the rack, for either compressing or extending the limbs; all of which might be regulated so as to produce every possible degree of pain.

Suffocation was produced by drenching, and was practised by tying a wet linen cloth over the mouth and nostrils of the individual, and continually supplying it with water, in such manner, that every time the individual breathed, he was obliged to swallow a portion of water, till his stomach became visibly distended. In the infamous transactions of the Dutch at

Amboyna, this species of torture was practised upon the English who fell into their power.

It would be useless to pursue this afflicting detail any further. How variously soever the causes may be diversified, the effect is still one and the same; viz. organical [*sic*] pain, whether of the acute or uneasy kind. This effect is common to all these modes of punishment. There are other points in which they may differ:—1. One of them may carry the intensity of the pain to a higher or lower pitch than it could be carried by another. 2. One may be purer from consequences which, for the purpose in question, it may or may not be intended to produce.

These consequences may be:—1. The continuance of the organical pain itself beyond the time of applying the instrument—2. The production of any of those other ill consequences which constitute the other kinds of corporeal punishment—3. The subjecting the party to ignominy.

In the choice of punishment, these circumstances, how little soever they are attended to in practice, are of the highest importance.

It would be altogether useless, not to say mischievous, to introduce into the penal code a great variety of modes of inflicting this species of punishment. Whipping—the mode which has been most commonly in use, would, if proper care were taken to give to it every degree of intensity, be sufficient, if it were the only one. Analogy, however, in certain cases, recommends the employment of other modes. The multiplication of the instruments of punishment, when not thus justified, tends only to render the laws odious.[320]

Among other works undertaken by order of the Empress Maria Theresa for the amelioration of the laws, a description was compiled of the various methods of inflicting torture and punishment in the Austrian dominions. It formed a large folio volume, in which not only all the instruments were described, and represented by engravings, but a detailed account was given of the manipulations of the executioners. This book was only exposed for sale for a few days, Prince Kaunitz, the prime minister, having caused it to be suppressed. He was apprehensive, and certainly not without reason, that the sight of such a work would only inspire a horror of the laws. This objection fell with its whole force upon the instruments for the infliction of torture, which has since been abolished in all the Austrian dominions. It is highly probable that the publication of this work contributed to produce this happy event. If so, few books have done more good to the world, if compared with the time they continued in it.

[321]A valuable service would be rendered to society by the individual, who, being properly qualified for the task, should examine[322] the effects produced by these different modes of punishment, and should point out the greater or smaller evil consequences resulting from contusions produced

by blows with a rope, or lacerations by whips, &c. In Turkey punishment is inflicted by beating the soles of the feet. Whether the consequences are more or less severe, I know not. It is perhaps from some notion of modesty that the Turks have confined the application of punishment to this part of the human body.

If the suffering produced by a punishment of this class is rendered but little more than momentary, it will neither be sufficiently exemplary to affect the spectators, nor sufficiently efficacious to intimidate the offenders. There will be little on the chastisement but the ignominy attached to it; and this would have but little effect upon that class of delinquents upon whom such punishments are generally inflicted; the quantity of suffering ought, therefore, if possible, to be regulated by the laws.

Of all these different modes of punishment, whipping is the most frequently in use; but in whipping not even the qualities of the instrument*[323] are ascertained by written law: while the quantity of force to be employed in its application is altogether intrusted [sic] to the caprice of the executioner. He may make the punishment as trifling or as severe as he pleases. He may derive from this power a source of revenue, so that the offender will be punished, not in proportion to his offence, but to his poverty. If he has been unfortunate, and not able to secure his plunder, or honest, and has voluntarily given it up, and this has nothing left to make a sop for Cerberus, he suffers the rigour—perhaps more than the rigour—of the law. Good fortune and perseverance, in dishonesty, would have enabled him to buy indulgence.

The following contrivance would, in a measure, obviate this inconvenience:—A machine might be made, which should put in motion certain elastic rods of cane or whalebone, the number and size of which might be determined by the law:[324] the body of the delinquent might be subjected to the strokes of these rods, and the force and rapidity with which they should be applied, might be prescribed by the Judge: thus everything which is arbitrary might be removed. A public officer, of more responsible character than the common executioner, might preside over the infliction of the punishment; and when there were many delinquents to be punished, his time might be saved, and the terror of the scene heightened, without increasing the actual suffering, by increasing the number of the machines, and subjecting all the offenders to punishment at the same time.

---

*The Chinese, owing perhaps to the extensive use they make of this mode of punishment, have attempted to, by fixing the length and breadth at the extremities, and weight of the bamboo, to render uniform the amount of the suffering produced by this mode of punishment; but one material circumstance that they have omitted to regulate, and certainly the most difficult to regulate, is the degree of force with which the stroke is to be applied; an omission that leaves the uncertainty nearly in the same state as in this country.—See the *Penal Code of China*, translated by Sir G. T. Staunton, p. 24.

SEC. II. EXAMINATION OF
SIMPLE AFFLICTIVE PUNISHMENTS.

The examination of a punishment consists in comparing it successively with each of the qualities which have been pointed out as desirable in a lot of punishment, that it may be observed in what degree some are possessed and the others wanted; and whether those which it possesses are more important than those which it wants; that is to say, whether it is well adapted for the attainment of the desire end.

It will be remembered, that the several qualities desirable in a lot of punishment are—variability, equability, commensurability, characteristicalness [*sic*], exemplarity, frugality, subserviency to reformation, efficiency with respect to disablement, subserviency to compensation, popularity, and remissibility.[325]

That any species of punishment does not possess the whole of these qualities, is not a sufficient reason for its rejection: they are not all of equal importance, and indeed no one species of punishment will perhaps ever be found in which they are all united.

[326]Simple afflictive punishments are capable of great variability: they may be moderated or increased at will.[327] Their effects, however, are far from equable: the same punishment will not produce the same effects when applied to both sexes,—when applied to a stout young man, and an infirm old man. These punishments are almost always attended with a portion of ignominy, and this does not always increase with organic pain, but principally depends upon the condition of the offender. For this reason, there is scarcely a punishment of this description which would be esteemed slight, if inflicted upon a gentleman.[328]

It was inattention to this circumstance that was one cause of the dissatisfaction occasioned by the Stat. 10 Geo. III, called the Dog Act, passed to restrain the stealing of Dogs:[329] among the punishments appointed was that of whipping. There is one thing in the nature of this species of property which renders the stealing of it less incompatible with the character of a gentleman than any other kind of theft. It is apt therefore to meet with indulgence from the moral sanction, for the same reason that enticing away a servant is not considered as a crime, on account of the rational qualities of the subject of property in these cases. An individual also may be innocent, notwithstanding appearances are against him. A dog is susceptible of volition, and even of strong social affections, and may have followed a new master without having been enticed.

The same inattention has been observed to be remarkably prevalent throughout the whole system of penal jurisprudence in Russia. In the reign which preceded that of the mild and intelligent Catherine II, neither rank nor sex bestowed an exemption from the punishment of whipping.[330] The institutions of Poland[331] were also chargeable with the same roughness; and it was no uncommon thing for the maid of honour of a Polish princess to be disciplined in public by the *Maitre d'Hôtel*.[332]

Nothing more completely proves the degradation of the Chinese than the whips which are constantly used by the Police. The mandarins of the first class, the princes of the blood, are subjected to the bamboo, as well as the peasant.[333]

[334]The principal merit of simple afflictive punishments, is their exemplarity. All that is suffered by the delinquent during their infliction may be exhibited to the public, and the class of spectators which would be attracted by such exhibitions, consists, for the most part, of those upon whom the impression they are calculated to produce would be most salutary.[335]

Such are the most striking points to be observed with respect to these punishments. There is little particular to be remarked under the other heads. They are of little efficiency as[336] to intimidation or reformation, with the exception of one particular species—*penitential diet*; which, well managed, may possess great moral efficacy. But as this is naturally connected with the subject of imprisonment, the consideration of it is deferred for the present.[337]

CHAPTER II.
OF COMPLEX AFFLICTIVE PUNISHMENTS.

Under the name of complex afflictive punishments, may be included those corporeal punishments, of which the principal effect consists in the distant and durable consequences of the act of punishment. They cannot be included under one title. They include three species, very different the one from the other in their nature and their importance.

The permanent consequences of an afflictive punishment may consist in the alteration, the destruction, or suspension of the properties of a part of the body.

The properties of a part of the body consist of its visible qualities, as of colour and figure, and its uses.[338]

Of these three distinct kinds of punishments, the first affects the exterior of the person, its visible qualities: the second affects the use of the organic faculties, without destroying the organ itself: the third destroys the organ itself.*

SEC. I—OF DEFORMATION, OR PUNISHMENTS WHICH ALTER THE EXTERIOR OF THE PERSON.

It was an ingenious idea in the first legislator who invented these external and permanently visible punishments,—punishments which are inflicted without destroying any organ—without mutilation—often without physical pain; in all cases without any other pain than what is absolutely necessary,—which affect only the appearance of the criminal, and render that appearance less agreeable, which would not be punishments if they were not indications of his crimes.[339]

The visible qualities of an object are its colour and figure; there are therefore two methods of altering them:—1. Discolouration—2. Disfiguration.

1. Discolouration may be temporary or permanent. When temporary, it

---

*The first may be included under the general name of *Deformation*,—the second under the name of *Dishabilitation*:—they render the organ impotent and useless. The third already has a proper name—*Mutilation*.

may be produced by vegetable or mineral dyes. I am not acquainted with an instance of its use as a punishment. It has always appeared to me that it might be very usefully employed as a precaution to hinder the escape of certain offenders, whilst they are undergoing other punishments.

Permanent discolouration might be produced by tattooing; the only method at present in use is branding.*

Tattooing is performed by perforating the skin with a bundle of sharp-pointed instruments, and subsequently filling the punctures with coloured powder. Of al methods of discolouration, this is the most striking and the least painful. It was practised by the ancient Picts, and other savage nations, for the purpose of ornament.

Judicial branding is effected by the application of a hot iron, the end of which has the form which it is desired should be left imprinted on the skin. This punishment is appointed for many offences in England, and among other European nations. How far this mark is permanent and distinct, I know not; but every one must have observed that accidental burnings often leave only a slight cicatrix—a scarcely sensible alteration in the colour and texture of the skin.

If it is desired to produce deformity, a part of the body should be chosen which is exposed to view, as the hand or the face; but if the object of the punishment is only to mark a conviction of a first offence, and to render the individual recognisable in case of a relapse, it will be better that the mark should be impressed upon some part of the body less ordinarily in view, whereby he will be spared the torment of its infamy, without taking away his desire[340] to avoid falling again into the hands of justice.

2. Disfigurement may in the same manner be either permanent or transient. It may be performed either on the person, or only on its dress.

When confined to the dress, it is not properly called disfigurement; but, by a natural association of ideas, it has the same effect. To this head may be referred the melancholy robes and frightful dresses made use of by the Inquisition, to give to those who suffer in public a hideous or terrible appearance. Some were clothed in cloaks painted to represent flames; others were covered with figures of demons, and different emblems of future torments.

Shaving the head has been a punishment formerly used. It was part of the penance imposed upon adulterous women by the ancient French laws.[341]

The Chinese attach great importance to the length of their nails; cutting them might therefore be used as a penal disfigurement. Shaving the beard might be thus employed among the Russian peasants, or a part of the Jews.

---

*Scarification and corrosion might be employed for the same purpose. The first is attended with this inconvenience,—the form which the cicatrix will take cannot be determined beforehand; it may leave none, or an accidental incision may leave a similar one. Corrosion by chymical caustics may not be liable to the same inconvenience; but its effects have not been tried.

The permanent means of disfigurement are more limited. The only ones which have been in use, and which may yet be employed in certain countries, were applied to certain parts of the head, which may be altered without destroying the functions which depend on those parts. The common law of England directs the nostrils to be slit, or the ears cut off, as the punishment for certain offences. The first of these punishments has fallen into disuse: the second has been rarely employed in the last century. In the works of Pope, and his contemporary writers, may be seen how far their malignity was pleased by allusions to this species of punishment, which had been applied to the author of a libel in their times.

The cutting off and slitting of the nose, the eyelids, and the ears, were once in common use in Russia, without distinction of sex or rank. They were the common accompaniments of the knout and exile: but it ought to be observed that the punishment of death was very rare.[342]

SEC. II.—OF DISABLEMENT, OR PUNISHMENTS CONSISTING IN DISABLING AN ORGAN.

To disable[343] an organ is either to suspend or destroy its use without destroying the organ itself.

It is not necessary here to enumerate all the organs, nor all the methods by which they may be rendered useless. We have already seen that it would not be useful to have recourse to a great variety of afflictive punishments, and that there would be many inconveniences in so doing. If we were to follow the law of retaliation, the catalogue of possible punishments would be the same as that of the possible offences of this kind.

I. *The visual organ.*—The use of which may be suspended by chymical [*sic*] applications, or by mechanical means, as with a mask or bandage.[344] The visual faculty may also be destroyed by chymical or mechanical means.

No jurisprudence in Europe has made use of this punishment. It has heretofore been employed at Constantinople, under the Greek emperors, less as a punishment, it is true, than as a politic method of rendering a prince incapable of reigning. The operation consisted in passing a red hot plate of metal before the eyes.

II. *The organ of hearing.*—This faculty may be destroyed by destroying the tympanum. A temporary deafness may be produced by filling the passage of the ears with wax. As a legal punishment, I know of no instance of its use.

III. *The organ of speech.*—Gagging has more often been employed as a means of precaution against certain delinquents, rather than as a method of punishment. General Lally[345] was sent to his punishment with a gag in his mouth; and this odious precaution perhaps only served to turn public opinion against his judges, when his character was re-established. It has sometimes been employed in military prisons. It has the merit of analogy, when the offence consists in the abuse of the faculty of speech.

Gagging is sometimes performed by fixing a wedge between the jaws, which are rendered immoveable: sometimes by forcing a ball into the mouth, &c.

IV. *The hands and feet.*—I shall not speak of the various methods by which these members may be rendered for ever useless. If it were necessary to be done, it would not be difficult to accomplish.

Handcuffs are rings of metal, into which the wrists are thrust, and which are connected together with a bar or chain. This apparatus completely hinders a certain number of movements, and might be employed so as to prevent them all.

Fetters are rings of metal, into which the legs are fixed, united in the same manner by a chain or bar, according to the species of restraint which it is desired to produce. Handcuffs and fetters are often employed conjointly. Universal use is made of these two methods, sometimes as a punishment, properly so called, but more frequently to prevent the escape of a prisoner.

The pillory is a plank fixed horizontally upon a pivot, on which it turns, and in which plank there are openings, into which the head and the hands of the individual are put, that he may be exposed to the multitude. I say to the gaze of the multitude—such is the intention of the law; but it not unfrequently happens, that persons so exposed are exposed to the outrages of the populace, to which they are thus delivered up without defence, and then the punishment changes its nature;—its severity depends upon the caprice of a crowd of butchers. The victim—for such he then becomes—covered with

---

*De infibulatone non tacendum. In maculis usitatum est apud antiques, non quidem in pœnam sed in custodiam. Servis a quibus ministerium exigebatur cui nocere existimabatur usus veneris, solebant domini in penem trans præputium instrumentum cudere quod vocabant fibulam. Id dum manebat coïtum penitus impediebat. Hunc ad morem innuit Martialis cum in aliis locis, tum in hoc.

Delapsa est misero fibula, verpus erat.

    Atque iterum

Menophili penem tam grandis fibula vestit

Ut sit Comœdis omnibus una satis.

Fœminarum fibulationem sollicitudo maritalis cum apud barbaros nonnullos invenisse dicitur, tum etiam apud Hispanos recentiores. Apud Turrem Londinensem, ni fallor, instrumentum cernere est ut inter Armadæ Hispanicæ spolia, huic usui, ut prædicant, destinatum. Est annulus quem clavis aperit a marito custodienda. [This note was added at this point to Dumont's edition, Théorie des peines, vol. I p. 118. It does not appear within Smith's edition of 1830.]

filth, his countenance bruised and bloody, his teeth broken, his eyes puffed up and closed, no longer can be recognized. The police, at least in England, used to see this disorder, nor seek to restrain it, and perhaps would have been unable to restrain it. A simple iron trellis, in the form of a cage, placed around the pillory, would, however, suffice for stopping at least all those missiles which might inflict any dangerous blows upon the body.

The Carcan, a kind of portable pillory, is a species of punishment which has been used in many countries, and very frequently in China, it consists of a wooden collar, placed horizontally on the shoulders, which the delinquent is obliged to carry without relaxation for a longer or shorter time.*

SEC. III.—OF MUTILATIONS.

I understand by *mutilation*, the extirpation of an external part of the human body, endowed with a distinct power of movement, or a specific function, of which the loss is not necessarily followed by the loss of life; as the eyes, the tongue, the hands, &c.

The extirpation of the nose and of the ears is not properly called mutilation, because it is not upon the external part of these organs that the exercise of their functions depends; they protect and assist that exercise, but they do not exercise these functions. There is, therefore, a difference between that mutilation which causes a total loss of the organ and that which only destroys its envelope. The latter is only a disfigurement which may be partly repaired by art.

Everybody knows how frequently mutilations were formerly employed in the greater number of penal systems. There is no species of them which has not been practised in England, even in times sufficiently modern. The punishment of death might be commuted for that of mutilation under the Common Law. By a statute passed under Henry VIII, the offence of maliciously drawing blood in the palace, where the king resided, was punished by the loss of the right hand. By a statute of Elizabeth, the exportation of sheep was punished by the amputation of the left hand. Since that time, however, all these punishments have fallen into disuse, and mutilations may now be considered as banished from the penal code of Great Britain.

Examination of complex afflictive Punishments.

The effects of simple afflictive punishments are easily estimated, because their consequences are all similar in quality, and immediately produced. The effects of all other punishments are not ascertained without great difficulties, because their consequences are greatly diversified, are liable to great uncertainty, and are often remote. Simple afflictive punishments must always be borne by the parties on whom they are inflicted: all other punishments are deficient in point of certainty: the more remote their consequences, the more these consequences escape the notice of those who are deficient in foresight and reflection.

Around a simple afflictive punishment a circle may be drawn, which shall inclose [sic] the whole mischief of the punishment; around all other punishments the mischief extends in circles, the extent of which is not, and cannot be marked out. It is mischief in the abstract, mischief uncertain and universal, which cannot be pointed out with precision. When the effects of punishments are thus uncertain, there is much less ground for choice, for the effects of one punishment may be the same with those of another. The same consequences often resulting from very different punishments. The choice must therefore be directed by probability, and be governed by the presumption that certain punishments will more probably produce certain penal consequences than any other.

Independently of the bodily sufferings resulting from them, punishments which affect the exterior of the person, often produce two disadvantageous effects, the one physical—the individual may become an object of *disgust*; the other moral—he may become an object of *contempt*; they may produce a *loss of beauty or a loss of reputation*.

One of these punishments, which has a greater moral than physical effect, is a mark producing only a change of colour, and the impression of a character upon the skin; but this mark is an attestation that the individual has been guilty of some act to which contempt is attached, and the effect of contempt is to diminish goodwill, the principle that produces all the free and gratuitous services that men render to one another; but in our present state of continual dependance [sic] upon each other, that which diminishes the goodwill of others towards us, includes within itself an indefinite multitude of privations.*

When such a mark is inflicted on account of a crime, it is essential that a character should be given to it, which shall clearly announce the intention with which it was imposed, and which cannot be confounded with cica-

---

*Stedman relates a fact which proves what has been above said of the indefinite consequences of these punishments. Speaking of a Frenchman, named *Destrades*, who had introduced the culture of Indigo into Surinam, and who, during many years, had enjoyed general esteem in that colony. He states, that being at the house of one of his friends in Demerara, he became ill of an abscess, which formed in his shoulder. He would not suffer it to be examined: it became dangerously worse, but his resistance remained still the same: at last, not hoping for a cure, he put an end to his life with a pistol-ball, when the secret was revealed, it was found that his shoulder was marked with a letter *V*, or *Voleur*.—*Narrative of an Expedition against the Revolted Negroes of Surinam, by Major Steadman,* chap. xxvii.

trices of wounds or accidental marks. A penal mark ought to have a determinate figure—and the most suitable, as well as the most common, is the
initial letter of the name of the crime. Among the Roman, slanderers were
marked on the forehead with the letter K. In England, for homicide, committed after provocation, offenders were marked in the hand with the letter
M (for manslaughter), and thieves with the letter T. In France, the mark for
galley-slaves was composed of the three letters GAL.

In Poland, it was the custom to add a symbolical expression: the initial
letter of the crimes was enclosed in the figure of a gallows. In India, among the
Gentoos [*sic*], a great number of burlesque symbolical figures are employed.

A more lenient method, which may be referred to the same head, is a
practice too little used, of giving to offenders a particular dress, which
serves as a livery of crime. At Hanau, in Germany, persons condemned to
labour on the public works were distinguished by a black sleeve in a white
coat. It is an expedient which has for its object the prevention of their
escape; as a mark of infamy, it is an addition to the punishment.[346]

On the score of frugality, deforming punishments are not liable to any
objection; disablement and mutilation are; if the effect of either is to prevent
a man getting his livelihood by his own labour, and he has no sufficient
income of his own, he must either be left to perish, or be supplied with the
means of subsistence; if he were left to perish, the punishment would not be
mere disablement or mutilation, but death. If he be supported by the labour
of others, that labour must either be bestowed gratis, as would be the case if
he were supported on the charity of relations and friends, or paid for, at public
cost; in either case it is a charge upon the public. This consideration might of
itself be considered a conclusive objection against the application of these
modes of punishment, for offences that are apt to be frequently committed,
such as theft or smuggling; the objection applies, however, in its full force, to
such of these modes of punishment only as have the effect of depriving the
particular individual in question of the means of gaining his livelihood.

In respect of remissibility, they are also eminently defective; a consideration which affords an additional reason for making a very sparing use of them.

[347]In respect also of *variability*, these punishments are scarcely in a less
degree defective. The loss of the eyes, or of the hand, is not to a man who can
neither read or write, the same degree of punishment as it would be to a
painter, or an author. Yet, however different in each instance may be the
degree of suffering produced by the mass of evil to which the infliction of the
punishment in question gives birth, all who are subject to it will find themselves more or less affected; of these inequalities, and therefore of the aggre-
gate amount of the punishment in each particular instance, it is impossible to
form any estimate; it depends on the sensibility of the delinquent, and other

circumstances, which cannot be foreseen. By a slothful man, the loss of a hand might not be regarded as a very severe punishment, it has not been uncommon for men to mutilate or disable themselves to avoid serving in the army.

In point of variability, the several classes of punishment now before us, when considered all together, are not liable to much objection; there is a gradation from less to more, which runs through the whole of them. The loss of one finger is less painful than the loss of two, or of the whole hand. The loss of the hand is less than the loss of an arm. But when these punishments are considered singly, the gradation disappears. The particular mutilation directed by the law, can neither be increased or diminished, that it may be accommodated to the different circumstances of the crime or of the delinquent. This objection recurs again under the head of Equability. The same nominal punishment will not always be the same real punishment.[348]

In respect of *exemplarity*, the punishments in question possess this property in a higher degree than simple afflictive punishments, this latter species of punishment not being naturally attended with any distant consequences (their infamy excepted), the whole quantity of pain it is calculated to produce is collected, as it were, into a point, and exposed at once to the eyes of the speculator; while of the other, on the contrary, the consequences are lasting, and are calculated perpetually to awaken in the minds of all, to whose eyes any person that has suffered this species of punishment may happen to present himself, the idea of the law itself, and of the sanction by which its observance is enforced. For this purpose it is necessary, however, as has been already observed, that the penal mark should be such as at first glance to be distinguished from any mark that may have been the result of an accident—that misfortune may be protected from the imputation of guilt.

The next property to be desired in a mode of punishment, is subserviency to *reformation*. In this respect the punishments under consideration, when temporary, have nothing in themselves that distinguishes them from any other mode of punishment; their subserviency to reformation is as their experienced magnitude. It is the infamy attendant on them that gives them those effects which are apt in this respect to distinguish them to their disadvantage.

Infamy, when at an intense pitch, is apt to have this particular bad effect: it tends pretty strongly to force a man to persist in that depraved course of life by which the infamy was produced. When a man falls into any of those offences that the moral sanction is known to treat with extreme rigour, men are apt to suppose that the moral sanction has no hold upon him. His character, they say, is gone. They withdraw from him their confidence and goodwill. He finds himself in a situation in which he has nothing to hope for from men, and for the same reason nothing to fear: he experiences the worst already. If, then, he depend upon his labour for subsistence, and his business is of such sort as requires confidence to be reposed in him, by losing that necessary portion of confidence he loses the means of providing himself with subsistence, his only remaining resources are then mendicity [*sic*] or depredation.

From these observations it follows, that mutilations ought to be reserved as punishments for the most mischievous offences, and as an accompaniment of perpetual imprisonment. An exception to this rule may perhaps be found in the case of rape, for which analogy most strongly recommends a punishment of this kind.

CHAPTER III.[349]
OF RESTRICTIVE PUNISHMENTS— TERRITORIAL CONFINEMENT.

Restrictive punishments are those which restrain the faculties of the individual, by hindering him from receiving agreeable impressions, or from doing what he desires. They take from him his liberty with respect to certain enjoyments and certain acts.

Restrictive punishments are of two sorts, according to the method used in inflicting them. Some operate by moral restraint, others by physical restraint. Moral restraint takes place when the motive presented to the individual to hinder him from doing the act which he wishes to perform, is only the fear of a superior punishment; for, in order to be efficacious, it is necessary that the punishment with which he is threatened, must be greater than the simple pain[350] of submitting to the restraint imposed upon him.

The punishment of restraint is applicable to all sorts of actions in general, but particularly to the faculty of *loco-motion*. Everything which restrains the locomotive faculty, confines the individual, that is to say, shuts him up within certain limits, and may be called *territorial confinement*.*

In this kind of punishment the whole earth, in relation to the delinquent, is divided into two very unequal districts; the one of which is *open* to him, and the other *interdicted*.

If the place in which he is confined is a narrow space surrounded with walls, and the doors of which are locked, it is imprisonment.

If the district in which he is directed to remain is within the dominions of the state, the punishment may be called *Relegation*. If it is without the dominions of the state, the punishment is called *Banishment*.

The term *relegation* seems to imply, that the delinquent is sent out of the district in which he ordinarily resides. This punishment may consist in his confinement in that district where he ordinarily resides, and even in his own house. It may then be called *quasi imprisonment*.

---

*These two relationships are expressed very clearly in Latin: *Locus in quo—Locus a quo*. [This note appears within Dumont's edition, *Théorie des peines*, vol. I, p. 130, but not within Smith's edition of 1830.]

If it refers to a particular district, which he is prohibited from entering, it is a sort of exclusion, which has not yet a proper name, but which may be called *local interdiction.*

Territorial confinement is the genus which includes five species:—imprisonment, quasi imprisonment, relegation, local interdiction, and banishment.[351]

CHAPTER IV.
IMPRISONMENT.

Imprisonment makes a much more extensive figure than any other kind of hardship that can be inflicted in the way of punishment.[352] Every other kind of hardship (death alone excepted) may be inflicted for two purposes—*punishment* and *compulsion*. Imprisonment, besides these two purposes, may be employed for another. Safe custody; when thus employed, it is not a punishment, properly so called. It is intended only to ensure the forthcomingness of an individual suspected of having committed an offence, that he may be present to undergo the punishment appointed[353] for that offence, if he be found guilty. When thus employed, it ought not to be more severe than is necessary to insure forthcomingness. Whatever exceeds this, is so much misery in waste.[354]

When imprisonment is intended to operate as a punishment, it may be rendered more or less severe, according to the nature of the offence and the condition of the offender. It may be accompanied by forced labour, which may be imposed upon all; but it ought not to be so imposed without reference to the age, the rank, the sex, and the physical powers of the individuals. Other punishments, which may be employed in addition to hard labour, and of which we shall have occasion to speak in a future chapter, are—diet, solitude, and darkness.[355]

When imprisonment is inflicted for the purpose of *compulsion*, the severer it is, the better, and that for various reasons.

When it is protracted, but slight, the danger is that the prisoner may come by degrees to accommodate himself to it, till at last it ceases in a manner to operate upon him. This is found not uncommonly to be the case with insolvent debtors. In many of our gaols[356] there are so many comforts to be had by those who have money to purchase them, that many a prisoner becomes in time tolerably well reconciled to his situation. When this is the case, the imprisonment can no longer be of use in any view.

The severer it is, I mean all along in point of intensity, the less of it, in point of magnitude, will be consumed upon the whole; that is, in point of intensity and duration taken together; the more favourable, in short, will it be to the sufferer: it will produce its effects at a cheaper rate. The same quantity of painful sensations, which, under the milder imprisonment, are diffused through a large mass of sensations, indifferent or pleasurable, being, in the severer imprisonment, brought together, will act with collected force, and produce a stronger impression: the same quantity of pain will therefore go farther this way than in any other. Add to this, that in this way the same quantity of suffering will not have so pernicious an influence on his future life. In the course of a tedious confinement, his mental faculties are debilitated, his habits of industry are weakened, his business runs into other channels, and many of those casual opportunities which might have afforded the means of improving his fortune, had he been at liberty to embrace them, are irrecoverably gone. These evils, which, though they may come eventually to be felt, are too distant and contingent to contribute anything beforehand to the impression it is intended to produce, are saved by placing the magnitude of the punishment in intensity rather than in duration.[357]

By the fundamental constitution of man's nature, without anything being done by any one to produce a change in his situation, if left to himself, in a situation in which he is debarred from exercising the faculty of loco-motion, he will in a short time become a prey to various evils, to the action of various causes producing various organical pains, which, sooner or later, are sure to end ultimately in death. If duration and neglect be added to imprisonment, it necessarily becomes a capital punishment. Since, therefore, it is followed by an infinite variety of evils which the individual is unable himself to guard against, and against which precautions must be taken by others to preserve him, it follows, that to form a just notion of imprisonment, it must be considered, not simply by itself, but in common with different modes and consequences. We shall then see that, under the same name, very different punishments may be inflicted. Under a name which presents[358] to the mind only the single circumstance[359] of confinement in a particular place, imprisonment may include every possible evil; from those which necessarily follow in its train, rising from one degree of rigour to another, from one degree of atrocity to another, till it terminates in a most cruel death; and this without being intended by the legislator, but altogether arising from absolute negligence—negligence as easy to be explained as it is difficult to be palliated.

We shall class under three heads the penal circumstances which result from this condition. 1. *Necessary* inconveniences, which arise from the condition of a prisoner, and which form the essence of imprisonment. 2. *Accessory* inconveniences, which do not necessarily, but which frequently follow in its train. 3. Inconveniences arising from *abuses*.

SEC. I.—NEGATIVE EVILS, INSEPARABLE FROM IMPRISONMENT.[360]

1. Privation of the pleasures which belong to the sight, arising from the diversity of objects in town and country.

2. Privation of the liberty of taking pleasurable exercises that require a large space, such as riding on horseback or in a carriage, hunting, shooting, &c.

3. Privation of those excursions[361] which may be necessary even for health.

4. Privation of the liberty of partaking of public diversions.

5. Abridgement of the liberty of going out to enjoy agreeable society, as of relations, friends, or acquaintance, although they should be permitted to come to him.

6. Privation of the liberty, in some cases, of carrying on business for a livelihood, and abridgment of such liberty in all cases.

7. Privation of the liberty of exercising public offices of honour or trust.

8. Privation of accidental opportunities of advancing his fortune, obtaining patrons, forming friendships, obtaining a situation, or forming matrimonial alliances for himself or children.

Although these evils may in the first instance be purely negative,—that is to say, privation of pleasures, it is evident that they bring in their train of consequences positive evils, such as the impairing of the health and the impoverishment of the circumstances.

SEC. II.—ACCESSORY EVILS, COMMONLY ATTENDANT ON THE CONDITION OF A PRISONER.

1. Confinement to disagreeable diet. The want of *sufficient* food for the purpose of nourishment, is a distinct mischief, which will come under another head.

2. Want of comfortable accommodations for repose:—hard bedding, or straw, or nothing but the bare ground. This hardship alone has been thought to have been productive, in some instances, of disease, and even death.

3. Want of light. By the exclusion of the natural light of the sun by day, and the not furnishing or not permitting the introduction of any artificial means of producing light by night.

4. Total exclusion from society. This evil is carried to its height when a prisoner is not permitted to see his friends, his parents, his wife, or his children.

5. Forced obligation of mixing with a promiscuous assemblage of his fellow prisoners.*[362]

---

*This inconvenience would be apt to be attended with effects of the most serious nature in the case of an Hindoo [*sic*] of any of the superior castes; an association, however involuntary, with persons of an inferior rank, or contaminated character, causing a forfeiture of caste, which, among the Hindoos, is productive of the same afflictions as excommunication at its first institution was intended to produce amongst Christians—extreme infamy, and an utter

6. Privation of the implements of writing,[363] for the purposes of correspondence. A useless severity, since everything which is written by a prisoner may be properly submitted to inspection. If ever this privation is justifiable, it is in cases of treason and other party crimes.

7. Forced idleness, by the refusal of all means of necessary occupation: as of the brushes of a painter, the tools of a watchmaker, or of books, &c. This has sometimes been carried to such a degree of rigour as to deprive prisoners of all amusement.

These different evils, which are so many positive evils in addition to the necessary evils of simple imprisonment, may be useful in penal and penitential imprisonment. We shall hereafter shew [*sic*] in what manner they ought to be used. But with respect to the fifth evil, the forced obligation of mixing with a promiscuous assemblage of prisoners, it is always an evil, and an evil which cannot be obviated without a change in the system and construction of prisons.[364]

We proceed to the consideration of evils purely abusive: of those which exist only by the negligence of the magistrates, but which necessarily exist, where precautions have not been taken to prevent their existence. We shall present two catalogues; one of the evils, the second of their remedies.

Evils[365]	*Remedies*
1.	1.
Pains of hunger and thirst: *general debility—death.*	Sufficient nourishment.[367]
2.	2.
Sensation of cold in various degrees of intensity: *stoppage of the circulation—mortification*[366] *of the extremities†—death.*	Sufficient clothing, adapted to the climate and the season—fire.
3.	3.
Sensation of heat: *habitual debility—death.*	Shelter from the sun in hot weather—fresh air.
4.	4.
Sensation of damp and wetness: *fevers and other disorders—death*	The ground everywhere covered with boards, or bricks, or stone—fresh air—tubes for conveying heated air.

---

exclusion from society, but that of persons marked with the same stigma. It has been said, I hope without truth, that by some unhappy neglect, when the Rajah Nuncomar, a man of the first rank in Bengal, was in custody for the forgery for which he was afterwards tried under the laws of Great Britain, and executed, proper care was not taken to protect him from this ideal contamination. If this be true, before he was proved guilty, he was made to suffer a punishment greater perhaps than that to which he was afterwards sentenced. [This note appears at the end of the parallel chapter of Dumont's edition, *Théorie des peines*, vol. I, I p. 143.]

†Howard, p. 39. [This reference does not appear within Dumont's edition.]

5.

Noisome smells, collections of putrifiable [sic] matter: *habitual debility—falling off of the members by gangrene—gaol-fever—contagious diseases—death.*

6.

Pain or uneasiness resulting from the bites of vermin: *cutaneous [sic] diseases—want of sleep—debility—inflammation—fever—death.*

7.

Various diseases.

8.

Painful sensations arising from indelicate practices.

9.

Tumultuous noises—indecent practices—indelicate conversations.

10.

Evils resulting from the religious sanction—from the non-exercise of the ceremonies prescribed by it.

5.

Fresh air—change of clothes—water and other implements of washing—fumigations—whitewashing the walls—medicines and medical assistance.

6.

Chymical applications to destroy them—cleanliness—a person with proper implements[368] for their destruction and removal.

7.

Medicines and medical advice.

8.

Partitions to keep the prisoners separate during the hour of rest, at least those of one sex from those of the other.

9.

Keepers to be directed to punish those guilty of such practices. The punishment to be made known to the prisoners by being fixed up in the prison.

10.

In Protestant countries, a chaplain to perform divine service. In Roman Catholic countries, a priest to perform mass, and to confess the prisoners, &c.*

---

*It was mentioned as a circumstance of peculiar distress attending the fate of many of the numerous state prisoners confined in Portugal, during the Marquis of Pombal's administration, their being debarred, during a course of years, the comforts of confession. When this circumstance was brought to light, it produced a considerable degree of public indignation.

IMPRISONMENT—FEES.

Another way in which a man is often made to suffer on the occasion of imprisonment, is the being made to pay money under the name of fees.[370] This hardship, on the very first inspection, when deduced as a consequence from a sentence or warrant of imprisonment, can be classed under no other title than that of an abuse; for naturally it has just as much to do with imprisonment as hanging has.[371]

This abuse is coeval with the first barbarous rudiments of our ancient jurisprudence; when the magistrate had little more idea of the ends of justice than the freebooter; and the evils he inflicted were little more than a compensation for the evils he repressed. In those times of universal depravity, when the magistrate reaped almost as much profit from the plunder of those who were, or were pretended to be, guilty, as from the contributions of those who were acknowledged innocent; no pretext was too shallow to cover the enterprises of rapacity under the mask of justice.[372]

All the colour which this abuse is capable of receiving, seems to have been taken from a quibbling and inhuman sarcasm. "Since you have lodging found you," says the gaoler to the prisoner, "it is fit, like other lodgers, you should pay for it." Fit it certainly would be, if the lodger came there voluntarily; the only circumstance in the case which is wanting to make it a just demand instead of a cruel insult.

But the gaoler, like every other servant of the state, it will be said, and with perfect truth, must be satisfied for his trouble; and who more fit than the person who occasions it? I answer any person whatever; if contrary to the most obvious principles of justice,[373] some one person must bear the whole charge of an institution, which if beneficial to any, is beneficial to all. I say anybody; because there is no person whose clear benefit from the punishment of the criminal (I am speaking here of the judicial, appointed punishment, the imprisonment; and I mean clear benefit after the inconvenience has, been deducted) is not greater than the criminals. This would hold good were the peculiar circumstances of the criminal out of the question; but when these come to be considered, they add considerable force to the above conclusion. In the case of nineteen delinquents out of twenty, the utter want of all means of satisfying their lawful debts was the very cause and motive of the crime. Now then, whereas it is only possible in the case of a man taken at random that he has not wherewithal to pay, it is certain that in nineteen cases out of twenty the delinquent has not.

So powerful is the force of custom, that for a long series of years, Judges of the first rank, and country magistrates, none of whom but would have taken it ill enough to have had their wisdom or their humanity called in question, stand upon record as having given their allowance to this abuse. If any one of these magistrates had ever had the spirit to have refused this allowance, the gaoler would for a moment have remained unpaid, and from thenceforward the burthen would have been taken up by that public hand which, from the beginning, ought to have borne it.*[374]

So far is this hardship from being justifiable on the score of punishment, that in most, if not in all our prisons, it is inflicted indiscriminately on all who enter, innocent or guilty.[375] It is inflicted at all events, when it is not known but they may be innocent: for it is inflicted on them at first entrance when committed only for safe custody. This is not all; it is inflicted on men after they have been proved to be innocent. Even this is not all; to fill up the measure of oppression, it is inflicted on them *because* they have been proved innocent. Prisoners, after they have been acquitted, are, as if to make them amends for the unmerited sufferings they have undergone, loaded with a heavy fine, professedly on the very ground of their having been acquitted. In some gaols, of a person acquitted of murder a sum of money is exacted, under the name of an acquittal, equal to what it costs an ordinary working man to maintain himself for a quarter of a year: a sum such as not one man in ten of that class, that is, of the class which includes a great majority of the whole people, is ever master of during the course of his whole life.[376]

---

*By the old law, when money was recovered against a Hundred, the Sheriff laid hold of the first Hundredor he met, and made him pay the whole. Even this was a better expedient for providing for the public burthen than the one in question.

CHAPTER VI.
IMPRISONMENT EXAMINED.[377]

[378]

W e now proceed to examine the degree in which imprisonment possesses the several properties desirable in a lot of punishment.

1. Imprisonment possesses the property of *efficacy with respect to disablement* in great perfection. The most dangerous offender, so long as his confinement continues, is deprived of the power of doing mischief out of doors; his vicious propensities may continue at their highest pitch, but he will have no opportunity of exercising them.[379]

2. Imprisonment is generally exceptionable on the score of frugality;[380] none of the inconveniences resulting from it being convertible to profit. It is also generally accompanied with expense, on account of the maintenance of the persons confined.[381] In these calculations of expense, that loss ought not to be forgotten which results from the suspension of the lucrative labours of the prisoner, a loss which is often continued beyond the period of imprisonment, owing to the habits of idleness it has induced.*[382]

3. Imprisonment is objectionable in respect of equality. If we recur to the catalogue of privations of which it consists, it will be seen that the inequality is extreme, when one prisoner is sickly, and the other healthy; when one is the father of a family, and the other has no relations; when the one is rich and accustomed to all the enjoyments of society, and the other poor, and his usual condition is one of misery.[383]

One party may be deprived of his means of subsistence; another may be scarcely affected in this respect. It may be said, is not this loss merely temporary? May it not be considered as a forfeiture which forms a part of the punishment? If the individual belong to a profession, the exercise of which cannot be interrupted without great risk of its total loss; the consequence may be his absolute ruin. This is one of those cases in which a latitude may properly be left to the Judge of commuting this punishment for another. A pecuniary punishment may frequently, with propriety, be substituted. The greater number of offenders, however, are not in a condition furnish this equivalent. It would therefore be necessary to have recourse to simply afflictive punishments. The degree of infamy attached to these punishments

---

*This objection to imprisonment is carefully removed in the plan of Panopticon Imprisonment, an account of which is given in Book V, ch. 3. [This note is not found within Dumont's edition.]

would, however, not be an objection in case the offender consented to the exchange; and this consent might be made a necessary condition.

Among the inconveniences which may be attached to imprisonment, there is one which is particularly inequable [*sic*]. Take away paper and ink from an author by profession, and you take away his means of amusement and support. You would punish other individuals, more or less, according as a written correspondence happened to be more or less necessary for their business or pleasure. A privation so heavy for those whom it affects, and at the same time so trifling for the greater number of individuals, ought not to be admitted in quality of a punishment. Why should an[384] individual who has received instruction in writing, be punished more than another. This circumstance ought rather to be a reason for indulgence; his sensibility has been augmented by education; and the instructed and cultivated man will suffer more from imprisonment than the ignorant and the clownish.[385]

On the other hand, though the punishment of imprisonment is inequable, it should be observed, that it naturally produces an effect upon every one. There is no individual insensible to the privation of liberty—to the interruption of all his habits, and especially of all his social habits.

4. Imprisonment is eminently *divisible* with respect to its duration. It is also very susceptible of different degrees of severity.[386]

5. Under the present system, the exemplarity of imprisonment is reduced to the lowest term. In the Panopticon, the facility afforded to the admission of the public, adds much to this branch of its utility.

However, if the prisoners are not seen, the prison is visible. The appearance of this habitation of penitence may strike the imagination and awaken a salutary terror. Buildings employed for this purpose ought therefore to have a character of seclusion and restraint, which should take away all hope of escape, and should say, "This is the dwelling place of crime."[387]

6. *Simplicity of description.*—Under this head there is nothing to be desired. This punishment is intelligible to all ages,[388] and all capacities. Confinement is an evil of which everybody can form an idea, and which all have, more or less, experienced. The name of a prison at once recalls the ideas of suffering[389] as connected with it.

Let us here stop to examine three auxiliary punishments, that under special circumstances, and for a limited time only, may be usefully made to accompany afflictive imprisonment. These auxiliaries are *solitude, darkness*, and *hard diet*.[390] Their distinguishing merit consists in their *subserviency to reformation*.[391]

That the three hardships, thus named, have a peculiar tendency to dispose an offender to penitence, seems to be the general persuasion of mankind. The fact seems to be pretty generally acknowledged; but the reasons are not altogether obvious, nor do they seem to be very explicitly developed in the minds of those who show themselves strenuously convinced of the fact. An imperfect theory might naturally enough induce one to deny it. "What is it," it may be said, "that is to produce in the offender that aversion to his offence which is stiled penitence? It is the pain which he experiences to be connected with it. The greater then that pain, the greater will be his aversion; but of what kind the pain be, or from what source it issues, are circumstances that make no difference. Solitude, darkness, and hard diet, in virtue of a certain quantity of pain thus produced, will produce a certain degree of aversion to the offence; be it so. But whipping, or any other mode of punishment that produced a greater pain, would produce a stronger aversion.[392] Now, the pain of whipping may be carried to as high a pitch as the pain produced by this group of hardships altogether. In what respect then can these have a greater tendency to produce penitence than whipping?"

The answer is, that the aversion to the offence depends, not merely upon the magnitude of the pain that is made to stand connected with it; but it depends likewise upon the strength of the connection which is made to take place between those two incidents in the patient's mind. Now that solitude, darkness, and hard diet have a greater tendency than any other kind of hardship to strengthen this connection, I think, may be satisfactorily made out.

Acute punishment, such as whipping, at the time it is inflicted, leaves no leisure for reflection. The present sensation, with the circumstances that accompany it, is such as engrosses the whole attention. If any mental emotion mixes itself with the bodily sensation, it will rather be that of resentment against the Executioner, the Judge, the Prosecutor, or any person whose share in the production of the suffering happens to strike the sufferer most, than any other. The anguish is soon over, and as soon as it is over, the mind of the patient is occupied in the eager pursuit of objects that shall obliterate the recollection of the pain that he has endured; while all the objects by which he is surrounded contribute to repel those salutary reflections upon which his reformation depends.[393] Indeed, as soon as the anguish is over, a new emotion presents itself, and emotion of joy which the patient feels at the reflection that his suffering is over.

The gradual and protracted scene of suffering produced by the combination of punishments we are now considering, is much more favourable to the establishment of the wished for effect. By solitude a man is abstracted from those emotions of friendship or enmity which society inspires, from the ideas of the objects their conversation is apt to bring to view: from the apprehension of the disagreeable situations their activity threatens to expose him to, or the pleasures in which they solicit him to engage. By confinement[394] he is abstracted from all external impressions but such as can be afforded him by the few and uninviting objects that constitute the boundaries, or compose the furniture, of a chamber in a prison, and from all ideas which, by virtue of the principle of association, any other impressions are calculated to suggest.[395]

By darkness, the number of the impressions he is open to is still further reduced, by the striking off all those which even the few objects in question are calculated to produce upon the sense of sight. The mind of the patient is, by this means, reduced, as it were, to a gloomy void; leaving him destitute of all support but from his own internal resources, and producing the most lively impression of his own weakness.

In this void, the punishment of hard diet comes and implants the slow but incessant and corroding pain of hunger, while the debility that attends the first stages of it, (for the phrensy [sic] that is apt to accompany the last stages is to be always guarded against) banishes any propensity which the patient might have left, to try such few means of activity as he is left undeprived [sic] of, to furnish himself with any of the few impressions he is still open to receive. Meantime, the pain and this debility, however irksome, are by no means so acute as to occupy his mind entirely, and prevent altogether its wandering in search of other ideas. On the contrary, he will be forcibly solicited to pay attention to any ideas which, in that extreme vacancy of employment, are disposed to present themselves to his view.[396]

[397]The most natural of all will be to retrace the events of his past life; the bad advice he received, his first deviations from rectitude, which have led to the commission of the offence for which he is at the time undergoing punishment; a crime, all the pleasures derived from which have been already reaped, and of which all that remains is the melancholy suffering that he endures. He will recall to his recollection those days of innocence and security which were formerly his lot, and which, contrasted with his present wretchedness, will present themselves to his imagination with an increased and factitious degree of splendour. His penitent reflections will naturally be directed to the errors of which he has been guilty: if he has a wife, or children, or near relations, the affection that he once entertained for them, may be renewed by the recollection of the misery that he has occasioned them.

Another advantage attendant on this situation, is, that it is peculiarly fitted to dispose a man to listen with attention and humility to the admonitions and exhortations of religion. Left in this state of destitution in respect of all external pleasures, religious instructions are calculated to take the stronger hold of the mind. Oppressed by the state of wretchedness in which he finds himself, and by the unlooked-for or unknown events that have led to the detection of his crime, the more he reflects upon them, the more firmly he will be convinced of the existence of a providence which has watched over his actions, and defeated his best concerted contrivances. The same God that punishes him, may also save him; and thenceforward the promises of eternal bliss or torment will more anxiously engage his attention—promises of happiness in another state of being, in case of repentance, and denunciation of torments prepared for the guilty in the regions of eternal night, of which the present situation seems a prelude and a foretaste, will fix his regard. In a frame of mind such as this, to turn a deaf ear to the admonitions and consolations afforded by religion, a man must be very different from the ordinary caste of men. Darkness, too, has, in circumstances like this, a peculiar tendency to dispose men to conceive, and in a manner to feel, the presence of invisible agents. Whatever may be the reason, the fact is notorious and undisputed. When the external senses are restrained from action, the imagination is more active, and produces a numerous race of ideal beings. In a state of solitude, infantine superstitions, ghosts, and spectres, recur to the imagination. This, of itself, forms a sufficient reason for not prolonging[398] this species of punishment, which may overthrow the powers of the mind, and produce incurable melancholy. The first impressions will, however, always be beneficial.[399]

If, at such a time, a minister of religion, qualified to avail himself of these impressions, is introduced to the offender thus humiliated and cast down, the success of his endeavours will be almost certain, because in this state of abandonment he will appear as the friend of the unfortunate, and as his peculiar benefactor.

This course of punishment,[400] thus consisting of solitude, darkness, and hard diet, is, as has been observed, when embodied, a sort of discipline too violent to be employed, except for short periods: if greatly prolonged, it would scarcely fail of producing madness, despair, or more commonly a stupid apathy. This is not, however, the place for fixing the duration of the punishment proper for each species of offence: it ought to vary according to the nature of the offence, the degree of obstinacy evinced by the offender, and the symptoms of repentance which he exhibits. What has been already said, is sufficient to shew that the mass of punishments in question may be employed with the greatest advantage simultaneously: they mutually aid each other. In order to produce the desired effect most speedily, even the sort of food allowed may be rendered unpalatable as well as scanty, otherwise, there would be danger lest to a young and robust person the constantly recurring gratification afforded to the palate, might render him insensible to the loss of all other pleasures.[401]

If any punishment can in itself be popular, this, I think, promises to be so. It bears a stronger resemblance than any other to domestic discipline. The tendency which it has to lead the offender to acknowledge the evil of his offence, and the justice of his sentence, is the same which an indulgent father desires his punishments to possess, when he inflicts them upon his children; and there is no aspect which it is more desirable the law should assume than this.[402]

The effects produced by solitary confinement, are not matters of mere conjecture; they have been ascertained by experience, and are reported upon the best authorities.

Speaking of the cells in Newgate, "I was told," says Mr. Howard,* "by those who attended me, that criminals who had affected an air of boldness on their trial, and appeared quite unconcerned at the pronouncing sentence upon them, were struck with horror, and shed tears, when brought to these darksome, solitary abodes."[403]

"I remember an instance," says Mr. Hanway,† "some years before the law for proceeding to sentence upon evidence, of a notorious malefactor, who would not plead. It was a question, whether he should be brought to the *press*; but the jailor privately recommended to the magistrates to try solitary confinement in prison. This produced the effect, for in less than twenty-four hours, the daring, artful felon chose to hold up his hand at the bar, and quietly submit to the laws, rather than remain in such a solitary state without hope."

The same gentleman mentions‡ a set of cells, provided for the purpose of solitary confinement, in Clerkenwell Bridewell, by order of the Justices of the Peace for that division. One of those magistrates, he says, assured him, "That every person committed to those solitary apartments, had been in a few days reformed to an amazing degree." The apartments, though solitary, were not dark, nor is anything said about the circumstance of diet.

Directly opposed to solitary imprisonment is the promiscuous association of prisoners. The suffering which results from this circumstance, is not the result of direct intention on the part of the magistrate. It is an evil acknowledged, and yet suffered still to exist to a very considerable extent.[404] It is evidently not so much inflicted as admitted, from the supposed inability of Government to exclude it; the great and only objection to its exclusion being the expense of the arrangements necessary to the accomplishment of that purpose. The advantage by which it is recommended, is that of frugality. It is less expensive to shut up prisoners in one room, than to provide separate apartments for each one, or even to keep them divided into classes.§

This promiscuous assemblage of prisoners, considered as part of the

---

*Page 152. [Dumont's edition cites p. 132, *Théorie des peines*, vol. I p. 154.]
†Page 75. [Dumont's edition cites p. 74.]
‡Page 74.
§It must be acknowledged that this difficulty was very great before the invention of the plan of central inspection.

punishment, has no penal effect upon the most audacious and the most perverse. On the contrary, with reference to them, it renders imprisonment less painful,—the tumult with which it surrounds them, diverts them from the misery of their situation, and from the reproaches of their consciences. It is therefore an evil most severe for the prisoner of refinement and sensibility. It is an addition to the punishment of imprisonment, evidently unequable, unexemplary [*sic*], and unprofitable, producing a variety of unknown sufferings, such as that those only who have experienced them, can be fully acquainted with their extent.[405]

But the great and decisive objection to the promiscuous association of prisoners, considered as a punishment, is, that it is directly opposed to their reformation. Instead of rendering a delinquent better, its evident tendency is to make him worse. The ill effect which, in the instance of indelible infamy, is only problematical, is, in the instance of this species of hardship, certain; it obliterates the sense of shame in the mind of the sufferer: in other words, it produces insensibility to the force of the moral sanction.

The ill effect of the promiscuous association of prisoners, is too obvious not to strike even the most superficial spectator. Criminals, confined together, are corrupted, it is said, by the society of each other: there are a thousand[406] ways of diversifying the expression, and it is generally set off with great exuberance of metaphor. The word *corruption*, and the greater part of the terms that compose the moral vocabulary, are not calculated, of themselves, to convey any precise import, but serve rather to express the disapprobation which he who uses them happens to entertain of the practices in question, than the tendency to produce mischief, which is, or at least ought to be, the ground of it. In order then to form a precise idea of the phœnomena in which this corruption displays itself, let us examine the mischievous habits produced by this promiscuous intercourse, and the way in which it tends to produce mischief in society.

The ill consequences of the association in question, may be comprised under the following heads:—

1. It strengthens, in the minds of all parties concerned; the motives which prompt to the commission of all sorts of crimes.
2. It diminishes the force of the considerations which tend to restrain them.
3. It increases their *skill*, and by that means their *power*, of carrying their obnoxious propensities into practice.

Crimes are the sort of acts here in question. Now, the names of crimes are words, for which precise ideas have, or might at least be found: they are evils of a certain description. The names of the motives that prompt a man to the commission of a crime, are also the names of pains and pleasures. In examining, therefore, the consequences of the association of delinquents, under the foregoing heads, we tread upon clear and palpable ground, unobscured by metaphor and declamation.

[407]1. As to the motives by which men are prompted to the commission of crimes. These are the expectation of the pleasures which are the fruit of them. By far the greater number of the offences which bring men to a prison, are the offspring of *rapacity*. Crimes issuing from any other motive, are so few as scarcely to demand in this view any separate notice. The bulk of offenders will be of the poorer sort; among them the produce of a little plunder will go in the purchase of pleasure much beyond that which the ordinary produce of their labour would enable them to purchase, such as more food, more delicate liquors, in greater plenty and more delicious,— finer clothes; and more expensive pleasures. These things naturally form the subject of conversation among the prisoners, and an inexhaustible subject of boasting on the part of those who by their skill or good fortune have acquired the means of enjoying them. These recitals give a sort of superiority which those who possess it are fond, from a principle of vanity, to display and magnify to the humble and admiring crowd of their less fortunate associates. They inflame the imagination of the hearers; and, in a word, their propensity to gratify their rapacity by all sorts of crimes, is increased by the prospect of the pleasures of which the means are furnished by these crimes. The more numerous the association, the more varied the exploits to be recounted; and what subject more naturally the subject of conversation, than the circumstances which have brought them together.[408]

2. While, on the one hand, as has been just observed, all the vicious propensities are nourished and invigorated—on the other hand, all considerations tending to restrain the commission of offences, are repelled and enfeebled. These considerations belong to the one or the other of the three sanctions—the political, the moral, or the religious.

Those derived from the political sanction, are the various punishments appointed by law; amongst these, that which they are actually undergoing, have undergone, or are about to undergo. Of these sufferings it will naturally be the study of them all to make as light as possible; to which end the society of each other will afford them many powerful assistances. From pride, each man will endeavour to make his own sense of his own sufferings appear to others as slight as possible: he will undervalue the afflicting circumstances of his situation: he will magnify any little comforts which may attend it, and, as the common phrase is, will put as good a face upon the matter as he can. Thus the most intrepid and proud become a pattern for all others. The sensibilities of all are gradually elevated to the same pitch: it would be a matter of shame to them not to bear their misfortunes with equanimity. Even from mere sympathy, many will derive a powerful motive to soothe the sufferings of their partners in affliction—to congratulate them on the termination of such as are past, to relieve them under such as are present, and to fortify them against such as may be to come. It may possibly be observed, that to ascribe to persons of the class in question any such benevolent affections, is to attribute to them virtues to which they are altogether strangers.[409] But to suppose that men consist only of two classes, the altogether good, and the altogether bad, is a vulgar prejudice. The crime which subjects a man to the lash of the law, may leave him possessed of a thousand good qualities, and more especially of sympathy for the misfortunes of others. Daily experience may convince us of this, and lead us to believe that the criminal are not always altogether vicious.

[410]The considerations derived from the *moral sanction*,[411] are the various evils, positive and negative, apprehended from the ill-will of such persons with whom the person in question is in society. [412] Whilst a man remains in general society, though his character may be the subject of a general suspicion, he will be obliged to keep a guard upon his actions, that he may not too strongly confirm these suspicions, and render himself altogether despicable. But in a prison the society is unmixed, having interests of its own, opposite to the former, governed by habits and principles opposite to those which are approved in general society. The habits and practices which were odious there, because they were mischievous there,—not being mischievous, are not odious here. Theft is not odious among thieves, who have nothing to be stolen. It is in vain for them to make pretensions to probity; they agree, therefore, by a tacit convention, to understand this virtue. The mixed qualities of patience, intrepidity, activity, ingenuity, and fidelity, which are beneficial or not according as they are subservient to the other, will be magnified to the prejudice of the former. A man will be applauded for his patience, though it were exerted in lying in wait for a booty; for his intrepidity, though manifested in attaching the dwelling of a peaceable householder, or in defending himself against the ministers of justice; for his activity, though employed in seizing the unwary traveller; for his ingenuity, though displayed in working upon the sympathetic feelings of some deluded, compassionate benefactor; for his fidelity, though employed in screening his associates in some enterprise of mischief from the pursuit of the injured. These are qualities which enjoy the highest estimation in such society, and by their possession. That thirst for sympathy and applause is gratified, of which every man, in whatever situation he is placed, is desirous.

The probity which is held in honour, in such society, is not intended to be useful to mankind at large: its rules may be strictly observed in the society in which it is established, and disregarded to the prejudice of all persons not connected with that society. The Arabs, who live by plunder, are remarkable for their honesty towards the members of their own tribe. Thus also, that there is *honour among thieves*,[413] has become proverbial.*

The considerations derived from the *religious sanction*, are the sufferings apprehended from the immediate will of the Deity, in some degree perhaps in the present, but chiefly in a future life. This displeasure is, under the Christian religion, and particularly the Protestant, invariably believed to be annexed, with few or no exceptions, to all those malpractices which bring men into prisons. The considerations, therefore, which that sanction affords are to be numbered among the considerations which tend to restrain men from committing crimes. Now the force of this sanction, acting in opposition to that of the local moral sanction, which is generated and governs in a prison, will naturally have the whole force of this latter exerted against it to overthrow it. Not that a prison is the region of acute and scrupulous philosophy. The arguments there made use of, will be addressed to the passions rather than the judgment. The being of a God, the authority of Revelation, will not be combated by reason. The force of this sanction will be eluded rather than opposed; the attention will be diverted from the idea of God's displeasure, to the improbability of its being manifested. The authority of revelation will be combated by satires upon its ministers; and that man will be pronounced brave, who shall dare to deny the one, and despise the other. And arguments of this kind will be found to have most influence upon the members of such societies.

[414]3. The third and last of the ways in which the association of malefactors in prisons contributes to corrupt them, is by increasing their skill, and by that means their power of carrying their mischievous propensities, whatever they may be, into practice.

That their conversation will naturally turn upon their criminal exploits has been already observed. Each malefactor will naturally give a detail of the several feats of ingenuity which, in the course of those exploits, the occasion led him to practice. These facts will naturally be noted down,

---

*The influence of a man's conduct on the happiness of the whole race of sensitive beings, must be taken into the account, before it can with propriety be termed virtuous of vicious, simply and without addition. The same conduct which is pernicious, and on that account is or ought to be disreputable in society at large, is beneficial to, and on that account, held in honour by, a smaller society included within the former. The member of parliament who solicits or defends for his borough a privilege detrimental to the nation, is called a patriot in his borough. The man who devised the oath by which the candidates for degrees were made to engage not to propagate [*sic*], elsewhere than at Oxford and Cambridge, the seeds of what was thought useful learning, was probably thought a man of great merit in those Universities.

were it only on the score of curiosity. But as a means of gratifying those propensities, which the situation in question has a strong tendency to strengthen and confirm, they will make a much more forcible impression. An ample mass of observations will be soon collected, drawn from the experience of the whole society, and each particular member of it will soon be wise with the wisdom of the whole. Prisons, therefore, have commonly and very properly been stiled *schools of vice*.[415] In these schools, however, the scholar has more powerful motives for, and more effectual means of, acquiring the sort of knowledge that is to be learnt there, than he has of acquiring the sort of knowledge that is taught in more professed schools. In the professed school he is stimulated only by fear, he strives against his inclination. In these schools of vice he is stimulated by hope, acting in concert with his natural inclination. In the first, the knowledge imparted is dispensed only by one person; the stock of knowledge proceeds from one person: in the others, each one contributes to the instruction of all the others. The stock of knowledge is the united contribution of all. In professed schools the scholar has amusements more inviting to him than the professed occupations of the school. In these he has no such amusements, the occupation in question is the chief of the few pleasures of which his situation admits.

To the most corrupt, this promiscuous association is mischievous. To those committed for a first offence, who have yielded to the temptations of indigence, or have been misled by evil example; who are yet young and not hacknied [*sic*] in crimes; punishment, properly applied, might work reformation. This association can only render such more vicious; they will pass from pilfering to greater thefts, till they are guilty of highway robbery and murder. Such is the education yielded by promiscuous association of criminals in prison.[416]

CHAPTER VII.
GENERAL SCHEME OF IMPRISONMENT.

Let there be three kinds of imprisonment, differing one from another in the degree of their severity.

The first for insolvents: in case of rashness or extravagance, in lieu of satisfaction. The second, for malefactors whose imprisonment is to be temporary. These may be stiled second-rate malefactors. The third, for malefactors whose imprisonment is perpetual. These may be stiled first-rate malefactors.[418]

1st. Let all insolvents be upon the footing of bankrupts; compellable to discover, under pain of death, or other heavy penalty; on discovery not liable to imprisonment of course, but liable in case of rashness or extravagance; or else let rashness or extravagance be presumed in the first instance; and let it lie upon the insolvent to exculpate himself. To the same prison let such persons be committed as are arrested upon *mesne* process. On persons of this class the imprisonment[419] comes in before judgment to enforce; after judgment to stand in lieu of satisfaction. Here let there be no mark of infamy. Nor let there be here any rigour, either real or apparent.

The second kind of imprisonment[420] is designed for correction as well as for example. The real, therefore, and the apparent punishment ought to be upon a par. Here, let labour be added to imprisonment, and for the last week, or fortnight, or month, solitude, darkness, and spare diet. Here let a stigma be inflicted; but let that stigma be a temporary one. It will answer two purposes: first, that of example, as increasing the apparent punishment: second, that of security, by preventing escape.[421]

The third kind of imprisonment is destined for example only. The end of correction is precluded; since the delinquent must never to mix with society again. Here too, for the same purposes as in the former case, let a stigma be inflicted; and let that stigma be perpetual. Here let the apparent condition of the delinquent be as miserable, and the real as comfortable, as may be. Let the gentleman occupy himself as he pleases. Let the yeoman who has an art, exercise his art, and let him be a sharer in the profits. Let the labour of the yeoman who knows no art be more moderate than in the temporary prison.[422]

The diet in many prisons is in part provided for by private benefactions.[423] Such benefactions are of use only upon supposition of that gross negligence on the part of Government, of which they are a pregnant testimony. The demand a man in the situation in question has for food, is not at all varied by the happening of a casual act of humanity by a chance individual. Whatever be the proper allowance, he ought to have as much, although no private benefaction were given for that purpose; he ought not to have more, were the amount of such benefactions ever so considerable.[424] If ever the legislature should fulfil this obvious and necessary duty, all such private benefactions should be taken into the hands of the public.[425] Such resumption, far from being a violation of the wills of the benefactors, would be a more complete execution of them than any they could have hoped for.[426]

For the same reason all casual benefactions of particular persons, to particular delinquents, should be prevented. The way to do this, is not to prevent the money's being given; but to prevent it being spent, at least, in food and liquors; the introduction of money could not be prevented without establishing a search too troublesome and humiliating to be executed with the strictness requisite to answer the purpose. But articles so bulky as those of food and liquors might easily be excluded.[427] Such an institute would tend in no inconsiderable degree to promote restitution. At present, in all offences of rapacity, that is in nineteen out of twenty, of the crimes that are committed,* the greater a man's guilt has been, the more mischief he has done, the better he fares while he is in prison. It is seldom that the whole produce of the crime is found upon the delinquent at the time of his being apprehended; and though it be found on him, if it consists in money, it is seldom that it can be identified in such manner as to warrant the restitution of it against the consent of the delinquent. Commonly, if it is not spent, it is in the hands of some friend of the delinquent; an associate in iniquity, a wife or mistress. Thus secured, it is disposed of at his direction, and either lavished in debauchery, or in feeing lawyers to obstruct the course of justice.

When, therefore, the plunder is of no use to him, it will require a much less effort, on his part, to restore it to the right owner. The workings of conscience will be powerfully seconded by such an institution.

Whatever, therefore, is found upon the person, or in the possession of any one who, by virtue of a charge upon oath, is apprehended for a felony, should be impounded in the hands of the officer. As much of it as consists in money, or other articles that include a considerable value in a small compass, should be sealed up with the seal of the magistrate; who should have it in his option to keep it in his own custody, or commit it to that of the ministerial officer, giving, in either case, a receipt to the suspected felon.

---

*See Howard's Tables. [This note is not included within Dumont's edition.]

An objection to imprisonment,[428] when all are upon equal footing with respect to entertainment, is that the punishment is apt to be disproportionate. The rich are punished more than the poor; or, in other words, those who have been accustomed to good living, more than those who have been accustomed to hard living. On the other hand, to allow those who are committed for crimes of rapacity to give in to any expence [*sic*] while any part of the booty they may have made remains unrestored, is to allow them to enjoy the profit of their crimes; to give the criminal an indulgence at the expense of those whom he has injured.[429]

Here, then, arises a difference in the treatment proper to be given in this respect to different crimes. Persons committed for crimes of rapacity, should, in the case where the profit of the crime has been reaped, be debarred, until complete restitution shall have been made, of the liberty of procuring themselves those indulgences that are to be had for money. Persons committed for any other crimes may be allowed it.

With respect to restitution, a further caution is to be observed. It will happen very frequently that a person apprehended for one offence, has been guilty of many others. For this reason it is not the restitution of the booty gained by the first offence for which the malefactor is apprehended, that ought to be deemed sufficient to entitle him to the liberty of purchasing indulgences. A time ought to be limited, (suppose a month or six weeks) and notice given for any persons who, within a certain time, (suppose a year) have been sufferers by him, to come in and oppose the allowance of such liberty. Very light proof in such case ought to be held sufficient.[430]

Let us return for a moment to the different kinds of prisons: the different purposes for which they are destined ought to be very decidedly marked in their external appearance, in their internal arrangements, and in their denomination.

The walls of the first sort ought to be white—of the second, grey—of the third, black.

On the outside of the two last kinds of prisons may be represented various figures, emblematical of the supposed dispositions of the persons confined in them. A monkey, a fox, and a tiger, representing mischief, cunning, and rapacity, the sources of all crimes, would certainly form more appropriate decorations for a prison than the two statues of melancholy and raving madness, formerly standing before Bedlam. In the interior let two skeletons be placed, one on each side of an iron door: the occasional aspects of such objects is calculated to suggest to the imagination the most salutary terrors. A prison would thus represent the abode of death, and no youth that had once visited a place so decorated could fail of receiving a most salutary and indelible impression. I am fully aware, that to the man of wit, these emblematical figures may serve as matter for ridicule: in poetry they are admirable, in reality despicable. Fortunately, however, they are more assailable by ridicule than by reason.*

Distinguishing the several species of prisons by characteristic denominations, is far from being a useless idea. Justice and humanity to insolvent debtors, and to persons detained upon suspicion, require that they ought to be screened even from the apprehension of being confounded with delinquents, a risk to which they are naturally exposed, where all places of confinement bear the same appellation. If no such sentiment were found to be already in existence, the legislator ought to make it his business to create it: but the truth is, that it does exist, and it is the most valuable classes of the community that are most severely wounded by this want of discrimination.

A difference in the situation and name affords another means of aggravating one of the most important parts of the punishment—the apparent punishment.

The first sort of prison may be called the *House for Safe Custody*—the second, the *Penitentiary House*—the third, the *Black Prison*.

The first of these names does not convey any idea of misconduct; the second does, but at the same time presents the idea of reformation; the third is calculated to inspire terror and aversion.

With a view to reformation in the case of offences punished by temporary imprisonment, part of the punishment may consist in learning by heart a certain part of the criminal code, including that part which relates to the offence for which the party is punished. It might be digested into the form of a Catechism.

[431]In second-rate felonies and misdemeanors, where, after being punished, the offender is returned into society, it is of importance to lighten as much as possible the load of infamy he has been made to bear. The business is to render infamous not the offender, but the offence. The punishment undergone, upon the presumption of his being reclaimed, he ought not, if he is returned into society, to have his reputation irretrievably destroyed. The business is, then, for the sake of general prevention, to render the offence infamous, and, at the same time, for the sake of reformation, to spare the shame of the offender as much as possible. These two purposes appear, at first, to be repugnant: how can they be reconciled? The difficulty, perhaps, is not so great as it at first appears. Let the offender, while produced for the purpose of punishment, be made to wear a mask, with such other contrivances upon occasion as may serve to conceal any peculiarities of person. This contrivance will have a farther good effect in point of exemplarity. Without adding anything to the force of the *real* pun-

---

*Of the importance of symbols, and the uses that have been made of them, by the Catholic clergy, after the example of ancient Rome, see *Emile*, tom. iv.

ishment, on the contrary, serving even to diminish it, it promises to add considerably to the force of the *apparent*. The masks may be made more or less tragical [*sic*], in proportion to the enormity of the crimes of those who wear them. The air of mystery which such a contrivance will throw over the scene, will contribute in a great degree to fix the attention by the curiosity it will excite, and the terror it will inspire.[432]

CHAPTER VIII.

OF OTHER SPECIES OF TERRITORIAL CONFINEMENT— QUASI-IMPRISONMENT— RELEGATION—BANISHMENT.[433]

434 *Quasi-Imprisonment* consists in the confinement of an individual to the district in which his ordinary place of residence is situated.

Relegation consists in the banishment of an individual from the district in which his ordinary place of residence is situated, and his confinement to some other district of the state.

Banishment consists in the expulsion of a man from the country in which he has usually resided, and the prohibition of his return to it.[435]

These three species of punishment may be either temporary or perpetual.

Relegation and banishment are punishments unknown to the English law. Transportation, as we shall presently have occasion to observe, is in its nature totally different.[436] The exclusion of Papists from a certain district about the court is to be considered rather as a measure of precaution than of punishment.[437]

It is true, that the condition of persons living within the rules of a prison corresponds pretty accurately with the idea of territorial confinement. But this kind of territorial confinement is not inflicted in a direct way as a punishment. The punishment inflicted by the law is that of imprisonment, which the prisoner is allowed to commute upon paying for it. A man is not committed to the rules: he is committed to the prison, and upon paying what the jailor chooses, or is permitted to demand, he has the liberty of the rules; that is, of being in any part of a certain district round about the jail.*

The several inhabitable districts which are privileged from arrest, may be considered as scenes of territorial confinement with respect to offenders who resort to them to escape being arrested, and sent to prison. A man in such cases voluntarily changes the severer species of restraint into a milder.

---

*It appears from Mr. Howard, that in England there are six prisons that have *Rules* belonging to them. In London, two, the Fleet (p. 156), and the King's Bench (p. 196): in Carmarthen, two (pp. 422, 468); one in the Cornish borough of Lostwithiel (p. 386); and one in Newcastle-upon-Tyne (p. 422).

In France, instances of relegation were not unfrequent [*sic*]. Under the old regime, a man was ordered to confine himself to his estate, or to quit his estate and go and live at another place. A punishment, however, of this sort, almost always fell upon a man of rank, and generally was rather an arbitrary expression of the personal displeasure of the sovereign than a regular punishment inflicted in the ordinary course of justice. The person on whom it fell was commonly a disgraced minister, or a member of parliament. It has repeatedly happened that a whole parliament has been relegated[438] for refusing to register a particular edict. In these cases, however, it was often employed, not so much as a punishment, as a means of prevention—to prevent what were called intrigues. The exercise of such an act of authority was a symptom of apprehension and weakness on the part of the minister.

When a man is banished from all the dominions of his own state, he has either the whole world besides left for him to range in, or he is confined to a particular part of it. In the first case it may be said to be indefinite, with respect to the *locus ad quem*, in the other definite.*[439]

It might seem at first sight as if the defining the *locus ad quem* in banishment would be an operation nugatory and impracticable. For banishment is one of those punishments that are to be carried into effect, if at all, only by the terror of ulterior punishment. Now to be liable to ulterior punishment at the hands of his own state, a man must be still in the power of that state; which, by the supposition, it would appear as if he could not be. There are three cases, however, in which he may be so still—1. Where the banishment is only temporary.—2. Where, though his person is out of the dominions of his own state, his property, or some other possession of his, is still within its power.—3. Where the foreign state to which he is exiled is disposed on any account to co-operate with his own, and either to punish, or give up to punishment, such persons as the latter shall deem delinquents.[440]

---

*Instances of definite banishment are what one would not expect to find frequent in any system of legislation. In banishment, the object in general is to get rid of the malefactor; and what becomes of him afterwards is not minded. If it were an object of choice with the Government, what country the delinquent should betake himself to, the circumstances that could not but serve to determine such a choice would naturally be such as were of a temporary nature. This, accordingly, was the case with an Act of the British Parliament, which furnishes the only instance that occurs to me of a punishment of this nature. By statute 20 Geo. II, c. 45, the king is empowered to commute the punishment incurred by persons engaged in the late rebellion, into transportation to America, and the persons this dealt with are made subject to the pains of capital felony, not only as usual in case of their returning to any part of Great Britain or Ireland, but besides that, in case of their going into any part of the dominions of France or Spain, nations with whom the British was then at war. [Dumont's edition does not include this note.]

The inconveniences of territorial confinement, whether by relegation or banishment, are for the most part of the same description as those of simple imprisonment; they are apt in some respects to be greater, in others less severe than simple imprisonment.

Territorial confinement[441] is, however, susceptible of such infinite diversity, arising from the nature of the place—the extent of the district—the circumstances of the delinquent—that nothing like uniformity can be met with, and scarce any proposition can be laid down respecting it, that shall be generally true.

In case of relegation, the liberty of beholding the beauties of nature and of the arts, of enjoying the company of one's friends and relations, of serving them and advancing one's own fortune, is liable to be more or less abridged.

The liberty of exercising any public power, and of taking journies for the sake of health or of pleasure, are subject to be entirely taken away.

The liberty of carrying on business for a livelihood will be subject to be more or less abridged, according to its nature; and in respect of some particular species of business or trade, the opportunity of exercising it will be subject to be entirely taken away.

In respect to *banishment*, the inconveniences are liable to vary to such a degree, both in quality and species, that nothing can be predicated of this mode of punishment that shall be applicable to all cases.

The sort of evils with which it will be found to be most generally accompanied, may be arranged under the following heads:—

Separation from one's friends, relations and countrymen.

Loss of liberty the of enjoying objects of pleasure or of amusement to which one has been accustomed, as public diversions, or the beauties of nature or art.

Loss of the opportunity of advancement in the way of life in which one had engaged, as in the military line or in public offices.

Loss of the opportunity of advancing one's fortune, and derangement in one's affairs, whether of trade or any other lucrative profession. But under this head scarce anything can with certainty be said till the business of each delinquent is known, and the country to which he is relegated. All opportunity of advancing one's fortune may be totally taken away, or may be changed more or less for the worse, but it may even be improved. A workman acquainted with only one branch of a complicated manufacture, if relegated to a country in which no such manufacture was carried on, would lose the whole of his means of subsistence, so far as it depended upon that manufacture. A man engaged in his own country in the profession of the law, relegated to a country governed by different laws, would find his knowledge altogether useless. A clergyman of the church of England would lose the means of subsistence derivable from his profession, if relegated to a country in which there were no members of that sect to be found.

The quantity of suffering incident to banishment, and, in some cases, to relegation, will depend upon the individual's acquaintance, or want of acquaintance, with foreign languages. For this purpose it ought to be borne in mind that in every country the great majority of the people know no other language than their own. A great deal will depend upon the language a man speaks. A German, or an Italian, merely by being banished in his own state, would suffer nothing in this respect, because in other states he will find the bulk of the people speaking precisely the same language. Next to a German or an Italian, a Frenchman would be least exposed to suffer, on account of the popularity of the French language in other European nations. An Englishman (except in America), a Swede, a Dane, and a Russian, would find themselves worse off in this respect than inhabitants of other European countries.

A man being among people with whose language he is unacquainted, is liable to be exposed to the most serious evils. A difficulty in conversation imports a difficulty in making known all one's wants; in taking the necessary steps for procuring all sorts of pleasures, of warding off all sorts of pains. Though so much of the rudiments of a language should be acquired as may be sufficient for the common purposes of life, a man rarely acquires it in such perfection as to enable him to enjoy, unembarrassed, the pleasure of conversation; he will feel himself condemned to a perpetual state of inferiority, which must necessarily interfere with, and obstruct his engaging in any profitable employment.

To some people, banishment may be rendered in the highest degree irksome by the manners and customs of the people among whom the individual is cast. The words, manners and customs are here employed in their greatest latitude, and are considered as comprising every circumstance upon which a state of comfortable existence depends. The principal objects to which they refer are diet, cloathing [*sic*], lodging, diversions, and everything depending on difference of government and religion; which last has, among the lower classes at least, no inconsiderable influence upon the sympathies and antipathies of persons in general.

Throughout Europe, especially among persons of the higher ranks of life, a certain degree of conformity in manners and customs prevails: but a Gentoo,[442] banished from his own country, would be rendered extremely wretched, especially on the score of religion.

Change of climate is another circumstance of importance; the change may be for the better, but the bulk of mankind, from the effects of long habit, with difficulty accustom themselves to a climate different from that of their native country; the complaints of expatriated persons usually turn upon the injuries their health sustains from this cause.

With respect to all these several evils which are thus liable to arise out of the punishment of banishment, no one of them is certain to have place; they may or may not exist; in respect of severity they are liable to unlimited variation, and it may even happen that the good may preponderate over the evil.*

[443]In point of frugality, it seems as if these several punishments were all of them more eligible than imprisonment, at least than the system of imprisonment as at present managed; and that quasi-imprisonment and relegation are more frugal than banishment.

Under imprisonment, a man must at all events be maintained. Simple imprisonment adds nothing to the facility which any man has of maintaining himself by his labour. It takes from that facility in many cases. By imprisonment some people will always be altogether debarred from maintaining themselves. These must be maintained at the expense of the public. An imprisoned man, therefore, is, on an average, a burthen. His value to the state is negative. A man at liberty is, at an average, a profit. His value to the state is positive; for each man, at an average, must produce more than he consumes, else there would be no common stock. A banished man is neither a burthen nor a profit. His value to the state is 0. It is greater, therefore, than that of an imprisoned man.

The value of a man under quasi-imprisonment and relegation, may, it should seem, be taken as equivalent or not in any assignable degree, less than that of a man at large. In the only instances in which these modes of punishment occur in England, the sufferer, instead of receiving anything from the public, pays.†[444]

In point of certainty, they have none of them anything to distinguish them from other punishments.

---

*Gallio having been exiled to the isle of Lesbos, information was received at Rome that he was amusing himself there, apparently very much to his satisfaction; and that what had been imposed upon him as a punishment, had, in fact, proved to him a source of pleasure; upon this they determined to recal [sic] him to the society of his wife and to his home, and directed him to confine himself to his house, in order that they might inflict upon him what he should think a punishment.—*Essais de Montaigne*, liv. i, c. 2.

So far the French writer: Tacitus says—

Italia exactus: et quia incusabature facile toleraturus exiliium, delecta Lesbo, insula nobile et amena retrahitur in urbem, custoditurque domibus magistratuum.—*Ann.* Liv. vi, c. 3.

†I am speaking of the rules of the six jails in England that have rules. The public is not at the expense of finding lodging. The houses are the property of private individuals, who get somewhat more for them than could be got for houses in the same condition out of the rules. Besides this advanced rent, the prisoner pays fees for the indulgence, which goes towards the jailor's salary.

In point of equality, they are all of them deficient,* but especially the two latter, and most of all the last.

To be confined to within the circuit of a small town[445] can scarcely but be a punishment in some degree to almost all, though to some more, to others less. To live out of one's own province, or out of one's own country, is a very severe punishment to many; but to many it is none at all.

It is impossible to state with any accuracy the difference in this respect between relegation and banishment. In one point of view it should seem as if banishment were the more penal. For the difference in point of laws, language, climate and customs, between one's own province and another province of one's own state, is upon an average not likely to be so great as between one's own province and a foreign state. In nations, however, that have colonies, it will generally happen that there are provinces more dissimilar to one another on the whole in those respects than some of those provinces may be to other provinces of neighbouring nations. How small a change, for instance, would an Englishman find in crossing from Dover to Dunkirk, and how great a change in going from the first of those places to the East or the West Indies?

In point of variability, except in respect of time, no punishment of the chronical kind can be more ineligible than these. But in point of intensity, although the degrees of suffering they are liable to produce in different persons are so numerous, yet they are not by any means subject to the regulation of magistrate. It is not in his power to fix the quantity of punishment upon the whole to anything near the mark he may pitch upon in his own mind.[446]

In point of exemplarity they all yield to every other mode of punishment, and banishment to the other two. As to banishment, what little exemplarity it possesses, it possesses upon the face of description.[447] The descriptions of orators and poets have rendered it in some degree formidable upon paper. On the score of execution, it is the essential character of it to have none at all. Removed out of the observation of his countrymen, his suffering were they ever so great, can afford no example to his countrymen. This is the lowest degree of inexemplarity [sic] a punishment can possess, when even the person of the sufferer is out of the reach of observation. The two others are upon a footing with pecuniary punishment: in which the person of the sufferer is under observation, and occasionally perhaps his sufferings; but there is no circumstance to point out the derivation of the latter from the

---

*This inequability [sic] may be illustrated by the history of the young Venetian noble delegated to the Isle of Candia. Despairing of being allowed to revisit the walls of his native city, and of again embracing his friends and his aged father, he committed another crime, unpardonable by the laws of the State, because he knew that he should be reconveyed [sic] to Venice for trial, and to suffer death.—Moore's *View of Society and Manners in Italy*, tom. i, lett. xvi.

punishment that produced them. They are inferior to imprisonment because there the main instrument of punishment, the prison, is continually before his eyes. To quasi-imprisonment and relegation there belongs no such instrument—the punishment as we have observed, being produced in the first instance not by any *material* but merely by *moral* means.*

On the score of subserviencey [*sic*] to reformation there seems to be a considerable difference among these three punishments. Quasi imprisonment is apt to be disserviceable in this view: relegation and banishment rather serviceable than otherwise, more especially the latter.

1. Quasi imprisonment is apt to be disserviceable. The reasons have been already given under the head of Imprisonment. The property which we mentioned as being incident to imprisonment, I mean of corrupting the morals of the prisoners by the accumulating, if one may so say, of the peccant [*sic*] matter, is incident to quasi imprisonment only in a somewhat less degree. Under the former they can have no other company than that of each other: under the latter there may be room for some admixture of persons of repute. Under the former they are forced into the company of each other: under the latter they may choose to be alone.

2. Relegation is apt to be rather serviceable than otherwise: as in solitary imprisonment, if the delinquent has formed any profligate connections, it separates him from them and does not, like simple imprisonment, lead him to form new ones of the same stamp. Turned adrift among strangers he cannot expect all at once to meet with a set of companions prepared to join with him in any scheme of wickedness. Should he make advances and be repulsed, he exposes himself to their honest indignation, perhaps to the censure of the law. Should the company he happens to fall in with be persons as profligate as himself, it would be some time before he could establish himself sufficiently in their confidence. If he continues to make war upon mankind it must be with his own single strength. He may find it easier to betake himself to charity or to honest labour. He is separated not only from the objects which used to supply him with the *means* to commit crimes, but from those which used to furnish him with the *motives*.[448] The company he meets with in the new scene he enters upon[449] will either be honest, or at least, for aught he can know to the contrary, will for some time seem to be so. In the meantime the disapprobation he may hear them express for habits resembling those which subjected him to the punishment he is undergoing, may co-operate with that punishment, and contribute to the exciting in him that salutary aversion to those habits which is styled repentance.

---

*The little benefit that banishment, in so far as it operates as a punishment, can be of in the way of example, is reaped by foreign states; by that state to wit which the banished man chooses for his asylum.

3.[450] In this respect banishment is apt to be rather more serviceable than relegation. If the delinquent be still of that age at which new habits of life are easily acquired, and is not insensible to the advantages of a good reputation, his exile, if the character in which he appears is not known, will be the more likely to contribute to his reformation, from his finding himself at a distance from those who were witnesses of his infamy, and in a country in which his endeavours to obtain an honest livelihood, will not be liable to be obstructed by finding himself an object of general suspicion. But even though he were to carry with him to the place of his banishment his original vicious propensities, he would not find the same facilities for giving effect to them, especially if the language of the country were different from his own. The laws also of the foreign country being new to him, may on that account strike him with greater terror than the laws of his own country, which he had perhaps been accustomed to evade. And even in case of meeting with success in any scheme of plunder, the want of established connections for the disposing of it would render the benefit derivable from it extremely precarious. The consideration of all these difficulties would tend to induce him to resort to honest labour as the only sure means of obtaining a livelihood.[451]

But, taking all the above sources of uncertainty into consideration, it will be found that the cases are very few in which banishment can be resorted to as an eligible mode of punishment. In what are called state offences it may occasionally be employed with advantage, in order to separate the delinquent from his connections, and the remove him from the scene of his factious intrigues. In this case, however, it would be well to leave him the hope of returning as a stimulus to good conduct during his banishment.[452]

CHAPTER IX.
OF SIMPLY RESTRICTIVE PUNISHMENTS.[453]

[454]

Having now considered the several punishments which restrain the faculty of locomotion, we proceed to the consideration of those which restrain the choice of occupations. These may be called simply restrictive punishments, and consist in a simple prohibition of performing certain acts.

Upon this occasion we may recur to a distinction already explained, which exists between restraint and punishment. The Civil Code and Police Code are full of restraints, which are not punishments. Certain individuals are prohibited from selling poison. Innkeepers are prohibited from keeping their houses open after a certain hour. Persons are prohibited from exercising the professions of medicine or of the law, without having passed through certain examinations.[455]

Simply restrictive punishments consist in the preventing an individual from enjoying a common right, or a right which he possessed before. If the prohibition respects a lucrative occupation, if for example an innkeeper or a hackney-coachman is deprived of his licence, the prohibition acts as a pecuniary punishment, in its nature very inequable and unfrugal. If a man is deprived of the means of earning his subsistence, he must still be supported; the punishment therefore falls not upon the individual alone, but upon others whom it is not intended to affect.[456]

Employments which are not lucrative may be of an agreeable nature; their variety is infinite: but there is one point in which they all agree, and which will render it unnecessary to submit them to a detailed discussion. There are none of them, or at least scarcely one, which by its deprivation furnishes a sufficient portion of evil to enable us to rely upon its effect.

As respects pleasures, the mind of man possesses a happy flexibility—one source of amusement being cut off—it endeavours to open up another, and always succeeds; a new habit is easily formed; the taste adopts itself to new habits, and suits itself to a great variety of situations. This ductility of mind, this aptitude to accommodate itself to circumstances as they change, varies much in different individuals; and it is impossible beforehand to judge, or even to guess, how long an old habit will retain its dominion, so that its privation shall continue a real punishment.

149

This is not the only objection—Restrictive laws are very difficult of execution: they always require a subsidiary punishment of which the effect is uncertain. If you prohibit an individual from gaming, drunkenness, dancing and music, it becomes necessary to appoint an inspector for all these things, in all places, to see that your prohibition is observed. In a word, punishments of this kind are subject to this dilemma: either the attachment to the object prohibited is very weak or very strong: if strong, the prohibition will be eluded; if weak, the object desired will not be obtained.

In respect of exemplarity they are equally defective: the privations they occasion are not of a nature to be generally known, or if known to produce a strong effect upon the imagination: the misery they produce rankles in the mind; but is completely hidden from the public eye.[457]

These are some of the circumstances which have reduced the employment of these punishments within so narrow a compass: they are too uncertain in their effects, and to easily eluded, to allow of their use, as the sanction to a general law. It is true that if Judges were acquainted with the characters and circumstances of individuals, they might avail themselves of them with good effect; but this knowledge can scarcely ever be expected.

This species of punishment is well suited to domestic government. There is no pleasure which a parent or teacher cannot employ as a reward, by permitting its enjoyment, or convert into a source of punishment, by restricting its use.

But though restraints of this nature, that is to say, prohibition of agreeable occupation, do not alone form effective punishments, there is one case in which they may be usefully employed in addition to some other punishment—analogy recommends such employment of them. Has an offence been committed at some public exhibition, it may be well to prohibit the delinquent from attending such public exhibitions for a time.

Among simply restrictive punishments, there is one of which a few examples are found, and which has not received a name: I have called it *banishment from the presence*. It consists in an obligation imposed upon the offender immediately to leave the place in which he meets with the offended party. The simple presence of the one is a signal for the departure of the other. If Silius, the party injured, enters a ball or concert room, a public assembly or public walk—Titius is bound instantly to leave the same. This punishment appears admirably well suited for cases of personal insult, attacks upon honour, and calumnies, in a word—in all crimes which render the presence of the offender particularly disagreeable and mortifying to the party offended.[458]

[459]In the employment of this punishment care must be taken that power be not given to the party injured to banish the offender from places in which

he is carrying on his habitual operations, or where his presence may be necessary for the discharge of any particular duty. Hence it will, in many cases, be found indispensable to make exceptions in respect of churches, courts of justice, markets, and political assemblies.

Instances in which this mode of punishment has been employed may be found in the decrees of the French Parliaments. It will be sufficient to mention one instance. A man of the name of *Aujay* having insulted a lady of rank in the most gross manner, among other punishments, he was ordered, under pain of corporal punishment, to retire immediately from every place at which this lady might happen to be present.*

In the 'Intrigues of the Cabinet' may be seen the account of a quarrel between Madame de Montbazon and the Princess de Condé, in the course of which the former was guilty of very gross insults towards the Princess. The Queen, Ann of Austria, ordered that Madame Montbazon should retire from every place at which the Princess was present.†

Under the English law there are various instances in which, though not under the name of punishment, restrictions are imposed upon certain classes of persons. Catholics were formerly not allowed to exercise either the profession of the law or that of medicine. Persons refusing to take the sacrament according to the rites of the Church of England were excluded from all public offices.

Such was the law: the practice was always otherwise: in point of fact, a very large proportion of offices, civil and military, were filled by persons who had never taken the oaths required, but who were protected from the penalties to which they would otherwise have been subjected by an annual bill of indemnity. In point of right, the security thus afforded was a precarious one, but the uninterrupted practice of nearly a century left little room for apprehension on the part of the persons interested.

The restrictions here in question were not designed to operate as punishments; they were originally imposed with a view of avoiding the danger which, it was apprehended, might be incurred by vesting in the hands of persons of certain religious persuasions, situations of public trust. This, at least, was the avowed political reason: the true cause of the exclusion was however religious animosity: they were acts of antipathy.[460]

But these were not the only motives: self-interest had its share in producing the exclusion. Exclude one set of persons, and you confer a benefit on another set: those to whom the right is reserved have to contend with a smaller number of competitors, and their prospect of gain is increased: these restrictive laws, originating in religious hatred, were afterwards

---

*Causes Celèbres, tom. iv. p. 307.

†Anquetil, tom. iii.

maintained by injustice; the persecution began by misguided bigotry, was persisted in long after the original inducement had been forgotten, from the most sordid injustice.[461] This is the short history of the persecutions in Ireland. For the benefit of the Protestants, the restrictive laws against the Catholics were kept in force: out of eight millions of inhabitants, a selection was made of one million, on whom were conferred all offices of power or of profit. In this state of things, whilst privileges are, by the continuance of the persecuting laws, placed in the hands of the persecutors, the procuring their abolition may be expected to be attended with no small difficulty. The true motive—the sordid one—will long be concealed under the mask of religion.

Though it may be said that these restrictions are not designed to operate as punishments, and that, in the making of this general law, no particular individual was aimed at, yet there results from it a distinction injurious to the particular class of persons affected by it—necessarily injurious, since the continuance of the law can be justified only by supposing them to be dangerous and disloyal. Such laws form a nucleus around which public prejudice collects; and the legislator, by acquiescing in these transient jealousies, strengthens them, and renders them permanent. They are the remnants of a disease which has been universal, and which, after its cure, has left behind it deep and lasting scars.[462]

CHAPTER X.
OF ACTIVE OR LABOURIOUS PUNISHMENT.[463]

464

Active punishment is that which is inflicted on a man by obliging, or to use another word, compelling him to act in this or that particular way, to exert this or that particular species of action.[465]

There are two kinds of means by which a man may be compelled to act, physical and moral; the first applies itself to his body, the other to his mind, to his faculty of volition.

The actions which a man may be compelled to perform by physical means are so few, and so unprofitable, both to the patient and to others, as not to be worth taking into account.

When the instrument is of the moral kind, it is by acting on the volition that it produces its effect. The only instrument that is of a nature to act immediately upon the volition, is an idea; but not every idea; only an idea of pleasure or of pain, as about to ensue from the performance or non-performance of the act which is the object of the volition.

It cannot be an idea of pleasure which can so act upon the volition as to give birth to an act the performance of which shall be a punishment; it must therefore be an idea of pain,—of any pain, no matter what, so it be to appearance greater than the pleasures of abstaining from the performance of the penal act.[466]

It is manifest, therefore, that when a punishment of the laborious kind is appointed, another punishment must necessarily be appointed along with it. There are, therefore, in every such case, two different punishments at least necessarily concerned. One, which is the only one directly and originally intended, the laborious punishment itself; which may be styled the *principal* or *proper* punishment: the other, in case of the former not being submitted to, is called in to its assistance, and may be styled the *subsidiary* punishment.

This subsidiary punishment may be of any kind that, in point of quantity, is great enough. It ought not, however, to be likewise of the laborious kind; since in that case, as well as in the case of the principal punishment, the will of the patient is necessary to constitute the punishment; and to determine the will, some incident is necessary that does not depend upon the will. It will be necessary, therefore, to employ such punishments as are purely passive, or those restrictive punishments in which the instrument is purely physical.[467]

In regard to this class of punishments, one thing is here to be noted with reference to the instrument. In punishments of this kind, there is a link or two interposed between the instrument and the pain produced by means of it. The instrument first produces the volition, that volition produces a correspondent external act: and it is that act which is the immediate cause by which the pain here in question is produced. This punishment, then, we see, has this remarkable circumstance to distinguish it from other punishments, it is produced immediately by the patients own act: it is the patient who, to avoid a greater punishment, inflicts it on himself.

What then is the sort of act that is calculated to produce pain in the case of active punishment? It admits not of any description more particular than this: that it is any act whatever that a man has a mind not to do; or in other words that on any account whatever is disagreeable to him.[468]

An occupation is a series of acts of the same kind, or tending to the same end. An occupation may be disagreeable on a positive or a negative account; as being productive, in a manner more or less immediate, of some positive pain, or as debarring from the exercise of some more agreeable occupation.

Considered in itself, an occupation may be either painful, pleasurable, or indifferent; but continued beyond a certain time, and without interruption (such is the constitution of man's nature,) every occupation whatsoever becomes disagreeable: not only so, but such as were in the beginning pleasurable become, by their continuance, more disagreeable than such as were originally indifferent.*

To make the sum of his occupations pleasurable, every man must therefore be at liberty to change from one to another, according to his taste. Hence it is that any occupation which, for a certain proportion of his time, a man is compelled to exercise, without the liberty of changing to another, becomes disagreeable, and in short becomes a punishment.

Active punishments are as various as the occupations in which, for the various purposes of life, men can have occasion to be employed. These being usually inflicted on all offenders indiscriminately, have been such as all offenders indiscriminately have been physically qualified to undergo. They have consisted commonly in various exertions of muscular force, in which there has been little or not dexterity required in the manner of its application. In general, they have been such as to produce a *profit*: a collateral benefit in addition to that expected from the punishment as such.

---

*To eat grapes, for instance, is what, at certain times at least, will probably be to most men rather an agreeable occupation: to pick them an indifferent one. But in two or three hours, for example, the eating them will become intolerable, while the picking them may still remain, perhaps, in itself nearly a matter of indifference.

Among the modes of penal labour, a very common one has been that of rowing. This is an exercise performed chiefly by main strength, with very little mixture of skill, and that presently attained. Some vessels, of a bulk large enough to bear any sea, have been made so as to be put in motion in this manner, even without the help of sails. This occupation is more unpleasant in itself than that of an ordinary seamen, as having less variety, besides that the rowers are confined by chains. Such vessels are called gallies, and the rowers galley-slaves. This punishment, though unknown in England, is in use in most of the maritime states of Europe, and particularly in the Mediterranean and Adriatic Seas.

In many countries, malefactors have been employed in various public works, as in the cleansing of harbours* and the streets of towns, in making roads, building and repairing fortifications, and working in mines.

Working in the mines is a punishment employed in Russia and in Hungary. In Hungary the mines are of quicksilver, and the unwholesome effects of that metal, upon a person who is exposed to the effluvia of it for a length of time, may be one reason for employing criminals in that work, in preference to other persons.

Beating hemp is the most common employment which delinquents are put to in our workhouses. Persons of both sexes being subjected to it, without distinction.

From the nature of the service, active punishments may be distinguished into two sorts, specific and indiscriminate. I call it specific, when it consists in the being obliged to do such and such a particular kind or kinds of work: indiscriminate, when it consists in being obliged to do not any kind of work in particular, but every kind of work in general, which it shall please such or such a person to prescribe. If such person take all the profit of the work, he is called a master. If the profit is received by some other person, he is called a keeper, or overseer. There are cases of a mixed nature, in which, in certain respects, the servitude is indiscriminate, as to other respects, specific.

At Warsaw, before the partition of Poland, there was a public workhouse, in which convicts were confined in ordinary to particular employments determined by the laws or custom of the place. To this workhouse, however, any person who thought proper might apply, and upon giving security for their forthcomingness, and paying a certain stipulated price for their use, a certain number of the convicts were allotted to him, to be employed in any piece of work for a given time. The services they were

---

*The employment of malefactors for the cleaning of harbours was, for the first time, introduced into this country in the year 1776, by stat. 16 Geo. III. c. 43. [This note does not appear within Dumont's edition.]

employed upon were generally of a rough kind, such as digging a ditch, or paving a court; and a soldier, or a party of soldiers, according to the number of convicts thus employed, was placed over them as a guard.

This custom was in use in Russia.*

[469]This distinction between specific and indiscriminate servitude, may be illustrated by two examples derived from the English law.

The example of specific punishment is afforded by the statute which directs the employment of certain malefactors on board the hulks, in improving the navigation of the Thames. The statute determines the kind of labour, and the subsidiary punishments by which it is to be enforced.

Indiscriminate servitude is part of the punishment inflicted by our laws under the name of transportation. This servitude is sometimes limited as to its duration, but is without limitation, and without restriction, in respect of the services which may be required.[470]

All these kinds of labour, whether indiscriminate or specific, require as a necessary accompaniment that the individual should be upon that spot where the business is to be done. Some import imprisonment; all of them import restraint upon occupations, to wit, upon all occupations incompatible with those in which they constrain a man to employ himself. The degree of this restraint is in a manner indefinite. To lay a man, therefore, under a particular constraint of any kind, is for that time to lay him under an almost universal restraint. The clear value then of the pleasure which a man loses by being compelled to any particular occupation, is equal to that of the greatest of all the pleasures which, had it not been for the compulsion, he might have procured for himself.

[471]Upon examining laborious punishment, we shall find it to possess the properties to be wished for in a mode of punishment, in greater perfection, upon the whole, than any other single punishment.[472]

1. It is *convertible to profit*. Labour is in fact the very source of profit. Not that, after all, its power in this way is so extensive as that of pecuniary punishment. For, from the punishment of one man in this way, all the profit that is to be reaped is that which is producible by the labour of one man; a limited and never very ample quantity. On the other hand, from the punishment of a man in the pecuniary way, it may happen that a profit shall be reaped equal to the labour of many hundred men. The difference, however, in favour of this punishment is, that money is a casual fund; labour one that cannot fail. Indeed, upon the whole, though pecuniary punishment be in

---

*See Abbé Chappé's travels in that country. The Abbé had particular reason to remember it. Wanting, for the purpose of some experiment, to have the earth dug, he was complimented with the use of a dozen of these poor prisoners. Having given them some money to purchase liquor, they employed it in making their guard drunk, and then took to flight.—Vol. I, page 149.

particular instances capable of being more profitable, yet, considering how large a proportion of mankind, especially of those most liable to commit the most frequent and troublesome kinds of crimes, have no other possession worth estimating than their labour: laborious punishment, if managed as it might and ought to be, may perhaps be deemed the most profitable upon the whole.

2.[473] In point of *frugality* to the state, laborious punishment, considered by itself, is as little liable to objection as any other can be. I say, considered by itself: for, when coupled with imprisonment, as it can hardly but be in the case of public servitude, it is attended with those expenses to the public which have been noticed under the article of imprisonment. These, however, are not to be charged to the account of the laborious part of the punishment: so that[474] the advantage which laborious punishment has on this score over simple imprisonment is quite a clear one. But the former of these two punishments, though separable from the latter in idea, is not separable in practice. Imprisonment may be made to subsist without labour: but forced labour cannot be made to subsist without imprisonment. The advantage then, which servitude has in this respect, when compared with imprisonment, ceases when compared with any other mode of punishment. However, the profit gained by the one part is enough, under good management, to do more than balance the expense occasioned by the other. So that upon the whole it has the advantage, in point of economy, over any other mode of punishment but pecuniary.

3.[475] It seems to stand equally clear of objection in point of equability. As to the restraint it involves, it accommodates itself of itself to each man's circumstances. For, with respect to each man, it has the effect of restraining him from following those occupations, whatever they may be, which are to him most pleasurable. The positive servitude itself will be apt to sit heavier on one man than another. A man who has not been used to any kind of labour will suffer a good deal more, for some time at least, than one who has been used to labour, though of a different kind or degree from that in question. But this inconvenience may be pretty well obviated by a proper attention to the circumstances of individuals.

4. In point of variability, though it is not perfect throughout, yet it is perfect as far as it goes. In a very low degree it is not capable of subsisting; on account of the infamy it involves, at least in a country governed by European manners. One of the most odious acts of the reign of the Emperor, Joseph II, was the sentencing persons of high rank to labour in the public works. The Protestants of France considered the condemnation of their religious ministers to the galleys as a personal insult done to themselves: in this respect then it falls short of pecuniary punishment. After that

exception it is capable of being varied to the utmost nicety: being variable as well in respect of intensity, as of duration.

5. In point of *exemplarity* it has no peculiar advantage; neither is it subject to any disadvantage. Symbols of suffering it has none belonging to itself: for the circumstance which distinguishes penal servitude from voluntary labour is but an internal circumstance—the idea of compulsion operating on the patient's mind. The symbols, however, that belong necessarily to the punishment it is naturally combined with, I mean imprisonment, apply to it of course; and the means of characterising the condition of the patient by some peculiarity of dress are so obvious, that these may be looked upon as symbols naturally connected with it.

6. In point of *subserviency to reformation*[476] it is superior to any other punishment, except that mode of imprisonment which we have already insisted[477] on as being peculiarly adapted to this purpose.* Next to the keeping of malefactors asunder, is the finding them employment while they are together. The work they are engaged in confines[478] their attention in some measure: the business of the present moment is enough to occupy their thoughts; they are not stimulated by the impulse of *ennui* to look out for those topics of discourse which tend, in the manner that has been already explained, to fructify the seeds of corruption in their minds: they are not obliged, in search of aliment for speculation, to send back their memory into the field of past adventures, or to set their invention in quest of future projects.[479] This kind of discipline does not indeed, like the other, pluck up corruption by the roots:[480] it tends however to check the growth of it, and render the propensity to it less than powerful. Another circumstance, relative to the nature of this discipline, contributes to check the progress of corruption: to insure the performance of their tasks it is necessary that the workmen should be under the eye of overseers.[481] The presence of these will naturally be a check to them, and restrain them from engaging in any criminal topics of discourse.

So much for the tendency which this punishment has to keep men from growing worse. It has besides this a positive tendency to make them better. And this tendency is more obvious and less liable to accident than the other. There is a tendency, as has already been observed, in man's nature to reconcile and accommodate itself to every condition in which it happens to be placed. Such is the force of habit. Few occupations are so irksome that habit will not in time make them sit tolerably easy. If labour then, even though forced, will in time lose much of its hardship, how much easier will it become when the duration and the mode are in some measure regulated by the will of the labourer himself; when the bitter ideas of infamy and compulsion are

---

*Supra, p. 114. [A similar note does not appear within the manuscript or Dumont's edition.]

removed, and the idea of gain is brought in to sweeten the employment? in a word, when the labourer is left to work at liberty and by choice?[482]

7.[483] This mode of punishment is not altogether destitute of *analogy*, at least of the verbal kind, to that class of crimes which are the most frequent, and for which an efficacious punishment is most wanted: crimes, I mean, that result from a principle of rapacity or of sloth.[484] The slothful man is constrained to work. The vagabond is confined to a particular spot. The more opposite the restraint thus imposed is to the natural inclination of the patient, the more effectually will he be deterred from indulging his vicious propensities by the prospect of the punishment that awaits him.

8. With regard to the popularity of this species of punishment in this country, the prejudices of the people are not quite so favourable to it as could be wished. Impatient spirits too easily kindled with the fire of independence have a word for it, which presents an idea singularly obnoxious to a people who pride themselves so much upon their freedom. This word is slavery. Slavery they say is a punishment too degrading for an Englishman, even in ruins. This prejudice may be confuted by observing, 1st, That public servitude is a different thing from slavery, 2nd, That if it were not, this would be no reason for dismissing this species of punishment without examination. If then upon examination it is found not to be possessed, in a requisite degree, of the properties to be wished for in a mode of punishment that, and not the name it happens to be called by, is a reason for its rejection: if it does possess them, it is not any name that can be given to it that can change its nature. But these observations have been more fully insisted on in the Chapter on Popularity.[485]

Having thus spoken of this species of punishment in general, let us stop a moment to consider the different kinds of labour which ought to be preferred.

The principle distinction is that of public and private labour.

In public works, the infamy of their publicity tends to render the individuals more depraved than the habit of working tends to reform them. At Berne there are two classes of forced labourers, the one employed in cleaning the streets, and in other public works; the others employed in the interior of the prison. The latter, when set at liberty, rarely fall again into the hands of justice; the former are no sooner set at liberty than they are guilty of new crimes. This difference is accounted for at Berne by the indifference to shame they contract in a service, the infamy of which is renewed day by day. It is probable that after the notoriety of this disgrace, nobody in the country would like to hold communication with or to employ them.

The rough and painful kinds of labour which are ordinarily selected for this kind of punishment do not generally seem suitable. It is difficult to measure the powers of individuals, or to distinguish real from simulated weakness. Subsidiary punishments must be proportioned to the difficulty of the labour and to the indispositions to perform it. The authority with which an inspector must be armed is liable to great abuses; to rely upon his pity, or even upon his justice, in an employment which hardens the heart, betrays an ignorance of human nature; so soon as it becomes necessary to inflict corporal punishment, the individual who is charged with its execution will become degraded in his own opinion, and he will revenge himself by the abuse of his authority.

Nam nil asperius humili qui surgit in altum. *

Labour which require great efforts ought to be performed by free labourers. The labour obtained by the force of fear is never equal to that which is obtained by the hope of reward. Constrained labour is always inferior to voluntary labour; not only because the slave is interested in concealing his powers, but also because he wants that energy of soul upon which muscular strength so much depends. It would be a curious calculation to estimate how much is lost from this cause in those states where the greater portion of labour is performed by slaves. It would tend greatly to prove that their gradual emancipation would be a noble and beneficial measure.

Labour in mines, except in particular circumstances, is little suitable for malefactors, partly for the reason above given, and partly from the danger of degrading this occupation. The ideas of crime and shame will soon be associated with it; miner and criminal would soon become synonymous; this would not be productive of inconvenience if the number of malefactors were sufficient for working the mines, but if the contrary is the case, there might be a lack of workmen, from the aversion inspired towards this kind of labour in those who used to exercise it voluntarily, or who are at liberty to choose respecting it.

---

*Claudian.

CHAPTER XI.[486]
CAPITAL PUNISHMENT.

Capital punishment may be distinguished into—1st, simple; 2nd, afflictive.

I call it *simple* when, if any bodily pain be produced, no greater degree of it is produced than what is necessary to produce death.

I call it *afflictive*, when any degree of pain is produced more than what is necessary for that purpose.

It will not be necessary, upon the present occasion, to attempt to give an exhaustive view of all the possible modes by which death might be produced without occasioning any, or the least possible quantity of collateral suffering. The task would be almost an endless one: and when accomplished, the only use to which it could be applied would be that of affording an opportunity of selecting out of the catalogue the mode that seemed to possess the desired property in the greatest perfection, which may readily be done without any such process.

The mode in use in England is far from being the best that could be devised. In strangulation by suspension, the weight of the body alone is seldom sufficient to produce an immediate and entire obstruction of respiration. The patient, when left to himself, struggles for some time: hence it is not uncommon for the executioner, in order to shorten his sufferings, to add his own weight to that of the criminal. Strangling by the bowstring may to some, perhaps, appear a severer mode of execution; partly from the prejudice against every usage of despotic governments, partly by the greater activity exerted by the executioners in this case than in the other. The fact however is, that it is much less painful than the other, for it is certainly much more expeditious. By this means the force is applied directly in the direction which it must take to effect the obstruction required: in the other case, the force is applied only obliquely; because the force of two men pulling in that manner is greater than the weight of one man.[487]

It is not long, however, even in hanging, before a stop is put to sense; as is well enough known from the accounts of many persons who have survived the operation. This probably is the case a good while before the convulsive strugglings are at an end; so that in appearance the patient suffers more than he does in reality.

With respect to beheading, there are reasons for supposing that the stop put to sensation is not immediate: a portion of sensibility may still be kept up in the spinal marrow a considerable time after it is separated from the brain. It is so, at least, according to all appearance, for different lengths of time in different animals and insects, which continue to move after their heads are separated from their bodies.

SEC. II.—AFFLICTIVE CAPITAL PUNISHMENT.

To exhaust this part of the subject it would be necessary to make a catalogue of every various punishment of this description of which, in practice, there has been any example, adding to them such others as the imagination could be made to supply; but, the ungrateful task performed, of what use would it be? We shall the more willingly refrain from any such labour as in the more modern European codes these punishments have been altogether discarded; and in those in which they have not been formally abolished, they have long fallen into disuetude [sic]. Let us rejoice in these improvements: there are few opportunities in which the philosopher can offer to the governors of the world more just or more honourable congratulations. The importance of the subject, however, will not admit of its being passed over in perfect silence. The system of jurisprudence in question has been too long established, it has had too many apologists, and has had for its supporters too many great names, to allow of its being altogether omitted in a work expressly treating on the subject of punishment. It may besides be of use to shew that reason concurs with humanity in the condemning punishments of this description, not merely as being useless, but as producing effects contrary to the intention of the legislator.[488]

If the particular nature of the several species of punishments of this description be examined, as well as those that have for a long time past been abolished, such as crucifixion[489] and exposure to wild beasts, as those that have been in use in various parts of modern Europe, such as burning, empaling [sic], tearing to pieces, and breaking on the wheel, it will be found in all of them that the most afflictive part consists in their *duration*: but this circumstance is not of a nature to produce the beneficial effect that may have been expected from it.[490]

When any particular species of punishment is denounced, that part of it which takes the strongest hold of the imagination is its *intensity*: its duration makes a much more feeble impression. A slight apparent addition of organical suffering made to the ordinary mode of inflicting the punishment of death, produces a strong effect upon the mind: the idea of the duration of its pains is almost wholly absorbed by the terrors of the principal part of the punishment.[491]

In the legal description of a punishment, its duration is seldom (distinctly) brought to view; it is not mentioned, because in itself it is naturally uncertain: it depends partly upon the physical strength of the patient, and partly upon various other accidental circumstances. To this remarkable and important feature of this species of punishment there is no means by which the attention can be drawn and fixed upon it: upon those who reflect, it produces no impression; upon those who do not reflect, it is altogether lost.

It is true that the duration of any particular punishment might be fixed by law; the number of hours or minutes might be determined, which should be employed in performing the several prescribed manipulations. This obviously would be a mode of fixing the attention upon this particular feature of the punishment: but even this mode, perfect as it may appear to be, would be found very inadequate to produce the desired effect. By the help of pictures, the intensity of any particular species of punishment may be more or less faithfully represented; but to represent its duration is impossible. The flames, the rack and all the engines of torture, together with the convulsive throes of the half-expiring and wretched sufferer, may be depicted, but time cannot. A punishment that is to be made to last for two hours will not appear different from a punishment that is to last only a quarter of an hour. The deficiencies of art may, to a certain degree, be compensated for by the imagination: but even then the reality will be left far behind.

It is true that upon bystanders the duration of the punishment is calculated to make a strong impression: but even upon them, after a certain time, the prolongation loses its effect, and gives place to a feeling directly opposite to that which it is desirable to produce—sentiments of pity and sympathy for the sufferer will succeed, the heart of the spectator will revolt at the scene he witnesses, and the cry of suffering humanity will be heard. The physical suffering will not be confined to the offender: the spectators will partake of it: the most melancholy accidents, swoonings, and dangerous convulsions will be the accompaniments of these tragic exhibitions.[492] These sanguinary executions, and the terrific accounts that are spread concerning them, are the real causes of that deep-rooted antipathy that is felt against the laws and those by whom they are administered; an antipathy which tends to multiply offences by favouring the impunity of the guilty.

The only reason that can be given by any government, that persists in continuing to employ a mode of punishing so highly penal, is, that the habitual condition of the people is so wretched that they are incapable of being restrained by a more lenient kind of punishment.

Will it be said that crimes are more frequent in countries in which punishments such as those in question are unknown. The contrary is the fact. It is under such laws that the most ferocious robbers are found: and this is readily accounted for. The fate with which they are threatened hardens them to the feelings of others as well as their own. They are converted into the most bitter enemies, and every barbarity they inflict is considered as a sort of reprisal.

Upon this subject, as upon so many others, Montaigne was far beyond the age in which he lived. All beyond simple death (he says) appears to me to be cruelty.[493] The legislator ought not to expect that the offender that is not to be deterred by the apprehension of death, and by being beheaded and hanged, will be more effectually deterred by the dread of being exposed to a slow fire, or the rack. And I do not know indeed but that he may be rendered desperate.*

By the French Constituent Assembly afflictive punishments were abolished. In the *Code Napoléon*, beheading is the mode prescribed for inflicting the punishment of death. And it is only in the case of parricide, and of attempts made upon the life of the sovereign, that to the simple punishment of death the characteristic afflictive punishment of cutting off the hand of the offender is added.

In this country, the only crime for which afflictive punishment is in use, is that of high treason. The judgment in high treason consists of seven different operations of the afflictive kind. 1. Dragging at a horse's tail along the streets from the prison to the place of execution. 2. Hanging by the neck, yet not so as entirely to destroy life. 3. Plucking out and burning of the entrails while the patient is yet alive. 4. Beheading. 5. Quartering. 6. Exposure of the head and quarters in such places as the King directs. This mode of punishment is not now in use. In favour of nobility, the judgment has been usually changed into beheading: in favour of the lower classes, into hanging.

I wish that upon this part of our subject we could end here; but unfortunately there remains to be mentioned an afflictive mode of punishment most excruciating, and more hideous than any of which we have hitherto spoken, and which is still in use. It is not in Europe that it is employed, but in European colonies—in our own West India Islands.[494]

The delinquent is suspended from a post by means of a hook inserted under his shoulder, or under his breast bone. In this manner the sufferer is prevented from doing anything to assist himself, and all persons are prohibited, under severe penalties, from relieving him. He remains in this situation, exposed to the scorching heat of the day, where the sun is almost vertical, and the atmosphere almost without a cloud, and to the chilling dews of the night; his lacerated flesh attracts a multitude of insects, which increase his torments, and under the fever produced by these complicated

---

*Liv. ii. ch. 27.—Cowardice the mother of cruelty.
   Et lapus et turpes instant morientibus ursi
   Et quæcunque minor nobilitate fera est.

                                                        OVID.

sufferings, joined to hunger and thirst, all raging in the most intense degree, till he gradually expires.

When we reflect on this complication of sufferings, their intensity surpasses everything that the imagination can figure to itself, and consider that their duration continues not merely for many hours, but for many days, it will be found to be by far the most severe punishment ever yet devised by the ingenuity of man.

The persons to whom this punishment has been hitherto appropriated, are negro slaves, and their crime, what is termed rebellion, because they are the weakest, but which, if they were the strongest, would be called an act of self-defence. The constitutions of these people are, to their misfortune, in certain respects so much harder than ours, that many of them are said to have lingered ten or twelve days under these frightful torments.

It is said that this punishment is nothing more than is necessary for restraining that people, and keeping them in their servile state; for that the general tenor of their lives is such a scene of misery, that simple death would be generally a relief, and a less excruciating would scarce operate as a restraint.

This may perhaps be true. It is certain that a punishment to have any effect upon man must bear a certain ratio to the mean state of his way of living, in respect of sufferings and enjoyments. But one cannot well help observing where this leads. The number of slaves in these colonies is to that of freemen as about six to one; there may be about three hundred thousand blacks and fifty thousand whites; here there are three hundred thousand persons kept in a way of life that upon the whole appears to them worse than death, and this for the sake of keeping fifty thousand[495] persons in a way of life not remarkably more happy than that which, upon an average, the same number of persons would be in where there was no slavery; on the contrary, it is found that men in general are fond, when they have the opportunity, of changing that scene for this. On the other hand, it is not to be disputed that sugar and coffee, and other delicacies, which are the growth of those islands, add considerably to the enjoyments of the people here in Europe; but taking all these circumstances into consideration, if they are only to be obtained by keeping three hundred thousand men in a state in which they cannot be kept but by the terror of such executions: are there any considerations of luxury or enjoyment that can counterbalance such evils.

At the same time, what admits of very little doubt is, that the defenders of these punishments, in order to justify them, exaggerate the miseries of slavery, and the little value set by the slaves upon life. If they were really reduced to such a state of misery as to render necessary laws so atrocious, even such laws would be insufficient for their restraint; having nothing to lose, they would be regardless of all consequences; they would be engaged in perpetual insurrections and massacres. The state of desperation to which they would be reduced would daily produce the most frightful disorders. But if existence is not to them a matter of indifference, the only pretence that there is in favour of these laws falls to the ground. Let the colonists reflect upon this; if such a code be necessary, the colonies are a disgrace and an outrage on humanity: if not necessary, these laws are a disgrace to the colonists themselves.

CHAPTER XII.[496]
CAPITAL PUNISHMENT EXAMINED.

In making this examination, the following plan will be pursued. The advantageous properties of capital punishment will in the first place be considered: we shall afterwards proceed to examine its disadvantageous properties.

We shall, in the last place, consider the collateral ill effects resulting form this mode of punishment: effects more remote and less obvious, but sometimes more important, than those which are more immediate and striking.

The task thus undertaken would be an extremely ungrateful and barren one, were it not that the course of the examination will lead us to make a comparison between this and other modes of punishment, and thus to ascertain which is entitled to the preference. On the subject of punishment, the same rule ought in this respect to be observed as on the subject of taxes. To complain of any particular tax as being an injudicious one, is to sow the seeds of discontent, and nothing more: to be really useful, this in itself mischievous discovery, should be accompanied by the indication of another tax which will prove equally productive, with less inconvenience.

SEC. I.—ADVANTAGEOUS PROPERTIES OF THE PUNISHMENT OF DEATH.

1. The most remarkable feature in the punishment of death, and that which it possesses in the greatest perfection, is the taking from the offender the power of doing further injury. Whatever is apprehended, either from the force or cunning of the criminal, at once vanishes away. Society is in a prompt and complete manner delivered from all alarm.

2. It is *analogous* to the offence in the case of murder; but there its analogy terminates.

3. It is *popular* in respect of that same crime, and in that alone.

4. It is *exemplary* in a higher degree perhaps than any other species of punishment, and in countries in which it is sparingly employed, an execution makes a deep and lasting impression.

It was the opinion of *Beccaria* that the impression made by any particular punishment was in proportion to its duration, and not to its intensity. "Our sensibility" (he observes) "is more readily and permanently affected by slight but reiterated attacks than by violent but transient affection. For this reason the putting an offender to death forms a less effectual check to the commission of crimes than the spectacle of a man kept in a state of confinement, and employed in hard labour, to make some reparation by his exertions for the injury he has inflicted on society."*

Notwithstanding such respectable authority, I am apt to think the contrary is the case. This opinion is founded principally on two observations. 1. Death in general is regarded by most men as the greatest of all evils, and they are willing to submit to any other suffering whatever in order to avoid it. 2. Death, considered as a punishment, is almost universally reckoned too severe, and men plead, as a measure of mercy, for the substitution of any other punishment in lieu of it. In respect to duration, the suffering is next to nothing. It must therefore, I think, be some confused and exaggerated notion of the intensity of the pain of death, especially of a violent death, that renders the idea of it so formidable. It is not without reason, however, that with respect to the higher class of offenders, M. Beccaria considers a punishment of the laborious kind, moderate we must suppose in its degree, will make a stronger impression than the most excruciating kind of death that can be devised. But for the generality of men, among those who are attached to life by the ties of reputation, affection, enjoyment, hope, capital punishment appears to be more exemplary than any other.

5. Though the *apparent* suffering in the punishment of death is at the highest pitch, the real suffering is perhaps less than in the larger portion of afflictive punishment. In addition to their duration, they leave after them a train of evils which injure the constitution of the patient, and render the remainder of his life a complication of sufferings. In the punishment of death the suffering is momentary: it is a negation of all sensation.

When the last moment only is considered, penal death is often more gentle than natural death, and, so far from being an evil, presents a balance of good. The suffering endured must be sought for in some anterior period. The suffering consists in *apprehension*. This apprehension commences from the moment the delinquent has committed the crime; it is redoubled when he is apprehended. It increases at every stage of the process which renders his condemnation more certain, and is at its height in the interval between sentence and execution.

The more solid argument in favour of the punishment of death, results from the combined force of the above considerations. On the one hand, it

---

*Des Delits et des Peines.—Sect. xvi.

is to men in general of all punishment of the greatest apparent magnitude, the most impressive and the most exemplary; and on the other hand, to the wretched class of beings that furnish the most atrocious criminals, it is less rigorous than it appears to be. It puts a speedy termination to an uneasy, unhappy, dishonoured existence, stript [*sic*] of all true worth:—*Heu! Heu! quam male est extra legem viventibus.**

SEC. II.—DESIRABLE PENAL QUALITIES WHICH ARE WANTING IN CAPITAL PUNISHMENT

1. The punishment of death is not *convertible to profit*: it cannot be applied to the purpose of compensation. In so far as compensation might be derived from the labour of the delinquent, the very source of the compensation is destroyed.

2. In point of *frugality*, it is pre-eminently defective. So far from being convertible to profit, to the community it produces a certain loss, both in point of wealth and strength. In point of wealth, a man chosen at random is worth to the public that portion of the whole annual income of the state which results from its division by the number of persons of which it consists. The same mode of calculation will determine the loss in respect of strength. But the value of a man who has been proved guilty of some one or other of those crimes for which capital punishment is denounced, is not equal to that of a man taken at random. Of those by whom a punishment of this sort is incurred, nine out of ten have divested themselves of all habits of regular industry; they are the *drones*[497] of the hive: and with respect to them, death is therefore not an ineligible mode of punishment, except in comparison with confinement and hard labour, by which there is a chance if their being reformed and rendered of some use to society.

3.[498] *Equability* is another point, and that a most important one, which this punishment is eminently deficient. To a person taken at random, it is upon an average a very heavy punishment, though still subject to considerable variation. But to a person taken out of the class of first-rate delinquents, it is liable to still greater variation. To some it is as great as to a person taken at random; but to many it is next to nothing.

[499]Death is the absence of all pleasures indeed, but at the same time of all pains. When a person feels himself under temptation to commit a crime punishable with death, his determination to commit it or not to commit it is the result of the following calculation. He ranges on one side the clear portion of happiness he thinks himself likely to enjoy in case of his abstaining:

*Petron Satyr.

on the other, he places the clear happiness he thinks himself likely to enjoy in case of his committing the crime, taking into the account the chance there appears to him to be, that the punishment threatened will abridge the duration of that happiness.

Now then, if in the former case there appears to be no clear happiness likely to accrue to him, much more if there[500] appears to be a clear portion of unhappiness; in other words, if the clear portion of happiness likely to befall him appears to be equal to*, 0,[501] or much more if it appears to be negative, the pleasure that constitutes the profit of the crime will act upon him with a force that has nothing to oppose it. The probability of seeing it brought to an abrupt period by death will subtract more or less from the balance; but at any rate there will be a balance.

Now this is always the case with a multitude of malefactors. Rendered averse to labour by natural indolence[502] or disuse, or hurried away by the tide of some impetuous passion, they do look upon the pleasures to be obtained by honest industry as not worth living for, when put in competition with the pains: or they look upon life as not worth keeping, without some pleasure or pleasures which, to persons in their situation, are not attainable but by a crime.

I do not say that this calculation is made with all the formality with which I have represented it. I do not say that in casting up the sum of pains on the one side and pleasures on the other, exact care is always used to take every item into the account. But however, well or ill, the calculation is made: else a man could not act as he is supposed to do.

Now then, in all these cases, which unhappily are but too frequent, it is plain the punishment of death can be of no use.[503]

It may be said, no more would any other punishment. For any other punishment, to answer its purpose, must have the effect of deterring or otherwise disabling the person in question from committing the like crimes in the future. If then he is thus deterred or disabled, he is reduced to a situation in which, by the supposition, death was to him an event desirable[504] upon the whole. Being then in his power, he will produce it.

The conclusion, however, is not necessary. There are several reasons why the same impulse which is strong enough to dispose a man to meet death at the hands of justice should not be strong enough to dispose him to bring on himself that event with his own hand.

In the first place, the infliction of it as a punishment is an event by no means certain. It is in itself uncertain; and the passion he is supposed to be influenced by, withdrawing his attention from the chances that are in favour of its happening, makes it look still more uncertain.

---

*Zero. [Dumont's edition does not include a similar qualifying note. It may indicate, again, an insight into difficulties associated with translation regarding this genre.]

In the next place, although it were certain, it is at any rate distant: and the mortification he undergoes, from the not possessing the object of his passion, is present.

Thirdly, Death is attended with much more pain when a man has to inflict it on himself with his own hand, than when all he does is simply to put himself in a situation in which it will be inflicted on him by the hands of another, or by the operation of some physical cause. To put himself in such a situation, requires but a single and sudden volition, and perhaps but a single act in consequence, during[505] the performance of which he may keep his eyes shut, as it were, against the prospect of the pain to which he is about to subject himself. The moment of its arrival is at an uncertain distance. The reverse is the case where a man is to die by his own hand. His resolution must be supported during the whole period of time that is necessary to bring about the event. The manner is foreseen and the time immediate. It may be necessary that even after a part of the pain has been incurred, the resolution should go on and support itself, while it prompts him to add further pain before the purpose is accomplished.

Accordingly, when people are resolved upon death, it is common for them, when they have an opportunity, to choose to die rather by the hand of another than by their own. Thus Saul chose to die by the hand of his armour-bearer; Tiberius Gracchus by that of his freeman. So again the Emperor Nero by one of his minions.[506]

Fourthly, when a man is prompted to seek relief in death, it is not so much by the sudden vehemence of some tempestuous passion, as by a close persuasion that the miseries of his life are likely to be greater than the enjoyments; and, in consequence, when the resolution is once taken, to rest satisfied without carrying it immediately into effect; for there is not a more universal principle of human conduct, than that which leads a man to satisfy himself for awhile with the power, without proceeding immediately, perhaps without proceeding ever, to the act. It is the same feeling which so often turns the voluptuous man to a miser.[507]

Now this is likely enough to be the condition of those who, instead of death, may have been sentenced to another punishment.[508] They defer the execution of their design from hour to hour: sometimes for want of means, sometimes for want of inclination, till at last some incident happens that puts in their heads a train of thought which in the end diverts them from their resolution. In the mental as well as in the material part of the human frame, there is happily a strong disposition to accommodate itself by degrees to the pressure of forced and calamitous situations. When a great artery is cut or otherwise disabled, the circumjacent smaller ones will stretch and take upon themselves the whole duty of conveying to the part affected the necessary supplies. Loss of sight improves the faculty of feeling. A left hand learns to perform the offices of the right, or even the feet, of both. An inferior part of the alimentary[509] canal has learned to perform the office, and even to assume the texture of the stomach.

The mind is endowed with no less elasticity and docility, in accommodating itself to situations which at first sight appeared intolerable. In all sufferings there are occasional remissions, which in virtue of the contrast are converted into pleasure. How many instances are there, of men who, having suddenly fallen from the very pinnacle of grandeur into gulphs [sic] of misery, have, when the old sources of enjoyment were irrecoverably dry, gradually detached their minds from all recollections of their customary enjoyments, and created for themselves fresh sources of happiness. The Comte de Lauzin's Spider, the straw-works of the Bicêtre, the skilfully wrought pieces of carved work made by the French prisoners, not to mention others, are sufficient illustrations of this remark.

Variability is a point of excellence in which the punishment of death is more deficient than in any other.[510] It subsists only in one degree; the quantity of evil can neither be increased or lessened. It is peculiarly defective in the case of the greater part of the most malignant and formidable species of malefactors—that of professed robbers and highwaymen.*[511]

4. *The punishment of death is not remissible.*†[512] Other species of afflictive punishments it is true are exposed to the same objection, but though irremissible they are not irreparable. For death there is no remedy.

No man, how little soever he may have attended to criminal procedure, but must have been struck at the very slight circumstances upon which the life of a man may depend; and who does not recollect instances in which a man has been indebted for his safety to the occurrence of some unlooked-

---

*"Are you not aware that we are subject to one disease more than other men?" said a malefactor upon the rack to his companion, who shrieked from pain. When one observes the courage or brutal insensibility, when in the very act of being turned off, of the greater part of the malefactors that are executed at Newgate, it is impossible not to feel persuaded that they have been accustomed to consider this mode of ending their days as being to them a natural death—as an accident or misfortune, by which they ought no more to be deterred from their profession than soldiers or sailors are from theirs, by the apprehension of bullets or of shipwreck. [This note appears as a paragraph within the main text of Dumont's edition, *Théorie des peines*, vol. I, pp. 293–94.]

†There is an evil resulting from the employment of death as a punishment which may be properly noticed here.—*It destroys one source of testimonial proof.* The archives of crime are in a measure lodged in the bosoms of criminals. At their death, all the recollections which they possess relative to their own crimes and those of others perish. Their death is an act of impunity for all those who might have been detected by their testimony, whilst innocence must continue oppressed, and the right can never be established, because a necessary witness is subtracted.

for accident, which has brought his innocence to light. The risk incurred is doubtless greater under some systems of jurisprudence than under others. Those which allow the torture to supply the insufficiency of evidence derived from other sources: those in which the proceedings are not public, are, if the expression may be used, surrounded with precipices. But it may be said, is there or could there be devised any system of penal procedure which could insure the Judge from being misled by false evidence or the fallibility of his own judgment? No; absolute security in this branch of science is a point which, though it can never be attained, may be much more nearly approached than it has hitherto been. Judges will continue fallible, witnesses to depose falsehood or to be deceived; whatever number may depose falsehood or to the same fact, the existence of that fact is not rendered certain; as to circumstantial evidence, that which is deemed incapable of explanation, but by supposing the existence of the crime, may be the effect of chance or of arrangements made with the view of producing deception. The only sort of evidence that appears entitled to perfect conviction, is the voluntary confession of the crime by the party accused, but this is not frequently made, and does not produce absolute certainty, since instances have not been wanting, as in the case of witchcraft, in which individuals have acknowledged themselves guilty, when the pretended crime was impossible.

These are not purely imaginary apprehensions drawn from the region of possibility: the criminal records of every country afford various instances of these melancholy errors; and these instances, which, by the concurrence of a number of extraordinary events have attained notoriety, cannot fail to excite a suspicion, that though unknown, many other innocent victims may have perished.

It must not be forgotten either, that the cases in which the word of evidence is most apt to be employed, are not unfrequently those in which the

---

Whilst a criminal process is going forward, the accomplices of the accused flee and hide themselves. It is an interval of anxiety and tribulation. The sword of justice appears suspended over their heads. When his career is terminated, it is for them an act of jubilee and pardon. They have a new bond of security, and they can walk erect. The fidelity of the deceased is exalted among his companions as a virtue, and received among them for the instruction of their young disciples, with praises for his heroism.

In the confines of a prison this heroism would be submitted to a more dangerous proof than the interrogatories of the tribunals. Left to himself, separated from his companions, a criminal ceases to possess this feeling of honour which unites him to them. It needs only a moment of repentance to snatch from him those discoveries which he only can make; and without his repentance, what is more natural than a feeling of vengeance against those who caused him to lose his liberty, and who, though equally culpable with himself, yet continue in the enjoyment of liberty! He need only listen to his interest, and purchase by some useful information some relaxation of the rigour of his punishment. [This note does not appear within Dumont's edition.]

testimony adduced is exposed to most suspicion. When the pretended crime is among the number of those that produce antipathy towards the offender, or which excite against him a party feeling, the witnesses almost unconsciously act as accusers. They are the echoes of the public clamour. The fermentation goes on increasing, and all doubt is laid aside. It was a concurrence of such circumstances which seduced first the people and then the Judges in the melancholy affair of *Calas*.

These melancholy cases in which the most violent presumptions, which fall little short of absolute certainty, are accumulated against an individual whose innocence is afterwards recognized, carry with them their own cause: they are the cruel effects of chance, and do not altogether destroy public confidence. To produce any such effect we must be able to detect in such erroneous decisions proofs of temerity, ignorance, and precipitation, an obstinate and blind adherence to vicious forms, and of those determined prejudices which the very situation of Judge is apt to generate. A Judge, whose business it is to deal with human nature in its worst forms, having daily before his eyes the false pretences and mendacity to which the guilty have recourse, perpetually contriving expedients for unveiling imposture, gradually ceases to believe in the innocence of those accused, and by anticipation expects to find a criminal using all his arts to deceive him. That it is the character of all Judges to be actuated by these prejudices I am far from thinking; but when the propriety of arming men with the power of inflicting the punishment of death is the question under consideration, it ought not to be forgotten, before putting into their hands the fatal weapon, that they are not exempted from the weaknesses of humanity, that their wisdom is not increased, neither are they rendered infallible by thus arming them.

The danger attending the use of capital punishment appears in a more striking point of view when we reflect on the use that may be made of it by men in power, to gratify their passions, by means of a Judge easily intimidated or corrupted. In such cases, the iniquity covered with the robe of justice may escape, if not all suspicion, at least the possibility of proof. Capital punishment, too, affords to the prosecutor as well at to the Judge, an advantage that in all other modes is wanting: I mean greater security against detection, by stifling by death all danger of discovery arising from the delinquent, at least: while he lives, to whatever state of misery he may be reduced, the oppressed may meet with some fortunate event by which his innocence may be proved, and he may become his own avenger. A judicial assassination, justified in the eyes of the public by a false accusation, with almost complete certainty assures the triumph of those who have been guilty of it. In a crime of an inferior degree, they would have had everything to fear; but the death of the victim seals their security.[513]

If we reflect on those very unfrequent occurrences, but which may at any time recur, those periods at which the Government degenerates into anarchy and tyranny, we shall find that the punishment of death, established by law, is a weapon made ready prepared, which is more susceptible of abuse than any other mode of punishment. A tyrannical Government, it is true, may always re-establish this mode of punishment after it has been abolished by the Legislature. But the introducing what would then become an innovation, would not be unattended with difficulty: the violence of which it was to be the precursor, would be too much exposed, the tocsin would be sounded. Tyranny is much more at its ease when exercised under the sanction of law, when there is no appearance of any departure from the ordinary course of justice, and when it finds the minds of people already reconciled and accustomed to this mode of punishment.[514] The Duke of Alba, ferocious as he was, would not have dared to sacrifice so many thousand victims in the Low Countries, if it had not been a commonly received opinion that heresy was a crime which merited the punishment of death. Biren, not less cruel than the Duke of Alba, Biren, who peopled the deserts of Siberia with exiles, caused them previously to be mutilated, that being the most severe punishment that was in use in that country; he very rarely ventured to punish them capitally, because capital punishment was not in use. So little do even the most arbitrary despots dare to violate established customs. Hence we may draw a strong reason for seizing upon periods of tranquillity for destroying these dangerous instruments, which, though no longer dreaded when covered with rust, are with such facility brought into use again, when passion invites their employment.[515]

The objection arising from the irremissibility of the punishment of death, applies to all cases, and can be removed only by its complete abolition. Upon this occasion it is necessary to bear in mind that there are two branches of security, for each of which it is necessary to make provision. Security against the errors and corruptions in judicial procedure, and security against crimes. If the latter were not to be attained but at the expense of the former, there would be no room for hesitation. With respect to crimes, from whom is it that the terror is felt? From every person that is capable of committing a crime, that is to say, from all men, and at all times. With respect to the errors and corruptions of justice, these are the exceptions, the accidental and rare occurrences.[516]

This punishment is far from being popular; and it becomes less and less so every day in proportion as mankind becomes more enlightened, and their manners more softened. The people flock in crowds to an execution; but this eagerness, which at first might appear so disgraceful to humanity, does not proceed from the pleasure expected from the sight of men in the agonies of death, it arises from the pleasure of having the passions strongly excited by a tragic scene. There is, however, one case in which it does seem to be popular, and that in a very high degree; I mean the case of murder. The attachment seems to be grounded partly on the fondness for analogy, partly on the principle of vengeance, and partly perhaps by the fear which the character of the criminal is apt to inspire. Blood it is said will have blood, and the imagination is flattered with the notion of the similarity of the suffering, produced by the punishment, with that inflicted by the criminal.[517]

In other cases, the punishment of death is unpopular, and this unpopularity produces different dispositions, all equally contrary to the ends of justice; a disposition on the part of individuals injured not to prosecute the offenders, for fear of bringing them to the scaffold; a disposition on the part of the public to favour their escape; a disposition on the part of the witnesses to withhold their testimony, or to weaken its effect; a disposition on the part of the Judges to allow of a merciful prevarication in favour of the accused; and all these anti-legal dispositions render the execution of the laws uncertain, without referring to that loss of respect which follows upon its being considered meritorious to prevent their execution.

SEC. III.—RECAPITULATION AND COMPARISON OF THE PUNISHMENT OF DEATH, WITH THOSE PUNISHMENTS WHICH MAY BE SUBSTITUTED FOR IT.

The punishment of death, it has been observed, possesses four desirable properties.

1. It is in one case analogous to the offence.
2. In that same case it is popular.
3. It is in the highest degree efficacious in preventing further mischief from the same source.
4. It is exemplary, producing a more lively impression than any other mode of punishment.

The two first of these properties exist in the case of capital punishment when applied to murder; and with reference to that species of offence alone are they sufficient reasons for persevering in its use; certainly not: each of them, separately considered, as of very little importance. Analogy is a very good recommendation, but not a good justification. If in other respects any particular mode of punishment be eligible, analogy is an additional advantage: If in other respects it be ineligible, analogy alone is not a sufficient recommendation: the value of this property amounts to very little, because, even in the case of murder, other punishments may be devised, the analogy of which will be sufficiently striking.

In respect also of *popularity*, the same observations apply to this mode of punishment. Every other mode of punishment that is seen to be equally or more efficacious will become equally or more popular. The approbation of the multitude will naturally be in proportion to the efficacy of the punishment.

The third reason, that it is efficacious *in preventing further mischief from the same source*, is somewhat more specious, but not better founded. It has been asserted, that in the crime of murder it is absolutely *necessary*; that there is no other means of averting the danger threatened from that class of malefactors. This assertion is, however, extremely exaggerated: its groundlessness may be seen in the case of the most dangerous species of homicide. Assassination for lucre, a crime proceeding from a disposition which puts indiscriminately the life of every man into immediate jeopardy. Even these malefactors are not so dangerous nor so difficult to manage as madmen; because the former will commit homicide only at the time that there is something to be gained by it, and that it can be perpetrated with a probability of safety. The mischief to be apprehended from madmen is not narrowed by either of these circumstances. Yet it is never thought necessary that madmen should be put to death. They are not put to death: they are only kept in confinement; and that confinement is found effectually to answer to the purpose.

In fine, I can see but one case in which it can be necessary, and that only occasionally: in the case alleged for this purpose by M. Beccaria, the case of rebellion or other offence against government of a rebellious tendency, when, by destroying the chief you may destroy the faction, where discontent has spread itself widely through a community, it may happen that imprisonment will not answer the purpose of safe custody. The keepers may be won over to the insurgent party, or if not won over, they may be overpowered. They may be won over by considerations of a conscientious nature, which is a danger almost peculiar to this case; or they may be won over by considerations of a lucrative nature, which danger is greater in this case than in any other, since party projects may be carried on by a common purse.

What, however, ought not to be lost sight of in the case of offences of a political nature is, that if by the punishment of death one dangerous enemy is exterminated, the consequence of it may be the making an opening for a more formidable successor. Look, said the executioner, to an aged Irishman, shewing [*sic*] him the bleeding head of a man just executed for rebellion: "Look at the head of your son."—"My son (replied he) has more than one head." It would be well for the legislator before he appoints capital punishment, even in this case, to reflect on this instructive lesson.[518]

The fourth reason is the strongest. The punishment of death is exemplary, pre-eminently exemplary: no other punishment makes so strong an impression.

This assertion, as has been already noticed, is true with respect to the majority of mankind, it is not true with respect to the greatest criminals.[519]

It appears however to me that the contemplation of perpetual imprisonment, accompanied with hard labour and occasional solitary confinement, would produce a deeper impression on the minds of persons in whom it is more eminently desirable that that impression should be produced, than even death itself. We have already observed that to them life does not offer the same attractions as it does to persons of innocent and industrious habits. Their very profession leads them continually to put their existence in jeopardy; and intemperance, which is almost natural to them, inflames their brutal and uncalculating courage. All the circumstances that render death less formidable to them, render laborious restraint proportionably more irksome. The more their habitual state of existence is independent, wandering, and hostile to steady and laborious industry, the more they will be terrified by a state of passive submission and of laborious confinement, a mode of life in the highest degree repugnant to their natural inclinations.

Giving to each of these circumstances their due weight, the result appears to be that the prodigal use made by legislators of the punishment of death has been occasioned more by erroneous judgements [arising from the situation in which they are placed with respect to other classes of the community] than from any blameable cause. Those who make laws belong to the highest classes of the community, among whom death is considered as a great evil, and an ignominious death as the greatest of evils. Let it be confined to that class, if it were practicable, the effect aimed at might be produced; but it shews a total want of judgment and reflection to apply it to a degraded and wretched class of men, who do not set the same value upon life, to whom indigence and hard labour is more formidable than death, and the habitual infamy of whose lives render them insensible to the infamy of the punishment.

If, in spite of these reasons, which appear to be conclusive, it be determined to preserve the punishment of death, in consideration of the effects it produces *in terrorum*, it ought to be confined to offences which, in the highest degree, shock the public feeling—for murders, accompanied with circumstances of aggravation, and particularly when their effect may be the destruction of numbers; and in these cases expedients by which it may be made to assume the most tragic appearance may be safely resorted to, in the greatest extent possible, without having recourse to complicated torments.[520]

SEC. IV.—COLLATERAL EVIL EFFECTS OF THE FREQUENT USE OF THE PUNISHMENT OF DEATH.[521]

The punishment of death, when applied to the punishment of offences in opposition to public opinion, far from preventing offences, tends to increase them by the hope of impunity. This proposition may appear paradoxical; but the paradox vanishes when we consider the different effects produced by the unpopularity of the punishment of death. In the first place it relaxes prosecution in criminal matters, and in the next place foments three vicious principles. 1. It makes perjury appear meritorious, by founding it on humanity; 2. it produces contempt for the laws, by rendering it notorious that they are not executed; 3. it renders convictions arbitrary and pardons unnecessary.

The relaxation of criminal procedure results from a series of transgressions on the part of the different public functionaries, whose concurrence is necessary to the execution of the laws: each one alters the part allotted to him, that he may weaken or break the legal chain by which he is bound, and substitutes his own will for that of the legislator;* but all these causes of uncertainty in criminal procedure are so many encouragements to malefactors.[522]

---

*"Observe that juryman in a blue coat," said one of the Judges at the Old Bailey to Judge Nares. "Do you see him?" "Yes." "Well, there will be no conviction of death to-day." And the observation was confirmed by the fact.

BOOK III.
OF PRIVATE PUNISHMENTS, OR FORFEITURES.

CHAPTER I.
PUNISHMENT ANALYZED.[523]

W e now come to the last of the two grand divisions of Punishments—*Private Punishments*, or *Forfeitures*.

The word forfeiture is never used but with reference to some *possession*.*[524]

Possessions are either substantial or ideal—substantial when it is the object of a real entity (as a house, a field) ideal, when it is the object of a fictitious entity (as an office, a dignity, a right.)

The difficulty of dealing with cases of this description will immediately be seen. Real entities have all a common genus, to wit, *substance*. Fictitious entities have no such common genus, and can only be brought into method in virtue of the relation they bear to real objects.[525]

Possessions, of whatsoever nature they be, whether real or fictitious, are *valuable*; and to forfeit them can never otherwise be a punishment, than as far as they are instruments of pleasure or security. By specifying then the sort of persons or things from which the benefit said to belong to a fictitious possession is actually derived, all will be done that can be done towards giving a methodical view of those possessions, and of the penal consequences of forfeiting them.†

To investigate, therefore, the several kinds of proper forfeiture, it is necessary to investigate the several kinds of possessions. On this subject, however, as it comes in only collaterally on the present occasion, it will not be necessary to insist very minutely.[526]

---

*As all our ideas are derived ultimately from the senses, almost all the names we have for intellectual ideas, seem to be derived ultimately from the names of such objects as afford sensible ideas: that is, of objects that belong to one or other of the three classes of real entities. Insomuch that, whether we perceive it or not, we can scarce express ourselves on any occasion but in metaphors. A most important discovery this in the metaphysical part of grammar, for which we seem to be indebted to M. d'Alembert.—See his *Mélanges, tom.* 1, *Disc. Prelim.* &c.

The way in which the import of the word forfeiture is connected with sensible ideas seems to be as follows: the words to forfeit come either immediately, or through the medium of the old French, from the modern Latin word *forisfacere. Foris* means out of doors, or out of the house; *facere*, is to make or to cause to be. The conceit then is that, when any object is in a man's possession, it is as it were within doors; within his house; any act, therefore, which, in consequence of some operation of law, has the effect of causing the object to be no longer in his possession, has the effect of causing it, as it were, to be out of his doors, and no longer within his house. [Dumont's edition frequently modifies these notes by specifying their particular relevance to English jurisprudence.]

Possessions are derived either from things only, or from persons only; or from both together. Those of the two first sorts may be styled simple possessions: those of the other complex.

Possessions derived from things may consist either—1. in money: these may be called pecuniary; 2. in other objects at large. The former may be styled pecuniary, the latter quasi-pecuniary. Accordingly, forfeiture of money may be styled pecuniary forfeiture: forfeiture of any other possession derived from things, quasi-pecuniary. Quasi-pecuniary forfeitures are capable of a variety of divisions and subdivisions: but as these distinctions turn upon circumstances that make no difference in the mode of punishment, it will not be necessary, on the present occasion, to enter into any such detail.

Possessions derived from persons, consist in the *services* rendered by those persons. Services may be distinguished into *exigible* and *inexigible* [*sic*]. By exigible I mean such as a man may be punished (to wit, by the political sanction) for not rendering; by inexigible, such as a man cannot be punished for not rendering; or, if at all, not by any other sanction than either the moral or the religious.‡

The faculty of procuring such as are exigible is commonly called *power*, to wit power over persons: the faculty or chance of procuring such as are inexigible depends, in great measure, upon *reputation*; hence result two farther kinds of forfeiture: forfeiture of power and forfeiture of reputation.§

Reputation may be distinguished into natural and factitious; by factitious I mean that which is conferred by rank or dignity.

Credibility is a particular species of reputation: the reputation of veracity. Hence we have two further kinds of forfeiture, both subordinate to that of reputation: forfeiture of rank or dignity, and forfeiture of credibility.[527]

---

†Forfeiture is, in some cases, though rarely, applied to corporal punishments. Thus capital punishment is called forfeiture of life; mutilation, forfeiture of limbs or members. It is also, with the addition of the word liberty, applied to corporal punishments of the restrictive classes, as in the case of imprisonment and quasi imprisonment. The other modes of confinement require further additions to be made to them: as to express foreign banishment, forfeiture of the liberty of residing in any part of the dominions of the state: to express domestic banishment, forfeiture of the liberty of being any longer in the place of his abode. The infinite variety of specific restraints may also be expressed by the phrase of forfeiture of liberty, with so many different additions: forfeiture of the liberty of exercising such or such an operation, forfeiture of the liberty of pleading, &c.

‡To services inexigible, but by the force of these auxiliary sanctions, correspond what are called imperfect rights. Whatever right a man may have to a service, which the party is not punishable by law for not rendering him, is what is called by writers on the pretended law of nature, an imperfect right; and the obligation to render any such service, an imperfect obligation.

§Of services that are altogether inexigible, such as are strictly spontaneous, gratuitous, depend altogether upon goodwill: upon the goodwill of the party rendering them to the party to whom they are rendered. This goodwill depends, in great measure, upon the reputation of the party to whom they are rendered.

As to complex possessions, and the forfeitures that relate to them, these are too heterogeneous to be arranged in any systematic method: all that can be done is to enumerate them. Thus much only may be said of them in general, that the ingredients of each of them are derived from both the classes of objects which we have mentioned as being the sources from which the several kinds of simple forfeitures are derived.

It should seem, however, that they might all of them, without any great violence, be brought under the title of *conditions*. Conditions then may in the first place be distinguished into *ordinary* and *peculiar*.

Ordinary conditions or modes of relationship, may be distinguished into *natural* and *acquired*. By natural conditions I mean those which necessarily belong to a man by birth: to wit in virtue of either his own birth or that of some other person to whom he stands related. Such as that of son, daughter, father, mother, brother, sister, and so on through the several modes of relationship, constituted by the several degrees of consanguinity. To stand in any of these relations to such or such a person may be the source of various advantages. These conditions, it is plain, cannot themselves be forfeited; a man, however, may, and in some instances has been said to have forfeited them, and may actually be made to forfeit many of the advantages attending them.

Acquired conditions may be distinguished in the first place into *political* and *religious*; and political again into *domestic* and *public*. Domestic conditions may be distinguished into *family* conditions and *professional*. Family conditions are—1st. The matrimonial; or that of being husband or wife to such a person; 3d and 4th,[528] that of being guardian or ward; 5th and 6th, that of being master or servant to such a person.

By public political condition, I mean that of belonging to any voluntary society of men instituted on any other than a religious account.

By religious condition, I mean that of belonging to any society or sect instituted for the sake of joining in the performance of religious ceremonies.

Of conditions that may be termed peculiar, the several sorts may, it should seem, be all comprised under the head either 1st, by offices; or 2dly, by corporation privileges.[529] A right of exercising an office is an exclusive right to render certain services.

Conditions constituted by offices may be ranked in the number of complex possessions, inasmuch as they are apt to include the three simple possessions following: to wit, a certain share of power, a certain rank, and a certain salary, or fees or other emoluments coming under the head of pecuniary or quasi-pecuniary possessions.

Of offices there is an almost infinite variety of kinds, and a still greater variety of names, according to the almost infinite modifications of rank and power in different countries, and under different governments. This head is, consequently, susceptible of a great variety of divisions and subdivisions; but these it will not be necessary, on the present occasion, to consider.

Corporations may be distinguished into political and religious. Under the head of religious corporations may be included the various monastic orders established in countries professing the Roman Catholic religion.

As to political corporations, the catalogue of the possessions that may be annexed to the condition of one who is a member of those bodies are so various, that no other account need, on the present occasion, or indeed can be given of it, than that there are scarce any of the simple possessions above enumerated, but may be included in it.*

To the condition of one who is a member of a religious order or corporation may be annexed, besides the above possessions others, the value whereof consists in such or such a chance as they may appear to confer of enjoying the pleasures of a future life, over and above such chance of enjoying the same pleasures as appears to be conferred by the condition or privilege of being an ordinary professor of the same religion.

As an appendix to the above list of possessions[530] may be added two particular kind of possessions, constituted by the circumstance of contingency, as applied in different ways to each one in that list. These are the legal capacity of acquiring, as applied to those articles respectively, and the protection of the law, whereby a man is secured against the chance of losing them, if acquired.[531] These abstract kinds of possessions form the subject of so many kinds of forfeiture: forfeiture of legal capacity and forfeiture of the protection of the law: forfeiture of legal capacity with respect to any possession, taking away from a man whatever chance he might have of acquiring it; forfeiture of protection, subjecting him to a particular chance of losing it.†

---

*A share beneficial or fiduciary in the use of such a quantity of money, of such an estate in land: a share in such an office of power or trust: an exemption from such a tax or other public burthen: the exclusive privilege of such or such an occupation.

†Forfeiture of protection may be considered also, in another point of view, as being the forfeiture of the services of such ministers of Justice, whose office it is to afford a man protection in the enjoyment of the possession in question.

CHAPTER II.
OF THE PUNISHMENTS BELONGING TO THE MORAL SANCTION.

⁵³²

Punishments of this class admit of no distinctions: and this, however paradoxical it may seem, for no other reason than their extreme variety.[533] The way in which a man suffers who is punished by the moral sanction is, by losing a part of that share which he would otherwise possess of the esteem or *love* of such members of the community as the several incidents of his life may lead him to have to do with. Now it is either from the esteem they entertain for him, or the love they bear him, or both, that their *good-will* towards him, in a great measure,[534] depends: moreover, the way in which this good-will displays itself, is by disposing the person who entertains such affection, to render good offices, and to forbear doing ill offices (or in other words, to render *inexigible services*) to the party towards whom it is entertained; the way in which the opposite affection, *ill-will*, displays itself, is accordingly by disposing the former to forbear doing good offices, and if it has risen to a certain degree, by disposing him to render ill-offices, as far as may be consistent with his own safety, to the latter.[535]

Now then, from the good offices of one man to another, may all sorts of possessions, and through them, or even more immediately, all sorts of pleasures, be derived. On the other hand, from the withholding of the good offices one man might have expected from another, may all sorts of pains, and death itself, be also derived; much more may they from positive ill-offices added to those other negative ones. And what are the good offices which you may be disposed to withhold from me, or the ill offices you may be disposed to do to me, from my having become the object of your ill-will? It is plain not one or other[536] particular species of good or ill office, but any species whatever, just as occasion serves, that shall be proportionate to the strength of your ill-will and consistent with your own safety. This consideration will make our work short under the head which respects the several modes or species of punishment subordinate to the mode in question.[537]

The same consideration will make it equally short under the second head, relative to the evils producible by the mode or modes of punishment in question. These, it must have been already seen, may be all sorts of evils: all the different sorts of evils which are producible by any of the punishments belonging to the political sanction; by any punishment properly so called: in a word, all the different sorts of evils to which human nature is liable.[538]

But though the punishments belonging to the moral sanction admit not of any varieties that are separable from one another, there are two distinct parcels, as it were, into which the evils produced by any lot of punishment issuing from this source, on the occasion of any offence, may be divided. One (which, as being the basis of the other, may be mentioned first, though the last in point of time) consists of the several contingent evils that may happen to the offender[539] in consequence of the ill-will he has incurred; the other consists of the immediate pain or anxiety, the painful sense of shame, which is grounded on the confused apprehension of the unliquidated assemblage of evils above-mentioned. It is this last which is referable in a peculiar manner to the moral sanction, and which cannot be produced by the political, any otherwise than as far as those who have the management of that sanction can gain an influence over the moral: it may therefore, for distinction sake, by styled the *characteristic evil* of the moral sanction. This must obtain, in a greater or less degree, upon every instance of detected delinquency, unless in those callous and brutish natures, if any such there be, in whom all sense of disgrace, and all foresight of the consequences, is utterly extinguished. The others above spoken of may be styled the casual evils.

These casual evils, (as we have already intimated) owing to their extreme uncertainty, admit not of any determinate variations in point of *quality*; in point of *quantity*, however, they do admit of some distinction resulting from,[540] 1st, their *Intensity*; 2dly, their *Extent*. This distinction ought not to be overlooked, since we shall have occasion to make frequent application of it to practice.

These two lots of evils, howsoever distinguishable, intermix with and aggravate one another. I have done an immoral act: I am discovered: I perceive as much. Now then, before I happen to have occasion to avail myself of the good offices of such of my acquaintance as come to know of it, before I happen to be in a way to suffer from the denial of those good offices, in a word, before I have experienced any of the *casual* evils annexed by the moral sanction to my delinquency, I already foresee more or less clearly, and apprehend more or less strongly, the loss of those good offices and of that good will: I feel the painful sense of shame, the pain of ignominy; I experience, in a word, the *characteristic* evil of the moral sanction as the punishment of my misbehaviour. This sense of shame stamps the marks of guilt upon my deportment. This being the case, either out of despair I avoid my acquaintance, or else I put myself in their way. If I avoid them, I by that means already deprive myself of their good offices: if I put myself in their way, the guilt which is legible in my countenance, advertises and increases their aversion: they either give an express denial to my request, or what is more common, anticipate it by the coldness of their behaviour. This reception gives fresh keenness to the sting of shame, or (in the systematical language I have ventured to make use of,) the experiment I have made of the *casual* evils adds force to the *characteristic* evils of this sanction.

We have already intimated the distinction between positive and negative ill offices; to the former, and even in a few instances to the latter, it is the duty, and a great part of the business, of the political magistrate to set limits. These limits, however, may come accidentally to be transgressed, as there are scarce any laws that can be made but what may come accidentally to be disobeyed. On this account, the evils that may result from this source remain still indeterminate and unlimited. But were the laws that might be made in this behalf ever so certain in their operation, those evils would still remain indeterminate and unlimited, notwithstanding. For so uncertain and unforeseeable may be the connection between the refusal of a good office, and the miseries which in particular circumstances may be the consequences of such a refusal, that no law could make a secure provision against those miseries in every case, without such a subversion of all liberty and all property as would produce much greater miseries. Your giving me a shilling to buy me food, or taking me twenty miles to a physician, may on a critical occasion save me from an excruciating disease; but no law, without leaving it to the determination of the person in want, can with sufficient certainty describe such occasions; nor can any law, without depriving you of all liberty and all property, oblige you to give money to, or take a journey for every man who shall determine himself to be in want of such assistance.[541]

Howsoever this be with regard to negative ill offices, positive ill offices not only may be limited, but in most cases may be and commonly are forbidden. In no settled state of government is private displeasure permitted to rise so high as to vent itself indiscriminately in any of those direct ways of inflicting pain which the political magistrate himself may have thought it expedient to recur to. However flagrantly immoral[542] may have been the conduct of a delinquent, persons at large are never permitted, of their own authority, to punish him by beating or maiming, or putting him to death. Positive ill offices may be divided into such as display themselves in actions at large, and such as display themselves in discourse. Now, it is to speech that the latitude which is still left to the right of rendering positive ill offices in a *direct* way, is principally confined:* and even this right

---

*I am conscious that the distinction here stated, between the direct and indirect way of rendering ill offices is far enough from being explicit; but there would be no way of making it so without despatching a large and intricate title of the doctrine of offenses. [This note does not appear within Dumont's edition.]

is commonly subject to a number of limitations. But ill offices which are confined to speech are not, if they stop there, productive of any evil. When they are, it is ultimately by disposing other persons to entertain a displeasure against the same person, and manifest it by actions of another kind. If then such positive ill offices as display themselves in actions at large be excluded, all that remains is resolvable ultimately into *negative* ill offices. And of these, those which a delinquent has in ordinary cases to apprehend amount only to such as are not *illegal*.[543]

Nor is even this a contemptible and inconsiderate source of suffering. Dependent as men in a state of society are upon one another, the punishment derived from the source in question, even when narrowed by all these restrictions, may, and, indeed, frequently does rise to a tremendous height. It admits of no evasion: it comes upon a man from all quarters: he can see no end to its duration, nor limits to its effects. It is not unusual for it to bereave him of the chief pleasures and sources of profit he has set his heart upon: it may deprive him of all those profits and enjoyments he had been accustomed to expect at the hands of his friend or his patron: by setting his common acquaintance at a distance from him, it may fill the detail of his life with a perpetual train of disappointments and rebuffs. It leaves him joyless and forlorn: and, by drying up the source of every felicity it embitters the whole current of his life.

Were we indeed to enquire minutely into the distinction between the nature of the political and moral sanctions, it would come out that, of the evils which when considered as issuing from the moral sanction I have stiled [*sic*] *casual* evils, some are even more *likely* to be brought upon a man by the action of one of these sanctions, and some others by that of the other. But as to the species of evil, this is all the distinction we shall be able to make out; for there is not any evil which the exertion of one of these forces may bring upon a man, but which may also be brought upon him by the action of the other.[544]

The most studied and artificial torments, for instance, that can be invented by a political magistrate, and the most unlikely for a man to be exposed to suffer by the unassisted powers of nature, or even from the unauthorized resentment of an individual, are what he may by accident be exposed to from the latter source. It may be for want of some evidence that an individual might furnish, and from ill-will forbears to furnish, that I may have been doomed to these torments by a Judge; or if the like torments be supposed to be inflicted by the unauthorized violence of an enemy, they may be attributed in the first place indeed to the vengeance of that enemy; but in the second place, to the dis-esteem and ill-will borne me by some stranger, who having it in his power to rescue me, yet exasperated against me on account of some real or supposed instance of immorality in my behaviour, chose rather to see me suffer than to be at the pains of affording me his assistance.

On the other hand, the whole sum of the evils depending upon the moral sanction, to wit, not only the casual evils, but the sense of infamy which constitutes the characteristic evil, is liable in many instances to be brought upon a man by the doom of the political magistrate. This is what we have found it unavoidably necessary, on various occasions, to give imitation of, and what we shall have need more particularly to enlarge upon hereafter.

3.[545] It is the *manner*, then, in which the evils that come alike under the department of each of the two sanctions come to be inflicted, that the only characteristic difference discernible between these two sanctions are to be seen. With regard to punishment issuing from the political sanction, the species, the degree, the time, the place, the person who is to apply it, are all assignable. With regard to that which may issue from the moral sanction, none of these particulars are assignable.[546]

When I say assignable, I must be understood to speak with reference to some particular time coincident with or subsequent to that of the commission of the offence. At that very time, then, with respect to political punishment, that is, with respect to personal punishments and forfeitures, many of those particulars, and sometimes all of them, are assignable, and may be foreseen. At the time the offence, theft suppose, is committing, it may be foreseen that a number of stripes given with such an instrument, not more than so many nor fewer than so many, will be inflicted (in case of detection) so many days or weeks hence, at such a place and by the hands of such an executioner: and *vice versa*, when they come to be inflicted, the punishment will be seen to be the consequence of such an offence. Now when the organical pain produced by the punishment thus inflicted is over, all the punishment for that offence, as far as depends upon the political sanction, is commonly over and at an end. But as to the ill offices, as well negative as positive, which constitute the substance and groundwork of the moral sanction, no man can tell what they will be, what particular evils they will subject a man to, when they will commence, or when they will end, where they will display themselves, nor who will render them. Nor *vice versa*, when they have actually been rendered, when such or such a neighbour has shut his door against me, and I am pining with hunger or shivering with cold, can I always know for certain that the immorality I was guilty of at such or such a time was the occasion of this unkindness. In a word, *determinateness* is the perfection of the punishments belonging to the political sanction: *in*determinateness is the very essence of those issuing from the moral.[547]

A word or two may be of use in this place with respect to the nomenclature employed in speaking of the punishments belonging to this sanction.

The expressions made use of on this occasion are singularly various: a whole legion of fictitious entities are created for the purpose of representing the one fundamental idea in question, under the different aspects of which it is susceptible. The names of these fictitious entities are many of them disparate; they require different sets of words to enable them to make a meaning: and the coincidence lies not between the import of these names when separately taken, but between certain sentences or propositions, in which they may respectively be made to bear a part. Among these words may be reckoned reputation, honour, character, good name, dishonour, shame, infamy, ignominy, disgrace, aversion, and contempt. In speaking then of a man as suffering under a punishment of the moral sanction, it may be more or less convenient, according to the occasion, to use amongst others any of the following expressions. We may say that he has forfeited his reputation, his honour, his character, his good name; that his fame has been tarnished; that his honour, his character, or his reputation has received a stain; that he stands disgraced; that he has become infamous; that he has sunk under a load of infamy, ignominy, or disgrace; that he has fallen into disgrace, into disesteem, into disrepute; that he has incurred the ill-will, the aversion, the contempt of the neighbourhood, of the public; that he is become an object of aversion or contempt. It were the task rather of the lexicographer than the jurist to exhaust the catalogue of these expressions. Those which have been already exhibited may be sufficient to advertise the reader of the similarity there may be in point of sense between a variety of other expressions of like import, however dissimilar they may be in sound.[548]

Hitherto we have considered the punishment belonging to the moral sanction in no other point of view than that in which it appears when sanding singly, uncombined with and uninfluenced by the political. In this state the direction given to it, and the force with which it acts, are determined altogether by the persons to whom it belongs ultimately to dispense it,[549] unassisted and uncontrolled by the political magistrate. In this state it acted before the formation of political society, before the creation of that artificial body of which the political magistrate is the head. In this state, by its connection with the various modes of conduct which happened to be employed to prohibit or recommend, it gave birth to that fictitious set of rules which are what some moralists have sometimes at least in view, when they speak of the *law of nature*. In this state it was an engine, to the power of which the political magistrate was a witness, before the construction of that which is of his own immediate workmanship. It then was, it still is, and it ever must be, an engine of great power in whatever direction it be applied; whether it be applied to counteract or to promote his measures. No wonder then he should have sought by various contrivances to press it into his service. When thus fitted up and set to work by the political magistrate, it becomes part of the vast system of machinery to which we have given the name of the political sanction. And now then we are in a condition to discuss the nature of that genus of political punishment which, in systems of jurisprudence, is commonly spoken of under the name of infamy, or forfeiture of reputation.[550]

SEC. II.—ADVANTAGES AND DISADVANTAGES OF THE PUNISHMENTS BELONGING TO THE MORAL SANCTION.

We will not proceed to examine the punishments belonging to the moral sanction itself, independently of any employment of it by the magistrate to aggravate or guide the effect of his designs.

Punishments of this class, as has already been said, admit of no distinctions; they comprise all sorts of evils: the ill-will produced manifests itself in a variety of modes, that can neither be calculated or foreseen. They admit then of no precise description; for it is only when the effects are determinate that a punishment admits of a description. Will they be analogous to the offence, or unfrugal, or excessive? upon these points nothing can be said.

Our observations will be comprised under three heads—their divisibility, equability, and exemplarity.

1. These punishments admit of minute division: they have all the degrees possible from mere blame to infamy, from a temporary suspension of goodwill, to active and permanent ill-will: but these several degrees depend altogether upon accidental circumstances, and are incapable of being estimated by anticipation. Punishments of the pecuniary or chronical class, as, for example, imprisonment, are susceptible of being exactly measured: punishments that depend on the moral sanction, not. Before they are experienced, the value put upon them is necessarily extremely inaccurate. In respect of intensity they are liable to be inferior to the greater part of those belonging to the political sanction; they consist more in privations of pleasure than in positive evils. This it is that constitutes their principal imperfection; and it is solely for supplying this imperfection that penal laws were established.

[551]One of the circumstances by which their effect is weakened, is the *locality* of their operation. Do you find yourself exposed to the contempt of the people with whom you are in the habit of associating? to exempt yourself from it, all that you have to do is change your abode. The punishment is reduced to the giving a man the option to remain exposed to the inconveniences resulting from this contempt, or to inflict on himself the punishment of banishment, which may not be perpetual. He does not abandon the

hope of returning, when by lapse of time the memory of his transgressions shall be effaced, and the public resentment appeased.

2.[552] In respect of *equability* these punishments are really more defective than at first sight they might appear. In every condition in life each man has his own circle of friends and acquaintance. To become an object of contempt or aversion to this society is a misfortune as great to one man as to another; this is the result that may at first view present itself to the mind, and which, to a certain extent, is really correct; it will, however, upon a more narrow scrutiny of the matter, be found, that in point of intensity this class of punishment is subject to extreme variation, depending as it does upon the condition in life, wealth, education, age, sex, and other circumstances; the casual[553] evils resulting from the punishments belonging to this sanction are infinitely variable: shame depends upon sensibility.

Women, especially among civilized nations, are more alive to, and susceptible of, the impression of shame than men. From their earliest infancy, and even before they are capable of understanding the object of it, one of the most important branches of their education is, to instil into them principles of modesty and reserve; and they are not long in discovering that this guardian of their virtue is at the same time the source of their power. They are, moreover, physically weaker, and more dependent than men, and stand more in need of protection; it is more difficult for them to change their society, and to remove from the place of their abode.[554]

At a very early age, generally speaking, sensibility to the moral sanction is not remarkably acute: in old age it becomes still more obtuse. Avarice, the only passion that is fortified by age, subdues all sense of shame.

A weak state of health, morbid irritability, any bodily defect, any natural or accidental infirmity, are circumstances that aggravate the suffering from shame as from every other calamity.

Wealth, considered of itself, independently of rank and education, has a tendency to blunt the force of these impressions. A rich man has it in his power to change his residence, to procure fresh connections and acquaintance, and by the help of money to purchase pleasures for which other people are dependent upon goodwill. There exists a disposition to respect opulence on its own account, to bestow on the possessor of it gratuitous services, and, above all, external professions of politeness and respect.

Rank is a circumstance that augments the sensibility to all impressions that affect the honour: but the rules of honour and morality are not always calculated upon the same scale: the higher ranks are, however, in general more alive to the influence of opinion than the inferior classes.

Profession and habitual occupation materially affect the punishments proceeding from this source. In some classes of society, the point of honour is at the very highest pitch, and any circumstance by which it is affected produces a more acute impression than any other species of shame. Courage, among military men, is an indispensable qualification: the slightest suspicion of cowardice exposes them to perpetual insults: thence, upon this point, that delicacy of feeling among men who, upon other points, are in a remarkable degree regardless of the influence of the moral sanction.[555]

The middle ranks of society are the most virtuous, it is among them that in the greatest number of points the principles of honour coincide with the principles of utility: it is in this class also that the inconveniences arising from the forfeiture of esteem are most sensibly felt, and that the evil consequences arising from the loss of reputation produce the most serious ill consequences.[556]

Among the poorer classes, among men who live by their daily labour, sensibility to honour is in general less acute. A day labourer, if he is industrious, though his character is not unspotted, will be at no loss for work. His companions are companions of labour, not of pleasure: from their gratuitous services he has little to expect and as little to ask. His wants are confined to the mere necessaries of life. His wife and his children owe him obedience, and dare not withhold it. The pleasures which arise from the exercise of domestic authority fill up the short intervals of labour.

3.[557] The greatest imperfection attending punishments arising from the moral sanction, is their want of *exemplarity*. Their effect, in this respect, is less than that of any of the punishments of the political sanction. When a man is exposed to suffering from loss of reputation, it may be unknown to all the world, or at least the knowledge may be confined to those who are the instruments of his punishment, and to the immediate circle of his friends and acquaintance. But these are witnesses only of a small part of his sufferings. They perceive that he is treated with indifference or disdain—they observe that he does not find protection or confidence; but all these observations are transitory. The individual, wounded by these signs of coldness or aversion, shuns the company of the authors or the witnesses of his shame; he retires to solitude, where he suffers in secret, and the more unhappy he is, the smaller is the number of the spectators of his punishment.

[558]Punishments, connected with the moral sanction, are advantageous with reference to *reformation*. When a man suffers in consequence of a violation of the established rules or morality, he can only refer the evil he experiences to its true cause; the more sensible he is to shame, the more he will fear to increase it: he will become either more prudent that he may avoid detection, or more careful to save appearances, or he will in future submit to those laws which he has been unable to break without suffering. Public opinion, with the exception of a few cases, is not implacable. There

is among men a reciprocal need of indulgence, and a levity and ease in forgetting instead of forgiving faults, when the resemblance of them is not renewed by fresh failures.

On the other hand, with respect to dishonourable actions for which there is neither appeal or pardon, the punishment of infamy acts as a discouragement, and not as a motive to reformation. *Nemo dignitate perditæ parcit.*

These disadvantages are in measure compensated, and this sanction receives a degree of force which is often wanting in the political sanction, from the *certainty* of its action. There is no offending against it with impunity—an offence against one of the laws of honour, arouses all its guardians.[559] The political tribunals are subjected to a regular process, they cannot pronounce a decision without proof, and proofs are often defective. The tribunal of public opinion possesses more liberty and more power; it is liable to be unjust in its decisions, but they are never delayed on that account; they can be reversed at pleasure. Trial and execution proceed with equal steps, without delay or necessity for pursuit. There are everywhere persons ready to judge and to execute the judgment. This tribunal always inclines to the side of severity; its Judges are interested by their vanity and their love of display in making its decisions severe; the more severe they appear, the more they flatter themselves with the possession of the good esteem of others. They seem to think that the spoliation of one character forms the riches of another. Thus, although the punishments of the moral sanction are indeterminate, and, for the most part, when estimated separately, of little weight, yet by the certainty of their operation, their frequent recurrence, and their accumulation, from the number of those who have authority to inflict them, they possess a degree of force which cannot be despised by any individual, whatever may be his character, his condition, or his power.[560]

The power exercised by the moral sanction varies according to the degree of civilization.

In civilized society there are many sources of enjoyment, and consequently many wants, which can be supplied only from considerations of reciprocal esteem; he who loses his reputation is consequently exposed to extended suffering in all these points.[561]

The exercise of this sanction is also favoured or restrained by different circumstances. Under a popular Government it is carried to the highest degree, under a despotic Government it is reduced almost to nothing.

Easy communications, and the ready circulation of intelligence, by means of newspapers, augments the extent of this tribunal, and increases the submission of individuals to the empire of opinion.

The more unanimous the decisions of the moral sanction the greater their force. Are its decisions different among a great number of different sects or parties, whether religious or political, they will contradict each other. Virtue and vice will not use the same common measure. Places of refuge will be found for those who have disgraced themselves, and the deserter from one sect or party will be enrolled in another.[562]

CHAPTER III.
FORFEITURE OF REPUTATION.[563]

We now come to consider the Punishment of Infamy or Forfeiture of Reputation.* The nature of this punishment we have already had occasion to discuss, in treating of the moral sanction from which it derives its origin. All that remains for us to do in this place, is to state the various contrivances by which the political magistrate has gone about to modify its direction and to augment its force.[564]

In point of *direction* the way in which he influences the action of this punishment is very simple; it is this, by annexing it to the commission of any act which, by prohibiting, he has constituted an offence.

In point of *force*, he may influence it by various means.

The methods by which this may be done may be divided in the first place into *legislative* or *executive*. 1st. It may be done by methods simply legislative, without any of that interference which, in the case of ordinary punishments, is necessary of the executive power: the law in this case commits to each individual, in as far as he himself is concerned, the office of Judge and Executioner.—2nd. But in this case, as in any other, the law may carry itself into execution in the ordinary methods of procedure; authorising the Judge either in imitation of his predecessors, or in conformity to the letter of positive law, to direct and animate the resentment of the community at large.[565]

By the simple exercise of the legislative office, the law may annex to any mode of conduct a certain quantity of disrepute in the following ways:—[566]

1. By simply prohibiting any mode of conduct; although no political penalty be also employed to enforce the prohibition. This is the lowest

---

*Though infamy is the more common, forfeiture of reputation is the more convenient expression of the two. Infamy is a term which appears forced, when applied to any other than the very high degrees of the punishment in question: the phrase forfeiture of reputation is accommodated to one degree as well as another; for the quantity of reputation may be conceived to be divided into as many lots or degrees as there can be reason for.

The turn and structure of language having put a man's reputation, like his estate, upon the footing of his possessions, men have considered and spoken of the subject as if it were a quantity alike determinate, and as if a man might be made to forfeit the whole of his reputation at a single stroke, as he may the whole of his estate. But that this, though possible in the latter instance, is impossible in the former, will presently be seen by tracing up these fictitious objects of possession to the real objects from whence they are respectively derived. A man's estate is derived out of *things*: out of certain determinate allotments of things moveable or

degree in which the political magistrate can be instrumental in applying the force of the several sanctions. This slightest exertion of the force of the moral sanction is inseparable, we see, from an exertion of that of the political. A few words may be of use on this occasion, to shew what causes it is owing that a certain share of the former of these forces is become, as it were, appurtenant to the other.

2. If no political penalty is denounced, the community finds in this circumstance a stronger or additional reason for annexing their disesteem to the breach of it.[567] For since it must be evident to the legislator, as it is to every man, that no rule can have any effect without a motive to prompt a man to observe it, his omitting to annex any other penalty is naturally understood to be a kind of tacit warning to the community at large to take the execution of the law into their own hands. All he does in such case is to give *direction* to the moral sanction, trusting to its native force for the execution of his law.

3. If the ordinance be accompanied by an express exhortation to obey it, or, what comes to much the same thing, if the terms in which it is delivered savour of exhortation, this is another and more express declaration of his persuasion of the utility of the ordinance he promulgates. And the more anxious he is that it should meet with obedience, the more pernicious [it shews] he appears to deem the conduct of any one who disobeys it, or at least the more convinced he shews himself to be, that to a certain degree at least the non-observance of it would be pernicious to the community.†

5.[568] A fifth expedient, by which the moral sanction is called upon in a manner still more express to enforce political ordinance,[569] is by censure

---

immoveable; or if any part of it be derived immediately out of persons, it is derived out of the services of a few persons, and those persons (and very frequently those services due from each person) determinate and certain. But a man's reputation is derived immediately out of *persons*: out of the services of persons; out of any services of any persons whatsoever: out of the services of as many persons, be they who they may, as choose to render him any. This is a stock which the political magistrate can never perhaps by any one operation, nor indeed by any number of operations of any kind, be certain of exhausting: much less by any such vague and feeble operations as those are by which an offender is commonly understood to have been made to incur the forfeiture of reputation, that is, the punishment of infamy.

If there be, it is that punishment which, if the vulgar tradition is to be depended upon, was inflicted by Richard III on Jane Shore: the direct prohibiting of all persons from rendering to the offender any kind of service. But this is but in other words the punishment of *starving*. The same punishment has sometimes been denounced in other countries where, being strictly executed, it has been, as it could not but be, attended with that effect. [A version of the first paragraph and a condensed version of the second paragraph, appear within Dumont's edition, *Théorie des peines*, vol. I, p. 349, but not the third paragraph or its additional note.]

Case of the Albigenses.—See Rapin (Montfort).—See Watson's Phil. 2d.

†This anxiety may be grounded or excited not solely by a supposed utility of the law, but in some degree by a supposed propensity in the people to disobey it.

directly levelled at him, whosoever he shall prove to be, that shall infringe it. This censure may be levelled at the offender either immediately, or else mediately, by being immediately pointed at the offence.*[570]

6. A sixth expedient is by transferring, or at least endeavouring to transfer, upon one offence, the measure of disrepute that naturally attends upon another. The way in which this is done, is by affecting to regard the obnoxious practice in question as an evidence of another practice of which men are already in the habit of bestowing a superior degree of disrepute.† It is plain that the cases in which this can be attempted with any prospect of success must necessarily be limited. To warrant the inference, some appearance in connection, however superficial, there must be between the two offences. But any little connexion, however slight, is ordinarily sufficient. In such a case, men in general are not apt to be very difficult with regard to the evidence. The vanity of being thought sagacious, the pride of sitting in judgment and condemning, the hope of earning a certain measure of reputation on the score of virtue at an easy rate. The love of novelty and paradox, and the propensity to exaggeration, especially on the unfavourable side, second the aim of the legislator.

So much for the ways in which the political magistrate may exert an influence over the moral sanction by the bare exercise of his *legislative* powers: we now come to the instances in which he requires the assistance of the Executive.[571]

[572]Of all the expedients[573] that may be classed under this head, the least severe is that of *publication*, the making public the fact of the offence,

---

*Of the terms of condemnation applied directly to the offense, the *improbè factum* of the Lex Valeria may serve for an example. "Valeria Lex, quum eum qui provocâsset virgis cædi securique necari voluisset, siquis adversus ea fecisset, nihil ultra quam *improbè factum* adjecit."—Livy, 1. 10, ch. 9. [Dumont's edition uses this note as a generally "remarkable example," *Théorie des peines*, vol. I p. 350.]

The laws of Greece and Rome afford several examples, where for different offenses, the offender is pronounced infamous.§

†Of this we have an example in certain laws of Zaleucus the Locrian Legislator, pretended to have been preserved (say my authority) by Diodorus Siculus. "Let not a free woman go forth from the city in the night, *unless* when she goes to prostitute herself to her gallant. Let her not wear rich ornaments or garments interwoven with gold, unless she be a courtesan."—Princ. of Pen. Law, c. 26.

This was a much as to say, that if he knew of a woman's going abroad in a lone place at the unseasonable hour he is speaking of, the legislator should take it for granted that such was the errand she went out upon. If she dressed in a manner in which it was particularly the business of courtesans to dress, he should take for granted her being of that stamp. [The contents of this note are incorporated into the main text of Dumont's edition of this chapter. *Théorie des peines*, vol. I, p. 351.

§So by 9 Ann. c. 14, §5, a loss at play, if prosecuted on that statute, is to be declared infamous.—Vide etiam stat. Ed. 6.

accompanied with a designation of the offender. It is principally in point of *extent* that a measure of this sort tends to add to the natural *quantum* of disrepute: though something likewise may be supposed to be contributed by it in point of *intensity*, on account of the certainty which it gives to men's opinions of the delinquency of the offender. Even this mode of proceeding, mild as it may appear, is capable of various degrees of publicity that may be given to the fact. It may be registered in a written instrument to which few people have access; it may be registered in a written instrument to which any person may have access. It may be notified by proclamation, by sound of trumpet, by beat of drum. Since the invention of printing, it may be recorded in indelible characters, and circulated through the whole state.* It is obvious that the discredit reflected by this expedient must be greater or less in point of intensity as the offence is esteemed more or less disreputable.

[574]The censure which in the law is pronounced in general terms upon such uncertain persons as may chance to become offenders, may, upon conviction, by the assistance of the executive power, be brought home to, and personally levelled at any individual offender. And this may be done in a manner more or less public, and either in a settled form of words, or with more latitude in a speech *ad libitum*,[575] to be delivered by the Judge.†[576]

[577]But the severest expedient for[578] inflicting infamy is that which consists in the applying of some political punishment, which, by its influence on the imaginations of mankind, is in possession of the power of producing this effect. This leads us to enquire into the different measures of infamy that stand naturally annexed to the several modes of punishment; and in the course of this enquiry we shall find reason to distinguish certain punishments from the rest by the special epithet of infamous.

A certain degree of infamy or disrepute, we have already remarked, is what necessarily attends on every kind of political punishment. But there are some that reflect a much larger portion of infamy than others.‡ These, therefore, it is plain, are the only ones which can be stated properly by that name.[579]

Upon looking over the list of punishments we shall find that it is to

---

*In certain offenses against the Police,—for instance, in selling bread by short weight, it is not an uncommon thing, where the degree of delinquency appears to be considerable, for the magistrate to threaten the offender, that upon the next conviction he shall be advertised in the newspapers. Such a punishment seems to be looked upon as more severe than the fine imposed by statute.

†When the punishment is capital, or the sentence discretionary, it is common with us in England to preface it with such a speech.

‡Aware of this circumstance, the Roman lawyers have taken a distinction between the *infamia facti* and the *infamia juris*: the natural infamy resulting from the offense, and the artificial infamy produced through the means of the punishment by the law. See Keinecc. Elementa Jur. Civil. Pand. 1.3. tit. 2. § 399, whose explanation however is not very precise.

those which come under the name of corporal punishments that this property of reflecting an extraordinary degree of infamy is almost exclusively confined. Pecuniary punishments, which are the most common, are attended with a less degree of infamy than any other; unless it be quasi-pecuniary punishments; which in this respect, as in most others, are pretty much upon a par with pecuniary. Next to these come the several modes of confinement; among which, if there be any difference, *quasi* imprisonment and local interdiction[580] seem the mildest in this respect, next to them banishment, and imprisonment the severest. Of specific restraints and active punishments at large, they are so various, that it is not easy to give an account. In general they seem to be on a footing with those punishments that are mildest in this respect, unless where, by means of analogy, they are so contrived as to reflect and aggravate in a peculiar manner the infamy of the offence.* The same account may be given of all the other kinds of forfeiture.

With regard to corporal punishments short of death, there is no punishment of this class but is understood to carry with it a very high degree of infamy. The degree of it, however, is not by any means in proportion to the organical pain or inconveniences that are respectively attendant upon those punishments. On the contrary, if there be any difference, it seems as if the less the quantity is which a punishment imparts, of those or any other kind of inconveniences, the greater is the quantity which it imports of infamy. The reason may be, that since it is manifest the punishment must have been designed to produce suffering in some way or other, the less it seems calculated to produce in any other way, the more manifest it is that it was for this purpose it was made choice of. Accordingly, in regard to punishments to which the highest degrees of infamy are understood to be annexed, one can scarcely find any other suffering which they produce. This is the case with several species of transient disablement; such as the punishments of the stocks, the pillory, and the carcan: and with several species of transient as well as of perpetual disfigurement; such as ignominious dresses and stigmatisation. Accordingly, these modes of punishment are all of them regarded as neither more nor less than so many ways of inflicting infamy. Infamy thus produced by corporal punishments, may be stiled corporal ignominy or infamy.

According as the corporal punishment that is made choice of for the sake of producing the infamy is temporary or perpetual, the infamy itself may be distinguished into temporary or indelible. Thus the infamy pro-

---

*Such as the obligation to ask pardon, an instance of active punishment: the forbearing to carry on an employment which the offender has exercised fraudulently, an instance of restrictive punishment: the forbearing to come into the presence of the party injured, an instance of ambulatory confinement. [This note does not appear within Dumont's edition.]

duced by the stocks, the pillory, and the carcan, is but temporary; that which is produced by an indelible stigma is perpetual. Not but that any kind of infamy, howsoever inflicted or contracted, may chance to prove perpetual; since the idea of the offence, or what comes to the same thing, of the punishment, may very well chance to remain more or less fresh in men's minds to the end of the delinquent's life: but when it is produced by an indelible stigma, it cannot do otherwise than continue so long as the *mark* remains, whatsoever happens to him. Wheresoever he goes, and how long soever he lives,[581] he bears about him the evidence of his guilt.

Mutilation and the severer kinds of simple afflictive punishments, discolourment, disfigurement and disablement, are all attended likewise with a very intense degree of infamy; that is in as far as the effects produced on purpose in the way of punishment. But with regard to many of the sorts of punishment that come under the three latter heads, as the effects of them are, upon the face of them, no other than might have been produced by accident, they are therefore the less certain of producing the effect of infamy. This infamy produced by these punishments is, in point of duration, of a mixed nature, as it were, between temporary and perpetual. At the time of the execution it stands upon a par in this respect with the pillory or the stocks, with whipping, or any other kind of simple afflictive punishments: after that time it is greater than what is produced by any of these punishments, because the visible consequences still continue: it is not however so great as what is produced by stigmatization, because it does not of itself, like that galling punishment,[582] make known the guilt of the delinquent to strangers at the first glance.

[583]Nearly allied to corporal infamy[584] are two other species of infamy, which as they derive their influence altogether from that which is possessed by corporal infamy, may be stiled quasi-corporal. The one is inflicted by an application made, instead of to a man's body, to some object, the idea of which, by the principle of association, has the effect of suggesting to the imagination, the idea of a punishment applied actually to the body itself. This, inasmuch as it operates by the force of symbols or emblems, may be styled symbolical or emblematical corporal infamy.* The other is inflicted by a punishment applied indeed to the body, but not till after it has ceased to be susceptible of punishment, I mean not till after death; this may be styled *posthumous* or post-orbitory [*sic*] corporal infamy.†

[585]To the head of forfeiture of reputation must be referred a forfeiture

---

*Among the ancient Persians, in some cases, when the criminal was of high rank, instead of whipping the man himself, it was the custom to whip his clothes. To this head may also be referred the custom which prevails in France and other nations upon the continent of executing criminals in effigy. The feigned punishments inflicted on the effigy is commonly, I suppose,

of a very particular kind, forfeiture of credibility; that is, in effect, forfeiture of so much of a man's reputation as depends upon the opinion of his veracity. The effect of this punishment (as far as it can be carried into effect) is to cause people to bestow on the delinquent that share of ill-will which they are naturally disposed to bear to a man whose word they look upon as not being to be depended upon for true.[586]

This punishment is a remarkable instance of the empire attempted, and not unsuccessfully, to be exercised by the political magistrate over the moral sanction. Application is made to the executors of that sanction, that is the public at large, to bestow on the delinquent not so much of their dis-esteem[587] in general, nor yet so much of their dis-esteem as they are disposed to annex to some particular offence of which he has been found guilty, but such a share as they are disposed to annex to another offence of which he has not been proved guilty, and which, unless by accident, has no connection with that of which he has actually been proved guilty.

The method too which is taken to inflict this punishment is equally remarkable. It is inflicted not by any restraint or other punishment applied to the delinquent, but by a restraint laid upon another person, a Judge, or by an inconvenience which may be of any kind whatsoever, thrown (as the case may require) upon any person whatsoever. The Judge is forbidden to interrogate him, or to permit him to be interrogated as a witness in any cause, as also to pay any regard on any such occasion, to any instrument purporting to contain his written attestation. The party who may have stood in need of his evidence for the preservation of his life, liberty, or fortune, or the public who may have stood in need of it to warrant the punishment, and guard itself against the enterprises of another, perhaps more atrocious, criminal, are precluded from that benefit.[588]

---

the same that would have been really inflicted upon the man's person for the same offense; nor is it usual, I believe, to employ this punishment where the delinquent is forthcoming.

In Portugal, several of the persons who were concerned in the attempt upon the late king's life were punished in this manner. [A version of this note appears as part of the main text within Dumont's edition which adds another example relating to an assassination committed by the Duke of Medina-Celi in Spain, punished in a similar manner. *Théorie des peines*, vol. I, pp. 358–59.]

†To this head may be referred a part of the punishment in use in England for High Treason, according to the Common Law; the taking out and burning of the entrails, the cutting off the head, and the dividing the body into four quarters, which are disposed of at the King's pleasure. 2 *Hawkins*, 443.

By an English statute, in cases of murder, the Judge is rejoined to order the body (after the criminal has been put to death by hanging) to be publicly dissected, and is empowered to order it to be hung in chains, as the phrase is: which is practised by suspending it from a gibbet in an iron frame. [This note appears within the main text of Dumont's edition, *Théorie des peines*, vol. I p. 359.]

I know not of any instance in which it is absolutely clear that a man has been made to incur this singular kind of forfeiture in the express view of punishment. In all the cases in which it has been adopted, it is not impossible but that the restraint which it imports may have been imposed in no other view than that of improving the rules of evidence, and guiding the Judge against error in his decision[589] upon the questions of fact brought before him.

Be this as it may, it is certain that in the English law it stands annexed in many instances to offences which have not the remotest connection with the veracity or mendacity of the offender.*[590]

[591]To this head also must be referred the punishment of forfeiture of rank, otherwise entitled degradation.[592] For the purpose of understanding this modification of ignominious punishment, reputation must be distinguished into natural or *ordinary*, and factitious or extraordinary. By *natural* share of reputation and goodwill, I mean that which each man possesses in virtue of his own personal conduct and behaviour. By factitious,[593] I mean that extraordinary share of these possessions which, independently of a man's personal conduct, is bestowed on him by the institution and contrivance of the political magistrate.[594]

This kind of factitious reputation is commonly annexed to office or employment: but it sometimes exists by itself.[595] This is the case, for instance, in England, with the ranks of gentleman, esquire, knight, and baronet, and the ranks derived from academical [*sic*] degrees.[596]

Rank may be conferred either by custom or by authority. When derived from custom, it is annexed either to family or to occupation. When derived from authority, it is annexed to the person. But whether it were conferred by authority or no, it is in the power of authority to diminish the reputation belonging to it, if not wholly to take it away. A sentence of a Judge degrading a man from the rank of gentleman, cannot cause a man not to have been born of a father that was a gentleman, but it may divest him of a greater or less share of that respect which men were disposed before to pay him on that account.[597]

As to the mode of inflicting degradation, it may be inflicted by any process that serves to express the will of the magistrate, that the delinquent be no longer considered as possessing the rank in question, with or without corporal ignominy.

---

*For instance, to High Treason, or the adherence to the unsuccessful side in a competition for the Crown; to Homicide committed in revenge, on a sudden quarrel, or in the course of a duel, by consent: to Rape and other irregularities of the venereal appetite. This, however, seems to proceed not so much from design as from inattention in the authors of our Common Law; and is one of the many absurd and mischievous consequences that follow from the lumping together offenses of the most heterogeneous natures under the name of Felonies.

Degradation, did it answer precisely to the definition given of it, when it is stiled forfeiture of rank, should take away from a man that precise quantity of reputation, and consequently of good offices, and consequently of happiness, for which he stands indebted to his rank. But as these quantities are incapable of being measured, or even estimated with any tolerable degree of exactness, the punishment of degradation can never with any certainty be made to answer precisely to such definition. It seems probable that a man who has once been possessed of a certain rank, can never be totally deprived of all the reputation, respect, and good offices that are commonly rendered to that rank: the imaginations of mankind are too stubborn to yield instant and perfect obedience to the nod of power. It seems probably, notwithstanding that the condition of a man who has undergone a degradation of rank is thereby commonly rendered worse upon the whole than if he had never been possessed of it; because in general simply not to possess, is not so bad as having possessed to lose. To speak with more precision, it should seem that the characteristic pain of the moral sanction produced by such a punishment, is in general more than equivalent to the sum of such of the casual benefits of that sanction as the punishment fails to take away.

It is common enough to speak of a *total* loss of reputation; and some Jurists speak of such a loss as if it could easily be, and were frequently incurred. But such a notion is not compatible with any precise idea of the import of that term. To understand this, it will be necessary to conceive in idea a certain average or mean quantity of reputation equal to Zero, from whence degrees of good reputation may be reckoned on one side, and of bad reputation on the other. This mean quantity of reputation, or goodwill call that which any given member of the community may be deemed to possess, who has no rank, and who either has neither merits nor demerits, if such a human being be conceivable, or rather whose merits stand exactly upon a level with his demerits. All *above* this average quantity may be stiled *good* reputation, all *below* it *bad* reputation. In one sense then, a total forfeiture of reputation should consist of nothing more than a total forfeiture of good reputation, as thus defined. Now then, according to this account of the matter, a total forfeiture of reputation would be nothing more than what is very possible, and indeed must be very frequent. But it is plain that this is not what the Jurists, nor indeed what persons in general, in speaking of a total forfeiture of reputation, have in view. For all that this would amount to, would be the reducing the delinquent to a level with a man of ordinary merit and condition: it would not put his reputation upon so low a footing as that to which a man of ordinary merit and reputation would be reduced by the slightest instance of moral or political delinquency. What they have in view is the acquisition, if one may so term it, of a certain share of ill reputation, the quantity of which they view in a confused manner, as if it were determinate, and consisted of all the ill reputation a man could possibly acquire. But this, it is plain, it never can do, at least in the cases to which they apply it. For they speak of such an event as if it could be and commonly were the effect of a single instance of delinquency; for instance, a robbery or ordinary murder. This, it is plain, it can never be, unless it should be maintained that an act of parricide, for example, would not make a man worse looked upon than he was before, after having committed only a robbery or ordinary murder. It is plain that the maximum of bad as well as that of good reputation is an infinite quantity, and that in this sense there is no such thing within the sphere of real life as a total forfeiture of reputation.[598]

[599]SEC. II.—SIMPLE IGNOMINIOUS PUNISHMENTS EXAMINED.

The infliction of ignominious punishment[600] is an appeal to the tribunal of the public—an invitation to the people to treat the offender with contempt, to withdraw from him their esteem. It is (to speak in figurative language) a bill drawn upon the people for so much of their ill-will as they shall think proper to bestow. If they look upon him in a less favourable light than they would otherwise, the draft is honoured: if they do not, it is protested, and the charge is very apt to fall upon the drawer. Ignominious punishments are like those engines which are apt to recoil, and often wound the hand that unadroitly [sic] uses them.[601]

But if skilfully managed, what important services may they not be made to render! The legislator, by calling in to his aid, and trusting to the moral sanction, increases its power and the extent of its influence: and when he declares that the *loss of honour* is to be considered as a severe punishment, he gives to it in the eyes of every man an additional value.*

1. This species of punishment, so far as it goes, is not without some commodious properties: it is *variable* in quantity from the paternal admonition of the Judge, to a high degree of infamy. Accompanied with more or less publicity, with various circumstances of disgrace and humiliation, the legislator may proportion the punishment to the malignity of the offence, and adapt it to the various circumstances of age, rank, sex, and profession. Every station in life will, for this purpose, afford facilities that are peculiar to it, and in particular the military.

---

*See Traités de Legislation, tom. iii. c. 17. Emploi du Mobile de l'Honneur.

In point of variability, punishments of this kind have an advantage over every other mode of punishment. This quality is desirable in a mode of punishment that it may be capable of being made to bear a due proportion to every offence to which it is annexed. With regard to all other kinds of punishments that are constituted solely by the law, the proportion must be settled by the law; whereas this mode has a tendency to fall into that proportion itself. The magistrate pronounces—the people execute. The people, that is, as many of the people as think proper: they execute it, that is, in whatever proportion they think proper. The malignity towards the delinquent is in general proportionate to the malignancy of his offence. It is not,[602] however, like corporal punishment, capable of being universally applied to all offences. In many cases an offence may be productive of real mischief, but a mischief which the people, the executioners of this mode of punishment, are not qualified to perceive. On this part of the subject we shall have occasion to speak further presently.

2. In point of *exemplarity*, this mode of punishment cannot be excelled. Whatever it is that a man suffers by the publication of his offence, whether by degradation or by being subject to ignominious exposure; it is evident that he suffers it from the infamy attached to his character under the sanction of the legislator.

3. In point of *frugality* it is advantageous enough.[603] The mischief apprehended from the ill-will annexed to a disreputable act, bears, I suppose, at least as high a ration to the eventual mischief, as the mischief apprehended from any other mode of punishment does to the eventual.

4. In point of *popularity* it cannot be excelled. For what objection can the people have to a man's being punished in this manner, when all that is done to him is the giving them notice that within the bounds which the law allows, they themselves may punish him as they please, when they themselves are both Judges and executioners?[604]

5. They are *remissible*. An erroneous sentence may be annulled. A greater degree of notoriety may be given to the justification than accompanied the condemnation. The stain that had been thus affixed on his character will not only be completely effaced, but the supposed offender, from the unjust persecution that he will have undergone, will become a general object of sympathy, and especially to those who have been instrumental in inflicting the punishment.

What is more, even though justly inflicted, the patient, by the stimulus he will have received, may be excited to exertions to recover the esteem he has lost, and to earn fresh honours to hide his disgrace. In the army it has happened that the whole body of troops, after having been stigmatized by their officers, have atoned for their offence by distinguished acts of valour, and have received the highest marks of honour.

This advantage is not possessed by ignominious corporal punishments: the stain that they leave is indelible; and unless the patient expatriates himself, his lost reputation is irrecoverable.

Having thus stated the properties that belong to punishments of this kind, we proceed to notice a difficulty which arises in their application, and which is peculiar to them. The legislator cannot at pleasure attach to any given species of offence the degree of infamy that he may be desirous of affixing to it. There are some classes of offences really detrimental to the country, such, for example, as election bribery and smuggling, for the punishing of which the legislator has no means of pressing the great bulk of the people into the service. Upon other points the popular sentiments are in direct opposition to those of the legislature: there are others in which they are wavering, neutral, or too feeble to serve his purpose. The case of duelling may serve as an example.

"So far" (says Rousseau) "is the censorial tribunal from leading the public opinion, it follows it: and when it departs from it, its decisions are vain and nugatory."*

Be it so; but what follows from this? Is it that the legislator is to be the slave of the most mischievous and erroneous popular notions? No. This would be to quit the helm while the vessel was surrounded with rocks. His greatest difficulty will consist in conciliating the public opinion, in correcting it when erroneous, and in giving it that bent which shall be most favourable to produce obedience to his mandates.

The legislator is in an eminent degree possessed of the means of guiding public opinion. The power with which he is invested gives to his instructions, whenever he may bestow them, far greater weight than would be attributed to them if falling from a private individual. The public, generally speaking, presumes that the government has at its command more completely than any private man, the requisite sources of information. It is presumed also that in the great majority of cases its interest is the same with that of the people, and that it is unbiased by personal interest, which is so apt to misguide the opinion of individuals. If things go on unprosperously, the responsible agents become subject to the animadversion of the public: if prosperously, they have the credit and the advantage. Of this people in general have a confused notion, and it is the ground of their confidence.

In extirpating prejudices that appear to him to be mischievous the legislator has the means of laying the axe to the root of the evil. He may form institutions which, without inculcating doctrines in direct repugnance to received opinions, may indirectly attack them. Instead of planting against them a battery he may sink a mine beneath them, the effect of which will be infallible.

Contrat Social. Liv. iv. c. 7.

The legislator is clothed not only with political but with moral power. It is what is commonly expressed by the words consideration, respect, confidence. There are not wanting instances in which, by means of such instruments, the most important effects have been produced.[605]

[606]A certain degree of infamy, it is obvious, must naturally result upon a conviction for any offence which the community are accustomed to mark with their displeasure: thus much results from the bare conviction, indeed from the bare detection, without any express designation of the magistrate. The only way, therefore, in which the magistrate can produce any additional degree of infamy, I mean all along pure and simple infamy, is by taking extraordinary measures to make public the fact of the offence. In this way it is only in point of *extent* that the magistrate adds to the actual portion of infamy that flows from the offence.

In point of intensity, there is but one way in which the law can contribute anything to the infliction of simple infamy. This is by bestowing on the act in question some opprobrious appellation: some epithet, calculated to express ill-will or contempt[607] on the part of him who uses it. Thus, a legislator of ancient Rome, (in a passage of Livy, quoted by the Author of Principles of Penal Law,*) after describing a particular mode of offence, is said to have done nothing more towards punishing it, than by subjoining these words, *improbè factum.* Here the legislator begins the song of obloquy, expecting that the people will follow in chorus. The delinquent is to be pelted with invectives, and the legislator begins and casts the first stone.[608]

But when the object of the legislator is to conciliate the public opinion, and especially when that opinion is opposite to the one he would establish, he must address himself to their reason.[609]

I hope it will not be supposed that under the name of *reasons*, I have here in view those effusions of legislative babbling, those old-womanish aphorisms, mocking the discernment of the people, degrading the dignity of the legislature, which stuff up and disgrace the preambles of our statute-books. "Whereas it has been found inconvenient—Whereas great mischiefs [sic] have arisen"—as if it were endurable that a legislator should prohibit a practice which he did *not* think "inconvenient," which he did *not* think "mischievous," and as if, without his saying as much, the people would not give him credit for wishing that it might be believed he thought it.[610]

Of what sort then should the reasons be which the legislator ought to employ to back and justify an epithet of reproach? They should be such as may serve to indicate the *particular* way in which the practice in question is thought liable to do mischief; and by that means, point out the analogy there is between that practice, and those other practices, more obviously but

---

*P. 290, 1st edit.

perhaps not more intensely mischievous, to which the people are already disposed to annex their disapprobation. Such reasons, if reasons are to be given, should be simple and significant, that they may instruct, energetic[611] that they may strike, short that they may be remembered.

Take the following as an example in the case of smuggling. *Whosoever deals with smugglers let him be infamous. He who buys uncustomed goods defrauds the public of the value of the duty. By him the public purse suffers as much as if he had stolen the same sum out of the public treasury. He who defrauds the public purse defrauds every member of the community.**

As the legislator may lay the hand of reproach upon him who counteracts the purposes of the law, so may he take it off from him who forwards them. Such is the informer: a sort of man on whose name the short-sightedness and prejudice of the people, inflamed by the laws themselves, have most undeservedly cast an odium. The informer's law might be prefaced in the following manner:

It is the artifice of bad men to seek to draw contempt upon them who, by executing the laws, would be a check upon their misdeeds. If the law is just, as it ought to be, the informer is the enemy of no man, but in proportion as that man is an enemy to the rest. In proportion as a man loves his country he will be active in bringing to justice all those who, by the breach of the laws, entrench on its prosperity.[612]

It will be remarked, that in this new part of the law—in this struggle to be made against the errors of the moral sanction—there is work for the dramatist as well as the legislator, or else, that the politician should add somewhat of the spirit of the dramatist to all the information of the lawyer. Thus wrote the legislators of ancient days, men who spoke the significant and enchanting language of ancient Greece. Poetry was invited to the aid of law. No man had ever yet thought of addressing the people in the barbarous language that disgraces our statute-book, where the will of the legislator is drowned in a sea of words. Habited in a Gothic accoutrement of

---

*I say the public purse, I do not say the public simply. Far from the pen of the legislator be that stale sophistry of declaiming moralizers, which consists in giving to one species of misbehaviour the name and reproach of another species of a higher class, confounding in men's minds the characters of vice and virtue. Pure from all taint of falsehood should the legislator keep his pen; nor think to promote the cause of utility and truth by means which only tyranny and imposture can stand in need of. In what I have said above there is nothing but what is rigorously and simply true. But it were not true to say that a theft upon the public were as mischievous as a theft upon an individual; from this there results no alarm, and the more the loss is divided the lighter it falls upon each other. [A version of this note appears as a separate paragraph within the text of Dumont's edition, following the paragraph to which this note is attached which appears in quotation marks within Dumont's edition. A citation for the source of that quote is not offered, suggesting that it merely indicates a rhetorical device. *Théorie des peines*, vol. I, pp. 369–70.]

RATIONALE OF PUNISHMENT

antiquated phrases, useless repetitions, incomplete specifications, entangled and never-ending sentences, he may merely, from incomprehensibility, inspire terror, but cannot command respect. It may be matter of astonishment, why the arbiters of our life and of our property, instead of disporting themselves in this grotesque and abject garb, cannot express themselves with clearness, with dignity, and with precision: the best laws would be disfigured if clothed in such language.

[613]"In a moderate and virtuous government," says an elegant and admired writer, "the idea of shame will follow the finger of law."

Yes, so as his finger be not so employed as to counteract and irritate the determined affections of the people.[614] He goes on and says, "whatever species of punishment is pointed out as infamous, will have the effect of infamy." True, whatever is appointed by the legislator as a mark to signify his having annexed his disapprobation to any particular mode of conduct, will have this effect;[615] it will make the people sensible that he wishes to be *thought* to disapprove of that mode of conduct; in most cases, that he does really disapprove of it. But to say that whatever the legislator professes to disapprove of, the people will disapprove of too, is, I doubt, going a degree too far.

We may direct his attention[616] to an instance of an offence which, under as moderate and virtuous a government, I dare believe, (all prejudices apart) as ever yet existed, laws have rendered penal, magistrates have endeavoured to render infamous, by a punishment which in general marks the patient with infamy, but which no laws, no magistrate, no punishments, will in this country ever render infamous. I mean state-libelling.[617]

The offence of libelling, as marked out by the law as it stands at present, is this;[618] it is the publishing respecting any man anything that he does not like. This being the offence of libelling in general, the offence of state-libelling is the publishing respecting a man in power anything which he does not like.

A libel is either *criminative* or *vituperative*. By criminative, I mean such an one as charges a man with having done a specific act (determinable by time and place,) of the number of those that are made punishable by law. By *vituperative*, simply vituperative, I mean such an one as, without charging a man with any specific fact, does no more than intimate, in terms more or less forcible, the disapprobation in which the libeller holds the general conduct or character of the party libelled. Such are all those epithets of vague reproach, liar, fool, knave, wicked profligate, abandoned man, and so forth: together with all those compositions which in the compass of a line or of a volume intimate the same thing. A criminative libel therefore is one thing: a vituperative is another. The law knows not of these terms: but it acknowledges the distinction they are here intended to express.

Of these two, a libel of the criminative kind admits, we may observe, of another much more confined and determinate definition: a vituperative libel will admit of no other than that which is given above.

[619]Now then so it is, that for a libel simply vituperative, against a private person, the law will not let a man be punished by what is called an action to the profit of the party, unless it be under particular circumstances, which it is not here the place to dwell upon. But by imprisonment, or to the profit of the Crown, by what is called an indictment, or more especially what is called an information, it will let him be punished at the caprice, (for no rules are or can be laid down to guide discretion) at the caprice, I say, and fancy of the Judges. For a libel of the criminative kind, against a private person, the law will not let a man be punished, if the libeller can prove his charge to be a true one. But for a libel against a man in power, criminative or vituperative, true or false, moderate or immoderate, it makes a man punishable at all events, without distinction. If it be true, it is so much the worse; Judges, thinking to confound reasoning by paradox, have not scrupled to hazard this atrocious absurdity. The Judges of antiquity broached it long ago; succeeding Judges have adhered to it; present Judges, whose discernment cannot but have detected it, present Judges, as if borne down by the irresistible weight of authorities, recognize it; and it triumphs to this hour.[620]

This being the case, he who blames the proceedings of a man in power, justly or unjustly, is a libeller: the more justly, the worse libeller. But for blaming the proceedings of men in power, and as they think justly, never will the people of this country look upon a man as infamous. Lawyers may harangue, juries may convict; but neither those juries, nor even those lawyers will, in their hearts, look upon him as infamous.*[621]

The practical conclusion[622] resulting from this is, that the legislator ought never to oppose the public opinion by his measures, by endeavouring to fix a stain of ignominy upon an act of the description of those in question, which are equally liable to originate in the most virtuous as in the most vicious motives, and which consequently escape general reprobation.

But it is not less true, that in a very extensive class of cases, an argument addressed to the understandings and sentiments of the people, would,

---

*In 1758, Dr. Shebbeare, was pilloried† for writing a libel against the then King under a Whig administration. He stood in triumph. The people entertained him with applause. At another time, J. Williams, bookseller, was pilloried for publishing a libel against his Majesty George the Third, under an administration charged with Toryism: the people made a collection for him. At another time, W. Beckford, Lord Mayor of London, replied extempore, in an unprecedented and affrontive [sic] manner, to a speech from the throne: the citizens put up a statue in Guildhall. Shame did not then, I think, follow the finger of the law. [This last sentence is not included within the parallel note within Dumont's edition. *Théorie des peines*, vol. I, p. 375.

†2 Bur. 792. [This additional reference is not found within Dumont's edition.]

if properly applied, have some considerable effect, as well as on arguments addressed to their fears. If he thought the experiment worth trying, the legislator might do something by the opinion of his probity and his wisdom, and not be forced to do everything by the terror of his power. As he creates the political sanction so he might lead the moral. The people even in this country are by no means ill-disposed to imagine great knowledge where they behold great power. A few kind words, such as the heart of a good legislator will furnish without effort, will, if the substance of the law be not at variance with them, be enough to dispose the people to be not uncharitable in their opinion of his benevolence.

[623]Not that the legislator in our days, and in those countries which, on the subject of government, one has principally in view, ought to expect to possess altogether the same influence over the moral sanction as was exercised by the legislators of such small states as those of Greece and Italy in the first dawnings [sic] of society. The most prominent reason of this difference is, that in monarchical governments it is birth, and not any personal qualifications, that fix a man in this office. It is rare that the person in whose name laws are issued is the person who is believed to make them. It is one thing to make laws, and another to touch them with a sceptre.

[624]The Catherines and Gustavuses govern, and are seen to do so. Other Princes are either openly governed, or locking up their bosoms from the people—reign as it were by stealth.

In a mixed government like our's [sic], where the sovereign is a body, he has no personal character. He shows himself to the people only in his compositions, which are all that is known of him. By those writings he may doubtless give some idea of his character. But as his person is in a manner fictitious and invisible, it is not to be expected that the idea of his character should make so strong an impression upon the imagination of the people, as if they had the idea of this or that person to connect it with.

In the small states of Greece the business of legislation stood upon a very different footing. The Zaleucuses, the Solons, the Lycurguses, were the most popular men in their respective states. It was from their popularity, and nothing else, that they derived their title. They were philosophers and moralists as well as legislators: their laws had as much of instruction in them as of coercion: as much of lectures as of commands. The respect of the people has already placed the power of the moral sanction in their hands, before they were invested with the means of giving direction to the political. Members of a small state, the people of which lived as if they were but one family; they were better known to the whole people, for whom they made laws, than with us a member ordinarily is by the people of the country he is chosen for.

In those days, men seem to have been more under the government of opinion than at present. The word of this or that man, whom they knew and reverenced, would go further with them than at present. Not that their passions, as it should seem, were more obsequious to reason; but their reason was more obsequious to the reason of a single man. A little learning, or the appearance of it, gleaned from foreign nations, gave a man an advantage over the rest, which no possible superiority of learning could give a man at present. *Ipse dixit* is an expression that took its rise from the blind obsequiousness of the disciples of Pythagoras: and not ill characteristic of the manner of thinking of those who pretended to make any use of their thinking faculty throughout ancient Greece.*[625]

---

*Let me be permitted here to illustrate what has been said of the power possessed by ancient legislators, by a modern example, borrowed from what to some persons will appear a frivolous person. The legislator in question was a master of ceremonies. For a long series of years, by the authority of opinion, *Nash*, commonly called *Beau-Nash*, regulated at Bath, the conduct of the company assembled at that place during the season: sovereign arbiter [*sic*] and director of all points pertaining to the custom and etiquette of the place, of the order in which balls, concerts, &c. were to succeed each other. How did he go to work? "*Let such a thing be done*," said the legislator of the Bath Assemblies. "*Let not such a thing be done.*" "*Let such an Assembly take place on such a day: that it begin at such an hour, that it finishes at such an hour*," &c. &c. Setting aside the extreme disparity of the object, the resemblance is striking between these ordinances of fashion, and such laws of antiquity as have been handed down to us. There were no punishments properly so called. The company assembling met there, confiding in his prudence and experience in the concerns he had to regulate, put into his hands a certain quantity of the power of the moral sanction, and the public voice was ready to be raised against the infractors [*sic*] of his rules; and laws the weakest in appearance, were most strictly obeyed. [This note is not found within the manuscript. A version of it can be found within Dumont's edition, *Théorie des peines*, vol. I pp. 378–79.]

CHAPTER IV.
OF PECUNIARY FORFEITURES.[626]

We now come to consider the several kinds of Forfeitures, and first, the sorts of forfeiture that bear the name of pecuniary and *quasi*-pecuniary: forfeiture of money, and what is exchangeable for money.[627]

A pecuniary forfeiture is incurred when a man is, by a judicial sentence, compelled to pay a sum of money to another, or, as it is in some cases called, a fine.[628]

As to the methods which may be taken by the law to inflict a punishment of this sort; they are as follows:—

1. The simplest course is to take a sum of money,[629] to the amount in question, out of the physical possession of the delinquent, and transfer it into the physical possession of the person who is to receive it; after which, were he to meddle again with the money so taken, he would be punished just as if he had meddled with any other parcel of money that never was in his possession. This course can only be taken when it happens to be known that the delinquent has such a sum in his possession, and where it lies. But this is seldom the case.

2. The next and more common expedient is to take such and such a quantity of what other corporeal effects he may have in his physical possession as, if sold, will produce the sum in question, and to make sale of them accordingly, and bestow the produce as before.

3. Another expedient is, to make use of compulsive means to oblige him to produce the sum himself. These means will be either, 1st, the subjecting him to a present punishment, to be taken of as soon as he *has* done the thing required: 2d, the threatening him with some future punishment, to be applied at such or such a time in case of his *not* having done by that time the thing required.[630]

4. A fourth expedient is to take such property of his, whether in money or other effects, or whereof, though the legal right to them, or in a certain sense the legal possession of them, is in him, the physical possession is in other people. As the existence of such legal right, and the place here the effects in question are deposited, are circumstances that can seldom be known but by his means, this makes it necessary to apply compulsion to him to oblige him to give the requisite information.

Of these four expedients, the first and second commonly go together, and are put in practice indiscriminately at one and the same operation. The officer to whom the business is entrusted, if he finds money enough, takes money: if not, he takes other effects to make up the deficiency. The first then may, in future, be considered as included under the second.

In England, the second and the third have both of them been in practice from time immemorial: not indiscriminately however, but according to the name that has been given to the punishment by which the money has been exacted. When this punishment has been called a *fine*, the third method has been exclusively employed: when it has been called damages, the second and third have been employed together, not indeed in their full force, but under certain restrictions too particular to be here insisted on.

The fourth is comparatively of late invention. It was first applied to traders by one of the Bankrupt Laws,[631] and has since been extended by the Insolvent Acts to persons at large, where the obligation they are under to pay money bears the name of debt. Such is the case in many instances where that obligation is imposed in a view to punishment.[632]

SEC. II.—PECUNIARY FORFEITURES EXAMINED.

1. As to the evils produced by a punishment of this kind, they are all reducible to the *pain of privation* occasioned by the loss of so much money.*[633]

2. Pecuniary forfeiture shares with penal servitude in the striking advantage of being *convertible to profit*.[634]

The quantity of profit is not limited in this case as in that. This is its peculiar excellence; and this it is that adapts it particularly to the purpose of compensation.

3. In respect of *equality*, it is not less advantageous. No punishment can be made to sit more equally than this can be made to sit on different individuals; so as the quantum of it be proportioned to the means which the delinquent has of bearing it. For money (that is, the ratio of a given sum of money to the total sum of a man's capital) we have already shewn to be the most accurate measure of the quantity of pain or pleasure a man can be made to receive. The pleasures which two men[635] will be deprived of, by being made to lose each a given part (suppose a tenth) of their respective fortunes, will in *specie* perhaps be very different; but this does not hinder but that, on taking into the account quantity on the one hand and actual

---

*See Introd. To Morals and Legislation, Ch. 3. [This note does not appear within Dumont's edition.]

expectations and probable burthens [*sic*] on the other, they may be the same; they will be the same as nearly as any two quantities can be made to be so by any rule of measuring.[636] It is from his money that a man derives the main part of his pleasures; the only part that lies open to estimation. The supposition we are forced to follow is, that the quantities of pleasure men are capable of purchasing with their respective capitals are respectively equal. This supposition is, it must be supposed, very loose indeed, and inaccurate, because the quantity of a man's capital is subject to infinite fluctuations, and because there is great reason to suppose that a richer man is apt to be happier upon an average[637] than a poorer man. It is, however, after all nearer to the truth than any other general suppositions that for the purpose in question can be made.[638]

4. In point of *variability*, it is evident nothing can excel this mode of punishment, as far as it extends. It commences at the very bottom of the scale. In this respect it has greatly the advantage over corporal punishments, which are always complicated with a certain degree of infamy; while in the instance of pecuniary punishments, no other infamy is produced than what is necessarily attached to the offence.

5. In respect of *frugality*. Pecuniary punishment, especially when the relative quantum of it is great, is liable to a disadvantage which balances in some degree[639] against the advantage which it has of being convertible to profit. Along with the delinquent, other parties who are innocent are exposed to suffer; *to wit*, whatever persons were comprised within the circle of his dependents. This suffering is not the mere pain of sympathy, grounded on the observation of his suffering: if it were, there would be no reason for making mention of it as belonging in a more especial manner to the present mode of punishment. It is an original pain, produced by a consciousness of the loss which they themselves are likely to incur by the impoverishment of their principal. This evil again is not a mere negative evil; the evil which consists in the not being to have the comforts which had it not been for his impoverishment they would have had.[640] If it were, there could be no more reason for taking it into the account on this occasion than the pain of sympathy. For, whatever it be, it is balanced, and that exactly, by the pleasure that goes to those persons, whosoever they be, to whose profit the money is applied. The pleasure resulting from the use of that money is neither diminished nor increased by the operation: it only changes hands. The pain then, that is peculiar to this species of punishment, is neither more nor less than the pain of disappointment produced by the destruction of those expectations which the parties in question had been accustomed to entertain, of continuing to participate in the fortune of their principal, in a measure proportioned to that in which they had been accustomed to participate in it.[641]

6. In point of *exemplarity*, it has nothing in particular to boast of. At the execution of it, no spectacle is exhibited: the transfer of a sum of money on this account has nothing to distinguish it from the case of an ordinary payment. It is not furnished with any of those symbolical helps to exemplarity which belong to most punishments of the corporal kind. Upon the face of the description,[642] the exemplarity it possesses is in proportion to the quantum of it: that is, in the ratio of the quantum of the forfeiture to the capital of him whom it is to affect.[643]

There is one case, however, in which it is particularly deficient in this article. This is when it is laid on under the shape of costs. Upon the face of the law nothing occurs from whence any adequate idea can be drawn of what eventually turns out to be the quantum of the punishment.[644]

[645]7. In point of *remissibility* it is in an eminent degree advantageous.[646] Under no other mode of punishment can reparation be made for an unjust sentence with equal facility.

8. In point of *popularity* this punishment exceeds every other. It is the only one of any consequence against which some objection or other of the popular cast has not been made.[647]

In point of quantity pecuniary forfeitures are susceptible of varieties which may have considerable influence on their effects.

The quantum of such a forfeiture, as inflicted by statute or common law, may be either discretionary or indeterminate: or if determinate, it may be either limited or fixed; and in either case it may be determined, either absolutely or by reference. In the latter cases with regard to the standards by which it is determined, it would manifestly be in vain to attempt to set any bounds to their variety. The circumstances most commonly made choice of for this purpose are—1. The profit of the offence; 2. the value of the thing which is the subject matter of the offence; 3. the amount of the injury; 4. the fortune of the offender.[648]

In England a punishment of this kind is known in different cases by different names, which have nothing to do with the nature of the punishment (that is of the suffering) itself, nor essentially with the manner in which it is inflicted. They are taken only from the accidental circumstance of the manner in which the produce of the punishment is disposed of.

When this produce is given to the King or his grantee, the punishment being left unlimited by the legislature, after the quantum of it has been settled by a Judge, it is called Fine.

When, after being limited by the legislature, it has been settled by the Judge, the name employed to denote it by, howsoever applied, has commonly been the general term of Forfeiture.

When the *quantum* of it has been left unlimited by the legislature, and the produce of it given to a party injured by the offence, the punishment is called Damages. In this case the settling of the quantum has generally been committed to a jury.

SEC. III.—OF QUASI-PECUNIARY FORFEITURES.

By quasi-pecuniary forfeitures I mean the forfeitures of any kind of property that is not money, but is of such a nature as admits of its being exchanged for money.

The enumeration of the different species of property belongs more to a treatise upon civil law than to a work upon punishments. As many species of property, so many species of forfeiture.

The observations we have made upon pecuniary punishments may in general be applied to quasi-pecuniary punishment. The evil produced by their infliction may be estimated according to the pecuniary value lost; but there is one exception to be made with respect to objects possessing a value in affection. An equivalent in money will not represent any of the pleasures attached to these objects. The loss of patrimonial lands, of the house which has passed from father to son in the same family, ought not to be estimated at the price for which those lands or that house would sell.

Punishments of this kind are in general more exemplary[649] than pecuniary punishments. The confiscation of lands, of a manor, for instance, more visibly bears the marks of a punishment, attracts the attention of a greater number of persons than a fine of the same or of a greater value. The fact of the possession is a fact known through all the district: a fact of which the recollection must be recalled by a thousand circumstances, and perpetuated from generation to generation.

These considerations open a vast field for reflection, upon the use of confiscations of territorial property, especially in the case of those equivocal crimes called rebellions or civil wars. They perpetuate recollections which ought to be effaced. We shall recur to this subject when we speak of *Punishments misplaced.*—Book IV.

CHAPTER V.[650]
FORFEITURE OF CONDITION.[651]

W hen the property under consideration consists of a real tangible entity, as a house or lands, it presents itself under its most simple and intelligible shape: but when it is of an *incorporeal* nature, it can only be designated by abstract terms; and to explain those terms it is necessary to have recourse to those real entities[652] from which those fictitious entities derive their name and their signification. In order to explain the nature of any particular condition in life, for example that of husband,[653] it is necessary to state the right conferred upon him by the law, over the person, the property, and the services of an existent being—the woman to whom he is married. To explain the nature of *rank*[654] it is necessary to explain the rights that it confers—the exclusive privilege of using a certain title, of being habited in a particular manner, of being entitled to priority upon certain occasions; in short, to enjoy such honours as are attached to the particular rank in question. So far the effect produced is produced by the operation of the law. As to the honour itself, which is the source of their value, depends upon the moral sanction. It is, however, a species of property.[655] A man invested with a certain rank is entitled to receive from persons at large unexigible [*sic*] services, services of respect, and which will be generally rendered to him in consideration of his rank.[656]

In respect of *offices*, public offices, we may point out the power possessed by the person holding them over his subordinates, the emoluments that are attached to them, and the unexigible services that may result from the possession of them, that is to say, benefits resulting from the disposition that may be supposed to be felt by persons at large to render services to a man placed in an official station.

By the same process we may explain the nature of all rights; for example, the right of voting in a Parliamentary election. Every person in possession of this right has the privilege of giving a vote, by which he influences the choice of the person to be invested with a particular species of power. The value of this interest, under the present state of things, consists principally in giving the elector a certain power over the candidate and his friends. An honest and independent exercise of this right is a means of acquiring reputation. To generous and benevolent minds there also accrues from it a pleasure of sympathy, founded on the prospect of public happiness, that is to say, upon the influence that the choice of a virtuous and enlightened candidate may have upon the public welfare.

The value of a condition in life, of a right, of a privilege,[657] being explained to consist in power, profit, and reputation, that is to say, the pleasures resulting from the possession of it, we are in possession of all the necessary elements for estimating the evil accruing from their loss, or, in other words, the magnitude of the punishment occasioned by their forfeiture.[658]

To give an analytical view of all the modifications of which property is susceptible, and every species of forfeiture to which it may be exposed, would be a work of almost endless labour. We shall content ourselves here with giving a few examples, beginning with,

SEC. I.—THE MATRIMONIAL CONDITION.

The evils liable to be experienced by the husband from the forfeiture of this condition consist in the loss of the pleasures belonging to it.

1. The pleasures, which are the principal objects in the institution of marriage, may be divided into, 1st Pleasures of sense; and 2nd—Pleasures proceeding from the perception of an agreeable object, which depends partly on the senses, and partly on the imagination.

2. The innumerable minor pleasures of all kinds resulting from those inexigible services which belong to a husband's authority. Notwithstanding their variety, they may be all of them comprised under the head of pleasures of possession.

3. The pleasures resulting from the use of the property derived from the wife: these belong to the same head as the preceding.

4. Where the wife has separate property, over which a power of disposal is reserved to her, pleasure resulting from the hope of becoming possessed of this part of her property. Pleasure of expectation founded on the pleasures derivable from the possession of wealth.

5. The pleasure resulting from the persuasion of being beloved. This affection producing a variety of uncompellable [sic][659] services, which have all the charms of appearing to be spontaneous, as those that are the result of friendship. These pleasures may be referred to the pleasures of the moral sanction.

6. The pleasure resulting from the good repute of the wife which is reflected upon the husband, and which has a natural tendency, as honour derived from any other source, to conciliate to him the esteem and goodwill of persons in general. This may also be referred to the pleasures arising from the moral sanction.

7. The pleasure of witnessing her happiness, and especially that part of it which he is most instrumental in producing. This is the pleasure of benevolence or goodwill.

8. The pleasure resulting from the several uncompellable [*sic*] services received at the hands of the family of which he has become a member. This may be referred to the pleasures of the moral sanction.

9. The pleasure of power, considered generally, independently of any particular use that may be made of it, with which he is invested, in virtue of the exclusive controul [*sic*] he possesses over the fund for reward and punishment. This may be referred to the pleasures of the imagination.

10. The pleasure resulting from the condition of father. This we shall have occasion to notice in considering the evils resulting from the forfeiture of the condition of the father.

This same catalogue, with such slight variations, as the reader will find no difficulty in making, is applicable to the condition of wife.

The task of coolly analysing and classifying feelings of this nature may appear tedious, but it is not the less necessary if we would estimate the amount of evil resulting from the loss of this condition.[660]

SEC. II.—THE PATERNAL CONDITION.

The evils resulting from the forfeiture of the condition of father may be referred most of them to the loss of the following pleasures:—

1. The pleasures derived frown the imagining his own existence perpetuated in that of his child. This is a pleasure of the imagination.

2. The pleasure of having at his command, during the child's minority, the services that he may be in a condition to render. This is a pleasure of power.

3. The pleasure of employing, in so far as it can be done without diminution, the separate property of this child. This is a pleasure referable to two sources, that of father, and of guardian (of which presently).

4. The pleasure of filial affection, a pleasure of the moral sanction.

5. The pleasure reflected upon him by the good repute of his child. This also is a pleasure of the moral sanction.

6. The pleasure of advancing the happiness of his child: pleasure of benevolence or goodwill.

7. The pleasure derived from the several unexigible[661] services that he may hope to receive from the connections that his son, as he grows up, may form in the world. Pleasure of the moral sanction.

8. The pleasure resulting from the sentiment of paternal power. This is a pleasure of the imagination.

9. In some cases the pleasure derived from the expectation of becoming possessed of the whole or a part of the property the child may have acquired, or in case of his death the actual possession of such property. Pleasure in the one case of expectation founded on the pleasures derivable from the possession of wealth, in the other case from the actual possession of wealth.

SEC. III.—CONDITION OF CHILD.

Pleasures belonging to the condition of child:—

1. The pleasure derived from the use of the exigible services of the parent.

2. The pleasure resulting from the power of using certain parts of the property belonging to the father.

3. The pleasure resulting from the persuasion of being beloved by him.

4. The pleasure derived from the good repute of the father, which is reflected upon the child.

5. The pleasure of witnessing the father's happiness, and of contributing to promote it: a pleasure rendered more vivid by being accompanied with sentiments of gratitude.

6. The pleasure resulting from the connections of the father, and the right he may have to certain services at their hands.

7. The pleasure derived from the hope of inheriting the whole or a part of his father's property, or if he be dead, from the possession of the property.

SEC. IV.—PLEASURES DERIVED FROM THE CONDITION OF TRUSTEE.

The pleasures resulting from standing in the condition of trustee, are the following:—

1. The pleasure resulting from the hope of contributing to the happiness of the individual whose interest is in question. This is a pleasure of benevolence or goodwill.

2. The pleasure derived from the hope of the inexigible services to be expected from the gratitude of the individual in question. Pleasure of the moral sanction.

3. Pleasure founded on the hope of receiving inexigible services at the hands of persons benefited by the being entrusted with the use of the trust property. This also is a pleasure of the moral sanction.

4. Pleasure founded on the hope of sharing in the esteem, the goodwill, and the inexigible services of the different persons to whom his capacity

and probity in the management of the trust property may have become known. This is also a pleasure of the moral sanction.

5. When a salary is annexed to the duty: pleasure of pecuniary profit.

It is but too well known, that the pleasures respectively belonging to these conditions are liable to vanish, and at any rate to be alloyed by a corresponding set of pains. These pains are too obvious to need insisting on. The value of any such condition may therefore be either positive or negative; in plain terms, a man may either be the better for it or the worse. Where the value of it is positive, it will consist of the sum of the values of the several pleasures after that of the several pains had been deducted: when negative, as the sum of the value of the pains after that of the pleasure has been deducted. When therefore the value of any such condition happens to be negative, a sentence taking a man out of it, must needs operate not as a punishment but as a reward.

With regard to those pleasures or benefits which are common to several of the above conditions, it is manifest that, though the pleasure is in each of these several cases nominally the same, they are liable to be very different in point of value. Thus the pleasure of contributing to the happiness of the person who forms the other term in the relation, is incident to the condition of parent, and also that of a guardian: but it is more certain and more vivid in the case of the father than in that of the guardian. To engage, however, further in such details, besides their being so obvious, would lead us from the subject of politics to that of morals.

Let us now proceed to consider the manner in which the several forfeitures may be produced, or, as the case be, any part of them may be employed as an instrument of punishment.

The advantages of the conjugal condition may be substracted [*sic*] as a punishment by a judicial sentence, declaring that the offender is not, or shall not be any longer considered as the husband or wife of the person in question.

The consequence of such sentence would be, not completely to destroy the advantages of that condition, but to render them precarious.

If after this sentence has been pronounced they cohabit, or are suspected of cohabiting together, the woman is considered as a concubine. When this sort of connexion is known to subsist, it is in some countries punished by the moral sanction, in others, both by the moral and political.*

---

*By the laws of the State of Connecticut (North America) "If a man and woman who have been divorced shall again cohabit together as man and wife, they shall be punished as adulterers;" and "the punishment for adultery is discretionary whippings branding in the forehead with the letter A, and wearing a halter about the neck on the outside of the garments so as to be visible. On being found without the halter, on information and proof made before an assistant or justice of the peace, he may order them to be whipped not exceeding thirty stripes."—Swift's Laws of Connecticut, vol. ii, p. 328. [This note does not appear within Dumont's edition.]

By legal divorce, a man is also deprived in the whole or in part of the inexigible services derived from the right he has over the property of his wife, and especially of those services derived from cohabitation, it would make him dependant upon her with respect to the testamentary disposition over such part of her property of which she might have an absolute power of disposal.

With respect to the pleasures derivable from the relation of father, the law, it is true, cannot deprive a man altogether of the pleasures connected with this condition, but it may be greatly embittered; as, for example, by a retrospective sentence, declaring his children to be illegitimate. Upon those who might be born subsequent to the sentence of divorce, the punishment would fall with much greater certainty, for the public opinion, which would not be forward in supporting the degradation of children born under the faith of lawful wedlock, would not exercise the same indulgence towards those who were born after a divorce.

The paternal and filial condition may, in so far as the nature of the case admits of it, be in the same manner substracted by a judicial sentence, declaring that the offender is not, or shall no longer be considered as, the father or the son of the person in question.

The certain effects of a sentence of the kind in question, in respect of the father, would be to deprive him of all legal power over the person of his child: in respect of the child, to deprive him of taking by inheritance or representation the property of his father.

As to the other advantages derivable from these relations, the sentence may or may not have any effect, according to the feelings of the parties interested: its operation will depend upon the father and the son—upon their more immediate connections, and upon the public in general.

As to the office of guardian and other offices of a fiduciary nature, the sentence will operate to the whole extent of those offices: a legal interdiction of all the acts annuls all the advantages issuing from them.

It may at first sight appear extraordinary that a power should be attributed to the magistrate, of destroying relations founded in nature. It is, it may be observed, an event—an event that has already happened; and how can it be in the power of any human tribunal to cause that which has taken place, not to have taken place? This cannot be accomplished; but the magistrate may have power to persuade people to believe that an event has happened in a manner different from what it actually did happen. It is true that, upon the parties themselves, and upon the persons who have a direct knowledge of the fact, the power of the magistrate, as to this purpose, is altogether nugatory, but with the public at large an assertion so sanctioned would have the greatest weight. The principal obstacle to the exercise of any such power, however, is, that a declaration to this effect as a penal instrument would, upon the face of it, bear marks of its own falsehood. This is a dilemma from which there is no escaping. If the offender is not the father of the person in question, to declare that he is not is not an act of punishment: if he is his father, the declaration is false.

The idea of employing as a mode of punishment the subtraction of any of the rights attached to the several conditions as above, is not however so extravagant as at first might be imagined. If not the same thing, what approaches very near to it is already in use.[662]

This object may be effected in two modes; one, the endeavouring to cause it to be believed that the offender does not stand in the relation of father or of son, as the case may be, to the person regarded as such: the other is in endeavouring to cause it to be believed that from the non-observance of some legal form, the progeny is illegitimate.

A case somewhat analogous to this, is that famous one upon which so many volumes have been written—*corruption of blood*; or, in other words, the perfection of inheritable blood. The plain object, stripped of all disguise, is to prevent a man from inheriting, as he would have done if this punishment had not been pronounced: but what is endeavoured to be done by the help of this expression is, to cause it to be believed that the blood of the person in question undergoes some real alteration, which is a part of the punishment.

Another example in which, at least in words, a control is assumed over events of the description of those in question, is by that barbarous maxim that a *bastard is the son of no one*; a maxim which has a tendency, as much as it is in the power of words to give it, to deprive a man of all parental connexions. It is not, however, ever employed as a punishment.

Another example, opposite to the preceding one, is that other legal maxim, *pater est quem nuptiæ demonstrant*: a maxim by which sanction is frequently given to a palpable falsehood. By recent decisions, the severity of this rule has however been relaxed, it being now settled that though marriage is to be considered as presumptive proof of filiation [*sic*], it may be rebutted by evidence of the impossibility of any connexion having taken place.

In France, a mode of punishment has been employed which, it is true, without any such pretence as that of destroying the fact of parentage, endeavoured, as far as might be, to abolish all trace of it, by imposing on the person in question the obligation of changing his name.*

The same punishment has been employed in Portugal.†

The punishment, consisting in the forfeiture of credibility, is another example, no less remarkable, of an attempt to exercise a despotic control over the opinions of men. As part of the punishment for many sorts of

---

*This was done in the case of Damiens and Ravaillac.

†In the case of certain persons convicted of an attempt against the life of the King.

offences, which do not import any want of veracity, the offender is declared to have lost all title to credence: the visible sign of this punishment is the not being permitted to depose in a court of justice.

The forfeiture of the conjugal condition, at least to a certain extent, is frequently among the consequences of imprisonment, especially when with imprisonment is combined penal labour. This part of the punishment is not formally denounced, but it is not the less real. It is not ever in express terms declared that a man is divested of this condition; but he is in fact precluded from the principal enjoyments of it, and the condition separate from the pleasures that belong to it is evidently nothing more than a mere name. The forfeiture is temporary or perpetual, according as the imprisonment is either one or the other.

SEC. V.—CONDITION OF LIBERTY.

Liberty being a negative idea (exemption from obligation,) it follows that the loss of liberty is a positive idea. To lose the condition of a freeman is to become a slave. But the word slave or state of slavery, has not any very definite meaning which serves to designate that condition, as existing in different countries. There are some countries in which slavery is unknown. In countries in which slavery is in use it exists under different forms, and in different degrees. The pain of servitude would be different, according to the class to which the offender might be aggregated.

Slaves are of two classes—they may belong to the government or to individuals.

The condition of public slaves, determined by regulation, fixing the nature and amount of the work, and the coercive punishments by which the performance of it may be compelled, is not distinguishable from the condition of persons condemned for life to penal labour: if there exist no such regulations, it varies little from private slavery. A public slave, unprotected by any such regulations, is placed under the despotic controul of an overseer, who is bound to employ him, for the benefit of the public, in a certain sort of occupation: this power, arbitrary as it is, does not extend to life and death. This condition varies very little from that of private slavery. A negro, for example, employed upon a plantation belonging to the crown is not from this circumstance in a condition greatly superior to what he would be in if standing in the same relation to a private individual, who, instead of being his own overseer, employed an agent for that purpose.

The most ready means of forming a correct conception of the condition of slavery, is by considering it in the first instance as absolute and unlimited. In this situation the slave is exposed to every possible species of evil. The punishment designated then by the expression—forfeiture of liberty,[663] is no other than the being exposed to a greater or less chance, according to the character of the master, of suffering all sorts of evils: that is to say, of all evils resulting from the different modes in which punishment may be inflicted. To form an accurate notion of this situation, all that is required, is to glance the eye over all the possible varieties of punishment. The slave, with respect to the individual standing in the condition of master, is absolutely deprived of all legal protection.*

Such is the nature of slavery under its most simple form: such is the nature of the total deprivation of liberty. The different restrictions that may be imposed on the exercise of this power, renders the state of servitude more or less mild.[664]

There are then two heads to which the evils resulting from this condition may be referred.

1. The risk, on the part of the slave, of being subject to every possible evil: with the exception of such only as the master is expressly prohibited from inflicting. 2. The continuity of the pain founded on the apprehension of these sufferings.[665]

SEC. VI.—CONDITION OF POLITICAL LIBERTY.

I shall say but one word upon a subject that would require a volume.

The loss of political liberty is produced by a change in the condition: not merely of any particular individual, but of the whole community. The loss of liberty is the result of a fresh distribution of the power of the governing body; a distribution which renders the choice of the persons, or their measures, less dependant upon the will of the persons governed. A fresh distribution of power depends absolutely upon a corresponding disposition to pay obedience to that fresh distribution. When superior physical force is in the possession of those from whom obedience is demanded, it is evident that the power of commanding can be exercised only in so far as that obedience is rendered. As this disposition to pay obedience may be produced by the conduct of a single individual of the governing class, it may be, and has frequently been said, that a single man has destroyed the constitutional liberty of a whole nation. But if the analysis of such events be followed out, it will be found, that this liberty can be destroyed only by the people themselves.[666]

---

*Such a condition would be too rigorous for criminals: it is for innocent men that it is reserved.

CHAPTER VI.[667]
FORFEITURE OF THE PROTECTION OF THE LAW.[668]

A class of forfeitures as miscellaneous and extensive as any, and the last that we shall now take notice of, is that of the *protection*, whatever it be, that the law affords a man for the enjoyment of the objects of possession. This is not altogether the same thing with a forfeiture of the possessions themselves. In the instance of some of them, the law, by taking from him the possessions themselves, excludes him, by sure and physical means, from the enjoyment of them. In the instance of others, the law, without taking away from him altogether the physical capacity of enjoying them, punishes him in the case of his attempting to enjoy them. In the remaining cases, the law uses not either of those compulsive methods: it, however, does an act by which the parties on whose choice the enjoyment of the object in question depends, are disposed, on pre-established principles, to put an end to it. It therefore, in this case, likewise becomes still the author of the punishment. This is the case with the forfeitures in which the political sanction produces its effect: not by its own immediate energy, but by the motion it gives, if one may so say, to the moral and religious sanctions.

In the case of forfeiture of protection, the law takes no such active part. All it does is this. It simply withdraws in part, or altogether, that punishment by means of which it protects a possessor in the enjoyment of those several possessions. If then, every man refrain from disturbing him in the enjoyment of any such possession, it is well the law does nothing of itself to prompt them to it. But if any persons of their own notion choose to disturb him, it is also well the law does nothing of itself to hinder them. Forfeiture of protection is in short neither more nor less than the forfeiture of the use of the ministers of justice, that is, of such persons whose business it is to protect the several members of the community in the enjoyment of their respective rights.[669]

Between forfeiture of protection, and forfeiture of capacity, the difference is, that by the latter, the law *does* what is necessary to prevent a man's acquiring a possession: in the former, it *forbears* to do anything to prevent his losing it. When considered with reference to the individual who has forfeited the protection of the law, this species of punishment may be called forensic disability; it forms part of the artificially complex punishment of outlawry; the consideration of which will be subsequently resumed.*

---

*Book v. ch. v.

BOOK IV.
OF THE PROPER SEAT OF
PUNISHMENT: OR SAY,
OF MIS-SEATED PUNISHMENT.

WHAT is here meant by mis-seated punishment is *not* that which in another place was meant by groundless punishment.[671]

The case in which the epithet *groundless* was applied to the subject punishment, is that in which by the supposition there was no offence in the case, no act to which, by the annexation of eventual punishment, any such character as that of an offence ought, by the legislatures to have been superinduced [*sic*].

The case in which the epithet *mis-seated* is applied to the same subject, the case which on the present occasion is in view—is that in which there exists an offence, that is, an act fit to be, as above, converted into an offence—an act to which it is fit that punishment be accordingly attached, and in which case punishment is attached accordingly. Thus far all is right: but what there is wrong in the case consists in this, that punishment is to be found, which, *in consideration of the same offence*, has been attached to a *wrong* person: that some persons, one or many, are to be found on whom, in respect of that same offence, no punishment from which they could have been saved ought to have been attached, but on whom punishment, of some sort or other, from which they might have been saved, does notwithstanding stand attached.

When, in so far as by appointment of the legislator or of the Judge, acting (as in all cases of unwritten or judge-made law) in the place of the legislator, punishment is inflicted on any person by whom no part has been borne in the offence, it may be said to be mis-seated: seated in a place which is not its proper place.

In this case, if along with the non-offender, no offender suffers, the mis-seated punishment may be, as in practice it has been termed, *vicarious*: if in the contrary case, extravasated [*sic*] punishment—that is, flowing in a wrong channel.

Punishment ought naturally to be the work of reflection: but whether it be vicarious or extravasated, should there be found an instance in which the infliction of it appears to have been the result, not so much of reflection and thought, as of want of thought, (and the mass of such instances will be found but too extensive) in such case it may be termed *random* punishment.

Punishment (which is mis-seated, and in particular that which is in an extravasated state), may be so unavoidably or avoidably.[672]

First, as to the case in which the extravasation [*sic*] is unavoidable. On another occasion, in another work, and for another purpose, this case has already been brought to view: viz. under the head of *"Circumstances influencing sensibility.**

Whether in the way and for the purpose of punishment, or in any other way, and for any other purpose, a man cannot be made to suffer, but his connections, if he have any—always his connections in the way of sympathy, frequently his connections in the way of interest, (understand self-regarding interest) are made to suffer along with him: and forasmuch as it can only be by some rare accident, that a man can be found, who has not in either of those ways any connections; thence it follows, that if where it is unavoidable, the certainty or probability of its extravasation were regarded as a sufficient cause for forbearing to inflict punishment, it would only be by a correspondently rare accident, that any thing could be done for the prevention of offences of any sort; the consequence of which would be general impunity to crimes and other offences of all sorts, and with it the destruction of society itself.

In so far as it is mis-seated, and is not unavoidably so, punishment, it is almost needless to observe, is, with reference to the person on whom it is thrown, *groundless*: as such it is thrown away: it is so much evil expended in waste:—reformation, determent, disablement—it contributes not any thing to any one of the proper ends of punishment; not so much as to vindictive satisfaction for injury, at least to any mind that is not more or less deranged; it is repugnant to utility, inconsistent with humanity, inconsistent with justice.[673]

To all these it is repugnant; but what it is not repugnant to, is English law, written as well as unwritten; for under both these dispensations, instances of it are to be found—instances altogether deplorable in extent as well as abundance.

When the epithet *unavoidable* is on this occasion, employed, some such limitative clause as is expressed by the words *without preponderant inconvenience* must be understood. For, in point of possibility, punishment, i.e. the infliction of suffering on that score, being on the part of the legislator and the Judge an act of the will, to avoid inflicting it will on this as on every other occasion, be respectively in their power at all times, not only on this but on every occasion. On so simple a condition as that of seeing government, and with it society itself, perish, you may avoid inflicting punishment altogether.

---

*Introduction to Morals and Legislation. [This reference is to *IPML*, ch. 6]

Bearing continually in mind this necessary and not unobvious limitation, in answer to the question, what, in regard to mis-seated punishment, ought to be the conduct of the legislator, two simple propositions may be laid down without difficulty.

1. One is—Where it is unavoidable, mis-seated punishment may be employed.

2. Where it is avoidable, mis-seated punishment ought in no case to be employed.

Unhappily there exists not a system of established law which does not exhibit instances in which mis-seated punishment is thus wrongfully employed.[674]

First, as to the case when the application thus made of the matter of punishment is unavoidable: not to be avoided without letting in, in some other shape, evil in such a quantity, as after deduction made of the evil saved on the score of punishment, shall leave a net balance on the side of evil upon the whole.

Now, taking the matter on the footing of the principles of utility, punishment, however mis-seated, not only may be, but ought to be introduced: and on the part of him by whom that principle is embraced, and taken for his constant guide, to say that of punishment so circumstanced that it ought not to be introduced, would be equivalent to a contradiction in terms.

But, says an objector, punishment in so far as it is inflicted falls upon the guiltless, and to inflict punishment on the guiltless is to violate one of the most important, and fundamental, and universally recognized principles of justice.

The answer is—this being one of those principles which in substance are continually alluded to, but which in truth are not any where to be found, cannot with propriety be employed in the character of an objection to any rule which, standing expressed in a determinate form of words, is seen to be unexceptionable.

To inflict punishment when, without introducing preponderant inconvenience, the infliction of such punishment is avoidable, is, in the case of the innocent, contrary to the principle of utility. Admitted:—and so is it in the case of the guilty likewise.

To punish where, without introducing preponderant inconvenience, such punishment, is unavoidable, is not in either case contrary to the principle of utility:—not in the case of the guilty: no, nor yet in the case of the innocent.

What then are the cases in which the application of punishment to the innocent is avoidable? What the cases in which it is unavoidable?

Answer. Wheresoever, punishment not being, in the case in question, in itself undue, it is in your power to apply to the guilty punishment as great a quantity as (supposing it actually administered) is commensurate to the end of punishment—namely, without having recourse to the innocent, there the evil, whatsoever it be, that would be produced by the infliction of punishment on the innocent is avoidable.[675]

Now the fact is, and so it will be found, that (with the exception of such suffering as extravasates [sic] and overflows upon the innocent, in consequence of their connexion in the way of sympathy or particular and casual interest) wheresoever the nature of the case admits of the distinguishing who is innocent from who is guilty, the infliction of suffering on the innocent is avoidable.

Define punishment in a certain way, and even the above limitation need not be made. Say that to give it the character of punishment, it is necessary that the suffering that is inflicted should, the whole of it, be directly intentional; that is, either mediately [sic] or ultimately intentional; and in that case, such part of the suffering as, in virtue of their connexion with the guilty person, falls unavoidably upon third persons (a wife or husband, children, relations, dependants, friends or creditors, and so forth) is not punishment—does not come under the denomination of punishment.

This, however, is but a question of words. Take any lot of evil you will, such as it is, it is, whatsoever be its name. Say that it *is punishment*, the reason for avoiding to produce it, if unavoidable, will not be the stronger; say that it is *not* punishment, the reason for avoiding to produce it, if avoidable, will not be the weaker.[676]

SEC. I.[677]—NATURALLY EXTRAVASTING PUNISHMENT.—RULES CONCERNING IT.

In regard to such punishment as comes under the denomination of derivative or naturally extravasating punishment, the following seem to be the rules that may be laid down.

1. The consideration that the lot of punishment in question comes under the denomination of derivative or extravasating punishment—punishment overflowing upon the guiltless from the guilty—can never of itself constitute a sufficient reason for forbearing to inflict such punishment.

For were that a sufficient reason, punishment could not, in the way of legislation, be appointed in any case.

2. In so far as punishment not coming under this denomination is capable of being inflicted to a sufficient amount, without the addition of any punishment which comes under this denomination, in other words, in as far as properly seated punishment to a sufficient amount is capable of being inflicted without the addition of derivative or extravasating punish-

ment, no such addition ought by the legislator to be appointed, viz. either prescribed or authorized.

3. For so far as, without prejudice to the sufficiency of the remainder, the lot of punishment actually to be inflicted is capable of being cleared of derivative or extravasated punishment (punishment or suffering borne by those who have had no share either in the commission of the offence or in the benefit of the offence)—such clearance ought always to be made.

4. In the account taken of the suffering for the purpose of any punishment which is about to be inflicted by the Judge, such derivative suffering ought always to be comprised: comprised, in the first place, in respect of what it is in itself and of itself; in the next place, in respect of the pain which, if inflicted on the innocent connexions of the guilty person, it may be expected to produce, viz. in the shape of a pain of sympathy, in the bosom of the guilty person himself.

5. Accordingly, in the case of a delinquent having such connections, to the end that the *real* quantity of punishment may not be greater than in the case of a delinquent in the same degree of delinquency having no such connections, the *nominal* may be,—and so far as the deduction is capable of being made with sufficient precision, ought to be,—made by so much the less.

6. For the purpose of making any such allowance as may be requisite on this score, proceed thus: In the first place, settle with yourself what would be a sufficient punishment, on the supposition that the delinquent had no connexions: then, enquiring into such connexions, if any, as he has, proceed to make such abatement, if any, as may be requisite on this score.

7. For any such purpose, the view of the Judge must not absolutely confine itself to the connexion itself, the outward and visible sign and presumptive evidence of the internal and invisible sympathy, viz. the fact that the delinquent has a wife, has children, has other persons in his dependence. Of the existence of the degree of sympathy naturally and usually attached to the species of relationship in question, the existence of the relationship itself may, it is true, be received in the character of *primâ facie* or presumptive evidence. Such evidence as, in default of evidence to the contrary, may be taken for conclusive.

But supposing any such contrary evidence to be offered, or to be capable of being, without preponderant inconvenience, collected, such presumptive evidence as above mentioned ought not to be taken and acted upon as if conclusive.

If for example it appear that in consequence of ill usage inflicted by him, his wife has been separated from him, it is not right that, on that account, he should be let of with a less punishment, merely because he has a wife: if it appear that, in consequence of ill usage, or desertion, or neglect, on his part, children of his have been taken in hand and provided for by some relation or private friend, or some public institution, it is not right that, merely because he has children, he should be let off with a less punishment, as above.

8. In so far as it is in the nature of the punishment to extract and provide any quantity of matter applicable to the purpose of compensation, the legislator and the Judge, respectively acting within their respective spheres, ought not, in the care taken by them to avoid the production of unnecessary mis-seated punishment, to confine themselves to negative measures.

If, for example, either by the general nature of the appointed punishment, imprisonment, for example, or banishment, or death, a separation is made, or to the purpose in question, by special appointment, can be made, between the lot of the delinquent and the lot of his guiltless connexions, it may be right, out of and to the extent of the pecuniary means of the delinquent, to make a provision for his guiltless connexions.

9. In other words. So far as can be done, without reducing to too low a pitch the suffering inflicted on the delinquent, the claims of any guiltless connexion of his, to be saved harmless from such mis-seated punishment, as would otherwise be made to overflow upon them from the punishment inflicted upon him, should have the preference over the interest of the public purse.

This rule may, without reserve or difficulty, be in its full extent applied to ordinary creditors, to persons whose connexion with the delinquent is accordingly a connexion purely in the way of interest, unaccompanied with any such connection as in the case of wife and children, or other near relatives, has place in the way of sympathy. For example, to speak particularly and precisely, on the score and for the purpose of punishment, money extracted from the pocket of a delinquent ought not to be poured into the public purse, such sum excepted as, if any, remains to be disposed of, after satisfaction of all just and *bona fide* demands made, or capable of being made, by creditors.

SEC. II.—PUNISHMENT APPARENTLY, BUT NOT REALLY MIS-SEATED—CIVIL RESPONSIBILITY.[678]

One class of cases may be marked out in which a punishment to which it may happen in appearance to be mis-seated is not mis-seated in reality. The offence is committed by A, who is a person under power; the punishment is inflicted on B, in whom the power resides. In other words, the super ordinate [*sic*] is made responsible for the subordinate.

To this class of cases may be aggregated the following:

Responsibility of
{
the husband for the wife.
the father for the children.
the guardian for his ward.
the madman's keeper for madman.
the gaoler for prisoners.
the sheriff for the gaoler.
the military commander for
subordinates.
the master for his servants.
}

In all these cases, though to appearance the punishment may be misseated, yet in point of fact the punishment is inflicted on the person having the power, not under the notion of innocence on his part, but in contemplation of delinquency on the score of negligence for an ill choice of, or want of attraction to, his subordinates. It is on his part a transgression of the negative cast, consisting in the omitting to take proper precautions for the prevention of the positive offence committed by his subordinates.[679]

Under our law, the sheriff is punished if any of the prisoners under the gaoler's custody escape. The sheriff has not the immediate custody of the prisoners; his other duties are incompatible with that. From this circumstance alone then there is no reason for supposing any complicity on his part. But the gaoler is appointed by him; and the object of the law is to render him circumspect, in his choice. The gaoler himself is the person immediately responsible, but as the safe custody of prisoners is a matter of the highest importance, the punishment levelled at the sheriff is in the highest degree expedient, and the more so as the amount of it is in certain cases left to the discretion of the Judge.

The responsibility thus imposed on superiors for the acts of their subordinates is founded not only on the reasons above mentioned, but on others equally substantial, which have been more particularly developed in another work.*

SEC. III.—MIS-SEATED PUNISHMENT, VARIETIES OF.

Punishment is mis-seated in either of two cases 1. Where the delinquent himself is not made to suffer at all, but some other is in his stead.—2. When the delinquent himself is punished and some other guiltless person with him in virtue of an express provision by law.

---

*Traités de Legislation, tom. ii, p. 362. [This subject also is given a much more thorough and detailed treatment in *IPML*, ch. 16, para. 34–55.]

If the delinquent himself is not punished, but some other person is in his stead, the punishment may be called vicarious punishment. It is thus that in the case of a suicide, who is of course removed beyond the reach of human punishment, suffering is inflicted on his wife, his children, or his dependants.

When in virtue of a social connexion between the delinquent and some other person, it passes from the delinquent upon that other, it may be stiled *transitive punishment*. It is thus that in our law the children and other descendants in many cases are punished with their parents, for the delinquencies of their parents and other ancestors.

Where a large body of persons are punished at once, upon a presumption that the delinquent or delinquents are to be met with in that body, it may be stiled *collective punishment*. Thus it is, in our law, corporations are in several cases punishable for the delinquencies of the co-corporators [*sic*].

Lastly, where along with the delinquent a person is punished who is a total stranger to him; the punishment in this case may, as far as the stranger is concerned, be stiled *random punishment*. Thus it is that by our law a person who, after certain acts of delinquency secretly committed, has bought land of the delinquent, loses his money and the land.

Punishment by lot, as is sometimes practised where the delinquents are numerous, as in large bodies of soldiery, comes not within this case. The persons who are made to cast lots are all supposed to be delinquents. There is therefore, no punishment but what is *in propriam personam* in this case. It is not random *punishment*, but random *pardon*.

In *vicarious punishment*, we see it is a third person, as the phrase is, that is punished alone. In *transitive punishment*, a third person with the delinquent in virtue of his connection with him. In *collective punishment*, a large body of third persons, uncertain and indeterminate, because probably the delinquent is of the number. In *random punishment*, a single third person, who, for certain is not the delinquent, and with whom the delinquent has nothing to do.

SEC. IV—VICARIOUS PUNISHMENT.

The case in which punishment is in the most palpable degree mis-seated, is that in which it has received the name of *vicarious*: Upon the person who has had any share in the offence, no punishment is inflicted, yet upon the same occasion, punishment is inflicted upon this and that person, who has not had any share in the offence.

In the reign of James I, there lived a Sir Kenelm Digby, who besides being a person of quality, was an adept in the science of medicine. Dressing of wounds is among the number of those operations that are attended with pain and trouble. By means of a powder of Sir Kenelm's invention, this inconvenience was saved. In addition to this powder, all that he required for the cure of the most desperate wound, was a little of the blood that had been made to flow from it. To this blood a competent dose of the powder being applied, the wound closed, and the cure was radical. The presence of the patient was no more necessary, than to our present quack doctors. While the compound of powder and blood, was lying upon Sir Kenelm's shelves the patient might be at the antipodes.

Exactly of a piece with the therapeutics that invented this *sympathetic powder,* for such was the name which by the author was applied to it, are the politics that gave birth to vicarious punishment.

I was about to exhibit the absurdity and mischief of this mode of punishment, but what end would it answer? A simple statement, that one man is punished for the offence of another, is calculated to produce a stronger impression on the mind, than could be produced by the aid of logic and rhetoric. An error so extravagant could never have been acted on, but from confusion of ideas, or upon suppositions, the improbability of which was altogether lost sight of.[680]

In the English law, the only instance which is to be seen of a case of mis-seated punishment, which is clearly and palpably vicarious, is that of the punishment attached to suicide. It may perhaps be said, that the man himself is punished as much as the case will admit of; that his body used to be pierced with a stake, that he is still buried with ignominy, and that with respect to him, everything that could be done, is done; that this is not found sufficient, and that as an additional check to the commission of this offence, it is necessary to call in aid the contemplation of the sufferings that his wife and children may endure by his death. But the effect of this contrivance is obviously very trifling. The prospect of the pain he shall suffer by continuing to live, affects him more than that of the pain it seems to him they will suffer upon his putting himself to death. He is more affected then with his own happiness than with theirs. The selfish predominate in his mind over the social affections. But the punishment of forfeiture, that is the punishment of those relations and friends, can have the effect of preventing his design upon no other supposition, than that the social affections are predominant in him over the selfish, that he is more touched by their suffering than by his own; but this is shewn [*sic*] by his conduct not to be the case.

Nor is this all; it is not only nugatory as to its declared purpose, but in the highest degree cruel. When a family has thus been deprived of its head, the law at that moment steps in to deprive them of their means of subsistence.

The answer to this may be, that there is some species of property, which upon this occasion is not forfeited, that the law is not executed, that the Jury elude it, by finding the suicide to be insane, and that, moreover, the King has the power of remitting the forfeiture, and of leaving to the widow and orphans the paternal property.

That such is the disposition of Juries, and of the Sovereign is undeniable: but is that a reason for preserving in the penal code, a law that it is considered a duty invariably to elude? And by what means is it eluded? By perjury. By a declaration made by twelve men, upon oath, that the suicide was deranged in his mind, even in cases in which all the circumstances connected with the case exhibit marks of a deliberate and steady determination. The consequence is, that every suicide who dies worth any property, is declared to be *non compos*. It is only the poorest of the poor, who, after making the same calculation that was made by Cato, and, finding the balance on the same side, act accordingly, that are ever found to be in their senses, and their wives and children to be proper victims for the rigour of the law. The cure for these atrocious absurdities is perjury: perjury is the penance, that at the expense of religion, prevents an outrage on humanity.[681]

In speaking of vicarious punishment,[682] in order to avoid the confusion that might be produced by its liability to be ranked under this head, it may be necessary to mention a case belonging to the subject of international law. The case of reprizals [*sic*] in war. By a foreign nation, innocent persons are subjected to the most rigorous punishment—to confinement, and even to death, the real author of the offence not being in the jurisdiction of the foreign state. The exercise of this power is justified by necessity, as a means of preventing the infliction of injuries not warranted by the rules of war.[683]

This is not strictly speaking vicarious punishment. The reprizals inflicted on his subjects, operate upon the Sovereign himself, either by the compassion felt for their suffering, or by the fear, if patiently submitted to, of alienating the affections of his people. It is more particularly useful between contending armies. Honour is the principal sanction of the laws of war, but the power of making reprizals is a very necessary coadjutor. In these cases, what humanity dictates, is, that the sufferings inflicted on the innocent should be the least possible, consistent with the production of the desired effect, that they should be remissible, and that the utmost degree of publicity should be given to them, either by public declarations or in any other more effectual manner.[684]

One word more, and I have done. Instances have not been wanting in history, when an innocent person has offered to satiate the resentment of the person injured, and his self-devotion has been received in expiation. What satisfaction did the offended person reap from this sacrifice?—the degradation and shame belonging to it. The glory of the sufferer was the disgrace of the Judge.

It may be asked. Is it possible to find any case in which one person may, with propriety, be allowed spontaneously to subject himself to the punishment designed for another—a son for his father—a husband for his wife—a friend for his friend. Such cases might perhaps be imagined, but it is useless to enter upon the consideration of such deviations from the ordinary course of things.

SEC. V.—TRANSITIVE PUNISHMENT.

It has already been observed, that it is the nature of all punishments, to affect not only those that are the immediate objects of them, but also those that are connected with the offender, in the way of sympathy, and their participation in his suffering is unavoidable. With these we have nothing to do. What we have to do with are those that the legislator by an express provision of the law inflicts upon persons connected with the delinquent—punishments, the existence of which depends entirely upon the legislator, and which, as he has created, he can abrogate them. Thus under the English law, with respect to property of a particular description, the innocent grandson, by the delinquency of his father, is made to lose the chance he had of succeeding to his grandfather, because no title can be deduced through the corrupt blood of the father: this is what, by English lawyers, is called *corruption of blood.**

The strength of the argument lies in the metaphor: this cabalistic expression serves as an answer to all objections; the justice of the metaphor turns upon two suppositions.

The one is, that where a man has committed a felony,[685] (stolen a horse for instance) his blood immediately undergoes a fermentation, and, (according to the system of physiology in use upon this occasion) becomes really corrupt.

The other is, that when a man's blood is in this state of putrescency [*sic*], it becomes just and necessary to deprive his children not only of all

---

*As the subject is involved in a good deal of obscurity, it may be necessary, in order that the expediency of this mode of punishment may be understood, to state the nature of it a little more explicitly. [This part of the note does not appear within Dumont's edition.]

By a rule of positive law, founded on the most obvious dictate of utility, so obvious as to have been received with little variation over the whole world, a man is permitted to succeed in case of death to the property undisposed of by his next relation.

This general rule is, with a variety of caprice, with which the conceptions and expectations of the people can never keep pace, differently narrowed and modified by the different laws of various States. With us it is not in every instance that a man is permitted to succeed to his relation. And the misery produced by the unintelligible exceptions to the general provision of the law, is in all cases, in proportion to the strength of the expectation that is thus disappointed.

Forfeiture is more penal in its consequences than escheat. By both forfeiture and escheat, an individual and his descendants are made to lose their chance of coming to the estate of him,

real property, of which he was in the enjoyment, but of what might thereafter be derived through him.[686]

The end of punishment, is to restrain a man from delinquency. The
question is, whether it be an advantageous way of endeavouring at this, to
punish in any, and what cases, in any, and what mode, to any, and what
degree, his wife, his children, or other descendants; that is, with a direct
intention to make them sufferers.

If a man can be prevented from running into delinquency, by means of
punishment hung over the heads of persons thus connected with him, it is
not, as in the cases above-mentioned, because it is expected that they
should have it in their power to restrain him, by any coercion, physical or
mental, of their imposing. It is not that they are likely to have it in their
power, by anything they can *do*. In the case of the wife, it is not very likely:
in the case of children already born, it is still less likely: in the case of children not yet born, it is impossible. What is expected to work upon him, is
the image of what they may be made to *suffer*. The punishment then upon
theme may be, and it is expected it will be, without any act of theirs, a punishment upon him. It will produce in him a pain of sympathy.

First, we will consider the case of the wife, where the punishment consists in being made to lose what is already in specific prospect: viz. The
immoveable property in which she had her dower.

It has been doubted whether it were possible for a man to love another
better than himself; that is to be affected, not merely momentarily, but for
a length of time together, more by the pains and pleasures of another than
by his own. Some have denied the possibility, all will admit that it is
extremely rare. Suppose it then to happen in one case out of five hundred,
and to do all possible honour to the marriage state, let us suppose that this

---

to whom they stood as next immediate descendants. But corruption of blood goes further. By
corruption of blood, the party in question, and his descendants, are made to lose the chance
they had of succeeding either to a remote ancestor, or to any collateral relation.

Offenses by which the blood is said to be corrupted, are stiled [*sic*], how different soever
[*sic*] in their nature, by one common appellation, felonies.—Between my brother and me, the
common ancestor is my father.—If then, my father commit a felony, the consequence is, I am
prevented from succeeding not only to whatever real property was my father's, but to whatever was my brother's also, or that of any one descended from him: and this, because in
making out my title to the property in question, in virtue of any relationship to my brother, I
must reckon through my father, although my father (such is the provision made by the law)
could not himself have taken it. Between my paternal uncle and me, the common ancestor is
my grandfather. If then my father commit a felony, I lose the chance of succeeding, not only
to whatever real property was his, but also to whatever was either my grandfather's or my
uncle's. So also if my grandfather commit a felony, I lose the chance of succeeding not indeed
to the property that was my father's, but however, to whatever was either my grandfather's, or
my uncle's, or any descendant of my uncle's.

person whom a man loves better than he does himself, is never any other than his wife. But it is not so many as half the number of men of an age to commit crimes, that have wives. Nor is there above one in a hundred who has lands of which a wife is endowed. Upon this calculation, there is not above one man in 50,000 of those that are liable to this mode of punishment, on whom it would operate in as great a degree as if laid on himself. In the remaining 49,999 instances, in order to produce the same effect, more punishment must be laid upon the innocent wife, than would need to be laid upon the offending husband. Let us suppose, for the purpose of the argument, that every man loves his wife half as much as he does himself, on this supposition, ten degrees or grains (or by what other name soever [*sic*] it shall be thought proper to call so many aliquot parts of punishment, must be laid upon the wife, in order to produce) the effect of five grains laid directly upon the husband. On this supposition, then in 49,999 out of 50,000, half the punishment that is laid on in this way, is laid in waste.*

What has been said with regard to the wife, may, without any very considerable variation, be applied to the children. In this latter case, however, generally speaking, the affection is likely to be more uniform and certain, and consequently the contemplation of the suffering they may be exposed to more certainly effacious [*sic*], in restraining the commission of the act intended to be guarded against. The same method, making due allowance on this score, will therefore apply to this, as to the preceding case.

What follows from this, therefore, is that till the whole stock of direct punishment be exhausted upon the offender himself none ought in this way to be attempted to be applied through the medium of the innocent.

[687]If there is any case in which forfeiture can be employed with advantage, it would be that of *rebellion*. Rebellion, not treason, for treason is a name applied to a variety of offences that have nothing in common but their name. And if it were employed against the descendants of a rebel, it should not be in the way of transitive punishment, nor in the way of punishment at all, but as a measure of self-defence:[688] of self-defence against the mischief that might be expected, not from the criminal who is no more, but from his dependants. When the husband is engaged in rebellion, it is probable that the affections of his wife† are enlisted on the same side. Is it certain? By no means. But, however, it is probable. Is it probable that so also are his children? Is it certain? By no means. All rebellions, and particularly the last

---

*It will not, it is hoped, be understood that any stress is meant to be laid upon the particular number here employed: the reader may put in numbers for himself: they are merely given as a specimen of the manner in which such an enquiry ought to be conducted.

†Those who have read Lord Clarendon's History, will remember what grievous complaints that historians, in speaking of the Duke of Albemarle, makes of the Duke's Presbyterian wife. [This reference does not appear within Dumont's edition.]

Scotch rebellion, afford instances to the contrary. But, however, it is probable. What then should be done? Presume guilt, and make it require an effort to exempt the party from the consequences? No, but presume innocence, and make it require an effort on the part of the Crown to afflict him. Let the Crown be empowered immediately upon the attainder of a rebel, to seize into its hands the possessions, real as well as personal, of his wife, his children, and his other descendants too; with a power to continue the seizure from year to year upon special mention of each person, in so many proclamations to be issued for that purpose: and this too, property, under whatever title it might be held, without suffering the law, as it is now, to be turned into a dead letter, by expedients for giving to property such modification as to render it unforfeitable. This would be a remedy exactly analogous to the suspension of the *Habeas Corpus Act*: putting the near kindred of a convicted rebel upon the same footing, with respect to their fortunes, which by that Act all men without distinction are put upon, with respect to their liberties. This would be a certain, not a casual safeguard, giving strength to the Government, without bringing guiltless oppression upon the people.[689]

State crimes, with treason at the head of them, may issue from various sources: from indigence, from resentment, from ambition; but in many instances they are crimes of conscience. By lawyers in this country, it is spoken of as one of those almost incredible abominations, at which nature shudders: like murder, not to be committed by any man, but one who has sold himself to the devil. They see not, or would not seem to see, that the character of rebel or of loyalist, turns upon the accidents of war: that men may differ with the most perfect integrity, and with the purest intentions about the title to the Crown, or to such a branch of public power, as well as about a town, or a piece of land; and that it is only party prejudice that makes rebellion and wickedness synonymous. But in those difficult and distracted times, when right and duty are liable to lie confounded, the Hydes, the Falklands, the Seldons, and the Hampdens divide themselves: who can read the recesses of their hearts; men enlist front pure motives in the worse, and from sordid in the better cause. Now, when conscience is the motive, it is always probable that the same conscience which governs the principal may govern the dependants, or in other words, the same that governs the husband and the father, may govern the wife whom he cherishes and the children whom he educates. Rebellion then, is a family offence.

That treason, however, which consists in secretly conspiring in a united nation with a foreign enemy, stands upon a very different footing. This is always among offences against conscience. It can scarcely arise even from personal resentment: it arises from the most sordid of all sources— lucre. Every one acknowledges the baseness of such a crime; and a man could scarcely be more detested by the public at large, than he would be if discovered by his own family. This is no more a family offence than robbery or murder are family offences. In this kind of offence, therefore, there is not the same reason for casting the family upon the mercy of the crown. Whatever the family suffers is endured without reason and in waste.[690]

SEC. VI.—DISADVANTAGES OF THIS MODE OF PUNISHMENT.[691]

From what has been said, except in the above case of rebellion, it will be pretty apparent that in point of *certainty* this mode of punishment is eminently deficient. In by far the greater number of cases in which the offence has been committed, this punishment cannot take place for want of a subject on which to operate. A man that has no wife or children, cannot be punished in the persons of his wife and children. Couple this circumstance with the cases in which the offender will have nothing to forfeit, and it will be found that the punishment will be inoperative in nine hundred and ninety-nine cases out of a thousand. Now a punishment that is good in one case only out of a thousand is good for nothing. Some other punishment then must be adopted in its room. This punishment must be as much as is enough in those cases, otherwise there had as good be none. Now then as that punishment serves in all other cases, why may it not in this one? If it is enough in those cases, it is, when added to the particular punishment in question, more than enough in this one. Now then, if it is more than enough, it is misery in waste. It is, therefore, for the most part useless, and whenever it is not useless, it is mischievous.

2. After this it is saying little to observe, that in respect of *equability* it is not less defective, because, to a man who has no thought about his wife or children, or has taken a dislike to them, it is at least matter of indifference to him whatever may befall them; in this therefore the punishment of them is so much clear waste.

3. In respect of *Frugality* it is in a very remarkable degree defective, the quantity of evil that it is susceptible of producing is altogether boundless. Consider the chain of domestic connection, and calculate the number of descendants that a man may have; the suffering communicates from one to another, and destroys the peace of the most extensive families. To produce a direct punishment, which may be estimated as unity, indirect and mis-seated punishment must be created equal to ten, twenty, thirty, a hundred, or perhaps, a thousand, &c.

4. It is no less deficient in point of *exemplarity*. What the delinquent himself suffers is known always by the sentence, it is in many cases visible

in the execution. The woman or the child who is made to suffer for his crime, languishes in secret and unavailing misery.

5. The punishment thus withdrawn from its natural course, possesses not so much as the advantage of *popularity*; it is directly adverse to the general sentiments of sympathy and antipathy. When the delinquent himself is punished, the public vengeance is satiated, and receives no satisfaction from any ulterior punishment, if he is pursued beyond the tomb, and his innocent family are offered up as victims, feelings of pity are excited; an indistinct feeling accuses the laws of injustice, humanity declares itself against them, and on all sides the respect for the laws is weakened.

SEC. VII.—COLLECTIVE PUNISHMENTS.[692]

I now come to another case, of which examples are to be met with in the penal dispensations of most countries—that of *collective punishment*, or the punishment of large bodies of men for the delinquencies of a part of them. Under the English law one instance is the punishment inflicted on a whole corporation for the delinquency of some of its members.

When this mode of punishment is justifiable, it is only on the score of necessity. Now to prove this necessity two matters of fact must be made appear; one is, that the guilty could not be punished without the innocent: the other is, that the suffering of the innocent, when added to that of the guilty, will not, in the whole, compose a mass of evil more than equivalent to the benefit of the punishment.

Of these two matters of fact, the first is easy enough to be judged of; the latter must be left to vague conjecture.

Of the administering this mode of punishment there are some remarkable instances both by common law, and by statute. The above principles will enable us to form a judgment of the propriety of those several proceedings.[693]

By the common law it is settled that the privileges of a municipal corporation may be forfeited for the misconduct of the corporators: those privileges which are indiscriminately beneficial to all the persons who are free of the corporation, for the delinquency of the majority of any general assembly of those who form the governing part of it. The power, however, of adjudging such a forfeiture has been very rarely exercised, and the insidious and unconstitutional use that was attempted to be made of it in the reign of Charles II, has cast a stigma on the general doctrine; so that it is not likely to be ever more carried into practice. Such a mode of punishment is plainly unnecessary and inexpedient. The particular delinquents in this way may always be ascertained, and that much more easily and infallibly than in the case of ordinary offences; their acts being, in the very essence of them, public and notorious.

Our own times have exhibited several instances in which punishment, either in reality or to appearance, has been inflicted on a body of men for the misbehaviour of a part of it. I will mention them in their order.

The first I shall mention is the case of the city of Edinburgh, which happened in 1736. A very numerous mob rose up in arms, seized the City Guard, possessed themselves of the city gates, and in defiance of the public authorities, put to death a Captain *Porteous*, who lay under sentence of death, but had been reprieved. This outrage occasioned an Act of Parliament to be made.* By this Act a particular punishment is inflicted upon the Lord Provost of the town, for the particular neglect he is there charged with: but besides this, a fine is laid on the corporation.[694]

Of these punishments, that on the Provost, we may observe, was *in propriam personam*. The fine on the corporation was a collective punishment, falling on as many persons as might find themselves in any shape prejudiced by such fine. Now the ground of applying this latter punishment was not the absolute impracticability of applying any punishment of the proper kind at all. The Provost, as we see, was punished for the negative offence of his neglect. And it appears from another Act, which immediately follows that in question, that a number of persons were actually fugitives for the principal offence. By the second Act these fugitives, in case of their not surrendering within such a time, were to suffer death, as were also those who should conceal them. If then they never surrendered, they remained fugitives, and were punished by banishment. If they surrendered, the presumption was that they would be punished with the ordinary punishment for the offence of which they were guilty; this punishment, however, was not thought sufficient for so enormous and dangerous an outrage. As a supplement, operating in the way of *ex post facto* law, this fine upon the corporation was thought of. Now from such a punishment, considered in itself, it is not probable that any great effects could have been expected. It served, however, to point the moral sanction against the offence, and to help express, as in the words of the Act, the "highest detestation and abhorrence" of the criminal transaction.

In this case, as in that of rebellion, what may be presumed even though the fact be not capable of being established by evidence, is that there was a complicity of affection, in virtue of which all the inhabitants joined in endeavouring to protect the offenders from the visitation of the law.

The next statute I shall take notice of in this view is that for punishment of the corruption that prevailed in the borough of *New Shoreham*.* A

---

*10 Geo. II, c. 34. [This reference does not appear within Dumont's edition.]

society calling itself the Christian Society, consisting of a large majority of the electors, had formed itself and subsisted for several years, for the purpose of selling the seats in Parliament for that borough. On this account all who were members of that society, were, by name, with great propriety, laid under a perpetual incapacitation. So much, considered as a punishment, was a punishment *in propria personas.* But the proper light in which this measure ought to be considered seems not to have been that of a punishment; for in this light it seems hardly to be justified. If it was a punishment, it was an *ex post facto* punishment, which was the less necessary as there was already a punishment of the same kind provided by the law: to wit, incapacitation, though it be but temporary. But in truth, by much the greatest part of the efficacy which it was expected to have, was built on another ground: on it, as a measure of anticipation: calculated to prevent an evil which, but for such remedy, it was visibly in the power, and as visibly in the intention, of the parties thus disabled to introduce: viz. a succession of representatives brought in this corrupt and unconstitutional way. It was therefore not punishment for an evil past and gone, but self-defence against an evil still impending. Now the expense at which this benefit was purchased for the community, could not well be less in any instance than in this. The franchise of electorship, like any other branch of public power, is not an usufructuary [*sic*] possession, but a trust: an article of property which a man holds not for his own benefit alone, but for that of the whole community, of which he is himself but one. Those who are in possession of it find means, it is true, of deriving from it a personal benefit to themselves: but this is in direct repugnance to the interest of the community and the end of the institution; so that, with reference to the particular interest of the possessor, it may be truly said, it is of the less value to him the more conscientiously he discharges it. In truth, I see not why, with respect to the possessor himself, it ought to be looked upon as anything.

But the legislature went farther: besides incapacitating the electors there named, who were a majority, but not the whole, it went on and communicated the right of election to all the forty-shilling freeholders within a large district, of which the borough in question was but a part. In doing this they lessened the right of the innocent burghers who remained.† And as to such part of it, the measure, if it be to be considered as a measure of punishment, must be allowed to have been a punishment *in alienas personas.*

---

*11 Geo. III, c. 55. [Dumont's edition identifies it as "Statute II," rather than 11, *Théorie des peines*, vol. I, p. 435.

†The punishment, if any, that was thus inflicted on the innocent burghers, consisted in the pain of apprehension that among the new electors would be found some, and perhaps a majority of the whole, who would make an improper use of the power of which they were made partakers. [This note does not appear within Dumont's edition.]

Considered, in this light, it was not expedient, since it was not necessary, for the innocent not only could be but actually were distinguished from the guilty. But in whatever light it may appear, considered with reference to the particular persons subjected to that trifling disadvantage, as a measure of reformation it cannot be too highly praised. It stands as the pattern and ground-work of a great plan of constitutional improvement.*

[695]SEC. VIII.—RANDOM PUNISHMENT.

Random punishment is the epithet that may be applied to mis-seated punishment, in those cases in which, without previous design, it has fallen[696] upon the innocent by some caprice of the imagination taken up at the moment, when the occasion and the pretence has come for the infliction of it: not so much as even the wretched sort of pretence which had place in the case of extravasated punishment having place in the present case.[697]

For the illustration of this modification of mis-seated punishment[698] we may again refer to the law of forfeiture,[699] to that of deodands,[700] and that of the exclusion put upon testimony, when for the punishment of an inconjecturable [*sic*] number of innocent persons, through the sides of one delinquent, and by wounds of every imaginable breadth,[701] and depth, and nature, the fact of his delinquency forms the pretence.[702]

When a man who has a freehold interest in any lands commits an offence, part of the punishment for which is the forfeiture of such interest, and then sells, or mortgages, or in any other manner disposes of that interest, and is afterwards attainted for the offence, the law takes it back from those in whose favour it was disposed of, without deigning to enquire whether they knew anything of his having committed it. An individual commits a secret murder, and sells you an estate: twenty years after he is discovered,

---

*One thing let me be permitted to mention, which I think would have been an improvement, and would have done all that could be wanting to reconcile the measure to the strict principles of ordinary justice. A part of the electors stood in a meritorious light; they had either the merit to withstand, or the good fortune to escape, the temptation to which their co-electors yielded. Yet by the statute in question, the condition of this meritorious part so far from being bettered was rendered worse than it was before. There was a method by which these might, I think, have been prevented, without the least prejudice to the reforming part of the measure, and at the same time a signal encouragement held out to conscientious electors, and this without any prejudice to the reforming part of the measure. [This portion of the note appears as the final paragraph of this parallel section within Dumont's edition, *Théorie des peines*, vol. I p. 437. The rest of this note does not appear within that edition.] The expedient was a simple one. It was but the adding to the number of votes which each of the sound voters should have under the new constitution, in such manner that the weight of each man's suffrage should bear the same proportion

prosecuted, attainted. The King, that is, somebody who assumes his name, seizes the estate. If you have devised it, charged it, sold it, if, besides your's, it has passed through fifty other hands, it makes no difference. If it was your wife who had been murdered, it would make no difference. You would lose your wife by the crime and your fortune by the punishment.

It might be supposed that the law looked upon itself as driven to this expedient by the apprehension of fraudulent conveyances; but this is not the case. In the case of moveable and other personal property, it recognizes the practicability of distinguishing fraudulent conveyances from fair. It establishes the latter: it vacates only the former. Yet, it is obvious that immoveable property is much less obnoxious to such a fraud than moveable.

With all this the author of the Commentaries is perfectly well satisfied. "This *may* be hard," he says, "upon such as have unwarily engaged with the offender." But what of that? "the cruelty and reproach" continues he, "must lie on the part, *not* of the law, but of the criminal, who has thus knowingly and dishonestly involved others in his own calamities."[703] To one who can reason in this manner, nothing that is established can come amiss. So long as there is the least particle of guilt not only in him who is punished but in any one else, no law by which punishment is inflicted can be cruel, no law deserving of reproach.

Another instance of random punishment is that of Deodands.

You are a farmer. You employ a wagon. You send your son to drive it: he slips down, is run over and killed. The King, or somebody in his name, is to have your wagon. This is the consolation which the law of England gives you for your loss.

This idea might be improved upon. Let it be a law that when a man happens to break his neck, the people of his parish shall draw lots who shall be hanged to keep him company. The punishment would be greater, but the reason for punishment would be the same.

If instead of a wagon it had been a ship that was moving to your son's death, it would make no difference: though the ship were laden with the

---

to that of the rest under the new constitution as it had done under the old one. The benefit thus reserved would in such case have told for more than it was in reality. The men by being only not punished, would have seemed to be rewarded. They certainly would have been rewarded in point of honour. If a religious attention were constantly to be paid to private subsisting interests, which being temporary may always be provided for at a small expense, reformation would be delivered from much of that opposition which it is at present apt to meet with. One may say to reformers, *serve the whole but forget not that each member is a part of it.*

Strictly speaking, it is true that the electors have no reason to complain, except as above, upon the occasion of an extension of the elective franchise. The dilemma is clear: if you do not mean to discharge it conscientiously, you ought not to be trusted with it. If you do, it is of no benefit to you, and you can have no ground to complain of its being taken from you for the benefit of the State.

treasure of the Indies it would make no difference, the ship and its lading would be the King's.[704]

The source from whence this institution flowed is pretty generally known: but it is not perhaps so generally observed that the institution is not a just consequence, even from the ideas then received. It was established, it is not easy to say how early, but however in the days of Catholicism. In those days, as soon as a man's soul had left its body, it used to go to a place called Purgatory, there to be broiled for 20,000 years. Now in this life some souls love music, others not. But in that post, life which was then to come, all souls were fond of it alike. Luther himself, who ought to know, is positive of it.* Not that all music was to their taste. It was only a particular kind of music, such as priests know only how to sing. But it was not reasonable that priests should sing unless they were paid for it; for the labourer is worthy of his hire. Now when a man died thus suddenly, it was not probable that he should have made any provision by his will for paying them. Therefore it was necessary that somebody else should pay them. So far was in order. But why resort to any other fund than the man's own property? Was he the poorer for having died a violent death, than if he had died a natural one? or for dying by the effect of a thing in motion, than if he had died by a fall from a thing at rest? And if, after all, he had nothing to pay for himself, could not the parish, or the hundred, or the next abbey have paid for him?[705]

I would not swear but the sages who invented this notable institution might think to do a spite to the thing, the wagon, the ship, or whatever it was, by making it forfeited; as the Athenians exterminated a stone that struck a man and killed him, that is, carried it out of their country and threw it into another. Many a public institution, which the lawyer admires with humble deference, has had no better ground.[706]

The next instance of random punishment which I would give, consists in the exclusion put upon testimony.[707]

I could wish to give the reader a precise list of the offences to which this punishment is annexed, but this I find to be impossible. Every principle delivered on this subject teems with contradiction. The enumeration which is sometimes made includes nearly every principal crime, comprehending treason, perjury, forgery, and *such like crimes*, theft, all crimes considered infamous, and felony. As to felony, this is spoken of as if it were a particular species of crime: the case is, that felony is a collection of crimes as heterogenous [*sic*] as can be conceived, and which have nothing in common between them but the accidental circumstance of being punished with the same punishment. Crimes of mere resentment, or malicious mischief, are by scores of statutes made felonies. Homicide intentional, in the heat of

---

*See Sir J. Hawkin's History of Music. [This note does not appear within Dumont's edition.]

passion; or unintentional, by an unlucky blow, is felony.—Rape is felony.—Crimes of lewdness are felonies.—What is not felony?—The evidence of persons excommunicated is not received, the reason annexed by some has been, that these individuals not being under the influence of religion cannot be believed on their oath. By others it has been generally said, that those who converse with excommunicated persons are excommunicated with them, and consequently they cannot be admitted to receive any questions from a Court of Justice.[708] Of this nature are the reasons frequently given for existing laws in the books of English jurisprudence.

Without longer stopping, therefore, to ascertain in what cases testimony is refused, let us proceed to examine if this is a proper punishment, that is to say, if there is any case in which because a man has committed a crime his testimony ought to be rejected.

The only reason there can be for rejecting a witness is this, that it appears more probable that after every expedient that can be put in practice to get the truth of him, the account he gives of the matter would rather mislead those who are to judge than set them right. I say mislead the judges; I do not say be a false one: for whether it be true or not, is what to the purposes of justice is a matter of indifference. The point is for them to (be enabled to) form such a notion of the fact in dispute as shall prove a true one; by what means they come at it is no matter. He would commit perjury indeed, but that is quite another evil, and an evil for which there is another and more proper remedy than that of prematurely repelling his evidence. This want of veracity, therefore, is no objection to him, unless he has the faculty of maintaining to the last such a degree of consistency and plausibility as shall enable him to conceal it.[709]

As to want of veracity it should be considered that the greatest liar in the universe rarely swerves from truth (I mean what to him seems truth) in one instance out of a hundred. The natural bent of all mankind is to speak truth; it requires the force of some particular interest, real or imaginary, to overbalance that propensity. Some men, it is true, are made to deviate from it by very slender motives, but nobody tells a lie absolutely without a motive.

Now then, do but suppose him absolutely with out any interest to give a false account, and the most abandoned criminal that ever was upon the earth might be trusted to as safely as the man of the most consummate virtue. Where then lies the difference? In this, that the profligate man may easily be made to fancy he has such an interest in telling falsehood as shall preponderate over the interest he fancies he has in speaking truth; the easier, the more profligate he is: the man of virtue, not without difficulty; the more difficulty, the more he is confirmed in virtue.

Now a motive to speak truth, in cases where he is called upon by law to give his testimony, is what every man has, and unless he be insane must conceive himself to have; he has it from the political sanction, in the penalties which the law denounces against falsehood in such cases: he has it from the moral sanction, in the infamy annexed by men in general to such a conduct: he has it from the religious sanction, unless he be an atheist, and except in as far as dispensations or absolutions may intervene to take it off.

The interest which a man may have on the other hand to speak falsehood in such a case, may be distinguished into a natural interest, and an artificial one. What I mean by a natural interest need not be explained. I call that an artificial interest which he may derive in the way of reward, by the express act of him who has some natural interest. If you are at law for an estate, you have a natural interest in my telling any story, true or false, that may serve to establish your title. If you give me a reward for telling such a story, I have an artificial one, which is raised up in me by you.

Now whether a man has a natural interest or no in the fate of a contest, is in general pretty easy to be known; it is a question of itself: and if determined in the affirmative, the tendency of the law is, to reject a man as a witness, upon that distinct ground, and without regard to his probity or improbity.

The question is here concerning an artificial interest, the existence, or non-existence of which, does not so readily lie within proof; but the lights that are to be had, are to be drawn from such circumstances as may appear to affect the description of a man's general character. Thus much only is certain, that in proportion as a man is more or less confirmed in virtue, the less or the more likely is any artificial motive which may be presented to him, to preponderate over the motives he has to speak truth, and be effective, so as to determine him to speak falsehood.

It is here proper to be upon our guard against a vulgar error. Men of narrow experience, of hasty judgment, and of small reflection, in a word, the bulk of mankind, have in a manner but two classes in which to stow a man, in respect of merit: they know but of two characters, the good man and the bad man. If then they happen to view a man's conduct, in any instance, in a favourable light, up he goes among the good men; if in an unfavourable, down he goes among the bad men, and they fix a great gulph between the two. If their opinion, with respect to either, comes to change, as they have no intermediate stages, he is removed from his station, with the same violence as he was at first placed in it. But men of observation and cool reflection, who have had patience and sagacity to make a narrow search into human nature, learn to correct the errors of this indolent and hasty system; they know that in the scale of merit, men's characters rise one above the other, by infinite and imperceptible degrees; and, at the same time, that the highest is distant from the lowest, by a much less space than is commonly imagined.

Those who admit the truth of these observations will see how precarious and ill-contrived a means the law takes to come at truth, by giving into the error above noticed: by making one class of men, which it will hear, and another of men, whom it will not suffer to be heard in any case, or on any account. In a word, (for I own that the argument comes to this) that while it enjoins any class of persons to be excluded, at all events, to avoid a small degree of possible inconvenience, it embraces a great degree of certain inconvenience.

It is manifest, that the smaller the number of persons is whom it guards against, in proportion to those whom it remains still exposed to danger, the less is the advantage gained by it. Whom then does it guard against? a few hundreds, perhaps, in a nation. And from whom does it remain exposed to danger? all the rest of the nation. For who is it from whom it does not stand exposed, in any case, to a danger of this kind, I declare is more than I can imagine. If there be any man now living that can lay his hand upon his heart, and solemnly declare, that in no instance, trivial or important, has he ever departed from the rigid line of truth, upon the prospect of advantage, he has either more hypocrisy than I would wish to impute to any man, or more virtue than I can persuade myself to exist in any man. The only person about whom I can be sure, and who yet would not willingly yield the palm of integrity to any one that lives, nor barter any atom of it for any other honour the world has to bestow, is far, I know, from the thoughts of making any such pretensions.

There are cases in which the best man alive could scarcely be credited without danger: there are cases in abundance, in which the worst man alive might be believed with safety. Such are all those, where the circumstance of the case afford the witness no natural motive to speak falsely: and the circumstances of the parties are such as can afford him no artificial one. I am, for instance, as bad a man as, for the supposition's sake, you would choose to have me. I happen to see one man beating another, who afterwards seeks his remedy at law against the oppressor, and calls me as a witness, and the only witness. Now, it has happened, that I have been convicted of perjury, over and over again, as many times as you please: I would swear my father's life away for a penny. But the parties are, both of them, miserably poor: they neither of them have a penny to tempt me with. What then is there to induce me to give a false account of the matter? nothing. What then is the danger of admitting me? none at all. What the consequence of rejecting me? the triumph of oppression. Now, in a case like this, there is nothing singular nor improbable; a thousand such might a man figure to himself with ease.

Having proceeded thus far, I will venture to advance this position, that a man's testimony ought not to be rejected at all events, even for the crime of perjury: if not for perjury, it will follow, *à fortiori*, not for any other crime. I will just offer a farther consideration or two, in support of this opinion; I will then give a short sketch of the evil consequences that result from such an absolute rejection; I will thirdly offer an expedient, which, I think, would answer every good purpose of it; and lastly, I will state the different degrees of reason there may be, for extending the incapacity to the different crimes that may be proposed.

Now then, let the crime of which the witness has been convicted, be that of perjury. He has, however, no natural interest to speak false; if he has, that forms another ground of disability, which is not here in question. If then, he has an artificial interest, it is the party that must give it him. But in this case, the party must be a suborner: unless then, he stand already convicted of subornation on a former occasion, there can be no ground for repelling the perjured witness, without peremptorily attributing to another man, whose character stands unimpeached, a crime of a similar complexion: a supposition, which no rule, either of law or reason, seems to warrant.

I cannot help thinking,[710] that these rules of peremptory incompetency would never have been laid down, had those, who first started them, gone deliberately and circumspectly to work, and carefully examined the consequences on both sides of the question. The evil consequences of the rule, they seemed scarcely to have cast their eyes on. They seem to have gone to work, as if they had witnesses enough in every case to pick and choose out of; on which supposition, certainly, they would do well to discard the worst, to pick out and retain none but the best, and such as should be proof against all exception.[711] All this was mighty well, provided there was no danger on the other side. But the danger on the other side is terrible. It is a truth, however, which I can scarce help looking upon as very obvious, and certainly it is an important one, that to mark any man out as disabled from witnessing at all events, is to grant all men a license to do to him and before him all manner of mischief whatsoever. Now, as to what may be done *to* him, that indeed may be taken as so much punishment of the proper kind, though it would be a strange loose and inconsiderate method of laying a man under proscription.*

But as to mischief that may be done to others in his presence, or which, in any other way, others may suffer for want of his evidence,[712]—the case of Pendoch and Mackendar† may serve as an example. By the statute, which is called the Statute of Frauds and Perjuries, three witnesses are necessary to a will of land. In this case, the will had three witnesses as it ought to have. Two stood unimpeached; but it was found out, that the other, once upon a time, had been convicted of petty larceny, and been whipt [*sic*]. This was before the attestation, how long, it does not appear. The suit was com-

---

*It would be worse, in some respects, than forfeiture of reputation. [This note does not appear within Dumont's edition.]

†2. Wils. 18. [This reference is not provided within Dumont's edition.]

menced five years afterwards. This man being deemed a bad witness, (and as such, not to be heard) there wanted the requisite number, and the man, in whose favour the will had been made, lost the estate. One may imagine the shock to a person, who thought he had all the security for his estate which the law could give him; one may imagine the surprise and indignation the testator, were he to arise out of his grave, must feel, at seeing his disposition vacated, by an incident which common prudence could never have prompted him to guard against, unless, by looking in a man's face, he could have told, that once in his life he had been guilty of a trifling breach of honesty, and been whipt for it.[713]

The limits of this design will not permit me to expatiate upon this subject any further, by suggesting cases of like mischief that are liable to happen, or collecting such as are known actually to have happened. This general sketch of them being given, the intelligent reader will readily excuse me from entering into the detail.

Because a woman has been guilty of perjury, or any other offence which has rendered her testimony inadmissible, it is just that she should be punished; but is it just, is it proper, that she should be delivered over to the lust of whatever man to whom her beauty may become an object of desire? If the law were known to be, in this respect, as it is said to be, the nation would become a scene of lust, cruelty, and rapine; but it happens here, as it will sometimes happen in other instances, one mischief operates as a palliative to another: the extreme absurdity of the law is veiled by men's utter ignorance of its contents.

Let us turn back and look on the other side. What then would be the mischief of admitting the testimony of a man thus stigmatized? I see none: none at least that can for a moment stand in competition with the mischief on the other side. "But the person so stigmatized does not deserve to be believed!" Does he not? why am I to think so? because you say so? No; but because men in general will say so too! And will they then? Yes, surely will they. I do believe it, and therefore it is I say there is no danger. Let him be known for what he is, and a Jury will be under the strongest bias not to believe him. Their prejudice will bear strong against him; nor will any thing less than the strongest degree of probability, and the most perfect consistency in the whole narration be sufficient to induce them to believe it. I see not what it is that should justify the extreme distrust which Judges have shown of Juries in establishing this rule: especially, as in case of a conviction of an innocent person, which is the greatest danger the case is open to, it is so entirely in the power of the Judge to save the convict. The general prejudice of mankind, as we have before observed, leads them to exaggeration in the judgment they pronounce of the general tenor of a man's character, from a single action; in particular, to spread the stain that a single act of delinquency brings upon a man's character, farther than according to reason, it ought to go. It is from having been the dupes, as I take it, of this prejudice, that even Judges, the ancient Judges, who first laid down the law upon this point, first broached this rule. It may always be expected to work, at least as strongly as it ought to work, upon Juries taken from the body of the people.

Were it then abolished, the conduct of Juries, then you think, would nearly be the same as if it subsisted? I think it probable. What advantage then would you gain by the abolition? This great one: the chance that a delinquent might have of impunity in such a case, would no longer be visible upon paper; he would no longer see a formal license given him, by the letter of the law, to commit all manner of wickedness in presence of an object circumstanced like the party in question; if a guilty person were acquitted upon that ground, it would appear as if, upon the whole, the story was not credible, and that, in fact, no such crime was committed as was charged, not that having been committed, it was suffered to go unpunished. This then is the advantage, and I think a more conclusive one cannot well be required to justify any institution.

All that prudence requires in such a case is, that the character of the witness, that is to say, the offence of which he was formerly guilty, should be known, that those who are called upon to inveigh his testimony, may be able to judge how far he is to be believed.[714]

Suppose the party has been guilty of perjury, this crime most particularly affects his credibility.—There is a great difference to be observed in the quality of the crime when committed in self-defence, in one's own cause, and when committed on the subornation of a stranger, and in an attack upon the life of an innocent person; such distinctions are most important, and readily offer themselves to those who consult the dictates of common sense, and do not suffer their eyes to be blinded by the mist of technical jargon.

The time which has elapsed since the offence was committed is a consideration of importance.—A man in his youth, at fourteen or fifteen years of age, was led to take a false oath, and was convicted—he becomes reformed, during thirty or forty years, he maintains an unimpeachable character. His reformation is of no consequence, the record of his forgotten crime is dragged from the dust with which it had been covered; in accordance with this rule, his testimony must be rejected; upon every principle of common sense and of utility, it would have been equally admissible with any other.

In the prosecution of criminals, the testimony of those who have a manifest interest in their condemnation, is not refused, whether that interest be pecuniary, or arising from a desire of vengeance. Such testimony is, however, received with distrust and caution.—This is well;—be equally distrustful of a witness, whose previous conduct has rendered him suspected; but hear him, and examine whether the circumstances of his crime are of a nature to affect his credibility on each particular occasion.[715]

SEC. IX.—CAUSE OF THE FREQUENCY OF MIS-SEATED PUNISHMENT.[716]

As to the cause of the abuse thus made of punishment, it lies not very deep below the surface. It lies partly in the strength of the self-regarding, and dissocial passions, partly in the weakness of the intellectual faculties on the part of legislators, and of Judges acting in the place of legislators.

It lies more particularly in the strength of the dissocial passions, and in that one of the false principles, rivals to the principle of utility, viz. in the principle of sympathy and antipathy, in the production of which the dissocial affections, influenced and swollen to that pitch in which they assume the name of passion, have so large a share.

Urged on by the dissocial passion of antipathy, misguided by the principle of sympathy and antipathy, men in power have punished, because they hated: taking as a sufficient warrant for the infliction of the sufferings which they proposed to themselves to inflict, the existence of that hatred, of which, as towards the person in question, the existence was demonstrated to them by their own feelings.

That which was the cause, became naturally the measure of what was done: punishing, because of this hate, it was, to the man with the strong hand, matter of course to punish in proportion to his hate.

A lot of punishment, in which so much suffering and not more, would fall upon the innocent, as consistently with the application of punishment to the guilty, was unavoidable, sufficed not for the gratification of his hate: of that satisfaction which consists in his contemplation of another's suffering, he would have as much more as was to be had; and frequently there was scarce a price, so as it was at the expense of others only that that price was made up, and not any part at his expense—there was scarce a price at which he was not content to purchase it.[717]

BOOK V.[718]
OF COMPLEX PUNISHMENTS.

CHAPTER I.[719]
INCONVENIENCES OF COMPLEX PUNISHMENTS.

W e have before us observed that a penal act is not simple in its effects, does not produce one single evil, that it produces many masses of evil at once. A punishment, considered as an act, may be simple, considered in its effects, complex.

A man is imprisoned, here is a simple punishment as respects the act on the part of the Judge: but as respects the individual the evils resulting from it may be very various, affecting in different ways his fortune, his person, his reputation and his condition in life.

A simple punishment is that which is produced by a single act of punishment: a compound punishment, is that which requires more than one operation; the punishment for an offence may include imprisonment, a fine, a mark of infamy, &c. if all these are announced by the law; if each of these punishments is expressed by a clear and familiar term, the punishment, though compound or complex, may be a good one.

Improper[720] complex punishments are those of which the integral parts are not known, those which include evils that the law does not announce, which are only expressed by obscure and enigmatical names which do not exhibit their penal nature in clear characters, and which are only understood by lawyers; of this kind are transportation—felony with and without benefit of clergy—præmunire outlawry—excommunication—incompetency as a witness, and many others.

Everything which is uncertain, everything which is obscure, offends against the first condition in framing a good law.

The inconveniences attached to complex punishments when thus defined are very great, but they may be explained in a few words—the legislator knows not what he does—the subject knows not what is meant by the punishment threatened.—It becomes impossible for the legislator to do what is proper in each case, he therefore does either too much or too little—every obscure expression veils from his eyes the nature of the punishment or punishments he employs: he strikes blindfolded, and scatters suffering at hazard.—The Jury and the Judges who witness the inconveniences of the law in each particular case, allow themselves to employ all possible means to avoid them, they usurp the authority of the legislator, and perjury becomes the habitual palliative of his injustice or improvidence.[721]

If the law is executed, what happens?—the Judge in inflicting one useful punishment, is obliged to inflict a multitude of useless punishments:—punishments of which the offenders had only an imperfect idea, which produce mischief in pure waste, oftentimes the mischief spreads over persons who are entire strangers to the offence, and the consequences are such that the legislator would have trembled had he foreseen them.

We have already spoken of incompetency as a witness, we shall now direct our attention to the other punishments above-named.

CHAPTER II.
OF TRANSPORTATION.[722]

723

Among the advantages which the North Americans[724] have derived from their independence, there is one that cannot fail to strike every man who has any feeling of national pride; it has saved them from humiliating obligation of receiving every year an importation of the refuse of the British population, of serving as an outlet for the prisons of the mother country, whereby the morals of their rising people were exposed to injury, by a mixture with all possible kinds of depravity.[725] North America, after having been exposed to this scourge for upwards of a century, no longer serves as a receptacle for these living nuisances; but can any limits be assigned to the moral effects that may have been produced by this early inoculation of vice?[726]

I shall have occasion again to recur to this important topic, when in speaking of the Colony at New South Wales,[727] and of the population now forming there.—I shall point out the inconveniences which result from sending thither these periodical harvests of malefactors.[728]

The present object is to show that the system of transportation, as now managed, is essentially different from what it was under the old system, and that with the change of scene, the punishment itself has in many respects been materially altered; in some respects for the better, in many others for the worse.

Under the old system of transportation to America, power being given for that purpose by Parliament, the convicts[729] destined for transportation were made over by the government to a contractor, who, for the profit to be made by selling their services for the penal term to a master in America, engaged to convey them to the scene of banishment. To banishment, the banishment prescribed by law, was thus added in all cases in which the individuals were not able to purchase their liberty, the ulterior and perfectly distinct punishment of *bondage*. But wherever it happened that through the medium of a friend, or otherwise, the convict could bid more for himself than would be given for his services by a stranger, he was set at liberty in the first port at which he arrived. The punishment was limited, as respected him, to simple banishment, the individual was therefore punished with bondage rather for his poverty than for the crime he had committed.[730] Thus the most culpable, those who had committed great crimes and who had contrived to secure the profits of their crimes, were least punished.—The minor thieves, novices, and inexperienced malefactors, who had not secured their plunder, bore the double chain of banishment and slavery.

Under the system of transportation to Botany Bay, the whole expense is borne by the Government. The Governor of the Colony always retains an authority over the convicts, and acts as their gaoler; he provides them with habitations, employment, and food; they are placed under his sole controul; he may employ them either in public or private works. Hard labour, with some few exceptions, is the lot of all; exemption from it cannot be purchased by money. In this respect the inequality above spoken of, has been greatly corrected, and the punishment having been rendered more certain is consequently more efficacious.

Transportation to America was attended with another inconvenience,—that country presented too many facilities for the return of the convicts. A great number of them availed themselves of these opportunities, and returned to the mother country to exercise their fatal talents with superior skill. Some when their terms of banishment[731] had expired, many before that period had arrived. As to the latter, the facility of return was one among the disadvantages attending transportation to America; as to the others, in the eyes at least of those who conceive that the commission of one offence ought not to operate as a forfeiture of all title to justice, this facility of return could not fail to appear as an advantage. On the other hand, the distance of Botany Bay afforded a better security against illegal returns, being situated at the antipodes of Britain, with scarcely any existing commerce when first selected, the return of any of the convict population was an event hardly to be looked for:—whilst however a security thus effectual was provided against the return of convicts whose terms had not expired, an equally effectual barrier was raised against the return of those whose terms had expired, and thus, at one stroke, all inferior degrees of this punishment were, in nearly all eases, indiscriminately converted into the highest; whether such an effect was intended or not it is needless to enquire, but that such was the effect is indisputable.[732]

Transportation under the present system, is a complex punishment, composed, first, of banishment, and, second, of hard labour,—banishment, a punishment eminently defective, particularly in respect of its inequality: hard labour, a punishment in itself eminently salutary, but when connected with banishment, and, as in this case, carried on under every possible disadvantage, failing altogether to produce any beneficial effects.[733]

In order to show how completely adverse the system of transportation to New South Wales is to the attainment of the several objects or ends of penal justice, it will be necessary shortly to recapitulate what those ends or objects are, and then to show from the accounts which have been furnished, respecting the state of the convict population of that Colony, in what degree these ends or objects have been respectively fulfilled.

The main object or end of penal justice is *example*; prevention of similar offences, on the part of individuals at large, by the influence exerted by the punishment on the minds of bystanders, from the apprehension of similar suffering in case of similar delinquency; of this property transportation is almost destitute. This is its radical and incurable defect. The punishment is not seen by, it is hidden, abstracted from, the eyes of those upon whom it is desirable it should operate in the way of example. Punishments which are indicted at the antipodes, in a country of which so little is known, and with which communication was so rare, could make only a transient impression upon the minds of people in this country. "The people," says an author, who had deeply considered the effects of imagination, "the mass of the people make no distinction between an interval of a thousand years and of a thousand miles."[734] It has been already said, but cannot be too often repeated and enforced, that the utility and effect of example is not determined by the amount of suffering the delinquent is made to endure, but by the amount of apparent suffering he undergoes. It is that part of his suffering which strikes the eyes of beholders, and which fastens on their imagination, which leaves an impression strong enough to counteract the temptation to offend. However deficient they may be in respect of exemplarity, the sufferings inflicted on persons condemned to this mode of punishment are not the less substantial and severe; confinement for an unlimited time in prisons or in the hulks, a voyage of from six to eight months, itself a state of constant sufferance from the crowded state of the ships and the necessary restraint to which convicts are subjected—the dangers of the sea—exposure to contagious diseases which are often attended with the most fatal consequences. Such are some of the concomitants of the system of punishment in question, which serves as the introduction to a state of banishment and bondage in a distant region, in which the means of subsistence have been extremely precarious, and, where by delay in the arrival of a vessel the whole colony has been repeatedly exposed to all the horrors of famine. It is scarcely possible to conceive a situation more deplorable than that to which the convicts thus transported have been exposed. Constant hard labour, and exposure to depredation, (if they have anything of which they can be plundered,) and occasional starvation; without the means of mending their condition while they remain there, without the hope of ever leaving it; such has been the condition to which persons banished to this Colony, for periods that in pretence were limited, have found themselves exposed. Here then is punishment, partly intentional, partly accidental, dealt out with the most lavish profuseness; but compared with its effects in the way of example, it may be considered as so much gratuitous suffering inflicted without end or object. A sea of oblivion flows between that country and this. It is not the hundredth, nor even the thousandth part of this mass of punishment that makes any impression on the people of the mother country—upon that class of people who are most likely to commit offences, who neither read nor reflect, and whose feelings are capable of being excited, not by the description, but by the exhibition of sufferings. The system of transportation has moreover this additional disadvantage, which not merely neutralizes its effects in the discouragement of offences, but renders it, in many cases, an instrument of positive encouragement to the commission of offences. A variety of pleasing illusions will, in the minds of many persons, be connected with the idea of transportation, which will not merely supplant all painful reflections, but will be replaced by the most agreeable anticipations. It requires but a very superficial knowledge of mankind in general, and more especially of the youth of this country, not to perceive that a distant voyage, a new country, numerous associates, hope of future independence, and agreeable adventures, will be sufficiently captivating to withdraw the mind from the contemplation of the painful part of the picture, and to give uncontrolled sway to ideas of licentious fascinating enjoyment.*[735]

II. The second end or object of punishment is *Reformation*:[736] prevention of similar offences, on the part of the *particular individual* punished in each instance, by taking from him the *will* to commit the like in future—under this head what has been done in the colony of New South Wales? By referring to facts, we shall find, not only that in this respect it has been hitherto radically defective, but that from the nature of things it ever must remain so.[737]

Connected with the system of transportation to the American colonies, there were two circumstances highly conducive to the reformation of the convicts transported—their admission, upon landing in the country, into families composed of men of thrift and probity—their separation from each other.

When a master in America had engaged a convict in his service, all the members of the family became interested in watching his behaviour. Working under the eye of his master, he had neither the inducements nor the means of giving loose to his vicious propensities. The state of dependence in which he was placed, gave him an obvious interest in cultivating the goodwill of those, under whose authority he found himself placed; and if he still retained any principle of honesty, it could scarcely fail to be invig-

---

*Not many years ago, two young men, the one about 14 the other about 16 years of age, were condemned for a petty theft, to be transported. Upon hearing this unlooked for sentence, the youngest began to cry. "Coward," said his companion with an air of triumph, "who ever cried because he had to set out upon the grand tour?" This fact was mentioned to me by a gentleman who was witness to this scene, and was much struck with it.

orated and developed under the encouragement that it would find in the society with which he was surrounded.

Thus it was in America. How is it in New South Wales? To receive the convicts upon their landing, a set of brutes in human shape, a species of society beyond comparison less favourable to colonization than utter solitude. Few other inhabitants, but the very profligates themselves, who are sent by thousands, from British goals, to be turned loose to mix with one another in this desert, together with the few taskmasters who superintend their work in the open wilderness, and the military men who are sent out with them in large but still unequal numbers, to help keep within bounds the mischief they would otherwise be sure to occupy themselves with, when thus let loose. Here then there were not, as in America, any families to receive the convicts, any means of constantly separating them from each other, no constant and steady inspection. *Field-husbandry* is, under this system, the principal employment; hence general dispersion—field-husbandry carried on by individuals or heads of families, each occupying a distinct dwelling, the interior of which is altogether out of the habitual reach of every *inspecting* eye. It is true that the Police officers occasionally go their rounds to maintain order and keep the convicts to their work; but what is to be expected from a system of inspection at long intervals, and which is as disgusting to the inspectors as to the inspected. Can this be regarded as a sufficient check against sloth, gaming, drunkenness, incontinence, profaneness, quarreling [*sic*], improvidence, and the absence of all honourable feeling. Immediately the back of the inspector is turned, all the disorder which his actual presence had suspended, is renewed. It may easily be imagined how completely all controul may be set at defiance by a set of men who have regularly organized among themselves a system of complicity, and who make it a matter of triumph and agreeable pastime to assist each other in escaping from inspection.

On this subject, the public have long been in the possession of a very valuable document: it is a complete history of the first sixteen years since the establishment of this colony, which in respect of fidelity possesses every title to confidence, and which states the events as they happened, in the form of a journal, accompanied with the necessary details. What gives the work the highest claim to confidence, is that the historiographer is also the panegyrist, the professed panegyrist of the establishment: a character which, when accompanied, as in this instance, with that candour and those internal marks of veracity, with which it is so rare for it to be accompanied, renders the testimony, in this point of view, more than doubly valuable.

The general impression left by a perusal of this work, is one of sadness and disgust: it is a history of human nature in its most degraded and depraved state—an unmixt [sic] detail of crimes and punishments. The men constantly engaged in conspiracies against the government, always forming plans for deceiving and disobeying their task-masters, forming among themselves a society of refractory and wily profligates—a society of wolves and foxes. The women everywhere else, the best part of humanity, prove in New South Wales a remarkable exception to this general rule. The late chief magistrate says "the women are worse than the men, and are generally found at the bottom of every infamous transaction that is committed in the colony."* His work abounds with passages to the same effect. Of such materials is it that the foundation of the colony is formed. From such a stock, and under such auspices, is it that the rising generation is to be produced.[738]

The historian has not confined himself to vague imputations of general immorality and profligacy, but has particularized the acts of delinquency on which those imputations rest. The crimes that are committed at New South Wales,[739] in spite of the alertness of the government and the summary administration of justice, surpass, in the skill and cunning with which they are managed, every thing that has been ever witnessed in this country: almost every page of his work contains the description of offences against persons, or against property, either of individuals or of the public. Gaming and drunkenness produce perpetual quarrels, which usually end in murder. The crime of incendiarism [sic] is there practised to an extent altogether unexampled in any other country. Churches, prisons, public and private property, are all alike subjected to the devouring element, without any regard to the extent of the loss that may be occasioned, or the number of lives that may be sacrificed. "When the public gaol was set on fire," says the historian, "it will be read with horror, that at the time there were confined within the walls, twenty prisoners, most of whom were loaded with irons, and who with difficulty were snatched from the flames. Feeling for each other was never imputed to these miscreants; and yet, if several were engaged in the commission of a crime, they have seldom been known to betray their companions in iniquity."† The bond of connection is not sympathy for each other, but antipathy to the government, the common enemy. For the natives they manifest as little feeling, as towards each other. Spite of the rigour of the law, these European savages, are guilty of the most wanton acts of barbarity towards the natives of the country; instead of cultivating a good understanding with them, which might have been attended with many advantages, they have converted them into the most determined enemies.

---

*Collins, vol. II. p. 218. [Citation of this book appears only as a general reference at the end of the previous parallel paragraph of Dumont's edition, *Théorie des peines*, vol. I p. 223.
†Collins, vol. II, p. 197. [Again, Dumont's edition does not quote this source, directly.]

So far from exhibiting any symptoms of reformation, the longer they are subjected to the discipline of the colony, the worse they become. Whatever may be the degree of viciousness ascribed by the historian to the convicts during the continuance of their term, they appear in his history to be in a certain degree honest, sober, and orderly in comparison with those whose term is expired and who afterwards become settlers: they then become the prime instigators of all the crimes committed in the colony, and constitute the principal source of the embarrassment to which the government is subjected.

In proof of this assertion, the historian furnishes a most satisfactory piece of evidence. During the first five years subsequent to the establishment of the colony, and when there were no convicts whose terms had expired, the conduct of the convicts was in general orderly, and such as to give hopes of a disposition to reformation; but in proportion as, by the expiration of their respective terms, the number of the emancipated colonists increased, the most ungovernable licentiousness was introduced: not only those that were thus recently emancipated, as if to make up for the time they had lost, abandoned themselves to every species of excess, but they encouraged the natural viciousness of those who still remained in a state of bondage. The convicts finding among these independent settlers, who were their old companions and associates, receivers of stolen property, and protectors from the punishments denounced by the law, always ready to receive them in their retreat from justice, and to conceal them from detection, became more insolent and refractory, anxiously waiting for the time when they also would be entitled to assume this state of savage independence.

What possible means can be devised to neutralize this perpetually increasing influx of vice. All the expedients that have hitherto been employed have proved completely fruitless, and there would be no difficulty in shewing [*sic*] that so they must ever be. Instruction, moral and religious, seems almost altogether vain: the very nature of the population bids defiance to the establishment of an effectual system of police, or to an uniform administration of the laws: *rewards* were found as inefficient as goodwill in procuring evidence;—the enormous consumption of spirituous liquors, the principal cause of all the disorders in the colony, has from local circumstances, hitherto been found altogether irrepressible. Under each of these heads a few remarks may suffice.

With respect to religious instruction, little could be expected from two or three chaplains for a colony, divided into eight or ten stations, each to appearance at too great a distance from the rest to send auditors to any other. To minds so disposed as those of the convicts, of what advantage was the attendance on divine service for one or two hours on one day in the week? And with what profit could religious instruction be expected to be received by men who were "*made* (as the historian expresses it*) to attend divine service?" To rid themselves of the occasional listlessness they were thus *made* to endure, the Church was got rid of by an incendiary plot. To punish them (if by accident another building fit for the purpose had not been already in existence) they were to have been employed on the Sunday in the erecting another building for the purpose.† To work on Sunday they might be made, but will they ever be made to lend an attentive ear and a docile heart to authoritative instruction. Even the women, says the historian, were extremely remiss in their attendance on divine service, and were never at a loss for mendacious pretenses [*sic*] for excusing themselves. In short, instead of being observed as a day dedicated to religious duties, Sunday appears in that colony to have been distinguished only by the riot and debauchery with which it was marked: those who did not attend divine service, taking advantage of the absence of those who did, to plunder their dwellings and destroy their crops.

It has just been seen with how very sparing a hand, religious instruction for the Protestant part of the establishment was supplied. For the spiritual instruction of the Catholic part of the colony, which, from the large importations made from Ireland must now have become very numerous, it does not appear that any provision whatever was made. It is true, that in one of the importations of convicts from Ireland, a priest of the Catholic persuasion, whose offence was sedition, was comprised.‡ If, instead of a seditious clergyman, would not the expense have been well bestowed in sending out a loyalist clergyman of the same religious persuasion.§[740]

As to the police, it is necessarily in an extreme degree debilitated by the corrupt state of the subordinate class of public functionaries. In a population that warranted the utmost distrust on the part of the government, it was found necessary to restrain the free intercourse between the several parts of the colony. *All persons*, officers excepted, were forbidden to travel from one district of the settlement to another without passports. These regulations proved, however, altogether nugatory: the constables whose duty

---

*Col. II. p. 122.

†Collins, II. p. 129.

‡Collins, II. p. 293.

§There is a passage in Collins (II. p. 51) highly characteristic of the light in which the securing the means of attendance, and thence attendance itself on divine worship, on the part of the convicts, was regarded by the constituted authorities.—A church-clock having been brought to the settlement in "The Reliance," and no building fit for its reception having been since erected, preparations were now making for constructing a tower fit for the purpose, *to which might be added a church*, whenever at a future day the increase of labourers might enable the governor to direct such an edifice to be built.

it was to inspect these passports,* either from fear or corruption, neglected to do their duty, whilst, as has been already mentioned, a most effectual bar to the preservation of any well regulated system of police, was found in those convicts whose terms had expired, and who were ever ready to give protection and assistance to the criminal and turbulent.[741]

With regard to all classes of offences committed in this colony, justice was paralyzed by a principle which ensured impunity, and which it seems impossible to eradicate. With the historian, who was also Judge Advocate, it is a matter of perpetual complaint, that it was scarcely possible to convict an offender who was not taken in the very act of committing an offence. Evidence was on almost all occasions altogether as inaccessible, as if there had been a combination and tacit agreement among the majority of the inhabitants of the colony to paralyze the arm of justice, by a refusal to bear testimony. He speaks of five murders in one year,† (1796) which were left unpunished, notwithstanding the strong presumptions which indicated the guilty parties, because the necessary witnesses would not come forward, even though extraordinary rewards were offered. One such fact is sufficient: it is superfluous to cite others of the same nature.

The most prominent cause of this state of abandoned profligacy, is the universal and immoderate passion for spirituous liquors: it is the exciting cause which leads to every species of vice—gaming, dissoluteness, depredation, and murder—servants, soldiers, labourers, women, the youth of both sexes, prisoners and their gaolers, all are alike corrupted by it; it was carried to such a pitch, that numbers of the settlers were in the practice of selling the whole of their crops, as soon as they were gathered, in order to purchase their favourite liquor. The attempts made from time to time by the government, to check this practice, have proved altogether unavailing: the policy of the government upon this point appears not to have been quite steady: sometimes it has allowed the trade in spirituous liquors, at other times it has been forbidden. But whatever may be the policy of the government, experience shows that from the diffusiveness of the population, as well as from other causes, no precautions within its power will ever diminish the quantity of this liquid poison consumed in any part of the colony. The greater the population, and the more distant the stations from the seat of government, the more easy will it be to carry on private distilleries, and to prevent them from being detected. And even if the supply thus produced were unequal to the demand, it would be impossible to prevent smuggling on an extent of coast which the whole navy of England would be unequal to guard. If it were found impossible to restrain this evil when the colony was confined to a single station, and

---

*Collins, II. p. 139.
†Collins, II. p. 4.

a single harbour, can any better success be looked for now that the settlements are spread wide over the face of the country, when there are numerous settlers constantly[742] employed in the manufacture of this article, and every ship that arrives is provided with an abundant supply, the sale of it being more certain and more profitable than that of any other commodity.

Such has been the state of the convict population of this colony—past reformation none—future reformation still more hopeless. We have perhaps dwelt too long upon this part of the subject: fortunately the topics which remain may be compressed into a narrower compass.[743]

III. The third object or end of punishment is incapacitation; taking from the delinquent the power of committing the same crimes—

Transportation accomplished this object, with relation to a *certain place*. The convict, whilst in New South Wales, cannot commit crimes in England; the distance between the two places in a considerable degree precludes his illegal return, and this is the sum of the advantage.

Whilst the convict is at Botany Bay, he need not be dreaded in England, but his character remains the same, and the crimes which are mischievous in the mother country are mischievous in the colony—we ought not, therefore, to attribute to this punishment an[744] advantage which it does not possess. That an inhabitant of London should rejoice in the removal to a distance of a dangerous character, is easily comprehended; his particular interest is touched. But a punishment ought not to meet the approbation of a legislature, which, without diminishing the number of crimes committed, only changes the place of their commission.

The security, great as it may appear to be, against returns both legal and illegal, has not been so effectual as might have been expected. The number of convicts who left the colony between the years 1790 and 1796, the accounts of which are scattered over the whole of Collins' work, amount in the whole to 166, of which, 89 consisted of those whose terms had expired, and 76 of those whose terms had not expired. This is, however, very far from being the total amount of either description of those that had quitted the colony with or without permission. Escapes are in various parts of the work mentioned as being made in clusters, and the numbers composing each cluster not being stated, could not be carried to the above account.

The number of escapes will, most probably, increase as commerce extends, and as the convicts become more numerous, and consequently possess greater facilities for escaping.

IV. The fourth end or object of punishment is the making *compensation* or *satisfaction* to the party injured.

On this head there is but one word to be said.—The system of transportation is altogether destitute of this quality. It is true that this objection has no weight, except in comparison with a system of punishment in which provision is made out of the labour of the offender for the compensation to the party injured.

V. The fifth end or object proper to be kept in view in a system of penal legislation, *is* the collateral object of *Economy*.

If it could be said of the system in question, that it possessed all the several qualities desirable in a plan of penal legislation, its being attended with a certain greater degree of expence [*sic*] would not afford a very serious objection to it; but in this case this system, the most defective in itself, is, at the same time, carried on at a most enormous expence.

Upon this subject the 28th Report of the Committee of Finance contains the most accurate and minute information. From that Report it appears, that the total expence incurred during the ten or eleven first years of the establishment, ending in the year 1798, amounted to £1,037,000, which sum being divided by the number of convicts, will be found to amount to about £46 a-head. A possible reduction is in that Report contemplated, which might in time cut down the expence to about £37 per head. To this expence, however, must be added the value of each mans' labour, since, if not considered as thrown away, the value ought to be added to the account of expence.

Consider New South Wales as a large manufacturing establishment; the master manufacturer, on balancing his accounts, would find himself *minus* £46 for every workman that he employed.

What enhances the expence of this manufacturing establishment beyond what it would be in the mother country, are, 1, the expence incurred in conveying the workmen to a distance of between two and three thousand leagues; 2, the maintenance of the civil establishment consisting of Governors, Judges, Inspectors, Police Officers, &c.; 3, the maintenance of a military establishment, the sole object of which is to preserve subordination and peace in the colony; 4, the wide separation of the workmen, their untrustworthiness, their profligacy, favoured by the local circumstances of the colony, and the trifling value of the labour that can be extracted by compulsion from men who have no interest in the produce of their labour; 5, the high price of all the tools and raw materials employed in carrying on the manufactory, which are brought from Europe at the risk and expence of a long voyage.

If it be impossible to find a single clerk in Manchester or Liverpool who would not have taken all these circumstances into his consideration in making such a calculation as that in question, and if after, or without having made it, there is not one man of common sense who would have undertaken such a scheme, a necessary conclusion is, that the arithmetic of those who risk their own property, is very different from that of those who speculate at the expence of the public.[745]

In addition to the evils above enumerated as attending the system of transportation to New South Wales, the punishment thus inflicted is liable to be attended with various species of aggravation, making so much clear addition to the punishment pronounced by the legislator.

When a punishment is denounced by the legislature, it ought to be selected as the one best adapted to the nature of the offence; his will ought to be that the punishment inflicted should be such as he has directed; he regards it as sufficient; his will is that it should not be made either more lenient or more severe; he reckons that a certain punishment, when inflicted, produces a given effect, but that another punishment, if by accident coupled with the principal one, whether from negligence or interest on the part of subordinates, exceeding the intention of the law, is so much injustice, and being nugatory in the way of example, produces so much uncompensated evil.[746]

The punishment of transportation, which, according to the intention of the legislator, is designed as a comparatively lenient punishment, and is rarely directed to exceed a term of from seven to fourteen years, under the system in question is, in point of fact, frequently converted into capital punishment. What is the more to be lamented is, that this monstrous aggravation will, in general, be found to fall almost exclusively upon the least robust and least noxious class of offenders—those who, by their sensibility, former habits of life, sex and age, are least able to contend against the terrible visitation to which they are exposed during the course of a long and perilous voyage. Upon this subject the facts are as authentic as they are lamentable.

In a period of above eight years and a half, viz: from the 8th of May 1787, to the 31st December 1795, of five thousand one hundred and ninety-six embarked, five hundred and twenty-two perished in the course of the voyage; nor is this all, the accounts being incomplete. Out of twenty-eight vessels, in twenty-three of which, the mortality just spoken of, is stated to have taken place; there are five in respect of which the number of deaths is not mentioned.*

A voyage, however long it may be, does not necessarily shorten human existence. Captain Cook went round the world and returned without the loss of a single man. It necessarily follows, therefore, that a voyage which decimates those that are sent upon it must be attended with some very peculiar circumstances. In the present case, it is very clear that the mortality that thus prevailed arose partly from the state of the convicts, partly from the discipline to which they were subjected. Allow them to come on deck, everything is to be apprehended from their turbulent dispositions: confine them in the hold,

---

*The mortality attendant upon these first voyages to New South Wales appears greatly to have originated in negligence. Cargoes of convicts have in many latter instances been carried out without a single death occurring. [This note is not found within Dumont's edition.]

and they contract the most dangerous diseases. If the merchant, who contracts for their transportation, or the captain of the ship that is employed by him, happens to be unfeeling and rapacious, the provisions are scanty and of a bad quality. If a single prisoner happens to bring with him the seed of an infectious disorder, the contagion spreads over the whole ship. A ship (*The Hillsborough*) which, in the year 1799, was employed in the conveyance of convicts, out of a population of 300 lost 101.* It was not, says Col. Collins, a neglect of any of the requisite precautions, but the gaol fever, which had been introduced by one of the prisoners, that caused this dreadful ravage.

Whatever may be the precautions employed, by any single accident or act of negligence,[747] death, under its most terrific forms, is at all times liable to be introduced into these floating prisons—which have to traverse half the surface of the globe, with daily accumulating causes of destruction within them, before the diseased and dying can be separated from those who, having escaped infection, will have to drag out a debilitated existence in a state of bondage and exile.

Can the intention of the legislator be recognised in these accumulated aggravations to the punishment denounced? Can he be said to be aware of what he is doing when he denounces a punishment, the infliction of which is withdrawn altogether from his controul, which is subjected to a multiplicity of accidents—the nature of which is different from what it is pronounced to be—and in its execution bears scarce any resemblance to what he had the intention of inflicting? Justice, of which the most sacred attributes are certainty—precision, and which ought to weigh with the most scrupulous nicety the evils which it distributes, becomes under the system in question a sort of lottery, the pains of which fall into the hands of those that are least deserving of them. Translate this complication of chances and see what the result will be—"I sentence you," says the Judge, "but to what I know not—perhaps to storm and shipwrecks—perhaps to infectious disorders—perhaps to famine—perhaps to be massacred by savages—perhaps to be devoured by wild beasts—Away, take your chance, perish or prosper, suffer or enjoy; I rid myself of the sight of you, the ship that bears you away saves me from witnessing your sufferings, I shall give myself no more trouble about you."

But it may perhaps be said that, however deficient in a penal view, New South Wales possesses great political advantages: it is an infant colony, the population will by degrees increase, the successively rising generations will become more enlightened and more moral, and after the lapse of a certain number of centuries, it will become a dependent settlement of the highest political importance.

The first answer to this is, if it be thought to require any, that of all the expedients that could have been devised for founding a new colony in this

---

*Coll. Vol. II, p. 222.

or in any other place, the most expensive and the most hopeless, was the sending out as the embryo stock, a set of men of stigmatized character and dissolute habits of life. If there be any one situation more than another that requires patience, sobriety, industry, fortitude, intelligence, it is that of a set of colonists transported to a distance from their native country, constantly exposed to all sorts of privations, who have everything to create, and who, in a newly formed establishment, have to conciliate a set of savage and ferocious barbarians, justly dreading an invasion on their lives and property. Even an old established and well organized community would be exposed to destruction, from an infusion of vicious and profligate malefactors, if effectual remedies were not employed to repress them: such characters are destitute of all qualities, both moral and physical, that are essential in the establishing a colony, or that would enable them to subdue the obstacles opposed by nature in its rude and uncultivated state.[748]

Where colonization has succeeded, the character of the infant population has been far different. The founders of the most successful colonies have consisted of a set of benevolent and pacific *Quakers*, of men of religious scruples who have transported themselves to another hemisphere, in order that they might enjoy undisturbed liberty of conscience; of poor and honest labourers accustomed to frugal and industrious habits.*[749]

---

*That New South Wales has, since these papers were written, become a flourishing colony, is owing not so much to convict transportation, but to the admission of free settlers. The evils above pointed out continue to exist, but their influence is lessened by the infusion of honest and industrious settlers.

The following quotation confirms the reasoning of Mr. Bentham, and shows that the greater portion of the evils he points out, continue unabated.—Ed.

"If convicts are still to be transported hither, the only chance of their reformation consists in scattering them widely over the country, and giving them pastoral habits. Convict transportation is at best a bad system of colonization; and Governor Macquarrie, by his preference of the convict to the free, made it worse for the plantation, and totally inoperative as the penalty of felony, or the penitentiary of vice.

"The evils and expense of the transportation system would certainly be lessened by placing the convicts more in the service of farming and grazing settlers, out of the reach of the temptations and evil communications of large towns, the establishment of which was too much the policy of the late governor. The salutary life of a shepherd or a stockman, would gradually soften the heart of the most hardened convict; but instead of this, Governor Macquarrie's system was to keep them congregated in barracks, and employed, at a ration of a pound and a half of meat and the same quantity of flour per diem, upon showy public buildings. Of wretches possessed of no better means of reformation than these, it could not be expected that industrious colonists should ever be made. When their period of transportation expired, or was remitted by favour, they would therefore take their grant of land and allowances for settling, and sell them the next hour for spirits."

Journal of an Excursion across the Blue Mountains of New South Wales.—Edited by Baron Fields, p. 457. Lond. 1825. [This note does not appear within Dumont's edition.]

CHAPTER III.[750]
PANOPTICON PENITENTIARY.[751]

T he plans of Mr. Bentham upon this subject[752] are already before the public: for the purpose of the present work, it will be only necessary shortly to explain the three fundamental ideas which he lays down.

I. *A Circular, or Polygonal Building*, with cells on each story in the circumference; in the centre, a lodge for the Inspector, from which he may see all the prisoners without being himself seen, and from whence he may issue all his directions, without being obliged to quit his post.

II. *Management by Contract.* The contractor undertaking the whole concern at a certain price for each prisoner, reserving to himself the disposal of all the profit which may arise from their labours, the species of which is left to his choice.

Under this system, the interest of the Governor is, as far as possible, identified with his duty.—The more orderly and industrious the prisoners, the greater the amount of his profits. He will, therefore, teach them the most profitable trades, and give them such portion of the profits as shall excite them to labour. He unites in himself the characters of Magistrate, Inspector, Head of a Manufactory, and of a family; and is urged on by the strongest motives faithfully to discharge all these duties.[753]

III. *Responsibility of the Manager.* He is bound to assure the lives of his prisoners. A calculation is made of the average number of deaths in the year, among the mixed multitude committed to his care, and a certain sum is allowed to him for each; but at the end of the year, he is required to pay a similar sum for everyone lost by death or escape. He is, therefore, constituted the assurer [*sic*] of the lives and safe custody of his prisoners; but to assure their lives is, at the same time, to secure the multitude of cares and attentions, on which their health and well-being depend.[754]

Publicity is the effectual preservative against abuses—under the present system, prisons are covered with an impenetrable veil; the Panopticon, on the contrary, would be, so to speak, transparent. Accessible at all hours, to properly authorised Magistrates; accessible to everybody, at properly regulated hours, or days. The spectator, introduced into the central lodge, would behold the whole of the interior, and would be a witness to the detention of the prisoners, and a judge of their condition.[755]

Some individuals, pretending to a high degree of sensibility, have considered this *continual inspection*, which constitutes the peculiar merit of Mr. Bentham's plan, as objectionable. It has appeared to them as a restraint more terrible than any other tyranny: they have depicted an establishment of this kind as a place of torment. In so doing, these men of sensibility have forgotten the state of most other prisons, in which the prisoners heaped together, can enjoy tranquillity neither day nor night.[756] They forget, that under this system of continual inspection, a greater degree of liberty and ease can be allowed, that chains and shackles may be suppressed, that the prisoners may be allowed to associate in small companies, that all quarrels, tumults, and noise, bitter sources of vexation, will be prevented; that the prisoners will be protected against the caprices of their gaolers, and the brutality of their companions; whilst those frequent and cruel instances of neglect which have occurred, will be prevented by the facility of appeal which will be afforded to the principal authority. These real advantages are overlooked by a fantastic sensibility which never reasons.[757]

Let us suppose a prison established upon this plan; and then observe in what manner it contributes to the several ends of punishment.

FIRST END—Example.

It would be placed in the neighbourhood of the metropolis, where the greatest number of persons are collected together, and especially of those who require to be reminded, by penal exhibitions, of the consequences of crime. The appearance of the building, the singularity of its shape, the walls and ditches by which it is surrounded, the guards stationed at its gates, would all excite ideas of restraint and punishment, whilst the facility which would be given to admission, would scarcely fail to attract a multitude of visitors—and what would they see?—a set of persons deprived of liberty which they have misused; compelled to engage in labour, which was formerly their aversion, and restrained from riot and intemperance, in which they formerly delighted; the whole of them clothed in a particular dress, indicating the infamy of their crimes. What scene could be more instructive to the great proportion of the spectators? What a source of conversation, of allusion, of domestic instruction. How naturally would the aspect of this prison lead to a comparison between the labour of the free man and the prisoner, between the enjoyments of the innocent and the privations of the criminal. And, at the same time, the *real* punishment would be less than the apparent:—the spectators, who would have only a momentary view of this doleful spectacle, would not perceive all the circumstances which would effectively soften the rigours of this prison. The punishment would be visible, and the imagination would exaggerate its amount, its relaxations[758] would be out of sight, no portion of the suffering inflicted would be lost. The greater number even of the prisoners, being taken from the class of unfortunate and suffering individuals, would be in a state of comfort—whilst *ennui*, the scourge of ordinary prisons, would be banished.[759]

SECOND OBJECT—REFORMATION.

Idleness, intemperance, and vicious connections, are the three principal causes of corruption among the poor; when habits of this nature have become to such a degree inveterate, as to surmount the tutelary motives, and to lead to the commission of crimes, no hope of reformation can be entertained but by a new course of education, an education that shall place the patient in a situation in which he will find it impossible to gratify his vicious propensities, and where every surrounding object will tend to give birth to habits and inclinations of a nature altogether opposite. The principal instrument which can be employed on this occasion is, perpetual superintendence [*sic*]. Delinquents are a peculiar race of beings, who require unremitted [*sic*] inspection. Their weakness consists in yielding to the seductions of the passing moment. Their minds are weak and disordered, and though their disease is neither so clearly marked nor so incurable as that of ideots [*sic*] and lunatics, like these, they require to be kept under restraints, and they cannot, without danger, be left to themselves.

Under the safeguard of[760] this continual inspection, without which, success is not to be expected, the Penitentiary House described, includes all the causes which are calculated to destroy the seeds of vice, and to rear those of virtue.[761]

I. *Labour.*—It is admitted that constraint, instead of inspiring[762] a taste for labour, is calculated to augment the aversion to it. It must, however, be recollected, that in this case, labour is the only resource against ennui; that being imposed upon all, it will be encouraged by example, and rendered more agreeable by being carried on in the company of others; it will be followed by immediate reward, and the individual being allowed a share in the profits, it will lose the character of servitude, by his being rendered, in measure, a partner in the concern. Those who formerly understood no lucrative business, will, in this new course of education, obtain new faculties and new enjoyments; and when they shall be set free, will have learned a trade, the profits of which are greater than those of fraud and rapine.

II. *Temperance.*—We have already had occasion to show that nearly all the crimes committed at Botany Bay, either originate[763] or are increased by the use of spirituous liquors, and that it is impossible to prevent their use. Here the evil is arrested in its source, it will not be possible to smuggle in a drop of this poison—transgressions will therefore be impossible. Man yields to necessity—difficulties may stimulate his desires, but an absolute impossibility of satisfying them, destroys them when they are not supported by long established habits. There is much humanity in a strict rule, which prevents not only faults and chastisements, but temptations also.

III. *Separation into classes.*—The Panopticon is the only practicable plan which admits of the prisoners being divided into little societies, in such manner as to separate those whose vicious propensities are most contagious. These associations can hardly fail to afford opportunities for the performance of reciprocal services, for the exercise of the affections, and the formation of habits favourable to reformation. The relation of master and scholar will gradually be formed among them; opportunities will thus be given for bestowing rewards for instruction;[764] for exciting emulation in learning, and the creation of a sentiment of honour and self-esteem, which will be among the first fruits of application. Ideas of improvement and lawful gains will, by degrees, supplant those of licentiousness and fraudulent acquisition. All these advantages arise out of the very nature of the establishment.

Why should not unmarried prisoners be allowed to inter-marry. It would operate as a powerful spur to those who aimed at attaining this reward, which should only be bestowed on account of orderly conduct and industry.

These little societies present an additional security, arising from their mutual responsibility.[765] It is both just and natural to say to them, "You live together, you act together, you were able to have prevented this crime, and if you have not so done, you are accomplices in it." Thus the prisoners would be converted into guardians and inspectors of each other. Each cell would be interested in the good conduct of every one of its members. If any one of them should be distinguished for its good order, some distinction might be bestowed upon it, which should be visible to all. By such means, a feeling of honour might be excited even in the abode of ignominy.[766]

IV. *Instructions.*—Indigence and ignorance are the parents of crime.[767] The instruction of those prisoners, who are not too old to learn, confers upon them many benefits at once; it affords great assistance in changing the habits of the mind, and elevating them, in their own estimation, from the class of beings who are degraded on account of the inferiority of their education. Different studies may usefully fill up the intervals of time, when mechanical operations are suspended; both prudence and humanity dictating the occupation of those intervals, instead of abandoning to themselves minds to whom idleness is a burthen difficult to bear. But the object is much more important, especially with regard to young offenders, who form the largest proportion of the whole. The prison should be their school, in which they should learn those habits, which should prevent their ever entering it again.[768]

The services of religion ought to be rendered attractive, in order that they may be efficacious. They may be performed in the centre of the building, without the prisoners quitting their cells. The central lodge may be opened for the admission of the public, the worship adapted to the nature of the establishment, may be accompanied with solemn music to add to its solemnity. The Chaplain engaged in its performance would not be a stranger to the prisoners; his instructions should be adapted to the wants of those to whom they are[769] addressed; he would be known to them as their daily benefactor, who watches over the progress of their amendment; who is the interpreter of their wishes, and their witness before their superiors. As their protector and instructor, as a friend who consoles and who enlightens them, he unites all the titles which can render him an object of respect and affection. How many sensible and virtuous men would seek[770] a situation which presents, to a religious mind, opportunities for conquests more interesting than the savage regions of Africa and Canada.[771]

There is, at all times, great reason for distrusting the reformation of criminals. Experience too often justifies the maxim of the poet,

"L'honneur est comme une île escarpée et sans bords:
On n'y peut plus rentrer des qu'on en est dehors."[772]

But those who are most distrustful and incredulous of good, must acknowledge at least, that there is a great difference to be made in this respect, on account of the age of the delinquents and the nature of their offences; youth may be moulded like soft wax, whilst advanced age will not yield to new impressions. Many crimes are not deeply rooted in the heart, but spring up there from seduction, example, and above all, indigence and hunger.[773] Some are sudden acts of vengeance, which do not imply habitual perversity. These distinctions are just and not controverted,—it must also be admitted, that the plan we have described presents the most efficacious means for the amendment of those who have preserved some remains of honest principle.[774]

THIRD OBJECT—Suppression of power to injure.

Whatever may be its effects in producing internal reformation and correcting the will. The Panopticon unites all the conditions requisite for the prevention of the commission of new offences.

Under this head, the prisoners may be considered at two periods—the period of their imprisonment; the period posterior to their liberation.

During the first, suppose them as wicked as you will, what crimes can they commit whilst under uninterrupted inspection, divided by cells at all times sufficiently strong to resist a revolt, unable to unite or to conspire without being seen; responsible the one for the other; deprived of all communication with the exterior; deprived of all intoxicating liquors (those stimulants to dangerous enterprises); and in the hand of a governor who could immediately isolate the dangerous individual. The simple enumeration of these circumstances inspires a feeling of perfect security. When we recall the picture of Botany Bay, the contrast becomes striking as it can be rendered.[775]

The prevention of crimes on the part of delinquent prisoners, is also[776] in proportion to the difficulty of their escape; and what system affords in this respect a security comparable to that of the Panopticon.

With respect to discharged prisoners, the only absolute guarantee is in their reformation.

Independently of this happy effect, which may be expected in this plan more than upon any other, the liberated prisoners would, for the most part, have acquired, by the savings made for them out of their part of the profit[777] of their labour, a stock which will secure them from the immediate temptations of want, and give them time to avail themselves of those resources of industry, which they have acquired during their captivity.

But this is not all. I have reserved for this Chapter the mention of an ingenious plan, which the author of the Panopticon has proposed as a supplement to this scheme of punishment. He has paid particular attention to the dangerous and critical situation of discharged prisoners, when re-entering the world after a detention, perhaps, for many years: they have no friends to receive them; without reputation to recommend them; with characters open to suspicion; and many times, perhaps, in the first transports of joy for recovered liberty, as little qualified to use it with discretion as the slaves who have broken their fetters. By these considerations, the author was led to the idea of an auxiliary establishment, into which the discharged prisoners might be admitted when they leave the Panopticon, and be allowed to continue for a longer or shorter period, according to the nature of their crimes, and their previous conduct. The details of the plan would be foreign to the present subject. It must suffice to say, that in this privileged asylum, they would have different degrees of liberty, the choice of their occupations, the entire profit of their labour, with fixed and moderate charges for their board and lodging, and the right of going and returning, on leaving a certain sum as a security; they would wear no prisoner's uniform, no humiliating badge. The greater number, in the first moment of their embarrassment, whilst they have no certain object in view, would, themselves, choose a retreat so suitable to their situation. This transient sojourn, this noviciate, would serve to conduct them by degrees to their entire liberty; it would be an intermediate state between captivity and independence and afford a proof of the sincerity of their amendment. It would afford a just precaution against individuals in whom an immediate and absolute confidence could not be reposed without danger.[778]

FOURTH OBJECT—Compensation to the party injured.

In most systems[779] of jurisprudence, when a delinquent has been corporally punished, justice is thought to have been satisfied; it is not in general required that he should make compensation to the party injured.

It is true that, in the greater number of cases, compensation could not be exacted of him. Delinquents are commonly of the poorer class, *ex nihilo, nihil fit.*

If they are idle during their imprisonment, far from being able to render satisfaction, they constitute a charge upon society.

If they are condemned to public works, these works, rarely sufficiently lucrative to cover the expense of undertaking them, cannot[780] furnish any surplus.

It is only in a plan like the Panopticon, in which, by the combination of labour and economy in the administration, it is possible to obtain a profit sufficiently great to offer at least some portion of indemnity to the parties injured—Mr. Bentham had made engagements upon this head in his contract with the ministers. In the prisons of Philadelphia, they levy upon the portion of profit allowed to the prisoner, the expenses of his detection and prosecution. One step more, and they will grant indemnity to the parties injured.[781]

FIFTH OBJECT—Economy.

To say that of two plans of equal merit, the most economical ought to be preferred, is to advance a proposition which must appear trivial to all those who do not know that the expense of an enterprise is often its secret recommendation, and that economy is a virtue against which there exists a general conspiracy.

In the contract for the Panopticon, one thousand convicts were to have cost the state £12 per head, without including the expense of constructing the prison, which was estimated at £12,000 and the ground at £10,000, upon which reckoning interest at £5 per cent., £1, 10s. ought to be added for the annual expense of each, making the total expense of each individual, £13, 10s. per annum.

It should be recollected that at this time the average expense of each convict in New Holland, was £37 per annum, nearly three times as much. Besides the author of the Panopticon assured

I. An indemnity to the parties injured.

II. He allowed a fourth part of the profits of their labour to the prisoners.

III. He was to make a future reduction in the expense to government.

A new undertaking like that of the Panopticon, intended to embrace many branches of industry, would not yield its greatest profits at first; it would be expensive at first and only become profitable by degrees. Time would be required for establishing its manufactories, and for the cultivation of the grounds applicable to the support of the establishment; for forming its pupils, and regulating their habits, in a word bringing to perfection the whole economy of its system. Mr. Bentham had expressly stipulated for the publicity of his accounts; and if the advantages, as was expected, had become considerable, the government would have been enabled to take advantage of them in obtaining more favourable terms in its subsequent contracts. Mr. Bentham reckoned, from the calculations he had made, and respecting which he had consulted experienced persons, that after a short time the convicts would cost the government nothing.[782]

Laying aside everything hypothetical, it is clear that a Penitentiary at home ought to be less expensive than a colonial establishment. The reasons for this opinion have been given when speaking of transportation to Botany Bay.

I have shewn the excellence of this plan with reference to all the ends of punishment, it remains to be observed that it attains its object without producing any of those collateral inconveniences which abound in colonial transportation. There is no prolonged sojourn in the hulks.—None of the dangers of a long sea voyage—no promiscuous intercourse of prisoners—no contagious sickness—no danger of famine—no warfare with the savage natives—no rebellions—no abuse of power by the persons in authority—in short an entire absence of the accidental and accessory evils, of which every page of the history of the penal colony affords an example. What an immense economy in the employment of punishment. It will no longer be dissipated and lost upon barren rocks, and amid far distant deserts, it will always preserve the nature of legal punishment; of just and merited suffering, without being converted into evils of every description which excite only pity. The whole of it will be seen. It will all be useful; it will not depend upon chance;—its execution will not be abandoned to subordinate and mercenary hands—the legislator who appoints it may incessantly watch over its administration.

The success which may be obtained from a well regulated Penitentiary, is no longer a simple probability founded upon reasoning. The trial has been made; it has succeeded even beyond what has been hoped. The Quakers of Pennsylvania have the honour of making the attempt;—it is one of the most beauteous ornaments of the crown of humanity which distinguishes them among all other societies of Christians. They had a long time to struggle with the ordinary obstacles—of prejudice and indifference on the part of the public—the routine of the tribunals, and repulsive incredulity of frigid reasoners [*sic*].

The Penitentiary house at Philadelphia, is described not only in the official reports of its governor, but also in the accounts of two disinterested observers, whose agreement is the more striking, as they brought to its examination neither the same prejudices nor views—the one was a Frenchman, the Duke de Liancourt, well acquainted with the arrangements of hospitals and prisons—the other an Englishman, Captain Turnbull, more occupied with maritime affairs than politics or jurisprudence.

Both of them represent the interior of this prison as a scene of peaceful and regular activity. Hauteur and rigour are not displayed on the part of the gaolers, nor insolence nor baseness on the part of the prisoners. Their language is gentle, a harsh expression is not permitted. If any fault is committed, the punishment is solitary confinement, and the registration of the fault in a book, in which every one has an account opened as well for good as for evil. Health, decency, and propriety reign throughout. There is nothing to offend the most delicate of the senses; no noise, no boisterous songs nor tumultuous conversation. Every one engaged with his own work, fears to interrupt the labours of others. This external peace is maintained as favourable to reflection and labour, and well calculated to prevent that state of irritation, so common elsewhere among prisoners and their keepers.

"I was surprised" said Captain Turnbull, "at finding a woman exercising the functions of gaoler; this circumstance having excited my curiosity, I was informed that the husband having filled the same situation before her, amidst the attentions he was paying to his daughter, he was seized with the yellow fever and died, leaving the prisoners to regret that they had lost a friend and protector. In consideration of his services, his widow was chosen to succeed him. She has discharged all the duties with equal attention and humanity."

Where shall we find similar traits in the registers of a prison. They call up the pictures of a future golden age depicted by a prophet, when "the wolf shall lie down with the lamb, and a little child shall lead them."

I cannot refuse to transcribe two other facts, which do not stand in need of any commentary:—"During the yellow fever in 1793, there was much difficulty in obtaining nurses for the sick in the hospitals at Bush Hill. Recourse was had to the prison. The question was asked, the danger of the service was explained to the convicts, as many offered themselves as were wanted. They discharged their duties faithfully till the conclusion of that tragic scene, and none of them demanded any wages till the period of their discharge."

The females gave another proof of good conduct during the course of the contagion. They were requested to give up their bedsteads for the use of the hospital—they willingly offered their beds also.

Oh Virtue! where wilt thou hide thyself, exclaimed the philosopher,[783] upon witnessing an act of probity on the part of a beggar. Would he have been less surprised at this act of heroic benevolence in a criminal prison?

Had this good conduct of the prisoners been only a simple suspension of their vices and crimes, it would have been a great point gained; but it extended much further.

"Of all the criminals who have been found guilty," says Turnbull, "there has not been five in each hundred, who have been in the prison before."

At New York, although the result has not been so favourable, it exhibits the good effects of the system.—"During the five years, ending in 1801," says Mr. Eddy, the principal governor of the Penitentiary, in the account rendered to his fellow citizens, "of three hundred and forty-nine prisoners who have been set at liberty at the expiration of their sentences, or by pardons, twenty-nine only have been convicted of new offences; and of this twenty-nine, sixteen were foreigners. Of eighty-six pardoned, eight have been apprehended for new offences; and of this eight, five were foreigners."

It must, however, be remembered, that we may guard against exaggeration: that of these liberated prisoners, many may have expatriated themselves, and committed crimes in the neighbouring States, being unwilling to expose themselves to the austere imprisonment of New York or Philadelphia; for it is a fact, that the risk of death is less frightful to men of this temper, than laborious captivity.

The success of these establishments is, without doubt, owing in great measure to the enlightened zeal of their founders and inspectors; but it has permanent causes in the sobriety and industry established, and the rewards bestowed for good conduct.[784]

The rule which has ensured sobriety, has been the entire exclusion of strong liquors—no fermented liquor is allowed, not even small beer. It has been found more easy to insure abstinence than moderation. Experience has proved that the stimulus of strong liquors has only a transitory effect, and that an abundant and simple nourishment, with water for the only drink, fits men for the performance of continued labours. Many of those who entered the prison of New York with constitutions enfeebled by intemperance and debauchery, have regained, in a short time, under this regime, their health and vigour.[785]

The Duke de Liancourt and Captain Turnbull have entered into more precise details. We learn from them, that since the adoption of this system, the charge for medicines, which amounted annually to more than twelve hundred dollars, has been reduced to one hundred and sixty. This fact affords a still stronger proof of the salubrity [*sic*] of this prison.

This exposition, in which I have omitted many favourable circumstances, without suppressing anything of a contrary nature, is sufficient to show the superiority of Penitentiaries over the system of transportation. If the results have been so advantageous in America, why should they be less so in England? The nature of man is uniform. Criminals are not more obstinate in the one place than the other. The motives which may be employed are equally powerful. The new plan proposed by the author of the Panopticon, presents a sensible improvement upon the American methods—the inspection is more complete—the instruction more extended—escape more difficult; publicity is increased in every respect; the distribution of the prisoners, by means of cells and classes, obviates the inconvenient association which subsists in the Penitentiary at Philadelphia.[786] But what is worth more than all the rest, is, that the responsibility of the governor in the Panopticon system is connected with his personal interest in such manner, that he cannot neglect one of his duties, without being the first to suffer; whilst all the good he does to his prisoners redounds to his own advantage. Religion and humanity animated the founders of the American Penitentiaries: will these generous principles be less powerful when united with the interests of reputation and fortune? The two grand securities of every public establishment—the only ones upon which a politician can constantly rely—the only ones whose operation is not subject to relaxation—the only ones which always being in accordance with virtue, may perform its part, and even replace it when it is wanting.[787]

CHAPTER IV.
FELONY.[788]

Felony is a word of which the signification seems to have undergone various revolutions. It seems at first to have been vaguely applied to a very extensive mode of delinquency, or rather, (for delinquency in general: at a time when the laws scarce knew of any other species of delinquency cognizable by fixed rules, than the breach of a political engagement, and when all political engagements were comprised in one, that of feudal obligation. Upon feudal principles, everything that was possessed by a subject, and was considered as a permanent source of property and power, was considered as a gift, by the acceptance of which, the acquirer contracted a loose and indefinite kind of engagement, the nature of which was never accurately explained, but was understood to be to this effect: that the acceptor should render certain stipulated services to the donor, and should in general, refrain from everything that was prejudicial to his interests. It was this principle of subjection, in its nature rather moral than political, which at the first partition of conquered countries, bound the different ranks of men, by whatever names distinguished, to each other, as the Barons to the Prince, the Knights to the Barons, and the Peasants to the Knights. If then the acceptor failed in any of these points, if in any one of his steps he fell from the line which had been traced for him, and which at that time was the only line of duty, he was not such a man as his benefactor took him for, the motive for the benefaction ceased. He lost his fief, the only source of his political importance, and with it all that was worth living for. He was thrust down among the ignoble and defenceless crowd of needy retainers, whose persons and precarious properties were subject to the arbitrary disposal of the hand that fed them. So striking and impressive a figure did such a catastrophe make in the imaginations of men, that the punishment of death, when, in course of time, it came in various instances to be superadded to the other, showed itself only in the light of an appendage.* It came in by custom, rather than by any regular and positive institution: it seemed to follow rather as a natural effect of the impotence to which the inferior was reduced, than in consequence of any regular exertion of the public will of the community.[789]

---

*Blackst. Com. 95. [This note does not appear within Dumont's edition.]

This seems to have been the aspect of the times at the first dawnings [*sic*] of the feudal polity; but it was impossible things should long remain in so unsettled a state. It is in such times, however, that we are to look for the origin of a word, which sometimes as the name of a crime, sometimes as a punishment, is to be met with in the earliest memorials that are extant of the feudal law.[790]

Some etymologists, to show they understood Greek, have derived it from the Greek: if they had happened to have understood Arabic, they would have derived it from the Arabic. Sir Edward Coke, knowing nothing of Greek, but having a little stock of Latin learning, which he loses no opportunity of displaying, derives it from *fel*, gall. Spelman, who has the good sense to perceive that the origin of an old northern word is to be looked for in an old northern language, rejecting the Greek, and saying nothing of the Latin, proposes various etymologies. According to one of them, it is derived from two words, *fee*, which, in ancient Anglo-Saxon had, and in modern English has, a meaning which approaches to that of property or money; and *lon* [*sic*], which in modern German, he says, means *price*: fee lon is therefore *pretium feudi*. This etymology, the author of the Commentaries adopts, and justifies by observing, that it is a common phrase to say, such an act is as much as your life or estate is worth. But *felony*, in mixed Latin, *felonia*, is a word that imports action. I should therefore rather be inclined to derive it from some verb, than from two substantives, which when put together, and declined in the most convenient manner, import not any such meaning.

The verb *to fall*, as well as *to fail*, which probably was in its origin the same as the other, by an obvious enough metaphysical extension, is well known to have acquired the signification of *to offend*; the same figure is adopted in the French, and probably in every other language.*

In Anglo-Saxon there is such a word as *feallan*,† the evident root of the English word now in use. In German, there is such a word as *faellen*, which has the same signification. This derivation therefore, which is one of Spelman's, is what seems to be the most natural. So much for the origin of the word: not that it is of any consequence whence it came, so it were but gone.

---

*We say, he fell, as well as he swerved from the line of duty: he fell from his allegiance. The original sin of man is called the fall of man. Lord Clarendon says, somewhere, he fell from his duty and all his former friends. Let him who standeth, says the Gospel, take heed lest he fall. In Ecclesiastical Jurisprudence, a heretic relapsed, is one who, having once been convicted in heresy, *falls* into the same offense a second time. [This note does not appear within Dumont's edition. Instead, that edition presents a much briefer footnote, in English, at this parallel point of the chapter: "(1) To *fell*. He *fell* from his duty, he *fell* from his allegiance," *Théorie des peines*, vol. I p. 471.]

†*An* is nothing but the common termination of the infinitive mood. [This note does not appear within Dumont's edition.]

As the rigours of the feudal polity were relaxed, and fiefs became permanent and descendible, the resumption of the fief upon every instance of trivial delinquency, became less and less of course. A feudatory might commit an offence that was not a felony. On the other hand, it was found too, that for many offences the mere resumption of the feud was not, by any means, a sufficient punishment; for a man might hold different feuds of as many different persons. The Sovereign, too, interposed his claim on behalf of himself and the whole community, and exacted punishments for offences which, to the immediate Lord of the feudatory, might happen not to be obnoxious. In this way, for various offences, pecuniary and corporal punishments, in various degrees, and even death itself, came in some instances to be substituted; in others, to be superadded by positive laws to that original indiscriminating punishment, which used at first to follow from almost every offence. That punishment remained still inseparably annexed to all those offences which were marked by the highest degree of corporal punishment, the punishment of death: partly with a view of giving the Lord an opportunity of ridding himself of a race of vassals, tainted by an hereditary stain; partly, in order to complete the destruction of the delinquents' political as well as natural existence. The punishment of forfeiture, being the original punishment, still continued to give denomination to the complex mass of punishment of which it now constituted but a part. The word felony now came to signify a punishment: viz. the complex mode of punishment of which that simple mode of punishment, which anciently stood annexed to every delinquency a feudatory could incur, was a main ingredient.[791]

At this period of its history, when the above was its signification, the word felony was as a part of the Norman Jurisprudence imported into this country by the Norman conquerors; for among the Saxons there are no traces of its having been in use. At this period it stood annexed only to a few crimes of the grossest nature: of a nature, the fittest to strike the imagination of rude and unreflecting minds, and these not very heterogeneous. Theft, robbery, devastation when committed by the ruinous instrument of fire, or upon the whole face of a country with an armed force; these and homicide, the natural consequences of such enterprises, or of the spirit of hostility which dictated them, were included by it. At this time, the import of the word felony was not either as the name of a punishment, or as the name of an offence, as yet immeasureably [sic] extensive. But lawyers, by various subtleties, went on adding to the mass of punishment, still keeping to the same name. At the same time, legislators, compelled by various exigencies, went on adding to the list of offences, punishable by the punishment of that name; till at length it became the name not of one, but of an incomprehensible heap of punishments; nor of one offence only, but of as many sorts of offences almost as can be conceived. Tell me now that a man has committed a felony, I am not a whit the nearer knowing what is his offence: all I can possibly learn from it is, what he is to suffer. He may have committed an offence against individuals, against a neighbourhood, or against the state. Under any natural principle of arrangement, upon any other than that which is governed by the mere accidental and mutable circumstance of punishment, it may be an offence of any class, and almost of every order of each class. The delinquents are all huddled together under one name, and pelted with an indiscriminating volley of incongruous, and many of them, unavailing punishments.[792]

Felony, considered as a complex mode of punishment, stands at present divided into two kinds: the one styled *Felony without benefit of Clergy*, or in a shorter way, *Felony without Clergy*, or as capital punishment is one ingredient in it, *Capital Felony*; the other, Felony within benefit of Clergy, Felony within Clergy, or *Clergyable* [*sic*] *Felony*. The first may be styled the greater; the latter, the lesser felony. There are other punishments to which these are more analogous in quality, as well as in magnitude, than the one of them is to the other—such is the confusion introduced by a blind practice, and as the consequence of that practice, an inapposite and ill-digested nomenclature.[793]

How punishments so widely different came to be characterized in the first place by the same generic name, and thence by specific names, thus uncouth and inexpressive, shall be explained by and by, after we have analysed and laid open the contents of the greater felony, of which the other is but an off-set, detached from the main root.[794]

HISTORY OF THE BENEFIT OF CLERGY

The Christian religion, ere yet it had gained any settled footing in the state, had given birth to an order of men, who laid claim to a large and indefinite share in the disposal of that remote, but boundless mass of pains and pleasures, which it was one main business of that religion to announce. This claim, in proportion as it was acquiesced in, gave them power: for what is power over men: but the faculty of contributing in some way or other to their happiness or misery? This power, in proportion as they obtained it, it became their endeavour to convert, (as it is in the nature of man to endeavour to convert all power) into a means of advancing their own private interest. First, the interest of their own order, which was a private interest as opposed to the more public one of the community at large; and then of the individuals of that order. In this system of usurpation, a few perhaps had their eyes open; but many more probably acted under the sincere persuasion, that the advancement of their order above that of others, was beneficial to the community at large. This power, in its progress to those ends, would naturally seek the depression, and by degrees the overthrow of the political power, as of any other that opposed it. These operations, carried on by an indefinite multitude of persons, but all tending to the same end, wore the appearance of being carried on in concert, as if a formal plan had been proposed and unanimously embraced by the whole Clergy, to subdue the whole body of the Laity: whereas, in fact, no such plan was ever universally concerted and avowed, as in truth, there needed none. The means were obvious, the end was one and the same. There was no fear of clashing. Each succeeding operator took up the work where his predecessor had left off, and carried it on just so far as interest prompted and opportunity allowed.

In pursuance of this universal plan, not concerted, but surer than if it had been the result of concert, were those exemptions laid claim to which, by a long and whimsical concatenation of causes and effects, were the means of breaking down the punishment of felony into the two species of it that now subsist.

The persons of these favoured mortals, honoured as they pretended they were by a more immediate intercourse with the divinity, and employed as they were incessantly in managing the most important, and indeed, only important concerns of mankind, were of course to be accounted *sacred*: a word of loose and therefore the more convenient signification, importing at bottom, nothing more than that the subject to which it was attributed, was or was not to be accounted an object of distant awe and terror. They were therefore not to be judged by profane judgments, sentenced by profane mouths, or touched, in any manner that was unpleasant to them, by profane hands. The places wherein that mysterious intercourse was carried on, imbibed the essence of this mysterious quality. Stones when put together in a certain form became sacred too. Earth, within a certain distance round about those stones, became sacred too. Hence the privilege of sanctuary. In short, the whole of the material as well as intellectual globe became divided into sacred and profane; of which, so much as was sacred was either composed of themselves, or become subjected to their power. The rest of it lay destitute of these invaluable privileges, and as the name imports, tainted with a note of infamy.

I pass rapidly over the progress of their claim of exemption from profane judicature: the reader will find it ably and elegantly delineated in Sir W. Blackstone's Commentaries.

As to the causes, those which come under the denomination of felonies, are the only ones with which at present we have to do. Confining our consideration therefore to these causes; as to persons, it was first claimed, one may suppose, for those of their own order, by degrees, for as many as they should think fit for that particular purpose to recognise as belonging to that order. By degrees, the patience of profane judges was put to such a stretch, that it could hold no longer; and they seem to have been provoked to a general disallowance of those exceptions which had swelled till they had swallowed up in a manner the whole rule. This sudden and violent reformation wearing the appearance of an abuse, the clergy had influence enough in the legislature to procure an Act* to put a stop to it. By this Act it was provided, that all manner of Clerks, as well secular as religious, which shall be from henceforth convict before the secular Justices,—for any treasons or felonies touching other persons than the King himself, or his Royal Majesty, shall from henceforth freely have and enjoy the privilege of Holy Church, and shall be, without any impeachment† or delay, delivered to the Ordinaries‡ demanding them.

This Statute, one should have thought, would have been sufficiently explicit on the one hand, to secure the exemption to all persons in clerical orders, so, on the other hand, to exclude all persons not possessed of that qualification. To prove a person entitled to the exemption, the obvious and only conclusive evidence was, the instrument of ordination.[795] But the different ranks of persons who were all comprised under the common name of Clerks, and as such, partook more or less of the sacred character, were numerous: and some of these seem to have been admitted to their offices without any written instrument of ordination. Whether this omission was continued on purpose to let in a looser method of evidence, or whether it was accidental, so it is that the clergy had the address to get the production of that written evidence dispensed with. In the room of it, they had the address to prevail on the courts to admit of another criterion, which, ridiculous as it may seem at this time of day, was not then altogether so incompetent. "Orders," they said, or might have said, "may be forged, or may be fabricated for the purpose; but as a proof that the man really is of our sacred order, you shall have a proof that can neither be forged nor fabricated; he shall read as we do." The book was probably at first a Latin book: the Bible or some other book made use of in Church service. At that time, few who were not clergymen could read at all, and still fewer could read Latin. And the Judges, if they happened to see through the cheat, might in some instances, perhaps, not be sorry

---

*25 Edw. III. Stat. 3, c. 4.

†It should be *hindrance*: the French original is *empeschement*. [The precise word that Dumont's edition uses at this parallel point is *"empêchement," Théorie des peines*, vol. I p. 478.]

‡Meaning the Bishop, or other Ecclesiastical superior. [Dumont's edition uses the phrase *"supérieurs ecclésiastiques," Théorie des peines*, vol. I p. 478.]

to connive at it, in favour of a man possessed of so rare and valuable a qualification. But one book was easily substituted for another: a man might easily be tutored so as to get by rote a small part of a particular book; and as society advanced to maturity, learning became more and more diffused. We need not wonder therefore, if by the time of Henry VIIth, it was found that as many laymen as divines were admitted to the ecclesiastical privilege. I should suppose a great many more, for there is something in the ecclesiastical function, that in the worst of times will render them less liable than others of the same rank and fortune, to fall into open and palpable enormities. A Statute therefore* was made to apply a remedy to this abuse; and what would one imagine was that remedy? To oblige persons, claiming the benefit of Clergy, to produce their orders? No; but to provide, that persons claiming it, and not being in orders, should not be allowed it more than once; and that *all* persons who had once been allowed it, should have a mark set upon them, whereby they might be known. Real Clergymen, Clergymen who had orders to produce, were by an express provision of the Statute, entitled to claim it *toties quoties*, as often as they should have need, which privilege they have still.

When a felon was admitted to his clergy, he was not absolutely set free, but delivered to the Ordinary.[796] The great point then was, if we may believe Lay Judges, who it is to be confessed are not altogether disinterested witnesses, to prove him innocent, for this tended to discredit the profane tribunal. This business of proving him innocent, was called his *purgation*. If this were impracticable, he was put to penance: that is, subjected to such corporal punishment as the Ordinary thought proper to inflict upon him, which we may imagine, was not very severe. Thus it was that the clergy contrived to bind even the most stubborn spirits under the yoke of their dominion; the honest and credulous by their fears; the profligate, though incredulous, by their hopes.

Circumstances, however, are not wanting, which tend pretty strongly to make it probable, that when once a man got into the hands of the clergy, he almost always stood the purging, and proved innocent; and it is what the Lay Judges seem to have taken for granted would be the case of course.[797] When therefore they made a point of making the offender suffer the train of punishments that stood annexed to acknowledged guilt, (death excepted, which was too much for them to attempt) they knew no other way of compassing it, than by insisting on his not being admitted to make purgation. These punishments, the imprisonment excepted, consisted altogether of forfeitures and civil disabilities; penalties with which the Ecclesiastical Superior had nothing to do, and which it lay altogether within the province of the Temporal Judge to enforce. One should have thought then it would have been a

---

*4 Hen. VII. c. 13. [This note does not appear within Dumont's edition.]

much less apparent stretch of authority in the latter, to give effect to the proceedings of his own judicature, than to lay a restraint on the Ecclesiastical Judge in the exercise of what was acknowledged to be his. But it were too much to expect anything like consistency in the proceedings of those rude ages. The whole contest between the Temporal Judge and the Spiritual was, an irregular scramble, the result of which was perpetually varying, according to the temper of individuals and the circumstances of the time.

By the time of Queen Elizabeth it came to be generally understood that purgation, which originally meant trial, was synonymous to acquittal.*[798] This is so true, that when by a Statute of that reign,† purgation came to be abolished, the legislature, instead of appointing a trial, appointed punishment. Persons claiming the benefit of Clergy, instead of being delivered to the Ordinary to make purgation, were now, after being burnt in the hand, to be forthwith delivered out of prison, unless the Temporal Judge should think proper to sentence them to imprisonment, which he was now for the first time empowered to do for any time not exceeding a year.

It will here be asked what was done with the pecuniary punishments, the forfeitures, the corruption of blood, and the disabilities? The answer is, nothing at all—they were never thought of. However, by one means or other, there is now an end of them. The legislator neither then nor since has ever opened his mouth upon the subject. But the Judge, drawing an argument from that silence, has opened his and construed them away.

This bold interpretation is a farther proof[799] how entirely the ideas of purgation had become identified with that of acquittal. When a man was admitted to make purgation, he was acquitted: by that means he was discharged from these pecuniary penalties. Now then that the legislature has appointed that in the room of going free, the delinquent may now be punished by a slight pun-

---

*It is amusing enough to observe the continual struggle between the Spiritual and the Carnal Judge, as described in Staundford, title Clergy. It seems to have been a continual game of leap-frog, in which sometimes spirit, sometimes flesh was uppermost.(a)

A man, however, was not always so very kindly dealt with: he fared better or worse, according as he happened to be in favour with the Church. If they happened not to like him, although he had not been tried when delivered to them, they would not admit him to his purgation, but kept him in hard durance without trial . . . The Temporal Courts were then obliged to drive them on to trial. (a) If he was a favourite, although convicted, no guest could be better entertained: they used to cram him at both ends. This, a good Archbishop admits, who, being driven by the Parliament to make an ordinance to remedy this mischief, appoints, that in certain cases, they shall be dieted in a manner he prescribes; speaking all the while in much worse terms of the Lay Judges than of the malefactors, who met with this reception from their friends. [A version of this note does not appear within Dumont's edition.]

†18 Eliz. c. 7. [A version of this note does not appear within Dumont's edition.]

(a) Tale of a Tub. [Neither this note nor the following one appear within Dumont's edition.]

(a) Staundford Clergy, c. 48. Bracton.

ishment, and that not of course, but only in case the Judges should think fit to order it of their own accord, we cannot, said the Judges, suppose that it meant to subject him to a set of punishments so much severer than those it has named. Therefore, as to all but these, coming in place of an acquittal, we must look upon it as a pardon. Having by this chain of reasoning got hold of the word pardon, they went on applying it to other purposes in a very absurd manner; but as we have already had occasion to observe, with a beneficial effect.

One would imagine that being to suffer nothing (what has been mentioned only excepted), first, because he was acquitted, next, because he was pardoned, there was an end of all pecuniary penalties, of the one species of forfeiture as well as the other. This, however, neither was nor is the case. A man did then and does still continue subject to the forfeiture of his personal estate. The reason of this is of true legal texture, and altogether characteristic of ancient jurisprudence. Forfeiture of real estate is not to take place till after judgment; forfeiture of personal estate, without the least shadow of a reason for the difference, is to take place before judgment: to wit, upon conviction. Now, ever since the days of Henry VIth,[800] it has not been the way to admit a man to plead his Clergy till *after* conviction. Now, then, if a man comes and pleads his Clergy, whatever goods he had the King has got them. This being the case, having had your Clergy, you are innocent, or, what comes to the same thing, you are forgiven. All this is very true; but as to your money, the King, you hear, has got it, and when the King has got hold of a man's money, with title or without title, such is his royal nature, he cannot bear to part with it. For the King can do no man wrong, and the Law is the quintessence of reason. To make all this clear, let it be observed, there is a kind of electrical virtue in royal fingers, which attracts to it light substances, such as the moveables [*sic*] and reputed moveables of other men; there is, moreover, a certain glutinous or viscous quality, which detains them when they are got there.

Such are the grounds upon which the forfeiture of personal estate, in cases of clergyable felony, still continues to subsist.

This Act gave the finishing stroke to the abusive *jurisdiction* of the Clergy. The still more abusive exemption remained still, but so changed and depreciated by a lavish participation of it with the laity, that its pristine dignity and value was almost entirely obliterated. By the turn they had given to it, it was originally an instrument of unlimited dominion over others; it was now sunk into a bare protection, and that no longer an exclusive one for themselves.

At last, came the Statute of Queen Ann,* which gives the benefit of Clergy to *all* men whatsoever, whether they can read or cannot. This, together with a Statute of the preceding reign,† which had already given the

---

*5 Ann. c. 6. [This note and the following four notes do not appear within Dumont's edition.]
†3 & 4 W. & M. c. 9.

same benefit to *all women*, gave quite a new import to the phrase. In words, it confirmed and extended the abusive privilege; in reality, it abolished it. It put the illiterate altogether upon a footing with the literate; providing, at the same time, that in the case of the offences to which it extended, both classes alike should suffer, not the punishment which the unprivileged, but that which the privileged had been used to suffer before.

Since then, to allow the benefit of Clergy to any offence, is to punish all persons who shall have committed that offence, in the same manner as lettered persons were punished before. It is to punish in a certain manner all persons for that offence. To take away this benefit is to punish in a certain other manners much more severe, all persons for that offence. The difference between the having it and the taking it away, is now the difference between a greater and a lesser degree of punishment. The difference formerly was the allowing, or not allowing, an oppressive and irrational exemption.

But these entangled and crooked operations have been attended with a variety of mischiefs, which are not by any means cured as yet, and of which scarce anything less than a total revision of the Criminal Law can work a total cure. Such a veil of darkness, such a cob-web work of sophistry, has been thrown over the face of Penal Jurisprudence, that its lineaments can scarcely be laid open to public view but with great difficulty, and with perpetual danger of mischief.[801]

Of the mischief and confusion that has thus been produced, I will mention one instance, which will probably be thought enough.

In a statute of Henry VIIIth,* by a strange caprice of the legislature, the benefit of Clergy was taken away in the lump from all offences whatever, which should happen to be committed on the high seas. He might as well have said, or in such a county, or by men whose hair should be of such a colour. In point of *expediency*, of a provision like this, one knows not what to make. Considered with reference to other parts of the legal system, it is reasonable, as doing something towards abolishing an unreasonable distinction. Considered in the same point of view, it is unreasonable, as making that abolition no more than a partial one, and grounding it, as far as it went, on a circumstance totally unconnected with the mischievousness of the offence. Considered by itself, it is again unreasonable, as tending to subject to the punishment of death for a great many offences, a great many persons for whom a less punishment might suffice.

In point of fact, however, what the legislature meant by it, is clear enough: he meant, that all men, without exception, privileged persons as well as others, should suffer death and so forth, who should be guilty of any kind of felonies upon the high seas, instead of their being made, some of

---

*28 Hen. VIII. c. 15.

them, to suffer death, others a punishment beyond comparison less severe. Would any one imagine what has been the effect of this provision? The effect of it has been, that these privileged persons, instead of suffering death, have suffered no punishment at all. Yes, absolutely no punishment; not even that slight degree of punishment to which they before were subject. Now the case is, that at present, if one may be indulged in a solecism established by the legislature, all persons are privileged. So that now, all persons who may think proper to commit clergyable [*sic*] felonies on the high seas, are absolutely dispunishable [*sic*]. This situation of things, in itself, is not altogether as it ought to be; but the means whereby it has been brought about, are still worse. When a man is indicted of a clergyable offence within that jurisdiction, let his guilt be ever so plainly proved, the *constant course* is, for the Judge to direct the Jury to acquit him.* The man is proved to be guilty in such a manner, that no one can make a doubt about it. No matter; the Judges direct the Jury to say upon their oaths that he is not guilty.

In the Ecclesiastical tribunal, we have above been speaking of, things were so ordered, that according to the author of the Commentaries, "felonious clerks" were not constantly, but "almost constantly" acquitted. I do beseech the reader to turn to that book, and observe in what energetic terms (partly his own, partly adopting what had been said on the same subject by Judge Hobart) the learned author has chosen to speak of this unjustifiable practice†. Ibid. "Vast complication of perjury and subornation of perjury—solemn farce—mock trial—good Bishop—scene of wickedness—scandalous prostitution of oaths and forms of justice—vain and impious ceremony—most abandoned perjury." Such are the terms he uses, to the reader is left to make an application of them.[802]

FELONY WITHOUT BENEFIT OF CLERGY

As to felony without benefit of Clergy, I will, in the first place, state the ingredients of which this mode of punishment is compounded.

Of punishments included under the title of felony without benefit of Clergy, we must distinguish, in the first place, such as are made to bear upon the proper object—punishments *in personam propriam*—and in the second place, such as are thrown upon the innocent, punishments *in personam alienam*.[803]

Of punishments *in personam propriam*[804] it includes the following:—
    I. A total forfeiture of goods and chattels,[805] whether in possession or

---

*4 Comm. c. 28. Foster, 288. Moor, 756.
†Ibid.

in action at the time of the forfeiture taking place. It is a sweeping punishment of the pecuniary kind. It takes place immediately upon conviction: that is, upon at man's being found guilty, and does not wait for judgment, that is, for sentence being pronounced upon him.

II. Forfeiture of lands and tenements.[806] This also is a sweeping punishment of the pecuniary kind. It does not take place till after judgment. This and the other forfeiture between them include the whole of a man's property, whether in possession or in action at the time of the forfeiture taking place. If he does not lose it by the one, he loses it by the other.

III. The corporal punishment[807] of imprisonment till such time as the conclusive punishment is executed upon him. The length of it depends partly on the Judge, partly on the King.

IV. The disability to bring any kind of suit. This operates as a punishment in such cases only in which a long interval, as sometimes happens, intervenes between the sentence and the actual infliction of the ultimate punishment.[808]

V. The corporal punishment of death: viz. simple death by hanging.[809] As this punishment in general puts a speedy period to all the rest, the dwelling upon the elect of any other, is what may, at first sight, appear useless; but this is not absolutely the case. For the execution of this punishment may, at the pleasure of the King, be suspended for any length of time; and in some instances, has actually been suspended for many years.*

Thus much for punishment *in propriam personam*. Punishments *in alienam personam* included under it, are the following; some of them are instances of transitive, others of merely random punishment.[810]

I. His heirs general, that is, that person or persons of his kindred, who stand next to him, and so to one another in the order of succession to real property unentailed [*sic*], forfeit all property of that denomination which he had enjoyed, and which without an express appointment of his to the contrary, they would have been entitled to from him. This results as a consequence of the doctrine of corruption of blood.[811] This is an instant forfeiture: it is a sweeping punishment of the pecuniary kind upon the heir. It may amount to a forfeiture total or partial of all the immoveable property the heir would be worth, or to no forfeiture at all. If, previously to the commission of the offence the offender had settled upon his heir apparent the whole or any part of what property he had of the kind in question, this the heir will not be deprived of.[812]

II. His heir, as before, forfeits his hope of succession to all such real property as he must make title to through the delinquent, as standing before

---

*Sir Walter Raleigh was kept for many years with the halter about his neck: he had the command given him of an expedition; went to America, where he committed piracies on the Spaniards; came back again; and was hanged at last for the original offense. [This note does not appear within Dumont's edition.]

him in the order of consanguinity to the person last seised [*sic*]. This is a remote contingent forfeiture. Another pecuniary punishment of the sweeping kind. In this the uncertainty is still greater than in the former case.

III. Any creditors of his who have had real security for their debts, forfeit such security, in case of its having been granted to them subsequently to the time of the offence committed. This, where it takes place, is a fixed punishment of the pecuniary kind. It is uncertain as to the person, but if there be a person on whom it falls, it is certain as to the event.

IV. Any persons who may have purchased any part of his real property, forfeit such property, in case of this purchase having been made by them subsequently to the time of the offence.[813] This, again, is a fixed punishment of the pecuniary kind. It is uncertain whether it shall fall upon any person, because it is uncertain whether there be a person so circumstanced, but if there he, it is certain as to the event of its falling.

V. Any persons who hold lands or tenements of him under a rent, are obliged to pay over again to the person on whom the forfeiture devolves, whatever they may have paid to the delinquent subsequently to the time of the offence.[814]

These four last denominations of person are made to suffer in virtue of the doctrine of *back-relation*. According to legal notions, it is the delinquent that suffers, by the forfeiture being made to relate back to the time of the offence: as if it were a new suffering to a man to be made to have parted with what he had already parted with of his own accord. In plain English, it is the people themselves—the tenants, purchasers, and creditors that suffer. It is they who forfeit, and not he.

Again, by virtue of the forfeiture of what is called his personal property, the following denominations of persons are made to suffer:—

I. His wife: by being deprived of whatever she would have been entitled to under his will, or under the law of distributions.

II. His children, or others next of kin: by losing what they might, in the same manner, have become entitled to.

III. His creditors: by losing all claim upon his personal estate. By this forfeiture, added to what takes place in the case of real estate, all his creditors whatever are defrauded; such only excepted as may have been fortunate enough to have obtained a real security previous to the commission of the offence.

We now come to *Felony within Clergy*. The mass of punishments included within this title, are much less various as well as less severe.

Of punishments *in propriam personam*,[815] it includes only the first and third of those which are included under the other species of felony.

In the room of the 5th and last punishment, the punishment of death, there is one that takes place, or rather is said to take place, of course. I mean, marking in the hand:* others there are, which, besides the former, take place optionally, at the discretion of the Judge: conjunctively, with respect to the three former; disjunctively, with respect to one another.

This punishment of marking, is now become a farce. It is supposed to be inflicted in open court, immediately after the convict, in order to exempt himself from the punishment of the other felony, has been made: if a woman, to plead the statute; if a man, to tell the solemn lie that he is a clerk. The mark to be inflicted is, according to the statute, to be the letter T, unless the offence be murder, in which case it is to be an M; murder, at that time, not as yet having been taken out of the benefit of Clergy;[816] as it has, however, since, the mark ought now to be that of a T in all cases. The part to be marked is the brawn of the left thumb, so that if a man happens to have lost his left thumb, he cannot be marked at all; or, if afterwards he chooses to cut it off, he may prevent its answering the purpose it was meant to answer, that of distinguishing him from other men.

The instrument originally employed was a heated iron with a stamp upon it of the shape of the letter to be marked. To the Judges of that time, this was the only expedient that occurred for marking upon the human skin, such a mark as should be indelible. At present the practice is to apply the iron, but it is always cold: this is what is called burning with a cold iron; that is burning with an iron that does not burn; in consequence no mark at all is made. The Judge presides at this solemn farce; by no one is it complained of; by many, it is approved; it is mildness, humanity: it is true that the law is eluded, and turned into ridicule: but the Judge spares himself the pain of hearing the cries of a man, to whose flesh a red hot iron is applied. It may be asked, why do not the Judges propose that the law should be made conformable to the practice? I cannot tell.

The Judge that first disregarded the Statute was guilty of the assumption of illegal power: he who should now have the courage to obey it, might now affix the prescribed mark without putting the delinquent to any considerable pain.†

The other punishments which in all cases of felony within Clergy, may, at the discretion of the Judge, be superadded or not to those which we have seen, are those of imprisonment and transportation.[817]

For the second offence of a clergyable felony, capital felony is the punishment.‡

---

*4 Hen. VII. c. 13. [This note does not appear within Dumont's edition.]

†The statute directs that the convict shall be "marked:" the mode of marking is left altogether to the Judge. The author of the Commentaries (4 Comm. p. 367, ed. 1809) "burnt with a hot iron." It is plain by this that he had never read the statute: for the statute, which is a very short one, says not a syllable about burning, or about a hot iron.

‡4 Hen. VIIth, c. 13. [This note does not appear within Dumont's edition.]

Clerks in orders are alone exempted:* peers are not: women are expressly subjected to it. It is certainly a distinction highly honourable to the clergy that they may go on pilfering, while other people are hanged for it.

Why a man having been punished for one act of delinquency, should be punished more than ordinarily for a second act of the same species of delinquency, or even for any other offence of the same species of delinquency, there is at least an obvious, if not a conclusive reason. But why when a man has been punished by a certain mode of punishment, and then commits an offence as different as any offence can be from the former, the punishment for this second offence is, because it happens to be the same with that for the first, to be changed into a punishment altogether different, and beyond comparison more penal, is what it will not, I believe, be easy to say. Is it because the first mode of punishment having been tried upon a man, the next above it, in point of severity, is that of capital felony? That is not the case: for præmunire is greatly more penal than clergyable felony. I mention this as being impossible to justify, not as being difficult to account for, since nothing better could consistently be expected from the discernment of those early times.[818]

There is one thing which a clergyable felon does not forfeit, and which every other delinquent would forfeit for the most venial peccadillo—and that is reputation. I mean that special share of negative reputation which consists in a man's not being looked upon as having been guilty of such an offence.[819] This share of reputation, the law, in the single instance of clergyable felony, protects a delinquent, in so far forth as it is in the power of law, by brute violence, to counteract the force of the most rational and salutary propensities. If a man has stolen twelve-pence, and been convicted of it, call him a thief and welcome. But if he had stolen but eleven-pence-halfpenny, and been convicted of it, and punished as a felon, call him a thief and the law will punish you. This has been solemnly adjudged.

I say convicted and punished as a felon: for if he has not been convicted of it, in virtue of the general rule in case of verbal defamation, you may call him so if you can prove it; but when the law, by a solemn and exemplary act has put the matter out of doubt, then you must not mention it. Would any one suspect the reason? It is because the statute which allows the benefit of clergy operates as a pardon. It has the virtue to make that not to have been done which has been done: and it was accordingly observed, that a man could no more call another thief who had been punished for it in this way (thief say they *in the present time*) than say he *hath* a shameful disease when he had had it, and has been cured of it.†

---

*By 4 Hen. VIIth, c. 13. repealed in effect *quo ad hoc*, by 28 Hen. VIIth, c. 1, and 32 Hen. VIIIth, c. 3: and revived in effect *quo ad hoc* by 1 Ed. VIth, c. 12. p. 10. [This note does not appear within Dumont's edition.]

*. Hobart 81. [A version of this note does not appear within Dumont's edition.]

It is there also said, with somewhat more colour of reason, though in despite of the last mentioned rule, "that there is no necessity or *use* of slanderous words to be allowed to ignorants," and that though the arresting of a pardoned felon, by one who knows not of the pardon, may be justifiable, because this is in "advancement of justice; yet so it is not to call him thief, because that is neither necessary, nor advanceth nor tends to justice."[820] He who said this knew not, or did not choose to know, how mighty is the force and how salutary the influence of the *moral* sanction: how much it contributes to support, and in what a number of important instances it serves to control the caprices and supply the defects of the *political*. It was perhaps Sir Edward Coke: a man who from principle was a determined enemy, though from ill humour, upon occasion an inconsistent and unsteady friend to political liberty:[821] who in his favourite case, *de libellis famosis*, has destroyed, as far as was in his power to destroy, the safeguard of all other liberties, that of the press: proscribing all criticism of public acts; silencing all history; and vying in the extent of his anathemas with the extravagance of the most jealous of the Roman Emperors.

CHAPTER V.
OF PRÆMUNIRE.[822]

The punishment of Præmunire* consists in the being "put out of the King's protection," and "in the forfeiture of lands and tenements, goods and chattels;" but such is the uncertainty of English law, that some add to the above, imprisonment during the King's pleasure, and others say for life. Sir Edward Coke is for adding loss of credibility; he might as well have added loss of ears; but I do not find that this conceit has been taken up by anybody else.

The offences to which this punishment has been applied, are as heterogenous [sic] as any that can be imagined. The offence to which it was first applied, was an offence against Government; since that, besides a multitude of other offences against Government, it has been applied to various offences against the property, against the personal liberty of individuals, and against trade!†

What it is that in such a variety of laws should have tempted the legislature, instead of the known and ordinary names of punishment, to devise a new and unexpressive name to which no meaning whatever could be annexed, without rummaging over a confused parcel of old French statutes, is not easy to assign. There is nothing gained by it in any way, not in point of brevity, for in one of the statutes in which it is described with the most conciseness, I find more words are taken up by this uncouth description, than would be by the plain one: there is nothing gained by it in point of precision, for the word has no signification whatever, but by reference to the words of the old statute, and consequently cannot be more precise than they are.[823]

The only recommendation I can find for it is, that it is a Latin word: added to the notion, perhaps, that, as being less intelligible than most other names of punishments, it might be more tremendous.

If this has been the design, it has been in some measure answered—terrible indeed is the name of Præmunire. It is become a kind of bug-bear,

---

*This word, from being the name of nothing at all, first became the name of a writ, then the name of a punishment, and from thence, as was natural, the name of an offense: to wit, of many offenses as were punishable by that punishment.

†See a list of these offences in Blackstone's Commentaries. So difficult is it for any one to ascertain what the law is upon any subject, that though this punishment was adopted in the Regency, Act 5 George. III. c. 27. which was passed many years before the 4th vol. of the Commentaries was printed. This Act was not enumerated in that list.

in which shape it has descended even among the lowest mob. It is used as synonymous with a scrape: not that the sort of persons last mentioned have any much clearer idea of the particular sort of scrape, than those have who bring others into it by solemn acts of legislation.

CHAPTER VI.
OUTLAWRY.

The punishment known in practice by the name of Outlawry, consists of the following ingredients:

I. Forensic disability, which may be called simple outlawry.

II. Forfeiture of personal estate.

III. Forfeiture of the growing profits of the real estate.

IV. Imprisonment, &c.

This is the punishment inflicted for the offence of absconding from justice in all cases, except where the punishment for the principal offence amounts to felony: in this case, a man against whom a sentence of outlawry is pronounced, is punished as if he had been convicted of the principal offence.

As the offence of absconding is a *chronical* [*sic*] offence, the punishment applied to it should be a *chronical* punishment, such an one as being made to cease upon the cessation of the offence, may operate only as an instrument of compulsion. All these punishments are capable of being made so; but none are so upon the face of them. None were so originally. They are by this time, however, rendered so in great measure by modern practice, which has corrected the inordinate severity of the original institution.

This punishment applies in most cases, but not in all cases: in all cases where the prosecution for the original offence was in the criminal form, that is, in other words, in all criminal suits: it applies in most, but not in all civil suits. In the same civil suit, it applies or does not apply, according as the suit happens to be commenced before one court or another. In the same suit, and that carried on in the same court, it does or does not apply according as the suit happens to have been commenced by one kind of jargon or another. All this without the least relation to the merits.

[824]The punishment of forensic disabilities is applied to a multitude of offences: namely, to all those which are punished either by capital felony, or præmunire, or excommunication. In felony, it is useless, because the effect of it is merged in the punishment of death; in præmunire, it is justifiable, in as far as the punishment of total and perpetual impoverishment, is an eligible mode of punishment, for of this it makes a necessary part. In excommunication, it is ineligible, on account of its inequality. To make it answer in an equable manner the purpose of impoverishment, is impracticable, for want of the punishment of forfeiture, of which it can come in only as an appendage.

Taking it by itself, and laying aside what is necessary to make it answer the purpose of impoverishment, it is superfluous when added to the punishment of imprisonment.

Whatever may be the offences cognizable in the Ecclesiastical Court, either corporal punishment is enough for them without pecuniary, or it is not. If it be enough, simple outlawry in addition to it is too much; if not, it is too little. All this is upon the supposition that the delinquent is forthcoming for the purpose of undergoing imprisonment.

When a man absconds and has no property in possession, or none that is sufficient to answer the demand upon him, in this case, and in this only, the punishment of simple outlawry is expedient. Why? not because it is eligible in itself, but because it is the only one the case admits of. When a man has no visible property in his own country, and has made his escape into another, generally speaking, his own country has no hold of him. This may happen, suppose in nine instances out of ten; but in the tenth, it may happen that he may have a debt due to him, which he may want the assistance of the laws of his own country to recover. If this debt be more in value to him than what is equivalent to the punishment he would be likely to suffer for the original offence which made him fly, he will return and submit to justice. The punishment of simple outlawry in this case will answer its purpose. It is eligible, therefore, in this case, because it has some chance of compassing its end, and no other punishment has any.*

ADVANTAGES AND DISADVANTAGES OF FORFEITURE OF PROTECTION.

To this mode of punishment, the objection of inequality applies with peculiar force. The fund out of which a man who has a fund of his own subsists, is either his labour, or his property. If he has property, it consists either in immoveables, or in moveables. If in immoveables, it is either in his own hands, or in those of other persons; if in moveables, it is either in public hands, or in private: if in private, either in his own hands, or in those of other persons.

---

*An anecdote given us by Selden, in his Table Talk, (a) may serve very well to illustrate the influence this mode of punishment may have over a man who is out of the reach of every other. In the reign of James 1st, an English merchant had a demand upon the King of Spain, which he could not get the King to satisfy. The merchant had already brought his action, and Selden, who was his Counsel, advised him to proceed to Outlawry. Writ after writ was sent to the Sheriff to take his Majesty, and have his body before the Justices at Westminster. His Majesty was not to be found. Great outcry, as is usual, was made after him upon this in sundry ale-houses. His Majesty did not happen to be at any of the ale-houses. He was accordingly proclaimed an outlaw; and a wolf's head, in due form of law, was clapt [sic] upon his shoul-

A man who subsists by his labour, is in general scarcely at all affected by this punishment. He receives his pay, if not before he does his work, at least as soon as a small quantity of it is done.[825]

A man whose fund of subsistence consists in immoveable property, is very little affected by this punishment, if that property is in his own hands. The utmost inconvenience it can subject him to, is the obliging him to deal for ready money. If his property is in the funds, he is not at all affected. There seems no reason to suppose that those who have the management of those funds, would refuse a man his dividend on the ground of any such disability. They would have no interest in such a refusal; and the importance of keeping public[826] credit, would probably be a sufficient motive to keep them in this instance from departing from the general engagement.

If a man's property consists in moveable property which is in his own hands, for instance, stock in trade, it affects him indeed, but not very deeply. The utmost it can do, is to[827] oblige him to deal for ready money: to preclude him from selling upon credit. It does not preclude him from buying[828] upon credit[829], since, though others are not amenable to him, he is to others.

It is only where a man's property consists in credits: for example, in immoveables in the hands of a tenant, in a sum due for goods sold on credit, or in money, out upon security, that it can affect him very deeply. Of such a man it may be the utter ruin.

In this case, whether a man suffers to the extreme amount, or whether he suffers at all, depends upon what? upon the moral honesty of those he happens to have to do with.

There are two circumstances therefore, on which the quantum of this mode of punishment depends: 1st, the nature of the fund from whence he draws his subsistence; 2nd, the moral honesty of the people he happens to have to do with. But neither of these circumstances is any ways connected with the degree of criminality of any offence for which a man can be thus punished. Of two men, both guilty, and that in the same degree, one may be ruined, the other not at all affected. The greater punishment is as likely to

ders, (b) so that anybody might lay hold of him, and put him into jail, that had a mind for it.
(c) The case was, his Majesty happened at that time to have demands upon several merchants in England, for which demands, so long as he continued under judgment of outlawry, he could not have his remedy. Upon this consideration, his Ambassador, Gondamar, submitted and paid the money; upon which, the wolf's head was taken off, and the King's head put in its place.

(a) Title *Law*.

(b) *Caput Lupinum*,—C.Litt. 128.b. Lamb. Leg. Tax, ch.128. Fleta, L. 1. c.27. Bract. L.5. fol.421. Britt. fol.20. Mirror, c.4. *Defaults Punishable*.

(c) Antiently, when a man had a wolf's head upon his shoulders, he might be killed by anybody. But this was altered in Edward III.'s time. See C. Litt.

fall upon the lesser offender, as upon the greater:[830] the lesser upon the greater offender, as upon the lesser.

Another objection applies to this mode of punishment on the score of *immorality*. The punishment being of a pecuniary nature, there is a profit arising out of it, which accordingly is to be disposed of in favour of somebody. And in whose favour is it disposed of? in favour of anyone, who, having contracted an engagement with the delinquent, can, for the sake of lucre, be brought to break it.[831]

It may be said, that the engagement being by the supposition rendered void, these is no harm in its being broken. True, it is void, as far as concerns the political sanction, but it is not void by the moral. All that the law does is not to compel him to perform it;[832] but the interests of society require, and accordingly so does the moral sanction require, that a man should be ready to perform his engagement, although the law should not compel him. If a man can be brought in this way to break his engagement, it is a sign that the power of money over him is greater than that of the moral sanction.[833] He is therefore what is properly termed an immoral man; and it is the law that either has begotten in him that evil quality, or at least, has fostered it.

The dispensations, therefore, of the political sanction, are, in this case, set at variance with those which are and ought to be those of the moral sanction. It invites men to pursue a mode of conduct which the moral sanction, in conformity to the dictates of utility, forbids.

CHAPTER VII.
EXCOMMUNICATION.[834]

Various and manifold are the evils which the punishment of excommunication inflicts, or proposes to inflict: various are the sources from whence they flow.[835] It does not confine itself to the political sanction: it calls in, or makes as if it would call in, the two others to its assistance.[836]

Of Excommunication, there are two species, or degrees: the greater and the lesser. The greater contains all that the lesser does, and something more. I will first then give an account of those that are contained in the lesser, and then take notice of those that are peculiar to the other.

Those contained in the lesser are as follows:—

I. Imprisonment, the time unlimited, depending on the good pleasure of the Judge: the severity of it is determined by the circumstance of its being in the Common Jail.

II. Penance, as a condition to the termination of the other punishment. By penance is meant, a corporal punishment of the ignominious kind. The particular manner of inflicting it shall be considered hereafter.

III. In lieu of the penance, commutation money. The quantum of it is not limited in a direct manner, but is in an indirect manner; it cannot be more than a man chooses to give, in order to avoid the corporal penance.

These two last are accidental ingredients in this complex mass of punishment. Their infliction or omission depends, in some measure, upon the will of the prosecutor. Those which follow, are inseparable.

IV. Disability to sue, either in a court of law or equity. This is a punishment of a pecuniary nature, contingent in its nature, and uncertain as to time.

V. Disability of acting as an Advocate,* or as an Attorney, or Procurator, for another:† that is, I suppose, in the Ecclesiastical Courts, and not in any other. This is a punishment of the class of those that affect a man's condition; in the present instance, it affects a man chiefly on a pecuniary account.

VI. Disability of acting as a Juryman.‡[837]

---

*Gibs. 1050. [This footnote and the subsequent notes are not found within Dumont's edition.]

†2 Bacon's Ab. 674.

‡3 Blackst. Com. 101.

VII. Disability of being presented to an Ecclesiastical benefice:* of this, the same account may be given as of the last disability but one.[838]

VIII. Disability of bringing a suit, or action, as an executor.† This is a punishment *in alienam personam*: affecting those who have a beneficial interest under the will.

IX. Incapacity of being constituted or continued an administrator, or at least, danger of being subjected to that disability.

X. Disability of being a witness. This, likewise, is another punishment *in alienam personam*, affecting those persons to whom this evidence, if given, would be beneficial in respect of their lives, fortunes, liberties, and every other possession that is in the protection of the law.[839]

XI. The being looked upon as a heathen and a publican. This, I suppose, is meant as a sort of infamy.‡[840]

XII. Exclusion from all churches: this is a species of personal restraint, that involves in it consequences that belong to the religious sanction.[841]

XIII. Exclusion from the benefit of the burial service. I do not know under what class to rank this punishment: I do not very precisely know what benefit it is to a man after he is dead, to have the service read over his body: if it be anything, it belongs to the religious sanction.[842]

XIV. Exclusion from the benefit of the sacraments of Baptism and the Lord's Supper. This belongs altogether to the religious sanction.[843]

So much for the lesser excommunication. The greater adds two other circumstances to the catalogue:—

I. *Exclusion from the commerce and communion of the faithful.*§

II. *Disability of making a Will.*‖ This is a punishment that affects the power of the party: viz. in the present case, the investitive [*sic*] power performable in a particular manner, with respect to the ownership of such property as he shall die entitled to. In as far as the power of making a will includes that of appointing a Guardian to a child, as also that of an Executor to manage the property of a person, of whom the party in question was executor: it is a punishment *in alienam personam*. The child may suffer for want of a proper Guardian. The persons interested in the effects of the first testator may suffer for want of a proper person to manage those effects.[844]

This is the mode, and the only mode of punishment inflicted by those Courts that go by the name of Ecclesiastical, or Spiritual Courts. This they are forced to make serve for all occasions; they have neither less nor

---

*Gibs. 1050.
†God. O. L. 37, 8.
‡Burn, Penance, 6.
§Lenderb. 266.
‖Swinb. 109. God. O. L. 37.

greater: it is the only punishment they have. When this punishment is pronounced, they have exhausted their whole Penal Code. If its brevity be its recommendation, it must be confessed that it has no other.[845] Let us consider a little more particularly, the punishments of which it is composed. Of imprisonment, nothing in particular need be said at present.[846]

The punishment of penance demands more attention. It consists in the penitent being exposed bare-headed and bare-legged, with a white sheet wrapped round the body, either in the parish church, or in the cathedral, or in the public market,* there to pronounce a certain form of words containing the confession of his crime. This, as has been already observed, is a corporal punishment of the ignominious kind, and might, if defined with precision, be employed with the same advantage as are other punishments of that description. The time at which it should take place, and the duration of the penance, ought to be determined, but there is nothing fixed with regard to them, so that it may continue for several hours, or only for an instant. It may take place before a crowd of spectators, or in the most absolute solitude.—Besides this, there is a vast difference between the parish church of a village, and the cathedral of a great city, or the public market of a district. The larger or smaller concourse of spectators will render the punishment more or less severe.

The penitent ought to pronounce a formula containing an acknowledgment of his crime; a different formula ought therefore to be provided for every crime by law. This formula may be pronounced either distinctly or indistinctly—a man can hardly be expected, willingly, to proclaim his own shame. It would therefore be proper that he should only be required to repeat the words, which should be clearly and distinctly pronounced by an officer of Justice, as is practised with respect to the administration of oaths. Certain persons, also, should be nominated to preside over the ceremony, and ascertain that everything is done according to law.

Till these points are regulated, this mode of punishment, though good in itself, will always be subject, as it is at present, to the greatest abuses. It will be executed with inequality, and capriciously, according to the condition of the individuals, rather than according to their crimes, and according as the character of the Judge is more or less severe.[847]

Penance is the punishment usually imposed, says Dr. Burn, "in the case of incest or incontinency," these two offences are classed together by the ecclesiastical compiler, and opposed to what he calls smaller offences and scandals.—When we consider how far these two first offences are removed from one another, one is astonished to see them classed together, and visited with the same punishment. Far be it from me to treat lightly the expo-

---

*Godolph. Appendix, 18. Burn, tit. Penance.

sure of innocence to infamy, the disturbance of domestic felicity, or to degrade the chaste raptures of the marriage bed to a level with the bought smiles of harlots. But there are degrees in guilt, which I see not why it should be meritorious to confound.

It is not often that we hear of this punishment being put in practice: examples of it were more frequent in former times, but now it is most commonly commuted for by the payment of a sum of money.

II. As to the different legal incapacities which form part of this punishment, the objections to which they are liable have been pointed out elsewhere. (See Book IV. *Misplaced Punishments*.)

III. Part of the punishment consists in the delinquent's being looked upon, if men think fit to look upon him in that light, as a heathen and a publican.[848]

To try the effect of generals, the only way is to apply them to particulars. A. is not willing, or not able, to pay his Proctor's, or another man's Proctor's fees. He is in consequence excommunicated. Amongst his other punishments, he is to be looked upon as a heathen or a publican, that is, as being such a sort of man as Socrates, Cato Titus, Marcus Antoninus, a collector of taxes, or a Lord of the Treasury. The heaping of hard names upon a man might, at one time, have been deemed a punishment, but such legal trifling now a-days, serves only to render the laws ridiculous.[849]

IV. Exclusion from the churches. In our days an exclusion of this sort shows rather oddly under the guise of punishment. The great difficulty is now not to keep people out of the churches, but to get them in. The punishment, however, was not ill designed, if it were intended to increase the desire of attending there, by forbidding it. The general effect of every prohibition being, to give birth to a desire to infringe it. It affords a presumption, that what is prohibited is in itself desirable, or at least, desirable in the opinion of the legislator, or he would not have prohibited it: such is the natural supposition when the interdiction relates to an unknown object; but even when it relates to an object which has been tried, and neglected from distaste, the prohibition gives to it another aspect. The attention is directed to the possible advantages of the act: having begun to think of them, the individual fancies he perceives them, and goes on to exaggerate their value; on comparing his situation with that of those who enjoy this liberty, he experiences a feeling of inferiority; and by degrees, a most intense desire often succeeds to the greatest indifference.

Those who are forward to refer the propensity to transgress a prohibition of any kind to an unaccountable perversity, and unnatural corruption in human nature, as if it were not reconcileable [*sic*] to the known dominion of the ideas of pain and pleasure over the human mind, do an injustice to man's nature, in favour of their own indolence. Man, according to these superficial moralists, is a compound of inconsistencies: everything in him is an object of wonder—everything happens contrary to what they would expect; strangers to the few simple principles which govern human nature, the account they give of everything is, that it is unaccountable.[850]

With respect to those parts of the punishment of excommunication which belong to the religious sanction, such as exclusion from the sacraments, their most striking imperfection is, their extreme inequality: their penal effect depends on the belief and sensibility of the individuals. The blow which would produce torments of agony in one person, will only cause the skin of another to tingle. There is no proportion in these punishments, and nothing exemplary: those who suffer, languish in secrecy and silence; those who do not suffer, make a jest and a laughing stock of the law in public. They are punishments which are thrown at hazard among a crowd of offenders, without care whether they produce any effect or none.[851]

I speak of these punishments with reference only to the present life; for who is there that supposes that a sentence of excommunication can carry with it any penal consequences in a future state. For what man, reasoning without prejudice, can believe that God hath committed so terrible a power to beings so feeble and so imperfect, or that the Divine justice could bind itself to execute the decrees of blind humanity; that it could allow itself to be commanded to punish otherwise than it would have punished of itself. A truth so evident could only have been lost sight of by an abasement, which could only have been prepared by ages of ignorance.*[85]

---

*These observations might be much more extended, with reference to the details of Ecclesiastical Judicature, but the subject would not be of general interest. The foregoing observations may therefore suffice with respect to these laws, which are so generally condemned, and may serve to show the necessity for their formal abolition.

BOOK VI.
MISCELLANEOUS TOPICS.

CHAPTER I.[853]
CHOICE OF PUNISHMENTS— LATITUDE TO BE ALLOWED TO THE JUDGES.

The legislator ought, as much as possible, to determine everything relating to punishments, for two reasons: that they may be *certain*, and *impartial*.

I. The more completely the scale of punishments is rendered certain, the more completely all the members of the community are enabled to know what to expect.[854] It is the fear of punishment in so far as it is known, which prevents the commission of crime. An uncertain punishment will therefore be uncertain in its effects—since, where there is a possibility to escape, escape will be hoped for.[855]

II. The legislator is necessarily unacquainted with the individuals who will undergo the punishment he appoints; he cannot, therefore, be governed by feelings of personal antipathy or regard. He is impartial, or at least, appears to be so. A Judge, on the contrary, only pronouncing upon a particular case, is exposed to favourable or unfavourable prejudices, or at least, to the suspicion of such, which almost equally shake the public confidence.[856]

If an unlimited latitude be allowed to Judges in apportioning punishments, their functions will be rendered too arduous: they will always be afraid either of being too indulgent or too severe.[857]

It may also happen, that being able to diminish the punishment at discretion, they may become less exact in requiring proof, than if they had to pronounce a fixed punishment. A slight probability may appear sufficient to justify a punishment which they may lessen at pleasure.[858]

There may, however, often arise, either with regard to the offences themselves or the person of the delinquent, unforeseen and particular circumstances, which would be productive of great inconveniences, if the laws were altogether inflexible. It is therefore proper to allow a certain latitude to the Judge, not of increasing, but of diminishing a punishment, in those cases in which it may be fairly presumed, that one individual is less dangerous, or more responsible than another, since, as has been before

observed, the same nominal punishment is not always the same real punishment. Some individuals, by reason of their education, family connections, and condition in the world, presenting, if we may so speak, a greater
surface for punishment to act upon.[859]

Other circumstances may render it expedient to change the kind of
punishment; that which has been directed by the law may be incapable of
application, or it may be less suitable in other respects.

But whenever this discretionary power is exercised by a Judge, he
ought to declare the reasons which have determined him.[860]

Such are the principles. The details of this subject belong to the Penal
Code, and to the Legislative Instructions to the Tribunals.[861]

CHAPTER II.
OF SUBSIDIARY PUNISHMENTS.[862]

O f all the punishments which can be appointed by the law, there is none but what, from one accident or another, is liable to fail. It is obvious that against such an event it becomes the law, in every case,[863] to make provision. Such a failure may arise from either of two causes: unwillingness, that is, want of will to bear the punishment; or inability, that is, want of power.

The first cause, if no steps were taken to control it, would naturally occasion the failure of all punishments, the execution of which is dependant upon the will of the party to be punished. This,[864] among corporal punishments, is the case with all such as are either active or restrictive, one case of restrictive punishment excepted, that, to wit, in which the restraint is produced by physical means.

To give efficacy, therefore, to the mandate, of which any of these punishments is intended as the sanction, it is absolutely necessary that some further punishment should be appointed to back it through the whole of its continuance. In the first instance, this *backing*, or *subsidiary*, punishment as it may be called, may be taken from those two classes, as well as from the other; and so through any number of instances, one behind another. A punishment of the active kind, for instance, might be backed by quasi-imprisonment; that again by banishment; or any one of those punishments, for a certain term, by the same, or another, (kind of punishment) for a further term. Ultimately, however, every such series must be terminated by some punishment that may be inflicted without the concurrence of[865] the party's will; that is, by some punishment of the passive kind; or if of the restrictive kind, by such restraint as is compassed by physical means.

Even such punishments, to the execution of which (so the party be forthcoming) the concurrence of the party is not essentially necessary, may fail from his *want of power*, or in other words, from his *inability* to sustain them. This is the case with all corporal punishments not capital, that affect any parts of the body that are not essential to life. It is the case, therefore, with simply afflictive punishments, and with discolourment, disfigurement, disablement, and mutilation, in as far as they affect any of the parts just spoken of. It is also the case with forfeitures of all kinds. The only punishments therefore that are sure, and require no others to be subjoined to them,

321

are the above-mentioned corporal punishments, in the cases where the parts they affect are such as are essential to life; imprisonment, and such punishments, by which life itself is taken away.[866]

Even these, like any others, may come to fail by the want of will, (in the party to sustain them) to wit, by his not choosing to be forthcoming, which is a cause of failure common to all punishments; but then this cause does not necessarily produce its effect: it does not render the punishment of the man necessarily dependent upon his will, for he may be taken and punished in spite of his wishes and endeavours to prevent it; which, when a man does suffer any of these punishments, especially death, and those other acute and heavy punishments, is generally the case. In this case, the only resource is in forfeitures, upon the contingency of a man's having anything to forfeit, that is, within the reach of justice, or in the punishment of those whose feelings are connected with his own by sympathy, as in punishments *in alienam personam*.[867]

From the differences above-remarked respecting the cause of failure in the punishment *first-designed*, results a difference in what ought to be the quantity of the *subsidiary* punishment, concerning which we may lay down the following rules:—[868]

Rule I. *Where inability is manifestly the only cause of failure, the subsidiary punishment should be neither greater nor less than that which was first designed.* For no reason can be given why it should be either less or greater.[869]

Rule II. *Where want of will is manifestly the only cause of failure, the subsidiary punishment ought to be greater than that which was first designed.* For the punishment first designed is that which by the supposition is thought the best: to determine the delinquent then to submit to this, in preference to the other, there is but one way, which is, to make that other punishment the greater.

Rule III. *When the cause of failure may be want of power, or want of will, as it may happen, and it cannot be known which, the subsidiary punishment ought to be greater than the punishment first designed, but not so much greater as in the case last mentioned.* This is apt to be the case with pecuniary forfeitures. If, however, it can be ascertained which of these is the cause, it ought always to be done, otherwise, on the one hand, he who fails from mere inability, will be punished more than there is occasion; and he who fails wilfully, not enough.[870]

When a man fails wilfully to submit to the punishment first designed for him, such a failure may be considered in the light of an offence. Viewing it *in* this light, we shall immediately see the propriety of the following rule.

Rule IV. *The subsidiary punishment ought to be made the greater, the easier it is for the delinquent to avoid the punishment first designed*[871] *(without being detected and made amenable).* For the punishment, to be efficacious, must always be greater than the temptation to the offence; and the temptation to the offence is the greater, the greater is the uncertainty of that punishment which is the motive that weighs against[872] the profit of the offence.[873]

Imprisonment is the most convenient and natural kind of subsidiary punishment, in cases where the offender cannot or will not submit to a pecuniary punishment. A circumstance that renders these two modes of punishment particularly apt for being substituted to each other, is their *divisibility*: they admit of every degree that can be desired.[874]

Simple afflictive punishments, on account of the infamy they involve, cannot in general be eligibly employed as substitutes for pecuniary punishments.

In case of violation of boundaries of local confinement, the most eligible substitute is imprisonment. A single act of transgression may be taken as a sufficient warning that the penal mandate is not meant to be regarded.

Laborious punishments require an uninterrupted train of attention, in order to compel the delinquent to submit to them. A constant supply of fresh motives is required: to produce the desired effect, it is necessary therefore that these motives should be drawn from a stock of punishment that is susceptible of minute division, and capable of being applied at the moment it is wanted. Thus, whenever an Inspector is appointed in a House of Correction in which the individuals confined are employed in hard labour, power is tacitly given to him to inflict personal correction. The infamy by which it is accompanied, is not an objection: because, by the principal punishment—the penal labour—an equal degree of infamy is produced.

We have already observed, that to pecuniary punishment, in case of inability on the part of the patient, ought to be substituted imprisonment.

But by what standard are we to estimate a sum of money by a sum of imprisonment—for what debt, or part of a debt, is each day's imprisonment to be reckoned as an equivalent?

Let us say that the amount of the debt struck off by each day's imprisonment shall be equal to what each day the patient might have earned, had he remained in a state of liberty. The daily income of a mechanic, sailor, soldier, artist, labourer, servant, may be calculated according to the wages of persons employed in the same profession.

The daily income of a farmer may be estimated according to the 365th part of the rent of his farm. If, besides his farm, he is engaged in any other line of business, the daily benefit arising from that business must be added to the income arising from his farm.

The revenue of a man who is not engaged in any business, or is not a manufacturer, may be calculated as being eight times the rent of his house. If he is a manufacturer, at four times the rent of his house. If he is engaged in trade, at six times that rent.

The revenue of a man that boards and lodges in the house of another, may be estimated at double the sum that he so pays. If he lodges only, at four times that sum. If he is supported gratuitously in the house of a relation, as equal to the value of his board and lodging.*

The points that then require to be determined, are the three following:—

I. The income being given, what portion of the debt shall be considered as being abolished, by imprisonment of a certain duration?

II. From what period anterior to the contracting of the debt, ought the value of the income to be estimated?

III. What proofs ought to be required by which to fix the amount of the income in question? It would be the interest of the debtor to make it appear as great as possible. During the examination, the creditor ought to be present, and to be at liberty, either by himself or his counsel, to examine the defaulter.

The more exalted a man's rank, the greater in general are his annual outgoings; the greater, consequently, ought to be the debt abolished by a given period of imprisonment.

I confine myself then to the laying down the principles upon which the calculation may be made: the details of their application belong more properly to the Penal Code than to a work on punishment.

*Example.	Per Day.	Per Day.		£. s. d.
	£. s. d.	£. s. d.		£. s. d.
Labourer.	0 1 0	15 13 0	{ Debt discharged by seven years' imprisonment. }	109 11 0
Ensign.	0 3 8	66 18 4	{ Debt discharged by seven year's imprisonment. }	66 18 4

CHAPTER III.
OF SURETY FOR GOOD
CONDUCT.[875]

The obligation of finding sureties for good conduct is an expedient, the utility of which appears more problematical in proportion as it is examined more nearly. A condition which is essential to it is, that there be an ulterior punishment destined to replace this obligation, in case its fulfilment is found impossible. This subsidiary punishment is ordinarily imprisonment,—this imprisonment is ordinarily indefinite as to its duration: it may be perpetual, and it is natural that it should be so. Does the accused find himself without friends ready to risk their security upon his good conduct? Imprisonment, and the ignominy that accompanies it, are means little proper for enabling him to find friends so devoted.[876]

Suppose that he finds them; what happens then? To a properly seated punishment, a vicarious punishment is added, a punishment to be borne by the innocent for the guilty. In the nature of things, any punishment might be equally well enjoyed for this purpose. By custom, pecuniary punishment only is employed in the first instance, which, however, changes into imprisonment, in case of insolvability, according to a general rule. It is not, however, natural, that a man, especially a man who, by the supposition, has given proofs of misconduct, should find friends who will expose themselves to be punished for actions over which they have no power, unless he have wherewith to indemnify them for bearing this pecuniary punishment. Does he find them in this case? Then this expedient is useless; it would have been quite as well to have fixed the amount upon him directly. In order that this expedient may have an efficacy of its own, it will be necessary to limit its use to the case in which the incapacity of the accused to furnish this indemnity is known. Does he, after this, find any persons sufficiently generous thus to expose themselves for him? It is, without doubt, something gained in point of security, but it is a security very dearly bought. In all other cases, this expedient resolves itself into a question of account.[877]

The support which the law receives from this expedient, springs from two sources: it operates as an additional punishment, whereby the will of the accused is influenced; this punishment, consisting in the remorse which a generous mind would feel in seeing friends, who had devoted themselves for him, plunged into misfortune by his ingratitude. It is also an expedient whereby he is attacked upon the side of power: his sureties become guards, whom the danger to which they as exposed induces to watch over his conduct.

But will he, whom the fear of punishment to be inflicted upon himself has been found insufficient to restrain, be restrained by the fear of a less punishment to be inflicted upon another? Those passions which have stifled the voice of prudence, will they obey those of generosity and gratitude? they may obey it, but that they will not obey it is, I think, most natural; but if this is so, it is a very costly expedient. In the majority of cases, instead of insuring the good of prevention, it will produce the evil of punishment—of punishment borne by the innocent.

Whilst, as to this guard, it is a security much more verbal than real—it would be a very weak security, even if the individuals were his companions, and lived under the same roof with him at all times. But it is not among such as these that sureties are selected: they are, under the English law, required to be householders, having separate establishments. Is it then possible, that the passion which, by the supposition, had broken through the united restraints of prudence, gratitude, and honour, should be restrained by so loose a band. Besides this, is it natural that the extremes of confidence and mistrust should be united in the same person.

The bitterness of this punishment, to which the innocent are made to expose themselves, is not taken away by calling the exposure voluntary. This willingness is owing only to the constraint which the consideration of his friend being sent, or about to be sent, to prison for life, brings with it. It is a willingness produced by torture.

In conclusion, suretyship [sic] is a resource which ought not to be resorted to without very evident necessity, if it were unattended with any other inconvenience than this, of exposing the virtue of individuals to these combats, which, in a moment of weakness, may give birth to a remorse, which shall end only with life.[878]

This expedient is much employed under the English law; but custom has caused it to exist only in connexion with judicial communication [sic]. A certain fine is determined on, the accused is made to say, I consent to the payment of this fine, if I commit a certain offence. One or more sureties are made each to say, I consent on the same condition to owe the same, or a part of the same sum. In this manner, as if an inevitable punishment required an extorted consent to its infliction, the accused himself is made to contract an engagement, which, if it is not always ridiculous, it is that it is sometimes unjust. Implying a claim upon his property, it serves to rob his creditors of their just rights to payment of debts contracted between the period of the engagement and the contracting of the debt.

Of this ill-contrived compound mischief, what are the effects in practice? very commonly, none. This formality is complied with, as so many others are complied with, without thinking of what it means, partly from duty, and partly from habit. Sometimes it may be useful, because it always includes admonition, and sometimes threatening, according to the proportion between the fine threatened, and the punishment which would have had place without it; sometimes for want of sureties it may be believed that the accused himself may go to prison; sometimes, after having found them, it may equally be believed that they may incur the fine, and that they pay it, or go to prison, with or without him. Do these misfortunes frequently happen? I know not. How can I know? This is one of those thousand things on which everybody ought to be instructed, and of which no one can find an opportunity of learning the truth.

CHAPTER IV.
DEFEAZANCE OF PUNISHMENT.

SEC. I.—OF PARDON.

I t is necessary to increase the magnitude of a punishment in proportion as it is wanting in certainty. The less certain your punishments are, the more severe they must be; the more certain your punishments are, the more you may reduce their severity.

What shall we then say of a power expressly established for rendering them uncertain? I mean the power of pardoning: it has cruelty for its cause, it has cruelty for its effect.[879]

Among nations, as among individuals, the government of the passions precedes that of reason. The object of primitive punishments was, to assuage the rage of their authors. Of this there are two proofs: the first is drawn from the multitude of cases in which the most severe punishments have been lavished upon actions which have but a slightly hurtful influence upon the happiness of individuals or society, and with respect to which such evil influence was not sought to be established, till long after these punishments were appointed—of this kind are the punishments directed against heresy. The second is drawn from the praises lavished upon clemency: for whilst the effect of an offence is only to enrage the Sovereign, there is merit in his abstaining from punishing it. There is utility in his so doing, for by a privation which is borne by him alone, he spares the infliction of terrible evils upon a multitude of persons. In this consists the difficulty, for it is difficult to a man accustomed to follow the bent of his inclinations to restrain them. Suppose the effect of a crime is to interrupt his ease, and the effect of the punishment is to repress this crime; to abstain from the application of this punishment is a treason of which the most pardonable sources are feebleness or folly. To praise the clemency of the Sovereign upon this supposition, is to praise the surgeon, who allows his patient to perish by not cutting off a gangrened finger. Among Sovereigns, therefore, without cruelty, the use of unmerited pardons could not take place: the reason is, an enlightened love of the public welfare does not engage him in undoing with one hand what he had done with the other. If the punishments have not had for the cause of their establishment cruelty towards individuals, it is cruelty towards the public to render them useless, to violate his promise, the engagement which he has made to the laws to put them in execution.

I speak here of gratuitous pardons, such as all pardons have hitherto been. There are cases in which the power of pardoning is not only useful, but necessary. In all these cases, if the punishment were inflicted, the evil produced would exceed the good, and in some cases, almost infinitely. If the legislator could have known that certain individual cases would or would not be included in the general case in which he would have wished that the punishment should cease, he would act unwisely were he to rely upon any other person for its cessation. For why should he give to another a power to frustrate his designs?

But he does not possess this knowledge, unless in quality of legislator, he acts also in that of a prophet. It follows, therefore, that he must rely upon some other.

In English law, one method by which the law gives to a party injured, or rather, to every prosecutor, a partial power of pardon, consists in giving him the choice of the kind of action which he will commence. On this, or on the difference between the actions, depends a difference between the punishments—so far as the happening of this difference is concerned, the lot of the offender depends not on the gravity of his offence, but on some other foreign circumstances, such as the degree of the ill-will of the party injured, or other prosecutor, or of the knowledge of his legal advisers. The Judge is a puppet in the hands of any prosecutor, which he can cause to move at his pleasure and caprice.

There are many persons, as we have seen, who exercise the power of pardoning; there are many others who possess it who are not observed.

Among the latter class may be placed those who have the power of placing nullities in the course of procedure. In England, an attorney, or his clerk, any copying clerk at eighteen pence or two shillings per day, may grant or sell impunity to whomsoever it seems them good.

If the individual injured can directly, or indirectly, put an end to a criminal process, otherwise than by the punishment before the judgment has been pronounced, and in case of conviction, executed, he enjoys in effect this right of pardoning. The right of remission is then one branch of the power of pardoning. When the interest of the public requires that the punishment should take place, the individual injured ought not to enjoy this right; when this interest does not require it, he may enjoy it.

This power may be allowed in all cases, when the offence on which it operates, being founded only in a private quarrel, does not spread any alarm through society, or at least does not spread any alarm which the conduct of the parties does not destroy.

But in the case of corporal injuries, how trifling soever, and especially in the case of injuries accompanied with insult, this remission ought not to be allowed without the knowledge of the Judge, otherwise the weakness and good-nature of some minds would serve to draw down upon them vexation from hardened oppressors.

Homicide is a case in which the power of remission ought not to be allowed to any one in particular. It would, in effect, be to grant to him an arbitrary power over the life of those whose death he might thus pardon; he might boldly employ any assassin, by exercising in favour of that assassin his power of pardoning.

If to grant to any one whatsoever, the power of taking away a reward offered by the legislator would be regarded as an absurdity, to grant the power of taking away a punishment in the opposite case, with the reserve of specific exceptions, would be a more terrible absurdity.

This absurdity is not found in the system of rewards: no person proposes to take away a reward after the legislator has offered it; the nullities, however, allowed in prosecutions, when he has appointed a reward for offenders, operates to this effect in the case of punishment.

The frequency of capital punishment is one of the most probable causes of the popularity of pardons.

In England, it may therefore admit of debate, whether the legislature has done most evil by appointing so many capital punishments, or the Sovereign, by exercising his power of remitting them.

The essence of this power is, to act by caprice. The King, as it is falsely said,—the Deputy of the King, as it ought to have been said, does not act judicially; he does not act from a knowledge of the matter; he has not the power of doing so; he has not even the power of compelling the attendance of witnesses. Is a lie told before this powerless despot? it is an unpunishable [sic] lie.

The power of pardoning is often said to be one of the brightest jewels in the Royal Crown: it is burdensome as it is bright, not only to those who submit to the Crown, but still more so to him also who wears it.

Many cases have occurred in England in which the counsellors of the Crown have, from more or less praiseworthy motives, made use of this lawful despotism of the King, to soften the tyranny of the laws. Never was power so undoubtedly legal, though undue, employed for a more legitimate purpose,—the result, however, has been, not that the Minister has been applauded as he deserved, but he has become the object of clamour, libels, and threats. The most correct and legitimate exercise of the powers impoliticly attached to his character, has only served to draw down upon the King that treatment which a tyrant would have merited.

How much discontent and fear would have been spared, if a right, legally abusive, had given place to an enlightened and well ordered law.[880]

SEC. II.—BY LENGTH OF TIME.

Ought punishment in any cases, and in what, to be defeasible [*sic*] by length of time? By the time, I mean, that has elapsed since the commission of the offence.[881]

At first view, the answer seems to be clearly in the negative. For what, it may be said, has the circumstance of the length of time to do with the demand there is for punishment?

Upon a nearer view, however, it will be found, that the utility of prescription in certain cases is maintainable by specious, at least, if not conclusive, arguments.

As a foundation for these arguments, it must be admitted, that if in any case the suffering of the delinquent is not necessary for the attainment of the ends of punishment, the punishment ought not to be inflicted.

This being premised, it should seem, that in a view to one of the ends of punishment, to wit, reformation, the execution of it after a certain length of time, is not necessary. A certain number of years, suppose ten, has elapsed since he committed the offence: now then, in all this time; either he has committed similar offences, or he has not. If he has not, he has reformed himself, and the purpose of the law has been answered without punishment; if he has, he has been punished for subsequent offences, and the discipline he stood in need of, has been already administered to him, at a time when he stood more in need of it than he can be supposed to stand at present.[882]

Thus stands the argument upon the ground of Reformation: but of the facts alleged, one, it must be confessed, is rather problematical. If a man commit an offence, and is forthcoming ten years afterwards, it is by no means clear, from his not having been punished for any similar offences, that he has not committed any. In the same manner that he escaped detection or prosecution for the first, he may have escaped detection or prosecution for any number of other similar offences. The difficulty of detection, the death of witnesses, the subtleties of procedure, are circumstances that afford ample grounds for disputing the force of the inference, from his not having incurred punishment to his not having deserved it.*

Upon the ground of example, there is still less to be said in favour of

---

*Any one who is at all conversant with anecdotes of notorious criminals must have observed, that nothing is more common in this country than for a man to be guilty of twenty, thirty, or forty thefts or robberies, before punishment overtakes him.

prescription. If the prescription is not to take place till at the end of a long period, as ten years (the number above taken for an example), it will not contribute, in any assignable degree, to lessen the apparent value of the punishment. When a man meditates a crime, his great fear is the being detected and apprehended immediately almost upon the commission of it. The taking away the danger that would await him at the end of ten years, will add very little to his security.*

[883]When a crime has been committed, either the person only who committed it may remain unknown, or the fact† itself as well as the *person*. If either be unknown, it is plain no prosecution can have been set on foot. If both be known, then either a prosecution may have been set on foot, or not. It is only in case of there being no prosecution, that prescription has ever been allowed. The rule is, that a man shall not be prosecuted after that interval has elapsed, not that if he has been prosecuted and convicted, he shall not suffer.[884]

The apprehension of danger commences at the time of the discovery. Persons who are about the criminal now understand that they have among them a thief, a robber, or a murderer: this cannot but give them some alarm. If no punishment at all is to be inflicted on him, if he is suffered to go on and live where he did before, how is this alarm to be quieted.

In crimes the object of which is a pecuniary profit, prescription ought not in any case to operate so as to protect the delinquent in the enjoyment of his ill-gotten acquisition.

Neither ought[885] it not to operate in such manner as to leave innocent persons exposed to suffer from their terror or abhorrence of the criminal.[886]

There are also certain crimes, in respect of which prescription ought not to be adopted in any case. Such are three species of homicide: viz. homicide for lucre, through wantonness, or from premeditated resentment;[887] incendiarism [*sic*]; and the offence of sinking a vessel manned, or of laying a country under water. The mischief of crimes of these kinds is so great, that it seems paying too great a regard to the interests of the criminal, to adopt a rule that may contribute, though in ever so small a degree, to lessen the apparent certainty of the punishment; and the horror or terror, a fact of any of those kinds inspires when discovered, is[888] so great, that that circumstance alone seems enough to overweigh any good that could be gained by it.

What is the good in view in prescription? It is the interest of one single person that is in question: the delinquent. The sparing of that single person from a suffering which it is supposed it may, in the case in which it is pro-

---

†Mr. Bentham does not appear to have carried on his examination of this subject in respect to the other ends of punishment.—Ed.

‡Under the name of the fact, I would here include such and so many circumstances as are necessary to make the act in question come under the denomination of some crime.

posed the prescription should take place, not be necessary, at least not so necessary as formerly to the purposes of punishment to inflict. Now, when it is a crime by which men are exposed to suffer in their individual capacities, it can scarcely be detected, but a multitude of persons must begin to suffer: to wit, by the apprehension of his committing other such crimes in future, of which they may chance to be the objects; and this suffering of theirs will continue, till he be manifestly disabled to hurt them: the least penal method of doing which, is to send him out of the way.[889]

Upon this slight examination, we perceive that the utility of prescription will vary greatly in respect of different offences. To discuss this topic completely, it would be necessary, therefore, to consider it with a view to the several sorts of offences. To do this fully, belongs not to our present subject—all we can do in this place is, to offer a few general hints, just to put us in the way,[890] and to serve as a clew to indicate the principal points[891] upon which the enquiry ought to turn.[892]

Whether a given person, detected after such a length of time, of a crime of the sort in question, is or is not an object of terror to those around him, is a question that can be answered only by a particular enquiry: it is a matter, therefore, that ought rather to be committed to the Magistrate who has the power of pardoning, than to be provided for by a general law.[893]

SEC. III.—By death of parties.

In pursuit of (the means of making) compensation, the business of punishment is apt to be overlooked. When one man, the party injured, is presented with what another man, the injurer,[894] is made to pay, men are apt to take it for granted and at first asking, would be apt to answer, that there is no punishment in the case. They imagine, but hastily and erroneously,[895] that the only person who has suffered by the offence, is that party who is the immediate object of the injury. If then that person, by an operation of law, be made to enjoy as much as by the offence he had been made to suffer, they conclude (and justly enough were the foundation true) that everything is set to rights, and that the law has nothing more to do. The pain which the offender is made to suffer by being made to give up what the party injured is made to enjoy, they do not look upon in the light of punishment. They look upon it as a circumstance resulting, accidentally and unintentionally, out of the operation by which an indemnification is produced to the injured party, so that it would be but so much the better if that pain could be altogether spared; and it is for want of being able to save it, that it is suffered to exist. In short, so entirely is the idea of punishment lost in that of compensation, that a law which appoints the latter is not understood to appoint the former, is not looked upon as a *penal* law.[896]

Punish, however, it must—a penal law in one sense of the word, it must be, if it is to have any effect at all in preventing the practice which is productive of the mischief it means to cure; and it is by *punishing* that it does more good than by *indemnifying*.[897] For of the two ends, prevention and compensation,[898] the former, as has been proved, is by much[899] the most important.[900]

This neglect, however, of the principal end of laws made in restraint of private injuries, has not been attended with all the ill consequences that might at first sight be imagined. The indemnification being made to come out of the pocket of the aggressor, has produced the punishment of course. Now, under the laws of most nations, in most instances of acknowledged injuries, indemnification has been exacted, and by that means, in most cases, it has happened that punishment has been applied. Yet not in all: because compensation has been made defeasible by contingencies; I say in most, but it has not in all: for there are two events by which in all these cases indemnification is rendered not necessary in so great a degree as it was before, and, as it may appear upon a superficial glance, not necessary at all. In effect, upon the happening of either of these two events, under most laws, and particularly under our own, the obligation of making compensation has been cancelled. At the same time compensation being the only object in view, this being taken away, punishment has of course dropped along with it. But in these cases, as I hope soon to make appear, howsoever it may stand with compensation, the demand for punishment has not been lessened by either of the events in question.[901]

These are, 1st, the death of the injurer; 2dly, the death of the party injured.

I. The death of the injurer has been deemed to take away the occasion for indemnification. The reason that occurs is, that there is nobody to give it. Had he continued alive, he ought to have given it, doubtless; but as he is gone, who ought then? Why one person rather than another?[902]

To answer these questions at large, we must make a distinction according to the nature of the offence. The offence is either attended with a *transferable* profit, a fruit transmissible to the representatives[903] of the offender, or not. In the first case, the obligation of making compensation ought clearly to devolve on the representative on the score of punishment, if on no other. In the latter case, there would still be one use in its being made to devolve on the representative, as far as the possessions he inherits from the party deceased extend, though not so great a use as in the former case.[904]

Where the profit of a transgression is transmissible to a representative, the obligation of restoring the amount of it ought likewise to devolve on him; if not, the punishment would not, in the case in question, be equal to the profit: in fact, there would be no punishment at all, no motive for the party under temptation to abstain from it. It may occur for the first moment (but it will soon appear to be otherwise) that neither will there in contemplation of this case be any temptation: for if the injurer thinks himself about to die, there will be an end of the profit of the injury. But this is not the case: should he be made to lose it ever so soon himself, he may transmit it to those who are dear to him, so that the pleasure of sympathy, grounded on the contemplation of their enjoyment, is a clear force that acts without control, and impels him to transgression. Besides this, the delays and uncertainty of justice add still to the force of the temptation. If he can contrive to spin out the suit so long as he lives, the whole business from beginning to end is clear gain to him.905

II. Even though the profit of a transgression be not of such a nature as to be transmissible to a representative, there seems still to be a reason why the obligation of making amends ought to devolve on the representatives, as far as they have *assets*.* Such an arrangement would be eligible, as well on account of punishment as of compensation.906

On account of compensation, for the following reasons: the mischief of the transgression is a burthen that must be borne by somebody: the representative and the party injured are equally innocent in this respect, they stand upon a par; but the representative would suffer less under the same burthen than the party injured, as we shall presently perceive. From the moment when the injury was conceived, the party injured, in virtue of the known disposition of the law in his favour, entertained *expectations* of receiving amends. If these expectations are *disappointed* by a sudden and unforeseen event, like that of the delinquent's death, a shock is felt by the party injured, such as he would feel at the sudden loss of anything of which he was in possession. The eventual representative entertained no such determinate expectations. What expectation he could entertain in the life-time of his predecessor, respected only the clear surplus of his fortune; what should remain of it after the deduction of all charges that might be brought upon it by his misfortunes, his follies, or his crimes.907

On account of punishment, for the following reason: the punishment of the delinquent in his own person, is a punishment which fails upon his death. The burthen thrown upon those who are dear to him, extends his punishment, as it were, beyond the grave. Their suffering, it is true, will, for the reasons above given, not be very considerable; but this is what the bulk of mankind are not apt to consider. It will be apt therefore, in general, to appear to him in the light of punishment, and will contribute to impose a restraint on him in a case in which, otherwise, there would be none. Nor

---

*Assets: Effects descending to them from the ancestor, and liable to alienation.

will this advantage, in point of punishment, be charged with that *expense*, which renders punishments *in alienam personam* generally ineligible: for when the burthen is made to rest on the representative who has assets, there is less suffering, as we have shown, upon the whole, than if it were to rest upon any other person.[908]

The law of England on this head is full of absurdity and caprice. The following are the instances in which (the heir is permitted to enrich himself by the wrongdoing of his ancestor) a man is permitted to enrich his heir with the profit of his crimes.* By the wrongful *taking* and withholding of any kind of moveables, while, if it had been by only *withholding* money due, the heir must have refunded. By the waste committed on immoveables, in which he has only a temporary interested.†[909] By selling a prisoner for debt his liberty. By embezzling property entrusted to him by will: though, if he had not broken any such confidence, but had intruded himself into the management of the dead man's property without warrant, the heir must have refunded; in short, by any kind of injurious proceeding, where the compensation, instead of being left to the discretion of a Jury, is thought fit to be increased and liquidated by a positive regulation.

The death of the party injured is another event upon which the obligation of making amends is very commonly made to cease; but with full as little reason, it should seem, as in the former case. The death of the party in question[910] is a contingency which does not at all lessen the demand there is for punishment. For compensation, indeed, the demand is not altogether so strong in this case, as in the former: the person[911] who was the immediate object of the injury, entertained a prospect of reaping, in present, the whole profit of a compensation he expected to be adjudged to him; his representative did not, during the life-time of the principal, entertain so fixed a prospect: he, however, entertained a full prospect of some compensation to be made to his principal; and he entertained a prospect of a part, at least, of that compensation devolving upon himself, subject to the contingencies to which his general expectations from the principal were exposed. This expectation is more than any one else was in a situation to entertain, so that there is a better reason why he should reap the profit of the punishment, than why any one else should.[912]

The law of England has been more liberal in the remedies it has given *to* the heir of the party injured, than in those which it has given against the

---

*In all these points, I depend upon the authority of Comyn's Digest, I 262, 263.

†A person whom I know, having the immediate reversion of an estate, part in houses, part in land, rented the land of a person who had the life-interest in both. The life-owner letting the houses go to ruin, the reversionary, to indemnify himself, stop the rent of the land. The life-owner died without repairing the houses, as he was bound: the consequence was, that the reversioner [*sic*], (as he was advised, to his great surprise) though obliged to pay his rent, lost his remedy for the waste.

heir of a wrong-doer. It gives it to the heir in all cases, as it should seem, of injuries done to the *property* of the ancestor. It denies it however in the case of injuries to the person,* be they ever so atrocious; and probably, in the case of injuries to the reputation. This omission leaves an open door to the most crying evils. Age and infirmity, which ought, if any difference be made, to receive a more signal protection from the law, than the opposite conditions of life, are exposed more particularly to oppression. The nearer a man is to his grave, the greater is the probability that he may be injured with impunity, since, if the prosecution can be staved off during his life, the remedy is gone.†[913] The remedy, by a criminal prosecution, is but an inadequate *succedaneum*. It extends not to injuries done to the person through negligence, nor to all injuries to the reputation: it is defeasible by the arbitrary pleasure and irresponsible act of a servant of the Crown: it operates only in the way of punishment, affording no compensation to the heir.[914]

After so many instances where no satisfaction is exigible [*sic*] from the heir for transgressions, by which he profits, no one will wonder to find him standing exempt from that obligation in the case of such injuries as, being inflicted commonly, not from rapacious, but merely vindictive motives, are not commonly attended with any pecuniary profit. Such are those done to the person, or to the reputation, or in the way of mere destruction[915] to the property. So accordingly stands the law.‡ Though there are none of them by which the injurer may not, in a multitude of cases, draw indirectly a pecuniary profit: for instance, in the case of a rivalry in manufactures, where one man destroys the manufactory of his more successful rival.

THE END.

---

*1 Comyns's Dig. 261.

†A man may be kept in gaol, and his fortune ruined by it; and if he die under the imprisonment, his family are without remedy. In some cases, the wrong-doer may not even be punishable by a criminal prosecution; or he may be maltreated in such a manner, as to contract a lingering distemper, such as does not follow from the injurious treatment with sufficient speed and certainty to bring it within the crime of murder. If the prosecution can but be staved off till he dies, his family are without remedy. Many years ago, a butcher was committed to Newgate, at a time when the gaol distemper was raging in that prison, upon a false and malicious charge of theft. He died there, leaving a large distressed family, who were altogether without remedy for this atrocious injury.

‡I rest still on the authority of Comyns, except in the case of injuries to reputation, in which I conclude from analogy, Comyns being silent.

NOTES

INTRODUCTION

1. This group of disciples has been distinguished from the group of sycophants who, reportedly, flattered Bentham and approved of his ideas without challenge, unlike the earlier group (including, explicitly, Dumont) that addressed and compiled his work in a much more critically rigorous way. David Lieberman, "From Bentham to Benthamism," *The Historical Journal*, 28, no. 1 (March 1985): 261–202. An account of John Austin's critique and alteration of Bentham's ideas, despite his extremely high regard for his mentor's philosophical method, is provided in Wilfrid E. Rumble, *The Thought of John Austin: Jurisprudence, Colonial Reform, and the British Constitution* (London: Athlone, 1985), pp. 23–26.

2. Hedonic utilitarianism of this sort is famously associated with Henry Sidgwick, *The Method of Ethics* (Indianapolis: Hackett, 1981), pp. 119–61. Good critiques of that approach are provided in Jerome B. Schneewind, *Sidgwick's Ethics and Victorian Moral Philosophy* (New York: Oxford University Press, 1976), pp. 317–28; and (especially in terms of a consideration of the plural subjectivity of pleasure) Fred Feldman, "Two Questions About Pleasure," in *Philosophical Analysis*, David Austin, ed. (Dordrecht, The Netherlands: Kluwer, 1988), pp. 59–81.

3. This interpretation of utilitarian thought has been most famously advanced in Karl Popper, *The Open Society and Its Enemies* (London: Routledge and Keegan Paul, 1966), especially at vol. II, p. 304 n. 62.

4. At least two facsimile reproductions of the 1830 edition have been published but, obviously, these sorts of reproductions do not represent an actual new edition. Jeremy Bentham, *The Rationale of Punishment* (Boston: Elibron Classics, 2005); Jeremy Bentham, *The Rationale of Punishment* (Stockton, CA: University Press of the Pacific, 2004).

5. An excellent overview of all of the information pertaining to the general background of this book, its manuscripts, and its publication is Hugo Bedau, "Bentham's Theory of Punishment: Origin and Content," *Journal of Bentham Studies* 7 (2004).

6. That parallel is, especially, notable in Jeremy Bentham, *Introduction to the Principles of Morals and Legislation*, J. H. Burns and H. L. A. Hart, eds. (Oxford: Oxford University Press, 2005) 156–279.

7. That difficulty has been noted by many scholars. It is a theme that is acknowledged in J. H. Burns, "Jeremy Bentham: An Iliad of Argument," *Journal of Bentham Studies* 3 (2000).

8. Bentham addressed this project and the ideas that support it in much greater detail in other works, including Jeremy Bentham, *Proposal for a New and Less Expensive Mode of Employing and Reforming Convicts* (London 1798). An outstanding analysis of this aspect of his theory of a reformed penal system can be found in Janet Semple, *Bentham's Prison: A Study of the Panopticon Penitentiary* (Oxford: Clarendon Press, 1993).

9. An interesting overview of this controversy regarding the treatment of punishment as an extrinsic evil that is relative to the extrinsic good that it can produce (including the general criticisms toward utilitarian thought and the response that this criticism has elicited in this respect) is offered in Alan Brudner, "Retributivism and the Death Penalty," *University of Toronto Law Journal* 30, no. 4 (Autumn 1980): 337–55. Attempts to extricate a utilitarian approach to punishment from this criticism (especially in terms of an appeal to a rule-utili-

tarian interpretation) have been offered, in different ways, by H. L. A. Hart, *Punishment and Responsibility* (Oxford: Oxford University Press, 1968), pp. 44–49, 181–83; and John Rawls, "Two Concepts of Rules," *Philosophical Review* 64, no. 1 (January 1955): 3–32.

10. Compare, for example, Bentham, *Morals and Legislation*, ch. XIII with Jeremy Bentham, *The Rationale of Punishment*, Richard Smith, ed. (London: Robert Heward, 1830), bk. IV, sec. 2.

11. This approach is explored in Struan Jacobs, "Bentham, Science and the Construction of Jurisprudence," *Journal of the History of European Ideas* 12 (1990): 583–594.

12. The efforts of other utilitarian scholars in, effectively, collaborating upon the publication of Bentham's manuscripts are addressed in J. H. Burns, "The Bentham Project," in *Editing Texts of the Romantic Period*, John D. Baird, ed. (Toronto: AMS Press, 1987), pp. 73–87; J. H. Burns, "Dreams and Destinations: Jeremy Bentham in 1828," *The Bentham Newsletter* 1 (1978): 21–30, and and John R. Dinwiddy, "Bentham and the Early Nineteenth Century," in *Radicalism and Reform in Britain, 1780–1850* (London: Hambledon, 1992), pp. 291–99.

13. An overview of this widely accepted understanding of communication (including the communication of political ideas) is provided in Robert E. Denton and Gary C. Woodward, *Political Communication in America* (Westport, CT: Praeger, 1998), pp. 1–16; Brian McNair, *An Introduction to Political Communication* (New York: Routledge, 2003), pp. 3–15; and Marshall McLuhan, *The Essential McLuhan*, Eric McLuhan and Frank Zingrone, eds. (New York: Basic Books, 1996), pp. 89–106.

14. This interpretation is based upon the claim that, although Bentham's earlier works are best known, the vast corpus of his later works were appropriated by his disciples (especially James Mill) and transformed by them, thus more firmly linking Bentham's legacy to the cause of radical political reform through this indirect and passive (on his part) collaborative process. An excellent assessment and analysis of this claim is provided in Lieberman, pp. 199–224.

15. Those dates are ascribed to all of the available manuscripts that were transcribed into *The Rationale of Punishment* from Bentham's handwriting.

16. This relationship is described in Bedau.

17. These problems are discussed in Tony Draper, "An Introduction to Jeremy Bentham's Theory of Punishment," *Journal of Bentham Studies* 5 (2002). A fuller account of Dumont's relationship to Bentham and his work is provided in C. Blamires, "Étienne Dumont: Genevan Apostle of Utility," *Utilitas* 2 (1990): 55–70.

18. This information is derived from an examination of Jeremy Bentham, *Théorie des peines et des Récompenses*, Etienne Dumont, ed. and trans., second edition (Paris: Chez Bossange et Masson, 1818), vol. I.

19. One source that considers this relationship is Yoshio Nagai, "Smith and Bentham on Jurisprudence: English Utilitarianism in Contrast with the Scottish Enlightenment," *Enlightenment and Dissent* 19 (2000): 1–22.

20. This orientation of Blackstone's contribution to eighteenth-century legal theory is expounded in Duncan Kennedy, "The Structure of Blackstone's Commentaries," *Buffalo Law Review* 28, no. 1 (January 1980): 205–382.

21. Bentham, *Rationale of Punishment*, p. 213.

22. Ibid., pp. 4–5. Compare it with Bentham, *Morals and Legislation*, ch. XII.

23. Ibid., pp. 61–62. Compare this passage with Bentham, *Morals and Legislation*, ch. XV.

24. Dumont, in a note that he added to this chapter, commented that some people regarded it "only as fit subjects for ridicule and caricature," suggesting that Bentham's motive in making these analogies might, indeed, have been sarcasm. Ibid., p. 62.

25. That criticism is acknowledged in Hanna Fenichel Pitkin, "Slippery Bentham: Some Neglected Cracks in the Foundations of Utilitarianism," *Political Theory* 18, no. 1 (February 1990): 104–33.

26. This interpretation of utilitarian attitudes toward normative moral value and the controversy that ensues from it are examined in Stuart M. Brown, Jr., "Duty and the Production of Good," *The Philosophical Review* 61, no. 3 (July 1952): 299–311.

27. This "anti-hedonistic" interpretation of utilitarianism associated with John Stuart Mill's principle of "higher pleasures," is seminally explored in Sidgwick, pp. 93–94, 121–22 and further assessed in David O. Brink, "Mill's Deliberative Utilitarianism," *Philosophy and Public Affairs* 21, no. 1 (Winter 1992): 67–103, and Schneewind, pp. 185–86.

28. Some critics have argued that this consequentialist standard is unattainable because punishment as a rational deterrent would depend either upon its disproportionate severity or its intrusiveness, in either case affirming the hedonic principle and suggesting that utilitarian punishment standards must be more severe than normally assumed. Alvin Goldman, "The Paradox of Punishment," *Philosophy and Public Affairs* 9, no. 1 (1979), pp. 42–58.

29. Bentham's utilitarian critique of Blackstone's theories and his alternative propositions are presented in David Lieberman, *The Province of Legislation Determined* (Cambridge: Cambridge University Press, 1989), pp. 227–39, 257–76.

30. This uncertainty regarding the overall meaning of Bentham's theories is part of an ongoing debate, as discussed in James E. Crimmins, "Contending Interpretations of Bentham's Utilitarianism," *Canadian Journal of Political Science* 29, no. 4 (December 1996): 751–77.

31. *Cambridge History of English and American Literature* (Cambridge: Cambridge University Press, 1921), vol. XI, sec. 2.

32. This effort is described in Correspondence no. 678, Dumont to Bentham, *Correspondence of Jeremy Bentham*, Alexander Taylor Milne, ed. (London: Athlone, 1981), vol. IV, p. 93, and also noted in *Correspondence*, Stephen Conway, ed. (Oxford: Clarendon Press, 1989), vol. IX, p. 130 n. 36.

33. An excellent example of this attitude can be found in a letter in which Dumont declares that he has been diverted from his work upon one of Bentham's manuscript because of his discovery of another one that entirely "enchants" him, Correspondence no. 878, Dumont to Bentham, November 23, 1792, in *Correspondence*, Alexander Taylor Milne, ed. (London: Athlone, 1981), vol. IV, p. 405.

34. John Bowring and Richard Doane, eds., *The Works of Jeremy Bentham* (Edinburgh: William Tait, 1843), vol. X, pp. 185–86. This personal controversy in the relationship of the two men also is described in Leslie Stephens, *The English Utilitarians* (University Press of the Pacific, 2004), vol. I, ch. 5, sec. 2.

35. "Correspondence no. 1,085, Bentham to the Duc de Liancourt, October 11, 1795, in *Correspondence* Alexander Taylor Milne, ed. (London: Athlone, 1981), vol. V, p. 160.

36. Quoted in Ibid., vol. V, p. 201 n. 5.

37. "Correspondence no. 1,701, May 21, 1802, *Correspondence*, J. R. Dinwiddy, ed. (Oxford: Clarendon Press, 1988), vol. VII, p. 54. This particular letter concerned Dumont's efforts regarding the *Traités de legislation civile et pénale*.

38. Correspondence no. 857, Bentham to Dumont, August 16, 1792, *Correspondence*, vol. IV, pp. 385–86.

39. Correspondence no. 2,029, Dumont to Bentham, February 6, 1809, *Correspondence*, Stephen Conway, ed. (Oxford: Clarendon, 1988), vol. VIII, p. 15, Correspondence no. 2,044, Dumont to Bentham, May 11, 1809, *Correspondence*, vol. VIII, p. 28, and, especially, Correspondence no. 2,051, Dumont to Bentham, July 31, 1809, *Correspondence*, vol. VIII, p. 40, suggesting the necessity of relying upon inference on the part of Dumont.

40. Correspondence no. 2,532, Bentham to William Plumer, Jr., December 1818, *Correspondence*, vol. IX, p. 310.

41. An overview of the development of this attitude on the part of Rousseau (including insights into the influences that may have affected Dumont in this respect) can be found in

Helena Rosenblatt, *Rousseau and Geneva: From the First Discourse to the Social Contract, 1749–1762* (Cambridge: Cambridge University Press, 1997), pp. 10–45.

42. W. R. Sorley, "Bentham and the Early Utilitarians," *Cambridge History of English and American Literature* (Cambridge: Cambridge University Press, 1921), vol. XI, ch. 2.

43. Dumont's general governmental role in advising Mirabeau is addressed in H. O. Pappe, "Sismondi's System of Liberty," *Journal of the History of Ideas* 40, no. 2 (April 1979): 253–54. His general support for the goals of France's republican revolution was expressed within his memoirs of this relationship, Etienne Dumont, *Recollections of Mirabeau and the First Two Legislative Assemblies of France* (Philadelphia: Carrie & Lea, 1833), pp. 41–113.

44. An overview of Dumont's approach and contribution to Bentham's writings and early utilitarian thought is provided in Blamires, pp. 55–70. Additional insights are provided in Jonathan Harris, "Bernardino Rivadavia and Benthamite 'Discipleship,'" *Latin American Research Review* 33, no. 1 (January 1998): 131–133.

45. This fact is listed in the credits of Bowring's edition of Jeremy Bentham, "The Rationale of Punishment," vol. X, p. 548.

46. Gunhild Hoogensen, "Bentham's International Manuscripts versus the 'Published' Works," *Journal of Bentham Studies* 4 (2001), http://www.ucl.ac.uk/Bentham-Project/journal/hoogensn.htm, especially n. 15.

47. Bentham to Jean Baptiste Say, August 4, 1823, *Correspondence*, Catherine Fuller, ed. (Oxford: Clarendon Press, 2000), vol. XI, p. 274.

48. Ibid.

49. Some of these issues are addressed in Henry Schogt, "Semantic Theory and Translation Theory," in *Theories of Translation*, John Biguenet and Rainer Schulte, eds. (Chicago: University of Chicago Press, 1992), pp. 193–203.

50. This idea is explored in terms of the "mirror of the mind," as explained in Noam Chomsky, *Language and Politics*, Carlos P. Otero, ed. (Montreal: Black Rose Books, 1988), pp. 233–50.

51. Correspondence no. 3,154, Bentham to Dumont, December 14, 1824, *Correspondence*, vol. XII, Luke O'Sullivan and Catherine Fuller, eds. (Oxford: Clarendon Press, 2001), pp. 74–75.

52. Bentham to Jean Baptiste Say, August 4, 1823, *Correspondence*, Catherine Fuller, ed. (Oxford: Clarendon Press, 2000), vol. XI, p. 274.

53. This general problem is acknowledged in François Chevrette, "Les concepts de 'droits acquis,' de 'droits des groups,' et de 'droits collectifs,'" in *Les Droits linguistiques: rapport de la commission d'enquête sur la situation de la langue française et sure les droits linguistiques au Québec* (Québec: Gouvernement du Québec, 1972), pp. 403–49; Roda Roberts, "Legal Translator and Legal Interpreter Training in Canada," *Terminology Update* 20, no. 6 (1987): 8–10, and Claude-Armand Sheppard, ed., *The Law of Languages in Canada* (Ottawa: Information Canada, 1971), pp. 109–43.

54. This theme is addressed in greater detail in James T. McHugh, "Is the Law 'Anglophone' in Canada?" *American Review of Canadian Studies* 23, no. 1 (Autumn 1993): 407–24.

55. An excellent account of *lacunae* on the part of both Dumont and Smith can be found within the published texts and manuscripts (which are in Bentham's handwriting) concerning Bentham, *Rationale of Punishment*, Book VI, chapter 2, which appears within Dumont's edition as Bentham, *Théorie des peines*, Book II, chapter 15, pp. 317–23, and which can be found on the back page of Jeremy Bentham, Manuscripts for *The Rationale of Punishment*, MSS Portfolio 141, Folder 102, p. 3—subsequent references to these manuscripts will be designated as, per this example, RP MSS 141/102: 3.

For example, each contributor to the 1830 edition of this book offers a different version of the explanation and calculations of "subsidiary punishment." Bentham's interpretation of this concept (as reflected within the unadulterated manuscript version) that is particularly prominent within the first part of the 1830 published edition, while Dumont's interpretation (as reflected within the 1818 French edition) is prominent within the latter part of the 1830 edition, while other interpretive gaps, throughout the 1830 text, relating to the interpretation of this concept apparently were filled by Smith. In some cases, the discrepancies appear to be technical in nature, with each one being based upon different ways of explaining a particular concept for the sake of descriptive clarity, rather than evaluating it or subjecting it to a particular analysis regarding suitability or propriety. Nonetheless, the overall effect upon interpretation often is profound, as notes that have been included throughout this new edition of this work will emphasize.

56. RP MSS, back of 141/130: 5.

57. Smith resorts to this archaic language for this translation (possibly extracted from a contemporary edition of Molière's *Le Misanthrope*). Bentham, *Rationale of Punishment*, Book V, ch. 3, which appears in more conventional French within Bentham, *Théorie des peines*, vol. I, p. 263.

58. The effect of tone has been measured in political terms and used to explain shifts in public policy. Roger W. Cobb and Charles D. Elder, *Participation in American Politics: The Dynamics of Agenda-Building* (Baltimore: Johns Hopkins University Press, 1983); and William Riker, *The Art of Political Manipulation* (New Haven: Yale University Press, 1986).

59. Bentham, *Rationale of Punishment*, Book I, ch. 8.

60. Ibid., Book IV, sec. I.

61. Ibid., Book IV, section IV.

62. Bentham, *Théorie des peines*, vol. I, p. 423.

63. Bentham, *Rationale of Punishment*, Book IV, sec. V.

64. *Théorie des peines*, vol. I, pp. 426–29.

65. Bentham, *Rationale of Punishment*, Book III, ch. 2, sec. I.

66. Ibid., Book II, ch. 11, sec. Sec. II.

67. Ibid., Book II, chapter 11, section II.

68. Bentham, *Théorie des peines*, vol. I, p. 272

69. Ibid., vol. I p. 275.

70. David Lyons, *In the Interest of the Governed: A Study in Bentham's Philosophy of Utility and Law* (Oxford: Oxford University Press, 2003), pp. 32–39 appears to agree with the individual happiness approach, while Ross Harrison, *Bentham* (London: Routledge & Kegan Paul, 1983), pp. 263–77 supports the "greatest happiness" interpretation.

71. That theme is apparent within Jeremy Bentham, *A Fragment on Government*, Ross Harrison, ed. (Cambridge: Cambridge University Press, 1988), pp. 106–14. A good comment on that theme is provided in L. J. Hume, "Jeremy Bentham and the Nineteenth Century Revolution in Government," *The Historical Journal* 10, no. 3 (March 1967): 364–68.

72. That point appears to be made in Jeremy Bentham, "Pannomial Fragments," in *Collected Works of Jeremy Bentham*, John Bowring, ed. (Edinburgh: William Tait, 1843), vol. III, pp. 219–21. This theme is central to the concerns expressed in Pitkin, pp. 104–31.

73. Elie Halévy, *The Growth of Philosophical Radicalism* (Boston: Beacon Press, 1960), pp. 118–19 noted this apparent inconsistency.

74. Bentham, "Constitutional Code," *Works*, IX, 6.

75. Bentham, "Anarchical Falacies," *Works*, II, p. 497; and Pitkin, pp. 121–22.

76. Bentham, "Principles of Penal Law," *Works*, I, p.561.

77. This idea is suggested in C. W. Everett, *The Education of Jeremy Bentham* (New York: Columbia University Press, 1931), pp. 190–93.

78. Mary Peter Mack, *Jeremy Bentham: An Odyssey of Ideas, 1748–1792* (London: Heinneman, 1962), p. 292 makes reference to this idea and this quote.

79. Bentham, "Panopticon," *Works*, IV, p. 39.

80. This development and philosophical arguments surrounding it are addressed in B. Buchan, "Zero Tolerance, Mandatory Sentencing, and Early Liberal Arguments for Penal Reform," *International Journal of the Sociology of Law* 30, no. 3 (September 2002): 201–18.

81. The classic treatment of this historical development, especially in terms of the "Whig liberalism" that influenced it, can be found in E. P. Thompson, *Whigs and Hunters* (New York: Random House, 1975), pp. 245–69.

82. Examples of this tendency include Johannes Andenaes, "Does Punishment Deter Crime?" in *Philosophical Perspectives on Punishment*, Gertrude Ezorsky, ed. (Albany: State University of New York Press, 1972), pp. 346–54; and Gordon Tullock, "Does Punishment Deter Crime?" in *Public Interest* 36 (Summer 1974), pp. 103–11.

83. A good example of this tendency can be found in H. L. A. Hart, *Essays on Bentham: Studies in Jurisprudence and Political Theory* (Oxford: Oxford University Press, 1982), pp. 45–48.

Perhaps, a more accurate way to describe the general utilitarian approach toward penal law is in terms of its "reductionist" goal, as expressed in David Wood, "Retribution, Crime Reduction, and the Justification of Punishment," *Oxford Journal of Legal Studies* 22, no. 2 (June 2002): 301–21.

84. However, some scholars contend that the resort to personal moral values, as shaped by the subjective inclinations of society, make the introduction of these guiding principles into a utilitarian approach to public policy inescapable. Arguably, calculations of actual outcomes on the part of "reasonable" and "well-informed" individual agents are displaced by a subjective and, often, unsubstantiated anticipation of possible outcomes, making the imposition, by the state, of a rule-based system designed to produce predictable outcomes an inescapable requirement of a general utilitarian approach, as broached in William H. Shaw, *Contemporary Ethics: Taking Account of Utilitarianism* (Malden, MA: Blackwell, 1999), pp. 29–30.

85. This conclusion is drawn, for example, by David A. J. Richards, *The Moral Criticism of Law* Encino and Belmont, CA, (Dickinson: 1977), pp. 232–33.

86. An excellent analysis of this criticism is provided in E. F. Carritt, *Ethical and Political Thinking* (Oxford: Clarendon Press, 1947), pp. 64–69. An arguably more sophisticated evaluation of this particular utilitarian response that tends to deny this conclusion includes F. Rosen, "Utilitarianism and the Punishment of the Innocent: The Origins of a False Doctrine," *Utilitas* 9 (1997), pp. 23–37; David Lyons, *The Forms and Limits of Utilitarianism* (Oxford: Oxford University Press, 1965), pp. 70–73; and Rawls, pp. 10–13.

Nonetheless, the feasibility and desirability of an "act utilitarian" approach to human behavior and social control arguably would not produce better results. The reasonable capacity of individual agents to engage in a moral calculation of whether an action would yield as much "net utility" as any alternative action is addressed in Dale E. Miller, "Actual-Consequence Act Utilitarianism and the Best Possible Humans," *Ratio* 16, no. 1 (March 2003): 49–62.

87. That communitarian argument is particularly well articulated in Nicola Lacey, *State Punishment: Political Principles and Community Values* (London: Routledge, 1994), pp. 121–41, 151–55.

88. The moral appeal of retributivist approaches to the death penalty, for example, are discussed in Hart, *Punishment and Responsibility*, pp. 71–77. A discussion of retribution as not only a matter of desert but of equal treatment under the law is provided in Ted Honderich, *Punishment: The Supposed Justifications* (Cambridge: Polity Press, 1989), pp. 35–44. It is given a spirited defense in H. J. McCloskey, "A Non-Utilitarian Approach to Punishment," *Inquiry* 8 (Autumn 1965): 260.

89. A brief synopsis of his approach, in this respect, is offered in John Stuart Mill, "On the Connection Between Justice and Utility," in *Utilitarianism*, John Plamenatz, ed. (Oxford: Clarendon Press, 1949), pp. 226–28.

90. The utilitarian approach of Sidgwick is addressed in Shaw, pp. 77–90.

91. An excellent overview of the counter-criticisms of utilitarian scholars against this claim (although arguably weakened by the need for general knowledge of the actual innocence of a convicted person) is provided in C. L. Ten, *Crime, Guilt, and Punishment: A Philosophical Introduction* (Oxford: Clarendon Press, 1987), pp. 13–37.

92. Nonetheless, it is possible to claim that a state which is guided by the will of individual agents within a democratic system cannot escape the substitution of perceived outcomes that are evaluated by subject principles of a "higher morality." This outcome may be especially true when subjective values are mistaken, in the popular mind, for rational and disinterested calculations of utility. That possibility is suggested by the acknowledgement of difficulties in this aspect of the application of utilitarian principles to penal policy in Lyons, *In the Interest of the Governed*, pp. 69–74; Shaw, pp. 29–30; and J. C. C. Smart, "Extreme and Restricted Utilitarianism," *Philosophical Quarterly* 6, no. 25 (October 1956): 334–54.

93. This idea is presented in G. E. Moore, "The Conception of Intrinsic Value," in *Philosophical Studies* (London: Routledge and Keegan Paul, 1960), pp. 253–75. This perception as applied to Bentham is explained in Smart, pp. 335–36.

94. This belief is explored in Richard Brandt, *Ethical Theory: The Problems of Normative and Critical Ethics* (Englewood Cliffs, NJ: Prentice Hall, 1959), pp. 303–307.

95. This problem of interpreting pleasure as an intrinsic good (including logical inconsistencies in its actual application) is given an excellent treatment in Fred Feldman, "On the Intrinsic Value of Pleasures," *Ethics* 107, no. 3 (April 1997):. 448–66.

96. It appears that some critics would remain skeptical of any claims that Bentham, or any utilitarian, would be motivated by a desire to lessen or eliminate the pain of punishment as a primary objective. It has been argued, for example, that advocates of penal reform of the European Enlightenment merely sought to replace the brutality of medieval forms of punishment with a different, and more efficient, form of penal tyranny based upon a rationality derived from the labor needs of the emerging market economy. Michel Foucault, *Surveiller et punir: Naissance de la prison* (Paris: Gallimard, 1993), pp. 75–103.

97. An interesting application of this consideration to business relationships can be observed in M. J. McNamee, H. Sheridan, and J. Buswell, "The Limits of Utilitarianism as a Professional Ethic in Public Sector Leisure Policy and Provision," *Leisure Studies* 20, no. 3 (July 2001): 173–97.

98. That interpretation is essential to Henry Sidgwick's seminal analysis of utilitarian thought, as summarized in Henry Sidgwick, *Essays on Ethics and Methods* (Oxford: Oxford University Press, 2001), pp. 3–9, and as present as the underlying theme of Bentham's evaluation of those cases that are not suitable for punishment. Bentham, *Rationale of Punishment*, pp. 23–26.

99. Ibid., pp. 32–41.

100. An example of that tone can be found within the evaluation of the formal ends of punishment, Ibid., pp. 19–22.

101. Ibid., p. 1.

102. As with much of the text, Bentham's original manuscript version is lost. Therefore, much of Smith's 1830 edition of this book apparently relied upon Dumont's 1818 French edition, based upon his translation of Bentham's original manuscripts. One concern regarding the accuracy of Dumont's original translation (including in reference to sentences such as this one) was the observed tendency of Dumont to idolize and, thus, idealize Bentham's ideas, as noted in Sedgwick, pp. 197–98, 201.

103. Bentham, *Principles of Morals and Legislation*, chs. XIII–XV.

104. Ibid., pp. 170–71.

105. Bentham, *Rationale of Punishment*, p. 2.

106. That more predominant interpretation of a utilitarian definition of punishment as dependent upon "concrete circumstances or consequences" is addressed in C. J. Ducasse, "Scientific Method in Ethics," *Philosophy and Phenomenological Research* 14, no. 1 (Sept. 1953): 83–85.

107. Bentham, *Rationale of Punishment*, p. 23.

A belief that Bentham's intent was to treat punishment as intrinsically evil may have prompted Dumont's note at the end of the chapter regarding the analogy between crime and punishment. This note suggests that the articulation of these analogous punishments (including horrific forms of torture, dismemberment, abuse, and execution) was intended to be merely instructional of the repugnance of punishment, generally, and, perhaps, "only as fit subjects for ridicule and caricature." Dumont, note in Ibid., pp. 62–63.

108. This concept is expressed most powerfully through the "metaphor of the cave" that was articulated in Plato, *The Republic*, G. M. A. Grube, trans. (Indianapolis: Hackett, 1974), bk. VII. An analysis of these ideas in a manner that is relevant to this application of them can be found in John Wild, *Plato's Modern Enemies and the Theory of Natural Law* (Chicago: University of Chicago Press, 1968), pp. 138–50.

109. This concept is addressed, relative to this argument, in Aristotle, *The Politics*, T.A. Sinclair, trans. (Baltimore: Penguin, 1972), pp. 25–29; and Aristotle, *Nicomachean Ethics*, Martin Ostwald, trans. (Indianapolis: Bobbs-Merrill, 1962), pp. 4–18. An evaluation of this principle (especially in terms of its broadest application) can be found in Terrence Irwin, *Aristotle's First Principle* (Oxford: Clarendon Press, 1988), pp. 94–116.

110. This interpretation is well explained in F. Rosen, "Crime, Punishment, and Liberty," *History of Political Thought* 20, no. 1 (Spring 1999): 173–85.

111. This concept is explained in Sir Ernest Barker, *Greek Political Theory: Plato and His Predecessors* (London: Methuen, 1961), pp. 52–54; Edward Hussey, *The Presocratics* (London: Duckworth, 1974), pp. 69–73; G. S. Kirk and J. E. Raven, *The Presocratic Philosophers* (Cambridge: Cambridge University Press, 1957); and Paul E. Sigmund, *Natural Law in Political Thought* (Cambridge, MA: Winthrop, 1971), pp. 1–3.

112. This particular sort of result is, arguably, somewhat reflective of Beccaria's approach to the justification for state-sanctioned punishment, which is referenced at various places within *The Rationale of Punishment* and which provided stimulus for utilitarian thought. Cesare Beccaria, *On Crimes and Punishments*, Henry Paolucci, trans. (Indianapolis: Bobbs-Merrill, 1963) pp. 42–59. This Beccarian approach to proportionality in punishment is assessed in David A. J. Richards, "Rights, Utility, and Crime," *Crime and Justice* 3 (1981), pp. 249–53.

113. These evaluations are made in particularly relevant detail in Bentham, *Rationale of Punishment*, bk. II.

114. This measurement is given particular emphasis in Ibid., pp. 32–41.

115. Ibid., p. 38.

116. Ibid., p. 38.

117. References to this specific philosophical misdesignation of "intrinsic" evil can be found in John Hospers, *Human Conduct: An Introduction to the Problems of Ethics* (New York: Wadsworth, 1995), pp. 114, 119, 156–57. and (especially in reference to later utilitarians) Edward W. Strong, "Justification of Juridical Punishment," *Ethics* 79, no. 3 (April 1969) : 188–89. References to this misconception and the proper understanding of "intrinsic" evil as being independent of circumstance and consequence can be found in Vinit Haksar, "Coercive Proposals," *Political Theory* 4, no. 1 (February 1976): 73–74, and, especially; Aurel Kolnai, "The Thematic Primacy of Moral Evil," *The Philosophical Quarterly* 6, no. 22 (January 1956): 37–38.

118. Despite reevaluations in this area, the commitment of Bentham, James Mill, and

other early utilitarians, in particular, to the cause of penal reform and the elimination of a vindictive and harsh political environment regarding law and punishment is well established, even if subject to some criticism and modification, as discussed in James E. Crimmins, "Bentham's Philosophical Politics," *Harvard Review of Philosophy* 3 (Spring 1993): 18–22.

119. One way to avoid that conceptual difficulty is to claim (perhaps too semantically to be effective) that punishment of the innocent is not, technically, punishment at all but qualifies, instead, as "injury," "harm-infliction," or some other such category. H. J. McCloskey, "A Non-Utilitarian Approach to Punishment," in *Contemporary Utilitarianism*, Michael D. Bayles, ed. (Garden City, NY: Anchor Books, 1968), p. 244.

120. On a practical level, the approach of treating punishment as merely an extrinsic evil could, potentially, lead to other, "compensatory evils" such as jury nullification, bribery, mistrust of public institutions, and other consequences. James Wood Bailey, *Utilitarianism, Institutions, and Justice* (New York: Oxford University Press, 1997), pp. 154–56.

121. This severe criticism of negative utilitarianism is summarized in Matti Häyry, *Liberal Utilitarianism and Applied Ethics* (London: Routledge, 1994), pp. 66–67, 122–24; and R. N. Smart, "Negative Utilitarianism," *Mind* 67, no. 268 (October 1958): 542–43.

122. Negative utilitarianism, within that context, also has been described as the technique of preventing a greater evil (in this case, crime) with a lesser evil (in this case, punishment) that, ideally, will lead, ultimately, to the mutual elimination of both evils. That approach to understanding this interpretation is discussed in Bernard Gert and Charles M. Culver, "The Justification of Paternalism," *Ethics* 89, no. 2 (January 1979): 202–206.

123. This approach is more consistent with the interpretation of Popper's negative utilitarianism as being, essentially, an exercise in limiting the power of the strong over the weak. Popper, vol. II, pp. 124–25. This interpretation is examined in Michael Lessnoff, "The Political Philosophy of Karl Popper," *British Journal of Political Science* 10, no. 1 (January 1980), pp. 118–20.

124. It may be instructive to compare this ideal with the interpretation of negative utilitarianism (which has been assessed in relation to John Stuart Mill's political principles in this area) that has been expounded in David Lyons, *Forms and Limits of Utilitarianism* (Oxford: Oxford University Press, 1965), pp. 211–12.

ADVERTISEMENT

125. Manuscripts of neither this preface nor of this advertisement are available.

126. The untranslated version of Dumont's preface states, at this parallel point, "Le succes m'encourageoit à continuer," which would translate as "Success encouraged me to continue." Etienne Dumont, *Théorie des peines et des récompenses, Ouvrage extrait des manuscripts de M. Jérémie Bentham, jurisconsulte anglois*, 2nd ed. (Paris: Bossange et Masson, 1818), p. v. Subsequent references to this edition will be cited, simply, as *Théorie des peines*.

127. Dumont's edition uses the word "cited" at this point. Ibid., p. v.

128. Dumont uses the word "ralenti," which Smith translates with the colloquialism of "cooled," though the word, more precisely, means "slowed."Ibid., p. vi.

129. A more literal translation of this phrase might be "They were put aside, not as rejection, but to the side, like attending stones, to enter, one day, the system of general legislation or the studies that the author had made for himself."Ibid., pp. vi–vii.

A draft plan for such a book, dated 1775 and reportedly in Jeremy Bentham's handwriting, apparently outlined his own overall conception of this work:
"Plan.

"The subject of the present work is Punishment. It is divided into three parts.

"The first I call the *Descriptive* part: the 2nd the *selective* part: the third the historical part.

"The first inquires what is possible to be done in the way of punishment: the 2nd and 4th what *ought* to be done: the 3rd, what *has* been done, emphasizing it with what ought to be done.

"If the subject of pain is to induce me to do any act which otherwise I should not have done, it is an act of *coercion* or *constraint.*

"The military service, civil obligation, and taxes are acts of this description: the pain with which they are accompanied is not the result of any intention on the part of the legislator: it contributes not to the promotion of the object aimed at: acts of coercion then or constraint are not acts of punishment." Back of RP MSS 141/8: 1.

130. This reference appears as a footnote within the original version. *Théorie des peines*, p. viii.

131. Dumont's preface could translate as "one would not be astonished." Ibid., p. viii.

132. Dumont used a rhetorical question: "But why is it important?" *Théorie des peines*, p. ix.

133. Dumont uses the word "new," instead of "additional," at this point. Ibid., p. x.

134. This retort also might refer to Dumont's frustration over having his desire for assistance on a treatise of the Genevan penal code rejected by Bentham, who considered it to be too small and unimportant a topic. Ross Harrison, *Bentham* (London: Routledge and Keegan Paul, 1983), p. 25.

135. Bentham's overt intent was for Dumont to transform his rough manuscripts, in both English and French, into a finished work without his further assistance, though he complained about Dumont's persistent demand for guidance which Bentham, nonetheless, generally ignored. Bentham to the Duc de Liancourt, October 11, 1795 [no. 1,085], *Correspondence of Jeremy Bentham*, Alexander Taylor Milne, ed. (London: Athlone Press, 1981), vol. V, p. 160.

136. Dumont refers only to the theory of punishments within this sentence. *Théorie des peines*, p. xii.

137. Dumont used the more emphatic phrase "principal object,. Ibid., p. xii.

138. Dumont specified the "positive" science of jurisprudence. Ibid., p. xiii.

139. Dumont does not make reference to the previous work, nor does he refer to "giving them a separate form." Ibid., p. xv.

140. These terms are italicized by Dumont, *Théorie des peines*, p. xv.

141. The "editor" in this case is Richard Smith; this "advertisement" served as a preface to the 1830 edition. Bentham, *Rationale of Punishment*, pp. 5–11.

BOOK I, CHAPTER I

142. These first three paragraphs are not found within the manuscript.

143. Bentham has been criticized for not making a sufficiently clear distinction between actions (including legal ones) that are done and actions that ought to be done. It has been associated with the observation he makes in *Principles of Morals and Legislation* in distinguishing between the natural association of pain and pleasure with "[o]n the one hand the standard of right and wrong, and on the other the chain of causes and effects, [that] are fastened to their throne." Bentham, *Morals and Legislation*, ch. I. Some critics have noted that this analysis is the source of a persistent problem within Bentham's writings and early utilitarian thought, in which normative moral conclusions are derived from empirical functional ones. Halévy, pp.

11–13. Similar observations have combined this criticism with a charge that Bentham has attempted to combine a theory based upon a hedonistic assumption of human psychology with an apparently altruistic vision of the common good, as explored in Lyons, *In the Interest of the Governed*, pp. 12–13. These concerns were part of the earlier critique of Sidgwick, *Methods of Ethics*, pp. 412–16. These themes are apparent within this opening paragraph.

144. The use of this word can be semantically difficult to appreciate within this philosophical context. However, it is absolutely central for a meaningful understanding of this thesis. Bentham clearly used the word "evil" as representative of a subjective definition of pain, as evident in Bentham, *Morals and Legislation*, intro.; and Bentham, "Constitutional Code," in *Works*, IX, pp. 6–7. However, his preference for reward over punishment strongly suggests a general distaste for the imposition of any punishment, even if it is unavoidable. Therefore, Bentham appeared to prefer the use of a "moral," rather than a "legal" sanction in order to promote general happiness, spurring his desire to use education for that purpose. Bentham, *Morals and Legislation*, pp. 122–26.

This theme could have had a particularly profound influence upon his disciples, including Richard Smith and Etienne Dumont, thus influencing their overall interpretation of punishment as, arguably, an intrinsically, rather than solely an extrinsically, undesirable result.

145. An alternative beginning to this chapter was proffered, then crossed-out, within the manuscripts. It was written, apparently in Richard Smith's handwriting (including, within it, other corrections and deletions) and, also apparently, it represents a translation of the first paragraph of Jeremy Bentham, *Théorie des peines*, vol. I, pp. 1–2. This omitted paragraph deals directly with the most foundational definition:

"The word *punishment*, in the case in which it ought to be employed in the following pages, may not, at first sight, appear to stand in need of any definition. It might be very difficult to endeavor to give a more precise conception of it than that which is already preferred by every person by whom it happened to be employed. But this popular meaning of that word, however clear it may appear to be, does not really present the degree of accuracy that is required for the present occasion: it does not for instance serve to distinguish the act of punishment from a variety of other acts to which in many respects it bears considerable analogy, and with which it is liable to be confounded. It will be necessary therefore to explain distinctly at the outset the precise sense in which the word in here means to be employed, and for this purpose, as the misconception liable to be produced arises principally from the too great latitude in which the vulgar sense of the word is employed, all that will be required will be to distinguish those cases not meant to be considered as comprised within the meaning of the word punishment." Back of RP MSS 141/1:1.

146. The manuscript begins at this point, Ibid.. According to the notes on the original folder cover, this chapter was transcribed by Richard Smith. Compared to the other transcribed manuscripts, this chapter contains remarkably few corrections.

147. All italicized words and phrases within this book are underlined within the original manuscripts.

148. The psychological definition of pain assumed particular importance when it was imposed by the state, particularly as it competed with a form of pleasure, on the part of a criminal, that also imposed pain on other people. Thus, Locke's definition of pleasure and pain as movements toward and from "states of uneasiness" provided a useful way to understand the motivating effect of penal legislation, even though Bentham also was critical of the inconsistent and, often, metaphysical emphasis placed upon this psychological interpretation of human motivation by Locke and his successors, as propounded in John Locke, *An Essay Concerning Human Understanding* (Toronto: Collier-Macmillan, 1965), pp. 144–46, 156. The influence of Locke on Bentham in this area is discussed in Nancy L. Rosenblum, *Bentham's Theory of the Modern State* (Cambridge, MA: Harvard University Press, 1978), pp. 30–35.

149. Rather than dwelling upon definitions at this point in the first chapter, Dumont focused upon applied examples, particularly in the form of a person named Titius. This tendency to provide both a more applied tone and a sense of personalization offers an example of the tone that is present throughout Dumont's edition, *Théorie des peines*, vol. I, pp. 2–3.

150. Bentham, like Beccaria and Montesquieu, objected to the concept of a judge-made law. He strongly felt that the judge should apply the law that the legislature created and he was particularly critical of the frequent recourse of judges to insert their own interpretation of the common law in a manner that amounted to the imposition of an ex post facto form of "judicial legislation." This objection is explained, variously, in Bentham, *Works*, vol. I, pp. 323, ;5 and analyzed in Hart, *Essays on Bentham*, pp. 47–48.

It is useful to compare this argument with the approach of other philosophers who write from a similar perspective, including Beccaria, pp. 2–5; Claude Adrien Helvétius, *De l'ésprit: or Essay on the Mind and Its Several Faculties* (London, 1759), pp. 80–84 (in which he advocates the practical need for reformers to engage in critiques from the perspective of legislators); and Charles de Secondat, Baron de Montesquieu, *De l'esprit des lois*, Victor Goldschmidt, ed. (Paris: Flammarion, 1979), bks. 2, 11.

Bentham's objection in this area was criticized, though, by John Austin (upon whom Bentham's ideas on jurisprudence had, otherwise, a strong influence) as being short sighted, since it neglected the fact that judges are forced, sometimes, to compensate for the omissions or negligence of legislators by supplementing legal prescriptions with their own (though, he admitted, often severely inadequate) interpretations and rulings. John Austin, *The Province of Jurisprudence Determined*, Wilfrid E. Rumble, ed. (Cambridge: Cambridge University Press, 1995), p. 163.

151. Bentham's concern regarding proper definitions arose, in part, from his criticism of the uncritical way in which previous commentators on the law (especially English jurists such as Sir William Blackstone) presented definitions based upon loose practice and unquestioned common usage. Therefore, his preoccupation with the very meaning and scope of the word "punishment" is a seminal concern that this initial chapter expounds. This central theme of Bentham's analysis of the law is discussed in James Steintrager, *Bentham* (Ithaca, NY: Cornell University Press, 1977), pp. 25–28.

152. The importance of rehabilitation and general moral reformation as a social goal was advanced by Bentham in "Outline of a Work entitled Pauper Management Improvement," *Works*, VIII, pp. 369–74. It provides an example of the generally progressive spirit that frequently has been attributed to him, especially by his disciples, Gertrude Himmelfarb, "Bentham's Utopia: The National Charity Company," *Journal of British Studies* 10, no. 1 (November 1970): 80–125. This perception of him as a progressive force arguably shaped the perspective and motivations of the utilitarian reformers and writers who immediately proceeded him, as suggested in Mack, Mary Peter, *Jeremy Bentham: An Odyssey of Ideas, 1748–1792* (London: Heinneman, 1962), pp. 212–15, 315–18.

153. Dumont enters into a similar consideration toward the end of the first chapter of his book. In his case, though, he relates it, theoretically, to arguments concerning the liberty and the state of nature that are reminiscent of both Hobbes and Locke in this respect, *Théorie des peines*, vol. I, pp. 9–10. Interestingly, Hobbes and Locke both use this analogy to justify the need for a social contract and the establishment of a government to enact laws for the protection of society. Thomas Hobbes, *Leviathan*, Richard Tuck, ed. (Cambridge: Cambridge University Press, 1996), pp. 117–66; John Locke, *Second Treatise of Government*, C. B. Macpherson, ed. (Indianapolis: Hackett, 1980), pp. 42–65. But Bentham did not regard liberty in this way, though he accepted its importance as a necessary social condition that is, nonetheless, meaningless without a utilitarian context. Liberty may precede law and justify the coercive actions of the state, for Bentham, but it did not constitute the basis of any abstract agreement between

persons and government within society; indeed, for Bentham, liberty as a legal concept was, yet, another one of the legal fictions that he sought to eradicate. Douglas G. Long, *Bentham on Liberty: Jeremy Bentham's Idea of Liberty in Relation to his Utilitarianism* (Toronto: University of Toronto Press, 1977), pp. 55–62.

BOOK I, CHAPTER II

154. This manuscript of this entire chapter is missing. Peripheral references to the subject of this chapter are found in RP MSS 67/1: 1–9.

155. This chapter appears to have been identified in an early French draft of the table of contents for this book, dated 1785, found in Ibid., 143/4: 61. This chapter within Dumont's edition is a direct parallel with this version. Bentham, *Théorie des peines*, vol. I, pp. 11–13.

156. Bentham's interpretation of human free agency traditionally was understood to be a belief in human predictability, almost in a mechanistic manner, as noted by Hilda G. Lundin, "The Influence of Jeremy Bentham on English Democratic Development," *University of Iowa Studies in the Social Sciences* 7, no. 3 (November 1920): 15. The idea that humans, by their very nature, seek nothing but pleasure (though diversely defined) resulted in the assumption of humans as being, essentially, hedonistic. Bhikhu C. Parekh, "Bentham's Justification of the Principle of Utility," in *Jeremy Betham: Ten Critical Essays*, Bikhu C. Parekh, ed. (London: Routledge, 1974), p. 103. Bentham's assumptions regarding psychological hedonism have been widely debated, including a famous argument that psychological hedonism is merely a type of psychological egoism, since pain and pleasure can only be interpreted in terms of one's own experience. Lyons, *In the Interest of the Governed*, pp. 68–73. That specific interpretation has been widely criticized; a representative example of that critique can be found in Harrison, pp. 263–77; and Gerald J. Postema, *Bentham and the Common Law Tradition* (Oxford: Clarendon Press, 1986), pp. 383–85. It also has been noted that Bentham included the possibility that hedonistic expression could be other-regarding, rather than just self-regarding, as he suggested within Bentham, "Constitutional Code," *Works*, IX, pp. 6–7.

However, Bentham's understanding of free agency continues to be regarded as the capacity to choose from among diverse options in order to find the one that should, from the perspective of the rational and well-informed human mind, result in the maximization of pleasure in competition with a similar search among other humans. An excellent overview of these interpretations, resulting in an argument that Bentham's approach to this subject was not bound by a precise human calculation of anticipated pain and pleasure but by an appreciation of the non-rational aspects of human experience, is presented in Paul J. Kelly, *Utilitarianism and Distributive Justice* (Oxford: Clarendon Press, 1990), pp. 14–38.

BOOK I, CHAPTER III

157. This chapter is not found among the manuscripts. However, two draft versions, in Smith's handwriting, of the texts found within this chapter, though crossed-out, are present on the backs of RP MSS 141/1: 8–9. This chapter is, essentially, the same one that appears as the third chapter of Dumont's edition. Bentham, *Théorie des peines*, vol. I, pp. 14–17.

158. It is interesting to compare this opening paragraph to one that had previously been drafted and, then, discarded for the purpose: "Having defined what in the course of the ensuing pages is intended by the word punishment we come next to consider what ought to be the ends of punishment. For it is by the end that all our subsequent speculations relating

to punishment must be governed. In accordance with the principle of utility the general end ought to be the greatest good of the community in general," back of RP MSS 141/8: 1. The opening paragraph of Dumont's edition refers to "magistrates," in addition to "legislators." Bentham, *Théorie des peines*, vol. I, p. 14.

159. This sentence begins the second paragraph of the apparent original draft of this chapter as found on the back of RP MSS 141/1: 8.

160. The rough draft version of this text employed the word "importance" instead of the word "value" that appears in the published version, on the back of Ibid., 141/1: 9.

161. This "associative link" was central to Bentham's reform of the penal law, as it also was for Beccaria, and it made the need for punishment to be both "speedy" and "certain" particularly acute. H. L. A. Hart, *Essays on Bentham*, pp. 46–47.

BOOK I, CHAPTER IV

162. This chapter originally was designated within the manuscripts as "Chapter III."

163. An earlier draft of this chapter is found in RP MSS 143/2: 24–28. No version of this chapter is found within the Dumont edition.

164. An earlier, though similar, draft of this first paragraph is found on the back of Ibid., 141/2: 54.

165. This chapter follows closely (both in text and tone) Bentham, *Morals and Legislation*, ch. 13, sec. 5.

Bentham was particularly concerned about preventing private ethics from being substituted for well-reasoned ethics, whether by legislators or judges. Therefore, given the extreme difficulty of determining a proportional response to the offenses that he addresses by these particular categories, the most efficacious solution would be to exempt them from consideration for punishment at all. Long, pp. 111–13.

166. By the end of the nineteenth century, several industrial societies (particularly Britain) had concluded that criminals committed their acts because of inherent mental deficiency. Subsequently, penal reform was, increasingly, motivated by that belief during the early decades of the twentieth century. While this deficiency was not regarded as being sufficient to exclude punishment, it did prompt penal reform regarding the use of punishment as a means for uncovering and treating the underlying causes for this deficiency. This development is explored in Martin J. Wiener, *Reconstructing the Criminal: Culture, Law, and Policy in England, 1830–1914* (Cambridge: Cambridge University Press, 1990), ch. 6.

167. The matter of effectiveness in punishment is one that is much more particular to a utilitarian approach than to other approaches, especially a retributive one, as addressed in Strong, pp. 187–98. This theme is discussed in greater detail in John Hospers, *Human Conduct: An Introduction to the Problems of Ethics* (New York: Wadsworth, 1995), pp. 288–99.

168. Although this consideration of the proportionality of punishment in relation to crime is well-adapted to a utilitarian perspective, it also finds expression within retributivist theories. However, that latter perspective tends to emphasize the justification of responding to a more serious crime with a harsher penalty, rather than a desire to limit needless punishment, as discussed in Ten, pp. 50–51, 150–60.

169. This approach to punishment clearly differs from approaches that are based upon a moral notion of "desert," which is especially prominent within the writings of retributivist theorists, such as Hart, *Punishment and Responsibility*, pp. 1–27. An interesting consequentialist approach to this subject, inspired by utilitarian principles, is provided in Douglas N. Husak, "Why Punish the Deserving?" *Noûs* 26, no. 4 (December 1992): 447–64.

BOOK I, CHAPTER V

170. This chapter is identified as "Chapter IV" within both the manuscript, RP MSS 141/8: 1, and Dumont's edition. Bentham, *Théorie des peines*, vol. I, p. 18.

171. Originally, this line was written in the manuscript as "an offense which rises with a rise to" and crossed out in favor of "as it were a capital hazarded in RP MSS 141/8: 1.

172. A previous, crossed-out draft had this line, following the semi-colon, was phrased slightly differently, although it retained the same meaning as the line as it appears in this version, Ibid., 141/8: 1.

173. Dumont expresses this line as a rhetorical question: "What is it that constitutes the expense? It is real pain," Bentham, *Théorie des peines*, vol. I, p. 19.

174. The Smith manuscript for this chapter is missing at this point but the next two paragraphs are found as part of an earlier, crossed-out draft in RP MSS 141/10: 1.

175. This expression offers an interesting overlap of "hedonistic" and "ideal" versions of utilitarian thought. The former approach (associated with Bentham) emphasizes that "good" and "evil" are purely functions of pleasure while the latter approach seeks "good" from other outcomes, often relating to the benefit of an entire community, rather than a greater number of competing individual members. This passage suggests a modification of the hedonistic approach to utilitarianism that emphasizes individual good as a component of a larger good of the community. This consideration is connected to the contrasting approaches of "rule" and "act" utilitarian thought, as explored in J. C. C. Smart, pp. 344–54. This contrast offers implications for an interpretation of punishment as an intrinsic, as opposed to an extrinsic evil, by emphasizing its effect upon even an individual member of the community.

176. From this point to the end of the chapter, the MSS copy is missing. However, it is present within the Dumont edition. Bentham, *Théorie des peines*, vol. I, pp. 20–23.

177. This example raises, again, the problem of punishing the innocent. Bentham's position arguably has permitted such an outcome but only if it demonstrably results in a greater good, especially through deterrence. However, this utilitarian tendency could be countered by the anticipation of revulsion that would result from knowledge, or potential knowledge, of that outcome. However, this example suggests that any punishment always should be minimalized in fact, if not in appearance. It is possible, therefore, that pretending to punish someone who is, actually, innocent would be acceptable under this scheme. This conundrum and its relationship to the utilitarian tradition is addressed in William Lyons, "Deterrent Theory and Punishment of the Innocent," *Ethics* 84, no. 4 (July 1974): 346–48.

178. An excellent study that confirms this utilitarian argument that perceptions of the severity of a punishment, rather than merely the certainty of punishment, produces this deterrent effect (in terms of an empirically demonstrable inverse relationship between severity of punishment and involvement in illegal activity) is provided in Harold G. Grasmick and George J. Bryjak, "The Deterrent Effect of Perceived Severity of Punishment," *Social Forces* 59, no. 2 (December 1980): 471–91.

BOOK I, CHAPTER VI

179. This quote is not in the original manuscript but it appears within Dumont's edition, which also identifies the chapter as "Chapter V." Bentham, *Théorie des peines*, vol. I, p. 24.

180. This paragraph, and the following several ones, are not found in any of the final manuscripts. However, a crossed-out draft copy does include an apparently earlier version of these ideas, RP MSS 141/16: 1, and it appears within the Dumont edition. Bentham, *Théorie des peines*, vol. I, pp. 24–25.

181. Montesquieu does not formally embrace a specific theory of punishment. Instead, he promotes general ideas regarding reciprocity as an important component of a rational society and the enlightened, republican government it ought to produce. Despotism, by contrast, uses vengeance as the basis for punishment and the general threat of violence through which it imposes its authority. Montesquieu, bk. XIX. This connection is considered within the broader context of Enlightenment political thought in Pierre Saint-Amand, "Original Vengeance: Politics, Anthropology, and the French Enlightenment," *Eighteenth Century Studies* 26, no. 3 (Spring 1993): 404–407. Beccaria offers a theory of punishment that is more specific in this respect, especially regarding the theme of proportionality and the infliction of minimal penal pain. Beccaria, pp. 14–17, 23–27. An analysis of his general approach to this subject is provided in Marcello Maestro, "A Pioneer for the Abolition of Capital Punishment: Cesare Beccaria," *Journal of the History of Ideas* 34, no. 3 (July 1973): 463–68.

This text indicates a greater willingness of this study to place the theory of punishment within this broader Enlightenment context than found within Bentham's earlier publications, particularly Bentham, *Morals and Legislation*, ch. 15. References to Becarria suggest, in particular, a particular emphasis upon proportionality and an arguably greater desire to avoid punishment. This broader context may provide further indication of the different emphasis of second-generation utilitarians, such as Dumont and Smith, regarding this subject.

182. Dumont's edition does not precede the stating of the rule (identified not by a number but as the "first rule") with this preliminary statement. Bentham, *Théorie des peines*, vol. I, p. 25.

183. A previous draft identifies this rule as number "2," RP MSS 141/16: 1. The six rules that are expressed within the Dumont edition are extended to thirteen within the Smith edition. However, the latter enumerations appear to include extensions and elaborations upon those original six, rather than entirely new fundamental principles.

184. This footnote, below, is not found within the manuscripts but it does appear within the Dumont edition. Bentham, *Théorie des peines*, vol. I, p. 25.

185. The Smith manuscript for this chapter begins at this point, RP MSS 141/9: 1.

186. Originally phrased as "This same mistake is made," Ibid. This phrase within the Dumont edition can be translated, literally, as "one falls within the same error every time." Bentham, *Théorie des peines*, vol. I, p. 26.

187. The original word used was "Advocates," RP MSS 141/9: 1, though Dumont also uses the word "authors." Bentham, *Théorie des peines*, vol. I, p. 26.

188. It has been argued that Adam Smith was influenced by a concept of "contemplative utilitarianism" that was based upon an overall acceptance of hedonistic motivations as a basis for society. T. D. Campbell, *Adam Smith's Science of Morals* (London: Allen and Unwin, 1971), pp. 217–20. But other scholars have contended that Smith may have appeared to be influenced by utilitarian considerations but that influence was overshadowed by other principles. J. R. Lindgren, *The Social Philosophy of Adam Smith* (The Hague: Springer, 1973), pp. 80–85. This cursory appeal to utility could be secondary, for Smith, to the influence of normative theories of justice that could be characterized as retributive, T. D. Campbell and I. S. Ross, "The Utilitarianism of Adam Smith's Policy Advice," *Journal of the History of Ideas* 42, no. 1 (January 1981): 73–92. A broader assessment of these considerations (including the relative influence of utilitarian ideas upon Smith's writings) can be found in Keith Tribe, "Adam Smith: Critical Theorist?" *Journal of Economic Literature* 37, no. 2 (June 1999): 609–32.

189. The words "just so much" were originally expressed with the adjective "useless," RP MSS 141/9.

190. The remainder of this paragraph and the entire next paragraph are missing from the manuscript.

191. The entire section for "Rule II" is missing from the manuscript.

192. This rule and the subsequent explanatory paragraphs appear within the Dumont edition as the fifth rule. Bentham, *Théorie des peines*, vol. I, pp. 32–33.

193. The manuscript resumes with "Rule III."

194. A version of this rule appears within the Dumont edition but identified as the fourth rule. Bentham, *Théorie des peines*, vol. I, pp. 30–31.

195. The manuscript included, and then, crossed-out, at the beginning of the following paragraph, the following sentence: "This rule would be observed if for even, portion of mischief a corresponding portion of punishment were appointed. If the thief who steals 10 crowns is not punished more than he who steals only five crowns the stealing of those five crowns is an unprofitable offense," RP MSS 141/10: 1.

196. This explanatory paragraph is used within the Dumont edition to illustrate the third rule within that chapter, as explained within endnote 21, below. Bentham, *Théorie des peines*, vol. I, p. 29.

197. The manuscript is missing for this, and the following two paragraphs, including the note at the end of the third paragraph.

198. This rule, also identified as the sixth rule, is found within the Dumont edition, including the subsequent explanatory paragraphs. Bentham, *Théorie des peines*, vol. I, pp. 34–35.

199. A similar critique has been provided in terms of the effect of being able to afford bail as a practical determinant in successful defense in court. William M. Landes, "An Economic Analysis of the Courts," *Journal of Law and Economics* 14, no. 2 (April 1971): 69–75.

200. However, it has been argued that the "opportunity cost" of similar punishments can represent more profound consequences to wealthy defendants who have "more to lose" in terms of long-term social and economic damage. John R. Lott, Jr., "Should the Wealthy Be Able to 'Buy Justice?'" *Journal of Political Economy* 95, no. 6 (December 1987): 1307–16.

201. The manuscript resumes with this paragraph.

202. This tendency within utilitarian approaches to punishment has been, arguably, one of its strongest features in preferring it to retributive theories, especially in cases in which wrongful conviction may occur. Michael Lessnoff, "Two Justifications of Punishment," *Philosophical Quarterly* 21, no. 83 (April 1971): 141–48.

203. A version of this rule and the proceeding rule appear, in a combined form, within the Dumont edition as the third rule, including the subsequent explanatory paragraphs, Bentham, *Théorie des peines*, vol. I, pp. 29–30.

204. Sedgwick addressed the problem of "sane" persons committing "unreasonable actions" within a utilitarian scheme of punishment by urging the need for means for the justice system to improve individual recognition of self-deception and irrationality. Henry Sidgwick, "Unreasonable Action," *Mind* 2, no. 6 (April 1893): 174–87.

205. This rule and the first subsequent explanatory paragraph appear within the Dumont edition as the second rule, Bentham. *Théorie des peines*, vol. I, p. 28.

206. The words "of which he is convicted" originally were phrased "that he had committed" within the manuscript, then corrected, RP MSS 141/14: 1.

207. Bentham's supposed lack of interest in historical context (as opposed to historical anecdotes) in the development of his work may be an example of these other "circumstances and considerations," although at least one scholar has contended that some of Bentham's writings may have reflected a greater practical acknowledgment of the "utility of history" than previously acknowledged, especially regarding the authority of legislation. Eldon J. Eisenach, "The Dimension of History in Bentham's Theory of Law," *Eighteenth Century Studies* 16, no. 3 (Spring 1983): 290–316.

208. The phrase "as too great a nicety in establishing" replaced, within the manuscript,

the original, subsequently crossed-out phrase, "it will not always be possible to draw fully to attend to the establishment," RP MSS 141/15: 1.

209. The word "dogmatic" replaced, within the manuscript, the original adjective "imposing," Ibid., 141/16: 1. The word that appears at this point within the Dumont edition is *"tranchante"* and it often translates as "sharp" or "cutting." Bentham, *Théorie des peines*, vol. I, p. 36.

BOOK I, CHAPTER VII

210. This chapter originally was identified as "Chapter VI" within the manuscript, as the parallel chapter is within the Dumont version, *Théorie des peines*, p. 38.

211. This chapter appears to provide a stronger emphasis upon an evaluation of the quality of punishment than *Introduction to the Principles of Morals and Legislation* provides in its chapter 15, which appears to stress quantity as the prime source for this calculus, especially in the language found specifically at Bentham, *Morals and Legislation*, ch. 15, para. 1–2.

212. The parallel section in Dumont's edition is entitled "Certainty—Equality." Bentham, *Théorie des peines*, vol. I, p. 39. Dumont's edition adds to this section an analysis of that former characteristic to the exclusive analysis of equality of punishment found within the parallel section of the 1830 edition. Those paragraphs are noteworthy because of the rhetorical questions (such as the exclamation "Is punishment uncertain by its nature?", found in Ibid., vol. I, p. 40) that establish its own tone of moral uncertainty that appears to accompany that analysis. Ibid., vol. I pp. 39–41.

213. Originally, instead of "age," the word "circumstance" appeared within the manuscript, RP MSS 141/18: 1. Dumont's edition uses the word "age" at this point. Bentham, *Théorie des peines*, vol. I, p. 39.

214. Dumont begins this section with a statement ("punishment must be commensurable among themselves") rather than an explanation. Ibid., vol. I, p. 41. That difference in style between Dumont and Smith is typical for the entire chapter.

215. This theme was addressed by the Home Department Committee on Prisons, under Herbert Gladstone, in 1985 as part of a wider array of reforms. The establishment of categorization of sentences was subject to many influences but utilitarian principles of penology provided a foundational starting point, especially as instituted by the Home Secretary, Winston Churchill, during the early twentieth century. This process and the various ideas behind it is described in Victor Bailey, "English Prisons, Penal Culture, and the Abatement of Imprisonment, 1895–1922," *Journal of British Studies* 36, no. 3 (July 1997): 302–305.

216. Retributivist theories of punishment tend to reject utilitarian principles in this area and, yet, remain dependent upon a need to relate a crime to its consequences in order to determine an appropriate punishment. By default, therefore, even retributivists are forced to rely upon this sort of utilitarian principle as articulated within this passage, as noted in Michael Davis, "How to Make the Punishment Fit the Crime," *Ethics* 93, no. 4 (July 1983): 726–52; and S. I. Benn and R. S. Peters, *The Principles of Political Thought* (New York: The Free Press, 1965), pp. 218–22.

217. This characteristic is, of course, central to the entire retributivist approach toward punishment. Its persistent appeal, both from a scholarly and a popular perspective, is addressed in Alan Wertheimer, "Should Punishment Fit the Crime?" *Social Theory and Practice* 3 (1975): 403–23. The popularity of revenge as a distinct justification for punishment is offered in Charles K. B. Barton, *Getting Even: Revenge as a Form of Justice* (Peru, IL: Open Court, 1999), pp. 85–100. An excellent critique of this approach is provided in Susan Jacoby, *Wild Justice: The Evolution of Revenge* (New York: Harper, 1988), pp. 32–48.

218. It is interesting to contrast the sociological theory of punishment as a symbolic expression, as explored by critics such as Michel Foucault, with the utilitarian approach. Bentham sought to remove those ritualistic trappings of punishment that did not serve a useful outcome (especially in the *Introduction to the Principles of Morals and Legislation*), yet he recognized the reinforcing effect that symbolic punishment could have in making punishment more practically effective. An analysis of these contrasting approaches in relation to the socially symbolic role of punishment is provided in David Garland, "Frameworks of Inquiry in the Sociology of Punishment," *British Journal of Sociology* 41, no. 1 (March 1990): 1–15, especially 5–6.

219. Gaetano Filangieri grounded his general theory upon a concept of "relative goodness" that are connected to a particular civilizations moral precepts (and which echo Montesquieu's arguments regarding the relevance of climate to such precepts) but which also must correspond to universal moral laws that are relevant to all members of society and not just a legal elite. Gaetano Filangieri, *The Science of Legislation*, Richard Clayton, trans. (London: Emory and Adams, 1806), ch. I. This theory relates to utilitarianism in terms of its emphasis upon the practical usefulness of laws enacted under its principles. This theory is explained, particularly within the context of reform-oriented late-eighteenth century legal and political philosophy, in Marcello Maestro, "Gaetano Filangieri and His Laws of Relative Goodness," *Journal of the History of Ideas* 44, no. 4 (October 1983): 687–91.

220. The word "Subservient" appears within this heading of the manuscript, RP MSS 141/23: 1.

221. The parallel section within Dumont's edition is listed as number nine. Bentham, *Théorie des peines*, vol. I, pp. 47–48.

222. The word "intimidation" was used instead of "to deter" within an earlier draft of this part of manuscript, RP MSS 141/27: 1.

223. The word "indiscriminate" was inserted within the manuscript at this point of this sentence, Ibid., 141/24: 1.

224. Utilitarian arguments derived from this approach of Bentham would have a limited influence, in this respect, regarding this specific area of penal reform, particularly (though not exclusively) within American prison systems. Children would be classified and segregated from the main prison population when sent to prison during the eighteenth century but this trend would be based more upon Calvinist and Lockean values and principles than upon utilitarian concepts of rehabilitation. John R. Sutton, "Social Structure, Institutions, and the Legal Status of Children in the United States," *American Journal of Sociology* 88, no. 5 (March 1983): 915–47, especially 919–21.

225. Dumont uses a word indicating a more general "harm" for this heading. Bentham, *Théorie des peines*, vol. I, p. 46.

226. This passage should be considered within the context of the possible influence of Bentham's writings upon other influential philosophers. The late eighteenth century Russian scholar and critic, Alexander Nikolaevich Radischev, sought to affect change in this area as a member of the Commission for the Composition of Laws under Czar Alexander I. His opposition, in particular, to the frequent use of mutilation as a form of permanent punishment through disablement has been ascribed to the influence of Bentham's writing, including such works as Jeremy Bentham, *The Theory of Legislation*, C. K. Ogden, ed. (London: Routledge and Keegan Paul, 1931), pp. 271–73, 358–62, 442–45. Etienne Dumont, in a letter to Sir Samuel Romilly, had particularly high praise for Radischev and his work, further suggesting this influence. Bentham, *Theory of Legislation*, p. xxxiii. However, the extent to which Radischev was influenced by early utilitarian thought (as opposed to the ideas of Beccaria, Filangieri, Mably, or other contemporary critics) is unclear. David M. Lang, "Radischev and the Legislative Commission of Alexander I," *American Slavic and East European Review* 6, no. 3/4 (December 1947): 22–24.

227. The parallel section within Dumont's edition subsequently is listed as number ten. Bentham, *Théorie des peines*, vol. I, pp. 48–49.

228. This calculation depends upon the assumption that government is not motivate to punish the innocent. However, it can be argued that a concept of "efficient punishment" that takes into account the sort of cost/benefit analysis that can be associated with this utilitarian theme of compensation might not take matters of guild or innocence into consideration but only profit and loss. David Friedman, "Why Not Hang Them All? The Virtues of Inefficient Punishment," *Journal of Political Economy* 107, no. 6 (December 1999): S259-S269. This general theme is explored, further, in Randy E. Barnett, "Restitution: A New Paradigm of Criminal Justice," *Ethics* 87, no. 4 (July 1977): 279–301.

229. A previous draft included the heading "By Way of Supplement to Explanation to Rule I," followed by an elaboration upon this theme: "The profit of the crime is very often certain as being immediate: the event of punishment is liable to a multitude of contingencies relating to the difficulty of detection and to the formalities necessary or unnecessary of prosecution. That the value of the punishment may enter upon the profit of the offense it must be increased in point of magnitude in proportion as it falls short in point of certainty and proximity." back of RP MSS 141/14: 1.

230. The parallel section within Dumont's edition is listed as number twelve. Bentham, *Théorie des peines*, vol. I, pp. 51–53.

231. This sentence initially began with the words "In short," within the manuscript. Also, the commas were omitted from the first part of this sentence. RP MSS 141/26: 1.

232. Empirical demonstrations that capital punishment has no effect upon either deterrence of crime nor a general promotion of a cycle of violence (even when widely witnessed and well-publicized) appear to reinforce this observation. William C. Bailey, "Murder, Capital Punishment, and Television: Execution Publicity and Homicide Rates," *American Sociological Review* 55, no. 5 (October 1990):. 628–33.

233. The manuscript initially included the words "Invariably [great]" [*sic*] at the start of this sentence. RP MSS 141/27: 1.

234. This historical experience of popularity and practical rejection was prominent within the late eighteenth century, as explored in Frank McLynn, *Crime and Punishment in Eighteenth Century England* (New York: Routledge, 1989), pp. 257–76. The class conflict that lay at the root of this trend challenged its alleged "popularity" and offered a further challenge to its rationality, especially from the perspective of critics such as Bentham and his followers, including Dumont and Smith. That background is examined in Peter Linebaugh, *The London Hanged: Crime and Civil Society in the Eighteenth Century* (London: Verso, 2006), pp. 1–30.

235. The predominant sentiment against which Bentham and his followers were presenting these arguments were grounded upon elite adaptations of marketplace values, as critically explored in the classic historical study of Thompson, pp. 245–69.

236. An earlier draft of this section identified it as "X." RP MSS 141/31: 1.

237. This particular characteristic (which appears to be prompted by a desire to make the law accessible to all members of society, rather than just legal and political elites) represents an addition to the list of qualities originally provided in Bentham, *Morals and Legislation*, ch. 15, para. 27. Arguably, it is designed to make it easier to avoid committing crimes and, therefore, the need to inflict punishment at all.

238. This principle is a central tenet of legal positivism that displaced natural law as a foundation for law in general. It is applicable particularly in the sense that a "command of the sovereign" (which defines law, itself, under this tradition) cannot function as a law (especially in terms of being recognized and followed) unless it is intelligible. James T. McHugh, *The Essential Concept of Law* (New York: Peter Lang, 2002), pp. 18–19. This subject serves as part of the preliminary discussion for the application of utilitarian principles to a "science" of jurisprudence. Austin,

pp. xiv–xv, 21–25. A general analysis of Austin's contributions in this narrow, yet important, category is provided in Dennis Lloyd, *The Idea of Law* (London: Penguin, 1987), pp. 108–109.

239. A previous draft of this section adds an interesting comment at this approximate point in the discourse: "Penal nomenclature thus becomes an object of the very greatest importance. An uneven denomination threads over a map of punishments a cloud which the mind can rarely if ever penetrate." back of RP MSS 141/31: 1.

240. The parallel section within Dumont's edition is listed as number seven. Bentham, *Théorie des peines*, vol. I, pp. 45–46.

241. This concern has been central to many sources of opposition to capital punishment, as noted in Michael L. Radelet and Marian J. Borg, "The Changing Nature of Death Penalty Debates," *Annual Review of Sociology* 26 (2006): 50–52. Interestingly, one approach to this subject has critiqued an interpretation of utilitarian thought upon this subject, contending that such an approach could justify execution of innocent persons if the deterrent effect of preventing murders outweighs the pain inflicted upon the victim of mistaken execution, especially when calculated from the perspective of the innocence of the innocent executed party in comparison with the innocence of murder victims in general. A prominent scholarly analysis of this position is provided in Ernest Van Den Haag, "On Deterrence and the Death Penalty," *Ethics* 78, no. 4 (July 1968): 280–88. The idea that such a strategy might actually guide state action in this area is suggested in Austin Sarat, *When the State Kills: Capital Punishment and the American Condition* (Princeton, NJ: Princeton University Press, 2001), pp. 245–48.

This overall calculation and strategy is, of course, completely rejected from the Kantian perspective. Immanuel Kant, *The Metaphysical Elements of Justice*, John Ladd, trans. (Indianapolis: Hackett, 1999), pp. 137–44. However, it often has been employed as a practical matter by states that adopt a retributive approach toward their respective penal systems, as discussed in George Schedler, "On Telishing the Guilty," *Ethics* 86, no. 3 (April 1976): 256–60. Also, it is arguable that a utilitarian account of such a practice would note that, if it was discovered that the state punished the innocent, the result would be a breakdown of trust in the efficacy of the state and its penal system which would pose a greater "evil" than any deterrent gain that punishing the innocent would represent. William Lyons, pp. 346–48. An overview of this issue in terms of ethical attitudes and public policy implications is provided in James D. Unnever and Francis T. Cullen, "Executing the Innocent and Support for Capital Punishment: Implications for Public Policy," *Criminology and Public Policy* 4, no. 1 (February 2005): 3–38.

242. Dumont's version of this section differs from the version presented by Smith, both in terms of emphasis and in terms of the generally more sympathetic tone that Dumont's version appears to convey toward innocent victims, Bentham. *Théorie des peines*, vol. I, pp. 45–46.

Dumont adds a reference at the end of this section to chapter 14 of the second volume, entitled "Of Rewards for Informers, Offered to Accomplices," in which lies extensive reference to Beccaria's condemnation of informers and their use. Ibid., vol. II, pp. 129–35. The tone of this chapter (especially in terms of its sense of moral outrage) reflects a similar tone regarding remissibility within Dumont's edition and offers an interesting contrast to Bentham's more pragmatic and detached approach.

243. Originally, the words "but there will be" appeared instead of "and there are" within the manuscript. RP MSS 141/32: 1.

Book I, Chapter VIII

244. This chapter originally was identified as Chapter VII within the manuscript, as it is within the Dumont edition. Bentham, *Théorie des peines*, vol. I, p. 59.

245. The words "confine myself" were crossed out within the manuscript and replaced with the words "point out." RP MSS 141/32: 1.

246. The historical transition from symbolic and ritualistic punishments (including analogous ones) toward punishments intended to promote other social goals was an important part of the process of general penal reform (including in relation to Bentham's scheme for the Panopticon), as famously advanced by Foucault, pp. 11–31, 195–228. An argument that this interpretation has been too harsh and fails to account for the value of punishment as social and psychic reinforcement is provided in Randall McGowen, "The Body and Punishment in Eighteenth-Century England," *Journal of Modern History* 59, no. 4 (December 1987): 651–79.

247. Originally, the phrase "destruction of property" appeared within the manuscript, replaced by the word "waste." RP MSS 141/33: 1.

248. This paragraph, as presented within the 1830 version, did not include reference to a third offense of this nature. The paragraph was rewritten according to the version found within Dumont's edition (as translated by the editor of this edition). Bentham, *Théorie des peines*, vol. I, p. 61.

The subsequent footnote attached to this paragraph also was included within Dumont's edition but not within the 1830 edition of Smith. It appears to have been written by Dumont. Ibid., vol. I, pp. 61–62. It is included within this edition because it offers a good example of the sort of moral tone that not only was evident throughout Dumont's edition but which appears to have found its way, indirectly, into Smith's version of 1830 but which is not typical of Bentham's original writings.

249. Instead of the word "evident," the word "sensible" appeared within the manuscript but was crossed-out. RP MSS 141/35: 1.

250. A previous draft of this chapter included the following additional comment under the heading of "poisoning": "Of these circumstances the former adds to the strength of the temptation, and in some measure to the mischief of the offense: the latter indicates the probability that the offender, watchful to his own interest, may be attentive to any peculiarity with quantity and quality of the punishment." Back of Ibid., 141/36: 1.

251. It is interesting to compare the theme of this chapter to a Hegelian approach to this subject, in which the severity of punishment is a necessary indication of difference in terms of the scale of the respective crimes. The particular nature of the punishment should be left to the discretion of local authority but a general analogy of severity of crime with severity of punishment appears to be approved within his writings. Georg Wilhem Friedrich Hegel, *Elements of the Philosophy of Right*, Alan W. Wood, ed., H. B. Nisbet, trans. (Cambridge: Cambridge University Press, 1991), pp. 124–28, 245–51. This approach is assessed in Peter J. Steinberger, "Hegel on Crime and Punishment," *American Political Science Review* 77, no. 4 (December 1983): 865–67

252. Originally, the phrase "inflicted upon" was provided within the manuscript, then replaced with the word "making." RP MSS 141/36: 1.

253. A previous draft of this chapter included, at the beginning of this section, the following qualification: "I mean always with the proviso: that the injury was malicious and ultimately intentional: that the intention of the delinquent was not merely to do bodily hurt but that precise kind of bodily hurt (or one of equal mischief) that has actually taken place" Back of Ibid., 141/37: 1.

254. The manuscript begins a new paragraph at this point, which continues to the bottom of the page, at which point the remainder is lost: "In the dissemination of calumny and the dissemination of false reports the degree of instrument employed . . ." Ibid.

255. The text from this point is missing within the manuscript, although an earlier draft can be found on the back of Ibid., 141/39: 1. This earlier draft begins with the sentence: "In crimes imputing falsehood the offending member may be a characteristic circumstance." Back of Ibid.

256. This paragraph appears within the Dumont edition as an in-text citation, though I it follows the second paragraph of this section. Bentham, *Théorie des peines*, vol. I, pp. 66–67.

257. The final manuscript draft remains missing at this point. However, an earlier draft of this section can be found, crossed-out, on the back of RP MSS 141/38: 1. Its section title is phrased "Disguise Assumed for the Offense Similar Disguise Marked on the Offender." Back of Ibid. It is, essentially, the same as section IV of the Dumont edition, which is entitled, simply, "Disguising." Bentham, *Théorie des peines*, vol. I, pp. 67–68.

258. The final manuscript draft remains missing at this point. However, an apparent early draft (including examples of different phrasing) can be found, crossed-out, on the back of RP MSS 141/40: 1. The handwriting of this draft appears to be somewhat different from both Smith's and Bentham's handwriting. It could, possibly, be Dumont's handwritten translation of this section, especially since it is, essentially, the same as the version which appears within his edition. Bentham, *Théorie des peines*, vol. I, pp. 68–69.

259. The manuscript (including the translation of Dumont's note) resumes at this point. RP MSS 141/38: 1.

260. Different methods for translating all of the text from Dumont's edition could be addressed regarding Smith's entire 1830 edition, especially those sections for which no English manuscript can be found and/or which appear to rely upon a translation of Dumont's edition as a primary source of authority. However, a critical assessment of the translation of this note is particularly significant, not only because it represents an undeniably original interpretation of, and contribution to, Bentham's ideas but, also, because it provides an intriguing source of comparison regarding the potentially different tone and attitude brought (though generally in a subtle way) by each contributor to this cumulative text.

261. Dumont's original French version is limited to the word "against" at this point, rather than including the arguably more descriptive word "urged." Bentham, *Théorie des peines*, vol. I, p. 70.

262. A rhetorical, and somewhat imploring, question, "how do you come to apply it?" is added at this point within Dumont's original French version. Ibid.

263. Smith's 1830 edition does not identify the volume and page reference, although that information is included, in French, within the manuscript. RP MSS 141/38: 1.

264. The descriptive word "is," rather than the suggestive word "ought," appears within Dumont's original French version. Bentham, *Théorie des peines*, vol. I, p. 70.

265. The phrase from which the word "degrading," as derived within this translation, was based upon the French words *esprit minutieux*, which more literally translate as a "meticulous spirit" that appears to add a more profound and, perhaps, sarcastic tone to this passage. Ibid., p. 71.

266. Dumont's French version uses the generic term for whip (*fouet*) and Smith, apparently, substitutes the more descriptively accurate noun (especially in reference to English naval practice) "cat-o'-nine-tails," Bentham. Ibid.

267. The precise word used by Dumont at this point, *châtiment*, while a synonym for punishment, arguably reflects a more disapproving expression of the concept (such as in reference to a form of retribution, rather than a more value-neutral practice of correction) than the word "punishment" generally might convey in this context. Ibid.

268. Dumont added the phrase "if exceeding forty-eight hours, he lost two" at this point. Ibid., p. 72. Smith apparently chose to omit this part of the sentence as being superfluous.

269. The phrase "since softening the punishment" is added, at this point, within Dumont's original French version, arguably adding a more approving tone to the description of this example. Ibid.

BOOK I, CHAPTER IX

270. This chapter in the Dumont edition appears as "Chapter VIII." Ibid., p. 73.

271. The title appears within the parallel chapter of Dumont's edition as *Du Talion*. Ibid. Although it can be translated as retribution, its origin is more directly tied to the Latin term *lex talionis*, referring to the ancient category of law concerning this theme.

272. The manuscript is missing at this point but it is present within the Dumont edition. Ibid.Ibid., but the footnote attached to the end of it is not found within that edition.

273. This paragraph appears within the Dumont edition. Ibid. But the footnote attached to the end of it is not found within that edition.

274. This theme within Blackstone's writings is noted in Daniel J. Boorstin, *The Mysterious Science of Law: An Essay on Blackstone's Commentaries* (Chicago: University of Chicago Press, 1996), pp. 96–97.

275. No version of this paragraph appears within the Dumont edition.

276. The manuscript resumes at this point.

277. It has been argued that, if a criminal has no good objection to the threat of retaliation, that criminal should have no objection to implementing the retaliation being imposed. In other words, the authority to threaten retaliation is a source for the authority to punish. Warren Quinn, "The Right to Threaten and the Right to Punish," *Philosophy and Public Affairs* 14, no. 4 (Fall 1985): 327–73. A concern with the wider implication of this sort of justification for retaliation (including in terms of its extension to other behavior, both public and private) is provided in Richard Brook, "Threats and Punishment," *Philosophy and Public Affairs* 17, no. 3 (Summer 1988): 235–39.

278. Again, the use of a statement to begin this paragraph offers a subtle, yet interesting, contrast with the first sentence of the parallel paragraph within Dumont's edition, which employs (as frequently found within that edition) a rhetorical question. Bentham, *Théorie des peines*, vol. I, p. 74. This difference in style suggests a potentially more confident treatment within the English version of 1830 than within the French text.

279. The phrase "which affect a certain district" replaced, within the manuscript, the crossed-out phrase "against a neighborhood." RP MSS 141/41: 1.

280. A crossed-out draft passage addresses this same point in slightly greater detail:
"In the case of a self-regarding offense, consisting in acts in violation of morality, the attempt to apply it would be attended with manifest absurdity. If a man designedly does to himself what is considered to another person as an injury would be an act of punishment to sentence him to receive a repetition of the same supposed injury." Back of Ibid., 141/10: 1.

BOOK I, CHAPTER X

281. This chapter is identified, within the manuscript, as having been written in Bentham's handwriting. It appears as chapter IX within Dumont's edition. Bentham, *Théorie des peines*, vol. I, p. 78.

282. The word "To" is replaced, within the manuscript, by the phrase "The objections which." RP MSS 141/43: 1.

283. Retributivist penal policy that is grounded upon public popularity often is associated with the principle of *lex talionis*, which, in turn, often is associated with the biblical admonition of "an eye for an eye and a tooth for a tooth." The continuing influence of this principle upon penal policy and the ethical problems associated with it are reviewed in Hugo A. Bedau, "Classification-Based Sentencing: Some Conceptual and Ethical Problems,"

Nomos XXVII: Criminal Justice (1985): 102. A redefining and defense of this principle, especially in relation to the unfair advantage that a criminal allegedly assumes over society simply by committing a crime, is offered in Michael Davis, "Harm and Retribution," *Philosophy and Public Affairs* 15, no. 3 (Summer 1986): 536–57. This indirect treatment of the theme of popularity as a legitimate source of penal principles has been modified by some scholars with a utilitarian requirement that this sort of retribution still requires a proportionate relationship between crime and punishment. That approach is explained and defended in F. H. Bradley, *Ethical Studies* (Oxford: Oxford University Press, 1962), pp. 26–28.

284. Bentham believed that public opinion was inherently progressive, so the expansion of liberal democracy would evolve toward a recognition and acceptance of utilitarian principles. This belief would be advanced further by his immediate and later disciples. This aspect of early utilitarianism (which helps to explain Bentham's seeming tolerance for potential emotional public recidivism within this chapter) is explained and defended in Fred Cutler, "Jeremy Bentham and the Public Opinion Tribunal," *Public Opinion Quarterly* 63, no. 3 (Autumn 1999): 321–46.

285. It may be instructive to compare Bentham's handwritten manuscript with Dumont's apparent translation. This paragraph reflects, within Dumont's version, the essence of Bentham's meaning yet it includes differences in style and emphasis which, though subtle, suggest a slightly different stress. For example, the use of rhetorical questions ("what is it like, in effect?") within the French translation suggests a possibly more interactive and, perhaps, even Socratic style on the part of Dumont. Also, Dumont appears to address a continental audience with references such as "within the most advanced nations" rather than Bentham's more parochial reference to attitudes "in this intelligent and favoured country than perhaps in any other." Bentham, *Théorie des peines*, vol. I, p. 78. These contrasts of style can be found throughout Dumont's translation of the manuscript of this chapter.

286. This stronger word, "warped," originally was written within the manuscript as "swayed." RP MSS 141/43: 1. It is interesting to note the substitution of the stronger and more judgmental adjective, especially in Bentham's own handwriting. Dumont's translation does not provide an adjective of any sort at this point. Bentham, *Théorie des peines*, vol. I, p. 78.

287. The phrase "without regard to even" was originally written within the manuscript as "not founded even upon." RP MSS 141/43: 1.

288. Early utilitarians had to contend with an adherence to antiquated common-law principles regarding punishment that often were upheld merely because they were popular in a traditional sense, as demonstrated in Martin Madan, *Thoughts on Executive Justice* (London: J. Dodsley, 1785), pp. 1–29. A defense of proportionality in the law against such writings was provided within utilitarian writings such as Sir Samuel Romilly, *Observations on the Criminal Law of England* (London: T. Cadell and W. Davies, 1813), pp. 40–56. It included an appendix written by Benjamin Franklin entitled which, though not embracing specific utilitarian arguments, nonetheless addressed the theme of employing enlightened thought as a substitute for popularity based upon a traditional defense of the common law. Benjamin Franklin, "A Letter from a Gentleman Abroad to His Friend in England," in Romilly, pp. 76–107. This exchange of opinions upon this theme is described in Marcello Maestro, "Benjamin Franklin and the Penal Laws," *Journal of the History of Ideas* 36, no. 3 (July 1975): 557–59.

289. The phase "will be found" originally appeared, then was crossed-out, and the word "may" was substituted. RP MSS 141/43: 1.

290. The manuscript begins this paragraph with the sentence "Their objections to which a mode of punishment stands exposed seem but reduced to the lapses then of Humanity, Decency, Liberty, and Religion." Ibid. Dumont's translation appears to reflect that version at the beginning of the parallel paragraph within his edition. Bentham, *Théorie des peines*, vol. I, pp. 78–79.

291. The manuscript is missing at this point.

292. Bentham reportedly was particularly frustrated with the application of this principle against the development of a rational legal system, especially one based upon utilitarian values that must treat law, necessarily, as a coercive instrument dedicated to the maintenance of a level of security that will prevent the pain of crime and other dangers. This analysis is provided in John R. Dinwiddy, "The Classical Economists and the Utilitarians," in *Western Liberalism: A History in Documents from Locke to Croce*, E. K. Bramstead and K. J. Melhuish, eds. (London: Longmans, 1978), pp. 12–25, and Long, pp. 1–46.

293. Dumont's edition specifies England in reference to this example. Bentham, *Théorie des peines*, vol. I, p. 79.

294. The subject of "decency" could be associated with Bentham's general treatment of normative morality. He was very critical of common-law rulings that apparently were based upon a historically subjective (if not arbitrary) standard of concepts such as "decency" and "modesty," which opinion is particularly evident in his criticism of Sir William Blackstone's attempt to provide a "science" of common-law jurisprudence in Jeremy Bentham, *A Comment on the Commentaries*, J. H. Burns and H. L. A. Hart, eds. (London: Athlone Press, 1977), pp. 35–77. In his attempt to distance the common law from a natural law conception of morality, Blackstone emphasized the command function of law as a device for the sovereign to define moral content. However, the evolutionary quality of the common law necessitated a historic accounting of these moral standards which could fluctuate, greatly, as noted in Michael Lobban, "Blackstone and the Science of Law," *The Historical Journal* 30, no. 2 (June 1987): 328–33.

Yet Bentham could be accused of employing a "naturalistic" approach toward his own explanation of human sentiments and motivations, especially as described within Bentham, *Morals and Legislation*, chs. I–VI. The concept of "pleasure," itself (particularly as an equivalent for "good"), is subject to that potential interpretation, especially respecting the qualities of human sentiment and sympathy, an accusation that is advanced in G. E. Moore, *Principia Ethica*, Thomas Baldwin, ed. (Cambridge: Cambridge University Press, 1993), pp. 19–22, 69–72. However, this charge is critically assessed and generally rejected in Amnon Goldworth, "Bentham's Concept of Pleasure: Its Relation to Fictitious Terms," *Ethics* 82, no. 4 (July 1972): 334–43 and in Kelly, pp. 40–45.

295. Dumont's edition adds an additional paragraph at this point within the parallel section of his edition:

"We will find, in the second book [*Théorie des récompenses*] that there are very strong reasons against the death penalty, or that at most it is inappropriate except in extraordinary cases: but this illegitimate claim is a borrowed reason of a false principle." Bentham, *Théorie des peines*, vol. I, p. 81.

296. Dumont's edition emphasizes the word "will." Ibid., p. 82.

297. The compatibility of utilitarian reason with the concept of a divine will would be explored by some utilitarians of the early to mid 19th century (despite Bentham's adherence to a strictly rationalist interpretation of his principles), especially as some of its adherents attempted to reconcile it to Victorian religious beliefs, as reviewed in J. B. Schneewind, *Sidgwick's Ethics and Victorian Moral Philosophy* (Oxford: Oxford University Online Monographs, 1986), pp. 122–52. Bentham's "raw" version of utilitarian thought has been contrasted with a theological version of this tradition that treated God as the ultimate font of "pleasure." Wilson Smith, "William Paley's Theological Utilitarianism in America," *William and Mary Quarterly* 11, no. 3 (July 1954): 402–24.

298. Dumont's edition makes no reference to Roman Catholicism within this example. Bentham, *Théorie des peines*, vol. I, p. 82.

299. Dumont's edition includes a note at this point: "*Pilati*. Histoire des revolution depuis l'accession de Constantin jusqu'a la chute de l'empire d'Occident." Ibid., p. 83.

300. The manuscript resumes at this point.

301. The first sentence of this paragraph was originally phrased within the manuscript as "Listen to the voice of reason which so often misleads us, as to the heart, that faithful and unerring guide, the heart." RP MSS 141/44: 1. This version is translated as the first sentence of the parallel section of Dumont's edition. Bentham, *Théorie des peines*, vol. I, p. 83.

302. Instead of the words "harrows up," the word "lacerates" appeared at this point of the manuscript. RP MSS 141/44: 1.

303. Originally, the phrase "in a painful shock" appeared within the manuscript, then was replaced by the phrase "in a more or less painful degree." Ibid. The French word used at this point, *douloureuse*, can be translated either way. Bentham, *Théorie des peines*, vol. I, p. 84.

304. The manuscript originally provided the following sentences instead of the text of this paragraph as it finally appeared, following the first semi-colon, which was a period within this phrasing of the manuscript: "If it were not averse to it, would it be calculated to attain its object? If no mode of punishment can be approved of that unfavorable approach with the idea of the offense." RP MSS 141/44: 1. A French version of this passage appears within the parallel paragraph within the Dumont edition. Bentham, *Théorie des peines*, vol. I, p. 84.

305. The manuscript originally concluded this sentence, following the second appearance of the word "antipathy," as "that it felt, as shall readily the rational difficult to detect." RP MSS 141/44: 1.

306. The phrase "more mischief than it prevents" originally was written within the manuscript as "preponderant evil." Ibid.

307. This evaluation of the relevance of "humanity" to the assessment of punishment is not inconsistent with the later development of non-hedonistic utilitarianism, as described in J. C. C. Smart, "An Outline of a System of Utilitarian Ethics," in *Utilitarianism: For and Against*, J. C. C. Smart and Bernard Williams, eds. (Cambridge: Cambridge University Press, 1973), pp. 12–26.

308. The phrase "satisfies the multitude" originally appeared as "flatters the people" within the manuscript. RP MSS 141/44: 1.

309. The phrase "being equally self-condemned" originally appeared as "accusing himself" within the manuscript. Ibid. Dumont's edition uses the French equivalent of the latter phrase at this point. Bentham, *Théorie des peines*, vol. I, p. 85.

310. The phrase "to the delinquent, and renders it a peculiar object of dread" originally was written as "and renders it inefficient [indecipherable] in the way of determent to a remarkable degree efficient." RP MSS 141/44: 1.

311. The manuscript originally included the following two paragraphs at this point:
"I maintain however though the judgment happen to be conformable to utility, it is not a matter of indifference from which of those principles they are derived: because giving judgment independent of utility this time, it may give judgment another time against her.

"The light of political and moral science will recover [?] this steadily in men's understanding, till they have taught themselves to employ this principle alone to the conclusion of all others. That the judgment is to decide the use of causatory or vituperative epithets is like the babbling of childhood. They ought cautiously to abstain from all philosophical disquisitions when the object is to instruct and convince the understanding and not to move the passions." RP MSS 141/44: 1.

312. The phrase "on any one occasion" originally was phrased "at one time" within the manuscript. Ibid.

313. Instead of the word "decide," the manuscript originally employed the phrase "approve or disapprove of any such measure." Ibid.

314. A note was added to the end of this parallel chapter within Dumont's edition, as translated by the editor of this edition:
"These impassioned terms include an entire petition of principle, an anticipated judgment

of approval or a disapproval implied by the same term. Anyone who makes use of it in an argument would make a species of trickery or violence to its reader. But when it is proved, when it is weighed for and against in the balance of utility, it appears to me neither possible nor proper to abstain from characterizing the good and evil by the epithets which are applied to them within ordinary language. This note is perhaps an apology prepared by the editor of these manuscripts; he made every effort not to need didactic parts; but to write without allowing any approving terms would be to walk a tightrope." Bentham, *Théorie des peines*, vol. I, p. 86.

It is interesting to compare the utilitarian treatment of this particular theme with the claim that Bentham could not decide whether his ideas displaced all previous ethical systems or, actually, subsumed them into a superior grand theory. This ambiguity is evident, throughout this chapter, particularly in terms of the way in which subjective sentiments and normative tendencies regarding the popularity of punishment as a supposedly legitimate property of punishment are legitimized. This ambiguity is addressed in Don Herzog, *Without Foundations* (Ithaca, NY: Cornell University Press, 1985), pp. 157–59.

BOOK II, CHAPTER I

315. Dumont's edition provides the following note at the end of this paragraph: "*Afflictive*, in this sense, conforms to the Latin word from which is derived: *Afflictatio*, as said Cicero in the Tuscalenes, est aegritudo cum vexatione corporis." Bentham, *Théorie des peines*, vol. I, p. 95.

316. Bentham's previous treatment of this subject tended to be more descriptive of its overall relationship to utilitarian principles than descriptive of specific methods. Bentham, *Morals and Legislation*, ch. 16, sec. 3, para. 33.

317. Originally, the word "hardly" appeared in place of "seldom." RP MSS 141/45: 2. The French word *malgré*, which can translate as "in spite of," appears at this point within the Dumont edition. Bentham, *Théorie des peines*, vol. I, p. 96.

318. The manuscript is interrupted at this point.

319. Dumont's translation of this paragraph appears to be a little awkward, apparently reflecting the colloquial difficulties and cultural differences. Ibid., p. 97.

320. Despite this seemingly non-committal treatment of this particular subject, the opposition to corporal punishment (particularly flogging) within the British military during the 19th century has been attributed, in part, to Benthamite utilitarian reformers such as Romilly, although many other factors (including evangelical agitation) combined with the advocacy of these principles to influence these changes, as discussed in J. R. Dinwiddy, "The Early Nineteenth Century Campaign against Flogging in the Army," *English Historical Review* 97, no. 383 (April 1982): 308–31.

321. The manuscript resumes at this point.

322. The words "and report" were added at this point in the manuscript but, later, crossed-out. RP MSS 141/46: 2.

323. This note does not appear within the Dumont edition.

324. Initially, instead of the word "law," the word "judge" had been applied within the manuscript. Ibid., 141/48: 2.

325. The em-dash following the phrase "in a lot of punishment are" was not present within the manuscript's version of this paragraph, [Ibid., 141/49: 2] offering an example of the occasional punctuation changes that appear to have been made during the preparation of the final galleys of the 1830 edition of this book. Generally, these punctuation changes are minor and have not altered the meaning of the text so other such alterations will not be specifically noted unless they prove to be significant in that sense. Dumont's edition employs numerous

em-dashes within the parallel section of this chapter, as well as slightly more elaborate explanations of each category. Bentham, *Théorie des peines*, vol. I, pp. 102–103.

326. Dumont's edition enumerates this explanation as number "1." Ibid., p. 103.

327. The word "pleasure" was used within the manuscript and, then, replaced with the "will." RP MSS 141/49: 2.

328. Instead of this sentence, Dumont's edition includes a sentence affirming the necessary discretion of judges. Bentham, *Théorie des peines*, vol. I, p. 103.

An entirely different paragraph follows at this parallel point within the Dumont edition on the subject of the variability of punishment and the ignominy of afflictive punishment. That paragraph (enumerated as number "2") concludes with the sentence concerning the effect of such punishments upon a "gentleman" (noting the different practice, in this respect, among European countries) along the lines of the sentence that concluded the previous paragraph within the 1830 Smith edition. Ibid., pp. 103–104.

329. The passage that originally began this paragraph within the manuscript was phased "Want of attention to this circumstance produced great discontent against an English act of Parliament called the Dog Act." RP MSS 141/49: 2.

330. Dumont's edition adds the following sentence at this point: "One knows that Peter I inflicted the punishment upon children as well as upon women of the first condition." Bentham, *Théorie des peines*, vol. I, p. 105.

331. Instead of reference to "The institutions of Poland," the manuscript originally used the words "This European." RP MSS 141/50: 2.

332. Dumont's edition elaborates further upon this example. Bentham, *Théorie des peines*, vol. I, p. 106.

333. The influence of Bentham, James Mill, and their subsequent disciples was cited as a primary basis for the codification of Indian law under the direction of Thomas Babington Macaulay, including a penal law that largely displaced flogging as a punishment upon grounds of utilitarian inefficacy, as described in David Skuy, "Macaulay and the Indian Penal Code of 1862: The Myth of the Inherent Superiority and Modernity of the English Legal System Compared to India's Legal System in the Nineteenth Century," *Modern Asian Studies* 32, no. 3 (July 1998): 513–57, and Eric Stokes, *The English Utilitarians and India* (Oxford: Clarendon Press, 1959) pp. 68–69, 225, 233.

334. Dumont's edition enumerates this explanation as number "3." Bentham, *Théorie des peines*, vol. I, p. 106.

335. That alleged exemplarity could be, arguably, most relevant within the context of childhood education. However, Bentham's influence upon educational reform (while challenged as being neither as progressive, original, or influential as often assumed) included a trend away from the use of corporal punishment in school, as noted in Elissa S. Itzkin, "Bentham's *Chrestomathia*: Utilitarian Legacy to English Education," *Journal of the History of Ideas* 39, no. 2 (April 1978): 303–16.

336. The phrase "are of little efficiency as" originally was written "have little tendency" in the manuscript. RP MSS 141/50: 2.

337. The back sides of these manuscript pages contain an earlier draft of this chapter. The tone, as well as the text, of that earlier draft differs from the final draft. That earlier draft appears to have placed greater emphasis upon the "certainty" of punishment in the broadest sense, with a tone that was more critical of the use of torture as a form of punishment, particular as found on the back of Ibid. Nonetheless, this earlier draft reveals, in its original introduction to this chapter, the same stress upon utilitarian cause and effect relationships that characterizes this chapter and the entire book:

"Simple afflictive punishments are easy enough to state and estimate, because their personal consequences are all of one kind and are seen to take place immediately with the application of the instrument. All others are much more difficult because their penal consequences are more various and of various degrees of uncertainty remoteness. Simple afflictive punishments produce pain pretty much alike in all persons: in every person some other modes of punishment are defective in respect of certainty. The more remote the consequences of any species of punishment, the less likely it is to operate upon those who neither calculate nor reflect." Back of Ibid., 141/46: 2.

Book II, Chapter II

338. These specific properties were not the focus of the earlier published texts of Bentham upon this particular subject but, rather, he emphasized their characteristics. Bentham, *Morals and Legislation*, ch. 16, especially sec. 5.

339. Following the first em-dash of this paragraph, the wording originally appeared in the manuscript as "which are so to speak external and long time visible—Punishments which without destroying any organ, which produce no mutilation, which are often not without physical pain or at least without any other pain than what is absolutely necessary for the operation which affects only the appearance less agreeably derived their principal value from being signs of the offense." RP MSS 141/51: 2.

340. The words "his desire" originally appeared within the manuscript as the phrase "therefore of the motive resulting from." Ibid., 141/52: 2. That latter phrase is more representative of the parallel phrase found within Dumont's edition. Bentham, *Théorie des peines*, vol. I, p. 112.

341. This paragraph is structurally connected to the following one within the Dumont edition, Bentham, *Théorie des peines*, vol. I pp. 112–13. This structural difference between the Dumont and Smith editions is a frequent occurrence, throughout all of the chapters of these texts.

342. The possibility that mutilation could be, hypothetically, an acceptable punishment under Bentham's utilitarian approach has been part of one of its most criticized features. This rejection of inhumane punishments as an in opposition to this utilitarian interpretation is articulated in Davis, "How to Make the Punishment Fit the Crime," pp. 737–38. An explanation of defining "inhumane" punishment within this context is provided in Michael Davis, "Death, Deterrence, and the Method of Common Sense," 7 *Social Theory and Practice*, no. 1 (1981), pp. 145–77.

343. Dumont's edition adds a note in reference to this word: "In English, *to disable* and *disablement.*—this word is absent from the French language. *Déshabiliter*, is unskillfully offered." Bentham, *Théorie des peines*, vol. I, p.114, as translated by the editor of this current edition.

344. From this point, the manuscript is missing.

345. Dumont's edition offers this general's name as de Lally. Ibid., vol. I, p. 115.

346. At the parallel point of Dumont's edition, additional material is included regarding such specific topics as punishments consisting of the ineffectiveness of markings that do not disfigure, the moral condemnation that this sort of punishment imposes, the greater sensibility of inflicting such punishments upon men, rather than women, and exceptions to the effect of these sorts of marking, such as the disfigurement of war wounds, which often results in sympathy and admiration. Ibid., pp. 124–25.

347. The manuscript resumes at this point.

348. The manuscript is missing at this point for the remainder of the chapter.

BOOK II, CHAPTER III

349. The manuscript resumes with this chapter.

350. The word "punishment" originally was used instead of "pain" within the manuscript.

351. This emphasis upon the utility of punishment as a policy is consistent with the sort of rule-utilitarian approach that is favored in Richard F. Bernstein, "Legal Utilitarianism," *Ethics* 89, no. 2 (January 1979): 127–46.

BOOK II, CHAPTER IV

352. A version of this opening sentence does not begin the parallel chapter within Dumont's edition, Bentham. *Théorie des peines*, vol. I, p. 132.

353. Instead of "appointed," the manuscript originally used the verb "awarded." RP MSS 141/58: 2.

354. The promotion of imprisonment as a punishment by Bentham was intended to rationalize and "humanize" penal law, providing a substitute for the brutality of execution and offering a source of efficient and beneficial reform. Barbee-Sue Rodman, "Bentham and the Paradox of Penal Reform," *Journal of the History of Ideas* 29, no. 2 (April 1968): 197–210.

355. The manuscript is missing from this point.

356. Dumont's edition specifies that this example refers to "England." Bentham, *Théorie des peines*, vol. I, p. 133.

357. The manuscript resumes from this point.

358. Instead of "presents," the manuscript originally used the verb "recalls." RP MSS 141/59: 2. Dumont's edition uses the phrase "does not recall" at this approximate point within the text. Bentham, *Théorie des peines*, vol. I, p. 135.

359. The phrase "only the single circumstance" originally was phrased "only the idea" within the manuscript. RP MSS 141/59: 2. Dumont's edition uses the phrase "simple circumstance." Bentham, *Théorie des peines*, vol. I, p. 135.

360. An earlier draft of this section originally identified it with the heading "Inconveniences," rather than "Imprisonment" as the 1830 edition presents it. Back of RP MSS 141/57–59: 2. Additional text of the previous draft of this chapter also can be found on the back of Ibid., 141/61–62. Dumont's edition uses the word "l'Empisonnement" within this heading. Bentham, *Théorie des peines*, vol., I, p. 135.

361. Instead of "excursions," the manuscript originally used the word "voyages." RP MSS 141/60: 2. Dumont's edition uses the word "exercises." Bentham, *Théorie des peines*, vol. I, p. 136.

362. The footnote to this paragraph was placed within a later section of the manuscript (suggesting that it was added at a later time), although a cross-reference to this paragraph was provided, RP MSS 141/61: 2.

363. The phrase "means of correspondence per ink and paper" originally appeared within the manuscript, replaced by "implements of writing." Ibid.

364. This discussion illustrates the tension that exists between act-utilitarian and rule-utilitarian interpretations of this philosophical tradition in terms of whether a particular penal policy is, "as a rule," acceptable, regardless of the particular evil that could be imposed upon a particular person by a particular "act" of punishment. A classic defense of rule utilitarianism as being more protective of moral rights in a consistent manner is provided in Rawls, pp. 9–16. A classic defense of act utilitarianianism in terms of a consequentialist analysis is provided in

J. J. C. Smart, *An Outline of a System of Utilitarian Ethics* (Melbourne: Melbourne University Press, 1961), pp. 4–41.

365. An earlier draft outline of this section regarding correlations appeared as a separate French manuscript (possibly in the handwriting of Dumont) in a different portfolio. RP MSS 143/45–46: 4

366. Instead of the word "mortification," the manuscript initially used the phrase "falling off of the extremities by the." Ibid.,S 141/62: 2.

367. Dumont's edition adds the following note at the end of this item: "A general rule of this sort is trivial and futile. It requires a succession of regulations for determining the number of ounces of bread or other food to supply to prisoners." Bentham, *Théorie des peines*, vol. I, p. 139.

368. The phrase "with proper implements" originally appeared within the manuscript as "responsible for." RP MSS 141/62: 2.

BOOK II, CHAPTER V

369. The parallel chapter within Dumont's edition appears as chapter six of the second book, Bentham. *Théorie des peines*, vol. I, pp. 168–71.

370. Dumont's edition uses the word *libération* at this point, followed by the English word "fees" in parenthesis. Ibid., p. 168.

371. This deterrent effect of punishment is consistent with an economic theory of law enforcement that has been lauded as a feature of Bentham's writings, though it was not resumed by scholars until the 1960s, according to A. Mitchell Polinsky and Steven Shavell, "The Economic Theory of Public Enforcement of Law," *Journal of Economic Literature*, no. 1 (March 2000): 45–46.

372. The manuscript continued this paragraph with an incomplete sentence: "A quibbling and inhuman person seems to have been." RP MSS 141/63: 2.

373. The manuscript originally used the phrase "instance of political economy" and replaced it with the phrase "principles of justice," Ibid., which conforms more closely to the phrase found at the parallel point of Dumont's edition. Bentham, *Théorie des peines*, vol. I, p. 169.

374. The manuscript includes, at the end of this paragraph, the additional sentence "There is no one of the Magistrates who contributed to the continuance of this abuse, but were much more objects of it than those wretched innocents on whom they laid the burthen." RP MSS 141/63: 2. The parallel paragraph of Dumont's edition ends with a footnote: "These rights, these fees of the gaolers, have nothing in common with the fees of justice to those to which the judge can condemn the delinquent." Bentham, *Théorie des peines*, vol. I, p. 170.

375. The parallel paragraph of Dumont's edition begins, in a tone of indignation, with the following exclamation: "Apologists of this practice will say that it is part of the punishment of the delinquent!" Ibid.

376. An additional note to this chapter was included within the manuscript but, apparently later, crossed-out: "[a] But this is only one among many instances in our law in which public charges instead of being levied upon affluence are laid upon distress. The taxes upon Low Proceedings, laid as they are upon both parties, before it is known which is the oppressed and which is the oppressor, falls under the same censure." RP MSS 141/63: 2. It appears as the final paragraph of the parallel chapter of Dumont's edition. Bentham, *Théorie des peines*, vol. I, p. 171.

BOOK II, CHAPTER VI

377. This chapter appears as the fifth chapter of the second book of Dumont's edition. Ibid., pp. 144–67.

378. The manuscript from the beginning of this chapter is missing.

379. The beginning of the trend toward reformation of the penal law in this respect (especially away from transportation and wide application of capital punishment) was prompted, in part, by the growth of similar attitudes among jurists, politicians, and the public in general, as recounted in J. M. Beattie, *Crimes and the Court in England, 1660–1800* (Princeton: Princeton University Press, 1986), pp. 538–48.

380. Dumont's edition refers more specifically to "profit," rather than "frugality," within this parallel item. Bentham, *Théorie des peines*, vol. I, p. 144.

381. Bentham's approach to the subject of imprisonment was preoccupied with this particular characteristic, particularly within the context of poor relief as a more useful alternative and his proposals concerning the National Charity Company and, later, Panopticon prison, as emphasized in Charles F. Bahmueller, *The National Charity Company: Jeremy Bentham's Silent Revolution* (Berkeley: University of California Press, 1981), pp. 1–33.

382. The chapter which this referred note cites as "Book V, ch. 3" is identified in a previous draft as "Ch. XII." Back of 141/123: 4.

383. It has been argued that Bentham differed from his disciples, especially beginning in the 1830s, in terms of his emphasis upon the "sociological salvation" of prisoners, rather than his disciples emphasis upon deterrence of crime. Robert Alan Cooper, "Jeremy Bentham, Elizabeth Fry, and English Prison Reform," *Journal of the History of Ideas* 42, no. 4 (October 1981): 675–81, thus contributing to some of the purported contrasts in tone, especially within sections (such as this one) in which the original manuscript appears to have been missing and *lacunae* may have been necessary.

384. The manuscript resumes at this point. A note on the folder identifies the manuscript for this chapter as being in Bentham's handwriting.

385. Dumont's edition uses the words "ignorant" and "gross" in place of "clownish" at this parallel point of the text. Bentham, *Théorie des peines*, vol. I, p. 146.

386. Dumont's edition adds headings at the beginning of the paragraphs beginning each enumerated item. Ibid., vol. I, p. 147.

387. Prevention was the principal end of punishment for Bentham and its exemplary nature (including in terms of imprisonment) was particularly important toward achieving that end. However, his disciples (arguably influenced by Beccaria in this respect) were more inclined toward other methods of prevention in this respect, rather than using punishment, itself, as an "exemplary" method. Donald Clark Hodges, "Punishment," *Philosophy and Phenomenological Research*, no. 2 (December 1957): 212–14. It may be significant, therefore, that the manuscript for this chapter, which stresses the relative benefits of imprisonment toward achieving utilitarian goals, is in Bentham's handwriting with less opportunity for *lacunae* upon the part of his disciples, Dumont and Smith, until the end of this chapter within Dumont's edition.

388. The phrases "the lowest understanding" and "every degree of" were written within the manuscript and crossed-out, finally replaced with the words "all ages." RP MSS 141/65: 2. Dumont's edition phrases this point of the text as "all degrees of intelligence and all ages." Bentham, *Théorie des peines*, vol. I, p. 147.

389. The manuscript originally used the word "punishment" instead of "suffering." RP MSS 141/65: 2. Dumont's edition uses the word "penal" at this point of the text. Bentham, *Théorie des peines*, vol. I, p. 148.

390. Dumont's edition does not use an adjective with the word "diet." Ibid.

391. The following sentences originally were written at the end of this paragraph within the manuscript: "The distinguishing excellence of this group of punishments of the 1st, 2nd, and 3rd is their subserviency to reformation. They may be all comprised with sufficient merit under these three particular appellations: Solitude, Darkness, and Hard Diet." RP MSS 141/66: 2.

392. A note was added to the manuscript (with a reference to this point) that subsequently was not included within the text of either Smith's edition or Dumont's edition: "III— For the purpose of general example of prevention when the design is by means of a certain quantity of pain to make an impression on men who have not experienced it a pain of one quality may be preferable to the same quantity of pain of another quality: in [indecipherable] the first by an equal quantity of real pain may produce more apparent. But that is not the case. It is the real pain that is to do the business. The [indecipherable] knows precisely what it is for [indecipherable] experienced it." Ibid.

393. The following sentences were included at this point in the manuscript but, subsequently, omitted from the published text: "Before any time has been given for reflection to [indecipherable] and cement the idea of the goals to that of the punishment. For the idea of the punishment to be firmly connected to that of the guilt which gave occasion to it requires a certain time of leisure during which the mind may be continually occupied in holding them up to view as it were at once speaking from the one of them to the other. But where whipping only is the punishment no such leisure time presents itself. Indeed, as some of the anguish is over a new emotion presents itself from opposite to the sensation it succeeds but still less favorable to that state of calm reflection which is requisite to give a firm union to the two ideas above spoken of which is the object to produce." Ibid., 141/66–67: 2.

394. The additional phrase "and within the narrow space of a chamber in a prison," originally was included within the manuscript. Ibid., 141/67: 2.

395. This sentence does not appear within Dumont's edition, Bentham. *Théorie des peines*, vol. I, p. 150.

396. The following sentence was begun, at the end of this paragraph, within the manuscript and discontinued at the bottom of the manuscript page: "Among the foremost of these, as being the most nearly related to that of his personal suffering will be the idea of that obvious passage in his conduct . . ." RP MSS 141/67: 2.

397. The manuscript is missing at this point.

398. The manuscript resumes at this point.

399. Dumont's edition adds an additional paragraph at this parallel point within the text: "If a minister of religion, upon this auspicious situation, comes bearing books of religious instruction to a humble and dispirited convict, the success is all the more certain that, in that state of abandonment, he will be presented as the only friend in his unhappiness, and will appear always as a benefactor." Bentham, *Théorie des peines*, vol. I, pp. 152–53.

400. Dumont's edition uses the word "discipline" instead of "punishment" at this point of the text. Ibid., p. 153.

401. However, under his scheme for Panopticon, Bentham would regard solitary confinement as unnecessary to achieve these ends under its system of close and perpetual scrutiny and inspection. Halévy, pp. 83–85.

402. However, some critics would charge that Bentham's approach, contrary to the paternalistic tone of this passage, was designed to advance "the greatest misery of the few." Gertrude Himmelfarb, *Victorian Minds* (New York: Knopf, 1968), pp. 76–77.

403. A previous draft of the manuscript includes the following sentence at a similar point in the text: "And the tendency can never be represented under a more popular and engaging character, than that of a parent watching with equal anxiety over all her children—consulting the happiness of the offender as much as that of the offended." Back of 141/124: 4.

404. Another sentence originally was included within the manuscript at this point: "The principal reason of this subject is that of economy." Ibid., 141/69: 2. This sentence appears within Dumont's edition. Bentham, *Théorie des peines*, vol. I, p. 155.

405. Versions of these five previous paragraphs appear within Dumont's edition but they are placed within a different order. Ibid., p. 154–56.

406. The manuscript is missing at this point.

407. The manuscript resumes at this point.

408. The manuscript is missing at this point.

409. The manuscript resumes at this point to the end of the chapter.

410. A previous draft of this section of the chapter can be found on the back of RP MSS 141/74: 2.

411. The words *"moral sanction"* originally were capitalized within the manuscript. Ibid., as it is within Dumont's edition. Bentham, *Théorie des peines*, vol. I, p. 160.

412. Dumont's edition begins this parallel paragraph with a different sentence: "The *moral sanction* is founded upon the public tribunal." Ibid.

413. The words *"honour"* and *thieves"* originally were capitalized within the manuscript. RP MSS 141/73: 2.

414. A prior draft of this entire chapter that is similar (especially in terms of these final sections) to the final published text can be found on the back of Ibid. 141/70–75: 2.

415. The words *"school"* and *"vice"* originally were capitalized within the manuscript. Ibid.,S 141/75: 2. Dumont's edition uses the phrase "school of perversity." Bentham, *Théorie des peines*, vol. I, p. 165.

416. A previous draft of this chapter particularly emphasized the enumeration of these characteristics, such as "4. *Variability.* In respect to duration . . . 5. Exemplarity: In respect of exemplarity, under the actual system of imprisonment, the advantages . . . are very inconsiderable." Back of RP MSS 141/68: 2.

Dumont's edition does not end this parallel chapter with this paragraph. The final three paragraphs of that chapter do not find an equivalent within the manuscripts or Smith's edition:

Perhaps it will be said that dishonest people always seek those who resemble them and who in prison, or out of prison, always will live in bad company.

Let us observe, initially, that it is not exactly true. That a dishonest person prefers to live with dishonest people does not prevent a thousand incidents that bring him closer to honest people, who at least point out to him the concepts of justice and virtue. In the most common conversations, he hears the judgments that one relates to dishonest actions and the contempt that one has for these rascals. If he does not receive moral lessons from the church, he will receive them in some village tavern.

In this world, there is a mixture of good and evil; but in prison, all of society is composed of more or less damaged individuals. It is still so for the most dangerous man. What will it be for the class of prisoners who were brought there for a first offense? They yielded to the temptation of indigence; they were drawn by a bad example; they are still at an impressionable age when the heart is not hardened by evil. A well managed punishment has been salutary to them. If, instead of reforming themselves, they become more vicious, if they pass from small rogues to great thieves, if they proceed to armed robbery and assassination—that is an indictment of prison education." Bentham, *Théorie des peines*, vol. I, pp. 166–67.

BOOK II, CHAPTER VII

417. The folder indicates that the manuscript for this chapter was written in Bentham's handwriting.

418. Recommendations for prison reform that reflected the spirit of this chapter had been advanced with particular success by John Howard and other reformers at the same time that Bentham was writing this original manuscript. An account and evaluation of these activities and reforms is provided in Robert Alan Cooper, "Ideas and their Execution: English Prison Reform," *Eighteenth Century Studies* 10, no. 1 (Autumn 1976): 73–93.

419. The word "punishment" originally was used instead of "imprisonment" and, then, replaced within the manuscript. RP MSS 141/76: 2.

420. The phrase "class of prisons" originally appeared within the manuscript and, then, was replaced with the phrase "kind of imprisonment." Ibid. The parallel phrase within Dumont's edition is closer in meaning to this omitted phrasing within the manuscript. Bentham, *Théorie des peines*, vol. I, p. 173.

421. Dumont's edition adds a paragraph at this point to which a parallel is not found within the manuscript:

> The end of their stay, the final week or the final month must be marked by a diet of penitence—solitude, darkness, bitter bread. It is important that the last impression be of sadness and gloom. An infamous mark is covenable in this prison, but only a temporary mark. It would be good toward two ends—*example*, joining much of apparent punishment—*surity*, as in the tendency to prevent evasion." Ibid., pp. 173–74.

422. A version of this final sentence of this paragraph does not appear within Dumont's edition. Ibid., p. 174.

Similar recommendations for distinctive forms of imprisonment to reflect different categories of crime were being proposed during the same period that Bentham was writing the manuscript for this chapter, as discussed in Ursula R. Q. Henriques, "The Rise and Decline of the Separate System of Prison Discipline," *Past and Present* 54 (February 1972): 61–93.

423. Dumont's edition identifies the prisons that conduct this practice as existing throughout Europe. Bentham, *Théorie des peines*, vol. I, p. 174.

424. This line of argument would be pursued from a more strictly medical perspective, beginning in the nineteenth century, as demonstrated in William A. Guy, "On Sufficient and Insufficient Dietaries, with Special Reference to the Dietaries of Prisoners," *Journal of the Statistical Society of London* 26, no. 3 (September 1863): 239–80.

425. The manuscript originally included the following sentence at this point: "Nothing could be farther that this [indecipherable] from a violation of the wills of the benefactor." RP MSS 141/76: 2.

426. Dumont's edition phrases this paragraph somewhat differently, concluding it with the sentence "Necessity must be provided by the state; more than necessity, it does nothing. The deficit is shocking, the superfluous is injurious." Bentham, *Théorie des peines*, vol. I, p. 175. Again, the tone of Dumont's translation suggests more than a strict utilitarian calculation.

427. The margins of the manuscript included, at this general point, the note "Prisoners to be prevented from spending money." RP MSS 141/76: 2.

428. The words "except in certain cases" originally were added to the manuscript at this point. Ibid., 141/77: 2.

429. The following sentence originally was added to the end of this paragraph within the manuscript: "This makes a distinction between the treatment which is proper to be given

to this belief in the case where the profit of the crime has been reaped, and that which is proper to be given to other persons." Ibid. A version of this sentence appears at this parallel point within Dumont's edition. Bentham, *Théorie des peines*, vol. I, pp. 176–77.

Accounts of these contrasts in prison conditions, in which the poor suffered more greatly than more affluent convicts, are provided in Sidney Webb and Beatrice Potter Webb, *English Prisons under Local Government* (London: F. Cass, 1963), pp. 22–48.

430. The manuscript is missing at this point.

431. The manuscript resumes from this point to the end of the chapter.

432. This last section of the manuscript of this chapter originally included the following, eventually crossed-out, text:

> Let the offenses be distinguished into three classes according to the three prisons. Offenses of the highest class may be termed Capital Felonies; those of the 2nd, Simple or second-rate Felonies: those of the lowest Misdemeanors. These denominations are not calculated to express any thing of the nature of the offense; they only serve to characterize the quantity and quality of the punishment.
>
> In the Black Prison a pair of Skeletons, one of each side of the gate (in whither the inner or outer gate), the one with the garment of a man; the other with that of a woman. They should be secured by a close grating to secure them from external injuries.
>
> Three prisons—Black, Grey, and White. The House of Confinement for Debtors to be called the Security House.
>
> Black Wash.
>
> Wormswood Head.
>
> Music previous to Execution. Dead March [indecipherable] or other and the most gloomy that can be found," RP MSS 141/78: 2.

BOOK II, CHAPTER VIII

433. A previous version of this chapter heading was phrased: "Territorial Confinement: Territorial Confinement Regulation and Banishment are none of them any more than Simple Imprisonment convertible to Profit" followed by the note that appears later in the final published version of this chapter, which begins with the words "instances of definite banishment are . . ." Ibid., 141/80: 2.

434. A note on the folder indicates that the manuscript for this chapter is in Bentham's handwriting.

435. Dumont's edition adds a note at this point: "Local interdiction naturally is related as the chief—but when it is ordinarily restricted to privations of some employment, it will be related under the *Simply Reflective Pains*." Bentham, *Théorie des peines*, vol. I, p. 181.

436. That distinction between transportation and banishment has been noted by other scholars, especially when contrasting English law, in this respect, with the practice in other countries, especially Latin America. Robert G. Caldwell, "Exile as an Institution," *Political Science Quarterly* 58, no. 2 (June 1943): 239–62.

437. This specific argument had been advanced, during the seventeenth century, by Lord Coke. Its application to the Jews and a rejection of the argument that such policies did not represent *de facto* banishment are presented in Ursula R. Q. Henriques, *The Jews and the English Law* (London: A. M. Kelley, 1974), pp. 58–63. It is curious that Bentham appeared to accept this position so uncritically.

438. Dumont's edition emphasizes this word in italics. Bentham, *Théorie des peines*, vol. I, p. 183.

439. The manuscript is missing at this point. As already noted in endnote 1 of this chapter, the note which is indicated at this point (RP MSS 141/79: 2) actually appears at another location (Ibid., 141/80: 2) within the manuscript for this chapter. Dumont's edition emphasizes the words "definite" and "indefinite" and does not include the Latin phrase in this description. Bentham, *Théorie des peines*, vol. I, p. 183.

440. Dumont's edition adds the following paragraph at this parallel point of this chapter: "For the rest, definite banishment cannot take place under very particular circumstances; in general, when one banishes a malefactor, it is for getting rid of him, and one hardly cares what becomes of him." Ibid., vol. I, p. 184.

441. Dumont's edition uses the word "banishment" in these cases without modifying it with the word "territorial," such as at Ibid., vol. I, p. 185.

442. This name refers to the Talibu people of Hyderabad in India.

443. The manuscript resumes at this point. Dumont's edition inserts a subheading, Ibid., vol. I, p. 189. Dumont's edition enumerates the following principal paragraphs. Bentham, Ibid., vol. I, pp. 189–91.

444. This paragraph and the note that is found at the end of it are not found within Dumont's edition.

445. The manuscript originally used the word "Quasi-Imprisonment" at this point but, then, replaced it with the phrase "To be confined to within the circuit of a small town." RP MSS 141/80: 2.

446. The previous three paragraphs do not appear within Dumont's edition.

447. Sir William Blackstone categorically disapproved of exile as being contrary to the traditions of the English common law, while some utilitarian arguments could be advanced which were more accepting in terms of the greater happiness of the community regarding the presence or absence of a particular person. Frederick G. Whelan, "Citizenship and the Right to Leave," *American Political Science Review* 75, no. 3 (September 1981): 644–46.

448. Instead of "*means*," the manuscript originally used, then crossed-out, the word "motives," without emphasis added, at this point. RP MSS 141/82: 2.

449. The manuscript originally began this sentence with the words "The tavern he used to drink at or the strumpet he used to cohabit with" but replaced it with the words "The company he meets with in the new scene he enters upon." Ibid.

450. Originally, the manuscript began, then omitted, this section with the following sentences:

> Banishment is apt to be rather more serviceable than Relegation. This is principally owing to the greater chance there is that the language of the foreign nation he is thrown into by Banishment should be stranger to him, than that of the province he is thrown into by Relegation. This circumstance would increase the difficulty he would be under in acquiring the confidence (above spoken of) necessary among partners in iniquity. The laws too of the foreign country being new to him, may on that account be more formidable to him than his nation's laws which perhaps he had been accustomed to evade." Ibid.

Furthermore, after the word "may" in the last sentence, the words "shock him with greater terror" were originally inserted at this point of the manuscript and, also, crossed-out.

451. Dumont's edition adds an additional paragraph at this parallel point of the chapter:

It follows from this examination that one finds little in the case of banishment to be decent. In certain political misdemeanors, of a rather doubtful nature, one can employ a like method of breaking relations with the delinquent, and of distancing him from the scene of intrigue and factions. He will do similarly in the case of leaving him the hope of returning, like a pledge of good conduct during his removal. Bentham, *Théorie des peines*, vol. I, p. 193.

452. At the end of the manuscript for this chapter, an assessment of Cesare Beccaria's treatment of the subject of banishment is begun but quickly abandoned. RP MSS 141/82: 2. Dumont's edition does add a sentence to that effect: "All of these reflections are exhausted in Becarria. It seems he had wanted banishment to be a universal punishment for all delinquents—*Treatise on Delinquents and Punishments*, chapt. VII." Bentham, *Théorie des peines*, vol. I, p. 193.

BOOK II, CHAPTER IX

453. A previous manuscript draft of this chapter can be found on the back of RP MSS 141/83–84: 2.

454. The manuscript for this chapter reverts to the handwriting of Richard Smith.

455. The manuscript originally referred to "lower grades" and, then, changed it to the word "examinations." Ibid., 141/83: 2.

456. During the period of Bentham's initial composition of this manuscript, the French government often engaged in particularly punitive disbarment practices against legal professionals that reflect this observations. David A. Bell, "Lawyers into Demagogues: Chancellor Maupeou and the Transformation of Legal Practice in France, 1771–1789," *Past and Present* 130 (February 1991): 114, 131–33.

457. A version of this paragraph does not appear within Dumont's edition.

458. Another crossed-out manuscript paragraph begins after the end of this sentence and continuing to the bottom of the page: It is not necessary that Banishment . . ." RP MSS 141/84: 2. It appears to offer an alternative drafting of the paragraph that follows this one within the text.

459. The manuscript is missing at this point through the end of the chapter.

460. A similar rationale was offered for excluding persons who refused to take a loyalty oath or who were, otherwise, suspected of being communists from assuming certain professional positions, such as professorships. Sidney Hook, "Academic Manners and Morals," *Journal of Higher Education* 23, no. 6 (June 1952): 323–26.

461. This opposition to religious tests and professional restrictions would be pursued with even more intellectual force by John Stuart Mill, as noted in Bernard Wishy, "Introduction," in John Stuart Mill, *Selected Writings of John Stuart Mill*, Bernard Wishy, ed. (Boston: Beacon Press, 1959), pp. i–x, 18.

462. A couple of sentences from a previous draft, beginning an apparently alternative section of this chapter, provide an intriguing reference to religious influence in this area: "Considerations arising from the *Religious Sanction* are the sufferings apprehended from the immediate will of the Deity either in the present or a future life or in both. Religious threats (particularly Protestant) may work on the greater number of criminals and particularly of the raw and inexperienced the conception of religion are rather forgotten than effaced." Back of RP MSS 141/83: 2.

BOOK II, CHAPTER X

463. A previous draft of this chapter, very similar in tone to the final manuscript version, can be found on the back of Ibid., 141/84–86: 2.

464. The manuscript for this chapter is identified by the folder as being in Bentham's handwriting.

465. Dumont's edition specifies such acts as being "repugnant." Bentham, *Théorie des peines*, vol. I, p. 202.

466. A similar sentiment (though apparently not inspired by Bentham's utilitarian arguments) accompanied the adoption of the Penitentiary Act of 1779 that would seek to displace the wide application of capital punishment with institutionalized hard labor, although the actual act, as finally passed, fell well short of those aspirations. Simon Devereaux, "The Making of the Penitentiary Act, 1775–1779," *The Historical Journal* 42, no. 2 (June 1999): 405–33.

467. The manuscript is missing at this point.

468. Versions of the previous eight paragraphs are not found within Dumont's edition. Instead, the following paragraph appears at the parallel point of this chapter:

> This method of punishment is distinguished from all others by a remarkable circumstance. The retribution is not inflicted by a foreign hand: the delinquent punishes himself. It requires the assistance of his will: but what determines that will is a much greater punishment with which one is menaced and one avoids only in overcoming the first—See *Subsidiary Punishments*, chap. XV.

The chapter that is cited does not appear within Smith's edition. Bentham, *Théorie des peines*, vol. I, p. 205.

469. The manuscript resumes at this point.

470. Dumont's edition specifies the example of HMS *Botany Bay*. Ibid., p. 206. Dumont's edition adds an explanatory paragraph at this parallel point of the chapter:

> Active punishments are not only a constraint upon doing what one would not want: it is also an impediment upon doing what one wants: these two parts of punishment are inseparable. The net value of pleasure which is lost upon an individual by a forced occupation is equal to the sum of all the pleasures which he would procure in a state of liberty." Ibid., pp. 206–207.

471. Dumont's edition treats this parallel part of this chapter as a separate section. It is identified by the title: "Second Section: An Examination of Active Punishments." Ibid., p. 207.

472. This apparent affection for this category of punishment is consistent with a non-liberal interpretation of Bentham's utilitarianism as an effort to affect individual behavior and personality through control and constraint that is advanced in Long, ch. 10, and Lea Campos Boralevi, *Bentham and the Oppressed* (Berlin: Walter de Gruyter, 1984), pp. 96–100. That non-liberal interpretation is countered by a liberal revisionist account of Bentham that reconciles utilitarian thought with principles of freedom and individual self-development that do not require the sort of constraint and compulsion that is represented by laborious imprisonment, Paul J. Kelly, "Utilitarianism and Distributive Justice: The Civil Law and the Foundations of Bentham's Economic Thought," *Utilitas* 1, no. 1 (May 1989): 88–95.

473. Dumont's edition does not enumerate this paragraph. Bentham, *Théorie des peines*, vol. I, p. 208.

474. The manuscript originally inserted, then crossed-out, the passage: "these expenses are to be set against the profit in comparing the complex punishment of Imprisonment coupled with hard labour to any other punishments." RP MSS 141/87: 2.

475. Dumont's edition numbers this paragraph as "3." Bentham, *Théorie des peines*, vol. I, p. 208.

476. Dumont's translation of "subserviency to reform" is, literally, "tendency toward moral reform" Ibid., p. 210.

477. The manuscript originally used the word "expected" before replacing it with "insisted." RP MSS 141/88: 2.

478. The manuscript originally used the phrase "serves to occupy" before replacing it with "confines." Ibid.

479. Dumont's version of this paragraph offers similar descriptions and arguments but in a different manner. For example, stress is placed upon the danger posed by these situations in creating a "school of perversity" and the benefit that "the principal fruit of this discipline is the acquisition of salutary habits." Bentham, *Théorie des peines*, vol. I, pp. 210–11.

480. The manuscript originally used the phrase "free up the mode of corruption altogether," replacing it with "pluck up corruption by the roots." RP MSS 141/89: 2.

481. The manuscript originally used the phrase "persons appointed for that purpose" and, then, replaced it with the noun "overseers." Ibid.

482. Versions of the preceding two paragraphs do not appear within Dumont's edition.

483. This paragraph is enumerated as item number "6" within Dumont's edition. Bentham, *Théorie des peines*, vol. I, p. 211.

484. The manuscript originally inserted, then crossed-out, the following sentences at this point: "In giving an account of this punishment as applicable to those crimes, the punishment one may say consists in there being subject to the law a hardship [indecipherable] by the prospect of the punishment that awaits him, the like hardship or rather portended hardship similar to like that to avoid which they plunged into delinquency. This punishment in this account [indecipherable] which in prospect to appear the heavier to them: and to others an account of their play of words and ideas, in some degree the more just." RP MSS 141/89: 2.

485. A version of the preceding paragraph does not appear within this chapter of Dumont's edition. It is possible that he deferred all mention of it to a separate chapter, as suggested by the last sentence of this paragraph. The manuscript is missing from this point through the end of the chapter.

BOOK II, CHAPTER XI

486. This chapter is missing from the manuscript. It appears as chapter 13 of the second book within Dumont's edition. Bentham, *Théorie des peines*, vol. I, pp. 269–81.

487. Dumont's edition identifies this method of strangulation (apparently use of the garrote) with a common execution in Turkey, followed by a note that indicates "It is in that place the honorable execution, such as decapitation among us." Ibid, p. 270.

488. This criticism of afflictive capital punishment contrasts with the claim that brutal capital punishment, performed in a conspicuous manner and for the purported good of the community may be (and, arguably, has been) justified by utilitarian principles, as advanced (especially in contrast with retributivist interpretations of punishment) in Igor Primoratz, *Justifying Legal Punishment* (Atlantic Highlands, NJ: Humanities Press International, 1989), pp. 44–50.

489. Dumont's edition adds a note at this point:

Everyone knows the reasons for abolishing this category of death among Christian nations. *Felix culpa*, we would say, along with a father of the Church, in another sense, if the same reasoning had been used to abolish all other cruel tortures. The exposition of ferocious animals is one which the Gospels well sought to destroy. It was sustained under the Christian emperors. Valentinian would throw criminals into the pit of two bears, which, by a barbarian derision, was given the name of Scrap of Gold and of Innocence: and even to reward the services of one of these animals, when in contemplation of this ferocious appetite, he would set it at liberty in the forest. *Gibbon*, vol. IV, chap. XXV." Bentham, *Théorie des peines*, vol. I, p. 272.

490. This suggestion that the relationship between the death penalty and cruelty (including in terms of torture) could, when juxtaposed, promote a social aversion toward both, including from a utilitarian perspective, is explored in Jeffrey H. Reiman, "Justice, Civilization, and the Death Penalty: Answering van den Haag, *Philosophy and Public Affairs* 14, no. 2 (Spring 1985): 134–42.

491. A version of this sentence does not appear within Dumont's edition.

492. Dumont's edition provides a note at this parallel point within this chapter:

This is a work cited by Mallebranche. (*Recherche de la vérité*, book II, chap. VII.)

Around seven or eight ago one could have seen, at the Incurables, a young man who was born insane, whose body had been broken in the same places in which one broke criminals. He lived nearly twenty years in that state: several people saw him there, and the late Queen Mother, having gone to visit the hospital, had been curious to see him, and even to touch the arms and legs of this young man at the places which had been fractured. According to the principles I have just established, the cause of this disastrous accident was that his mother, seeing how one broke a criminal, was content to see it carried out. All the blows inflicted upon this poor wretch, struck with imaginative force by this mother, and consequently upon the tender and delicate brain of this child, etc. Bentham, *Théorie des peines*, vol. I, p. 275.

493. A good assessment of Montaigne's beliefs in this area is provided in David Lewis Schaefer, "The Good, the Beautiful, and the Useful: Montaigne's Transvaluation of Values," *American Political Science Review* 73, no. 1 (March 1979): 139–54.

494. Dumont's edition does not specify the West Indies but only the European colonial "eastern islands." Bentham, *Théorie des peines*, vol. I, p. 278.

495. Dumont's edition specifies thirty thousand persons at this parallel point of the paragraph. Ibid., pp. 279–80.

BOOK II, CHAPTER XII

496. The manuscript is missing for the first section and part of the second section of the chapter. It appears as chapter XIV of the second book of Dumont's edition. Ibid., pp. 282–316.

497. Dumont's edition uses the word *frelon*, referring literally to a hornet, rather than the word *bourdon*, which is closer to the literal noun "drove." Ibid., p. 287. It is a minor discrepancy (and there are numerous discrepancies of this nature between the French and English texts) but it offers an interesting insight into the difficulties of translation regarding such manuscripts and texts, especially when the style of the original author is so elaborate and, frequently, pedantic.

498. Smith's edition identifies this subjection also as being "2" in an apparent typographical error.

499. The manuscript resumes that this point, reportedly in Bentham's handwriting.

500. The manuscript originally used the phrase "but on the contrary," followed by the phrase "the balance appears to be on the other side. These words were all crossed-out and replaced with the phrase "much more if there." RP MSS 141/90: 2.

501. In the manuscript, "0" is crossed-out and the note referring to it also is absent. Ibid. Dumont's edition refers to the word *nulle* at this parallel point. Bentham, *Théorie des peines*, vol. I, p. 288.

502. The manuscript originally began this sentence with the phrase "Seduced by the charm of indolence" but substituted "Rendered averse to labour by natural indolence" for it. RP MSS 141/91: 2. Dumont's edition uses the phrase "their existence is only one deplorable composite of many kinds of misery" at this parallel point of the text. Bentham, *Théorie des peines*, vol. I, pp. 288–89.

503. It has been argued that Bentham believed that justice generally was denied to the poor as a class, which is a factor that would explain the imposition of the death penalty for petty theft but not, necessarily, for other, more serious (especially non-property related) offenses. Harrison, *Bentham*, pp. 200–201. Such an attitude suggests a potential sympathy for the underlying goals (though not the means) of the French Revolution—a perspective that may have been particularly held by Dumont.

504. The manuscript is missing at this point.

505. The manuscript resumes at this point.

506. The manuscript originally extended this paragraph with an additional sentence: "So again the Emperor Nero to whom a pair of friends or lovers die together, it is common enough for them to receive from the hand of each other this last of all kind offices." RP MSS 141/92: 2.

507. Dumont's edition adds, at this parallel point, the sentence "Avarice is certainly the proof." Bentham, *Théorie des peines*, vol. I, p. 292.

508. The manuscript initially included, then omitted, at the end of this sentence a colon, followed by the phrase: "suffer rather than die is their motto." RP MSS 141/92: 2.

509. The manuscript is missing from this point through the end of the chapter.

510. As occurs in similar passages, Dumont's edition uses the term "inequality" to represent "variability," with a consequent emphasis upon the quality of modification that can make a punishment equitable. Bentham, *Théorie des peines*, vol. I, p. 293.
This characteristic appears to receive more consideration than other ones within this utilitarian assessment of capital punishment, which has been criticized because of an apparent lack of specific justification for giving greater weight to this characteristic than other ones that would be more favorably inclined (such as efficacy) toward the death penalty from a utilitarian perspective. Hugo Adam Bedau, "Bentham's Utilitarian Critique of the Death Penalty," *Journal of Criminal Law and Criminology* 74, no. 3 (1983): 1033–65. In the absence of Bentham's original manuscript, it is arguable that this stronger emphasis may be a result of editorial contributions (or, even, *lacunae*) by Dumont and Smith.

511. Dumont's edition inserts a different note at this parallel point:

Have you not known that we have been subject to an affliction more so than other men,'" said an assassin on the wheel to his companion in torture, who incited his cries.—*Tableau de Paris, by Mercier.* Bentham, *Théorie des peines*, vol. I, p. 293.

512. This sentence appears as a section title within Dumont's edition Ibid., p. 294.

513. This particular assessment reflects the later debate regarding "rule" and "act" util-

itarianism. It is not clear whether Bentham (or Dumont, Smith, and other second-generation disciples) were disinclined toward the penalty of death or, merely, its selective imposition. The proposition that capital punishment should be eliminated as a formal rule in the form of penal law, despite the fact that some particular instances of its greater utility could be determined, as opposed to an opposing proposition addressing its imposition (presumably by judges and legislators applying utilitarian reason) on a case-by-case basis does not appear to be resolved by this particular assessment. Indeed, whether this general treatise advances one perspective or the other one, in this respect, does not appear to be absolutely discernible. This broad and ongoing theoretical controversy is well framed in J. C. C. Smart, *Freedom and Reason* (New York: Oxford University Press, 1965), pp. 130–36; Donald C. Emmons, "Act vs. Rule Utilitarianism," *Mind* 82, no. 326 (April 1973): 226–33, and H. J. McCloskey, "A Note on Utilitarian Punishment," *Mind* 72, no. 288 (October 1963): 599.

514. This particular passage does appear to suggest that the death penalty ought to be eliminated as part of a "rule utilitarian" approach. That historical context and the political struggle against capital punishment on the part of Bentham is examined in James E. Crimmins, "Bentham's Political Radicalism Reexamined," *Journal of the History of Ideas* 55, no. 2 (April 1994): 277–78.

515. At this parallel point of Dumont's edition, the following paragraphs and note are added:

> One must arrange under the same heading another drawback, resulting from capital punishment, in the administration of justice: know, *the destruction of a source of testimonial proof.* The archives of crime is part of the memory of malefactors. With them perish all information that they possess in relation to other crimes and their accomplices. It is an impunity accorded to all those who could be detected or convinced only by the deceased: and innocence will be oppressed and good law will be incapable of being reached through the suppression of essential evidence.
>
> During the instruction of the criminal process, accomplices of the accused hide or run away: it is an interval of tribulation and agony: the sword is suspended over their head. Is that career finished? It is for them an act of jubilation and grace; they have a new lease on security, they march with raised heads. Fidelity is defunct for their companions and exalted like a virtue, and received, among them, for instruction of their young disciples, all the praises of heroism.
>
> During the time in prison, this heroism will be submitted to a more dangerous approval than the interrogation of the tribunal. Left to himself, separated from his accomplices, the delinquent soon ceases to be sensitive to this sort of honor which is associated with them. They will not have a moment from repenting to tear revelations from him: and similarly, without repenting, which is more natural than a desire for vengeance against those who conduct him to the loss of his freedom, and who, also culpable like himself, continues to play to them! He only needs to listen to his interest in buying, at the price of information, a lessening of his punishment.[1]
>
> [1] Like the example of these documents that one could find in a prison, I would cite a deed that I heard related in France. After an extraordinarily strong theft, committed in Lyon in 1780 or there about, the police, who could not obtain any information of the author of this offense, advised by an informer to Bicêtre an excuse to be disguised as a prisoner: he played his role well, he lively interested his audience by the recounting of his exploits in detail. Among this assembly were practitioners of crime, one

of whom exclaimed: *It is only Phillipe who could achieve such a great blow!* It was a luminous trait. This Phillipe was the leader of the plot; but he had taken measures to assure the flight of this prey." Bentham, *Théorie des peines*, vol. I, pp. 300–301.

516. This passage suggests a willingness to consider an act-utilitarian justification for applying the death penalty in selective cases, a general position attributed to Bentham (and criticized) in P. H. Nowell-Smith, "On Sanctioning Excuses," *The Journal of Philosophy* 67, no. 18 (September 1970): 610–12. A more general critique of act-utilitarian rationales of making exceptions (particularly within the context of Bentham's theory of punishment, including capital punishment) regarding the application of punishment is provided in David Lyons, "On Sanctioning Excuses," *Journal of Philosophy* 66, no. 19 (October 1969): 646–60.

517. Bentham and his disciples have been criticized as being naïve in holding this belief that the popularity of punishment would decline in the presence of the increased presence and application of reason within society because, it has been argued, this belief ignores the strong influence of vindictiveness within human motivation and toward a retributivist approach toward punishment in general, Bedau. "Bentham's Utilitarian Critique of the Death Penalty," p. 1043.

518. Dumont's edition includes the following note at this parallel point: "*History of the Penal Laws Against the Irish Catholics*, by H. Parnell, Esq." Bentham, *Théorie des peines*, vol. I, p. 307.

519. Again, this claim is not supported but merely asserted. In fact, in a report on the decline in crime in France at the end of the nineteenth century claimed that sentimentality, rather than reason, was more responsible for a decline in the imposition of the death penalty within that country. Note, "Criminality in France in 1895," *American Journal of Sociology* 4, no. 6 (May 1899): 847.

520. One possible exception, in this respect, is genocide, as argued (with a passing reference to this utilitarian approach, especially regarding a consequentialist justification) in Jens David Ohlin, "Applying the Death Penalty to Crimes of Genocide," *American Journal of International Law* 99, no. 4 (October 2005): 766.

521. Dumont's edition precedes the text of this parallel section of this chapter with a note:

At the moment when I was sending this article to the printer, I perceived that this subject does not benefit from innovation, and I am restricted to exposing its contents. It all relates to British jurisprudence." Bentham, *Théorie des peines*, vol. I, p. 309.

522. Dumont's edition continues this chapter with the following observations, followed by a contrasting table, none of which are found within Smith's edition. Ibid., pp. 309–16:

It is in the same principles, and somewhat under the same point of view, that Sir Samuel Romilly envisioned within the bills that he proposed, relative to certain minor offenses, for abolishing the death penalty. He always insisted that the non-execution of the law was the principal cause of the frequency of these offenses. He demonstrated that the law cannot be executed, because it has been outcast, not secretly and by a small number, but openly by the whole public: and in consequence of this disapproval, the injured parties, accusers, witnesses, juries, judges, the king himself, among others, discovered this plan of remission; however, one can imagine they were the most favorable to the delinquents, that a method of judicial administration offered them, to each step of this procedure, as many chances of escape from the law as disfavorable ones. But I would not test from recounting the arguments that were provided. Happily, he himself published where he had a summary of all the discourses in the House of Commons [*Observations on the criminal Law of England, as it relates to capital punishments, and on the mode in which it is executed.* 2d. ed., 1811.], and which contains, either for the principles and for the facts, all that is necessary to clarify the question. A similar work would mediate; the form, which is again somewhat like a discourse, carries the lecture too quickly; it is a return to previous reprises, that one feels all that is contained of mediation and experience: but it also is the fruit of a profound attention of a superior man who never lost this point of view, who studied criminal law throughout Europe and observed all the changes that have occurred for the past thirty years. And can one doubt that these comparisons of law, done upon a great ladder, does not provide this spirit more force, more attention than the isolated study of a single jurisprudence? Those who know nothing beyond England are surprised and nearly incredulous when they speak of the rarity of crime in a country where the death penalty is suppressed or reserved for extraordinary cases?

In reporting the bills of Sir Samuel Romilly, the first (abolition of the death penalty for robbery) obtained the approval of the legislature: the second failed, the next year, in the House of Lords. Five other bills of the same type would pass the Commons with an ever increasing majority. Final success is again doubtful. The spirit of reform is not in England a method which removes all. But this slowness of the march of reason is a characteristic of freedom. In a free country, all opinions have a force that they permit to struggle, and do not yield to conviction. How much time and effort did it cost to abolish the traffic in Blacks! Conquests are difficult in a country with many fortresses, but once you have won, you do not lose again. Relative to penal laws, abolished in fact, of which remains nothing more than the specter of defenders who would conserve them, it is sufficient to read the debates of the House of Lords, and particularly the discourse of Lord Lauderdale, Lord Holland, and the Marquis of Lansdowne [See *the Debates upon the bills for abolishing the punishment of death for stealing to the amount of forty shillings in a dwelling house, and of five shillings privately in a shop,* for an analytical tableau of the reasons for and against, published by Basil Montagu, Esq. Mr. Montagu published another very interesting collection: *The Opinions of different Authors on the punishment of death* (London, 1809). It very clearly exposes, in a preface one finds too short, the series of questions relative to this subject.], for predicting that criminal law, treated by men of state, will soon be worthy of figuring within the British Constitution.

"A first effect of these discussions well merits to be remarked. In England and Ireland, many leading manufacturers of textiles and cotton, exposed, by the nature of their work, to great depredations, have united to demand abolition of the death penalty against this category of theft in particular. Their reason is that the severity of the law protects them less well than it protects the malefactors. It does not act anymore than to declaim against rationalists, philosophers, and theorists. Thus are injured men, who feel their loss, who do not consult their interest, who solicit executable and executed laws.

But since one cries paradox, I could best finish in clearly establishing in what the paradox consists: after which nothing could be easier to refute. The refutation is all the same, when two colums of contradictory columns are arranged."

Paradoxical Opinion	*Refutation*
Everything within the law should be clear, and all of its laws should be executed.	Everything does not need to be clear within the law, and all laws need not be executed.
All is well when the law functions, it does not function as much as it is known, and as much as it is executed.	All is well with the working of the law, that it can function without being known and without being executed.
It must be the same for all, that it rules supreme, and the judge cannot be its dispenser and its agent.	It is not necessary that it be the same for all, nor that it rules supreme. The judge should not be prevented from being its dispenser and agent.
If the law determines a punishment that the tribunal habitually inflicts among others—if that law is so odious that the perjurer who evades appears to commit a meritorious act—if it is so disproportionate to the crime, that it requires a habitual palliative in the arbitration of judgments and pardons—the law is evidently vicious: and the more one needs to justify those who prevent its execution the more one condemns the law itself.	It is not necessary that the law be the same for all, nor that it rules supreme. The judge must not be constrained from being a dispensator and agent. The law is evidently good, if it determines a punishment, and the tribunal habitually inflicts it among others—if the same law is odious to the extent that the perjurer who evades appears to commit a meritorious act—if it is so disproportionate to the offense, that one needs a perpetual palliative in the arbitration of judgments and pardons. All of this does not prevent the law from being good: and one can approve of those who prevent its execution, without insinuating the least doubt in the excellence of the same law.

BOOK III, CHAPTER I

523. The manuscript for these first paragraphs of this chapter are missing. A general introduction to the analysis of punishment (apparently in Richard Smith's handwriting) offers an interesting metaphorical explanation of this theme:

I am not ignorant that in making use of the analytic method as a mystic doctrine, is concealing, if I may excuse myself, the anatomy, the muscles, and the nerves, great credit might be gained in respect of facility and brilliancy. In pursuing the analytic method, everything is foretold: the whole is luminous; but no surprises, no flights of the imagination, no flashes of genius which dazzle for one moment and the next and leave you in utter darkness. Great courage is required steadily to pursue so rigid a method: but it is the only one that can ever afford complete satisfaction to the understanding." RP MSS 141/93: 3.

However, another draft specifically identifies different opening paragraphs for this chapter which were, subsequently, crossed-out:

> It is not unusual however to take this method of expressing any modification of active punishments but that above mentioned: it being a much more ready way to speak, in the affirmative way, of the obligation to do a thing, than in the way of double negative: on, by speaking of the loss of the liberty (that is the not having any longer the liberty) of not doing it.
>
> The only case in which it would be natural to use this mode of expression if any such punishments were separately in use is one where men at large are being liable to the obligation not on the score of punishment, but as a *burthen* [an asterisk at this word refers to a margin note that states "see above Chap. I"] which for the purposes of society must be laid on somebody, a particular class of persons of which the party in question is in the way of punishment subjected to it anew. Such is the case in the instances above given. But in this case it is not only more precise but more common to use the word *exemption* or the more general word *privilege*, than the word liberty. Forfeiture of the exemption from serving in the militia: Forfeiture of the privilege of not being made to serve in the Militia.
>
> We are now in a condition to proceed with the Analysis of proper Forfeitures.
>
> To investigate therefore the several possible kinds of proper Forfeitures it is necessary to investigate the several possible kinds of Possessions. On this subject however, as it comes in only collaterally on the present occasion it will not be necessary to insist very minutely." Ibid.

Dumont's edition identifies this chapter with the title: "General Idea of the Book." Bentham, *Théorie des peines*, vol. I, p. 324.

524. Dumont's edition begins the note that appears at this parallel point of this chapter with a general explanatory paragraph:

> The English language has a generic word for these punishments, *forfeitures*. The French word *forfeiture*, which is distinguished by a single letter, and which derives its origin from the same root, does not correspond to the English word. *Forfeiture*, in French, is not the name of a punishment, but it is an offense or a class of offenses. Ibid.

525. This passage relates to Bentham's criticism of the use of "legal fictions" within the law, in which plain meaning and experience is displaced by legal metaphors that, ultimately, distort a reasoned response to legal conflicts and penalties. He makes particularly pointed reference to this practice in Jeremy Bentham, *Rationale of Judicial Evidence*, John Stuart Mill, ed. (London: Hunt and Clarke, 1827), p. 300, and Bentham, *Comment on the Commentaries*, pp. 58–59. This theme is explored in greater detail in Kim Lane Scheppele, "Facing Facts in Legal Interpretation," *Representations* 30 (Spring 1990): 42–77.

526. The manuscript, reportedly in Bentham's handwriting (which is elegantly scripted), begins after this sentence.

527. A Marxist critique of utilitarianism is centered upon this sort of distinction. That critique maintains that utilitarian policies (including civil punishment) treat various manifestations of human interests, efforts, labor, and considerations as mere external means of exchange in the pursuit of pleasure, rather than as an intrinsic expression of their own autonomy. Utilitarians generally counter this objection by noting that this process is a method

of decision making for rational agents and not an end in itself. Michael Green, "Marx, Utility, and Right," *Political Theory* 11, no. 3 (August 1983): 433–36. This chapter appears to confirm that interpretation, especially in terms of its recognition of "possession" as an abstraction (nonetheless, a tangible one that can result in pain or pleasure) that extends beyond legally narrow definitions of forfeitable personal property.

528. The second of these "family conditions" is missing in both the manuscript (RP MSS 141/94: 3) and the published text of the 1830 edition.

529. The manuscript originally used the word "rights" and, then, substituted the word "privileges," although the extent to which this change represented a strict theoretical distinction is not clear. Ibid. Dumont's edition uses the word *droit*, which can be roughly translated either way. Bentham, *Théorie des peines*, vol. I, p. 329.

530. The manuscript originally added the phrase "and of the forfeitures of which those possessions may respectively be the subject" but, then, omitted it. RP MSS 141/94: 3.

531. A note was added to the chapter at this general point but was, later, crossed-out within the manuscript:

I say in a great measure for mere sympathy with a man considered as a being endowed with sensibility and more particularly as a fellow-creature, will, whatever be his ill-deserts be sufficient to ensure to a man in the breasts of most men some small share at least of their good will. This share as far as it is out of the reach of being increased or lessened by his good or ill conduct being a quantity always the same may be all along laid out of the accounts.

As to the distinction there may be between love and esteem there is no need of entering into it upon the present occasion: since those affections unite and become indistinguishable in their eternal effects which are all we are concerned with" Ibid., 141/95: 3.

BOOK III, CHAPTER II

532. The manuscript for this chapter originally began with the words "First then in point of quality. As to the modes . . ." Ibid. Dumont's edition begins its parallel chapter in a similar fashion. Bentham, *Théorie des peines*, vol. I, p. 331.

533. These manuscript pages that appear in Bentham's handwriting include side-bar labels.

534. The manuscript is missing at this point.

535. A draft introduction, in apparently in Bentham's handwriting, was part of an earlier version (dated 1778) of this chapter that was, subsequently, omitted:

"If the several modes of punishment that issue solely from the political sanction we have just finished our account; we now come to the description of those which are referable to the Moral.

"To pursue the same plan throughout we set out upon, and give such an account of this class as shall correspond to the account already given of those which are referable to the former, we must continue to arrange our disquisitions under the same heads we have along adopted. We must accordingly consider, 1. The several kinds into which the punishments of this class may be distributed. 2ly. The evils which these several kinds of punishment are respectively adapted to produce. 3ly The several methods in which they may respectively be inflicted. On all these heads a word or two as we shall see presently will suffice and that for reasons which will presently appear" RP MSS 141/95: 3. This chapter expands upon the theme that was introduced in Bentham, *Morals and Legislation*, ch. 3, para. 10.

536. The manuscript resumes at this point.

537. Bentham admits, nonetheless, that the effectiveness of this moral sanction depends, largely, upon the value that a person places upon the opinion of other people and the community. Persons who are indifferent to those sentiments become, therefore, immune to its effect, as admitted in Ibid., ch. 10, n. 11.

538. The manuscript originally continued with, then excluded, a new paragraph:

Were we indeed to enquire minutely into the distinction between the natures of these two sanctions it would come out that, of the evils which when considered as issuing from the moral sanction I have stiled *casual* evils, some were more likely." RP MSS 141/95: 3.

539. The manuscript initially used the phrase "obnoxious person" instead of the noun "offender" at this point. Ibid., 141/96: 3.

540. A substantial alternative text was provided by the manuscript at this point and, later, omitted:

. . . the immediate source from whence they flow. This source (as we have already intimated) is the ill-will of the community; that is to consider it more minutely of such members of it as the delinquent may have to do with. In proportion then *coteris paribus*, to the total mass, if one may so say, of this that ill will, will be the total amount and value of these evils. Now the magnitude of this total mass of ill will, will depend upon two circumstances: 1st, The strength or intensity of the malevolent affection in each particular person, and 2. The number of persons who entertain it. This general sum of ill-will then may be estimated as being the product of two dimensions. 1st. Their *intensity*: resulting from its mean strength in the heart of each particular person. 2ly Their *extent* resulting from the number of persons thus concerned. This distinction ought not to be overlooked, since we shall have occasion to make frequent application of it to practice. It may be sufficient barely to mention the circumstance of *duration*—a circumstance the influence of which is too obvious to need insisting on." Ibid., 141/96–97: 3.

541. The parallel paragraph within Dumont's edition does not include this hypothetic example but, instead, concludes with a rhetorical question: "when the entire populous pours out an outrageous proposal for an individual, how do you apply this process to the entire public?" Bentham, *Théorie des peines*, vol. I, p. 334.

542. The manuscript originally used the adjective "obnoxious" and, then, replaced it with the phrase "flagrantly immoral." RP MSS 141/98: 3.

543. A version of this paragraph does not appear to have been included within Dumont's edition. In fact, several paragraphs within this manuscript appear to have been either omitted from the parallel chapter of Dumont's edition or assimilated into other paragraphs. This sort of occurrence is not uncommon and it will be noted only when the discrepancy appears to be sufficiently significant to have affected the overall understanding of the texts, themselves.

544. Measuring and assessing the "moral sanction" in relation to more empirically tangible "political sanctions" (including penal law) has been a difficult exercise for utilitarian scholars. A review of a nineteenth-century treatment of this subject by Henry Sidgwick (which

he labels as a "social" rather than a "moral" sanction) addresses that difficulty and challenges its suitability as an applied manifestation of this intellectual tradition. Henry Sidgwick, "Critical Notice: *Progressive Morality*, by Thomas Fowler," *Mind* 10, no. 38 (April 1885): 266–71. A twentieth-century treatment of this subject contends that the moral sanction is truly relevant to utilitarian thought and policy only to the extent that it is reducible to an "instrumental motive" of the fear of physical punishment. Jeffrey C. Alexander, *Theoretical Logic in Sociology* (Berkeley: University of California Press, 1982), vol. I, pp. 73–74, 183–86.

545. This enumeration does not appear at this parallel point within Dumont's edition. Bentham, *Théorie des peines*, vol. I, p. 336.

546. The manuscript adds to the end of this paragraph, in the margins, the following sentence: "It is in this point only that the two sanctions differ." RP MSS 141/99: 3.

547. The following lines were included within the manuscript as a continuation of this paragraph and, later, crossed-out: ". . . at the hands of his friend, his patron: by setting his common acquaintance at a distance from him it may fill the detail of his life with a perpetual train of disappointments and rebuffs. It leaves him joyless and forlorn; and by drying up the source of every felicity it embitters the whole current of his life." Ibid., 141/100: 3.

548. A considerable note is present within the margins of the manuscript at this general location of the text but it is too faint to be decipherable. Ibid.

549. The manuscript originally inserted, then omitted, the following phrase at this point: "that is to such members of the community at large as the offender shall happen to have concerns with." Ibid.

550. The words "forfeiture" and "reputation" are capitalized in the manuscript. Ibid., as are the parallel words *déshonneur* and *infamie* within Dumont's edition. Bentham, *Théorie des peines*, vol. I, p. 339. The manuscript is missing from this point.

551. This parallel paragraph within Dumont's edition is enumerated as number "2." Ibid., p. 340.

552. This parallel paragraph within Dumont's edition is enumerated as number "3." Ibid.

553. This word is emphasized in italics at this parallel point within Dumont's edition, as it is at other points within that chapter. Ibid., p. 341.

554. Despite this stereotypical observation, Bentham has been credited with having progressive beliefs regarding women within society. Mirian Williford, "Bentham on the Rights of Women," *Journal of the History of Ideas* 39, no. 1 (January 1975): 167–76. At least one noted critic has gone as far as the refer to Bentham as a "feminist." Halévy, pp. 20–21.

555. Dumont's edition refers, more specifically, to "the greatest moral indifference" at this parallel point of this chapter. Bentham, *Théorie des peines*, vol. I, p. 343.

556. This conventional sentiment regarding the relationship between "middle-class morality" and rational norms and public and private behavior could be related to James Mill's promotion of democratic reform (as championed by nineteenth-century utilitarians), as noted and discussed in Shannon C. Stimson and Murray Milgate, "Utility, Property, and Political Participation: James Mill on Democratic Reform," *American Political Science Review* 87, no. 4 (December 1993): 901–11, especially 907–908.

557. This parallel paragraph within Dumont's edition is enumerated as number "4." Bentham, *Théorie des peines*, vol. I, p.344.

558. This parallel paragraph within Dumont's edition is enumerated as number "5." Ibid., p. 345.

559. The manuscript resumes at this point but in a different handwriting from the previous section of this chapter, probably of Richard Smith. RP MSS 141/101: 3. It is entirely possible that this manuscript is derived directly from Dumont's edition, especially since it follows it, so closely, at this point, Bentham, *Théorie des peines*, vol. I, pp. 346–48. It also is pos-

sible to surmise that all of section two of this chapter was derived, likewise, from Dumont's edition in the preparation of Smith's edition.

560. This opinion provides an interesting contrast with John Stuart Mill's treatment of the subject of "self-regarding actions," especially as examined in Daniel Jacobson, "Mill on Liberty, Speech, and the Free Society," *Philosophy and Public Affairs* 29, no. 3 (Summer 2000): 298–301.

561. An excellent overview of this approach (including in terms of the broader idea of "virtue") within utilitarian thought, especially among nineteenth-century commentators (culminating with the utilitarian writings of John Stuart Mill) can be found in John Kilcullen, "Utilitarianism and Virtue," *Ethics* 93, no. 3 (April 1983): 451–66. This subject is addressed, more directly, in John Stuart Mill, "Utilitarianism," in *Collected Works of John Stuart Mill*, J. M. Robson and Michael Lane, eds. (New York: Routledge, 1991), pp. 235–36, 239.

562. The back of these manuscript pages contain an early draft version of the chapter "Of Subsidiary Punishments," specifically RP MSS 141/101–102: 3.

BOOK III, CHAPTER III

563. This chapter is identified by the folder as being in the handwriting of Jeremy Bentham. Its title appears within Dumont's edition as "Punishments which Affect Honor from Blame to Infamy." Bentham, *Théorie des peines*, vol. I, p. 349.

An early manuscript draft of a chapter entitled "Penal Code" is similar to this chapter, especially regarding enforcement of this specific form of punishment. RP MSS 67/256–74.

The first section of this parallel chapter within Dumont's edition is organized in a very different manner. Much of the same material can be found within it but in a different order and style than appears within the manuscript and Smith's edition. Bentham, *Théorie des peines*, vol. I, pp. 349–63.

The manuscript pages for this chapter includes margin notes, many of which are too faded to be decipherable, such as RP MSS 141/103: 3.

564. A previous draft of this chapter, apparently in Richard Smith's handwriting, offered an alternative introduction:

This mode of punishment, applied sparingly and with discretion, may be of no small use: if it be reserved to those cases in which the affections of the people are on the same side or at least neuter: especially where they already incline in some measure on the side of the law, but have not as yet attained to that degree of vigour which the force of the legislature's authority may serve to give them.

An epithet of this kind might be of use for example, with us is the case of Election-Bribery; as also that of smuggling. I will not look out for any more cases. There are enough to serve as instances. To compleat the collection would be to engage prematurely and irregularly on the vast topic of *Offenses*.

Where such epithets are employed, it may be necessary however that they should come backed with *reasons*. In no case can it do harm: but it is necessary where the affections of the people are either upon a looking pretty to that of pretty near to a neutrality or more, especially if they lean rather to the adverse side. Ibid., 141/113: 3.

565. A comparison with Bentham, *Morals and Legislation*, ch. 16, para. 34 indicates not only a more detailed and qualitative treatment within this chapter but, arguably, a better appreciation of the pain caused by loss of reputation.

566. A version of the following subsection of enumerated methods (one through six) does not find a parallel within Dumont's edition.

567. Dumont's edition entitles this parallel subsection as "Judicial Admonition." Bentham, *Théorie des peines*, vol. I, p. 353.

568. Number "4" in this enumeration is missing in both Smith's edition and the manuscript.

569. The manuscript used (in brackets) the phrase "to execute an ordinance of the political sovereign" instead of "to enforce political ordinance." RP MSS 141/105: 3.

570. Instead of this paragraph, Dumont's edition provides, at this parallel point of this chapter, the following summation of the preceding principles:

The legislature takes a step moreover when not limited to a simple defense but when accompanied by persuasive means, such as the exhortations of a legal observer, from reasons for showing the utility, from terms of censure or condemnation, applied to those who are violent, Bentham, *Théorie des peines*, vol. I, p. 350.

571. Parallel versions of the following several paragraphs within Dumont's edition are identified by separate headings. Ibid., pp. 352–62. The first section is labeled "Publication of the Offense." Ibid., p. 352.

572. This parallel subsection within Dumont's edition has the heading "Publication of the Offense." Ibid.

573. Instead of the word "expedients," the manuscript originally used the phrase "modes of proceeding." RP MSS 141/106: 3. Dumont's edition uses the words "Of all the measures belong to," Bentham, *Théorie des peines*, vol. I, p. 352.

574. The parallel subsection within Dumont's edition has the heading "Judicial Admonition." Ibid., p. 353.

575. Dumont's edition does not make reference to this Latin phrase at this parallel point but alludes to its principle of juridical discretion. Ibid.

576. Dumont's edition adds a "memento" at this parallel point of this chapter:

This operation, as simple as it is, is not useless. The first effect of passions is to regulate, so to speak, in obscurity the motives that oppose them. Recalled to the post from which they were expelled, these titular powers can regain all ascendancy that had been lost. However, what more proper to awaken in the heart the sentiment of virtue and respect for the law than the imposing sight of guardians of the law of public probity!

Admonishment is a punishment which is borne with honor. Recalling to the eyes of a man in public his duty and the laws, supposes that he could have forgotten them and the offense. But of all the honorable punishments, it is the most frivolous, considering that it offers for him that which is the object of a testament of esteem. It is, in point of honor, that which is a moderate fine of pecuniary punishment. The gravity depends upon its publicity, the number and the choice of the persons admitted to the ceremony. The more that the law will discern from these nuances, the more it will reveal to the eyes of citizens the importance of this salutary punishment: an importance which will be the indication and the gage of the person of status who obtains the moral sanction. Happy the people for whom the magistrates would make such a strong catch upon such a delicate wire!" Ibid., pp. 354–55.

577. The parallel subsection within Dumont's edition has the heading "Application of Punishments," Ibid., p. 355.

578. The manuscript originally used the phrase "method of" instead of "expedient for." RP MSS 141/106: 3. Dumont's edition includes the word *moyen* at this parallel point of the chapter. Bentham, *Théorie des peines*, vol. I, p. 355.

579. Blackstone argued that this consideration provides the basis for the sanctions of the common law against suicide, given the fact that reputation is (with the possible exception of the anticipation of being able to transfer one's fortune to heirs) the only interest that is retained by the successful perpetrator of this offense. Sir William Blackstone, *Commentaries on the Laws of England* (Chicago: University of Chicago Press, 1979), vol. IV, pp. 189–90.

580. The manuscript used the words "Imprisonment and Low-Exclusion" at this point, with all except the first of those words crossed-out. Unlike most of these differences, the words that finally appear within the published text ("*quasi* imprisonment and local interdiction") do *not* appear, at all, within the manuscript. RP MSS 141: 107: 3. Equivalent versions of those phrases also do not appear within Dumont's edition at this parallel part of this chapter. Bentham, *Théorie des peines*, vol. I, pp. 354–56.

581. The manuscript originally added, then eliminated, the following phrase at this point: "whatsovever happens to him." RP MSS 141/108: 3.

582. The manuscript originally inserted, then crossed-out, the following phrase at this point: "shew [*sic*] itself at first glance." Ibid., 141/109: 3. An equivalent phrase is found at this parallel point of the chapter within Dumont's edition. Bentham, *Théorie des peines*, vol. I, p. 357.

583. The parallel subsection found within Dumont's edition has the heading "Other Infamous Punishments.—Quasi-Corporal Punishments." Ibid.

584. In this paragraph and the following ones, the words "infamy" and "ignominy" are, frequently, crossed-out and substituted for each other. RP MSS 141/109: 3. Dumont's edition tends to use the word *infamie* in these instances, such as at Bentham, *Théorie des peines*, vol. I, pp. 357–59ff.

585. The parallel subsection of Dumont's edition appears at a slightly later point and has the heading "Forfeiture of Credibility." Ibid., p. 359.

586. Dumont's edition employs an even more condemnatory phrase at this parallel point, "an individual whose word merits no credence." Ibid., p. 362.

587. The manuscript originally used the phrase "general fund of" and replaced it with the words "their dis-esteem." RP MSS 141/109: 3.

588. In a word, his offense contains nothing which inculpates his truthfulness, and the punishment that one inflicts upon him is the annihilation of the privilege of having his testimony believed." Bentham, *Théorie des peines*, vol. I, p. 362.

589. The manuscript originally used the phrase "researches after litigated" but replaced it with "decision." RP MSS 141/110: 3.

590. This sentence, and the subsequent note attached to it, does not appear within Dumont's edition. Instead, that edition includes a different sentence to conclude this subsection: "It is an important point to which we will return in book IV, in speaking of the *Punishments of displacement*; because the evil, which results from the exclusion of testimony, can fall indistinctly upon each member of the community at risk." Bentham, *Théorie des peines*, vol. I, p. 363.

591. The parallel subsection of Dumont's edition has the heading "Degradation." Ibid., p. 359.

592. The terms "loss of rank" and "degradation" are emphasized with italics within Dumont's edition. Ibid.

593. The manuscript initially used the word "political" instead of "factitious" at this point., RP MSS 141/111: 3.

594. The careful distinction made between the application of corporal punishment in Russia during this time period illustrated this sentiment, with persons of noble or, otherwise,

elevated rank being immune from punishments that included public humiliation except under the most extreme circumstances until these punishments, in general, were curtailed, partly as a result of the influence of Enlightenment ideas from Europe. Abby M. Schrader, "Containing the Spectacle of Punishment: The Russian Autocracy and the Abolition of the Knout, 1817–1845," *Slavic Review* 56, no. 4 (Winter 1997): 613–44.

595. Within this sentence, the manuscript initially employed the words "or considerations" and "found pure" and replaced them with, respectively, the words "respectively" and "exists." RP MSS 141/111: 3.

596. A version of this sentence regarding English examples does not appear within Dumont's edition.

597. Dumont's edition adds an interesting elaboration to this theme at this parallel point: "The *false* consideration rests again, even when it is not supported by what I call *natural* reputation," Bentham, *Théorie des peines*, vol. I, p. 360.

598. A version of this paragraph is not found within Dumont's edition. The manuscript further includes the beginning of a new paragraph at this point: "The reader can hardly have traveled with one thus far without having seen frequent occasion . . ." RP MSS 141/113: 3.

599. The manuscript is missing at this point.

600. Dumont's edition refers, more specifically, to the concept (emphasized in italics) of *simply ignominious* punishment, to which term is added a note: "It is a simply ignominious punishment or simple infamy, 1st when this term is employed by law. *Quisquis in scaenam prodierit, infamis esto*; 2nd when, without infamy, the punishment would be nullified." Bentham, *Théorie des peines*, vol. I, p. 363.

601. In this sense, it is an example of *lex talionis* because it is based upon a desire for retribution on the part of the humiliated victim of crime against an offender who does not, otherwise, regard that action as humiliating. Thus the imposition of an "ignominious punishment" of this nature is intended to transfer that category of painful experience from one person to another one, as explored in William Ian Miller, *Humiliation and Other Essays on Honor, Social Discomfort, and Violence* (Ithaca, NY: Cornell University Press, 1995), pp. 53–92.

602. A very rough draft of this section, labeled "Infamy" and beginning at this approximate part of the text, can be found at RP MSS 141/114–118: 3.

603. The rough draft version of this section places the next paragraph's rhetorical question within this paragraph. Ibid., 141/114: 3.

604. Neither of these two preceding paragraphs or a version of their enumerated characterizations can be found within Dumont's edition. The subsequent paragraph, within that edition, consequently is enumerated as number "3." Bentham, *Théorie des peines*, vol. I, p. 365.

605. Dumont's edition deviates, at this parallel point, to a different subject:

I will say nothing here of the duel. The subject is amply discussed in the *Treatises of Legislation*.(1)
    In a law on venality, or on contraband, the legislator can characterize these offenses by any appropriate epithet, Bentham, *Théorie des peines*, vol. I, p. 368.

This theme is consistent with certain aspects of the legal defense of dueling, as addressed, indirectly, in Lance K. Stell, "Dueling and the Right to Life," *Ethics* 90, no. 1 (October 1979): 17–19.

606. This version of the manuscript, in a different handwriting (probably Richard Smith), resumes at this point.

607. The manuscript originally included the phrase "which ill-will naturally rises further" but, then, omitted it. RP MSS 141/114: 3.

608. A version of the previous two paragraphs does not appear within Dumont's edition.

609. The following paragraph appears, at this point, in the manuscript but was crossed-out:

There is one particular way in which the law can inflict infamy, besides these that have been already mentioned: but this applies only to particular individuals. As the law may take from a man's natural stock of reputation, so may it add to it: as is done by the Letters of Honour conferred by some person or persons in the state to whom that power is committed either by express law or usage. I am speaking at present of mere letters of honour unaccompanied by any share of emolument or power. Of this sort are the order of Baronetage, the several orders of knighthood conferred by the king, and the honorary degrees conferred by Universities. Now then when a man is in possession of any of these titles, to take it away from him will be a punishment. The honour being supposed to be accompanied by any share of emolument or power, this punishment will come properly under the name of simple Infamy. Simple Infamy inflicted in this manner to a person thus circumstanced is stiled Degradation, Ibid., 141/115: 3.

610. The manuscript originally added, then omitted, the following sentences and note at this point:
"It will one day be acknowledged as well as the Poet that the Legislator should either say something or be silent. It will be acknowledged; and the Statute-book will shrink into a tenth part of its present bulk.
a] Moliére Poet: 'Et mon vers, bien on mal, dit toujours quelque chose,'" Ibid., 141/114: 3.

611. The manuscript is missing at this point.

612. Dumont's edition also places this paragraph within quotation marks and, further, concludes it with the word "etc." Bentham, *Théorie des peines*, vol. I, pp. 370–71.

613. The manuscript resumes at this point.

614. This sentence does not appear within Dumont's edition.

615. This sentence was redrafted three times within the manuscript. The phrase "will have this effect" was initially phrased as "will at least have the effect of making" before settling upon its final form. RP MSS 141/115: 3.

616. Prior to beginning this sentence with the phrase "We may direct his attention," the phrase "It will tell this gentleman" was first written within the manuscript. Ibid.

617. The manuscript added, then eliminated, a semi-colon and the following phrase to the end of this paragraph: "a practise [sic] consistent with crying evils, but evils interwoven into the very offense of a free state." Ibid., a version of which line does appear within Dumont's edition. Bentham, *Théorie des peines*, vol. I, p. 372.

618. The manuscript originally included, then omitted, the following passage at this point: "I have made up the definition these many years. I have droned over law-books upon law-books. I have observed this practise [sic] of the champions of what is called liberty, and I can find no warrant for anything introducing it in the least: it is the crying any thing published of." RP MSS 141/115: 3.

619. The margin of the manuscript, at this approximate point, provides a note that appears to indicate a criticism of the lack of protection that libel laws offer common persons. However, the writing is faint and largely indecipherable and, thus, unquotable. Ibid.

620. The manuscript originally used the phrase "to this day" and, then, crossed-out that phrase and substituted "to this hour." Ibid.

621. The manuscript (including the note to which this asterisk refers) is missing from this point. However, a version of that note which is almost identical to the version found within the published text can be found following the end of this chapter of the manuscript. The final sentence of that draft version of the note adds a sentence at its conclusion that was, later, crossed-out, "The case of a regular accusation in a Court of Justice forms the only exception." Ibid., 141/118: 3.

622. Dumont's edition refers to the "only conclusion" at this parallel point of the chapter Bentham, *Théorie des peines*, vol. I, p. 375.

623. The manuscript resumes at this point. However, this first paragraph is phrased slightly differently within the manuscript and, then, crossed-out. RP MSS 141/117: 3.

624. The manuscript continues, at this point, with phrasing that is identical to the published text, although this particular paragraph (which is identical to the final published version) is crossed-out within the manuscript. Ibid.

625. Dumont's edition elaborates upon this final theme at the end of this chapter:

This hardly resembles our modern high schools. There is no more credibility, greater than the word: there are still from superior men; but in a higher degree, they are nearly neighbors. The summit of the pyramid has become, so to speak, a platform, and the empire of opinion has passed from a monarchy to a republic." Bentham, *Théorie des peines*, vol. I, p. 378.

BOOK III, CHAPTER IV

626. Dumont's edition entitles this parallel chapter as "Pecuniary Punishments and Quasi-Pecuniary. Forfeiture of Property." Ibid., p. 379.

627. This opening paragraph appears within the manuscript but it is crossed-out. RP MSS 141/119: 3.

628. The manuscript originally substituted the following (later crossed-out) paragraphs for this one:

Money is the representative of almost any thing that has a value: of all sorts of instruments, and of most individual instruments of pleasure or accounts.

As to the method whereby this punishment is inflicted, it is in the first place by obliging the parties under a sever penalty to deliver the sum of money in question to some person who is appointed to receive it: authorizing such officer to seize and sell such of as many of the other effects of the delinquent as shall produce it. Ibid.

The first two paragraphs of the parallel chapter within Dumont's edition appear to include phrases from the first two paragraphs of this chapter from both this manuscript version and Smith's edition. Bentham, *Théorie des peines*, vol. I, p. 379.

629. The summary of these methods within Dumont's edition does not comment upon their relative facility. Ibid., pp. 379–80.

630. The manuscript adds a note in reference to the end of this paragraph: "For a particular account of compulsive application see Ch. __ and B. II Ch. __." RP MSS 141/119: 3.

631. The manuscript indicates a note at this point within the text. The text of the note, which is incomplete, appeared within the manuscript as "[a—c. ff. a'16 The first of these in point of time is the first in which a clause for the purpose of interest is . . ." Ibid.

632. A version of the last two paragraphs of this chapter does not appear within Dumont's edition.

633. This paragraph, as well as the subheading that precedes it and the footnote attached to it, are missing within the manuscript. A version of both of them appears within Dumont's edition. Bentham, *Théorie des peines*, vol. I, p. 381.

634. An additional paragraph was added to this subsection within the manuscript but, later, was crossed-out:

The former is capable of producing this object in a greater degree but is not so certain of producing it as the latter. The former where the condition of the delinquent admits of its taking place very often be made to much more than the latter but it is not every delinquent in whom, altogether to be forthcoming, it is certain that the former can be made to take place: but if he be forthcoming, it is certain that the latter can be made to take place, and often an avenger of the whole number of delinquents to operate this effect. All men can not be made to pay: but all men may be made to work and that as it should seem in such manner as that the labour thus shall be made to produce clear profit. RP MSS 141/120: 3.

635. Dumont's edition identifies these hypothetical men as "Pierre" and "Paul." Bentham, *Théorie des peines*, vol. I, p. 381.

636. The manuscript initially used the phrase "method of operation" and, then, changed it to "rule of measuring." RP MSS 141/120: 3.

637. The manuscript included the phrase "for the most part" but substituted "upon an average" for it. Ibid.

638. The American constitutional approach to this issue has addressed only the subject of fines that are "so grossly excessive as to amount to a deprivation of property without due process of law," as established within the 1909 United States Supreme Court decision of *Waters-Pierce Oil Company vs. State of Texas*, 212 U.S. 86 (1909).

639. The manuscript originally used the phrase "which is preferable to the head of infrugality [*sic*]: a disadvantage which" but, then, replaced it with the phrase "which balances in some degree." RP MSS 141/120: 3.

640. The manuscript originally included, then omitted, an additional sentence at this point: "Whatever income a man who has dependants was accustomed to spend, a part of that income was spent to the profit of those dependents. It served as a general fund." Ibid., 141/121: 3.

641. The manuscript included and, then, omitted the following paragraphs at this point in the text:

Upon the supposition that the loss of the same proportion of their respective capitals will in different persons produce the same quantity of pain. Two men's fortunes being given, one may therefore make sure, as far as the above supposition holds good, of introducing the same quantity of pain in the one of them as in the other. It is by taking from each not the same sum; but the same part, that is the same proportion, of his capital. Of two delinquents one is worth a hundred pound, the other a thousand. To produce in these two persons the same quantity of pain the way is not to take from each of them what not the same sum (suppose 10,) but 10 from the 1st and a hundred from the other.

In point of variability it is evident nothing can excell this mode of punishment, as far as it extends. It extends down the lowest part of the scale and it is capable of existing in a lower degree than any corporal punishment, in as much as it stands uncomplicated with any degree of infamy, except with that which is necessarily attached to the offense. Ibid.

Versions of these paragraphs are found within Dumont's edition at the parallel point of the last paragraph describing method number 3 and the first paragraph describing method number 4. Bentham, *Théorie des peines*, vol. I, p. 382.

Bentham recognized that the imposition of fixed fines would fail to meet this standard so his assessment of the suitability of this punishment under this category is based upon the establishment of a rate of punishment that could be adjusted to a person's actual economic status, such as a fine that is determined by a proportion of any given income could provide. Bentham, *Morals and Legislation*, ch. IX. However, that sort of utilitarian calculation would depend solely upon consideration of a "marginal harm" and not upon all economic factors relating to a particular offender (for example, loss of ten percent of the salary of a wealthy person is less painful than the loss of the same proportion of the salary of a poorer person), including broader sociological ones. Gary S. Becker, "Crime and Punishment: An Economic Approach," *Journal of Political Economy* 76, no. 2 (March 1968): 190–98.

642. The manuscript is enumerated, on this page, as 257, which also is the page number of the published 1830 edition of this book on which the following text is found. RP MSS 141/122: 3.

643. The manuscript initially included, then omitted, at this point the following sentence as a separate paragraph: "In point of popularity, this punishment is remarkable for having almost the only one against which some popular objection or other has not been made." Ibid.

644. Dumont's edition concludes this description of this characteristic of "exemplarity" with a somewhat different example:

> There is a case, in England, where pecuniary punishment is like lost for the example. In a great number of minor offenses, ordinary punishment, often solitary punishment, is to be condemned to the costs and expenses. These expenses are not known; this masked punishment nearly entirely escapes the public. To him to whom it is submitted does not know its value until the moment it is executed. It wounds without warning. It is an inconvenience that would be easy to cure. Bentham, *Théorie des peines*, vol. I, pp. 383–84.

645. A version of the text of Smith edition, from this point to the end of this section of the chapter (including descriptions of the characterizations of remissibility and popularity), is not found within Dumont's edition.

646. The manuscript initially used the phrase "affords equal facilities for making reparations" and replaced it with "is in an eminent degree advantageous." RP MSS 141/122: 3.

647. The manuscript for this published text is missing from this point to the end of the chapter. However, the manuscript includes the following paragraph which is not included within the 1830 edition or any other published edition:

> This case is of very considerable extent and importance. In the case of the greater number of the offenses of all kinds that are committed, it constitutes the whole of the punishment that is inflicted. This is the case with all those offenses that are prohibited by laws which from their not being armed with a punishment formally described under that name, stand excluded in common speech from the catalogue of penal laws. Such are those by which men are restrained from the common run of offenses against property; such to wit as are not attended with any circumstances of aggravation. Even where there is a penalty expressly denounced, in many cases (thus the matter stands under our own jurisprudence at least) it bears a very small proportion to this marked penalty which is scarcely even, and never in its magnitude, still fell. Ibid.

648. The development of the "market model" for determining penal policy is an economic response to this utilitarian calculus that is particularly relevant to this category of pun-

ishment, as described in Isaac Ehrlich, "Crime, Punishment, and the Market for Offenses," *Journal of Economic Perspectives* 10, no. 1 (Winter 1996), pp. 43–67.

649. Dumont's edition emphasizes the words "more exemplary" in italics at this parallel point. Bentham, *Théorie des peines*, vol. I, p. 385.

BOOK III, CHAPTER V

650. This chapter is missing from the manuscript.

651. The parallel chapter within Dumont's edition is literally entitled "Forfeitures Affecting Condition." Ibid., p. 386.

652. Dumont's edition occasionally places an emphasis upon different words than Smith's edition provides. This chapter provides a particularly good and, arguably, revealing example of this contrast. For example, the term "real entities" is emphasized with italics at this parallel point within Dumont's edition, which does not emphasize the word "incorporeal." Ibid.

653. The phrase "conditions of a husband" is emphasized within Dumont's edition. Ibid.

654. Dumont's edition employs the more general phrase of "*dignité*," rather than the more precise word of *rang*, at the parallel point at which Smith's edition uses the word "rank," denoting, perhaps, a more precise continental understanding of the concept. Ibid.

655. The treatment of this specific source of pain as a form of punishment appears to be a particularly liberal interpretation (consistent with an abstract proprietary perception of non-tangible assets that can be subject to compensatory treatment), especially when contrasted with the cursory summary provided in Bentham, *Morals and Legislation*, ch. 16, para. 38. A classic analysis of the evolution of this concept is provided in C. B. Macpherson, *The Political Theory of Possessive Individualism* (Oxford: Oxford University Press, 1964), pp. 1–11.

656. This influence has been explored and affirmed in Donald Black, *The Behavior of Law* (San Diego: Academic Press, 1980), pp. 13–36.

657. Dumont's edition places the words "condition" (though not linked to the word "life"), "right," and "privilege" in italics for emphasis at this parallel point of the chapter. Bentham, *Théorie des peines*, vol. I, p. 388.

658. This specific theme and its various manifestations are explored in F. Y. Edgeworth, "The Hedonical Calculus," *Mind* 4, no. 15 (July 1879): 405–408.

659. At this parallel point and similar other ones, the word "uncompellable" is found within Dumont's edition as "*inexigibles*." Bentham, *Théorie des peines*, vol. I, p. 390.

660. Dumont's edition adds, at the end of this parallel paragraph, the sentence "It is the herbarium of the naturalist and the palette of the painter." Ibid., p. 391.

661. Interestingly, Dumont's edition does not use an adjective of any sort at this parallel point. Ibid., p. 392.

662. Dumont's edition provides an additional observation at this parallel point: "One should only observe how many similar things are done by the magistrate." Ibid., p. 398.

663. The parallel words for "punishment" and "forfeiture of freedom" are emphasized with italics within Dumont's edition. Ibid., p. 403.

664. The apparent ambiguity of this passage may reinforce arguments that utilitarianism could, under certain circumstances, provide a rational defense for the institution of slavery. However, the overall tone of this chapter and this book suggest otherwise. A refutation of the perception that utilitarianism could be employed in the defense of slavery is provided in R. M. Hare, "What is Wrong with Slavery," *Philosophy and Public Affairs* 8, no. 2 (Winter 1979): 103–21.

665. Utilitarian arguments and methods of analysis were employed in the defense of slavery among certain intellectuals within the American Deep South. An overview of this tra-

dition and its use of utilitarian principles can be found in Daniel Kilbride, "Slavery and Utilitarianism: Thomas Cooper and the Mind of the Old South," *Journal of Southern History* 59, no. 3 (August 1993): 469–86. However, sentiments in favor of abolition were associated with, if not directly inspired by, fundamental utilitarian arguments, especially as promoted by nineteenth-century disciples of this tradition as expounded in Louis S. Gerteis, *Morality and Utility in American Antislavery Reform* (Chapel Hill: University of North Carolina Press, 1987), pp. 145–55.

666. Bentham has been associated with those "neo-roman" intellectuals who ascribe a mere "absence of constraint" quality to liberty (a conception defined as "negative liberty") rather than a positive condition that, itself, contributes to human pleasure. Quentin Skinner, *Liberty Before Liberalism* (Cambridge: Cambridge University Press, 1997), pp. 82–83. This interpretation is consistent with a common belief that Bentham tended to disregard the intrinsic value of liberty, as discussed in Long, pp. 52–67.

This passage suggests a more subtle and textured approach to the subject of liberty that has been attributed to later utilitarian thought, culminating in the writings of John Stuart Mill, Herbert Spencer, and subsequent scholars. This subject is tied to the larger subject of "liberal utilitarianism" that contends that many utilitarians (including Bentham but increasingly apparent among subsequent generations) were ideologically liberal, even though utilitarian principles often can be found in conflict with certain liberal values. An excellent overview of this conflict and evolution within utilitarian thought is provided in David Weinstein, *Equal Freedom and Utility: Herbert Spencer's Liberal Utilitarianism* (Cambridge: Cambridge University Press, 1998), pp. 1–10, 79–82, 114–38.

BOOK III, CHAPTER VI

667. This chapter is missing from the manuscript.

668. The version of this chapter found within Dumont's edition is entirely different from this one. It begins with an enumeration of characteristics:

> Taking legal protection from an individual, or *outlawing* him, is a punishment in current use in many jurisdictions.
>
> In that of England, the *Ex-law* (Outlawry), includes the following punishments:
> 1st, Incapacity to resort to the protection of tribunals,
> 2nd, Forfeiture of personal property;
> 3rd, Forfeiture of profits from the accruing of real property;
> 4th, Life imprisonment.
>
> Such is the punishment inflicted for the offense of absconding from justice, so to speak, of not responding to a summons, to hide. It is imposed in all cases, except when the principal offense is a *felony*: in that case, the man who submits to a sentence of outlawry is punished as if he was convicted of the principal offense. Bentham, *Théorie des peines*, vol. I, p. 406.

The rest of this parallel chapter within Dumont's edition is organized into two sections. The first section provides an elaboration of the essential descriptions of this category of punishment as provided within Smith's edition. The second section, entitled "Examination of this Punishment," criticizes it in terms of "inequality," its difficulty in assessing and enforcing it, and its perceived moral deficiency. Ibid., pp. 406–12.

669. It may be interesting to contemplate this particular subject within the context of

general utilitarian objections to paternalism, as provided in Richard J. Arneson, "Mill *versus* Paternalism," *Ethics* 90, no. 4 (July 1980): 470–89.

BOOK IV

670. The manuscript is missing at this point.

671. Dumont's edition provides a different introduction for Book IV:

An offense has been committed. Who must bear the punishment?—This question addresses itself to reasonable men, and must it be replied seriously?

Before entering in an examination which will prove only too well the necessity of treating this subject, starting by explaining the term *misseated [sic] punishment*. Misseated punishment, or badly seated, or abberant [*sic*], is that which, instead of falling exclusive upon the author of the offense, falls in full or partly upon innocents. This punishment, which sort of his natural place, will not be always rigorously that which one calls a *punishment*, following the definition of the word (1). The law does not give it the name of punishment. It is rather absurd to declare that it punishes an innocent: but this is not a verbal dispute. The legislator, on the occasion of an offense of Titius, inflicted an evil upon those individuals who had no part in the offense, either to increase the punishment of Titius, maybe by a blind feeling of antipathy. It is that which I call a misseated punishment.

To avoid confusion, two cases must be distinguished, one where the responsibility for an offense must be borne by they who are not the authors; the other, where the evil of the punishment affects the innocents, without any intention on the part of the legislature, and without them being to prevent it. Bentham, *Théorie des peines*, vol. I, pp. 413–14.

672. This sentence and the five paragraphs following it find a parallel within Dumont's edition as the second section of that version of book IV: "Inevitable Evils Derived from Punishment." Ibid., pp. 416–18.

673. Some utilitarian critics would be even more distinct in this respect (though consistent with this tone) and argue that punishment of the innocent does not even merit the designation of "punishment" but, instead, should be redesignated as "injury," "harm infliction," or some other terminology. McCloskey, "A Non-Utilitarian Approach to Punishment," p. 244.

This passage is indicative of a tone that appears to be more critical of mis-seated punishment than its treatment in Bentham's previously published writings on the subject suggest. A comparison with Bentham, *Morals and Legislation*, ch. 13, sec. 1 (including n. 1), with its more functional evaluation, offers an interesting contrast in this respect.

674. These passages suggest a contemplation of the theme of "negative utilitarianism," in which the avoidance of pain is a greater priority than the promotion of pleasure. This approach is not generally associated with Bentham but may have been more readily embraced by later disciples. One critic who expressed sympathy for this approach (especially within the context of a hedonic interpretation of utilitarian thought) is Popper, vol. II, p. 304, especially n. 62.

675. One prominent interpretation of the utilitarian approach to this subject is that even Bentham believed in the promotion of an already present "harmony of interests," in which punishment served to affect motives, rather than interests, by allowing offenders to adjust their understanding of their own long-term interests. Therefore, "misseated" punishment of the innocent could not reinforce the general goals of utilitarianism. David Lyons, *In the Interest of the Governed*, pp. 61–69.

676. Again, the semantic issue regarding the proper definition of "punishment" remains a significant point. McCloskey, p. 244.

677. This section is numbered within the 1830 edition as section "III." The errata page for this edition identified this mistake and the subsequent dismembering of all of the sections within this chapter. The table of contents for that edition indicated, however, the correct numbering of these sections.

678. This section appears as the first one for Book IV within Dumont's edition. Bentham, *Théorie des peines*, vol. I, pp. 414–16.

679. The concept of punishing parents for the delinquency of their children arguably falls under this category of mis-seated punishment, especially as it has been raised and, occasionally, applied from a recidivist perspective, Note, "What's This About Punishing Parents?" *Federal Probation* 12 (March 1948): 237, Arthur L. Beeley, "Parenthood, the Police Power, and Criminal Justice Administration," *Western Political Quarterly* 12, no. 3 (September 1959): 801–802, and Quinn, pp. 354–55.

680. The final sentence of this paragraph does not appear at the parallel point of Dumont's edition. Bentham, *Théorie des peines*, vol. I, p. 421.

This interpretation of "vicarious punishment" has been characterized as a form of moral "absolutism," including in connection with utilitarian justifications, Gregory S. Kavka, "Some Paradoxes of Deterrence," *Journal of Philosophy* 75, no. 6 (June 1978): 287–88.

681. Another way of expressing this utilitarian objection is that mis-seated punishment can lead to other, compensatory evils, such as evasion of the law, jury nullification, bribery of public officials, mistrust of public institutions, and other substantive problems. Bailey, pp. 154–56.

682. Dumont's edition precedes this sentence with the phrase "I must not omit." Bentham, *Théorie des peines*, vol. I, p. 423.

683. The last sentence of this parallel paragraph in Dumont's edition is phrased "This law is yet justified by necessity; so to speak, in the case where there is not another method for repressing unusual violence, or for stopping acts of injustice." Ibid.

684. This argument is elaborated and explained as a conflict between rule-utilitarianism (which would prohibit military reprisals as a general principle) and act-utilitarianism (which might justify certain specific reprisals) in R. B. Brandt, "Utilitarianism and the Rules of War," *Philosophy and Public Affairs* 1, no. 2 (Winter 1972): 145–65.

685. The word "felony" is emphasized at this parallel point within Dumont's edition and the example of a "stolen horse" is not proffered. Bentham, *Théorie des peines*, vol. I, p. 425.

686. At this point, the versions of this section within the editions of Smith and Dumont diverge. The remainder of this section within Smith's edition does not appear within Dumont's edition. That edition, instead, appears to make a transition into the account of the "Disadvantages of this Mode of Punishment" that constitutes a separate section within Smith's edition. Ibid., pp. 427–32. These transitional paragraphs within Dumont's edition offer a commentary that emphasize this general tone of both rational and, seemingly, moral disapproval regarding the shifting of punishment to the family of a convict:

> Let us not enter into this polemic. Let us leave alone this shameful jargon. Let us see what one could say for justifying these transitive punishments.
>
> After my personal punishment, a punishment which falls upon those who are my loved ones is again a punishment against me. I participate in the suffering of those to whom I am attached with the most kindness. I can face the evils that would be only for me: I can be restrained by the fear to involve in my ruin those who are the first objects of my affections.
>
> Punishments against the family of a delinquent are thus punishments against himself.

This principle is true: but is it good? does it conform to utility (1)?

Asking whether a sympathetic punishment is as effective as a direct punishment is to ask whether the attachment that one bears for others is as strong as self-love.

If self-love is the stronger sentiment, it follows that one must resort to sympathetic punishments only after having suffered all that human nature can suffer in inflicting direct punishments. No torture is so cruel that one must not employ, before punishing the wife for the deeds of the husband, and the children for the deeds of the father.

(1) *Treatise of Legislation*, vol. II, p. 392. *Aberrant and misplaced* Punishments. Two or three paragraphs are transcribed here to avoid references. Bentham, *Théorie des peines*, vol. I, pp. 426–29.

687. At this point, Dumont's edition resumes its parallel with Smith's edition. Ibid., p. 429.

688. Dumont's edition emphasizes the word "self-defense" (more directly translated as "defensive measures" in italics. Ibid.

689. One response to this argument is that punishing the innocent could be constrained by "public uneasiness" but it would depend upon "side constraints" and other factors (such as public awareness and comprehension) as well as a reliance upon a rule-utilitarian approach (that might have "extreme results") rather than an "agent-centered optimization" of permitting a lesser evil in order to prevent a greater evil. Therefore, although utilitarians generally have rejected the punishing of the innocent, they have failed to provide a consistently satisfying theoretical premise for that position. Geoffrey Scarre, *Utilitarianism* (London: Routledge, 1996), pp. 166–72.

690. Bentham's observations (and, perhaps, the observations of his disciples) regarding the generally bad effects that mob behavior and attacks upon the state (which could include treasonous activities) could have in both Britain and, especially, France may have influenced the moral position that appears to be found within this passage regarding the crime of treason. Crimmins, "Bentham's Political Radicalism Reexamined," pp. 271–72.

691. A parallel version of this section appears as part of the previous section within Dumont's edition, though it is expressed in a somewhat different way:

I see in these misplaced punishments four principal vices.

1st What does one think of a punishment which one must often reject for want of objects that can be seated in it? There are many men who have neither father nor mother, wife not child. It is thus necessary to apply a direct punishment to this class of men; but as soon as there is a punishment levied against these men why wouldn't it be sufficient against others?

2nd And does not this punishment suppose feelings that may not exist? If a delinquent is concerned with neither his wife or her children, if he regards them with hatred, if he is indifferent at least to the evil that is related to them: this part of the punishment is null for him.

3rd But that which is the alarming in this system, it is the profusion, the multiplication of the evils. Consider the chain of domestic relations, calculate the number of descendants which men can have; punishment communicates from one to another, it envelopes a crowd of individuals. For producing a direct punishment which is equivalent to one, it is necessary to create an indirect punishment and improperly seated which is equivalent to twenty, thirty, one hundred, one thousand, etc.

4th Punishment, thus diverted from its natural course, does not have even the advantage of being in conformity with public feelings of sympathy or antipathy.

When a delinquent has paid his personal debt with justice, public vengeance is appeased, and does not ask anything more. If you pursue it beyond the grave, on an innocent and unhappy family, soon public pity is awakened: a confused feeling reveals your laws of injustice, humanity declares against you, the respect and confidence in government is weakened in all hearts.

But, one can say, compared to political offenses, the conspiracies, the rebellions where rich men are most dangerous, confiscation operates as a method of general security. Bentham, *Théorie des peines*, vol. I, pp. 427–29.

692. This section appears as the "sixth section" within Dumont's edition. Ibid., pp. 432–37.

693. Instead of versions of the preceding paragraphs of this section, Dumont's edition offers a different introduction:

By *collective* punishments, I understand punishments inflicted upon societies or corporations for offenses in which the authors are not separately known, but one can presume as belonging to the members of the corporation which is punished.

One finds punishments of this category in all jurisdictions.

For justifying this treatment, there are two points to prove: 1st that the culpable cannot be punished without the innocent. 2nd that the punishment of the innocent attached to those of the culpable is a lesser evil than the evil of the impunity.

Of these two points made, the first is susceptible to proofs: the second is a matter of conjecture. Ibid., p. 432.

694. At this parallel point, Dumont's edition does not include versions of the next three paragraphs but includes, instead, a different paragraph with a footnote:

The amendment was a collective punishment: it can fall upon the innocents: but like general punishment, destined to turn public opinion against the offense, it was useful, it tended to impress upon the spirit of the people a salutary idea that each one is interested in preventing seditious movements of the populace (1).

(1) After a riot in the city of Rennes, among other severities, one experienced one of these collective vengeances, which was described by Madame de Sévigné.

'One drove out and cleared all of a great street, and defended and collected under pain of life; so all these poor wretches were seen, pregnant women, the elderly, children, to wander in tears as they were driven from the city, without knowing where to go, without having food nor knowing where to sleep. This province is a good example for the others, and especially for respecting the governors and the governments, not to speak insults nor to throw stones in their garden,' *Letters*, 268. Ibid., p. 434.

695. The manuscript resumes at this point, reportedly in the handwriting of Jeremy Bentham. This section is not numbered within the manuscript, although it appears within the 1830 edition as section "VII," subject to the correction indicated within the errata page of that edition that makes it consistent with the table of contents for that edition. RP MSS 141/140: 8. This parallel section within Dumont's edition is identified as the "seventh section." Bentham, *Théorie des peines*, vol. I, p. 437.

696. The manuscript originally used the words "had to fall" and, then, replaced them with the words "has fallen." RP MSS 141/140: 8. The original words appear to be closer to

the literal sense in which they are found at the parallel point of Dumont's edition. Bentham, *Théorie des peines*, vol. I, p. 437.

697. Dumont's edition begins this section in a different tone: "I call *random punishment* or meting out by chance, that which the laws made to fall accidentally upon an innocent, who could be any individual as well as another, as much a stranger to the delinquent as to the offense." Ibid. It is interesting to compare this section with Bentham's treatment of the subject of "intentionality" within Bentham, *Morals and Legislation*, ch. 8.

698. The manuscript originally began a different phrase at this point, which subsequently was crossed-out, which stated "we may again refer to the law of forfeitures for that copious source of mischief as are not exhausted to the law of." RP MSS 141/140: 8. Dumont's edition begins this parallel paragraph "Here are drawn three examples from English law: 1st A scope of confiscation. 2nd The diodandes. 3rd Inadmissability of testimony." Bentham, *Théorie des peines*, vol. I, pp. 437–39. Dumont's edition divides this section into clearly enumerated and titled sections corresponding to each of these three divisions.

699. The manuscript originally started, then crossed-out, a different phrase at this point: "two cases may serve that of." RP MSS 141/140: 8.

700. A type of chattel servitude resulting from the causing of the death of another person. Blackstone, bk II, pp. 408–10.

701. The manuscript initially used the word "width" and, then, replaced it with "breadth." RP MSS 141/140: 8. Dumont's edition uses the general expression for "space" or "scope" at this parallel point. Bentham, *Théorie des peines*, vol. I, p. 438.

702. The manuscript is missing after this point to the end of the chapter.

703. Dumont's edition identifies the source of this quote, in a footnote, as Blackstone, book IV, chapter XXIX. Bentham, *Théorie des peines*, vol. I, p. 439.

704. Dumont's edition adds a footnote at this parallel point: "This does not take place if the vessel is at sea, in salt water." Ibid., p. 440.

705. This parallel paragraph is differently constructed within Dumont's edition:

The origin of this law comes from a time where one redeemed the soul of the dead from Purgatory, with the method of murmuring songs during the Mass. The power of the music over the souls in Purgatory was generally recognized. He had to pay the musicians who had the secret of this magic. The thing, which had caused the death of the deceased to whom one rendered this service, was the first seizable asset, and was used to pay it (2).

(2) *Omnia quae movent ad mortem sunt Deo danda.* See Blackstone, book I, chapter VIII. Ibid., p. 440.

706. In general, therefore, a properly applied punishment must interact with the motive of the offender, whose defective motive, in turn, is the product of a defective character that should be corrected in order to achieve pleasure for both the averted offender and the spared victims of the crime. Overall, a rational person, under this scheme, would exempt from punishment a person who was involved in an unlawful and painful action but who did not manifest a defective motive (as derived either from disinterest or an intention to produce a good result), thereby failing to demonstrate any defect of "standing motivation" related to character. Richard B. Brandt, *Morality, Utilitarianism, and Rights* (Cambridge: Cambridge University Press, 1992), pp. 228–32, 235, 262.

707. Dumont's edition provides, at this parallel point, a different introduction to this section:

There is a method of punishment, where, for making a scratch seem guilty, one passes an epee across the body of an innocent—I want to call this infamous punishment given to an individual *inadmissible testimony.*

The Romans, who transmitted this to us, who held it themselves from the Greeks; a nation singularly subject to be governed by caprice, by technicalities and refinements of the imagination.

The advantage of this punishment is null, because the same punishment is concealed. The law says nothing: the sentence is not mentioned. Exclusion is a blow drawn from darkness as an alleged consequence of other punishments. It is a secret which is not known to the legislators; and never is it revealed as doing evil, for giving impunity to a criminal, or for eluding good law by a nullity. Bentham, *Théorie des peines*, vol. I, pp. 440–41.

708. Dumont's edition adds a quote at this parallel point, though its source is not identified: "'Our laws go so far, says a jurist, to excommunicate also those who would discourse with them, and consequently, a judge cannot address their questions,'" Ibid., p. 442.

709. Bentham repeats this theme in Bentham, *Morals and Legislation,* XVI, ss. 20–24, and Jeremy Bentham, *Rationale of Judicial Evidence,* pp. 14–44.

710. Dumont's edition declares at this parallel point, more emphatically, "I am persuaded." Bentham, *Théorie des peines*, vol. I, p. 448.

711. Dumont's edition inserts the Latin phrase *"omni exceptione majores"* at this parallel point. Ibid.

712. Dumont's edition concludes the previous parallel paragraph with this narrative, though it assumes the form of a rhetorical and emotive statement and question: That he personally is placed beyond the protection of the law, it is a strange type of punishment! But the impunity given to crimes of which he is the only witness, how is that justified?" Ibid., pp. 448–49.

713. Dumont's edition emphasizes the concluding sentences of this parallel paragraph with exclamation points. Ibid., p. 449.

714. Bentham's influence regarding nineteenth century reforms of the laws concerning perjury and other, related rules of evidence has been extolled by prominent constitutional scholars such as A. V. Dicey and William Holdsworth. However, it has been argued that later utilitarian scholars and critics have been much more responsible for this development and the expansion of the sorts of arguments provided by this section of this chapter. Christopher Allen, *The Law of Evidence in Victorian England* (Cambridge: Cambridge University Press, 1997), pp. 1–13. Perhaps, this evolving influence began within this text with the contributions of two of his immediate disciples.

715. Dumont's edition concludes this section and book IV with the following paragraph:

Justinian attached this legal incapacity to a category of offense against manners. That one punishes this offense as severely as one wants, that is another question: but what offense can have a depraved taste for juridical truth? How can one conclude that a man infected by this vice will be disposed there to give a false testimony against an accused? It confuses ideas that have no rationale. Bentham, *Théorie des peines*, vol. I, pp. 453–54.

Interestingly, a somewhat similar argument was made by H. L. A. Hart within the context of his response to Lord Devlin's defense of the prosecution of acts of private morality. H. L. A. Hart, *Law, Liberty, and Morality* (Stanford, CA: Stanford University Press, 1972), pp. 48–52.

716. The Table of Contents of the 1830 edition identifies this section with a slightly differently phrased title. This section does not appear within Dumont's edition.

717. Within the context of this position, gratification, alone, is not sufficient to sustain a liberal utilitarian principle of punishment, including (perhaps especially) punishment of the innocent. Punishment that substantially reduces the well being of an agent (including torture) was increasingly rejected by nineteenth century utilitarians (especially in connection with the "harm principle" of John Stuart Mill), although that interpretation also has been associated with Bentham. Häyry, pp. 164–66.

BOOK V, CHAPTER I

718. The title of this book includes reference to a footnote within Dumont's edition:

(1) This book, which reports principally of English jurisprudence, is hardly of interest for *jurisconsults*. Bentham, *Théorie des peines*, vol. I, p. 455.

719. This chapter is not found within the manuscript.

720. Dumont's edition uses the adjective "vicious," instead of "improper," at this parallel point. Ibid., p. 456.

721. Social choice literature has attempted to explain the process by which legislators arrive at complex punishment strategies in establishing penal law in a manner that is compatible with utilitarian calculations. But another argument posits that this outcome is the result of non-cooperative legislative strategies, based upon the a different calculus, David P. Baron and John A. Ferejohn, "Bargaining in Legislatures," *American Political Science Review* 83, no. 4 (December 1989): 1181, 1186.

BOOK V, CHAPTER II

722. The parallel chapter of Dumont's edition is found at book II, chapter 11, entitled "Of Deportation to Botany Bay." Bentham, *Théorie des peines*, vol. I, pp. 215–41.

723. The manuscript is not present at this point.

724. Dumont's edition refers to them as "Anglo-Americans." Ibid., p. 215.

725. Dumont's edition adds a footnote at this parallel point:

(1) Franklin, in his capacity as an agent for the colonies, had advocated for the abolition of this practice. The minister pleaded with him the necessity of purging British soil of these malefactors. 'What would you say,' Franklin responded to him, 'if by the same reasoning, we would send you our rattlesnakes?' Ibid.

726. Excellent overviews of transportation to the American colonies and its effect (including economically) are provided in Bernard Bailyn, *Voyagers to the West: Emigration from Britain to America on the Eve of the Revolution* (New York: Random House, 1986), pp. 260–64, 292–95; and A. Roger Ekirk, "Bound for America: A Profile of British Convicts Transported to the Colonies, 1718–1775," *William and Mary Quarterly* 42, no. 2 (April 1985): 184–200.

727. Dumont's edition refers to New Zealand, instead of New South Wales, at this parallel point. Bentham, *Théorie des peines*, vol. I, p. 216.

728. This alternative destination for transported convicts became more attractive because of the conservative reaction to the French Revolution upon British policies, arguably even influencing Bentham (though this manuscript originally was written more than fifteen years prior to the start of that revolution) in this respect. Coleman Phillipson, *Three Criminal Law Reformers: Beccaria, Bentham, Romilly* (Glenridge, NJ: Patterson Smith, 1973), pp. 164–70; and Leon Radzinowicz, *A History of English Criminal Law and Its Administration from 1750* (London: Macmillan, 1948), pp. 232–38.

729. Dumont's edition adds a footnote at this parallel point: "(1) *Convicts* is the English word for designating malefactors, after the conviction for the offense, during the period of their imprisonment or banishment." Bentham, *Théorie des peines*, vol. I, p. 216.

730. The manuscript begins at this point, reportedly in Bentham's handwriting.

731. This noun is capitalized within the manuscript, RP MSS 141/124: 4.

732. The manuscript is missing from this point.

733. An excellent analysis of the motives and results of transportation to Botany Bay is provided in Alan Brooke, *Bound for Botany Bay: The Story of British Convict Transportation to Australia* (Toronto: Dundurn Press, 2006), pp. 13–36, 216–41.

734. Dumont's edition identifies this author as Racine, quoted in his preface to *Bajazet*. Bentham, *Théorie des peines*, vol. I, p. 219.

735. Bentham apparently had supported efforts to replace this penal option with increased use of hard labor (as a reforming measure, rather than as a deterrent) through adoption of the Hard Labour Bill, sponsored in Parliament by William Eden. Although the influence of Blackstone and Beccaria was more prevalent within this particular reform movement, Bentham was, at least peripherally, influential in its progress and disappointed with the ultimate shortcomings of these efforts. Devereaux, pp. 405–33.

736. Dumont's edition adds the word "correction" to reformation at this parallel point. Bentham, *Théorie des peines*, vol. I, p. 221.

737. Dumont's edition offers a somewhat different introductory paragraph to this section: "II. Second goal of punishments. *Correction, reformation* of individuals. Lets us consult the deeds, retrace the causes; we would see that the establishment of Botany Bay was fruitless and it always would be under that respect." Ibid.

738. Dumont's edition does not use the direct quote found within this paragraph of Smith's edition. Dumont's edition concludes this parallel paragraph with a biting rhetorical remark: "There are the mothers of the colony! The depositories of death of the nascent generation!" Ibid., p. 224.

739. Dumont's edition refers more specifically to Botany Day, rather than to the larger colony of New South Wales, such as at Ibid.

740. A version of this paragraph, including the notes, does not appear within Dumont's edition.

741. Dumont's edition refers to them, more pointedly, as "enemies of the government." Ibid., p. 228.

742. The manuscript resumes at this point.

743. Bentham's scheme for Panopticon would provide a distinct and, arguably, deliberate contrast with the experiment at Botany Bay, especially in terms of humane conditions and productive labor. James E. Crimmins, "Contending Interpretations of Bentham's Utilitarianism," pp. 761–62.

744. The manuscript originally began a new sentence, using the phrase "This punishment therefore does not possess this" but, then, replacing it with an emdash and the phrase "we ought not, therefore, to attribute this punishment an." RP MSS 141/125: 4.

745. Dumont's edition offers an additional paragraph at this parallel point that is not found within the manuscript:

One can make other objections, and quite seriously, against the establishment of Botany Bay, in relation to the constitutional law of Great Britain (1). I do not enter this examination, it would be foreign to my subject; but it is a final consideration which alone should make us abandon this system.

(1) See Mr. Bentham's work—*A Plea for the Constitution. Shewing the Enormities Committed, etc., etc. in New South Wales.* Bentham, *Théorie des peines,* vol. I, p. 234.

746. Dumont's edition uses a phrase at this parallel point that could be translated, more pointedly, as "an evil that is a pure waste." Ibid., p. 235.

747. Dumont's edition phrases this passage as "Should one multiply the regulations as much as one could, only one negligence is needed . . ." Ibid., p. 237.

748. An interesting overview of this general controversy in British penal policy is provided in Ged Martin, "The Alternatives to Botany Bay," *University of Newcastle Historical Journal* 3 (February 1975): 11–26.

749. Dumont's edition adds a few additional paragraphs at the end of this chapter:

Pirates, enriched from the pillage of nations, and which, by their number and by their wealth, had even established states, had been annihilated by their vices, and not left any historical trace of their existence.

If it had conformed to a healthy policy of founding a colony in New Zealand, it would have been thus necessary to send good laborers, industrious workers, honest families, and it would have brought the greatest care in spreading out the malefactors, who brought with them the seed of all the disorders, and who must have diverted from a similar establishment all of who ought preferably to have been invited.

It is ridiculous, at least in terms of the actual state of this colony, to speak of a single object of commerce. Far from producing an exchangeable surplus, it did not produce enough for their needs. It purchases a lot and sells nearly nothing. Its only method of commerce is specie; that specie, sent by the metropolitan authority for supporting civil and military government, passes entirely to national merchants or foreigners who wish to sell their produce to Botany Bay, at five hundred percent profit. Because of the specie, the government already is reduced to creating paper money, that is to say, establishing a colonial debt.

There without doubt it is shown that the political object is not fulfilled by the penal object." Bentham, *Théorie des peines,* vol. I, pp. 240–41.

BOOK V, CHAPTER III

750. A previous, crossed-out draft version of this chapter (apparently in the handwriting of Richard Smith) also, interestingly, makes reference to Bentham in the third person. That draft is very similar to the published text and is provided on the back pages of RP MSS 141/126–130: 5.

751. This parallel chapter appears as Book II, Chapter XII ("House of Penitence.— Panopticon.) within Dumont's edition, Bentham. *Théorie des peines,* vol. I, pp. 242–68.

752. Although this chapter is not present within the published 1818 French version, as edited and translated by Etienne Dumont, this previous English draft version of this chapter

makes reference to "Traités de Legislation, Tome III, art. Panoptique. Back of RP MSS 141/130: 5. Its second-person narrative offers an excellent example of the editorial and, possibly, substantive contributions that Smith and Dumont made to this work.

753. Bentham supported efforts to advance productive hard labor as a reforming measure for penal law, ultimately contributing to his ideas concerning Panopticon. Devereaux, pp. 432–33.

754. An excellent overview of this plan and the ideas that prompted in is provided in Semple, pp. 111–65.

755. The previous draft of this chapter includes, following this paragraph, an additional paragraph (with several words and phrases originally provided and replaced) that is not included within the published text:

> In France I have met with persons who, pretending to extreme sensibility have regarded as an objection what might Bentham's plan contribute to prominent merit the unremitted [*sic*] *inspection*. To their imagination it represents itself as a restraint more terrible than the most revolting tyranny: an establishment of this description was regarded by them as a prototype of Hell. By these men of delicate sensibility it had doubtless been forgotten; that under the present system of imprisonment, the prisoners are without any solution crowded together and have no place either by night or by day." Back of RP MSS 141/126–127: 5.

This passage is found at this parallel point of Dumont's edition. Bentham, *Théorie des peines*, vol. I, p. 244.

756. The manuscript resumes at this point in Richard Smith's handwriting, indicating at the word "may" the designation "A 353," RP MSS 141/126: 5.

757. An excellent study of this theme has been provided by Janet Semple. She disputes Foucault's analysis of Panopticon as a "laboratory of power" that anticipated the surveillance practices of the modern state, as argued in Foucault, pp. 195–229. She counters that assessment by noting that the conditions of this prison were intended to be much more humanitarian than the contemporary alternatives, providing a progressive source for modifying motivational behavior, providing meaningful labor and skills, and advancing the evolution of a rational prison system. Janet Semple, "Foucault and Bentham: A Defence of Panopticism," *Utilitas* 4 (1992), pp. 105–20.

Indeed, Bentham proposed that the structural scheme of the Panopticon could be applied to schools, also, as a method for improving educational supervision and direction. Bentham, *Works*, vol. IV (Letter XXI on Schools), pp. 63–64; and Itzkin, p. 305.

758. The manuscript originally used the word "relations" and replaced it with "relaxations." RP MSS 141/125: 5.

759. An overall analysis of this structure and design by its author, including its construction and functional advantages, can be found in Jeremy Bentham, *The Panopticon Writings*, Miran Božovič, ed. (London: Verso, 1995), pp. 43–48, 97–114.

760. The manuscript originally began this sentence with the words "By means of" but, then, substituted the words "Under the safeguard of." RP MSS 141/127: 5.

761. A liberal interpretation of Panopticon and its purpose asserts that it was intended to be a "school of motion" in which the intervention of the state in terms of constraining prisoners would be justified by its goal of shaping motivation through example and rational direction of action, especially regarding productive and instructive labor. Allison Dube, *The Theme of Acquisitiveness in Bentham's Political Thought* (Abingdon, England: Taylor & Francis, 1991), pp. 315–16.

762. The manuscript initially used the word "augmenting" and replaced it with "inspiring." RP MSS 141/127: 5.

763. The manuscript originally used the phrase "seen that all the disorders at Botany Bay are either caused" instead of "had occasion to show that nearly all the crimes committed at Botany Bay, either originate." Ibid. That first version is closer to the literal translation of the parallel phrase within Dumont's edition. Bentham, *Théorie des peines*, vol. I, p. 248.

764. The manuscript is missing from this point.

765. The previous draft underlined the word "responsibility" for emphasis at this point. back of RP MSS 141/128: 5.

766. This theme can be associated with a broader argument that Semple has advanced in relation to Bentham's overall scheme of penology in terms of identifying a dichotomy between a social system that advances the progress of rational persons (serving as a basis for democracy) and Bentham's understanding of the "criminal mind" as a distinct category that warrants segregation, especially in terms of isolating anti-social behavior from normal social interaction and activity. Semple, *Bentham's Prison*, pp. 152–54.

767. The previous, crossed-out draft began this section with the sentence "Indigence, ignorance, and crimes are very near akin." Back of RP MSS 141/128: 5.

768. This system would, thus, become part of the overall process of democratic reform, especially by advancing reason and adjusting human motivations regarding pleasure and pain. Semple, *Bentham's Prison*, pp. 309–23.

769. The manuscript resumes at this point.

770. The manuscript initially used the word "assume" but replaced it with "seek." RP MSS 141/128: 5. Dumont's edition uses the word *postuleroient* [*sic*] for this parallel phrase. Bentham, *Théorie des peines*, vol. I, p. 251.

771. Dumont's edition places additional emphasis upon this sentence with an exclamation point. Bentham, *Théorie des peines*, vol. I, p. 252.

772. "Honor an escarped island without edges; one cannot return as soon as one is outside," quoted from Nicolas Boileau-Despréaux, *Satires* (Paris: Les Belles Lettres, 1966), p. 167.

773. Dumont's edition uses the phrase *malesuada fames* instead of "hunger" (*faim*) at this point. Bentham, *Théorie des peines*, vol. I, p. 252.

774. Dumont's edition adds, at the end of this paragraph, another sentence: "I will soon cite proof in support of this theory." Ibid., p. 253.

775. Deprivation of choice is a necessary feature of any effective prison system, including one grounded upon utilitarian principles. Semple, *Bentham's Prison*, p. 157.

776. The manuscript substituted the word "also" for the original word "yet." RP MSS 141/129: 5.

777. The manuscript originally included, then crossed-out, the adjective "formal" in front of the noun "profit." Ibid.

778. These ideas anticipate, remarkably, the development of the halfway house system of transitioning convicts, through parole, back into society, as described in Oliver J. Keller, *Halfway Houses: Community Centered Correction and Treatment* (Lexington, MA: Lexington Books, 1970), pp. 1–10.

779. Dumont's edition specifies "In our systems." Bentham, *Théorie des peines*, vol. I, p. 256.

780. The manuscript initially used the words "could not" and, then, replaced it with the less tentative verb "cannot." RP MSS 141/130: 5.

781. The manuscript is missing from this point to the end of the chapter.

782. These third person references to Bentham are present within Dumont's edition, as they are within Smith's edition, such as at Bentham, *Théorie des peines*, vol. I, p. 259. This format of this chapter strongly suggests a presentation of Bentham's ideas, as interpreted first by Dumont and, then, by Smith.

783. Dumont includes a footnote at this parallel point: "(1) The philosopher of which I speak is the author of *Le Misantrope*." Ibid., p. 263.

784. The following sentence was included within the previous draft at this approximate place, which may offer an interesting insight into the tone of this section of the published chapter: "The Porter will be no stronger than his flock: they are the objects of his daily solicitude; he watches the prospect of their amendment and stands as their mediator and patron between them and their superior." Back of RP MSS 141/130: 5.

785. A rough overhead sketch of the physical outline of the Panapticon can be found within the margin of the previous draft at this approximate point of the published text, emphasizing its circular pattern with the observation tower in the center. Back of Ibid. This rough sketch may be based upon more detailed "blueprint" sketches found in Ibid., 119/119–130.

786. This type of argument would have particular appeal for the legislator, who not only is preoccupied with concerns about the safety and security of society but who also was increasingly inclined, at this time, to associate that security with the necessary conditions for social liberty. Dube, pp. 250–51.

787. This chapter represents a very brief summary of a much larger project that Bentham published, separately, Jeremy Bentham, *Panopticon; or, The Inspection House* (Dublin: T. Payne, 1791) and, as previously cited, a more recent version, edited by Miran Božovič. The outline for this project, itself, occupied 238 manuscript pages. RP MSS 119/131–315. A British House of Commons committee held hearings on Bentham's Panopticon proposal. The committee agreed with the Bentham's conclusion concerning the need for prison reform but not, specifically, to the model that he proposed. "Reports from the Committee on the Laws Relating to Penitentiary Houses," House of Commons, 31 May 1811–10 June 1811. A second report of this same committee included a response to, and copy of, Bentham's letter to the committee that included many of the same points raised within this chapter, except that it placed additional emphasis upon the safety and effectiveness of confinement that the Panopticon, he argued, would provide. "Second Report from the Committee on the Laws Relating to Penitentiary Houses," House of Commons, 10 June 1811. Although that second committee report is dated 1811, Bentham's letter is signed and dated "20th February, 1824."

BOOK V, CHAPTER IV

788. The manuscript for this chapter is not available. A version of it appears as book five, chapter three of Dumont's edition. Bentham, *Théorie des peines*, vol. I, pp. 468–95.

789. Dumont's edition ends this parallel paragraph with a somewhat different sentence: "It is established rather by custom than by a positive law: to remove life was a small thing after removing all that then can provide the prize." Ibid., p. 469.

790. This category is among those terms that Bentham criticized under the category of "legal fictions." Jeremy Bentham, *A Comment on the Commentaries*, pp. 58–59. This critique is noted in Scheppele, pp. 64–65.

791. The final sentence of this parallel paragraph within Dumont's edition is placed within parentheses. Bentham, *Théorie des peines*, vol. I, p. 472.

792. Bentham's emphasis upon etymology was central to the "preparatory principles" manuscripts that was an essential part of his overall philosophical scheme, especially in terms of eliminating errors in political and legal reasoning and debate through a better understanding of the meaning and application of words. Long, pp. 221–39.

793. Dumont's edition offers a different sentence at this parallel point: "These two punishments, thus contained under the same name by a routine blindness and an arrangement which confounds all principles of method, are very different from one to another, as we will soon see." Bentham, *Théorie des peines*, vol. I, p. 474.

794. A version of this concluding paragraph of this section does not appear within Dumont's edition.

795. This word is emphasized in italics within Dumont's edition Ibid., p. 478.

796. Dumont's edition adds, in parentheses, the clarification "ecclesiastical superiors" following the reference to "ordinary judge." Ibid., p. 481.

797. Dumont's edition offers, at this parallel point, a different passage that offers a semantic explanation: "for thus the word of *purging* had been the term employed for this procedure in the first revision." Ibid.

798. Dumont's edition emphasizes, in italics, the words "purgation," judgment," and "acquittal" at this parallel point. For the word "acquittal," Dumont's edition uses the French word "*absolution*." Ibid., p. 482.

799. Dumont's edition describes it as a "new proof." Ibid., p. 483.

800. Dumont's edition indicates Henry IV. Ibid., p. 484.

801. The text from this point to the end of the section does not appear within Dumont's edition.

802. English and Welsh developments in this area during the nineteenth century are reviewed in M. D. Stephen, "Gladstone and the Composition of the Final Court in Ecclesiastical Causes, 1850–1873," *The Historical Journal* 9, no. 2 (1966): 191–200.

803. Dumont's edition is more direct in identifying these broad categories: "It is necessary to distinguish within this punishment the part that falls upon the culpable, and that which is imposed upon the innocent." Bentham, *Théorie des peines*, vol. I, p. 487.

804. Dumont's edition does not use the Latin terms in identifying these two categories of punishment.

805. A version of the remainder of this paragraph is not found within Dumont's edition.

806. Dumont's edition distinguishes between the words "*tenure*" and "*tenemens*," applying both of them to this example. Bentham, *Théorie des peines*, vol. I, p. 487. Again, this edition presents a much simpler paragraph to describe this category in comparison with Smith's edition. Following the first sentence, Dumont's edition concludes this parallel paragraph with the following sentence and footnote:

This forfeiture of buildings is total(1) or partial following the nature of the good.

(1) It is not total in all cases. The wife of a delinquent has the right to her dowry taken from the confiscated goods. Bentham, *Théorie des peines*, vol. I, p. 487.

807. Dumont's edition does not qualify this category of punishment as "corporal" Ibid., p. 488.

808. This category is not included within Dumont's edition.

809. The remainder of this paragraph is not found within Dumont's edition, which is listed as category number four. Ibid.

810. Instead of this introductory paragraph to the next set of categories, Dumont's edition inserts the following sentence at this parallel point: "Punishment imposed upon the innocent, includes . . ." Ibid.

811. The term "corruption of blood" is emphasized in italics within Dumont's edition. Ibid.

812. Dumont's edition concludes this parallel paragraph with a different sentence: "Thus the forfeiture is casual, it is perhaps all or nothing." Ibid.

813. A version of the remainder of this paragraph does not appear within Dumont's edition.

814. A version of this paragraph does not appear within Dumont's edition.

815. Again, Dumont's edition does not employ this Latin term.

816. A version of the passage, phrased "unless the offense be murder, in which case it is to be an M; murder, at that time, not as yet having been taken out of the benefit of Clergy," appears as a footnote within Dumont's edition. Ibid., p. 490.

817. Dumont's edition emphasizes "transportation" in italics and does not use the word "imprisonment" at this parallel point. Ibid., p. 492.

818. Instead of this paragraph, Dumont's edition offers a different passage, which offers a good sense of the tone or moral disapproval (if not outrage) that frequently is evident (perhaps even more than in Smith's edition) within that text:

> It is undoubtedly a distinction that is very honorable to the clergy that the right to commit with very little risk several sorts of offenses, for which other members of society are hanged. One often intends to speak of adventurers who make considerable fortunes by taking five or six women at a time. Meanwhile, if a man is convicted of polygamy, one must be mindful of him, before hazarding there again. But ecclesiastics, by reason of the sanctity of their vocation, can enjoy a harem. I would recommend to young people who have good figures and graces, and who want to serve for their fortune, to follow these orders: those of a deacon will be sufficient, and they are not peasants, one can get rid of them when one wants. If they discover, they will be rid of a good bargain; cold iron will not provide a great evil; imprisonment for a few months is only a trifle when one is rich. It is better to be in prison and rich than free and indigent. It is true that there is a forfeiture of moveable effects: but so what? It is as easy to conceal ten thousand pounds sterling in a portfolio, and elsewhere what risk does one run, so far as one can convert moveable effects into good plots of land which are not prone to forfeiture? Ibid., pp. 492–93.

819. A version of this sentence does not appear within Dumont's edition.

820. These quotes do not appear within Dumont's edition.

821. Dumont's edition describes Sir Edward as "zealous partisan" in this respect. Ibid., p. 495.

A version of the remainder of this chapter, from this parallel point, does not appear within Dumont's edition, concluding both the chapter and this volume dedicated to the "Theory of Punishments." Volume two continues, of course, onto the separate, though related, subject of the "Theory of Rewards."

BOOK V, CHAPTER V

822. The manuscript for this chapter is not available.

823. An overview of the development of this category of law in England is provided in W. T. Waugh, "The Great Statute of Praemunire," *English Historical Review* 37, no. 146 (April 1922): 173–205.

BOOK V, CHAPTER VI

824. A subtitle at the start of this paragraph in the margin of the manuscript is entitled "Immorality." RP MSS 141/131: 5.

825. The following sentences originally were added to this paragraph within the manuscript but, later, crossed-out: "The lawyer views his files before he begins his work: the physi-

cian in a very short time after he has begun doing it. The common labourer in the customary way of dealing waits but a short time before he receives his hire: and in case of necessity it were an easy thing for him to stipulate its being paid him in advance." Ibid.

826. The manuscript identifies "D=401" at this point in the margin in Richard Smith's handwriting. However, the margin also makes reference to the titles "Forfeiture of Protection" and "Inequality." Ibid.

827. The manuscript originally used the phrase "It only" and replaced it with "The utmost it can do, is to." Ibid.

828. The manuscript uses the word "selling" instead of "buying," which does not appear within the manuscript at this place. Ibid.

829. The phrase "the benefit of such bargains" initially was included within the manuscript and, then, crossed-out and replaced with the words "upon credit." Ibid.

830. The manuscript initially used the phrase "a man who is guilty as to him who is not culpable" and, then, replaced it with the phrase "the lesser offender, as upon the greater." Ibid.

831. Bentham even compared the general resistance to codification of the law to a "confederated sinister interest" between lawyers and parliamentarians that was designed to reduce most of society to a condition of "outlawry." John R. Dinwiddy, "Bentham's Transition to Political Radicalism," *Journal of the History of Ideas* 36, no. 4 (October 1975): 288–89.

832. The manuscript originally used a period, rather than a semi-colon, at this point, making the next word the beginning of a new sentence. RP MSS 141/131: 5.

833. The manuscript originally used the phrase "money has more power over him than the morality" but replaced it with the phrase "the power of money over him is greater than that of the moral sanction." Ibid.

BOOK V, CHAPTER VII

834. This chapter does not appear within the manuscript. The parallel chapter within Dumont's edition appears as book five, chapter two. Bentham, *Théorie des peines*, vol. I, pp. 458–67.

835. The perspective of Bentham and Smith upon this subject would have been more directly informed through their exposure to canon law in the Church of England, while Dumont would have been more familiar with this subject from his own Calvinist experience, especially as having studied for the ministry at one time. Nonetheless, this subject has been most thoroughly developed through the Roman Catholic tradition. An overview of this subject from a traditional Catholic perspective is provided in Thomas J. Green, "Sanctions in the Church," in *New Commentary on the Code of Canon Law*, John P. Beal, James A. Coriden, and Thomas J. Green, eds. (Mahwah, NJ: Paulist Press, 2002), pp. 1533–73. An account of an approach to excommunication as it related to contemporaries of these utilitarian scholars can be found in Noah Porter, *Two Sermons on Church Communion and Excommunication, with a Particular View to Slaveholders in the Church* (Ithaca, NY: Cornell University Library, 2006), pp. 15–20.

836. The opening paragraph of this parallel chapter within Dumont's edition is somewhat different from this paragraph: "There is not a question here of excommunication in its relationship with English jurisprudence. The first point of this examination pivots on the punishments which are contained there, and which concerns enumeration." Bentham, *Théorie des peines*, vol. I, p. 458.

Bentham devoted himself to influencing the extirpation of religious beliefs from all aspects of public policy. This critique of the role of excommunication within the law fits within that theme. James E. Crimmins, "Bentham on Religion: Atheism and the Secular Society," *Journal of the History of Ideas* 47, no. 1 (January 1986): 95–110. This hostility was not, necessarily, shared by later utilitarians, as exemplified in John Stuart Mill, *Three Essays on Religion: Nature, the Utility of Religion, and Theism* (London: Prometheus Books, 1998), pp. 69–124. An assessment of this development is provided in Robert Carr, "The Religious Thought of John Stuart Mill: A Study in Reluctant Scepticism," *Journal of the History of Ideas* 23, no. 4 (October 1962): 475–95. Dumont's interpretation of this general category is uncertain, although his association with Mirabeau in France and his personal experiences in Geneva offer a ground for speculation in this respect; this chapter appears to be devoted to description, more than commentary, in this respect.

837. This category does not appear within the parallel chapter of Dumont's edition.

838. The parallel chapter within Dumont's edition combines this category with category V. Bentham, *Théorie des peines*, vol. I, p. 459.

839. The parallel chapter within Dumont's edition indicates this category as number eight. Ibid., pp. 459–60.

840. The parallel chapter within Dumont's edition indicates this category as number ten. Ibid., p. 460.

841. The parallel chapter within Dumont's edition indicates this category as number nine. Ibid.

842. The parallel chapter within Dumont's edition indicates this category as number eleven. Ibid., p. 460.

843. The parallel chapter of Dumont's edition indicates this category as number twelve. It makes references to the sacraments, especially stressing baptism, suggesting a particularly Catholic perspective. Ibid.

844. The parallel chapter of Dumont's edition explains this category, differently:

This is the sort of punishment employed by ecclesiastical courts, or according to a bizarre denomination, spiritual courts. They are forced to make use of it for all occasions, because they have neither largest nor smallest. (1) It is the whole of their penal code. If its brevity is a recommendation, it is necessary to acknowledge that it has no other. Let us dwell upon some of its imperfections.

(1) This excommunication is like the epee of Hudibras, who cleaves the giants, and who threads the lark. A man commits an incest? He is excommunicated. A fishwife gives injurious names to another fishwife? She is excommunicated. Ibid., pp. 460–61.

845. This observation appears to be consistent with Bentham's overall critique of the Church of England and its political establishment, including its "poisonous catechism." James E. Crimmins, *Utilitarians and Religion* (Bristol, England: Thoemmes Press, 1998), pp. 350–55. James Mill does not appear to have been quite as critical in this respect. Ibid., pp. 420–21.

846. This paragraph does not appear within the parallel chapter of Dumont's edition.

847. Punishment, overall, could be regarded as a "secularization of religious penance." Rodman, p. 210. Thus early utilitarians could have appreciated the relationship between normative moral sanction, as provided by religion, and the intrinsic qualities of punishment. Ibid., pp. 197–210

848. Dumont's edition offers a somewhat different version of this paragraph:

To be regarded like the pagans and the publicans, that is to say the public revenue collectors, is one of the punishments of excommunication. Of what import it has in that opinion, I am unaware. Of what import it has in the intention of those who pronounce it, is to envision the individuals as assimilated to the pagans and the publicans as condemned. Bentham, *Théorie des peines*, vol. I, pp. 463–64.

849. A version of this paragraph is not found within Dumont's edition. Instead, that edition offers a different paragraph at this parallel point:

> A man who, following the process of the spiritual court, will not or cannot pay his *proctor*, so to speak his *prosecutor* (for they are the same thing), is excommunicated. (1) Thus they are placed among the pagans, so to speak among the worshippers of Jupiter and the other gods of mythology; among the publicans, so to speak, the officers of public revenue, the financiers, the lords of the treasury, etc. It formerly had been a serious injury, but in our time, it is a burlesque epithet of ridicule that has been dropped from the law.

> (1) Excommunication is employed as a method of constraint in many cases for compelling a payment. Thus a man can be excommunicated for being poor. Blessed are they who are poor, said Jesus Christ. One sees that the language is not that of men who call themselves his successors. Ibid., p. 464.

850. Later utilitarians, especially John Stuart Mill, would be somewhat more sympathetic in evaluating the beneficial effects and value of religion upon individual and social life. Crimmins, *Utilitarians and Religion*, pp. 267–71.

851. One of the best surveys of the historical development of excommunication as a punishment is provided by F. Donald Logan, *Excommunication and the Secular Arm in Medieval England* (Toronto: Pontifical Institute of Medieval Studies, 1968).

852. Dumont's edition offers a somewhat different footnote to conclude this chapter:

> (1) I have, very nearly, followed my author in all of the observations regarding spiritual punishments. In several cases it would not have been comprised, without entering into many details of English jurisprudence. Elsewhere the subject is much less interesting, for ecclesiastical arms are rusted more and more by lack of use; and if it is important to continue fighting generally condemned laws, it remains necessary to abolish them. Formally, Bentham, *Théorie des peines*, vol. I, p. 467.

Nonetheless, the treatment of this subject within this chapter appears to be somewhat more sympathetic regarding the positive role and benefit of religion, in general, than suggested by Bentham's previous, though passing, published treatment of it within Bentham, *Morals and Legislation*, ch. 3, sec. 10.

BOOK VI, CHAPTER I

853. This chapter does not appear within the manuscript.

854. Civil-law systems, in which judges tend to acknowledge and apply, rather than interpret and declare, the law, often satisfy this desire for "certainty" much more readily than common-law systems. This distinction not only satisfies a utilitarian desire but, also, tends to make such systems more receptive to the municipal incorporation of international legal obligations. Mary Ann Glendon, Christopher Osakwe, and Michael W. Gordon, *Comparative Legal*

Traditions in a Nutshell (St. Paul: West, 1982), p. 234; and Beth Simmons, "Why Commit? Explaining State Acceptance of International Human Rights Obligations," *WCFIA: Weatherhead Center for International Affairs Working Papers* (November 2003): 13–15.

855. Even among those eighteenth-century defenders of natural law and the facility of common-law jurists in promoting these broad normative principles (whom Bentham tended to deride), the overriding authority of the legislature remains acknowledged. Sir Robert Chambers, with Samuel Johnson, *A Course of Lectures on the English Law, 1768–1773*, Thomas M. Curley, ed. (Madison: University of Wisconsin Press, 1986), pp. 89–93.

856. The role of the judge that Bentham critiqued is, of course, central to the working of the English common law tradition, distinguishing it from civil law traditions in which judges serve to administer, rather than interpret, the law. McHugh, *Essential Concept of Law*, pp. 60–64, 79–82. It is interesting that Bentham confines himself to an examination of the law of Britain as practiced in England and Wales and does not evaluate the "mixed-law" system of Scotland in this respect, although criminal law in Scotland does, largely, adhere to common-law practices regarding the role of judges, as discussed in Enid A. Marshall, *General Principles of Scots Law* (Edinburgh: W. Green and Son, 1978), pp. 213–15.

857. Even great defenders of the common-law tradition (of whom Bentham, in particular, was critical) have acknowledged the need for the legislature to curb the latitude of judicial discretion, such as in the area of defining and applying rights and liberties. Blackstone, *Commentaries on the Laws of England*, vol. I, pp. 122–44.

858. These general and persistent concerns regarding the relationship of judges to the legislature and the concept of "judicial law-making" are addressed (including in terms of a utilitarian critique) in Roscoe Pound and Neil Hamilton, *The Spirit of the Common Law* (Somerset, NJ: Transaction Publishers, 1998), pp. 170–72, 176–80.

859. This factor generally is acknowledged as an important feature of the common law tradition. Bentham's general attitudes in this, and other, respects are addressed in Postema, pp. 191–217.

860. A good overview of Bentham's attitude toward judges within a common-law system can be found in Pound and Hamilton, pp. 158–61.

861. An overarching tension continued to exist within the evolution of Britain's legal system regarding the competing principles of an independent judiciary and parliamentary supremacy, including in terms of the country's relationship to international conventions and legal arrangements. Andrew Moravcsik, "The Origins of Human Rights Regimes: Democratic Delegation in Postwar Europe," *International Organization* 54, no. 2 (Spring 2000): 239–41.

BOOK VI, CHAPTER II

862. The parallel chapter of Dumont's edition appears as book two, chapter 15. Bentham, *Théorie des peines*, vol. I pp. 317–23. The manuscript for this chapter is, reportedly (according to the folder cover), written in Jeremy Bentham's handwriting, circa 1775. Another draft, apparently in Richard Smith's handwriting, begins "It is evident that no penal law would be enforced if it depended upon the will of those who were to submit to it." Back of RP MSS 141/102: 3. That draft parallels the opening section of Dumont's version of this chapter, beginning with the fourth paragraph and extending for three additional paragraphs:

I call *Subsidiary Punishment* that which is assigned by the law for supporting a previous punishment which was in default because the delinquent *did not want* to subject himself to it.

I call *Subsidiary* or *Supplemental Punishment* that which is assigned for replacing a previous punishment, which was in default because the delinquent *cannot* submit to it.

The first law is in default. Here is what is common between these two cases: here, it is defaulted by the non-desire of the delinquent; there, by the non-capacity.

It is evident that no penal law will be executed, if one refered oneself to the will of that which must undergo it.

There are cases, as in passive punishments, where this will is beyond question; but there are many sorts of punishments which prescribe to the individual a certain control,—to do a certain thing,—to abstain from some other thing,—paying such a sum of money,—not to leave such a place, etc.; in all these cases where physical constraint is not implemented, it must necessarily, for giving full force to the mandate of the law, there is added the threat of a second punishment that will assure the execution of the first. This subsidiary punishment can be of the same sort as the original punishment: for example, for violation of temporary banishment, a new banishment;—but, in the last resort, all punishment which cannot be executed with the cooperation of the will of the individual, must be backed by some other punishment which is executed despite him.

The law is most particularly subject to be in default by the non-compliance of the delinquent, in the case of pecuniary punishments: but that can take place for passive punishments; such as if the law enjoins the mutilation of an organ, which, by accident, had not existed in the individual. Bentham, *Théorie des peines*, vol. I, pp. 317–18.

863. The manuscript originally used the word "constantly" and, then, replaced it with the phrase "in every case." RP MSS 141/132: 6.

864. The manuscript included, then crossed-out, the following phrase at this point: "is the case of all those punishments which in the grand division of corporal punishments into three classes are comprised under the names of *active* and *restrictive* punishments" Ibid.

865. The manuscript originally used the phrase "necessarily depends upon" but replaced it with "inflicted without the concurrence of." Ibid.

866. Bentham's ideas and recommendations regarding certain aspects of subsidiary punishment (including markings and other forms of discoloration) were subject to "ironic comments" within such contemporary publications as *Critical Review* 48 (1778): 138, as noted in Letter to Samuel Bentham [279], *Correspondence*, vol. II, (October 24, 1778), p. 180.

867. However, this approach also could result in an overwhelming proliferation of laws that are prompted by immediate experiences and desires and undermined by short-sighted and parochial drafting and implementation. MSS 140/92: 2. Both Romilly and Bentham were aware of this problem and consequence, and it served as an additional source of complaint regarding Blackstone's theories on the common law. David Lieberman, "Blackstone's Science of Legislation," *Journal of British Studies* 27, no. 2 (April 1988): 143–45.

868. Dumont's edition begins to parallel Smith's edition at this point. Bentham, *Théorie des peines*, vol. I, p. 318.

869. Dumont's edition offers a somewhat different presentation of this rule:

Is the first punishment a default because the delinquent is incompetent to submit? The subsidiary punishment must not be greater nor [*sic*] less than the first designation.

Here at least is the measure that one must seek, though difficult it is thus to reach. Ibid., pp. 318–19.

870. A version of the last two sentences of this paragraph do not appear within Dumont's edition. Ibid., p. 319.

871. The manuscript initially applied the phrase "more difficult it is for the delinquent to be detected and made amenable" and, then, replaced it with "easier it is for the delinquent to avoid the punishment first designed." RP MSS 141/132: 6.

872. The manuscript originally used the phrased "stands in the balance" and, then, replaced it with the words "weighs against." Ibid.

873. The manuscript is missing from this point to the end of the chapter. From this point, Smith's edition is reflected within the parallel chapter of Dumont's edition. Bentham, *Théorie des peines*, vol. I, pp. 320–23.

874. Arriving at an appropriate calculus for this sort of subsidiary punishment has been an emphasis of the "sanction hierarchy" approach to proportional punishment and the use of non-custodial penalties that was popularized by Andrew von Hirsch and Martin Wasik, "Punishments in the Community and the Principles of Desert," *Rutgers Law Journal* 20, no. 3 (Winter 1968): 595–618. In terms of the functional effectiveness of punishment, this method may work best for achieving the utilitarian goals of subsidiary punishment. This approach is explained and critiqued, in this respect, in A. Lovegrove, "Sanctions and Severity: To the Demise of Von Hirsch and Wasik's Sanction Hierarchy," *Howard Journal of Criminal Justice* 40, no. 2 (May 2001): 126–44.

BOOK VI, CHAPTER III

875. The manuscript for this chapter is not available.

876. Eighteenth-century Enlightenment thinkers often noted that the rise of commercial society prompted a distinction between self-interested relationships (which are most notably assumed within early utilitarian thought) and sympathetic relationships that are, arguably, less alienated from later utilitarian thought. This general development is addressed in Allan Silver, "Friendship in Commercial Society: Eighteenth-Century Social Theory and Modern Sociology," *American Journal of Sociology* 95, no. 6 (May 1990): 1474–1504.

877. The mandatory imposition of such surety has historical roots. Modern objections to the practice can be related to the broader concept of collective responsibility that distributes group liability (which might be associate with utilitarian objections to collective punishment) in contrast to individual liability, as explored in Joel Feinberg, "Collective Responsibility," *Journal of Philosophy* 65, no. 21 (November 1968): 679–80.

878. This concept has been applied to families of juvenile delinquents, in which parents of delinquent children for whom surety has been given may be liable (usually in terms of a lost bond) for future criminal acts of a child. Janet Gilbert, Richard Grimm, and John Parnham, "Applying Therapeutic Principles to a Family-Focused Juvenile Justice Model (Delinquency)," *Alabama Law Review* 52, no. 4 (Summer 2001): 1192–93.

BOOK VI, CHAPTER IV

879. An excellent overview of the traditional utilitarian position on pardons is offered in Kathleen Dean Moore, *Pardons: Justice, Mercy, and the Public Interest* (Oxford: Oxford University Press), pp. 35–46.

880. Bentham emphasized that the effectiveness of a pardon would be useless unless the conditions of moral order had been obtained first Beattie, pp. 604–605.

881. An explanation of the principle of the statute of limitations as applied to civil cases is provided in Marshall S. Shapo, *Principles of Tort Law* (St. Paul: West, 2003), pp. 27–28.

882. Transportation could be understood (as it may have been understood by Bentham and his contemporaries) as a form of pardon in which a convict, rather than being executed, was absolved of the consequences of the offense, provided that this person remain exiled for a prescribed number of years. Alan Atkinson, "The Free-Born Englishman Transported: Convict Rights as a Measure of Eighteenth-Century Empire, *Past and Present*, no. 144 (August 1994): 109.

883. The manuscript resumes at this point, reportedly in Bentham's handwriting.

884. A subheading in the manuscript margin indicates "Provide for the Innocent." RP MSS 141/133: 7.

885. The manuscript originally began this paragraph with the words "Prescription ought not" and, later, replaced it with "Neither ought it not." Ibid.

886. A subhead is inserted, then crossed-out, at this point in the manuscript: "3. Prescription not to be adopted in case of . . ." Ibid. The margin of the manuscript includes the subhead "In what offenses not to be admitted." Ibid.

887. The manuscript originally used the word "revenge" (which is crossed-out) instead of "replacement." Ibid.

888. The manuscript includes, at this point, the reference "ff–433=." Ibid.

889. The margin of the manuscript includes, near this point, the subhead "What is gained by it." Ibid.

890. The manuscript initially included the phrase "to guide us in the way of solving our researches," but, then, replaced it with "just to put us in the way." Ibid.

891. The manuscript originally included the phrase "to guide us in the detail of our research," and, then, replaced it with "to indicate the principal points." Ibid.

892. The margin of the manuscript includes, near this point, the subhead "meet for pardon." Ibid.

893. A previous draft of this chapter included a passage in Bentham's handwriting and written in red ink (except for the footnote, which was written in black ink) that elaborated upon the theme of this section, with the heading "Inf: Punishment whether defeasible by length of Time." Parts of it are faded and indecipherable yet still provide interesting insights into the attitude and approach of Bentham toward this subject:

> . . . the Civil Law and the Scotch Law and see the item on which Prescription is admitted. An account of Prescription as it *exists* should precede in this case the Inquisition concerning the prosperity of [indecipherable] obscure the Prescription in case of High Treason by a random Statute.*
>
> These prescriptions are necessary to prevent its doing great mischief. The good it can do that is the evil it can prevent harm in any case except that of forty misdemeanors is but very inconsiderable.
>
> In crimes of resentment it ought to be admitted only as far as concerns with respect to the extra punishment: it ought not to preclude the forty injured from exacting compensation if he pleases. Understand in this case when the resentment is vented upon the property: or where done to the person if the malefactor be unknown. Yet in this case to be allowed if no information was within such a time given to a Magistrate.
>
> None to be indicted unless within 3 years: nor prosecuted unless indicted within that time except for assassinating or designing to assassinate the King. Ibid.

894. The manuscript originally used the word "delinquent" and, then, replaced it with the word "injurer." Ibid., 141/134: 7.

895. The manuscript originally began this sentence with the phrase "Their notion is but it is a hasty and erroneous one" but used, instead, "They imagine, but hastily and erroneously." Ibid.

896. The margin of the manuscript includes, near this point, the subhead "The punishment included in the burthen of yielding compulation [*sic*] is apt to be overlooked." Ibid.

897. An assessment of a twenty-first century application of the general theme of compensation to international law can be found in Donald Francis Donovan and Anthea Roberts, "The Emerging Recognition of Universal Civil Jurisdiction," *American Journal of International Law* 100, no. 1 (January 2006): 148–60.

898. The manuscript initially used the word "indemnification" and, then, replaced it with "compensation." RP MSS 141/134: 7.

899. The manuscript initially used the words "beyond comparison" and, then, replaced it with the words "by much." Ibid.

900. The margin of the manuscript includes, near this point, the subhead "Yet compensation without punishment is an inadequate remedy." Ibid.

901. The margin of the manuscript includes, near this point, the subhead "The purpose of punishment is however in many instances answered without design." Ibid.

902. The margin of the manuscript includes, near this point, the subhead "1. by the death of the indemnifier." Ibid.

903. The manuscript originally included, then crossed-out, the noun "successor" and replaced it with "representative." Ibid.

904. The manuscript originally included, the omitted, at the end of this paragraph "I mean to the extent of the perceptions he inherits from the receipt." Ibid.

905. The margin of the manuscript includes, near this point, the subhead "2. Nor even where no pecuniary profit descends to him." Ibid., 141/135: 7.

906. The manuscript treats this paragraph and the one that follows as a single paragraph. Ibid.
The margin of the manuscript includes, near this point, the subhead "because there is no need of compensation" Ibid.

907. The margin of the manuscript includes, near this point, the subhead "and 2. of punishment." Ibid.

908. The margin of the manuscript includes, near this point, the subhead "Imperfection of the English law in this behalf." Ibid.
The manuscript, at this approximate point, indicates a change in the order of the paragraphs so they are not consistent with the order found within the published text, although those changes are noted in red ink in order to provide continuity. Ibid., 141/135–136: 7.

909. The footnote indicated here initially used the words "particular tenet" and, then, substituted the words "life-owner." It also originally used the phrase "was obliged to lose his remedy for the waste" but, then, replaced them with the phrase found within the parentheses. Ibid., 141/135: 7.

910. The manuscript originally started this sentence with the phrase "The punishment is by this means rendered upon," then began it with the phrase "The death of the party in question." Ibid.

911. The manuscript followed the colon with the words "for the expectation of the apparent representative" but, then, replaced it with the words "the person." Ibid.

912. Thus Bentham believed that unpunished crime could pose an expansive threat to the overall good of society. Eldon J. Eisenach, "Crime, Death and Loyalty in English Liberalism," *Political Theory* 6, no. 2 (May 1978): 214–15.

913. The manuscript, within this footnote, originally used the words "under imprisonment" and, then, substituted the words "in gaol." It also initially used the phrase "A year or

---

*7 Will. 3. C. 3. *ff* 5, 6.

two ago" to begin the sentence that ultimately begins with the words "Many years ago." RP MSS 141/136: 7.

914. This theme is expanded in Bentham, *Theory of Legislation*, pp. 73–74. This text also was translated from Dumont's original translation.

915. The manuscript originally used the phrase "done to the person, or" but, then, replaced it with the phrase "or in the way of mere." RP MSS 141/136: 7.

BIBLIOGRAPHY

BOOK CHAPTERS

Andenaes, Johannes, "Does Punishment Deter Crime?" in *Philosophical Perspectives on Punishment*, Gertrude Ezorsky, ed. Albany, State University of New York Press, 1972.

Bentham, Jeremy, "Anarchical Fallacies," in *Collected Works of Jeremy Bentham*, John Bowring, ed., Edinburgh, William Tait, 1843.

——, "Constitutional Code," in *Collected Works of Jeremy Bentham*, John Bowring, ed., Edinburgh, William Tait, 1843.

——, "Outline of a Work entitled Pauper Management Improvement," in *Collected Works of Jeremy Bentham*, John Bowring, ed., Edinburgh, William Tait, 1843.

——, "Pannomial Fragments," in *Collected Works of Jeremy Bentham*, John Bowring, ed., Edinburgh, William Tait, 1843.

——, "Panopticon," in *Collected Works of Jeremy Bentham*, John Bowring, ed., Edinburgh, William Tait, 1843.

——, "Principles of Penal Law," in *Collected Works of Jeremy Bentham*, John Bowring, ed., Edinburgh, William Tait, 1843.

——, "The Rationale of Punishment," in *Collected Works of Jeremy Bentham*, John Bowring, ed., Edinburgh, William Tait, 1843.

Burns, J. H., "The Bentham Project," in *Editing Texts of the Romantic Period*, John D. Baird, ed. Toronto, AMS Press, 1987.

Chevrette, François, "Les concepts de 'droits acquis,' de 'droits des groups,' et de 'droits collectifs,'" in *Les Droits linguistiques: rapport de la commission d'enquête sur la situation de la langue française et sure les droits linguistiques au Québec*. Québec, Gouvernement du Québec, 1972.

Dinwiddy, John R., "Bentham and the Early Nineteenth Century," in *Radicalism and Reform in Britain, 1780–1850*. London, Hambledon, 1992.

Dinwiddy, John R., "The Classical Economists and the Utilitarians," in *Western Liberalism: A History in Documents from Locke to Croce*, E. K. Bramstead and K. J. Melhuish, eds. London: Longmans, 1978.

Feldman, Fred, "Two Questions About Pleasure," in *Philosophical Analysis*, David Austin, ed. Dordrecht, The Netherlands, Kluwer, 1988.

Franklin, Benjamin, "A Letter from a Gentleman Abroad to His Friend in England," in Sir Samuel Romilly, *Observations on the Criminal Law of England*. London, T. Cadell and W. Davies, 1813.

Green, Thomas, J., "Sanctions in the Church," in *New Commentary on the Code of Canon Law*, John P. Beal, James A. Coriden, and Thomas J. Green, eds. Mahwah, NJ, Paulist Press, 2002.

McCloskey, H. J., "A Non-Utilitarian Approach to Punishment," in *Contemporary Utilitarianism*, Michael D. Bayles, ed. Garden City, NY, Anchor Books, 1968.

Mill, John Stuart, "On the Connection Between Justice and Utility," in *Utilitarianism*, John Plamenatz, ed. Oxford, Clarendon Press, 1949.

Mill, John Stuart, "Utilitarianism," in *Collected Works of John Stuart Mill*, J. M. Robson and Michael Lane, eds. New York, Routledge, 1991.

Moore, G. E., "The Conception of Intrinsic Value," in *Philosophical Studies*. London, Routledge and Keegan Paul, 1960.

Parekh, Bhikhu C., "Bentham's Justification of the Principle of Utility," in *Jeremy Betham: Ten Critical Essays*, Bhikhu C. Parekh, ed. London, Routledge, 1974.

Schogt, Henry, "Semantic Theory and Translation Theory," in *Theories of Translation*, John Biguenet and Rainer Schulte, eds. Chicago, University of Chicago Press, 1992.

Smart, J. C. C., "An Outline of a System of Utilitarian Ethics," in *Utilitarianism: For and Against*, J. C. C. Smart and Bernard Williams, eds. Cambridge, Cambridge University Press, 1973.

Sorley, W. R., "Bentham and the Early Utilitarians," *Cambridge History of English and American Literature*. Cambridge, Cambridge University Press, 1921.

JOURNAL ARTICLES

"Reports from the Committee on the Laws Relating to Penitentiary Houses," House of Commons, 31 May 1811—10 June 1811.

"Second Report from the Committee on the Laws Relating to Penitentiary Houses," House of Commons, 10 June 1811.

Note, "Criminality in France in 1895," 4 *American Journal of Sociology*, no. 6, May 1899.

Note, "What's This About Punishing Parents?" 12 *Federal Probation*, March 1948.

Arneson, Richard J., "Mill *versus* Paternalism," 90 *Ethics*, no. 4, July 1980.

Atkinson, Alan, "The Free-Born Englishman Transported: Convict Rights as a Measure of Eighteenth-Century Empire, *Past and Present*, no. 144, August 1994.

Bailey, Victor, "English Prisons, Penal Culture, and the Abatement of Imprisonment, 1895–1922," 36 *Journal of British Studies*, no. 3, July 1997.

Bailey, William C., "Murder, Capital Punishment, and Television: Execution Publicity and Homicide Rates," 55 *American Sociological Review*, no. 5, October 1990.

Barnett, Randy E., "Restitution: A New Paradigm of Criminal Justice," 87 *Ethics*, no. 4, July 1977.

Baron, David P., and John A. Ferejohn, "Bargaining in Legislatures," 83 *American Political Science Review*, no. 4, December 1989.

Becker, Gary S,, "Crime and Punishment: An Economic Approach," 76 *Journal of Political Economy*, no. 2, March 1968.

Bedau, Hugo, "Bentham's Theory of Punishment: Origin and Content," 7 *Journal of Bentham Studies*, 2004.

Bedau, Hugo, "Bentham's Utilitarian Critique of the Death Penalty," 74 *Journal of Criminal Law and Criminology*, no. 3, 1983.

Bedau, Hugo A., "Classification-Based Sentencing: Some Conceptual and Ethical Problems," *Nomos XXVII: Criminal Justice*, 1985.

Beeley, Arthur L., "Parenthood, the Police Power, and Criminal Justice Administration," 12 *Western Political Quarterly*, no. 3, September 1959.

Bell, David A., "Lawyers into Demagogues: Chancellor Maupeou and the Transformation of Legal Practice in France, 1771–1789," 130 *Past and Present*, February 1991.

Bernstein, Richard F., "Legal Utilitarianism," 89 *Ethics*, no. 2, January 1979.

Blamires, C., "Étienne Dumont: Genevan Apostle of Utility," 2 *Utilitas*, 1990.

Boileau-Despréaux, Nicolas, *Satires*. Paris, Les Belles Lettres, 1966.

Brandt, R. B., "Utilitarianism and the Rules of War," 1 *Philosophy and Public Affairs*, no. 2, Winter 1972.

Brink, David O., "Mill's Deliberative Utilitarianism," 21 *Philosophy and Public Affairs*, no. 1, Winter 1992.

Brook, Richard, "Threats and Punishment," 17 *Philosophy and Public Affairs*, no. 3, Summer 1988.

Brown, Stuart M., Jr., "Duty and the Production of Good," 61 *The Philosophical Review*, no. 3, July 1952.

Brudner, Alan, "Retributivism and the Death Penalty," 30 *University of Toronto Law Journal*, no. 4, Autumn 1980.

Buchan, B., "Zero Tolerance, Mandatory Sentencing, and Early Liberal Arguments for Penal Reform," 30 *International Journal of the Sociology of Law*, no. 3, September 2002.

Burns, J. H. "Dreams and Destinations: Jeremy Bentham in 1828," 1 *The Bentham Newsletter*, 1978

Burns, J. H., "Jeremy Bentham: An Iliad of Argument," 3 *Journal of Bentham Studies*, 2000.

Campbell, T. D., and I. S. Ross, "The Utilitarianism of Adam Smith's Policy Advice," 42 *Journal of the History of Ideas*, no. 1, January 1981.

Carr, Robert, "The Religious Thought of John Stuart Mill: A Study in Reluctant Scepticism," 23 *Journal of the History of Ideas*, no. 4, October 1962.

Cooper, Robert Alan, "Ideas and their Execution: English Prison Reform," 10 *Eighteenth Century Studies*, no. 1, Autumn 1976.

Cooper, Robert Alan, "Jeremy Bentham, Elizabeth Fry, and English Prison Reform," 42 *Journal of the History of Ideas*, no. 4, October 1981.

Crimmins, James E., "Bentham on Religion: Atheism and the Secular Society," 47 *Journal of the History of Ideas*, no. 1, January 1986.

Crimmins, James E., "Bentham's Philosophical Politics," 3 *Harvard Review of Philosophy*, Spring 1993.

Crimmins, James E., "Bentham's Political Radicalism Reexamined," 55 *Journal of the History of Ideas*, no. 2, April 1994.

Crimmins, James E., "Contending Interpretations of Bentham's Utilitarianism," 29 *Canadian Journal of Political Science*, no. 4, December 1996.

Cutler, Fred, "Jeremy Bentham and the Public Opinion Tribunal," 63 *Public Opinion Quarterly*, no. 3, Autumn 1999.

Davis, Michael, "Death, Deterrence, and the Method of Common Sense," 7 *Social Theory and Practice*, no. 1, 1981.

Davis, Michael, "Harm and Retribution," 15 *Philosophy and Public Affairs*, no. 3, Summer 1986.

Davis, Michael, "How to Make the Punishment Fit the Crime," 93 *Ethics*, no. 4, July 1983.

Devereaux, Simon, "The Making of the Penitentiary Act, 1775–1779," 42 *The Historical Journal*, no. 2, June 1999.

Dinwiddy, John R., "Bentham's Transition to Political Radicalism," 36 *Journal of the History of Ideas*, no. 4 (October 1975

Dinwiddy, John R., "The Early Nineteenth Century Campaign against Flogging in the Army," 97 *English Historical Review*, no. 383, April 1982.

Donovan, Donald Francis, and Anthea Roberts, "The Emerging Recognition of Universal Civil Jurisdiction," 100 *American Journal of International Law*, no. 1, January 2006.

Draper, Tony, "An Introduction to Jeremy Bentham's Theory of Punishment," 5 *Journal of Bentham Studies*, 2002

Ducasse, C. J., "Scientific Method in Ethics," 14 *Philosophy and Phenomenological Research*, no. 1, September 1953.

Edgeworth, F. Y., "The Hedonical Calculus," 4 *Mind*, no. 15, July 1879.

Ehrlich, Isaac, "Crime, Punishment, and the Market for Offenses," 10 *Journal of Economic Perspectives*, no. 1, Winter 1996.

Eisenach, Eldon J., "Crime, Death and Loyalty in English Liberalism," 6 *Political Theory*, no. 2, May 1978.

Eisenach, Eldon J., "The Dimension of History in Bentham's Theory of Law," 16 *Eighteenth Century Studies*, no. 3, Spring 1983.

Ekirk, A. Roger, "Bound for America: A Profile of British Convicts Transported to the Colonies, 1718–1775," 42 *William and Mary Quarterly*, no. 2 (April 1985

Emmons, Donald C., "Act vs. Rule Utilitarianism," 82 *Mind*, no. 326, April 1973.

Feinberg, Joel, "Collective Responsibility," 65 *Journal of Philosophy*, no. 21, November 1968.

Feldman, Fred, "On the Intrinsic Value of Pleasures," 107 *Ethics*, no. 3, April 1997.

Friedman, David, "Why Not Hang Them All? The Virtues of Inefficient Punishment," 107 *Journal of Political Economy*, no. 6, December 1999.

Garland, David, "Frameworks of Inquiry in the Sociology of Punishment," 41 *British Journal of Sociology*, no. 1, March 1990.

Gert, Bernard, and Charles M. Culver, "The Justification of Paternalism," 89 *Ethics*, no. 2, January 1979.

Goldman, Alvin, "The Paradox of Punishment," 9 *Philosophy and Public Affairs*, no. 1, 1979.

Goldworth, Amnon, "Bentham's Concept of Pleasure: Its Relation to Fictitious Terms," 82 *Ethics*, no. 4, July 1972.

Grasmick, Harold G., and George J. Bryjak, "The Deterrent Effect of Perceived Severity of Punishment," 59 *Social Forces*, no. 2, December 1980.

Green, Michael, "Marx, Utility, and Right," 11 *Political Theory*, no. 3, August 1983.

Guy, William A., "On Sufficient and Insufficient Dietaries, with Special Reference to the Dietaries of Prisoners," 26 *Journal of the Statistical Society of London*, no. 3, September 1863.

Haksar, Vinit, "Coercive Proposals," 4 *Political Theory*, no. 1, February 1976.

Hare, R. M., "What is Wrong with Slavery," 8 *Philosophy and Public Affairs*, no. 2, Winter 1979.

Harris, Jonathan, "Bernardino Rivadavia and Benthamite 'Discipleship,'" 33 *Latin American Research Review*, no. 1, January 1998.

Henriques, Ursula R. Q., "The Rise and Decline of the Separate System of Prison Discipline," 54 *Past and Present*, February 1972.

Himmelfarb, Gertrude, "Bentham's Utopia: The National Charity Company," 10 *Journal of British Studies*, no. 1, November 1970.

Hodges, Donald Clark, "Punishment," 18 *Philosophy and Phenomenological Research*, no. 2, December 1957.

Hoogensen, Gunhild, "Bentham's International Manuscripts versus the 'Published' Works," 4 *Journal of Bentham Studies*, 2001.

Hook, Sydney, "Academic Manners and Morals," 23 *Journal of Higher Education*, no. 6, June 1952.

Hospers, John, *Human Conduct: An Introduction to the Problems of Ethics*. New York, Wadsworth, 1995.

Hume, L. J., "Jeremy Bentham and the Nineteenth Century Revolution in Government," 10 *The Historical Journal*, no. 3, March 1967.

Husak, Douglas N., "Why Punish the Deserving?" 26 *Noûs*, no. 4, December 1992.

Itzkin, Elissa S., "Bentham's *Chrestomathia*: Utilitarian Legacy to English Education," 39 *Journal of the History of Ideas*, no. 2, April 1978.

Jacobs, Straun, "Bentham, Science and the Construction of Jurisprudence," 12 *Journal of the History of European Ideas*, 1990.

Jacobson, Daniel, "Mill on Liberty, Speech, and the Free Society," 29 *Philosophy and Public Affairs*, no. 3, Summer 2000.

Kavka, Gregory S., "Some Paradoxes of Deterrence," 75 *Journal of Philosophy*, no. 6, June 1978.

Keller, Oliver J., *Halfway Houses: Community Centered Correction and Treatment*. Lexington, MA, Lexington Books, 1970.

Kelly, Paul J., "Utilitarianism and Distributive Justice: The Civil Law and the Foundations of Bentham's Economic Thought," 1 *Utilitas*, no. 1, May 1989.

Kennedy, Duncan, "The Structure of Blackstone's Commentaries," 28 *Buffalo Law Review*, no. 1, January 1980.

Kilbride, Daniel, "Slavery and Utilitarianism: Thomas Cooper and the Mind of the Old South," 59 *Journal of Southern History*, no. 3, August 1993.

Kilcullen, John, "Utilitarianism and Virtue," 93 *Ethics*, no. 3,April 1983.

Kolnai, Aurel, "The Thematic Primacy of Moral Evil," 6 *The Philosophical Quarterly*, no. 22, January, 1956.

Landes, William M., "An Economic Analysis of the Courts," 14 *Journal of Law and Economics*, no. 2, April 1971.

Lang, David M., "Radischev and the Legislative Commission of Alexander I," 6 *American Slavic and East European Review*, no. ¾, December 1947.

Lessnoff, Michael, "The Political Philosophy of Karl Popper," 10 *British Journal of Political Science*, no. 1, January 1980.

Lessnoff, Michael, "Two Justifications of Punishment," 21 *Philosophical Quarterly*, no. 83, April 1971.

Lieberman, David, "Blackstone's Science of Legislation," 27 *Journal of British Studies*, no. 2, April 1988.

Lieberman, David, "From Bentham to Benthamism," 28 *The Historical Journal*, no. 1, March 1985.

Lobban, Michael, "Blackstone and the Science of Law," 30 *The Historical Journal*, no. 2, June 1987.

Lott, John R., Jr., "Should the Wealthy Be Able to 'Buy Justice,'" 95 *Journal of Political Economy*, no. 6, December 1987.

Lovegrove, A., "Sanctions and Severity: To the Demise of Von Hirsch and Wasik's Sanction Hierarchy," 40 *Howard Journal of Criminal Justice*, no. 2, May 2001.

Lundin, Hilda G., "The Influence of Jeremy Bentham on English Democratic Development," 7 *University of Iowa Studies in the Social Sciences*, no. 3, November 1920.

Lyons, David, "On Sanctioning Excuses," 66 *Journal of Philosophy*, no. 19, October 1969.

Lyons, William, "Deterrent Theory and Punishment of the Innocent," 84 *Ethics*, no. 4, July 1974.

Madan, Martin, *Thoughts on Executive Justice*. London, J. Dodsley, 1785.

Maestro, Marcello, "Benjamin Franklin and the Penal Laws," 36 *Journal of the History of Ideas*, no. 3, July 1975.

———, "Gaetano Filangieri and His Laws of Relative Goodness," 44 *Journal of the History of Ideas*, no. 4, October 1983.

———, "A Pioneer for the Abolition of Capital Punishment: Cesare Beccaria," 34 *Journal of the History of Ideas*, no. 3, July 1973.

Martin, Ged, "The Alternatives to Botany Bay," 3 *University of Newcastle Historical Journal*, February 1975.

McCloskey, H. J., "A Non-Utilitarian Approach to Punishment," 8 *Inquiry*, Autumn 1965.

———, "A Note on Utilitarian Punishment," 72 *Mind*, no. 288, October 1963.

McGowen, Randall, "The Body and Punishment in Eighteenth-Century England," 59 *Journal of Modern History*, no. 4, December 1987.

McHugh, James T., "Is the Law 'Anglophone' in Canada?" 23 *American Review of Canadian Studies*, no. 1, Autumn 1993.

McNamee, M. J., H. Sheridan, and J. Buswell, "The Limits of Utilitarianism as a Professional Ethic in Public Sector Leisure Policy and Provision," 20 *Leisure Studies*, no. 3, July 2001.

Miller, Dale E., "Actual-Consequence Act Utilitarianism and the Best Possible Humans," 16 *Ratio*, no. 1, March 2003.

Moore, Kathleen Dean, *Pardons: Justice, Mercy, and the Public Interest*. Oxford, Oxford University Press.

Moravcsik, Andrew, "The Origins of Human Rights Regimes: Democratic Delegation in Postwar Europe," 54 *International Organization*, no. 2, Spring 2000.

Nagai, Yoshio "Smith and Bentham on Jurisprudence: English Utilitarianism in Contrast with the Scottish Enlightenment," 19 *Enlightenment and Dissent*, 2000.

Nowell-Smith, P. H., "On Sanctioning Excuses," 67 *The Journal of Philosophy*, no. 18, September 1970.

Ohlin, Jens David, "Applying the Death Penalty to Crimes of Genocide," 99 *American Journal of International Law*, no. 4, October 2005.

Pappe, H. O., Sismondi's System of Liberty," 40 *Journal of the History of Ideas*, no. 2, April 1979.

Parnham, John, "Applying Therapeutic Principles to a Family-Focused Juvenile Justice Model (Delinquency)," 52 *Alabama Law Review*, no. 4, Summer 2001.

Pitkin, Hanna Fenichel, "Slippery Bentham: Some Neglected Cracks in the Foundations of Utilitarianism," 18 *Political Theory*, no. 1, February 1990.

Polinsky, A. Mitchell, and Steven Shavell, "The Economic Theory of Public Enforcement of Law," 38 *Journal of Economic Literature*, no. 1, March 2000.

Quinn, Warren, "The Right to Threaten and the Right to Punish," 14 *Philosophy and Public Affairs*, no. 4, Fall 1985.

Radelet, Michael L., and Marian J. Borg, "The Changing Nature of Death Penalty Debates," 26 *Annual Review of Sociology*, 2006.

Rawls, John, "Two Concepts of Rules," 64 *Philosophical Review*, no. 1, January 1955.

Reiman, Jeffrey H., "Justice, Civilization, and the Death Penalty: Answering van den Haag," 14 *Philosophy and Public Affairs*, no. 2, Spring 1985.

Richards, David A. J., "Rights, Utility, and Crime," 3 *Crime and Justice*, 1981.

Roberts, Roda, "Legal Translator and Legal Interpreter Training in Canada," 20 *Terminology Update*, no. 6, 1987.

Rodman, Barbee-Sue, "Bentham and the Paradox of Penal Reform," 29 *Journal of the History of Ideas*, no. 2, April 1968.

Rosen, F. "Crime, Punishment, and Liberty, 20 *History of Political Thought*, no. 1, Spring 1999.

———, "Utilitarianism and the Punishment of the Innocent: The Origins of a False Doctrine," 9 *Utilitas*, 1997.

Saint-Amand, Pierre, "Original Vengeance: Politics, Anthropology, and the French Enlightenment," 26 *Eighteenth Century Studies*, no. 3, Spring 1993.

Schaefer, David Lewis, "The Good, the Beautiful, and the Useful: Montaigne's Transvaluation of Values," 73 *American Political Science Review*, no. 1, March 1979.

Schedler, George, "On Telishing the Guilty," 86 *Ethics*, no. 3, April 1976.

Scheppele, Kim Lane, "Facing Facts in Legal Interpretation," 30 *Representations*, Spring 1990.

Schneewind, J. B., *Sidgwick's Ethics and Victorian Moral Philosophy*. Oxford, Oxford University Online Monographs, 1986.

Schrader, "Abby M., Containing the Spectacle of Punishment: The Russian Autocracy and the Abolition of the Knout, 1817–1845," 56 *Slavic Review*, no. 4, Winter 1997.

Semple, Janet, "Foucault and Bentham: A Defence of Panopticism," 4 *Utilitas*, 1992.

Shapo, Marshall S., *Principles of Tort Law*. St. Paul, West, 2003.

Sidgwick, Henry, "Critical Notice: *Progressive Morality*, by Thomas Fowler," 10 *Mind*, no. 38, April 1885.

———, "Unreasonable Action," 2 *Mind*, no. 6, April 1893.

Silver, Alan, "Friendship in Commercial Society: Eighteenth-Century Social Theory and Modern Sociology," 95 *American Journal of Sociology*, no. 6, May 1990.

Simmons, Beth, "Why Commit? Explaining State Acceptance of International Human Rights Obligations," *WCFIA: Weatherhead Center for International Affairs Working Papers*, November 2003.

Skuy, David, "Macaulay and the Indian Penal Code of 1862: The Myth of the Inherent Superiority and Modernity of the English Legal System Compared to India's Legal System in the Nineteenth Century," 32 *Modern Asian Studies*, no. 3, July 1998.

Smart, J. C. C., "Extreme and Restricted Utilitarianism," 6 *Philosophical Quarterly*, no. 25, October, 1956.

Smart, R. N., "Negative Utilitarianism," 67 *Mind* , no. 268, October 1958.

Smith, Wilson, "William Paley's Theological Utilitarianism in America," 11 *William and Mary Quarterly*, no. 3, July 1954.

Steinberger, Peter J., "Hegel on Crime and Punishment," 77 *American Political Science Review*, no. 4, December 1983.

Stell, Lance K., "Dueling and the Right to Life," 90 *Ethics*, no. 1, October 1979.

Stephen, M. D., "Gladstone and the Composition of the Final Court in Ecclesiastical Causes, 1850–1873," 9 *The Historical Journal*, no. 2, 1966.

Stimson, Shannon C., and Murray Milgate, "Utility, Property, and Political Participation: James Mill on Democratic Reform," 87 *American Political Science Review*, no. 4, December 1993.

Strong, Edward W., "Justification of Juridical Punishment," 79 *Ethics*, no. 3, April 1969.

Sutton, John R., "Social Structure, Institutions, and the Legal Status of Children in the United States," 88 *American Journal of Sociology*, no. 5, March 1983.

Tribe, Keith, "Adam Smith: Critical Theorist?" 37 *Journal of Economic Literature*, no. 2, June 1999.

Tullock, Gordon, "Does Punishment Deter Crime?" in 36 *The Public Interest*, Summer 1974.

Unnever, James D., and Francis T. Cullen, "Executing the Innocent and Support for Capital Punishment: Implications for Public Policy," 4 *Criminology and Public Policy*, no. 1, February 2005.

von Hirsch, Andrew, and Martin Wasik, "Punishments in the Community and the Principles of Desert," 20 *Rutgers Law Journal*, no. 3, Winter 1968.

Waugh, W. T., "The Great Statute of Praemunire," 37 *English Historical Review*, no. 146, April 1922.

Wertheimer, Alan, "Should Punishment Fit the Crime?" 3 *Social Theory and Practice*, 1975.

Whelan, Frederick G., "Citizenship and the Right to Leave," 75 *American Political Science Review*, no. 3, September 1981.

Williford, Mirian, "Bentham on the Rights of Women," 39 *Journal of the History of Ideas*, no. 1, January 1975.

Wishy, Bernard, "Introduction," in John Stuart Mill, *Selected Writings of John Stuart Mill*, Bernard Wishy, ed. (Boston: Beacon Press, 1959

Wood, David, "Retribution, Crime Reduction, and the Justification of Punishment," 22 *Oxford Journal of Legal Studies*, no. 2, June 2002.

MONOGRAPHS

Cambridge History of English and American Literature. Cambridge, Cambridge University Press, 1921.

Alexander, Jeffrey C., *Theoretical Logic in Sociology*. Berkeley, University of California Press, 1982.

Allen, Christopher, *The Law of Evidence in Victorian England*. Cambridge, Cambridge University Press, 1997.

Aristotle, *Nicomachean Ethics*, Martin Ostwald, trans. Indianapolis, Bobbs-Merrill, 1962.

Aristotle, *The Politics*, T. A. Sinclair, trans. Baltimore, Penguin, 1972.

Austin, John, *The Province of Jurisprudence Determined*, Wilfrid E. Rumble, ed. Cambridge, Cambridge University Press, 1995.

Bahmueller, Charles F., *The National Charity Company: Jeremy Bentham's Silent Revolution*. Berkeley, University of California Press, 1981.

Bailey, James Wood, *Utilitarianism, Institutions, and Justice*. New York, Oxford University Press, 1997.

Bailyn, Bernard, *Voyagers to the West: Emigration from Britain to America on the Eve of the Revolution*. New York, Random House, 1986.

Barker, Sir Ernest, *Greek Political Theory: Plato and His Predecessors*. London, Methuen, 1961.

Barton, Charles K. B., *Getting Even: Revenge as a Form of Justice*. Peru, IL, Open Court, 1999.

Beattie, J. M., *Crimes and the Court in England, 1660–1800*. Princeton, Princeton University Press, 1986.

Beccaria, Cesare, *On Crimes and Punishments*, Henry Paolucci, trans. Indianapolis: Bobbs-Merrill, 1963.

Benn, S. I., and R. S. Peters, *The Principles of Political Thought*. New York, The Free Press, 1965.

Bentham, Jeremy, *A Comment on the Commentaries*, J. H. Burns and H. L. A. Harts, eds. London, Athlone Press, 1977.

———, *A Fragment on Government*, Ross Harrison, ed. Cambridge, Cambridge University Press, 1988.

———, *An Introduction to the Principles of Morals and Legislation*, J. H. Burns and H. L. A. Hart, eds. (Oxford: Oxford University Press, 2005.

———, *Proposal for a New and Less Expensive Mode of Employing and Reforming Convicts*. London 1798.

———, *Rationale of Judicial Evidence*, John Stuart Mill, ed. London, 1827.

———, *The Limits of Jurisprudence Defined*, Charles Warren Everett, ed. Westport, CT, Greenwood Press, 1970.

———, *The Panopticon Writings*, Miran Božovi , ed. London, Verso, 1995.

———, *The Rationale of Punishment*, Richard Smith, ed. London, Robert Heward, 1830.

———, *Théorie des peines et des Récompenses*, Etienne Dumont, ed. and trans., second edition. Paris, Chez Bossange et Masson, 1818.

———, *The Theory of Legislation*, C. K. Ogden, ed. London, Routledge and Keegan Paul, 1931.

———, *The Works of Jeremy Bentham*, John Bowring and Richard Doane, eds., Edinburgh, William Tait, 1843.

Black, Donald, *The Behavior of Law*. San Diego, Academic Press, 1980.

Blackstone, Sir William, *Commentaries on the Laws of England*. Chicago, University of Chicago Press, 1979.

Boorstin, Daniel J., *The Mysterious Science of Law: An Essay on Blackstone's Commentaries*. Chicago, University of Chicago Press, 1996.

Boralevi, Lea Campos, *Bentham and the Oppressed*. Berlin, Walter de Gruyter, 1984.

Bradley, F. H., *Ethical Studies*. Oxford, Oxford University Press, 1962.

Brandt, Richard B., *Ethical Theory: The Problems of Normative and Critical Ethics*. Englewood Cliffs, NJ, Prentice Hall, 1959.

———, *Morality, Utilitarianism, and Rights*. Cambridge, Cambridge University Press, 1992.

Brooke, Alan, *Bound for Botany Bay: The Story of British Convict Transportation to Australia*. Toronto, Dundurn Press, 2006.

Caldwell, Robert G., "Exile as an Institution," 58 *Political Science Quarterly*, no. 2, June 1943.

Campbell, T. D. *Adam Smith's Science of Morals*. London, Allen and Unwin, 1971.

Carritt, E. F., *Ethical and Political Thinking*. Oxford, Clarendon Press, 1947.

Chambers, Sir Robert, with Samuel Johnson, *A Course of Lectures on the English Law, 1768–1773*, Thomas M. Curley, ed. Madison, University of Wisconsin Press, 1986.

Chomsky, Noam, *Language and Politics*, Carlos P. Otero, ed. Montreal, Black Rose Books, 1988.

Cobb, Roger W., and Charles D. Elder, *Participation in American Politics: The Dynamics of Agenda-Building*. Baltimore, Johns Hopkins University Press, 1983.

Crimmins, James E., *Utilitarians and Religion*. Bristol, England, Thoemmes Press, 1998.

Denton, Robert E., and Gary C. Woodward, *Political Communication in America*. Westport, CT, Praeger, 1998,

Dube, Allison, *The Theme of Acquisitiveness in Bentham's Political Thought*. Abingdon, England, Taylor & Francis, 1991.

Dumont, Etienne, *Recollections of Mirabeau and the First Two Legislative Assemblies of France*. Philadelphia, Carrie & Lea, 1833.

Everett, C. W., *The Education of Jeremy Bentham*. New York, Columbia University Press, 1931.

Filangieri, Gaetano, *The Science of Legislation*, Richard Clayton, trans. London, Emory and Adams, 1806.

Foucault, Michel, *Surveiller et punir: Naissance de la prison*. Paris, Gallimard, 1993.

Gerteis, Louis S., *Morality and Utility in American Antislavery Reform*. Chapel Hill, University of North Carolina Press, 1987.

Glendon, Mary Ann, Christopher Osakwe, and Michael W. Gordon, *Comparative Legal Traditions in a Nutshell* (St. Paul: West, 1982

Halévy, Elie, *The Growth of Philosophical Radicalism*. Boston, Beacon Press, 1960.

Harrison, Ross, *Bentham*. London, Routledge & Kegan Paul, 1983.

Hart, H. L. A., *Essays on Bentham: Studies in Jurisprudence and Political Theory*. Oxford, Oxford University Press, 1982.

——— *Law, Liberty, and Morality*. Stanford, CA, Stanford University Press, 1972.

———, *Punishment and Responsibility*. Oxford, Oxford University Press, 1968.

Häyry, Matti, *Liberal Utilitarianism and Applied Ethics*. London, Routledge, 1994.

Hegel, Georg Wilhem Friedrich, *Elements of the Philosophy of Right*, Alan W. Wood, ed., H. B. Nisbet, trans. Cambridge: Cambridge University Press, 1991.

Helvétius, Claude Adrien, *De l'ésprit: or Essay on the Mind and Its Several Faculties*. London, 1759.

Henriques, Ursula R. Q., *The Jews and the English Law*. London, A. M. Kelley, 1974.

Herzog, Don, *Without Foundations*. Ithaca, NY, Cornell University Press, 1985.

Himmelfarb, Gertrude, *Victorian Minds*. New York, Knopf, 1968.

Hobbes, Thomas, *Leviathan*, Richard Tuck, ed. Cambridge, Cambridge University Press, 1996.

Honderich, Ted, *Punishment: The Supposed Justifications*. Cambridge, Polity Press, 1989.
Hospers, John, *Human Conduct: An Introduction to the Problems of Ethics*. New York, Wadsworth, 1995.
Hussey, Edward, *The Presocratics*. London, Duckworth, 1974.
Irwin, Terrence, *Aristotle's First Principle*. Oxford, Clarendon Press, 1988.
Jacoby, Susan, *Wild Justice: The Evolution of Revenge*. New York, Harper, 1988.
Kant, Immanuel, *The Metaphysical Elements of Justice*, John Ladd, trans. Indianapolis: Hackett, 1999.
Kelly, Paul J., *Utilitarianism and Distributive Justice*. Oxford, Clarendon Press, 1990.
Kirk, G. S., and J. E. Raven, *The Presocratic Philosophers*. Cambridge, Cambridge University Press, 1957.
Lacey, Nicola, *State Punishment: Political Principles and Community Values*. London, Routledge, 1994.
Lieberman, David, *The Province of Legislation Determined*. Cambridge, Cambridge University Press, 1989.
Lindgren, J. R., *The Social Philosophy of Adam Smith*. The Hague, Springer, 1973.
Linebaugh, Peter, *The London Hanged: Crime and Civil Society in the Eighteenth Century*. London, Verso, 2006.
Lloyd, Dennis, *The Idea of Law*. London, Penguin, 1987.
Locke, John, *An Essay Concerning Human Understanding*. Toronto, Collier-Macmillan, 1965.
———, *Second Treatise of Government*, C. B. Macpherson, ed. Indianapolis, Hackett, 1980.
Logan, F. Donald, *Excommunication and the Secular Arm in Medieval England*. Toronto, Pontifical Institute of Medieval Studies, 1968.
Long, Douglas G., *Bentham on Liberty: Jeremy Bentham's Idea of Liberty in Relation to his Utilitarianism*. Toronto, University of Toronto Press, 1977.
Lyons, David, *The Forms and Limits of Utilitarianism*. Oxford, Oxford University Press, 1965.
———, *In the Interest of the Governed: A Study in Bentham's Philosophy of Utility and Law*. Oxford, Oxford University Press, 2003.
Mack, Mary Peter, *Jeremy Bentham: An Odyssey of Ideas, 1748–1792*. London, Heinneman, 1962.
Macpherson, C. B., *The Political Theory of Possessive Individualism*. Oxford, Oxford University Press, 1964.
Marshall, Enid A., *General Principles of Scots Law*. Edinburgh, W. Green and Son, 1978.
McHugh, James T., *The Essential Concept of Law*. New York, Peter Lang, 2002.
McLuhan, Marshall, *The Essential McLuhan*, Eric McLuhan and Frank Zingrone, eds. New York, Basic Books, 1996.
McLynn, Frank, *Crime and Punishment in Eighteenth Century England*. New York, Routledge, 1989.
McNair, Brian, *An Introduction to Political Communication*. New York, Routledge, 2003.
Mill, John Stuart, *Selected Writings of John Stuart Mill*, Bernard Wishy, ed. Boston, Beacon Press, 1959.
———, *Three Essays on Religion: Nature, the Utility of Religion, and Theism*. London, Prometheus Books, 1998.
Miller, William Ian, *Humiliation and Other Essays on Honor, Social Discomfort, and Violence*. Ithaca, NY, Cornell University Press, 1995.
Montesquieu, Charles de Secondat, Baron de, *De l'esprit des lois*, Victor Goldschmidt, ed. Paris, Flammarion, 1979.
Moore, G. E., *Principia Ethica*, Thomas Baldwin, ed. (Cambridge: Cambridge University Press, 1993

Phillipson, Coleman, *Three Criminal Law Reformers: Beccaria, Bentham, Romilly*. Glenridge, NJ, Patterson Smith, 1973.

Plato, *The Republic*, G. M. A. Grube, trans. Indianapolis: Hackett, 1974.

Popper, Karl, *The Open Society and Its Enemies*. London, Routledge and Keegan Paul, 1966.

Porter, Noah, *Two Sermons on Church Communion and Excommunication, with a Particular View to Slaveholders in the Church*. Ithaca, NY, Cornell University Library, 2006.

Postema, Gerald J., *Bentham and the Common Law Tradition*. Oxford, Clarendon Press, 1986.

Pound, Roscoe, and Neil Hamilton, *The Spirit of the Common Law*. Somerset, NJ, Transaction Publishers, 1998.

Primoratz, Igor, *Justifying Legal Punishment*. Atlantic Highlands, NJ, Humanities Press International, 1989.

Radzinowicz, Leon, *A History of English Criminal Law and Its Administration from 1750*. London, Macmillan, 1948.

Richards, David A. J., *The Moral Criticism of Law*. Dickinson, Encino and Belmont, CA, 1977.

Riker, William, *The Art of Political Manipulation*. New Haven, Yale University Press, 1986.

Romilly, Sir Samuel, *Observations on the Criminal Law of England*. London, T. Cadell and W. Davies, 1813.

Rosenblatt, Helena, *Rousseau and Geneva: From the First Discourse to the Social Contract, 1749–1762*. Cambridge, Cambridge University Press, 1997.

Rosenblum, Nancy L., *Bentham's Theory of the Modern State*. Cambridge, MA, Harvard University Press, 1978.

Rumble, Wilfred E., *The Thought of John Austin: Jurisprudence, Colonial Reform, and the British Constitution*. London, Athlone, 1985.

Sarat, Austin, *When the State Kills: Capital Punishment and the American Condition*. Princeton, NJ, Princeton University Press, 2001.

Scarre, Geoffrey, *Utilitarianism*. London, Routledge, 1996.

Schneewind, Jerome B., *Sidgwick's Ethics and Victorian Moral Philosophy*. New York, Oxford University Press, 1976.

Semple, Janet, *Bentham's Prison: A Study of the Panopticon Penitentiary*. Oxford, Clarendon Press, 1993.

Smart, J. C. C., *Freedom and Reason*. New York, Oxford University Press, 1965.

Shaw, William H., *Contemporary Ethics: Taking Account of Utilitarianism*. Malden, MA, Blackwell, 1999.

Sheppard, Claude-Armand, ed., *The Law of Languages in Canada*. Ottawa, Information Canada, 1971.

Sidgwick, Henry, *Essays on Ethics and Methods*. Oxford, Oxford University Press, 2001.

———, *The Method of Ethics*. Boston, Adamant Media, 2001.

Sigmund, Paul E., *Natural Law in Political Thought*. Cambridge, MA: Winthrop, 1971.

Skinner, Quentin, *Liberty Before Liberalism*. Cambridge, Cambridge Univeristy Press, 1997.

Smart, J. C. C., *An Outline of a System of Utilitarian Ethics*. Melbourne, Melbourne University Press, 1961.

Steintrager, James, *Bentham*. Ithaca, NY, Cornell University Press, 1977.

Stephens, Leslie, *The English Utilitarians*. Honolulu, University Press of the Pacific, 2004.

Stokes, Eric, *The English Utilitarians and India*. Oxford, Clarendon Press, 1959.

Ten, C. L., *Crime, Guilt, and Punishment: A Philosophical Introduction*. Oxford, Clarendon Press, 1987.

Thompson, E. P., *Whigs and Hunters*. New York: Random House, 1975.

Van Den Haag, Ernest, "On Deterrence and the Death Penalty," 78 *Ethics*, no. 4, July 1968.

Webb, Sydney, and Beatrice Potter Webb, *English Prisons under Local Government*. London, F. Cass, 1963.

Weinstein, David, *Equal Freedom and Utility: Herbert Spencer's Liberal Utilitarianism.* Cambridge, Cambridge University Press, 1998.

Wiener, Martin J., *Reconstructing the Criminal: Culture, Law, and Policy in England, 1830–1914.* Cambridge, Cambridge University Press, 1990.

Wild, John, *Plato's Modern Enemies and the Theory of Natural Law.* Chicago, University of Chicago Press, 1968.

MANUSCRIPTS AND LETTERS

Bentham, Jeremy, and Richard Smith, Manuscripts and Transcriptions of *The Rationale of Punishment* and Related Writings. Special Collections, University College London, catalogue 141.

Bentham, Jeremy, *Correspondence of Jeremy Bentham*, vol. IV, Alexander Taylor Milne, ed., London, Athlone, 1981.

———. vol. V, Alexander Taylor Milne, ed., London, Athlone, 1981.

———. vol. VII, J. R. Dinwiddy, ed., Oxford, Clarendon Press, 1988.

———. vol. VIII, Stephen Conway, ed., Oxford, Clarendon Press, 1988.

———. vol. IX, Stephen Conway, ed. Oxford, Clarendon Press, 1989.

———. vol. XI, Catherine Fuller, ed. Oxford, Clarendon Press, 2000.

———. vol. XII, Luke O'Sullivan and Catherine Fuller, eds. Oxford, Clarendon Press, 2001.

Photo of the editor conferring with the author
at University College, London.

GREAT BOOKS IN PHILOSOPHY PAPERBACK SERIES

ESTHETICS

❏ Aristotle—*The Poetics*
❏ Aristotle—*Treatise on Rhetoric*

ETHICS

❏ Aristotle—*The Nicomachean Ethics*
❏ Marcus Aurelius—*Meditations*
❏ Jeremy Bentham—*The Principles of Morals and Legislation*
❏ John Dewey—*Human Nature and Conduct*
❏ John Dewey—*The Moral Writings of John Dewey, Revised Edition*
❏ Epictetus—*Enchiridion*
❏ David Hume—*An Enquiry Concerning the Principles of Morals*
❏ Immanuel Kant—*Fundamental Principles of the Metaphysic of Morals*
❏ John Stuart Mill—*Utilitarianism*
❏ George Edward Moore—*Principia Ethica*
❏ Friedrich Nietzsche—*Beyond Good and Evil*
❏ Plato—*Protagoras, Philebus,* and *Gorgias*
❏ Bertrand Russell—*Bertrand Russell On Ethics, Sex, and Marriage*
❏ Arthur Schopenhauer—*The Wisdom of Life* and *Counsels and Maxims*
❏ Adam Smith—*The Theory of Moral Sentiments*
❏ Benedict de Spinoza—*Ethics* and *The Improvement of the Understanding*

LOGIC

❏ George Boole—*The Laws of Thought*

METAPHYSICS/EPISTEMOLOGY

❏ Aristotle—*De Anima*
❏ Aristotle—*The Metaphysics*
❏ Francis Bacon—*Essays*
❏ George Berkeley—*Three Dialogues Between Hylas and Philonous*
❏ W. K. Clifford—*The Ethics of Belief and Other Essays*
❏ René Descartes—*Discourse on Method* and *The Meditations*
❏ John Dewey—*How We Think*
❏ John Dewey—*The Influence of Darwin on Philosophy and Other Essays*
❏ Epicurus—*The Essential Epicurus: Letters, Principal Doctrines, Vatican Sayings, and Fragments*
❏ Sidney Hook—*The Quest for Being*
❏ David Hume—*An Enquiry Concerning Human Understanding*
❏ David Hume—*Treatise of Human Nature*
❏ William James—*The Meaning of Truth*
❏ William James—*Pragmatism*
❏ Immanuel Kant—*The Critique of Judgment*
❏ Immanuel Kant—*Critique of Practical Reason*
❏ Immanuel Kant—*Critique of Pure Reason*
❏ Gottfried Wilhelm Leibniz—*Discourse on Metaphysics* and the *Monadology*
❏ John Locke—*An Essay Concerning Human Understanding*
❏ George Herbert Mead—*The Philosophy of the Present*
❏ Michel de Montaigne—*Essays*
❏ Charles S. Peirce—*The Essential Writings*
❏ Plato—*The Euthyphro, Apology, Crito,* and *Phaedo*
❏ Plato—*Lysis, Phaedrus,* and *Symposium*

❑ Bertrand Russell—*The Problems of Philosophy*
❑ George Santayana—*The Life of Reason*
❑ Arthur Schopenhauer—*On the Principle of Sufficient Reason*
❑ Sextus Empiricus—*Outlines of Pyrrhonism*
❑ Ludwig Wittgenstein—*Wittgenstein's Lectures: Cambridge, 1932–1935*
❑ Alfred North Whitehead—*The Concept of Nature*

PHILOSOPHY OF RELIGION

❑ Jeremy Bentham—*The Influence of Natural Religion on the Temporal Happiness of Mankind*
❑ Marcus Tullius Cicero—*The Nature of the Gods* and *On Divination*
❑ Ludwig Feuerbach—*The Essence of Christianity* and *The Essence of Religion*
❑ Paul Henry Thiry, Baron d'Holbach—*Good Sense*
❑ David Hume—*Dialogues Concerning Natural Religion*
❑ William James—*The Varieties of Religious Experience*
❑ John Locke—*A Letter Concerning Toleration*
❑ Lucretius—*On the Nature of Things*
❑ John Stuart Mill—*Three Essays on Religion*
❑ Friedrich Nietzsche—*The Antichrist*
❑ Thomas Paine—*The Age of Reason*
❑ Bertrand Russell—*Bertrand Russell On God and Religion*

SOCIAL AND POLITICAL PHILOSOPHY

❑ Aristotle—*The Politics*
❑ Mikhail Bakunin—*The Basic Bakunin: Writings, 1869–1871*
❑ Jeremy Bentham—*The Rationale of Punishment*
❑ Edmund Burke—*Reflections on the Revolution in France*
❑ John Dewey—*Freedom and Culture*
❑ John Dewey—*Individualism Old and New*
❑ John Dewey—*Liberalism and Social Action*
❑ G. W. F. Hegel—*The Philosophy of History*
❑ G. W. F. Hegel—*Philosophy of Right*
❑ Thomas Hobbes—*The Leviathan*
❑ Sidney Hook—*Paradoxes of Freedom*
❑ Sidney Hook—*Reason, Social Myths, and Democracy*
❑ John Locke—*Second Treatise on Civil Government*
❑ Niccolo Machiavelli—*The Prince*
❑ Karl Marx (with Friedrich Engels)—*The German Ideology*, including *Theses on Feuerbach* and *Introduction to the Critique of Political Economy*
❑ Karl Marx—*The Poverty of Philosophy*
❑ Karl Marx/Friedrich Engels—*The Economic and Philosophic Manuscripts of 1844* and *The Communist Manifesto*
❑ John Stuart Mill—*Considerations on Representative Government*
❑ John Stuart Mill—*On Liberty*
❑ John Stuart Mill—*On Socialism*
❑ John Stuart Mill—*The Subjection of Women*
❑ Montesquieu, Charles de Secondat—*The Spirit of Laws*
❑ Friedrich Nietzsche—*Human, All-Too-Human*
❑ Friedrich Nietzsche—*Thus Spake Zarathustra*
❑ Thomas Paine—*Common Sense*
❑ Thomas Paine—*Rights of Man*
❑ Plato—*Laws*
❑ Plato—*The Republic*
❑ Jean-Jacques Rousseau—*Émile*

- ❑ Jean-Jacques Rousseau—*The Social Contract*
- ❑ Bertrand Russell—*Political Ideas*
- ❑ Mary Wollstonecraft—*A Vindication of the Rights of Men*
- ❑ Mary Wollstonecraft—*A Vindication of the Rights of Women*

GREAT MINDS PAPERBACK SERIES

ART

- ❑ Leonardo da Vinci—*A Treatise on Painting*

CRITICAL ESSAYS

- ❑ Desiderius Erasmus—*The Praise of Folly*
- ❑ Jonathan Swift—*A Modest Proposal and Other Satires*
- ❑ H. G. Wells—*The Conquest of Time*

ECONOMICS

- ❑ Charlotte Perkins Gilman—*Women and Economics: A Study of the Economic Relation between Women and Men*
- ❑ John Maynard Keynes—*The End of Laissez-Faire* and *The Economic Consequences of the Peace*
- ❑ John Maynard Keynes—*The General Theory of Employment, Interest, and Money*
- ❑ John Maynard Keynes—*A Tract on Monetary Reform*
- ❑ Thomas R. Malthus—*An Essay on the Principle of Population*
- ❑ Alfred Marshall—*Money, Credit, and Commerce*
- ❑ Alfred Marshall—*Principles of Economics*
- ❑ Karl Marx—*Theories of Surplus Value*
- ❑ John Stuart Mill—*Principles of Political Economy*
- ❑ David Ricardo—*Principles of Political Economy and Taxation*
- ❑ Adam Smith—*Wealth of Nations*
- ❑ Thorstein Veblen—*Theory of the Leisure Class*

HISTORY

- ❑ Edward Gibbon—*On Christianity*
- ❑ Alexander Hamilton, John Jay, and James Madison—*The Federalist*
- ❑ Herodotus—*The History*
- ❑ Thomas Paine—*The Crisis*
- ❑ Thucydides—*History of the Peloponnesian War*
- ❑ Andrew D. White—*A History of the Warfare of Science with Theology in Christendom*

LAW

- ❑ John Austin—*The Province of Jurisprudence Determined*

POLITICS

- ❑ Walter Lippmann—*A Preface to Politics*

PSYCHOLOGY

- ❑ Sigmund Freud—*Totem and Taboo*

RELIGION

- Thomas Henry Huxley—*Agnosticism and Christianity and Other Essays*
- Ernest Renan—*The Life of Jesus*
- Upton Sinclair—*The Profits of Religion*
- Elizabeth Cady Stanton—*The Woman's Bible*
- Voltaire—*A Treatise on Toleration and Other Essays*

SCIENCE

- Jacob Bronowski—*The Identity of Man*
- Nicolaus Copernicus—*On the Revolutions of Heavenly Spheres*
- Francis Crick—*Of Molecules and Men*
- Marie Curie—*Radioactive Substances*
- Charles Darwin—*The Autobiography of Charles Darwin*
- Charles Darwin—*The Descent of Man*
- Charles Darwin—*The Origin of Species*
- Charles Darwin—*The Voyage of the* Beagle
- René Descartes—*Treatise of Man*
- Albert Einstein—*Relativity*
- Michael Faraday—*The Forces of Matter*
- Galileo Galilei—*Dialogues Concerning Two New Sciences*
- Francis Galton—*Hereditary Genius*
- Ernst Haeckel—*The Riddle of the Universe*
- William Harvey—*On the Motion of the Heart and Blood in Animals*
- Werner Heisenberg—*Physics and Philosophy: The Revolution in Modern Science*
- Fred Hoyle—*Of Men and Galaxies*
- Julian Huxley—*Evolutionary Humanism*
- Thomas H. Huxley—*Evolution and Ethics* and *Science and Morals*
- Edward Jenner—*Vaccination against Smallpox*
- Johannes Kepler—*Epitome of Copernican Astronomy* and *Harmonies of the World*
- Charles Mackay—*Extraordinary Popular Delusions and the Madness of Crowds*
- James Clerk Maxwell—*Matter and Motion*
- Isaac Newton—*Opticks, Or Treatise of the Reflections, Inflections, and Colours of Light*
- Isaac Newton—*The Principia*
- Louis Pasteur and Joseph Lister—*Germ Theory and Its Application to Medicine* and *On the Antiseptic Principle of the Practice of Surgery*
- William Thomson (Lord Kelvin) and Peter Guthrie Tait—*The Elements of Natural Philosophy*
- Alfred Russel Wallace—*Island Life*

SOCIOLOGY

- Emile Durkheim—*Ethics and the Sociology of Morals*